THE POWER OF MONEY

THE POWER OF MONEY

Coinage and Politics in the Athenian Empire

THOMAS FIGUEIRA

PENN

University of Pennsylvania Press

Philadelphia

Printed in the United States of America on acid-free paper

10 9 8 7 6 5 4 3 2 1

Published by
University of Pennsylvania Press
Philadelphia, Pennsylvania 19104-4011

Library of Congress Cataloging-in-Publication Data

Figueira, Thomas J.
The power of money : coinage and politics in the Athenian Empire / by Thomas Figueira.
p. cm.
Includes bibliographical references and indexes.
ISBN 0-8122-3441-3 (alk. paper)
1. Coinage—Political aspects—Greece—Athens—History.
2. Monetary policy—Greece—Athens—History. 3. Greece—History—Athenian supremacy, 479–431 B.C. 4. Athens (Greece)—Politics and government. I. Title.
CJ459.A8F54 1998
737'.4938'5—dc21 97-50265
CIP

This work is dedicated to the memory of Dorothy Gentile Fields, my maternal aunt and godmother, whose love helped sustain me through forty-five years of my life. Born in New York City of immigrant parents, Dolly did not have the opportunity to attend college during the Depression years. Exploiting her natural wit and a civility and urbanity that were once the hallmark of the true Manhattanite, she enjoyed a varied, successful career in entertainment and the media (along with raising two sons). At different times, she pioneered in the earliest days of live television, was a TV casting director, represented actors as a talent agent, was a producer in radio, produced a play off-Broadway, worked on Broadway, and wrote plays and scripts. Her grace, glamor, and supple humor enchanted one little boy, born in a furnished room in Washington Heights, whom she once carried out of a smoky building into the night.

CONTENTS

TABLES

ABBREVIATIONS

BIBLIOGRAPHICAL ABBREVIATIONS

ATL = B.D. Meritt, H.T. Wade-Gery, and M.F. McGregor, *The Athenian Tribute Lists*, 4 vols. (Princeton 1939–1953)

Babelon = E. Babelon, *Traité des monnaies grecques et romaines* (Paris 1901–1933)

BGU = *Aegyptische Urkunden aus den koeniglichen Museen zu Berlin: Griechische Urkunden* (Berlin 1895–1912)

CAH^2 = *The Cambridge Ancient History* (Cambridge 1970–)

Cavaignac, *Études* = E. Cavaignac, *Études sur l'histoire financière d'Athènes au V*^{e} *siècle* (Paris 1908)

CH = *Coin Hoards* (London 1975–)

Coinage and Administration = I. Carradice (ed.), *Coinage and Administration in the Athenian and Persian Empires* (Oxford 1987)

CPG = E.L. von Leutsch and F.G. Schneidewin, *Corpus Paroemiographicorum Graecorum*, 2 vols. (Göttingen 1839–1851)

Erxleben *AfP* = E. Erxleben, "Das Münzgesetz der delisch-attischen seebundes," *Archiv für Papyrusforschung* 19 (1969) 91–139, 212; 20 (1970) 66–132; 21 (1971) 145–62

FD = *Fouilles de Delphes*, École française d'Athènes

FGH = F. Jacoby, *Die Fragmente der griechischen Historiker* (Leiden 1923–1958)

Figueira, *Aegina* = T.J. Figueira, *Aegina: Society and Economy* (New York 1981/82)

Figueira, *Colonization* = T.J. Figueira, *Athens and Aigina in the Age of Imperial Colonization* (Baltimore 1991)

Figueira, *Excursions* = T.J. Figueira, *Excursions in Epichoric History: The Aiginetan Essays* (Savage, MD 1993)

Finley, "Classical Greece" = M.I. Finley, "Classical Greece," in *Deuxième Conférence internationale d'histoire économique: Aix-en-Provence 1962* (Paris 1965) 11–35

Gaebler, *Münzen* = H. Gaebler, *Die antiken Münzen von Makedonia und Paeonia* in T. Wiegand (ed.), *Die antiken Münzen Nord-Griechenlands* 3 (Berlin 1935)

HCT = A.W. Gomme, A. Andrewes, and K.J. Dover, *A Historical Commentary to Thucydides*, 5 vols. (Oxford 1945–1981)

Head^2 = B.V. Head, *Historia Nummorum: A Manual of Greek Numismatics*^{2} (Oxford 1911)

IC = M. Guarducci (ed.), *Inscriptiones Creticae*, 4 vols. (Rome 1935–1950)

ID = F. Durrbach, P. Roussel, M. Launey (eds.), *Inscriptions de Délos* (Académie des Inscriptions et Belles-Lettres) (Paris 1926–1992)

IErythrai = H. Engelmann and R. Merkelbach, *Die Inschriften von Erythrai und Klazomenai* (Bonn 1972)

IG = *Inscriptiones Graecae*

I² = F. Hiller von Gaertringen (ed.), *Inscriptiones Atticae Euclidis anno anteriores, editio minor* (Berlin 1924)

I³ = D.M. Lewis, (ed.), *Inscriptiones Atticae Euclidis anno anteriores, editio tertia* (Berlin 1981, 1994)

II² = J. Kirchner (ed.), *Inscriptiones Graecae*, II–III, i–iv, editio minor, *Inscriptiones Atticae Euclidis anno posteriores* (Berlin 1913–1940)

IV = M. Frankel (ed.), *Inscriptiones Argolidis* (Berlin 1902)

IV.1 = F. Hiller von Gaertringen (ed.), *Inscriptiones Epidauri, editio minor* (Berlin 1929)

V.1 = W. Kolbe (ed.), *Inscriptiones Laconiae et Messeniae* (Berlin 1913)

VII = W. Dittenberger (ed.), *Inscriptiones Megaridis et Boeotiae* (Berlin 1892)

XI.2 = F. Durrbach (ed.), *Inscriptiones Deli liberae* (Berlin 1912)

XII.1 = F. Hiller von Gaertringen (ed.), *Inscriptiones Rhodi, Chalces, Carpathi cum Saro, Casi* (Berlin 1895)

XII.2 = G.R. Paton (ed.), *Inscriptiones Lesbi, Nesi, Tenedi* (Berlin 1890)

XII.5 = F. Hiller von Gaertringen (ed.), *Inscriptiones Cycladum* (Berlin 1903, 1909)

XII.7 = J. Delamarre (ed.), *Inscriptiones Amorgi et insularum vicinarum* (Berlin 1908)

XII.8 = C. Fredrich (ed.), *Inscriptiones insularum maris Thracici* (Berlin 1909)

XII.9 = E. Ziebarth (ed.), *Inscriptiones Euboeae insulae* (Berlin 1915)

XII Suppl. = F. Hiller von Gaertringen (ed.), *Supplementum* (Berlin 1939)

IGCH = M. Thompson, O. Mørkholm, and C.M. Kraay (eds.), *An Inventory of Greek Coin Hoards* (New York 1973)

Koch, *Volksbeschlüsse* = C. Koch, *Volksbeschlüsse in Seebundenangelegenheiten: Das Verfahrenrecht Athens im ersten attischen Seebund* (Frankfurt am Main 1991)

Kraay, *ACGC* = C.M. Kraay, *Archaic and Classical Greek Coins* (Berkeley and Los Angeles 1976)

Kraay-Mørkholm Essays = G. Le Rider, K. Jenkins, N. Waggoner, and U. Westermark (eds.), *Kraay-Mørkholm Essays: Numismatic Studies in Memory of C.M. Kraay and O. Mørkholm* (Louvain-la-Neuve 1989)

LSAG = L.H. Jeffery, *The Local Scripts of Archaic Greece* (Oxford 1961); *LSAG*² = revised edition by A.W. Johnston (Oxford 1990)

Mattingly, H.B.: The following articles will be cited according to abbreviated notation.

"The Athenian Coinage Decree," *Historia* 10 (1961) 148–88

"Epigraphically the Twenties are Too Late. . .," *BSA* 65 (1970) 129–49

"Periclean Imperialism," in E. Badian (ed.), *Ancient Society and Institutions* (New York 1967) 193–223; reprinted in G. Wirth (ed.), *Perikles und seine Zeit* (Darmstadt 1979) 312–49

"The Protected Fund in the Athenian Coinage Decree (ATL D 14, par. 7f)," *AJP* 95 (1974) 280–85

"The Second Athenian Coinage Decree," *Klio* 59 (1977) 83–100

"Coins and Amphoras—Chios, Samos and Thasos in the Fifth Century B.C.," *JHS* 101 (1981) 78–86

"The Athenian Coinage Decree and the Assertion of Empire," in *Coinage and Administration*, 65–71

"Methodology in Fifth-Century History," *EMC* 7 (1988) 321–28

Meiggs = R. Meiggs, *The Athenian Empire* (Oxford 1972)

Meiggs-Lewis = R. Meiggs and D. Lewis, *A Selection of Greek Historical Inscriptions to the End of the Fifth Century B.C.* (Oxford 1969; 2nd edition 1988)

OGIS = W. Dittenberger, *Orientis Graeci Inscriptiones Selectae* (Leipzig 1903–1905)

PA = J. Kirchner, *Prosopographia Attica* (Berlin 1901–1903)

P.Tebt. = B.P. Grenfell, A.S. Hunt, and J.G. Smyly (eds.), *The Tebtunis Papyri* (London 1902)

P.Cair.Zen. = *Catalogue Général des antiquités égyptiennes du Musée du Caire: Zenon Papyri* (Cairo 1925–1940)

PCG = R. Kassel and C. Austin, *Poetae Comici Graeci* (Berlin/New York 1989–1995)

Rhodes, *CAAP* = P.J. Rhodes, *A Commentary on the Aristotelian Athenaion Politeia* (Oxford 1981)

Robinson = E.S.G. Robinson, "The Athenian Coinage Decree and the Coinages of the Allies," in *Commemorative Studies in Honor of Theodore Leslie Shear*, *Hesperia* Suppl. 8 (1949) 324–40

Schoenhammer = M.O. Schoenhammer, *Coinage and Empire: The Athenian Standards Decree of the 5th Cent. B.C.* (Diss. City University of New York 1995)

Schuller, *Herrschaft* = W. Schuller, *Die Herrschaft der Athener im Ersten Attischen Seebund* (Berlin 1974)

SEG = *Supplementum Epigraphicum Graecum*. Vols. 1–25: J.J. Hondius (ed.), Leiden 1923–1971; Vols. 26–38: R. Stroud and H. Pleket (eds.), Leiden 1976–1988

Segre = M. Segre, "La legge Ateniese sull' unificazione della moneta," *ClRh* 9 (1938) 149(151)–78

*SIG*³ = W. Dittenberger, *Sylloge Inscriptionum Graecarum*, 3rd ed., 1915

SNG = *Sylloge Nummorum Graecorum*

*SVA*² 2 = H. Bengtson with R. Werner, *Die Staatsverträge des Altertums: Zweiter Band: Die Verträge der griechisch-römischen Welt von 700 bis 338 v. Chr.* (Munich 1962)

*SVA*² 3 = H.H. Schmitt, *Die Staatsverträge des Altertums: Dritter Band: Die Verträge der griechisch-römischen Welt von 338 bis 200 v. Chr.* (Munich 1969)

Tod, *GHI* = M.N. Tod, *A Selection of Greek Historical Inscriptions*, 2 vols. (Oxford 1933–1948)

ABBREVIATIONS OF PERIODICALS

AA = *Archäologischer Anzeiger*
AAA = Ἀρχαιολογικὰ Ἀνάλεκτα ἐξ Ἀθηνῶν
AAWW = *Anzeiger der Österreichischen Akademie der Wissenschaften in Wien, Philos.-Hist. Klasse*
AC = *L'antiquité classique*
AD = Ἀρχαιολογικὸν Δελτίον
AE = Ἀρχαιολογικὴ Ἐφημερίς
Aevum = *Aevum. Rassegna di scienze storiche, linguistiche e filologiche*
AfP = *Archiv für Papyrusforschung*
AHB = *Ancient History Bulletin*
AIIN = *Atti dell'istituto italiano di numismatica*
AJA = *American Journal of Archaeology*
AJAH = *American Journal of Ancient History*
AJN = *American Journal of Numismatics*
AJP = *American Journal of Philology*
AM = *Mitteilungen des Deutschen Archäologischen Instituts, Athenische Abteilung*
Annales = *Annales. Économie, sociétés, civilisations*
ANSMN = *American Numismatic Society Museum Notes*
AntJ = *The Antiquaries Journal: Being the Journal of the Society of Antiquaries of London*
ASNP = *Annali della scuola Normale Superiore di Pisa, Cl. di Lettere e Filosophia*
BAB = *Bulletin de la classe des Lettres de l'Académie Royale de Belgique*
BCH = *Bulletin de correspondance hellénique*
BE = *Bulletin épigraphique*
BICS = *Bulletin of the Institute of Classical Studies of the University of London*
BSA = *Annual of the British School at Athens*
BSFN = *Bulletin de la société française de numismatique*
C & M = *Classica et Mediaevalia. Revue danoise d'Histoire et de Philologie*
CA = *Classical Antiquity*
Cahiers = *Cahiers du Centre d'Études Chypriotes*
CENB = *Cercle d'études numismatiques, Bulletin*
Chiron = *Chiron. Mitteilungen der Kommission für alte Geschichte und Epigraphik des Deutschen Archäologischen Instituts*
ClRh = *Clara Rhodos*
CP = *Classical Philology*
CQ = *Classical Quarterly*
CR = *Classical Review*
CRAI = *Comptes rendus, Académie des Inscriptions & Belles-Lettres* (Paris)
CSCA = *California Studies in Classical Antiquity*
DialArch = *Dialoghi di archeologia*
DL = *Deutsche Literaturzeitung*
EHR = *The Economic History Review*
Eirene = *Eirene. Studia graeca et latina*

EMC = *Echos du monde classique/Classical Views*
GacNum = *Gaceta numismática [Barcelona]*
Gnomon = *Gnomon. Kritische Zeitschrift für die gesamte klassische Altertumswissenschaft*
G & R = *Greece and Rome*
GRBS = *Greek, Roman and Byzantine Studies*
Historia = *Historia. Zeitschrift für alte Geschichte*
ICN = *International Congress of Numismatics or International Numismatic Congress, Proceedings*
JdI = *Jahrbuch des Deutschen Archäologischen Instituts*
JEA = *The Journal of Egyptian Archaeology*
JHS = *Journal of Hellenic Studies*
JIAN = *Journal international d'archéologie numismatique*
JNG = *Jahrbuch für Numismatik und Geldgeschichte*
JOAI = *Jahreshefte des Österreichischen Archäologisches Instituts*
Klio = *Klio. Beiträge zur alten Geschichte*
KSIA = *Kratkije Soobščenija Inst. Akad. Nauk SSSR, Moskva*
Lactor = *Publication of the London Association of Classical Teachers*
Kretika Khronika = Κρητικὰ χρονικά. Κείμενα καὶ μελέται τῆς κρητικῆς ἱστορίας
Madrider Mitteilungen = *Mitteilungen des Deutschen Archäologischen Instituts, Madrider Abteilung*
Mém. Acad. Ins. et Belles-Lettres = *Mémoirs présentés par divers savants à l'Académie des inscriptions et belles lettres [Paris]*
MH = *Museum Helveticum*
MIGRA = *Miscellanea Graeca*
MMB =*Münzen und Medaillensammler. Berichte aus allen Gebieten der Geld-, Münzen-, und Medaillen-Kunde*
Mnem. = *Mnemosyne. Bibliotheca Classica Batava*
NAC = *Numismatica e Antichità classiche, Quaderni Ticinesi*
NC = *Numismatic Chronicle*
NCirc = *Numismatic Circular*
NM = *Numismatika Meddelanden*
NNM = *American Numismatic Society. Numismatic Notes and Monographs*
Nomisma = *Nomisma: Untersuchungen auf dem Gebiete der antiken Münzen*
Nomismatika Khronika = Νομισματικά Χρονικά (Athens)
NZNJ = *New Zealand Numismatic Journal*
OpAth = *Opuscula Atheniensia*
PACA = *Proceedings of the African Classical Association*
PAPS = *Proceedings of the American Philosophical Society*
PP = *La parola del passato*
RA = *Revue archéologique*
RBN = *Revue belge de numismatique et de sigillographie*
REA = *Revue des études anciennes*
REG = *Revue des études grecques*

RFIC = *Rivista di filologia e d'istruzione classica*
RhM = *Rheinisches Museum für Philologie*
RIN = *Rivista italiana di numismatica e scienze affini*
RN = *Revue numismatique*
RPh = *Revue de philologie, de littérature et d'histoire anciennes*
RSA = *Rivista storica dell'Antichità*
SAN = *Journal of the Society for Ancient Numismatics*
Sileno = *Sileno. Rivista di studi classici e cristiani*
SM = *Schweizer Münzblätter*
SNR = *Schweizerische numismatische Rundschau. Revue suisse de numismatique*
TAPA = *Transactions of the American Philological Association*
VDI = *Vestnik drevnej istorii*
YCS = *Yale Classical Studies*
ZfN = *Zeitschrift für Numismatik*
ZPE = *Zeitschrift für Papyrologie und Epigraphik*

NUMISMATIC ABBREVIATIONS

T = talent = 6000 drachms
mna = 100 drachms
dr. = drachm of 6 obols
didr., tridr., tetradr., etc. = didrachm, tridrachm, tetradrachm, etc.
ob. = obol
hemiob., diob., triob., tetrob., etc. = hemiobol, diobol, triobol, tetrobol, etc.
fr. = fraction
tetartēm. = tetartēmorion
st. = stater "standard coin"

Note: For abbreviations of ancient authors, consult the Index Locorum.

ACKNOWLEDGMENTS

I SHOULD LIKE to render thanks to the many friends and colleagues who gave so generously of their time and expertise to aid the researching and writing of this volume. I have tried to do justice to their suggestions and to correct or adjust where they have criticized. The reader will be the best judge of my success. In a far-ranging and synthetic work such as this, lacking any direct forerunner, I have had to make difficult (at least, to me) choices about the order of presentation and about the inclusion or exclusion of topics and supporting material. I apologize that I have not always adhered to the advice of my correspondents—offered to me at the cost of considerable exertion on their part—whether my failure was owed to the persuasion of other interlocutors or to my own hard-headed determination to cleave to a different ordering of the evidence and argument.

The earliest draft of this work was generously and helpfully read by John H. Kroll of the University of Texas at Austin, by Thomas R. Martin, then of Pomona College and now of Holy Cross College, and by Malcolm B. Wallace of the University of Toronto. I should like to restate here the gratitude that I have expressed in other acknowledgments for the consistent support offered me over the years by Mac Wallace, who has helped me with his advice concerning so many of my projects over the last twenty years. A much longer second draft was read in its entirety by A. John Graham, an emeritus professor of the University of Pennsylvania, who kindly provided me with many pages of criticisms, corrections, and suggestions. Another colleague, Mabel Lang, an emerita of Bryn Mawr College, undertook the same onerous task and was good enough to annotate my text most helpfully. Jack Kroll again showed great patience, not only in rereading this second draft closely but also in answering specific questions about (and supplying work in progress on) Athenian coinage, about which he is our greatest expert. In the midst of appraising my very different views on matters to which he had already made important contributions, Jack showed an exemplary balance between receptivity and advocacy. This work would be much the poorer without his intervention at many stages.

Martin Ostwald, emeritus of both Swarthmore College and the University of Pennsylvania, has been a friend and mentor since the years of my graduate studies, offering in this case sage criticism about the beginning of the second draft. Ernst Badian of Harvard University, whose patronage I readily acknowledge, took time out of his many commitments to read much of the second draft and to offer his thoughts, incisive and learned as always.

Leslie Beer-Tobey aided this project by offering advice about the treatment of Aiginetan coinage and about numismatic metallurgy. I thank her also for making her fine dissertation available to me. These are merely the latest in a succession of her kindnesses to me, going back to the time when Colin Kraay introduced us at Oxford in 1976. The late David Lewis of Oxford University, who will be much missed by all students of Athenian history, kindly answered several questions about *IG* I^3 1453 and provided part of his apparatus before the publication of the second fascicle of *IG* I^3. Dr. Andrey Eryomin, taking time from his Fulbright fellowship work in Spartan history, and his wife Kira, both of Samara State University in Russia, generously aided me with exposition and translation of Russian scholarship in epigraphy and metrology. Jonathan H. Kagan worked through the rewritten numismatic chapters, adducing invaluable amplifications, corrections, and clarifications. Jon Kagan has also been most generous in sharing with me his work in progress, as I have noted in my text, and in directing me to additional bibliography, sometimes providing the material out of his own personal library and offprints. Brunilde S. Ridgway, emerita of Bryn Mawr College, helped me with the Oxford and Salamis metrological reliefs, which assistance I acknowledge here. W.T. Loomis generously provided some of the scholarship from his forthcoming work on prices and salaries in the classical period.

This monograph was researched at several libraries whose staffs I should like to thank collectively: the Rutgers University libraries, and especially the staff of the Alexander library and its interlibrary loan office; the Princeton University libraries and particularly the persons staffing the Firestone and Marquand libraries; the library of the Institute for Advanced Study in Princeton and its director, Dr. Eliot Shore; and the library of the American Numismatic Society in New York City and its librarian Mr. Frank Campbell. The research and writing of this monograph was advanced by annual grants from the Faculty Research Council of Rutgers University, for which I am grateful.

My wife, Dr. Sarah George, was engaged in every aspect of this project from its inception and mightily aided its progress. She is responsible for the preparation of the text before you. My thanks are owed not only to her but also to the Publications Office of the American School of Classical Studies at Athens, for the use of their facilities. Finally, I should also like to thank both the staff of the University of Pennsylvania Press and its Director, Eric Halpern.

The availability of Attic epigraphical material on CD-ROM provided by the Packard Humanities Institute not only has been of enormous help in exploring parallel terminology and phraseology, but has helped open to view the arsenal of devices by which students of Athenian inscriptions of the fifth century have reconstructed the original texts. I have unapologetically availed myself of these weapons against the Coinage Decree; only an audacious approach seemed appropriate to break what I perceived to be an analytical impasse. While I trust that numismatists will find that my exposition of fifth-century monetary affairs builds on their work, they may also find some perspectives that have not been current in their investigations, such as hypotheses about separate minting authorities in the same *polis*, coin issues flowing along different channels of dissemination, and "private" money circulating alongside state issues. The vision integrating this work, I hope, is that of a historian of the classical economy, of Athenian administration, and of the institutionality of fifth-century Attic hegemony.

INTRODUCTION: GENESIS AND ORGANIZATION

THE MERE PHRASING of the title of my book could be thought to propound a fanciful interpretation of the interrelation between economic and political history during the fifth-century hegemony of the Athenians; at least, it could for anyone unversed in the scholarship on the Attic Coinage Decree. A historian innocent of that research might well protest the improbability of any classical city-state having a *monetary policy* in any respect. That phrase might conjure up modernizing images inconsonant with the regnant sensibility on ancient economic life. The "primitivist" spirit of much current interpretation is committed to emphasizing the disparities between Greek society and the modern "capitalist" order, while simultaneously stressing the analogies between the Greek economy and less differentiated, subsistence "peasant" economies.[1] To some interpreters of ancient economic life, the creation of an economic policy of any type would require the possession of an economic theory; to others it violates the principle that the ancient economy was "embedded" in contemporary social institutions.[2] Monetary policy might be taken to imply concerted efforts to promote the productivity of persons acting as private factors by manipulating characteristics of the monetary medium. Indeed, the most one would attribute to the makers of classical policy was an intention to facilitate *consumption* in an essential area like the procurement of foodstuffs.

The accidents of discovery of ancient documents inscribed on stone have permitted the epigraphists, numismatists, and political historians to wrest the subject of classical monetary policy away from the social and economic historians of antiquity. The former have interpreted the Coinage Decree, that great document that has been found in fragments

[1] On the continuing debate between "primitivists" and "modernists" (the two terms are meant neutrally and nonpejoratively here) on the nature of the ancient Greek economy, see E. Will, "Trois quarts de siècle sur l'économie grecque antique," *Annales* 9 (1954) 7–22; M.I. Finley (ed.), *The Bücher-Meyer Controversy* (New York 1979). See also Figueira, *Aegina* 13–18; Figueira, review of E.E. Cohen, *Athenian Economy and Society: A Banking Perspective* (Princeton 1992), *Bryn Mawr Classical Review* 5.2 (1994) 109–13.

[2] For a discussion of this terminology, see Figueira, "Karl Polanyi and Ancient Greek Trade: The Port of Trade," *Ancient World* 10 (1984) 15–30.

from sites within the fifth-century Attic *arkhē* and sphere of influence, as an instance of drastic intervention by the Athenians into the daily economic life of their allies—nothing less than a massive reshaping of the manner in which money was used in commerce and government in the whole Aegean basin.[3] Accordingly, the scholarly consensus exhibits little hesitation in coupling Attic monetary policy and fifth-century imperialism.[4]

Nonetheless, ambivalent points of view are vividly present in the controversies surrounding the Coinage Decree, for scholars have wavered in the face of choosing an appropriate etiology. Does monetary policy spring from observing and then conditioning economic behavior, or are the wellsprings of such decisions entirely partisan or ideological, with their ramifications for the daily business of life practically incidental? One baleful influence on ancient history of some Marxist interpretation in other historical fields—for Marxist analysis has seldom been applied systematically to the ancient world—is a legacy of economic determinism, even for philologically minded historians.[5] Attic monetary legislation could occupy a place of honor if one diligently prioritized economic factors in a hierarchy of causes, setting out on a search for the fundamental economic causation that shaped Athenian imperialism. That would, however, quickly become a disconcerting journey if one were then forced to conclude that the citizens of Periclean Athens showed their greatest awareness of economic conditions when they subordinated policy toward their allies to the pursuit of their own economic advantage. This posing of the problem has its own paradoxical air: by imputing economic considerations to fifth-century Athenian policy-makers, economic determinism is subverted, since we imply an articulated balancing of economic goods with other benefits. That is true unless we adduce a mode of false consciousness in which material factors win out despite the course of

[3] The term *arkhē* 'rule,' 'leadership,' or 'sway,' will be used for the allies whom the Athenians led militarily and whose foreign policy they directed, without prejudice to an assessment about the autonomy of the allies individually or in general (autonomy and coining will be addressed below). The intention is to avoid the more loaded term "empire," except where it cannot be avoided for the sake of general comprehension, as in my title. The term "hegemony" will used as an equivalent to *arkhē* as well as a convenient term for summarizing the authority exercised over the allies in the Delian League. I have not been so fastidious in my use of related adjectives; hegemonic and imperial are used as synonyms.

[4] Social historians have tended to follow the lead of the epigraphists and numismatists. They have filtered out some explanation of economic rationales with which they were uncomfortable in favor of raising the issues of the symbolism and the psychology of imperialism. See, for example, the summary by M.M. Austin and P. Vidal-Naquet, *Economic and Social History of the Ancient Greece* (Berkeley and Los Angeles 1977) 326–28.

[5] A fuller discussion of related issues (with citations) can be found in Figueira, "A Typology of Social Conflict in Greek Poleis," in A. Molho, K. Raaflaub, and J. Emlen (eds.), *City States in Classical Antiquity and Medieval Italy* (Stuttgart 1991) 289–307.

deliberation. Thus the reconstruction of Attic monetary policy forces us to classify the modes in which individual economic behavior and state decisions affect each other.

As so often in the investigation of ancient history, we do not have the evidence to analyze all the phenomena in this boundary zone between the private and public spheres. Nevertheless, the broadest canvas for the available evidence has not yet been essayed, that is, the investigation of the collective and individual decisions made by Athens and its allies about their use of money. The purpose of this work is to attempt to place the Coinage Decree within that framework of monetary policy in the fifth century. The results are notable not only for an appraisal of the Attic hegemony in the fifth century but also for the overarching questions of interpretation that have been raised in the preceding paragraphs (see pp. 227–39, 552–58 below).

THE COINAGE DECREE

The Coinage Decree is the name given to a piece of Athenian legislation that is attested by a group of partial inscriptions discovered over the last century in scattered locations.[6] An influential view propounded by that greatest of nineteenth-century German philologists, Ulrich von Wilamowitz-Moellendorff, held that the Coinage Decree was alluded to in the *Birds* of Aristophanes.[7] This supposition has pervasively conditioned interpretation and restoration of the epigraphical material. Von Wilamowitz-Moellendorff even suggested that he had predicted the existence of the decree attested by the fragments, basing himself on Aristophanes. This legislation is an interpretative mainstay in reconstructions of the evolution of Athenian hegemony over their allies in the Delian League during the Pentekontaeteia, the fifty-year period (as the Greeks referred to it conventionally) that lay between the defeat of Xerxes' invasion of the Greek homeland in 480–79 and the beginning of the Peloponnesian War in 431. Most scholars have evinced little doubt about its general significance. Athens had (perhaps by degrees) arrogated the

[6] For the sake of easy reference, we shall continue to use the denomination "Coinage Decree" (from *Münzgesetz*), despite the sensible appellation of this decree as the "standards decree" that is found most prominently and recently in M.H. Chambers, R. Gallucci, and P. Spanos, "Athens' Alliance with Egesta in the Year of Antiphon," *ZPE* 83 (1990) 38–57, esp. 55–56. The decree also involved the consolidation of metrological standards, but coinage remains its primary subject and thereby our unavoidable preoccupation. See pp. 263–64, 296–316 below.

[7] U. von Wilamowitz-Moellendorff, *Aus Kydathen* (Berlin 1880), *Philol. Untersuchungen* 1, 30–31 with note 56. See also Chapter 8 below.

supervision over a considerable range of the monetary and economic activities that had previously required the oversight of the officials of the allied cities.

The decree seems to have been the mechanism by which that imperial authority was consolidated. The cities belonging to the Delian League were the proud inheritors of traditions of coining in distinctive communal types. These advertisements of local pride, presumptive tokens of local autonomy, fell before the needs—be they perceived as commercial, administrative, or symbolic—of the hegemonic state. Not only did local silver issues lapse but allied states were compelled to abandon indigenous measures and weights, in a retreat on a wide front before an aggrandizement on behalf of Attic models and practices. The Coinage Decree belongs to a stage in the development of Attic imperialism when the role of Athens as *primus inter pares* in the Delian League had been left behind in favor of a blatant exultation in their state's power by the Athenian *dēmos* 'people.' Thus speaks the scholarly consensus.

Current Interpretations

An attentive and skeptical reader may already have recognized some discontinuities in this accepted interpretation, starting with disagreements on the rationale or motivations for this legislation. The very range of opinion becomes disquieting, for commentators will too readily reach the same conclusion, envisaging this legislation as an act of imperialism, from widely discrepant points of departure. The state of scholarship on monetary policy can be clarified if some categories of commentary on the Athenian *arkhē* are reviewed. Let us start by considering how the Coinage Decree is treated in three works on Greek history currently used in North America, starting with Russell Meiggs, who, in his revision of the venerable history of J.B. Bury, discusses the decree as follows (brackets in quotations mark my clarifications):[8]

> No less significant of Athens at this time [that is, during Periclean leadership in the early 440s] is a decree enforcing the use of Athenian coins, weights, and measures throughout the empire, and forbidding the minting of silver coins in allied cities, while allowing electrum coinages to be continued.[20] There had been an increasing tendency since the establishment of the Delian Confederacy for the smaller cities to adopt Athenian coinage with its wide commercial reputation, but many states still preferred to retain a coinage with their own state

[8] J.B. Bury and R. Meiggs, *A History of Greece to the Death of Alexander the Great*[4] (New York 1975) 226 (text); 533–34 (notes). J.V.A. Fine, *The Ancient Greeks: A Critical History* (Cambridge, Mass. 1983) 367, might also be noted.

> symbol. They were now forced to conform. Non-Attic coins were to be called in and brought to Athens to be reminted: henceforth Athenian coinage only was to be used. This sweeping act may have facilitated the development of trade in the Aegean, but it increased still further the economic dominance of the Piraeus. Silver for coinage could be secured at several points: Athenian coinage had to be bought with goods at Athens.

The note appended to Meiggs's first sentence, citing Meiggs-Lewis #45, makes three further points. First, the decree mentions silver coinage, while Cyzicene electrum staters are common from the second half of the fifth century. Their popularity in the Black Sea region may have privileged their continuation. Second, no exceptions are made among silver-minting states, so that the autonomous states of Samos, Chios, and Lesbos were included in the force of the decree. Finally, the date is controversial, but a date in the early 440s based on the Kos fragment in Attic lettering is widely preferred; it is also the better option—there was a dramatic increase in the minting of Attic tetradrachm coins around mid-century. The arguments for a later date, namely, that such strong imperialism is out of place before the death of Perikles and the epigraphical evidence from the other fragments, can be answered by noting that the 440s were the "critical period in the development of Athenian imperialism, when tough policies were deliberately pursued in order to prevent a dissolution of the alliance which peace with Persia might encourage." Difficulties may be resolved by opting for a decree of the early 440s that was revived in the late 420s (he notes the reference in Aristophanes' *Birds* 1040–41).

Raphael Sealey strikes only a slightly different note:[9] "at some time the Athenians passed a decree requiring the allies to use only Athenian coinage, weights and measures. Other coinage in circulation was to be brought to the mint at Athens and exchanged for Athenian coins." Sealey's discussion of the dating for the legislation starts with the allusion in the *Birds* and the letter forms of the Kos fragment, but he registers a reservation that "an argument which seeks to date an inscription from the forms of its letters has little force if it relies on the form of only one letter." Sealey raises the possibility that both the Coinage Decree and the Decree of Kleinias belong to the 420s. Yet, there is also stress on imperial control:

> The Coinage Decree speaks of Athenian supervisory officers as if they were commonly found in allied states. . . . It is possible . . . that Athens first sent out supervisory officers extensively after the Peloponnesian

[9] R. Sealey, *A History of the Greek City-States: ca. 700–338 B.C.* (Berkeley and Los Angeles 1976) 306.

> War began in 431. On the other hand, as Athens had to deal with widespread disaffection in the later years of the First Peloponnesian War [that is, the late 450s and early 440s], it is likely that Athenian officers were to be found in many cities of the Empire in the 440s.

The *World of Athens*, a background book for the Greek course of the Joint Association of Classical Teachers in Britain, opts for an early date and is firm on the decree's imperialism:[10]

> One final example of the politics of imperialism will illustrate both Athens' imperialistic mentality and at the same time the limits of Athenian imperial power. Somewhere between 450 and 446 (probably) Athens issued the so-called Coinage Decree, which sought to impose on the cities of the empire the use of Athenian coins, weights and measures to the exclusion of all others. The decree . . . has no very obvious economic significance for Athens. So the true significance of the decree is political: Athens further aimed to diminish her allies' sovereignty by removing their right to strike coins bearing the city's badge. However, archaeological evidence shows, the coinages of the allies were not all brought to a halt after 446. For whatever reasons, the decree was never fully enforced.

There is considerable common ground among these authorities (along with others who will be treated in Chapter 8), inasmuch as the decree is envisaged as a hegemonic measure that prohibited the allied minting of silver and usage of non-Athenian weights and measures and recalled allied coinage to Athens. There is disagreement whether the enactment had a constructive economic effect and thereby an economic rationale, but citing the benefits of monetary and metrological consolidation seldom exorcizes the imperialist aura surrounding the decree. Strangely, the Coinage Decree can be contributory to Athenian *and* allied economic gains through facilitation of trade, for example, but still bad because of its imperialistic purpose. Alternatively, the decree could advance economic interests of the Athenians exclusively and so be judged necessarily bad for this reason. Emphasis in general almost invariably falls on the Coinage Decree as a gambit in a struggle of political symbolism

[10] Joint Association of Classical Teachers' Greek Course Background Book, *The World of Athens: An Introduction to Classical Athenian Culture* (Cambridge 1984) 241. A similar approach is taken in the brief sketch of P.J. Rhodes, *The Athenian Empire* (Oxford 1985) 41: "states prevented from issuing their own coins and from using their own weights and measures (M&L 45) will have suffered a blow to their pride rather than to their economies . . . the use of the same coinage and standards in many states is likely to have encouraged trade among them, to the benefit of all."

over allied autonomy, because the supersession of traditional coin types dramatized Athenian domination.

In most general treatments, however, there is inevitably a discussion of (or, at least, a sidewards glance toward) the controversy whether the Coinage Decree is to be dated to the early 440s or the 420s. As shall be seen shortly, the emphasis on this debate mirrors epigraphical scholarship. Nonetheless, the dispute over chronology did not compel a reinterpretation of other aspects of the decree, a situation that is hardly surprising when one considers the views of H.B. Mattingly. He employed the decree as a centerpiece in his systematic efforts to redate a series of inscriptions dealing with Athenian jurisdiction over the allies to the period after the outbreak of the Peloponnesian War. Behind this effort is an intuitive judgment as to the degree to which Perikles and his associates practiced authoritarian hegemonism over the allied cities. That they would not have done so knits together the various direct arguments (not indeed necessarily insubstantial in themselves) for a late date for the decree. Mattingly has not appraised the legislation differently: "a political and imperial manifesto, a clear declaration of intent by Athens. . . . Here Athens was asserting its will, with no pretence of consultation, on the innermost territory of *polis* autonomy."[11]

Hence, where reservation on the historic role of the Coinage Decree is broached, it concerns chronology, or less frequently, a suggestion is made that the decree may not have been successfully enforced or did not achieve thorough compliance.[12] This discordant note is also struck above in the citation from the *World of Athens*, and it serves as one of the chief reservations that appears in the cautious discussion of D.M. Lewis in the second edition of the *Cambridge Ancient History*, the most prestigious overview of Greek history in English.[13] It has been on the basis of E.S.G. Robinson's study of the coinage of the allied states that such caution is customarily justified.[14] In *CAH*², the issue of the presence of Athenian

[11] H.B. Mattingly, "The Athenian Coinage Decree and the Assertion of Empire," in *Coinage and Administration* 65–71, esp. 65. See also that other prominent dissenter on chronology, Erxleben (*AfP* [1969] 162).

[12] See also D. Kagan, *The Outbreak of the Peloponnesian War* (Ithaca 1969) 116–17, who notes: "to be sure, the Athenians were unable to enforce this decree with total success." His treatment is otherwise close to the conventional interpretation, for he continues: "but the harshness of the language, the absence of reference to the alliance, the cool assumption that Athenian officials would be present in most cities show how far things had come since the settlement of Erythrae [in the 450s]."

[13] D.M. Lewis, "The Thirty Years' Peace," *CAH*² 5.121–46, esp. 130–31.

[14] "The Athenian Coinage Decree and the Coinages of the Allies," *Hesperia* Suppl. 8 (1949) 324–40.

officials in allied cities again provides a point of departure that leads into a discussion of the date, balancing *Birds* 1040–41 against the lettering of the Kos fragment. Nevertheless, Lewis characterizes the valence of the legislation in this way: "to forbid the allies to coin their own silver is clearly a political act of a fairly demonstrative nature." To the substantial credit of the author, he then goes beyond the usual to raise the subjects of "administrative convenience" and of exchange (see below, pp. 260–65).

One might expect to find in the major scholarly treatments of the Athenian *arkhē* the sustained investigations that would underpin the generalities that have been observed in the treatments aimed at a more general readership. That, however, is not the case. In Russell Meiggs's *Athenian Empire*, the familiar details are presented: allied mints are to close; non-Athenian money is to be reminted; a clause is to be added to the bouleutic oath punishing allied minting and any failure to use Athenian coins, weights, and measures; the ban did not extend to Cyzicene and Lampsacene electrum staters; and the ship-contributing allies were included in the prohibition.[15] The greater part of his discussion is devoted to a judicious summary of the question of chronology, with emphasis on the lettering of the Kos fragment and on W.K. Prichett's hypothesis concerning its inscription (see below, pp. 434–35, 449–51).[16] His brief judgment on the historical status of the decree deserves to be quoted for its distillation of prevailing views:[17]

> It issues sharp instructions and the Athenian officers overseas are to take the lead in seeing that they are carried out. There is no suggestion that Athens is thinking primarily of the good of the allies and that Attic coinage is being imposed on them all for their own economic benefit. The language leaves little doubt that the main interest is that of Athens; there is not the slightest hint that the allies have been consulted and the free threat of penalties seems to anticipate resistance. Perhaps Athens had various objects in mind. Uniformity of coinage over most of the Aegean would facilitate trade, and as Athens was the dominant trader she stood to gain most from the change. She would presumably attract more trade to the Piraeus, since Athens would in future exercise a monopoly in the issue of silver coinage, and cities and merchants who needed more coinage would find it convenient to bring goods to Athens to convert into Attic coins. Athens would also benefit when the tribute

15 Meiggs 168–69.

16 Meiggs 168–74. Numismatic support from Robinson and earlier authorities is adduced in corroboration (see below, pp. 49–51), and J.P. Barron's reconstruction of Samian politics and coining is recapitulated (pp. 166–74).

17 Meiggs 172–73. M.R. Cataudella, "Aspetti e strumenti della politica monetaria ateniese fra V e IV secolo," *Sileno* 12 (1986) 111–35, esp. 115–16, could also be cited.

> was paid only in Attic coin, apart perhaps from electrum staters; now that the principle had been decided to use League money for Athenian purposes most of the tribute would be spent in Athens, or at any rate paid to Athenians. We may also suspect that Athens was not thinking only in economic terms. The common Athenian coinage, together with the common obligations to the Great Panathenaea expressed the change from a Delian League to an Athenian Empire.

Note particularly the fusion of the ideas of selfish and altruistic economic motivations with the suspicion that an ideological goal was also in the minds of the Athenians.

In Wolfgang Schuller's useful overview of Athenian hegemony over their allies, the Coinage Decree is introduced to illustrate many specific details of Athenian imperial leadership. Here it is again useful to draw attention to the commonality of his general perspective with the material already discussed. Under the rubric "Leges generales," Schuller describes the decree:[18]

> und das Münze, Masse und Gewichte vereinheitlichte Münzgesetz ist das Musterbeispiel einer völlig einseitigen und ausserordentlich tief in die inneren Verhältnisse der Städte eingreifenden lex generalis
>
> and the Coinage Decree unifying coins, measures, and weights is the prime example of a general law, completely unilateral and interfering extraordinarily deeply in the internal affairs of the cities.

Problematical Perspectives

It is possible to place previous interpretations of the Coinage Decree along a spectrum, the poles of which are occupied respectively by economic and psychological motivations (see Chapter 9). Toward the "economic" pole are the sort of suggestions that were popular earlier in the century among scholars influenced by modern mercantilism. They held that the Athenians were creating an economic environment in the Aegean that favored their own mining industry or merchants to the disadvantage of others, whether allies or not. Thus, to Segre, the Coinage Decree is "un atto di imperialismo commerciale."[19] Others would see the economic motivations for Athenian monetary policy as serving the common good of the allies, but, as we have seen, they find imperialism elsewhere with their hints that, at the best, the Athenians sought an appropriate goal by improper means.

[18] Schuller, *Herrschaft* 107.

[19] From the first discussion of a mid-century date: M. Segre, "La legge Ateniese sull' unificazione della moneta," *ClRh* 9 (1938) 151–78, esp. 174.

More recent work has been less likely to see the Athenians making policy in order to favor the economic interests of private citizens. Where this scholarship discovers the influence of economic factors has been in the requirements of a hegemonic bureaucracy. These investigations focus attention on the streamlining effect for administration of forcing all the allies to deal in a single currency and to conduct business in Attic metrological standards, especially as a simplification for military procurement.[20] Still another variation on economic causation narrows the perspective to the subject of taxation. Accordingly, the Coinage Decree was meant to raise money by compelling the allies to exchange their own coins at the Athenian mint for Attic tetradrachms, which were called "owls" in the fifth century, a term that is also used now.[21] In this hypothesis, if all the silver coinage in circulation among the allies was at one time converted into Attic coins, the charges for minting could amount to a considerable sum.[22]

Contrasted with the hypotheses that envisage pragmatic motivations for the supersession of allied weights, measures, and coinage are interpretations in which it was the symbolic impact of the supersession that recommended the decree to the Athenians. If coinage is a form of coded political communication, the ubiquity of Attic coins manifested daily to the member states of the Athenian alliance the magnitude (even the universality) of Athenian authority. Conversely, the circulation of non-Athenian coins advertised that some activities were reserved for local prerogatives. The continuity of allied minting reminded cities like Samos and Aigina that they had themselves once been great commercial and thereby political powers. When the allies used coins that originated outside the *arkhē*, they were reminded that some entities of political and economic consequence still stood outside Athenian control.

Other medial positions lie along this simple continuum, and the mixed perspectives on Attic monetary legislation of the more general discussions, since they have not been subjected to extensive development, may intersect the spectrum at different points in the same explanation of the significance of this legislation. Notwithstanding the interpretative variety, their common appraisal should not be lost: for most scholars, a monopoly established among the allies for Attic weights, measures, and

20 For example, M.I. Finley, *The Ancient Economy* (Berkeley and Los Angeles 1973) 168–69; C.G. Starr, *Athenian Coinage: 480–449* B.C. (Oxford 1970) 69–70.

21 Philochorus *FGH* 328 F 200; Hesych. s.v. γλαῦκες Λαυριωτικαί, γ 615 Latte, cf. γ 610; *Suda* s.v. γλαὺξ ἵπταται, γ 282 Adler; Phot. s.v., γ 130 Th.; Lucian, *Nigrin.* "Prolog."; Schol. ΣArist. *Knights* 1093, *Birds* 301, 1106.

22 Note T.R. Martin, *Sovereignty and Coinage in Classical Greece* (Princeton 1985) 196–207.

coins deliberately marked a great symbolic watershed and dramatized the Athenian monopolization of political and military power in their alliance.

Much of the discussion below will thrash out the disagreements with the general interpretation. Suffice it to say here that it is disconcerting that an enactment dated to two contexts twenty or more years apart has the same valence under either chronology. Epistemological discomfort would persist even if we could convince ourselves that one chronology must be ruled entirely outside the bounds of probability. The gamut of motivations applied to the Coinage Decree provokes similar disquiet. Since scholars have not conclusively opted to consider its cause a hard-headed desire for material advantage, or, conversely, pure propaganda about the unquestioned supremacy of the Athenian *dēmos*—to posit just two rather polarized positions—certainly one should ask whether scholarship has not also missed something vital in the very significance of this law amid our vacillations over causation. Causations and rationales have seldom been analyzed systematically, and generalities and sketchiness prevail concerning the political function and economic context of monetary administration. Indeed, the early commentators on the epigraphical evidence staked out most of the historical interpretative positions still current in recent scholarship.

This scholarly consensus will be subjected to thorough criticism in the chapters below, but not because it is upheld foolishly. The reader must determine whether the traditional interpretation of the Coinage Decree should be discarded and then whether it should be replaced with the "revisionist" view proposed below. A few words are, however, appropriate on the tenacity of the received paradigm. Section xii of the Coinage Decree (following the division below) contains a clause that was added to the oath of the Attic Boulē or Council of the 500.

> xii. προσγράψαι δὲ πρὸς τὸν ὅρκον [τ]ὸν τῆς βολῆς τὸν γραμμάτεα τῆς [βολῆς τα]δί· ἐάν τις κόπτηι νόμισ[μα] ἀργυρίο ἐν τῆσι πό[λεσι κ]αὶ μὴ χρῆται νομ[ίσμασιν τοῖς] Ἀθη[να]ίων ἢ σταθμοῖς ἢ μέτ[ροις ἀλλὰ ξενικοῖς νομίσμασι]ν καὶ σταθμοῖς καὶ μέτροις, [τιμωρήσομαι καὶ ζημιώσω κατὰ τὸ πρότε]ρον ψήφισμα ὁ Κλέαρχ[ος εἶπεν]
>
> The Secretary of the Boulē is to add to the oath of the Boulē the following: if anyone mints silver coinage in the cities and does not use the coins or the weights or the measures of the Athenians [but foreign?] coins and weights and measures, [I shall punish him?] according to the earlier decree that Klearkhos proposed.

Those familiar with the conventions of epigraphical typography will note that the crucial words are a restoration. It is not difficult to appreciate how this conjecture of the first editors has been preserved so doggedly, as it was initially endorsed by epigraphists and philologists whose mastery of their subject exemplified the highest standards. Yet, uncertainty exists whether or not at least equally valid restorations of the same lacunae are possible. And any divergence from the received text has enormous ramifications.

As restored, this clause embodies a commitment by the councillors to take punitive action that seemed to be echoed elsewhere in the enactment. In fact, much will be said below about the tone of the provisions of the decree, especially in criticism of their supposed peremptory nature. Nonetheless, the threats of punishment for disobedience confirmed for the earlier commentators the validity of their approach to restoration, constituting the primary incentive for characterizing the decree as an act of imperialism.

Section xii has already been presented. Adding a clause to the bouleutic oath seems prima facie a serious step, and there is no way to determine the severity of the penalties that Klearkhos proposed. Next consider section viii in one version of the traditional restoration:

> viii. καὶ ἐάν τις εἴπηι ἢ] ἐπιψηφίσηι περ[ὶ τούτων ὅτι ἔστι ξενικῶι νομίσμα]τι χρῆσθαι ἢ δαν[είζεν, ἀπογραφέσθω αὐτίκα μάλα πρὸς] τοὺς ἕνδεκα· οἱ δ[ὲ ἕνδεκα θαν]άτωι ζ[ημιώσαντων· ἐὰν] δὲ ἀμφισβητῆι, ἐσ[αγαγόντων ἐς τὸ δικαστήρ]ιον.
>
> And if anyone proposes or puts to vote concerning [these matters that it is possible] to utilize foreign coinage or put out at loan, let him immediately be haled before the Eleven. The Eleven should punish him with death, but if he disputes his guilt, let them bring him before a dicasteric court.

So conventional thinking on the decree held that clause viii established the penalty of death for the usage of non-Athenian silver. Here again, however, the solidity of the restored text is deceptive. D.M. Lewis has shown that clause viii does not refer to allied offences in coining and utilizing non-Athenian coinage, but protects from tampering a fund of money in an "entrenchment clause" that has parallels in other Athenian legislation.[23] Once more, leaving the received text has a tremendous impact.

The traditional restorations underpin the conclusion that the achievement of metrological and monetary supremacy constituted a serious goal of Attic foreign policy. Many scholars of the decree apply its features

[23] D.M. Lewis, "Entrenchment-Clauses in Attic Decrees," in D.W. Bradeen and M.F. McGregor (eds.), ΦΟΡΟΣ: *Tribute to Benjamin Dean Meritt* (Locust Valley, NY 1974) 81–89.

(including the provisions for punishment) even to the autonomous, ship-contributing allies such as Samos, Chios, and the cities of Lesbos. The Coinage Decree would then be the most potent symbol of a transformed balance of power between Athens and the Delian League. To be sure, the authorities cited above were tempted by the possibility of altruistic reasons for the Coinage Decree based on economic factors, by envisaging the law as a measure to promote Aegean trade through simplifying both exchange and the terms of commerce. Not only, however, did this reaction collide with more cynical readings of the nature of Athenian leadership, but more significantly, it foundered on the gravity of the penalties supposedly imposed for disobedience and on the degree of intrusiveness implied by the scope of the decree's application. It remains to be seen whether other approaches to restoration can lead interpretation elsewhere.

Early students of this legislation did, however, sometimes evaluate the Coinage Decree as a stage in an extended sequence of Attic monetary laws affecting allied cities. The discarding of this position is not merely a function of the passage of time in which other examples of such lawmaking failed to appear. We do indeed have one prominent later discovery, the very fragmentary *IG* I^3 90, and epigraphical traces of postulated laws preceding 450 could not be anticipated with any assurance. Rather the Coinage Decree had become the standard corroborating item in a dramatization of a mid-century transformation of the Delian League into the Athenian Empire in the reconstruction of the Attic hegemony proposed in the influentual *Athenian Tribute Lists* (= *ATL*). Accordingly, the majority of comment on the decree now envisages it as a crucial watershed and the decisive act of Athenian legislation in its area of administration.

Impact on Epigraphy and Numismatics

Since the Coinage Decree stands at the moment of transformation of Attic hegemony, it is unsurprising that it has greatly affected epigraphical and numismatic scholarship on the fifth century. Two interrelated questions project the influence of the traditional interpretation throughout these two disciplines: a determination of the chronology of the surviving inscriptions (especially the fragment from Kos) and the identification of a break in allied coining that would correspond with the passage of the decree. Although other epigraphical arguments have been occasionally brought to bear, scholarly discussion has remained frustratingly fixed on the question whether the appearance of three-barred *sigmas* in the Kos fragment necessitates that this inscription and the promulgation of the Coinage Decree must antedate ca. 446. A group of other documents, rather like satellites in the grip of a larger body, can shift their chronology in consort with the Coinage Decree.

A second, numismatic axis along which investigation of the law has proceeded has probed the question whether clear traces of its impact can be found in the sequences of coining by mints within the Athenian *arkhē*. Although the mandating of weights, measures, and coins involves an imposition of Attic standards in each case, archaeological scholarship on metrology has heavily emphasized coinage (hence "Coinage Decree" or *Münzgesetz*). It is not hard to understand why this has been true in superficial terms. By their intrinsic worth, by their beauty (very often), and by their historical referentiality, coins attract much more attention than the other artifacts that may have been affected by this legislation. The small size and value of coins led to hoarding and thereby survival—not only in antiquity but thereafter. Common sense urges too that many more coins always existed (and will now survive) than, for example, commercial weights, another class of contemporary artifact. Coins are also items rich in information, archaeological, metrological, iconographic, symbolic, and bureaucratic. Naturally, a determination of the point in time for a hypothetical general cessation of coining has a bearing on a decision about the date for the imposition of Attic weights, measures, and standard of coinage, if again, that is taken to be its purpose. The evidence from coinage then would do duty for the entire series of administrative and economic changes set in motion by the decree.

Surveys of mints have attempted to verify one or another chronology for this legislation, and they have also sought to apply the prohibition enacted by the decree as a key distinction for unlocking the numismatic history of much of the fifth century. Numismatists have eagerly embraced the prospect that most allied mints could be divided into two phases, one before an interruption ca. 446 or ca. 425 and another, later period sometime thereafter (whether after the beginning of the Peloponnesian War, after the Syracusan debacle, or after the fall of Athens). Hence, even the most careful and detailed studies of particular mints have not been immune to the influence of the traditional paradigm on the contents, tone, and chronology of the Coinage Decree. As so often in ancient historical studies, where our evidence is imperfect, a circularity of explanation is prominent.

THE PLAN OF THIS WORK

This work argues that the traditional interpretation of the famous—or infamous—Attic Coinage Decree is inadequate in several crucial regards. In addition to the foregoing observations (especially concerning scholarly ambivalence on economic benefits and disadvantages), we note here the absence in the surviving sources of denunciations of the Coinage Decree as an instrument of imperialism. No speaker in Thucydides, for example, either condemns or defends Athenian monetary legislation. No Isocratean passage either apologetically casts the decree in defensible terms or deprecates it as an excess of the fifth-century democracy. Our one possible extant literary reference is an Aristophanic *joke* (*Birds* 1040–41; discussed in Part II).[24] The provisions of the fragments of the decree will be subjected to a thorough reinvestigation (in Part IV) and will yield important new clues to the contents and historical setting of Attic monetary legislation. For example, an examination of the surviving provisions of the decree will lead to substantial doubts about the decree's enactment of a prohibition on minting.

As a presumptive threshold in the exertion of Athenian control over the allies, this enactment is usually assumed to have had far-reaching ramifications, which we ought to be able to detect through archaeological data. Instead we shall discover that the monetary and metrological history (as far as the latter can be determined) of the fifth century appears to reflect a complexity of practices that look for all the world like the result of the manifold decisions of many political agents and do not demonstrably mirror an imposition of a single pattern, the result of an act of a hegemonic authority. As research has matured, the prospect of a single, dramatic numismatic or metrological boundary in the evidence has receded. We shall consider attempts to impose just such a single order on the archaeological evidence, but such simplification not only seems contestable in detail, but also wrong intuitively.

In contrast to earlier work, I shall also argue that the Coinage Decree was not an enactment that worked to any marked parochial advantage of the Athenians. Nor did it constitute a major tightening of imperial control to the disadvantage of the allies. Rather, as so often with economic legislation in Greek antiquity, economic conditions themselves promoted the likely provisions of the decree and of its forerunners in Athenian legislation—for after this analysis we can then admit the possibility of their existence. Consequently, this psephism probably acted to codify and order prevailing circumstances or to encourage their more desirable features. Therefore the Coinage Decree was no more or less advantageous to the Athenians or to their allies than the underlying monetary circumstances conditioning their policies. The system for the levying of

24 On the lack of references, compare for a start Martin, *Sovereignty* 206–207.

the tribute was the most important of these, and it probably had no small part in the creation of the Coinage Decree.

An examination of contexts in which the adoption of Attic standards could be significant helps us understand that we need not expect a total (or nearly complete) curtailment of allied minting in silver. Those ancient enemies of the Athenians, the Aiginetans, for instance, who might be expected to have been gravely affected by Attic monetary legislation, seem to have continued to mint throughout the period 457–31.[25] Nor is it necessary to adduce inveterate recalcitrance or some special dispensation in order to explain the phenomenon of continued Aiginetan minting or to account for the other cities that seem to have persisted in minting their own coins. Economic conditions provide an adequate understanding for this continuity.

Three types of source material can be brought to bear on the political history of money in the fifth century: literary, epigraphical, and archaeological. A case could probably be argued for taking up their exploration in any order, for none is methodically prior. I have tried to resist throughout the pretence that my discussion of any of these three areas could be uncontaminated by my interpretations in the others. The synthesis I reach below, whether *ignis fatuus* or flash of insight, informs its constituent elements in an investigative environment very poor in data. I have tried to provide as many cross references as feasible so that the reader may attempt his or her own ordering of the discussion.

I start with an exploration of the numismatic evidence on monetary practices during the fifth-century Attic hegemony (Part I). The reference of Aristophanes to Attic monetary legislation or diplomacy in *Birds* 1040–41 is then considered (Part II). By that point, I believe, the evidentiary bases for traditional views on the Coinage Decree will have been considerably undermined. From this cleared ground, the contours of a different topography for fifth-century monetary history will have begun to emerge. Before proceeding to an investigation of the epigraphical evidence, I thought it prudent to discuss the economic and fiscal environment in which Athenian policy was formulated, based on my readings of the numismatic and literary evidence (Part III). This approach has the advantage that it establishes a basis for integrating the evidence from metrological history in order to offer a combined monetary *and* metrological causation. Nevertheless, in the interests of an orderly discussion of theories on the background for Athenian monetary legislation,

[25] The brief discussion in Figueira, *Excursions* 288–92, previewed pp. 116–27 below.

successively commercial, fiscal, symbolic, and administrative rationales for the Coinage Decree will be explored in this part of the work.

The discussion of the fragments of the Coinage Decree has always been a process extremely sensitive to the assumptions with which the material has been approached. Those assumptions need to be evaluated and, to be frank, culled to establish a framework for an analysis of the inscriptions. Nonetheless, I believe that the epigraphical commentary on the fragments of the Coinage Decree (in Part IV) can be read independently of my reconstruction of its historical context. Two types of picture with varying degrees of sharpness emerge from that commentary. Some conclusions belong to a rougher-grained view of Attic monetary policy that derives from a close reading of the fragments in isolation. Compared to this conservative vision of the Decree is a finer-grained picture of a restored and recontextualized Coinage Decree seen through the lens provided by my treatment in Part III. A synthetic portrait of monetary consolidation closes out this work as Part V. Here it will be important to balance the monetary system of the *arkhē*, however imperfectly it is visualized, with its unraveling at the end of the fifth century.

PART I

NUMISMATIC EVIDENCE FOR MONETARY POLICY

1

NUMISMATIC BASICS AND HOARD EVIDENCE

THE EVIDENCE of coins can be used in several modes of analysis. One emphasizes the issues of a particular mint, whose coins reveal data about the circumstances of their issuance. The weight of coins can tell us about the standard that minters intended to embody, and this standard in turn may be revelatory about the coins of other mints that were meant to circulate in some conjunction with the issues in question. The fidelity of mints to underlying standards may be indicative of the presence of fiscal exigencies that could lead to underweight coins. Some underweight coining indicates value that government guarantees sought to add. Weight is also suggestive of wear, a factor witnessed by other physical qualities, all of which may provide material in two important areas, namely, the availability of newer coins and factors militating in favor of a coin being withdrawn from circulation by an ancient user. In addition, different denominations functioned in differing economic settings, so that the history of the range of denominations, or the relative proportions in emission between denominations, becomes significant.

The iconography of coin types can speak directly to the political situation through its allusiveness, while other features of design—such as the names of officials, letter sequences, and other symbols—may also reflect the administration of minting. Coin types are works of artistic representation whose esthetics may be studied both for art historical conclusions and for implications as to chronology and sequencing of issues. Countermarks created by punches are additions to coins made after striking. Notoriously elusive in interpretation, countermarking implies the existence of reviews and validations, which were memorialized in the countermarks, intended to affect the utilization of circulating coins.

Individual coins are the products of application to metal blanks of fixed obverse (anvil) and reverse (punch) dies that bore the hammer's impact. When a pair of coins shares the same die, die links are established, the study of which provides invaluable hints about not only the order of issues but also the percentage of coins that has survived from specific emissions. That proportion then permits estimations of the monetary output for a series or even for an entire mint. Sometimes the materials used in coining were not blanks but already minted coins (a process termed overstriking). Overstrikes offer information about the relationships of series and mints as well as hinting at mint administration.

A second mode of analysis explores coin aggregations, which are commonly called hoards (without respect to the intention or motivation of those who accumulated, placed, or abandoned them). Studying the composition of hoards allows for a chronological juxtaposition of the products of different mints. Hoards naturally reflect current or past circulation but do not necessarily provide a direct indication of the coins in usage in the local economy. The rationale by which the hoarder included any coin in an assemblage may vary from an automatic incorporation of items in near proportion to their appearance in the local market. The reconstruction of such rationales is thoroughly speculative in nature.

To portray the numismatic history of each city within the Athenian *arkhē* would be a colossal task, one probably impossible based on the present data. It is, however, uncertain whether any significant results for our purposes would justify either an exhaustive exploration of the archaeological record of each ally or an art historical evaluation of every allied coin. The latter task is (in any case) seriously complicated by such influences as esthetic or patriotic conservatism and archaizing. Our purposes are best served by examining the way the allies used money and by trying to account for the major thresholds in mint activity: the beginnings, terminations, and suspensions of minting; changes in standards and in the denominations being struck; and other significant demarcations in the emissions of individual mints. We shall start from the evidence provided by the hoards and then consider allied mints as they are grouped by numismatic and monetary phenomena. It turns out that redating a few series of coins would not change the basic conclusions about monetary policy and the nature of the Coinage Decree to be reached below.

Numismatists studying individual mints often account for changes in coining by relating them to political events. Such explanations seldom command much credence, because so little is usually known about the internal history of individual allied cities during the Attic hegemony. Moreover, an intrinsic flaw may lie at the heart of such "parochial" analysis because of its assumption that changes in minting are mainly driven by the interplay of politicians and factions, by constitutional changes or by the status of the relationship between an ally and the Athenians. If the dominant numismatic trend of the whole period after the defeat of Xerxes in 480–79 is discovered to be monetary consolidation through cessation or limitation of minting, more attention will have to be given to the general economic, and specifically fiscal, factors that promoted usage of nonlocal money (including Attic coins) in so many places.

In contrast, earlier students of Attic monetary legislation, and the Coinage Decree in particular, sought to find a temporal threshold in the record of minting that would solidify a date for a prohibition of allied minting in the decree, a chronology that they had also derived from epigraphical and literary evidence. Barring that optimal result, students of the Coinage Decree sought an interruption of minting that was experienced by a majority or a cross section of allied cities. In this reasoning, even ineffectual legislation could thus be considered to have left its mark on the archaeological material. In point of fact, the contradictory results of such analyses reveal that we risk finding more than one such threshold and facing the impalatable prospect of hypothesizing several rounds of nearly identical legislation, all partially ineffective.

Supporting the traditional interpretation of the Coinage Decree (and other similar legislation) as a prohibition on allied minting is a challenging exercise, much more demanding than has usually been conceded, inasmuch as the continuation of even a few series after the promulgation of a ban threatens the hypothesis. Accounting for such exceptions quickly leads to a gamut of special pleadings. Not only are such explanations often disturbingly ad hoc but they beg a very large question, whether Attic legislation (as a subcategory of political etiology) was the predominant cause for changes in allied minting practices as compared to the aforesaid economic or fiscal forces working directly on allied governments.

We must tweak a virtuous methodology out of a lamentable dearth of evidence. We lack the source material either to illuminate interstate trade and exchange or to investigate the actual status of the local money supplies. Because we shall never recreate the intuitive cost-and-benefit analysis of individual decisions about whether or not to coin, what denominations and what amounts were to be coined, and on what standard coins were to be struck, we are forced toward aggregate explanations—global rationales for a group of cities making the same decision about consolidating monetary and metrological standards at approximately the same time. That compulsory level of generality, however, may well fit a synthetic and synoptic investigation.

FIFTH-CENTURY COIN HOARDS

Let us start with an overview of the known coin hoards relevant to the period under our consideration.[1] There are in all 264–74 hoards containing

[1] My material has been compiled from M. Thompson, O. Mørkholm, and C.M. Kraay (eds.), *An Inventory of Greek Coin Hoards* (New York 1973); *Coin Hoards* 1–8 (1975–1994), and checked against E. Schönert-Geiss, "Die Geldzirkulation Attikas," *Klio* 56 (1974) 377–413 (note

Greek coins that are dated to the period 480–400 or, alternatively, are described as "classical" in *An Inventory of Greek Coin Hoards* or the fascicles of *Coin Hoards* and arguably belong to the fifth century.[2] Of these perhaps 147–75 were discovered on the territories of Greek *poleis* (if we set aside the Cypriot hoards).[3] There are just 43 hoards buried within the probable boundaries of the *arkhē* or within Attica, a number much less than might be expected given the population and wealth of the *arkhē*.[4] Most of the territory under Attic hegemony was less likely to experience hostile incursions during this period than before or after, although hostilities intensified as the century advanced. Thus the substantial group of hoards that were laid down in crisis and to which their owners were stopped from returning owing to military circumstances is perhaps less well represented in the Aegean during the Pentekontaeteia, the Archidamian War, and the Peace of Nikias (479–13). Therefore, the state of the hoard evidence lowers the expectation that dramatic proof

---

her earlier study: "Die Geldzirkulation Attikas im 4. Jahrhundert v. u. Z.," in E.C. Welskopf (ed.), *Hellenische Poleis* 1 [Berlin 1974] 531–50). See also C. Ehrhardt, "Greek Treasure Trove: Hoards and Hoarders," *NZNJ* 13 (1975) 169–73; M. Schoenhammer, "Some Thoughts on the Athenian Coinage Decree," in T. Hackens and G. Moucharte (eds.), *Proceedings of the XI International Numismatic Congress* 1 (Louvain-la-Neuve 1993) 187–91, esp. 187–88. The dates of hoards follows the chronology of *IGCH* and *CH*, unless specified otherwise.

[2] *IGCH* #13–44, #357–60, #695–713, #995–1003, #1178–99, #1234–36, #1250–56, #1272–77, #1481–84, #1644–48, #1881–1907, #2068–2113, #2259–60, #2310, #2352–53; *CH* 1.6–8, 10–15, 17–21; *CH* 2.13, 15–31; *CH* 3.5, 9–14; *CH* 4.9–10, 12–17; *CH* 5.2–4, 6–15; *CH* 6.4–5, 7–10; *CH* 7.12–26; *CH* 8.24, 39, 41, 46–48, 50–54, 56–59, 63–69, 71–73, 74. Hoards that are probably of the relevant period: *CH* 8.25–29, 33, 62. Note the following correspondences: *CH* 1.19 = *IGCH* #1904, 1.21 = *IGCH* #1255; *CH* 2.16 = *IGCH* #2088, 2.17 = *IGCH* #1644, 2.22 = *IGCH* #1905, 2.25 = *IGCH* #997, 2.31 = *CH* 1.17; *CH* 3.8 = *IGCH* #2352, 3.12 = *CH* 1.25; *CH* 4.13 = *IGCH* #1875 = *CH* 5.4, 4.16 = *CH* 3.14; *CH* 5.3 = *CH* 3.18, 5.7 = *CH* 1.13, 5.8 = *IGCH* #2078, 5.11 = *CH* 1.25; *CH* 7.13 = *IGCH* #13, 7.20 = *IGCH* #1179, 7.21 = *IGCH* #1184, 7.22 = *IGCH* #46; *CH* 8.30 = *IGCH* #1221, 8.34 = *IGCH* #362, 8.40 = *CH* 1.6, 8.42 = *IGCH* #1272, 8.43 = *IGCH* #1277, 8.44 = *IGCH* #1644, 8.49 = *IGCH* #1184, 8.55 = *CH* #7.17, 8.74 = *IGCH* #42. Following are possible linkages: *CH* 7.18 = *IGCH* #2073, 7.23 = *IGCH* #2103, 7.26 = *IGCH* #30.

[3] *IGCH* #13–44, #357–60; #696–99, #700(?), #710, #995–98, #1001–1003, #1179–80, #1182(?), #1183–88, #1189–90(?), #1191–95, #1196(?), #1198, #1199(?), #1254, #1881, #1882–83 (?), #1884–85, #1886–87(?), #1888–90, #1891(?), #1892–93, #1894(?), #1895–1902, #1904, #1906–1907, #2067–68, #2070, #2072, #2077–79, #2081, #2083–86, #2087(?), #2088–93, #2094(?), #2095–97, #2098(?), #2100–2104, #2105(?), #2106, #2107(?), #2108, #2110, #2111(?), #2113; *CH* 1.8–12, 1.13(?), 1.15(?), 1.18–19; *CH* 2.13, 2.16, 2.19–20, 2.23(?); 2.24–25, 2.26(?), 2.29–31; *CH* 3.5, 3.9–13; *CH* 4.10(?), 4.17(?); *CH* 5.2(?), 5.6, 5.7(?), 5.8–14; *CH* 6.9; *CH* 7.13–14, 7.17–18(?), 7.19–24, 7.26; *CH* 8.24, 8.41, 8.47, 8.50, 8.53, 8.63, 8.66, 8.69, 8.72.

[4] *IGCH* #13–14, #16, #26, #31, #32, #39, #42, #357–60, #696–699, #710, #1179–80, #1183–88, #1191–95, #1198; *CH* 1.18; *CH* 2.20, 2.24; *CH* 3.5, 3.9; *CH* 4.14; *CH* 6.9; *CH* 7.13–14, 7.20–22; *CH* 8.47(?), 8.50, 8.63, 8.69, 8.72(?). Note *CH* 7.13 = *IGCH* #13; 7.20 = #1179; 7.21 = #1184; 7.22 = #1184.

will be found for a hypothetical prohibition on minting or for any other item of monetary policy. Let us take a closer look at what the hoards can actually teach us.

Kraay observed a generation ago that hoards tended to be composed from coinages of their own region.[5] Coins were most valuable near their point of origin where they could be used for the most transactions including the payment of taxes. Coins tended to gravitate back to their place of issuance and to the region surrounding the political zones where they had their most solid standing in law. Coins were often minted below weight from the standpoint of the equivalent standard used for commercial weights (that is, the weight or stathmic standard).[6] This discrepancy was a part of the token value of coins where they had legal standing. Elsewhere smaller stocks of foreign coins were held by those who might use them for exchange or trade. Individuals held reserves of foreign coins, either treated as bullion or to be used abroad for trade, for travel, or for emergencies. Some odd or old coins may have settled into hoards deposited for the most extreme emergencies because they lacked any other easy utilization and were held virtually as bullion. The term "fractional coins" or "fractions" is used below for denominations less than the drachma. Such coins are systematically less well represented in the hoards, one assumes by virtue of the bias of hoarders.[7]

The Greek Colonial World and Its Hinterlands

West Greek hoards illustrate this phenomenon of localism particularly well, as so many contain issues exclusively from Magna Graecia.[8] North

[5] C.M. Kraay, "Hoards, Small Change and the Origin of Coinage," *JHS* 84 (1964) 76–91.

[6] See Figueira, *Excursions* 66–77.

[7] See, most recently, the overview of D. Bérend, "Réflexions sur les fractions du monnayage grec," in A. Houghton, S. Hurter, P.E. Mottahedeh, and J.A. Scott (eds.), *Festschrift für Leo Mildenburg* (Wetteren 1984) 7–30. Although long victims of neglect both by collectors and scholars, fractions are being increasingly studied and published, an evolution aided by the more careful attention paid to them in excavations, and perhaps by a greater use of metal detectors.

[8] Note *IGCH* #1881–98, #1900–1904 (#1904 = *CH* 1.19), #1906, #2067–70, #2072–91 (#2078 = *CH* 5.8; #2088 = *CH* 2.16), #2093–4, #2097, #2099–2102, #2104–13; *CH* 1.10; *CH* 2.19; *CH* 2.29–30; *CH* 3.13 (= *CH* 5.4); *CH* 4.14; *CH* 5.9, 12, 13; *CH* 7.17–18, 23; *CH* 8.46, 8.51, 8.56, 8.64(?), 8.66. The uniformity of these hoards' contents can be relieved by odd items like the group of Pegasi of Corinth and her colonies in *IGCH* #2098 or the coins of Corinth or Leukas in a small hoard (8+), *CH* 5.6, "Catania, 1978." An excellent overview of some of this material is offered by C. Arnold-Biucchi, *The Randazzo Hoard 1980 and Sicilian Chronology in the Early Fifth Century* B.C., *Numismatic Studies* 18, American Numismatic Society (New York 1990) 39–47.

African and Spanish hoards are also dominated by western Greek coins.[9] The presence of a small proportion of Athenian coins in some of these hoards results from several factors.[10]

Attic tetradrachms were a medium for the export of silver from Laureion, and a vast number were in circulation in the Aegean, the primary area of their currency or validity. Hence a certain degree of seepage into regions where they did not perform the role of a primary medium for local business might be expected. This judgment does not mean that merchants and other travelers leaving the Aegean did not at times carry resources westward in the form of Attic money, but these *individual* case histories of assemblages of coins are almost irrecoverable.[11] The relative, general absence of Attic coins merely indicates that the mechanisms for both the conversion of these coins into those more easily used in the west and the recirculation of the same Attic money back to its primary area of circulation were efficient enough that only a few coins that had moved westward found their way into local hoards.[12] Attic and other exotic coins stayed in the orbit of the *agora*, and in the possession of those most involved with its activities.[13] In this case, the underlying economic interaction between

[9] Classical hoards from Tunisia, Malta, and Spain share a similar pattern: *IGCH* #2259 (with Attic tetradrachms), #2260, and #2310. The admittedly fifth-century hoard from El Arahal near Seville (450–400) is western Greek in content (*IGCH* #2310). The earliest Spanish hoards with Athenian money are *IGCH* #2313 and #2315, which should be dated in the fourth century. Cf. Schönert-Geiss *Klio* (1974) 379.

[10] Cf. *IGCH* #1899, #1905 (= *CH* 2.22), #1907, #2071, #2089; *CH* 8.24. Cf. *IGCH* #2065, #2066 (with sizable Attic components). See K. Rutter, "Athens and the Western Greeks in the Fifth Century B.C.: The Numismatic Evidence," in *Kraay-Mørkholm Essays* 245–57.

[11] Note K. Rutter, "Early Greek Coinage and the Influence of the Athenian State," in B. Cunliffe (ed.), *Coinage and Society in Britain and Gaul: Some Current Problems* (London 1981) 1–9, esp. 4–5, who marks the appearance of Akanthian coins (in the absence of other northern Aegean mints) alongside Attic tetradrachms in *IGCH* #2065, #2066, two pre-classical hoards, as well as in #2071. This suggests a narrow and special line of conveyance westward, at least to these hoarders, for both these Attic and Akanthian coins. See also Schönert-Geiss *Klio* (1974) 380, 402.

[12] For my earlier thoughts on the constitution and abandonment of hoards, see *Aegina* 139–44.

[13] Suggestive exceptions to this general observation are provided by two large hoards that belong to the late archaic period, before the inception of the Delian League. *IGCH* #1874, "Taranto, 1911" (ca. 508), is a hoard of ca. 600 coins from ca. 28 mints, including seven northern Aegean mints and seven Aegean or Ionian mints, with Aigina, Athens, and Corinth. See E. Babelon, "Trouvaille de Tarente," *RN*[4] 16 (1912) 1–40. The second hoard is *CH* 8.35, "Selinunte, 1985" (ca. 490), with 170+ coins, including thirty-nine Corinthian and eighty Aiginetan coins. See C. Arnold-Biucchi, L. Beer-Tobey, and N.M. Waggoner, "A Greek Archaic Silver Hoard from Selinus," *ANSMN* 33 (1988) 1–35. *IGCH* #1874 may be the holdings of a merchant, silversmith, or money changer, someone who drew on the wider range of coins brought to southern Italy before their recirculation eastward. *CH* 8.35 indicates the

the west and the *arkhē* is essentially invisible monetarily and so of no use in reading the record of mint activity within the *arkhē*. The Attic coins that appear in hoards of the end of the century were carried west by the Athenian military during the Sicilian campaign, and not by travelers or traders, thus creating a phenomenon visible in the aggregate.[14]

A slightly different pattern of the circulation of coinage may prevail for southern France in places lying within the area of commercial activity centering on Massilia. This city was probably the western terminus of a nonintermediated trade route, the other end of which lay (at first) in Ionia (perhaps at Phokaia). The classical hoards from Auriol (*IGCH* #2352: 470–60 = *CH* 3.8, 5.5) and from Ollioules (#2353: ca. 470–60), and *CH* 8.64, "South France, 1982/83" (ca. 425) are mainly constituted from a characteristic coinage with Ionian affiliations that may have been issued by a number of mints, one of which was almost certainly Massilia.[15] The hoard of "Volterra, Etruria, 1868" (ca. 475) shows the penetration of this coinage into northern Italy, reminding us that the northern coasts of the Tyrrhenian Sea may have shared a similar pattern for the circulation of goods (*CH* 4.13 = *IGCH* #1875 = *CH* 5.4).

The northern Aegean and its Balkan hinterland reveal only some similarities with Magna Graecia in the constitution of coin hoards. This region, where land communications played a relatively greater role, was more compartmentalized economically. The composition of hoards in the north reflects the circumstances of Greek settlement in the region: except in the Chalcidice, *poleis* were located on the relatively narrow littoral fronting a large, barbarian (mainly Thracian) hinterland to which

---

commercial conveyance of Aiginetan and Corinthian coins to Selinos, a site that played an important role in intermediation between the Aegean and the western Mediterranean.

[14] *IGCH* #1910, "Vito Superiore" (ca. 387); #1911, "Reggio, 1913" (ca. 387); #2092, "Selinunte, 1885" (ca. 409); #2095, "Scornavache, 1949" (ca. 405–400); #2096, "Schiso" (ca. 403); #2103, "Falconera" (ca. 400?); #2114, "Campobello di Licata" (400–390?); #2117, "Lentini" (ca. 390?); #2120, "Ognina" (390–80); #2121, "Manfria" (390–80); #2123, "S. Maria di Licodia" (ca. 370); #2130, "Licata" (350–40). See S.C. Langher, "Problemi della circolazione moneta attica in Occidente," in *La circolazione della moneta ateniese in Sicilia e Magna Grecia*, *AIIN* 12–14 (1969) 165–99, esp. 172–98; cf. G. Manganaro, "Per la storia della circolazione della moneta attica nella Sicilia orientale," op. cit. 151–63; Rutter, *Kraay-Mørkholm Essays* 245. An earlier episode of infiltration of Attic coins into Magna Graecia through military activities took place in the 440s, when overstrikes of Attic coins at Rhegion and Messane are to be connected with the provision of supplies and a marshaling point for the Attic foundation of Thourioi. See C.M. Kraay, "Fifth-Century Overstrikes at Rhegium and Messana," in *La circolazione*, 141–50, esp. 146–49; Rutter, *Kraay-Mørkholm Essays* 249–50.

[15] See L. Breglia, "La monetazione 'tipo Auriol' e il suo valore documentario per la colonizzazione di Focea," *PP* 25 (1970) 153–65; G.E. Reynaud, "Un trésor de monnaies Massaliètes du Ve siècle," *RN*^{6} 25 (1983) 35–42. *IGCH* #2352 contains an Aiginetan hemiobol. Cf. *IGCH* #1875 = *CH* 4.13 = *CH* 5.4.

access was afforded by river valleys and passes. Compared with the west, there are a greater number of sites that offer us examples of purely local hoards.[16] There are also, however, a number of hoards of regional composition.[17]

Once we move beyond the territory of *poleis* and farther into Thrace, Thasian coins seem to have served as the chief repository of value for native hoarders (like Massiliot/Ionian coins in southern Gaul), as a group of hoards from Bulgaria demonstrates.[18] They were supplemented by Thracian copies that were possibly struck to compensate for the closing of the Thasian mint, whether after the surrender to the Athenians in 463 or after mid-century. Weaker evidence supports the performance of a similar role by the coinage of Parion (earlier in the century) in Hellespontine Thrace as approached through the northern shore of the Propontis.[19] The coins of Abdera and especially Maroneia may have come to share the role of Thasian currency in the interior, with the coinage of Maroneia particularly important in the fourth century.[20]

[16] *IGCH* #357, "Hierissos" (ca. 480–50?), where 150+ coins are from Akanthos (cf. *CH* 6.9, "Hierissos" with 4 Akanthian dr. in a tomb group); #358, "Kaliandra" (ca. 423) with ca. 400 Mendian tetradr.; #696, "Kiourpet" (Samothrace: ca. 470); #698, "Abdera" (ca. 460–50); #710, "Thasos?" (ca. 400).

[17] *IGCH* #359, "Olynthus" (ca. 421), but probably fourth-century; #360, "Nea Cassandra" (ca. 400), with a few coins from Boiotia; *CH* 1.11, "Pontolivado, 1972," which is split between coins of Thasos (10 st.; 29 fr.) and Neapolis (12 st.; 4 diobs.); *CH* 1.18, "Chalcidice, ca. 1962" (late fifth century), where a single Eretrian stater appears and analysis is hindered by appearance of issues from a number of uncertain mints; *CH* 8.75, "Drama, Macedonia, 1983" (ca. 400), with 23 coins from Eion, Aigai, Thasos, and Neapolis.

[18] *IGCH* #701, "Vaksevo" (fifth century); #702, "Benkovski" (fifth century); #705, "Pazardzik" (fifth century); #711, "Godjamo Belovo" (ca. 400); #712, "Dupnica" (ca. 400); #713, "Sofia" (ca. 400); *CH* 4.15, "Tigourovo, Bulgaria, 1971" (475–50); *CH* 6.7, "Akandjievo, Pazardjik" (ca. 450); *CH* 6.8, "Plovdiv" (no date). Note *IGCH* #695 from Krusovo near Plovdiv, with about a third of the hoard Thasian (51/153), and *CH* 7.25, "Gotze Deltchev" (400) with Thasian and Thracian tribal and dynastic coins. See J. Pouilloux, *Recherches sur l'histoire et les cultes de Thasos, Études Thasiennes* 3 (Paris 1954) 48–49. For later circulation, see M. Torbagyi, "The Circulation of Thasian Coins in the Carpathian Basin," in I. Carradice (ed.), *Proceedings of the 10th International Congress of Numismatics, London, September 1986* (London 1986) 23–25.

[19] At Krusevo, Parion contributed 101 dr. to a hoard of 153 coins, ca. 475 (*IGCH* #695), and the entire hoard both of 66+ at Tekirdag (Bisanthe) ca. 480–50 (*IGCH* #697) and of 13+ coins in a hoard found in Turkey (*CH* 2.21). Moreover, *CH* 8.71, "Asia Minor, 1984" (ca. 400), may indicate that the coins of Parion penetrated both northern and southern coasts of the Propontis.

[20] *IGCH* #708, "Sokolovci" (late fifth century) is all Abderan, while #709, "Haskovo" (late fifth century) contains coins from Maroneia. The best evidence for the influence of Maroneia on the interior of Thrace is fourth century. It includes the bronze coins with Odrysian dynastic affilations that may have been minted there and that probably supplemented civic issues in silver in the Thracian economy. See E. Schönert-Geiss, "Maroneia und seine Beziehungen zum Hinterland," in T. Hackens and R. Weiller (eds.), *Proceedings of the 9th International Congress*

More could be said about the more conventional utilization of Greek coins by native elites in the Balkans (see also the discussion of the usage of electrum coins on pp. 95–96 below). Suffice it to say here that nothing in the hoard evidence indicates a potentiality for a replacement of northern Aegean issues by Attic money in trade with non-Greeks. In political terms most of the mints of the northern Aegean fell within the *arkhē* (or the Athenians shared, if that is the right term, hegemony with the Odrysian kings). In terms of the circulation of money, however, we look in vain for signs of the achievement of an Attic monopoly over minting or for the results of the demonetization of local currencies. Athenian coins play a rather modest role in the hoards of the region in our period.[21] It is quite possible that a region that was a net exporter of silver was generally less affected by the infiltration of Attic silver coins that might have been treated by some of their non-Greek acquirers purely as bullion. If the hoards of the interior are any indication, Athenian money would not have replaced the issues of northern Aegean mints without causing substantial disruption.

The first hoard with a significant Athenian component may be *CH* 8.63, "Scione, 1991" (ca. 425), with 20 tetradrachms listed in a large hoard (ca. 250) that is otherwise conventionally regional. The composition of *CH* 8.63 probably reflects Athenian military operations in the Chalcidice during the 420s including the successful siege of Skione in 421. Another hoard from the north with a significant Attic component is *IGCH* #362 = *CH* 8.34, "Mount Athos, before 1842/43," but there are serious doubts whether it may be dated in the fifth century and whether a single hoard is at issue.[22] The Persian Darics in this hoard probably reflect in any case the Great King's erstwhile hegemony and later ambitions in Thrace.[23]

Farther north in the Balkans, the coins of Istros are the currency hoarded at Mahmudia (*IGCH* #700: ca. 450), a site that may have lain

of Numismatics, Berne, September 1979 (Luxemburg 1982) 177–86; Schönert-Geiss, "Maroneia und die Thraker-Wechselbeziehungen zwischen Polis und der Hinterland," *Eirene* 22 (1985) 39–53.

21 We find 1 dr. among 19 coins in *IGCH* #359 and 1 tetradr. among 153 in #695.

22 In *IGCH* #362, "Mt. Athos," there are ca. 100 Attic coins, along with 300 Darics. This hoard must be dated after 400: Starr, *Athenian Coinage* 87; C.M. Kraay, *Greek Coins and History* (London 1969) 49–51; I. Carradice, "The 'Regal' Coinage of the Persian Empire," *Coinage and Administration*, 73–95, esp. 77, 87; cf. Schönert-Geiss *Klio* (1974) 382, or later pieces may be misattributions or additions. See also H. Nicolet-Pierre, "Xerxes et la trésor de l'Athos (*IGCH* 362)," *RN*[6] 34 (1992) 7–22. Carradice notes the incongruity of envisaging an early fifth-century hoard in the bed of the canal.

23 Note also *CH* 8.33, "Tolbuhine district, Bulgaria, 1979" (ca. 500–400) containing ca. 10 Persian *sigloi*.

in Istrian territory, at Roksolany, ancient Nikonion (*IGCH* #704–707); and at Constanta (the site of ancient Tomi: *CH* 2.15 [fifth century]). Fifth-century hoards from sites in the Ukraine and Crimea are made up of local issues.[24] Treatment of the strictly contemporary hoards (from the standpoint of the duration of the Athenian *arkhê*) does appear to give a deceptive underestimation of the role of Cyzicene electrum staters in the region.[25] Several early and mid-fourth-century hoards have a significant segment composed of these staters (cf. *IGCH* #1011-13), and there are some finds not yet fully reported (such as the hoard from Orlovka near Odessa with 73 st.).[26] Schönert-Geiss reports that later hoards often contain earlier Cyzicenes that were perhaps imported into the Black Sea at a time nearer their date of issue.

Fifth-century hoards from northern Asia Minor can conveniently be discussed with their Black Sea counterparts. The hoard found at Isiklikåoy, the site of ancient Apamea-Myrlea, provides welcome early confirmation of the prominence of electrum coins in the trade of the Propontis and Pontus, as it contains electrum coins of Kyzikos and Lampsakos (*IGCH* #1234: ca. 460). Yet from the standpoint of its relative proximity to their point of emission, it is also unsurprising that the majority of its pieces are silver issues from Kyzikos (284) and Lampsakos (24).[27] The two hoards found farther east are exclusively Sinopean (*IGCH* #1235: ca. 450; #1236: fifth century).[28] Placing aside the circulation of electrum, one would conclude that the margins of the Black Sea and northern Asia Minor were divided into a series of monetary compartments for the regional circulation of silver coins. As in

24 Olbian coins are the sole constituent of hoards at Berezan island in the liman of the Bug and Dnieper (*IGCH* #995 [early fifth century?]; #998 [ca. 450]), nearby Kozyrka-Bogdanovka (#999), and at Olbia itself (#1001–1002; *CH* 7.24, "Olbia, 1968" [400]). Ancient Pantikapaion is modern Kerch, where local coins comprise a hoard (*IGCH* #996); neighboring Nymphaion has provided two hoards of the coins of Pantikapaion (*IGCH* #997 = *CH* 2.25, #1003). A hoard found in Georgia is unsurprisingly composed of Colchian coins (*IGCH* #1000).

25 E. Schönert-Geiss, "Die Wirtschafts- und Handelbeziehungen zwischen Griechenland und der nördlichen Scharzmeerküste im Spiegel der Münzfunde (6.–1. Jh. v. u.Z.)," *Klio* 53 (1971) 105–17. Cf. C.T.H.R. Ehrhardt, "Owls and Grain, an Archaeological Puzzle," *NZNJ* 17 (1988) 76–79.

26 The isolated archaic and classical finds of Cyzicene staters are well presented in M. Laloux, "La circulation des monnaies d'électrum de Cyzique," *RBN* 117 (1971) 31–69, esp. 38–45.

27 *CH* 4.14, "Gemlik, Bursa, Turkey, 1972" contains 30+ silver ob. of Kyzikos.

28 *CH* 1.15, "Black Sea, ca. 1970" (ca. 425) has a Sinopean core (65 dr.) with 16 Attic tetradr., 10 Persian *sigloi*, and a scatter of coins from other mints. See the discussion in C.M. Kraay and P.R.S. Moorey, "A Black Sea Hoard of the Late Fifth Century B.C.," *NC* 141 (1981) 1–19, esp. 16–19.

Sicily and Italy, any penetration of these compartments by silver minted in the Aegean was mostly counterbalanced by recirculation back to the Aegean (contrast *CH* 1.15).

Greek Money in the Near East and Egypt

As we move to consider the hoards that have been found beyond the area of extensive Greek settlement in Asia, a different economic context reveals itself. The Near East was under Persian control during the period of interest to us, and the Persians had inherited the political structures of the hierarchical "national" or ethnic monarchies that had preceded them. Our investigation has previously had to cope with either the motivations of (mainly Greek) hoarders who operated in monetized economies or individual members of native elites who were interested in exotic goods for reasons that were either practical or prompted by considerations of social status. Such partners in trade (and those subsequently exchanging goods with them) did not have elaborated state structures that constrained their economic behavior. In comparison, the silver coins comprising the hoards on Persian territory between 480 and 400 sometimes appear to be currency not only taken out of present usage in a money economy, but also (in all likelihood) currency permanently removed from the category of money and treated wholly as bullion.[29] So the intervention of state authorities, whose primary interest lay in capturing revenues through taxation, affected the usage of coins as money. On average, hoards found in areas without monetary economies tend to be more varied (relative to their size) than hoards found on the territories of *poleis* (and in adjoining native areas economically influenced by Greek colonies).

Hence, when Egyptian hoards are examined, the diversity of issues they contain is remarkable.[30] Even if we refrain from enumerating Cypriot mints and Lycian dynasts, the Asyut hoard has ca. 67 mints represented among 900 coins (*IGCH* #1644 = *CH* 2.17 = 8.44: ca. 475). Asyut's remarkable coverage of the Greek world is a function of its size, but the other pertinent hoards show similar variety: *IGCH* #1645, "Zagazig" (ca. 470) with 84 coins from 23+ mints; #1646, "Fayum" (ca. 460) with 15 coins and 11 mints; #1647, "Naucratis" (450–25) with 15 coins and mints.[31] *CH* 8.57, "Egypt, before 1857" (450–20) has been reconstructed

[29] The best overview is D. Schlumberger, "L'argent grec dans l'empire Achéménide," in R. Curiel and D. Schlumberger (eds.), *Trésors monétaires d'Afghanistan* (Paris 1953) 1–64.

[30] Cf. Price and Waggoner 13–22.

[31] The major archaic hoards exhibit the same composition: *IGCH* #1636, "Mit Rahineh" (ca. 500); #1637, "Demanhur" (500); #1638, "Delta" (ca. 500); #1639, "Sakha" (early fifth

to contain 17 coins from 14 or 15 mints.[32] These hoards contain damaged and destructively tested coins, issues belonging to an extended period of time, and nonmonetary silver in the form of ingots, jewelry, and scrap.

The Egyptian hoards may be taken to indicate the diversity of the coins that were carried to the only Greek *emporion* in Egypt at Naukratis, especially if one remembers that a tendency may have existed for a disproportionate treasurization of available but relatively rarer items in that mix of coins reaching Egypt.[33] The degree of economic sophistication differed substantially between Egyptian hoarders and the Greek traders that were their sources of silver, as the formers' crude methods of examination betray. Since the coinage in these hoards had lost much of its monetary function, at the very most the proportions of coinage from various Greek regions might help us gauge the overall availability of the coins of those regions, while not shedding much illumination on the currency of those coins as money within the Greek world. They are also assuredly nonillustrative about the commercial activities of the citizens of the cities of their mints. Hence the productive Attic, Aiginetan, and northern Aegean mints are well represented. The scale of importation of Egyptian grain to Athens, however, may have elevated the presence of Attic coins there relative to their proportion in the *total* Greek monetary circulation before 450. Eventually Athenian coins and their imitations would achieve a special role in the disbursements of Egyptian administrators, but that phenomenon belongs to the end of the fifth century and thereafter (pp. 528–35).

A similar variety typifies the two large fifth-century hoards from the Levant, *IGCH* #1482, "Jordan" (ca. 445) with 113 coins from over 28 mints,[34] and #1483, "Massyaf" (from northern Phoenicia: ca. 425–20) with 100 coins from 19+ mints.[35] Moreover, *CH* 6.4 + 6.5 = 8.45,

century?); #1640, "Benha el Asl" (ca. 485). A smaller hoard with considerable variety is *CH* 1.7, "Egypt, ca. 1955" (480?).

32 T.V. Buttrey, "Egypt, before 1879: Early 5th Century B.C., c. 14 AR," *CH* 8 (1994).

33 The appearance of a group of 4 owls from the same reverse die (in Robinson group F) in the "Zagazig" hoard (*IGCH* #1645) suggests a consignment imported into Egypt together rather than assembled there. The same conclusion may prevail on the basis of the die links of the northern Aegean mints in *IGCH* #1478, "Ras Shamra." See Rutter, *Coinage and Society* 3–4, with Kraay, *Coins and History*, 44–45; Kraay, "Archaic Owls of Athens: New Evidence for Chronology," *MIGRA* 1 (1975) 145–60, esp. 147–50.

34 See C.M. Kraay and P.R.S. Moorey, "Two Fifth Century Hoards from the Near East," *RN*[6] 10 (1968) 181–238, esp. 181–210. Note also H.B. Mattingly, "The Jordan Hoard (*IGCH* 1482) and Kimon's Last Campaign," in *10th ICN*, 59–64, but the effort there to find specific rationales for the contents of individual hoards in political events is disquieting.

35 Kraay and Moorey *RN* (1968) 210–22. *IGCH* #1483, "Massyaf," may be closer to 400; see A. Destrooper-Georgiades, "La Phénicie et Chypre à l'époque achéménide: témoignages

"Antilebanon, 1978" (ca. 480–75) has 70 coins from ca. 24 mints and a number of bun ingots.[36] Some smaller hoards found more recently also bear out this impression. For example, *CH* 1.14, "North Syria, 1974" (mid-fifth century) includes 16 coins from eight mints (n.b. Arados: 3; Sidon: 9); *CH* 7.12 may be related to *CH* 8.45, with its large consignment of ingots and chopped coins as well as 8 identifiable coins from different mints. The earliest known hoard, *IGCH* #1478, "Ras Shamra" (525–20) appears much like the earliest Egyptian hoards.[37] Naturally, Phoenician issues appear alongside Greek coins in the classical Levantine hoards, another illustration of the principle, now familiar to us, of hoards reflecting local circulation. Several hoards have the ubiquitous Attic tetradrachms as their significant exotic component.[38] *IGCH* #1252, "Asia Minor" (ca. 430) has its findspot variously given as Asia Minor or Egypt. The presence of Persian *sigloi* and the absence of coins from northern Aegean mints might incline a determination of the findspot toward Asia Minor (and perhaps to the Cilician or Pamphylian coast in particular), but it is striking that such an ambiguity could exist at all.[39]

This last-named hoard, as well as the Syrian hoards just noted, may be contrasted with hoards from Anatolia that are more truly reflective of *monetary* conditions rather than simply speaking to the relative rate of flow of silver from various regions of the Greek world toward the east and to the regional composition of final aggregates. In this regard, some Lycian hoards are overwhelmingly Lycian in composition.[40] The great

numismatiques," *Studia Phoenicia* 5 (1987) 339–55, esp. 349–50. Note also *IGCH* #1481, "Syria" (ca. 450), which contains three staters issued by Byblos and a Persian *siglos*. Finds of sixth- and fifth-century coins in Palestine are conveniently summarized in H.A. Cahn, "Stagira in Tel-Aviv," in *Festschrift Mildenberg* 43–50, esp. 45–49.

36 See S. Hurter and E. Pászthory, "Archaischer Silberfund aus dem Antilibanon," in *Festschrift Mildenberg* 111–25.

37 See R.A. Stucky, "Zum Münzschatz von Ras Shamra—Ugarit—Leukos Limen (Syrien)," *SNR* 63 (1984) 1–25.

38 *CH* 8.59, "Ramallah, Israel(?)" (ca. 430?), which contains Attic tetradrachms; and possibly *CH* 8.29, where two Athenian tetradr. were found among 14 Egypto-/Philisto-Arabian obols.

39 In general, note A. Davesne, "La circulation monétaire en Cilicie à l'époque achéménide," *REA* 91 (1989) 157–68, esp. 159–60.

40 *IGCH* #1250 (ca. 450): 63+ Lycian st.; #1251 (440–30): 100+ coins: Athens, 3+ tetradr.; 96+ st. of Lycian dynasts; *CH* 1.6: 150+ coins from various Lycian dynasts; *CH* 2.18, "Lycia, 1970" (470); *CH* 2.27, "Lycia, 1970" (440–30); *CH* 3.14 (= *CH* 5.3 = *CH* 4.16: 400), "Turkey, 1976"; *CH* 4.9, "Lycia, 1976" (480); *CH* 4.12, "Fethiye, Turkey, 1977" (475 or later); *CH* 8.32, "W. Lycia/ E. Caria, 1992?" (500–400); *CH* 8.39, "Lycia, 1981/82" (ca. 480). Cf. *IGCH* #1262, "Bucak" (ca. 375–70). Moreover, note J. Zahle, "Politics and Economy in Lycia during the Persian Period," *REA* 91 (1989) 169–82, esp. 172–75, suggesting further aggregation of these Lycian hoards.

exception is the "Decadrachm" or "Elmali" hoard, which was found at a site with good access to the sea and is analogous to the mixed hoards found in the regions of the *arkhē* in Asia Minor and will be discussed below with those hoards (*CH* 8.48).

Hoards from Cyprus have a markedly local or insular quality.[41] There are two large hoards, *IGCH* #1272 = *CH* 8.42, "Larnaca, 1933" (479–78), from the site of ancient Kition, with ca. 700 coins, and #1276, "Dali, 1869" (ca. 425–400), from the site of ancient Idalion, that are both exclusively Cypriot in their identified contents.[42] A late fifth-century Cypriot hoard (*CH* 6.10, "Cyprus" [ca. 400]) contains Cypriot staters (Paphos [5], Cition [1], Marion [2]), 1 Achaemenid st., and 1 st. from Side. A larger hoard that was also found at Idalion, *IGCH* #1275, "Dali, 1869" (ca. 425–400) is slightly variant but in a quite predictable style: 7 Athenian tetradr. supplement the coins of various civic and uncertain Cypriot mints in a hoard of 123+ items.

In Cilicia and Pamphylia, we find most hoards have a strong local coloration, although the practice of coining on the Persian standard presumably gave currency to monies that were in valid use outside their city of issue.[43] *IGCH* #1177, "Asia Minor, before 1961" (ca. 480) is from the Pamphylo-Cilician coast and resembles the mixed Ionian hoards that will be discussed below, as it contains 19 Attic tetradr. in 38 coins, with 10 Aiginetan st. (and one pseudo-aiginetan st.) as the next largest grouping. The pervasiveness of Attic tetradrachms in the

[41] In general, see Destrooper-Georgiades *Studia Phoenicia* (1987) 344–45. Four small hoards are exclusively Cypriot: *IGCH* #1273, "Cyprus, ca. 1929" (ca. 450) with 14+ st. from Marion; *IGCH* #1274, "Cyprus, 1924" (ca. 425) with 5+ st. from Kition and an unknown mint; *CH* 2.28, "Larnaca, Cyprus" (425), which has 17+ st. of Azbaal of Cition; *CH* 8.65, "Cyprus, 1987" (ca. 425), with 3 coins from Salamis and 2 uncertain mints. Another small hoard seemed initially to contain 2 non-Cypriot elements, 1 Thasian fr. and a fractional coin of the Lycian dynast Kheriga: *IGCH* #1277 = *CH* 8.43, "Cyprus, 1934–35" (ca. 425–400) with 9 coins from Cypriot mints. It now appears that the 2 non-Cypriot coins are intrusive. See M. Amandry, "A propos du trésor de Chypre, 1934/35 (*IGCH* 1277)," *Centre d'Études Chypriotes, Cahiers* 6 (1986) 37–38.

[42] A. Destrooper-Georgiades, "Le trésor de Larnaca (*IGCH* 1272) réexaminé," *Report of the Department of Antiquities: Cyprus, 1984* (Nicosia 1984) 140–61.

[43] In general, note Davesne *REA* (1989) 157–68. We may compare *IGCH* #1253, "Asia Minor" (ca. 420), composed entirely of staters of Aspendos, both with *IGCH* #1254 of ca. 400 (18+ coins in toto) from Selimiye, ancient Side in Pamphylia, with its double *sigloi* from Aspendos (2+), Side (12+), and Citium (1), and with *IGCH* #1255 (ca. 400), in which a large hoard of 1300+ coins is dominated by ca. 1,000 double *sigloi* of Kelenderis, but contains equivalent coins from 4–5 Cypriot mints and from Side, Mallos, and Soli (a few more coins are identified in *CH* 1.21, "Cilicia, 1957"). The small hoard *IGCH* #1256, "Cilicia" (ca. 400) is anomalous (Syracuse: 1 tetradr.; Athens: 6 tetradr. and coins from Tyre and Sidon). On *IGCH* #1254, see C.M. Kraay, "Notes on the Mint of Side in the Fifth Century B.C.," *NC*[7] 9 (1969) 15–20, esp. 19–20.

east is shown by the ca. 200 tetradr. that appear with coins on the Persian standard in *IGCH* #1255, as well as by the contents of *CH* 5.15, "Cilicia, 1977" (400), where over 300 Attic tetradrachms were buried.[44] As archaeological research in Anatolia has become more active and authorities have become more successful in achieving control over hoards that have been discovered, hoards of *sigloi* from territory that was not occupied by Greek *poleis* have been reported more often.[45]

To be sure, southern Anatolian, Syrian, and Egyptian hoards may provide invaluable evidence on the sequence of issues and on chronology but seem to offer us no real evidence about either monetary practices in the world of the *poleis* or a supposed extinction of the mints of Athenian allies. We do learn that Athenian coins were sufficiently prevalent in the eastern Mediterranean to be present regularly in the Egyptian hoards and sometimes in Anatolian and Near Eastern hoards. When the whole region is considered for the entire fifth century, this widespread and continuing, significant dissemination of coins is unique to the Athenian mint.

Homeland Greece

Hoarding in mainland Greece also shows a series of characteristic forms in our present evidence. Not unexpectedly, local coinage often appears prominently in hoards uncovered in the area of its issue. Corinth, with its large economy, substantial coinings, and commercial vitality, offers several instances of hoards exclusively local.[46] In the northwest, an area studded with Corinthian allies and dependencies during the fifth century, available hoards show a role for Corinthian money accompanying colonial issues. Notable companions are the coins of Leukas, struck on the Corinthian standard and very closely duplicating Corinthian Pegasi (pp. 489–93 below). A role for Corinthian coins alongside local issues is attested even at Corcyra, that Corinthian colony famous for its estrangement from its metropolis.[47] Unsurprisingly, this phenomenon

[44] Note also *CH* 8.73, "Asia Minor, 1990 or later" (ca. 400), which combines Attic tetradrachms and *sigloi*.

[45] *CH* 8.25, "Osmaniye, E. Asia Minor" (500–400); 8.26, "Burdur Region, S. Turkey, before 1989" (500–400); 8.27, "Near Dinar (= Apamea, Phyrgia), before 1989" (500–400) with ca. 6,000 coins; 8.28, "Bolu area(?), N. Turkey, before 1989" (500–400); 8.58, "Körez district, province of Manisa, W. Turkey" (450–350). See Carradice, *Coinage and Administration* 73–95, esp. 89–93 for discussion.

[46] *IGCH* #17 (ca. 470–60); #18 (ca. 470–50); #25 (430–15). In *IGCH* #41, "Peloponnesus" (late fifth century?), 50 Corinthian st. were accompanied by 4 Argive triob.

[47] Note *CH* 1.13 (= *CH* 5.7), "N.W. Greece, 1966" (ca. 460) with 136 coins, of which 48 st. from Corinth and 28 from Leukas have been identified. For Corcyra, contrast *CH* 8.41, "Near Stratia, near Paleopolis, (agora of ancient Corcyra), 1978" (ca. 480), a hoard of 157 coins of Corcyra and *IGCH* #38, "Corfu" (fifth century) and its 12 Corcyrean st., with *CH* 8.53,

of local monetary predominance varies only in its uniformity. There is a scatter of hoards exclusively local throughout the Greek homeland.[48] In Boiotia, where several mints operated within the same federal, political unit, the pattern of hoard deposition naturally reflects those conditions of regionality.[49]

Another category of classical hoards from the Greek homeland were collected under somewhat different conditions, inasmuch as these hoards possess a sizable Aiginetan component. Aiginetan staters were the first money of the Peloponnesos and their usage opened the way for an embryonic, archaic monetizing of the largely agrarian economies of that region.[50] Thus Aiginetan coins were the first repositories of wealth in the form of money for archaic elites in much of the Peloponnesos, central Greece, and Thessaly. These *poleis* collected their first taxes in money in Aiginetan coin. Although Aiginetan coins may have retained official recognition as well as elite acceptance in these areas, eventually local coins were minted, usually approximating the Aiginetic standard, that supplemented the Aiginetan "turtles" in the regional economy.[51] Although the hoard evidence is not much help, the Aiginetans produced a significant fractional coinage throughout the period and it is likely that Aiginetan fractions supplemented local heavier coins of the Aiginetic standard where required (contrast *CH* 3.9).[52] While Aiginetan

---

"Corfu (Corcyra), Greece, 1985" (ca. 450) with staters from Corcyra (5+); Leukas (1+), and Corinth (5+). *CH* 8.52, "Unknown findspot, before 1985" (ca. 450), a hoard of 152+ coins, with 73 Corinthian coins and 79 Corcyrean coins, not only belongs to the same pattern of circulation, but may even comprise a single hoard with *CH* 8.53.

48 Some examples of hoards exclusively local are *IGCH* #22, "Delphi" (ca. 450); #23, "Kyparissia" (450–25); #24, "Pyrgos" (450–25: both the latter are Elean); #27, "Melos" (ca. 416); #29, "Tegea" (ca. 430–400); *CH* 3.11, "Elis, 1933" (430) with Elean staters and hemidrachms; *CH* 7.19, "Olympia, 1948" (460) with Elean staters. A probable case is *IGCH* #20, "Peloponnesus, 1936" (ca. 460–50), that is entirely Elean. Compare also the Corcyrean hoards listed in the previous note.

49 Regional Boiotian hoards are *CH* 1.17 (= *CH* 2.31), "Boeotia, 1955" (late fifth century), the main body of which is Boiotian (Thebes: 9; Haliartos: 4; Orkhomenos: 11; Pharai: 1), and *CH* 5.10, "Agoriani, Boeotia" (450), with 35 coins that derive from Thebes, Tanagra, and Orkhomenos (and 1 Persian *siglos*).

50 Cf. Figueira, *Aegina* 81–88.

51 Following the terminology of numismatic handbooks, the term "Aiginetan" will be reserved for the coinage minted on the island of Aigina (for the most part) that bears the types of a turtle or a tortoise. The term "Aiginetic" will be used for all the coins, regardless of origin, minted on the standard associated with Aiginetan coins and first used monetarily in Aiginetan coinage. That these coins tend to be lighter than Aiginetan coins implies value added by local political authorities.

52 The persistence and evolution of these patterns is also illustrated by *CH* 8.147, "Near Cleitor" (340–30), a hoard in which the only large coins are 6 fifth-century worn turtle staters that were found along with 77 Aiginetic fr., many of which are fourth-century. It has been

coins continued to play an important role in circulation during the Pentekontaeteia, treasurized Aiginetan staters were sometimes older than the other coins deposited with them in the classical period. It is as though the staters represented a final reserve accumulated in the archaic period and later salted away by an *oikos* (often elite) against a household crisis.

Unsurprisingly, the hoards found on Aigina itself are exclusively Aiginetan and represent a strong manifestation of the dominance of local coins in hoards.[53] Other hoards containing Aiginetan coins with findspots scattered through Greece vary from exclusively Aiginetan ones,[54] in that Aiginetan hoards were supplemented by a few other coins,[55] to hoards possessing large Aiginetan and non-Aiginetan (often local) components.[56] The identity of some of such hoards as reserves for persons of means in agrarian states may also be demonstrated from the occasional appearance of Elean coins (on the Aiginetic standard) along with Aiginetan staters. They could be acquired through attendance at the festivals of Zeus at Olympia, and easily exchanged with other visitors to Olympia, or perhaps even expended in a political emergency. Like the Aiginetan staters,

suggested that the prevalence of Peloponnesian bronze coinage motivated the hoarder to put aside these fractions. See J. Warren, "The 1980 Kato Klitoria Hoard," in *Kraay-Mørkholm Essays* 291–300.

53 *CH* 1.8, "Greece, 1944?" (= the "Ritter Hoard": ca. 480) with 103+ Aiginetan st.; *CH* 1.12, "Aegina, 1965" (= the "Wells Hoard": ca. 460?); *CH* 3.9, "Angistri, Aegina" (450?) with 7 tortoise st. and 1 Phokian triob.; cf. *CH* 1.5, "Aegina, 1973" (ca. 500).

54 *IGCH* #15, "Olympia" (ca. 470); #21, "Koumares" (ca. 450), where an archaic Chian stater among 35 Aiginetan st. may be intrusive; #36, "Porto Cheli" (fifth century); *CH* 1.13, "Babes, Olympia, 1958–60" (480); *CH* 3.10 = 8.60, "Megalopolis, 1936" (ca. 430), a large hoard containing at least 350 coins; *CH* 7.26, "Peloponnesos" (= *IGCH* #30?). *CH* 1.15 = 3.12 = 5.11, "Myrina, Thessaly," was originally published with a fourth-century date of deposit, although it includes many archaic turtles. If, however, the tortoise staters which it also contains can be dated in the fifth century, the date for the hoard, more recently advanced, of 400 or even 440 may be accepted (see also below, pp. 124–25). See also the "Spink Hoard, ca. 1972" enumerated in L. Beer, *The Coinage of Aegina: A Chronological Reappraisal Based on Hoards and Technical Studies* (Diss., Oxford University 1980) 219–20.

55 See *IGCH* #28, "Charvari" where 2 Theban st. were found with 40 Aiginetan st.

56 *IGCH* #30, "Peloponnesus" (ca. 425–400): Boiotia 12 st.; Aigina 29 st.; Sikyon 2 st.; #35, "Lappa" (fifth century?): Aigina 40 st., 2 dr.; Elis 32 st., 17 dr., 9 triob.; Phocis 1 triob.; #37, "Agrinion" (fifth century?): a Tanagran stater; 19 turtles; 12 Elean st.; #44, "Olympia" (ca. 400?): Aigina 12 st., Elis 9+ st. *IGCH* #40, "Arcadia" (late fifth century), is rather more mixed: in 91 coins, there are 74 Arcadian triob., 4 Aiginetan st., and a selection of Peloponnesian coins with 3 Theban coins. See also *IGCH* #59, "Boiotia, ca. 1930" (ca. 350). *IGCH* #11, "Isthmia" (ca. 480) is not a true hoard but rather an aggregate of deposits, many dedicatory, closed after the burning of the archaic temple. As enumerated by Beer, *Coinage* 222–36, it contains 77 Aiginetan coins out of a total of 151. On the fourth-century circulation of Aiginetan coins in the Peloponnesus, see M. Oeconomides, "The IGCH 101 Hoard and the Circulation of the Tortoise in the Peloponnesus," in *Florilegium Numismaticum: Studia in honorem U. Westermark edita* (Stockholm 1992) = *NM* 38 (1992) 307–12.

the examples found in such mixed hoards are often countermarked, indicating that they have been revalidated.[57]

Because of the pioneering aspect of Aiginetan money in the growth of a monetary economy in mainland Greece, the primary area of circulation for Aiginetan coins far transcended that of other coinages of peninsular Greece. While the evolution of monetary integration within the Athenian *arkhē* will become noteworthy, we must also concede that a considerable degree of early monetary consolidation is indicated by the pattern of circulation of Aiginetan coins and the dissemination of the Aiginetic standard to other mints. As we have already seen in the discussion of the Egyptian hoards, the abundance of Aiginetan money and the commercial activity centered on the island ensured that considerable numbers of these coins were even carried beyond the Aegean.[58]

Aiginetan coins continued to play a substantial role in the areas of their traditional acceptance throughout the period that Aigina belonged to the Attic alliance as a tributary state. With the turtles and fifth-century tortoises can be grouped other issues on the Aiginetic standard that are prominent in local hoards that have already been noted (Arcadia and Mantineia, Argos, the Boiotian mints, Delphi, Elis, Opuntian Lokris, Phleios, Phokis, Sikyon).[59] Thus, when classical hoards from the Greek mainland, those outside the area of Athenian control, are reviewed from the perspective of their monetary standard, these hoards assume a greater degree of homogeneity than at first appears. There are not only many exclusively Aiginetan hoards, but additional hoards are wholly or nearly completely Aiginetic in standard.[60] Corinthian coins (and related allied issues) and the hoards in which they are the leading component stand as the most prominent exception.

[57] Note *IGCH* #35, where the Elean coins appear somewhat fresher than their Aiginetan counterparts (p. 124 below). See M. Oeconomides-Caramessini, "À propos du trésor de Lappa *IGCH* 35," in *Kraay-Mørkholm Essays* 9–22. In general see H. Nicolet-Pierre, "Remarques sur la chronologie relative des plus anciennes séries de statères éléens," *RN*[6] 17 (1975) 7–17.

[58] New accessions to this picture continue to occur. An important new hoard of Aiginetan staters (400+, of which 392 have been catalogued) from Albania has recently been announced: *CH* 8.67, "Hollmn, village of Quinam, S.E. Albania, 1991" (end of fifth century). See S. Gjongecaj, "Un trésor de statères éginètes trouvé à Hollm (Sud-est de l'Albanie)," in T. Hackens and G. Moucharte (eds.), *Proceedings of the XI International Numismatic Congress* 1 (Louvain-la-Neuve 1993) 107–12.

[59] The result would be still more impressive, if Corcyrean coins were included. The standard of Corcyra is sometimes described as "light Aiginetic" (cf. Head[2] 325–26).

[60] See *IGCH* #28; #30; #35; #37; #40; #44; *CH* 8.67. *IGCH* #19, "Naupactus" (ca. 460), containing 10 Elean st. in a silver box, might be considered a reserve hoarded for its Aiginetic standard coins, but the collection of such coins by an individual who might easily have visited Elis for any number of reasons is also possible.

Nevertheless, the complexities of economic interaction and the variety of political activity in classical Greece necessitate that there must appear in our evidence hoards that stand as exceptions to the general trends illustrated above. Gold and electrum coins were compact reserves of high value and several hoards seem expressly formed for their preservation, even in mainland Greece, far from any mint striking electrum.[61] Although it is possible to imagine idiosyncratic explanations for the composition of an exceptional hoard, we must also grant that such efforts are highly speculative.[62] But the occasional odd aggregation of coins should not distract from the main patterns. Some coins that are unlikely to have been valid or much used locally were (nonetheless) held by particular individuals. This phenomenon was doubtless influenced by the intrinsic value of silver coins as bullion.[63]

If the border into Athenian-controlled territory is crossed, there is no obvious sign from the pattern of hoarding that a different monetary regime has been entered. That a number of hoards were found in Attica is unsurprising. Given the pattern of exploration and excavation of sites there, it is rather more surprising that more have not been published, but the ease of disposal on the market is probably a factor. Such Attic hoards tend to be dominated by Athenian coins.[64]

Counterbalancing the dominance of Athenian coinage in Attica is its importance in neighboring areas, even in places where poor diplomatic relations might have implied that Attic money had little official standing.[65]

[61] One could not have predicted *IGCH* #43, "Elis" (ca. 400) from any comparative data. Containing 4 electrum Cyzicenes and 12 gold Darics, it is rather like the electrum hoards of Asia Minor to be discussed below. *IGCH* #32, "Athens" (fifth century?) is made up of several hundred Persian Darics. Such coins could have been acquired through military activity, and might have represented booty, ransom for a prisoner, or the profit from a sale of prisoners as slaves.

[62] One more anomalous hoard is *IGCH* #26, "Chalcis" (ca. 422–15); it is a hoard of ca. 51 bronze coins from Sicily (Himera: 1; Leontinoi: 4; Syracuse: 46) that has been suggested to be the property of fugitives from Leontinoi, an old Chalcidian colony, who found refuge in Euboia (note Thuc. 6.19.1, cf. 6.12.1; DS 12.83.1–3; Plut. *Nic.* 12.1). See P.R. Franke, "Leontinische ΦΥΓΑΔΕΣ in Chalkis?," *AA* (1966) 395–407. It might with equal likelihood be explained as a stock of coins accumulated in Sicily by a Euboian sailor with the Attic expeditionary forces on the island during 427–25.

[63] Schönert-Geiss, *Klio* (1974) 392, classifies as a hoard a group of Attic tetradrachms found at Goulas, ancient Lato, on Crete. See also G. Le Rider, *Les monnaies crétoises du Ve au Ie siècle av. J.C.* (Paris 1966) 263.

[64] *IGCH* #14, "Sunium" (ca. 480–70): 5 Attic coins; #16, "Attica" (ca. 465): 9 Attic coins; *CH* 5.14, "Piraeus, 1977" (404); *CH* 7.22, "Piraeus, 1902" (405/4).

[65] *IGCH* #33, "Megara" (fifth century) contained, along with 12 Attic tetradr., 100 dr., and 57 triob. The Megarians were not themselves minting at this time, and it is fairly obvious that the much larger and more "international" economy of their Athenian neighbors encouraged

In contrast, the common coin standard of the Euboians and Athenians undoubtedly furthered the early use of Attic money on Euboia, paralleling the circulation of Aiginetan coins alongside other coins on the Aiginetic standard. Thus there are Euboian hoards that antedate 480, showing that Athenian coins were in circulation on the island before Attic hegemony there (*IGCH* #3, 9–10). In addition, by 465 or, at the latest, by mid-century, the mints of Chalcis, Eretria, and Karystos had ended their activity. There are several mainly Attic hoards from fifth-century Euboia. *IGCH* #39, "Euboea" (late fifth century) is a hoard of 67 Attic tetradr. and *CH* 2.20, "Eretria, 1973" (fifth century) is a small deposit of Attic tetradrachms found in the course of excavation. *CH* 8.69, "Eretria, 1981" (ca. 411) contains 140 coins, of which all are Athenian save for 2 Eretrian tetradrachms.[66] *IGCH* #34, "Greece, central, ca. 1900" (fifth century), may be classed with these Atticizing hoards, although it has a few fractional coins from Phokian mints.[67]

The mainly Attic *IGCH* #39 can profitably be contrasted with a slightly later Euboian hoard, *IGCH* #42, "Euboea." The latter is a large hoard (ca. 350 coins) dated to ca. 400 and is dominated by Theban issues (68–70 st., with 1 Tanagran st.) and coins of the Euboian League (30 st.).[68] There are only 2 Athenian tetradr. included (as well as 1 Sicyonian st.). Here we clearly glimpse some of the monetary consequences of the Euboian defections of 411, as the hoard seems to reflect expenditures by the Euboians and their Boiotian allies in military efforts against Athens. As will be seen below, the termination of Athenian hegemony offers a far more dramatic and chronologically identifiable monetary watershed in some areas than does any stage of monetary evolution or consolidation during the existence of the *arkhē*.

As we shift our gaze eastward, the pattern of hoard deposition changes only gradually. A small hoard, *IGCH* #31, "Scyros" (fifth century), is like many mainland hoards: it is exclusively local. If it is truly to be dated around 475, *IGCH* #13 = *CH* 7.13, "Paros," made up of about 100 Parian coins, would be another example of localism. Aiginetan staters, however, have a significant presence in a massive hoard that was

---

(in the first place) the circulation and also perhaps an acceptance of Attic money on Megarian territory.

66 See A. Geiser, "Le trésor de monnaies classiques trouvé en 1981 sur l'agora d'Éretrie," in I.A. Carradice (ed.), *Proceedings of the 10th International Congress of Numismatics* (London 1986) 41–44.

67 The findspot could be Phokis: N. Langton, "Notes on Some Phocian Obols," *NC*[4] 3 (1903) 197–210; Schönert-Geiss *Klio* (1974) 385.

68 Its alternative findspot is Boiotia. See W.P. Wallace, *The Euboian League and Its Coinage*, *NNM* 134 (New York 1956) 49–50, 137–39.

also deposited on Paros.[69] These coins appear to have been hoarded in a fashion similar to that prevailing in contemporary mainland hoards, where they are the one common denominator in hoards from different regions. On Paros, as on the mainland, Aiginetan coins were hoarded in a setting where some local coins were emitted on the same Aiginetic standard (just as also on Keos, Naxos, and Siphnos). Two large archaic hoards are excellent illustrations of this phenomeneon, demonstrating that its beginning lay in the late archaic period.[70]

Ionia and Western Asia Minor

Somewhat farther east, in Ionia and its offshore islands, a majority of hoards exhibit once again either an exclusively local character[71] or a marked degree of dominance by local issues.[72] Moreover, even the interior of western Asia Minor was a zone in which the pattern of hoard composition partakes of characteristics of the "local" hoards already noted on *polis* territory, with the proviso that some hoards are regional in their composition (especially when we remember the parts played by Lydian and Persian coins). Carian hoards amply illustrate this phenomenon.[73] Satrapal territory in western Asia Minor did differ from most of the Great King's other dominions in the existence of a partially monetized economy. Just as Cilicia and Pamphylia produce

69 *CH* 2.24, "Eirini, Paros" (ca. 470) with 600 coins, of which 33+ were Aiginetan (the only group published).

70 *IGCH* #6, "Cyclades?, ca. 1889" (ca. 500), where the Aiginetan element is 114 st. out of 145+ coins and *IGCH* #7, "Santorin" (ca. 500–490) where there are 541 Aiginetan st. in a hoard of 760 coins. Other Aiginetic standard coins are present in both cases (ca. 21 in *IGCH* #6; at least 44 in *IGCH* #7).

71 *IGCH* #1179, "Chios?" (ca. 460); #1186, "Bodrum" (ca. 450) on the site of Halikarnassos, which is exclusively Knidian; #1187, "Lesbos" (ca. 450), all Methymnian; #1191, "Phanae on Chios" (ca. 450–40); #1192, "Mytilene" (ca. 450–400); #1193, "Caria?" (ca. 410), which is all Knidian; #1197, "Asia Minor" (ca. 400), all Milesian; #1198, "Samos" (ca. 400); *CH* 3.5, "Lesbos, 1960–69" (480), with 10+ Lesbian didr.; *CH* 7.14, "Chios, 1980" (475); probably *CH* 4.17, "Asia Minor, 1976" (late fifth century) containing Kolophonian dr.; *CH* 7.15, "Turkey, 1980" (475) containing Milesian diob.; *CH* 7.20 = *IGCH* 1179?, "Chios" (460); *CH* 8.47, "Ionia, 1983" (ca. 460), a hoard of 100+ Teian st.; *CH* 8.54, "Caria, 1987" (ca. 450), where 50+ Milesian ob. are deposited; *CH* 8.68, "Ionia" (ca. 415), all Kolophonian.

72 Consider *IGCH* #1195, "Ionia" (fifth century) with 21 Milesian ob. and 1 ob. from Ialysos; #1199, "Asia Minor" (ca. 400) with 19+ Milesian fr. and 5+ from Salamis; and perhaps #1190, "Asia Minor" (ca. 450) where 10+ coins are split among Kolpohon (6 tetartem.), Teos (1 st., 2 fr.), and an uncertain mint (1 fr.). *CH* 8.72, "Ionia, 1989" (ca. 400) is a little more varied: 133 diob., 22 hemiob., 41 other fr. from Miletos; 1 Teian coin; and 46 coins from Kebren.

73 *IGCH* #1181 is a small hoard that is exclusively Carian. *IGCH* #1180 is a hoard of 144+ pieces that is all Carian save for 2 st., one from Phaselis and another from an unknown mint. See also *CH* 8.50, "Izmir, Turkey" (ca. 455) with 3 Carian coins.

hoards consisting of coins on the Persian standard, the large "Çal dag" hoard (*IGCH* #1178: ca. 470), which was found near the site of Sardis, is made up of Lydian Croesiad hemistaters and Persian *sigloi.* The later "Izmir" hoard (*IGCH* #1197: ca. 400), from the environs of ancient Smyrna, contains 271 Persian *sigloi.* *CH* 2.26, "Asia Minor, 1975" (450–25), contains 350+ Persian *sigloi.*

Attic money first appears in Ionia in a group of hoards that are judged to precede slightly or to coincide with the establishment of the Delian League: *IGCH* #1172, "Chios, 1919" (ca. 480): 2+ Attic tetradr., 7+ Chian didr.; #1173, "Cos" (ca. 480): 1 Attic tetradr.; 1 Mende tetradr.; 3 Peparethos tetradr.[74] The small size of these hoards makes drawing conclusions difficult. These hoards around 480 holding Athenian coins, however, may indicate an infusion of Attic money into the hands of ordinary individuals through the military operations attendant upon Xerxes' invasion of mainland Greece and the subsequent advance of Hellenic League and especially Attic military forces into eastern Aegean waters in 479–76.

Two categories of hoards that are found in Ionia, however, are more distinctive in their makeup. One group is easily understood because these hoards are dominated by coins in electrum.[75] Electrum coins had an important function in overseas trade—they served as a monetary medium for trade with the Propontis and Black Sea region.[76] Electrum coins possessed much more value than coins of corresponding weights in silver. Thus electrum hoards may have served a purpose in Ionia similar to that performed by hoarded Aiginetan staters in mainland Greece. Because their general currency extended into the most obvious areas for overseas flight or exile for individuals leaving Ionia, hoards largely or exclusively composed of electrum coins may have served also

[74] Cf. *IGCH* #1165, "Asia Minor, western, before 1893" (ca. 500) with small presence of Attic Wappenmünzen.

[75] Instances are *IGCH* #1184 = *CH* 7.21 = 8.49, "Erythrae" (ca. 455), containing over 79 electrum coins: *hectae* 'sixth-staters' from Lesbos (57) and Phokaia (11); halves from a mint that is uncertain (11), and silver from Klazomenai (3 didr.), Erythrai (3 didr.), and Chios (10 dr.); *IGCH* #1194, "Vroula?" (ca. 410–400), a nonsilver hoard from the vicinity of Klazomenai that includes 70 Cyzicene st. and 20 Lampsacene st. (with a few gold Darics); *CH* 1.20, "Asia Minor, 1971" (late fifth century) with 26 electrum coins.

[76] For discussions of the circulation of electrum, see (for detail) Laloux *RBN* (1971); F. Bodenstedt, *Phökaisches Elektron-Geld von 600–326 v. Chr.* (Mainz 1976) 74–75 (including some finds not in *IGCH* or *CH*); in brief notice, see Cavaignac, *Études* 180–82; P. Gardner, "Coinage of the Athenian Empire," *JHS* 33 (1913) 154–57; J. Johnston, "An International Managed Currency in the Fifth Century," *Hermathena* 47 (1932) 132–57; Robinson 330–33; C. Seltman *Greek Coins*[2] (London 1955) 112–14; Erxleben *AfP* (1970) 98–99, 100–101; Kraay *ACGC* 260–67.

as emergency reserves. They were often to be dug out and used only *in extremis* (pp. 105–106 below).

A second category of Ionian hoards is virtually unique to this region within the *arkhē* for the degree of variety of its contents: *IGCH* #1182, "Asia Minor" (ca. 460); #1183, "Colophon" (ca. 450); #1185, "Rhodes" (ca. 450);[77] #1188, "Troas" (ca. 450). The *IGCH* listings for the hoards are reproduced in Table 1.1. *IGCH* #1189, "Asia Minor" (ca. 450), a small hoard of 11 coins that is not enumerated in Table 1.1, may be classed with these hoards (Athens: 1 fr.; Klazomenai?: 2 fr.; Kolophon: 5 fr.; Magnesia?: 2 fr.; Teos: 1 fr.).[78]

Although it probably does not derive from a site within the *arkhē*, but from its near hinterland, the "Decadrachm" hoard of Lycia, containing ca. 1700 coins (*CH* 8.48: ca. 460), offers several features for comparison despite its dating somewhat earlier than the established dates for these hoards.[79] Coins of northern Greece comprise 8 percent of this hoard by number and 15 percent by weight of silver, with the Bisaltai (68 coins), Akanthos (28), and Abdera (5 octadr. and 14 tetradr.) especially notable. There are 187 Attic coins in the hoard, comprising 11 percent by number and 16 percent by weight. Aigina makes a very modest contribution of 5 st., and Paros is the only Cycladic mint of significance (39 coins); various Ionian mints constitute 7 percent of the coins and 5 percent of the silver (note Samos: 41; Ephesos: 34). The Carian component of the hoard is significant (18 percent of the hoard by number and weight), but virtually all these Carian coins are from a single mint, Kameiros on Rhodes (289).[80]

A considerable variety of mints is represented in all these hoards, but that variety is modified by understandable local and (even) general conditions. For example, the coinages of Kolophon and nearby Teos are a significant component of *IGCH* #1183, "Colophon," just as the great "Decadrachm" hoard (*CH* 8.48) reveals its provenience by its ca. 1,000 coins minted by Lycian dynasts (56 percent of the hoard by number and 48 percent by weight). Attic tetradrachms seem to be important in *IGCH* #1182, as far as the scanty description of the hoard allows us to

[77] Cf. P. Naster, *La collection Lucien de Hirsch* (Brussels 1959) 148. The hoard is enumerated after J.H. Kagan, "IGCH 1185 Reconsidered," *RBN* 138 (1992) 1–24.

[78] Note also *CH* 5.2, "Asia Minor, pre-1965" (480), which is a small hoard holding coins from Abdera and Thasos along with Lindos and Phaselis.

[79] S. Fried, "The Decadrachm Hoard: An Introduction," in Carradice, *Coinage and Administration* 1–9.

[80] The coins of Kameiros are relatively tightly die linked and 121 st. are from one reverse die (Fried, *Coinage and Administration* 7–8).

Table 1.1 Mid-Century Ionian Hoards

AR = silver; EL = electrum; PL = plated; Unc. = uncertain

The entries that are italicized represent mints thought to have coined in the second half of the century.

#1182 (ca. 460)	#1183 (ca. 450)	#1185 (ca. 450)	#1188 (ca. 450)
"Asia Minor"	"Colophon"	"Rhodes"	"Troas"
ca. 50 AR	3 EL, 177 AR, 1 PL	46 AR	22 AR fr.
Abdera: 1 octadr.	*Kyzikos*: 1	*Abdera*: 1 tetradr.	*Kyzikos*: 1
Thasos: 1 didr.	Lampsakos: 2	Dikaia: 1 didr.	Lampsakos: 2
Akanthos: several tetradr.	Kyme: 1	*Thasos*: 8 didr.	*Kebren*: 11
Alex. I: 5+ octadr.	*Klazomenai?*: 13	Lete: 3 didr.	*Neandreia*: 1
Pantikapaion: 1 dr.	*Kolophon*: 74	*Mende*: 1 tetradr.	*Skepsis*: 1
Athens: many tetradr.	*Ephesos*: 10	Neapolis: 1 didr.	Tenedos: 2
Aigina: 2 didr.	*Erythrai?*: 1	Stagira: 1 tetradr., 2 didr.	Aigai: 1
Ephesos: 1 dr.	Magnesia?: 26	Unc. Thrac./Mac.: 2 didr.	Mytilene: 1
Phaselis: 1 double *siglos*	*Miletos*: 2	*Aigina*: 1 didr.	*Teos*: 1
Unc. Cypriot mint: 3 st.	*Phokaia*: 1	Tenos: 1 didr.	Unc. 1
	Teos: 38	Thera?: 1 didr.	
	Samos: 1	Kos: $\frac{1}{3}$ *siglos*	
	Caria: 1	*Ialysos*: 1 fr.	
	Persian kings: 2	Lycian dynasts: 3 st.	
	Unc. mints: 3 EL, 4 AR, 1 PL	Phaselis: 1 double *siglos*	
		———	
		Aigina: 2 didr.	
		Rhodes: 2 hemidr.	
		Soloi: 1 double *siglos*	
		Tarsos: 1 tetrob.; 1 double *siglos*	
		———	
		Cyrene: 3 tetrdr., 3 dr.	
		Barke: 1 dr.	
		Barke and Teukhira: 1 tetradr.	
		Euhesperides: 2 dr.	

determine. Otherwise, Attic money is only modestly represented in these "Ionian" hoards. The even smaller role for Aiginetan coinage contrasts significantly with Cycladic and mainland hoards.

Before the recent study of J.H. Kagan on *IGCH* #1185, it was tempting to treat the disparities between this hoard and the others that are listed in Table 1.1 as a function of its findspot. Rhodes was a nexus of various trading routes to an unusual degree, so that the appearance of coins of the Greek cities of Libya (for example), so seldom found in hoards outside North Africa, did not seem inconceivable. Kagan, however, has reacted to the anomalies of *IGCH* #1185 by adducing its similarity to Egyptian hoards such as *IGCH* #1637, "Demanhur" (500) or *IGCH* #1639, "Sakha" (early fifth century). He characterizes *IGCH* #1185 as a sort of Egyptian hoard *manqué*, one that did not make its destination.

Doubtless some hoards traveled around the Mediterranean before deposition in a particular site, but surely most varied assemblages of coins must have been amassed in the region in which they were hoarded. Strandings may have taken place, but there is no practical way to isolate them and ad hoc arguments are generally unsatisfactory. Egyptian hoards exhibit a particular mixture of issues, presumably as an accurate or even a partially distorted reflection of genuine flows of currencies toward the region. There is no reason to question prima facie that *IGCH* #1185 cannot mirror the variety of monies reaching the Rhodian cities, although the principles for inclusion or exclusion of the constituent coins by an *individual* hoarder necessarily remain unfathomable. Nonetheless, Kagan's suggestion that an archaic hoard, his group A, the first division in our list, was supplemented by one or two sets of inclusions, his group B, containing Rhodian hemidrachms, and group C with its Libyan issues (as divided on our list), is credible on the basis of his careful review of the coins. In any case, *IGCH* #1185 has a core that could be dated as early as ca. 500. That will be of no help to us in determining the status of allied mints at the mid-century or later. Yet it is not impossible that groups B and C are later inclusions in the same hoard. That the hoard may have been updated later in the century, however, could indicate that the proprietors of the hoard had not changed their appreciation of the utility of hoarding these disparate coins.

In the hoards dated to mid-century that are listed in Table 1.1, the proportions of different mints represented are not necessarily equivalent to the proportions of the coins from the same mints circulating in the markets of the Greek cities in the vicinity of their findspot.[81] Athenian coins are almost certainly underrepresented (nota bene) even from the standard established by the hoards of ca. 480. Rather, our emphasis in the analysis of these hoards (even excepting group A of *IGCH* #1185) should fall on the wide range of issues that seem to have continued in circulation throughout the region. The presence of coins from northern Aegean mints may be held to signal particularly this condition. A hypothesis in favor of the growing dominance of Attic money is in truth neither

[81] J.H. Kagan, "An Archaic Greek Coin Hoard from the Eastern Mediterranean and Early Cypriot Coinage," *NC* 154 (1994) 17–52, discusses a large, varied archaic hoard that contains a significant Cypriot component. It might be helpful to our discussion if its findspot could be solidly fixed.

substantiated nor disproved by these hoards.[82] The salient impression, however, is that there is little comfort here for the traditionalists on the Coinage Decree. Missing is the "smoking gun" of a hoard or hoards that exhibit the forced closing of allied mints and the demonetization of non-Attic silver. Even a minimalist interpretation of the economic ramifications of a ban on allied coining must hold that it should have altered the usage of *Attic* money in the cities of the *arkhē*, and for that there is no hoard evidence.

The dating of these hoards (save for group A of *IGCH* #1185) again around mid-century superficially appears to illustrate the disunity of coin standards and monies existing in the *arkhē* on the eve of the consensus date for the Coinage Decree. We may freely suspect, however, that there is more than a little circularity in such an argument, since the attraction of the dates for these hoards to 450 may be owed to the dominant mid-century date for the decree. A lower date for any one of these hoards would indicate that the Coinage Decree either must be downdated or that it did not close the allied mints in Ionia. For one thing, it is hard to see what would preclude the date of *IGCH* #1183 from creeping into the third quarter of the century.[83] It has the appearance of an archaic hoard that had been supplemented in the middle of the century. The coin of Neandreia in *IGCH* #1188 may also suggest a later date for that hoard or another late inclusion. These hoards contain a significant number of issues from mints thought to have coined in the second half of the century; they are italicized in Table 1.1.

The variety of coins in these hoards does in any case diminish the likelihood that any demonetization of allied money was practical. In contrast, legislation that did nothing more than enact that Attic coins were legal tender in the cities of the *arkhē* would not clash with the evidence of these hoards. Nothing here confutes the conclusion that Athenian coins were best reserved for spending and for returning to Attica in the form of payments of the tribute and in return for other goods. Many other mints supplied coins still in circulation that might more advantageously be hoarded, if they lay ready to hand. Electrum and disparate silver coins were possibly reserved for hoarding by some

82 Any growing significance of Athenian coins among the Greek coins circulating into Egypt and the Near East is a separate, though obviously related, topic. The evidence suggests two things: that Attic money was a larger proportion of the total pool of coins, out of which travelers' holdings were drawn, and that the holders of silver of Greek provenance exhibited a preference for Attic coins. Note *IGCH* #1482–83; 1645; 1647–49; 1651.

83 Cf. C.M. Kraay, "Monnaies provenant du site de Colophon," *SNR* 42 (1962/63) 5–13; E. Varoukha-Christodoulopoulou, *AD* 18, B′1 (1963) 6–7.

persons, because they served emergency purposes satisfactorily. In the settled conditions of the *arkhē*, a catastrophe for an affluent individual came most probably in the form of exile on some political charge, and against that eventuality there was no particular point in hoarding Attic tetradrachms.

Conclusion

The hoards in their present state tell us a handful of salient facts about the use of money during the Pentekontaeteia and the Peloponnesian War. Plentiful Aiginetan and especially Athenian coins can turn up almost anywhere that Greek coins penetrated. These didrachm staters and tetradrachms, along with other heavy coins, traveled to the Egypt and the Near East where nonmonetary hoarders included any silver that came ready to hand in reserves of precious metal. The ubiquity of Athenian money makes it hard to determine the areas in which Attic coins had utility in local transactions or even legal standing. It is obvious that hoarders were biased toward the preservation of local issues, a condition that is presumably reflective of local circulation. Nonetheless, the extent of regional currency for different series varied considerably, and disparate degrees of "localism" are manifested by the hoard evidence. The validity of the coins of some mints was restricted to the home city, while Aiginetan money, representing the other end of the spectrum of circulation, had validity through an extended area of the mainland and Cyclades. Where the Greek world abutted on non-Greek regions, the coins of particular mints often possessed a special influence as media of exchange or as repositories of wealth and status for native elites. The dynamics of this influence are usually mysterious in the present absence of anecdotal material. Yet native preferences for the utilization and possession of Greek coins probably limited the options for radical changes in Greek monetary policy.

The record of minting in the fifth century in the Aegean basin is one of the closure of mints (as shall soon be seen), but the hoards offer no support for the hypothesis of the intervention of hegemonic legislation in this process. No chronologically discrete *series* of hoards on allied territory from the later fifth century was composed exclusively of Athenian coinage or of Athenian and local coins of markedly different age or wear from usage. At present, no watershed is discoverable after which allied coins radically diminish in the record of hoards. Some, however, might object that such an expectation would be unreasonable even based on a far greater number of discovered hoards. The hoards discovered since the publication of the *IGCH*, however, have not altered the shape of our evidence.

Many hoarders tended to lay down reserves not for future ordinary consumption but as hedges against subsequent crises. Available coins that were less easy to use in daily business made good candidates for inclusion in some stocks of last resort, including large denominations, and odd, foreign, damaged, or obsolete pieces (sometimes in electrum or gold). Accepting this argument as pervasive and fundamental (in the spirit of a devil's advocate), however, leads to skepticism or caution in reading the evidence of the hoards rather than to advocating the traditional interpretation of the Coinage Decree.

2

CURTAILMENT OF ALLIED MINTING

NUMISMATIC CHRONOLOGY

An analysis of the chronology of the coin emissions of Athenian allies has had a long history in scholarship on the Coinage Decree. Current analysts owe debts to several generations of investigators: to the work of Weil, Babelon, Gardner, and Cavaignac in the infancy of the subject;[1] to the important mid-century review of Robinson, who wrote in reaction to the discovery of the Kos fragment of the Coinage Decree with its Attic letters;[2] and finally to the more recent survey by Erxleben.[3] Table 2.2 (following this chapter, pp. 84–87 below) organizes some minting dates synthetically (subdivided by the districts of the *arkhē*). From the earlier reconstructions, Robinson and Erxleben occupy deserved places of prominence, and they have therefore been accorded separate columns in this table. The work of the pioneers on the subject, writing against the background of a much smaller base of data, like Cavaignac[4] and Babelon,[5] are reserved for notes.

[1] R. Weil, "Das Münzrecht der ΞΥΜΜΑΧΟΙ im ersten attischen Seebund," *ZfN* 28 (1910) 351–64, esp. z357–64; E. Babelon, "La politique monétaire d'Athènes au Ve siècle avant notre ère," *RN*[4] 17 (1913) 457–85, esp. 469–80; P. Gardner, "Coinage of the Athenian Empire," *JHS* 33 (1913) 147–88, esp. 157–81; E. Cavaignac, *Études sur l'histoire financière d'Athènes au Ve siècle* (Paris 1908) 177–87.

[2] Robinson 328–37.

[3] Erxleben *AfP* (1970) 66–126.

[4] Cavaignac, *Études* 177–87. For comparison with the discussion below, Cavaignac categorized as follows: cities that ceased coining by 480: Chalcis, Eretria, all Keos, Seriphos, Siphnos, Paros, Naxos, Delos, Tenos, Andros, Kalymna?, Kos?, Karpathos?, Knidos, Phaselis, Tenedos?, Parion?, Khalkedon/Byzantion?, and Eion; those that ceased during the *arkhē*: Thera, Miletos (resumption after 450), Halikarnassos (resumption 425), and Lycia; and those that continued coining: Karystos, Samos, Chios, Mytilene, Methymna, Ephesos, Kolophon, Teos, Erythrai, Klazomenai, Phokaia, Kyme, Rhodes (Lindos, Ialysos, Kameiros), Iasos?, Termera, Kelenderis, Lampsakos, Kyzikos, Selymbria, Khersonesos, Sinope (Attic standard from ca. 453), Maroneia, Dikaia, Abdera, Neapolis, Akanthos (Attic standard to 423, then Milesian), Sermylie, Torone, Olynthos, Potidaia, Skione, Mende, Dikaiopolis, Skapsa, Ainos, and Thasos. For Ainos as an exception, see Cavaignac *RN* (1953) 3. For another early list of exceptions to the law, see Reinach, *Mém. Acad. Ins. et Belles-Lettres* (1911) 355–56.

[5] Babelon *RN* (1913) 469–78 argued for an almost universal suspension of minting or a reduction to drachmal and fractional issues at the time of entry into League. He notes the following examples, with the date of cessation or reduction noted in parentheses when the change did not occur at the foundation of the Delian League: Aigina (456), Karystos (470), Eretria, Andros, all Keos, Delos, Tenos, Siphnos, Naxos, Paros, Thera (426), Melos (416), Phaselis

Another column presents the dates offered by other authorities where they help to supplement, with the understanding that the reader will remember that earlier scholars were not (in most instances) necessarily suggesting dates for minting activity with an eye toward the Coinage Decree.[6] In this column, some dates from disparate sources are added without annotation, and the supporting scholarship may be found in the Appendix or in the discussion below. The specific scholarship exploring the fifth-century numismatic chronology of each mint is also listed under the individual ally in the Appendix (pp. 563–98 below).

Distinctions between the weight of the coins issued have been introduced where they are significant. The absence or presence of coining in tetradrachms and staters (and, of course, other heavy coins) cannot be overemphasized inasmuch as the heavier coins dominated all large purchases and transfers of funds, including the payment of the tribute to Athens. Moreover, heavier coins often served as a means for treasurization (whether secular or sacred, private or public). Fractional coins (below the drachma) obviously had a different mode of circulation than staters. The hoard evidence suggests that they traveled shorter distances and were less likely to be hoarded. The mediate position of drachm coins may also be noted: not only did drachms supplement fractions for larger or moderate retail purchases, but they may have had an important role in conveying wages or subsidies.

The dating of coin series is hardly an exact science, so that a degree of tendentiousness or "fudging" may be held excusable. Furthermore, numismatists have tirelessly invoked the Coinage Decree as an organizing principle in their reconstructions of fifth-century mints, as it seemed to be the most prominent external historical datum in their possession and, as such, to provide the obvious external "check" for application to their

---

(466), Knidos, Halikarnassos, Iasos, Miletos, Kolophon, Erythrai, Klazomenai, Kyme, Kebren, Dardanos, Gargara, Abydos, Astakos, Parion, Lampsakos, Tenedos, Khalkedon, Byzantion, Thasos (446), Torone, Olynthos(!), Poteidaia, and Peparethos. Exceptions under special convention: Assos, Ainos, Maroneia, Abdera, Akanthos, Rhodian cities, Kos, Samos, Chios, Ephesos, and Teos; electrum minters: Mytilene, Phokaia, and Kyzikos.

[6] The most important overviews are B.V. Head, *Historia Nummorum: A Manual of Greek Numismatics*[2] (Oxford 1911); C.M. Kraay, *Archaic and Classical Greek Coins* (Berkeley and Los Angeles 1976); M. Price and N. Waggoner, *Archaic Coinage: The Asyut Hoard* (London 1975); Mattingly *Historia* (1961) 186–87; Mattingly *BSA* (1970) 142–45; Mattingly *Klio* (1977) 92–100; Mattingly *JHS* (1981) 78–85; Mattingly *EMC* (1988) 324–28; M.J. Price, "The Coinages of the Northern Aegean," in Carradice, *Coinage and Administration* 43–51.

sequencing of emissions.[7] It should therefore stand as no sign of disrespect for the valuable work of Robinson and Erxleben and their predecessors that all are inclined to acquiesce in interruptions just where they would like to date the Coinage Decree, whether in the early 440s or in the later 420s.[8] The widely differing conclusions (based on a slowly evolving body of evidence) on the dating of an interruption in allied minting caution us about designing our own "improved" chronological systems. And we must also suspect that there has been a considerable degree of amalgamation in all such systems. Amalgamation has occurred in places where shifts or breaks in sequences of minting, which probably straggled over half decades and decades, have been made to cohere for the purpose of accommodating the necessarily punctuated effect of a legislative prohibition on minting in silver.

The chronologies for individual cities seem to leave us with no single window of opportunity for placing a decree ordering a cessation of coining in silver, unless we adopt some fairly desperate escape clause such as the existence of numerous exemptions, a limited period of validity, or massive resistance leading to a withdrawal of the legislation.[9] The summary by Kraay, who upholds a mid-century decree, betrays the fragile state of the evidence for any single line of division (my italics):[10] "Nevertheless a survey of all relevant mints has produced an overall picture of interruption of coinage during *the forties and thirties*, though there are anomalies which may be due to privileged exemption from the provisions of the decree or to insubordination in districts not easily controlled by naval power." The discussion below attempts to synthesize the evidence in a different way in order to clarify motives for continuing or ceasing to mint by mint administrators.[11]

[7] One might note the various reconstructions of May on the Thracian cities of Abdera, Ainos, and Maroneia (see below, pp. 130–38, 140–49). See also Kraay, *ACGC* 387, who, in his index, reflects earlier numismatic scholarship by invoking the Coinage Decree no less than fourteen times for confirmation of the chronology of individual mints; there are other examples in the pertinent literature that he does not happen to cite.

[8] Even though Erxleben notes that the numismatic evidence does not support a decree in the 440s or the 420s; see *AJP* (1970) 132.

[9] For a Coinage Decree that was partially ineffectual, see E. Will, *Le monde grec et l'orient* (Paris 1972) 209–10; Starr, *Athenian Coinage* 69. For discussion, see pp. 177–79, 455–57 below.

[10] Kraay, *ACGC* 71.

[11] Athenian allies have been grouped in categories by their numismatic histories, which are denoted by roman numerals. These categories appear in three compilations of evidence: the aggregate contribution of tribute to the Athenian government that was made by categories is noted in Table 2.1; the chronology of minting activities of cities (if any existed) is presented

MINTING, NONMINTING, AND LEGAL TENDER

A considerable number of allied states never coined at all before 400. They are listed in category I in the Appendix. Such cities form a virtually ignored component of the monetary history of the Attic alliance, although the decision not to mint and use local coins is as significant as any other action in monetary policy.[12] At all times these states include the majority of tributary communities in the *arkhē*. Out of all the states mentioned in the tribute lists, 227 (or 72 percent) out of about 316 tributaries did not mint coins before or during the Athenian hegemony.[13] In the chronological subdivisions into which payment of tribute has been analyzed here (starting from the actual assessment periods), about three fifths of the tributaries at any one time were states that never minted.[14] These states, however, contributed a much more modest proportion of the total attested tribute in any period, about a sixth or a fifth (note Table 2.1 [pp. 54–55 below], category I).

Thus, the absence of minting activity in an allied city, or for that matter, in any Greek *polis*, is partially a function of the size of the economy of the particular *polis*, for our assumption must always be that Attic tribute assessments generally reflect the scale of local economic activity.[15] There are naturally many exceptions (mainly small cities with mints), but in the aggregate the smaller the economy of the political entity the less likely it is to have minted at some time before 400. Concomitantly, the larger the

in Table 2.2; and the Appendix records tribute payments of individual allied states, the hoard evidence for their coinage, and a numismatic bibliography for each mint.

[12] Kraay's list of mints (*ACGC* 379–82) and B.V. Head, *Historia Nummorum: A Manual of Greek Numismatics* [2] (Oxford 1911) are supplemented to identify cities without fifth-century mints.

[13] This enumeration excludes the tributaries from the Black Sea region, which appear only in the assessment of 425/4. As noted, the Pontic region had a pattern of monetary circulation different from that of the Aegean, a condition that would permit a separation of the Pontic allies (attested in *IG* I^3 71.IV.126–72), even if the necessary information about their assessments was available. For these mints, see Erxleben *AJP* (1970) 123–24; *SNG* 9, *The British Museum: Part I: The Black Sea* (London 1993).

[14] Assessment periods rather than individual years are used to remove some of the uncertainties of missing, partial, or restored numbers for specific years. The regular assessment periods form a framework until 429 when a shift is made to two synthetic categories (7 and 8) for the data from the 420s, when the evidence becomes sketchier. Please consult the Appendix for the demarcation of the periods. Amounts of tribute are listed with some simplication of figures and notation, based on *ATL* 1 and Meiggs 540–59. All figures in Meiggs's table have usually been accepted for this purpose, without distinguishing complete numbers from restorations based on partial annotations or space considerations.

[15] See Figueira, *Aegina* 38–39, 122–25; Figueira, *Colonization* 193–94. See also L. Nixon and S. Price, "The Size and Resources of Greek Cities," in O. Murray and S. Price (eds.), *The Greek City: From Homer to Alexander* (Oxford 1990) 137–70.

polis the more probable it is to have struck coins (see below, pp. 481–82). Larger economies had better subsidized governmental apparatuses and so could afford to sustain minting activity. They could also procure sufficient stocks of silver to ensure the implementation of a program of coining.

It may well be true that smaller and poorer cities had more autarkic economies. One must consider, however, the monetized interactions within such autarkic, small, contained, or isolated local economies, disregarding consumption in the household, barter between *oikoi*, the role of dependent labor, and governmental or communal recirculation of goods. Thereupon, it may be seen that the proportion of transactions mediated monetarily that involved partners using nonlocal currencies was related to the size of the economy. In these transactions, the indigenous coinage of a small economy labored under the burden of its relative unattractiveness to those partners. Transactors would have been reluctant to carry away coins that had little value as money elsewhere, because the availability abroad of possible circulators of these coins back to the area of their main usage would have varied with the scale of the foreign trade of the issuing city. The coins of larger economies with greater activity (total and not necessarily proportional) in foreign trade kept more of their premium over their bullion value to the users of other currencies than did the coins of the smallest local economies; they recirculated more easily toward areas of their local validity. The participants in the smaller economies were accordingly under the continual pressure of circumstances to accept as legitimate tender the coins in use with or preferred by nonlocal transactors to mitigate the disadvantages of the unattractiveness of their own coins. Otherwise that unattractiveness levied a toll in goods in any exchange of currencies.

Furthermore, once a foreign currency achieved validity in an economy, it continued to compete with a local currency that may still have been relatively disadvantaged. That competition may have resulted in the dominance of the foreign currency even over the local market. Various factors may have diluted this impact; for example, there could have been competition among two or more foreign currencies. Second, legislation or social convention may have maintained the importance of the local money in paying certain taxes and supporting specific functions in religious or other ideological settings. All in all, however, cities with smaller economies had stronger incentives not to initiate minting or to terminate it after it had commenced. Compared to the situation of Athens' smaller allies, the size of the Attic economy, the scale of income and expenditures of the Athenian state, and the magnitude of the non-Attic economic

TABLE 2.1 Tribute Payments and Monetary Activity

(Roman numerals [for example, IIIB] denote categories of Athenian allies)

Format:

CATEGORY: Tribute amount (= talents.drachms)
Number of tributary states known to pay in period
Trib. %: Category's percentage of total tribute paid in period

Periods	1	2	3	4	5	6	7	8
No. of tributaries	152	172	148	173	71	164	99	121
I	75.3420	68.2860	53.5000	61.3210	29.3320	59.2370	37.2431	106.2040
	100 (66%)	102 (59%)	91 (61%)	101 (58%)	41 (58%)	101 (62%)	57 (58%)	89 (74%)
Trib. %	19%	17%	17%	16%	17%	17%	16%	20%
I+II	98.1760	93.4560	62.1500	83.5170	37.3320	88.3470	59.1331	107.2940
	109 (72%)	111 (65%)	99 (67%)	110 (64%)	44 (62%)	109 (66%)	62 (63%)	91 (75%)
Trib. %	25%	23%	20%	21%	21%	25%	25%	20%
IIIA	51.3000	46.5840	28.5000	31.2000	4	36.3000	15.1000	53.1500
	8 (5%)	10 (6%)	9 (6%)	11 (6%)	2 (3%)	10 (6%)	6 (6%)	8 (7%)
I+II+ IIIA	149.4760	140.4400	91.0500	115.1170	41.3320	125.0470	74.2311	160.4440
	117 (77%)	121 (70%)	108 (73%)	121 (70%)	46 (65%)	119 (73%)	68 (69%)	99 (82%)
Trib. %	38%	34%	29%	29%	23%	35%	32%	30%
IIIB	29.2320	51.2200	30.5200	46.4480	15.1180	27.4180	25.3280	65
	8 (5%)	12 (7%)	8 (5%)	12 (7%)	8 (11%)	11 (7%)	8 (8%)	5 (4%)
IIIC	32.1290	36.4000	32.4315	37.1000	22	43	18.5000	35
	7 (5%)	8 (5%)	9 (6%)	9 (5%)	3 (4%)	9 (5%)	5 (5%)	3 (2%)
III A–IIIC	113.0610	135.0040	92.2515	115.1480	40.1180	107.1180	59.3280	153.1500
	23 (15%)	30 (17%)	26 (18%)	32 (18%)	13 (18%)	30 (18%)	19 (19%)	16 (13%)

I+II+	222.2370	228.4600	154.4015	199.0650	77.4500	195.4650	121.4611	260.4440
III	122 (80%)	141 (82%)	125 (84%)	142 (82%)	57 (80%)	139 (85%)	81 (82%)	107 (88%)
Trib. %	56%	55%	50%	50%	43%	55%	52%	49%
IVA	21.4000	14.4000	20.0200	18.5200	10	29.3000	2.1000	6
	8 (5%)	8 (5%)	4 (3%)	7 (4%)	3 (4%)	7 (4%)	3 (3%)	1 (1%)
IVB	13.3500	11.1000	10.4000	11.2000	6.1000	3.1000	6.1500	24.0500
	7 (5%)	5 (3%)	6 (4%)	7 (4%)	3 (4%)	5 (3%)	5 (5%)	3 (2%)
IVC	41.3010	48.5440	15	32	6	24	28.1000	40
	5 (3%)	6 (3%)	2 (1%)	5 (3%)	1 (1%)	4 (2%)	3 (3%)	4 (3%)
IV A–IVC	76.4510	74.4440	45.4200	62.1200	22.1000	56.4000	36.3500	70.0500
	20 (13%)	19 (11%)	12 (8%)	19 (11%)	7 (10%)	16 (10%)	11 (11%)	8 (7%)
Trib. %	19%	18%	14%	16%	12%	16%	17%	13%
I–IV	299.1180	303.3040	200.2215	261.1850	99.5500	252.2650	158.2111	330.4950
	142 (93%)	160 (93%)	137 (93%)	161 (93%)	64 (90%)	155 (95%)	92 (93%)	115 (95%)
Trib. %	75%	73%	63%	66%	56%	71%	68%	63%
V	3	3	30	30	30	30	30	60
	1 (1%)	1 (1%)	1 (1%)	1 (1%)	1 (1%)	1 (1%)	1 (1%)	1 (1%)
VI	15	15.4320	1.5250	23	9	9	21	20
	2 (1%)	3 (2%)	1 (1%)	3 (2%)	1 (1%)	1 (1%)	2 (2%)	1 (1%)
VIIA	43.3000	43.3000	52	42	0	27.3000	0	2
	3 (2%)	3 (2%)	4 (3%)	3 (2%)	0 (0%)	3 (2%)	0 (0%)	1 (1%)
VIIB	36.3000	48.3000	34.3000	38,3000	40	36	24	116
	4 (3%)	5 (3%)	5 (3%)	5 (3%)	5 (7%)	4 (2%)	4 (4%)	3 (2%)
VII	80	92	86.3000	80.3000	40	63.3000	24	118
A+B	7 (5%)	8 (5%)	9 (6%)	8 (5%)	5 (7%)	7 (4%)	4 (4%)	4 (3%)
Trib. %	20%	22%	27%	20%	22%	18%	10%	22%
I–VII	398.1180	414.1360	317.5215	394.4850	178.5500	354.5650	233.2111	528.4950
	152	172	148	173	71	164	99	121

activity that was regularly and (one assumes) legally transacted in Athenian coins were all vastly greater during the height of the *arkhē*.

In the traditional interpretation of the Coinage Decree, the existence of these noncoiners has not received its due emphasis. To be sure, these cities never had mints to close down or to be closed down, but concomitantly they did not inaugurate coining during the Pentekontaeteia. A significant number of these states did indeed coin in silver and/or bronze after the period of the *arkhē*. As many as fifty of these states may have coined at some juncture in their later history. While it is hard to come to global judgments about the motivations to coin or not, the creation of a large political entity, the Delian alliance, arguably helped to integrate monetary usage in these states by virtue of one dominating political circumstance, the payment of the annual *phoros* to Athens and Athenian expenditure of *phoros*. In many places, the advantage of employing Attic coins and perhaps the coins of other allied mints of regional significance inhibited any motivation toward inaugurating a local coinage. The disinclination to coin is especially conspicuous in those cities that minted after the fall of the *arkhē*.

Although it is not an absolute certainty that these allies were all using Athenian money locally, it is important to stress that it cannot have been the case that sovereignty or administrative provision barred the acceptance of foreign money, such as the Attic owls, in their local markets and for the payment of taxes, because there was no local money to be privileged. It is overwhelmingly likely that among the other currencies in usage in many of these allied cities Athenian coins held a recognized place as tender accepted as appropriate by enactment or custom. As will be seen below, the greater availability of Attic coin in comparison to other currencies promoted its use. Even if some smaller places without their own money used the coins of larger neighbors with some frequency, in some cases possibly from a time before the inauguration of the alliance (cf. pp. 476–81 below), their failure to mint is still significant for the role of Attic coins. The common usage of a few international or regional currencies is a manifestation of consolidation of monies and, in particular, much simplified the process of conversion into Attic money.[16]

The issue of an officially recognized standing for Attic coins in allied cities—its status as legal tender—has been skirted above in favor of terms such as "legitimacy," "validity," "currency," and "utility" because one must not generalize to many cases without specific evidence. The legal

[16] Cf. Finley, "Classical Greece" 24, who notes that collection of tribute and payment of Athenians and armies abroad discouraged allied minting. See below pp. 260–73.

status of coins was a legitimate and regular legislative concern that was addressed in lawmaking that exhibits a varying degree of exclusivity. Our thin dossier of material does provide one important example of the legislation of a monopoly of the state currency. In a decree of Olbia usually dated to the middle of the fourth century, it is mandated that all business be conducted in Olbian silver and bronze (*SIG*[3] 218). Such a provision clearly represents the highest degree of privilege that may be accorded by a state to its own coins.

A somewhat lesser level of recognition was involved at Athens, as evidenced by the law proposed by Nikophon of 375/4 (*SEG* 26.72; discussed at length below, pp. 536–47). Here it is clear from the scrutiny of coins by a public slave (the *dokimastēs*) in the *bouleuterion* that payment to the government was made in Attic coins (lines 4–8). Tellingly, it was also compulsory that sellers receive payment in Attic coin that had been approved by the *dokimastēs* (lines 16–18). There is also, however, a suggestion here that the Athenian state did not interfere with transactions between private parties if they chose to use foreign coins or coins that were not approved (lines 8–10). As shall be seen below, there are some indications that foreign coins, particularly those of Aigina, Chios, and Kyzikos, were occasionally, but apparently legally, used at Athens in private business.[17] As we have just envisioned, other governments may have had greater difficulty than the Athenians in enforcing the rule that their own money had to be accepted by local transactors.

There are many attestations of the term *dokimos* 'approved' or 'valid' (and related words) as applied to coins (see pp. 398–400 below); most are literary but an early example is an archaic Eretrian inscription specifying the required medium for the paying of fines (*IG* XII.9 1273). This terminology establishes that rules often existed that limited the types of coins that could be used in dealings with the government of a *polis*. In many cases, this limitation validated only the local coins, just as Nikophon's law documents for Athens. Similarly, when the Corinthians, who were dispatching a contingent of colonists to Epidamnos in 435, allowed volunteers unable to travel with the expedition to reserve a place by payment, they specified an obligation for tendering 50 Corinthian staters (Thuc. 1.27.1). Likewise, when fines are cited in numbers of staters in sixth- and fifth-century contexts, it is natural to assume that payment was required in the "standard coin" of the local coinage.[18] Some states will,

[17] The restrictions or allowances for various coinages involved in the tribute system of the Delian League is a vitally important topic that will engage our attention below (pp. 273–95).

[18] Chios: Meiggs-Lewis #8B.3 (575–50); Corcyra: Thuc. 3.70.4 (427); Erythrai: *IErythrai* #2A.16–18, #2C.15–17 (pre-454); Thasos: *SEG* 18.347.5; *IG* XII Suppl. 347.I.3; cf. *IG* XII.8

however, have accepted receipts in foreign coins. Among them must have been the aforesaid states that did not mint. They had to denote which foreign money or monies would be acceptable for paying taxes,[19] unless one is prepared to grant that nonminting governments were ready to accept any coins of disparate origin and standard, a phenomenon that is in any case entirely unattested. In this eventuality, it would be also necessary to assume (improbably) that the disbursements of funds by such authorities were made in assorted currencies, presumably calculated by weight.

The principle that tribute assessments are grounded in the ability to pay and are thus reflective of underlying economic output is for us a central insight. There are no low assessments found among the mints in category VII, the ones that are the best candidates for inclusion among those continuously minting a range of denominations for the duration of the *arkhē*. Even when we compare the minters of drachms and fractions in category IV with the nonminters in category I, the former are still visibly larger than the latter. Thus, it is likely that a majority of the states in the *arkhē* that never minted before the fall of Athens made their choice not to coin based solely on economic factors (such as difficulties in managing exchange or a lack of access to stocks of silver) and not by virtue of any Athenian legislation. The tendencies of small cities not to mint or to cease minting and of larger cities to maintain local coinages teaches the priority of economic factors over legislation in shaping the monetary history of the Attic hegemony.

There has been a temptation to consider allied states that started coining during the duration of the *arkhē* from the standpoint of what their experiences can tell us about the chronology of the Coinage Decree. A group of these states, however, bears a strong resemblence to those nonminters who began minting only after the dissolution of the *arkhē*. This point will become clearer on a consideration of specific examples, which are isolated in category II. In the first place, there is considerable doubt surrounding the initiation of minting activity by some of these states. Did they begin coining during the existence of the tribute system (that is, before 413) or even during the Attic hegemony? For example, Schönert-Geiss, who has analyzed Byzantine money exhaustively is nonetheless

265.9; *IG* XII Suppl. 349A.7. The elaborate regulations concerning the Thasian *hieron* of Herakles contain a number of such references: lines 8–10, 28, 34, 39, 40, 46. See H. Duchêne, *La stèle du port: Fouilles du Port* 1, *Études thasiennes* 14 (Paris 1992).

19 Loans made to Arkesine on Amorgos indicate that this city accepted Attic coinage and secondarily the coinages of Alexander and of Demetrios: *IG* XII.7 69.21–23 (end of the fourth or beginning of the third century); *IG* XII.7 67B.53–57 (= *SIG*³ 955; second century or later).

in the minority opinion that the city began minting as early as 411. Moreover, a date after the end of Athenian hegemony was offered by Babelon for Lamponeia, Neandreia, Pitane, Pordoselene, Prokonnesos, and Tragilos.

In this regard, the first firmly attested appearance of the coins of these mints in a dated hoard ought to be carefully reviewed: Aphytis (*CH* 8.83, "Thasos, 1984/85": 400–300; *IGCH* #472, "Aphytis": 185–65); Bottiaioi (*IGCH* #380, "Olynthus": 348); Byzantion (*IGCH* #716, "Thrace?, 1933–34": ca. 357; #723, "Thasos, 1953": 340–35; #1259. "Cilicia, before 1914": ca. 380); Elaia (a bronze coin in *IGCH* #1227, "Lesbos?, 1936": fourth century?); Gargara (*IGCH* #1229, "Troas": fourth century); Idyma (*IGCH* #1639, "Sakha": early fifth century;[20] *CH* 5.17, "Caria": 375; *IGCH* #1289, "Mylasa": ca. 300); Lamponeia (no hoard evidence); Neandreia (*IGCH* #1188, "Troas": ca. 450); Pitane (no hoard evidence); Pordoselene/Nesos (*IGCH* #1227, "Lesbos": fourth century); Prokonnesos (no hoard evidence); Tragilos (no hoard evidence).

Fixing the dates of inaugurations or resumptions of coining during the Peloponnesian War is notoriously difficult. As we shall see elsewhere, the tendency to date changes or innovations in minting to changes in allegiance to the Athenians has been overwhelming in evidentiary environments poor in other points of political demarcation. Here, the first date of coining for some of these states, specifically Aphytis, Byzantion, Spartolos, and Gargara, has been determined following the hypothesis of its contemporaneity with a "defection" from Athens. The impression garnered from the hoards is that some of this class of mints are fourth-century; others may have started (fitfully or at a low level) during the Peloponnesian War at the earliest. Except for Byzantion, the scholarship on all these mints is quite outdated.

I argue below (pp. 247–52) that the inauguration of minting ought not to be considered an indispensable (or even strongly contingent) concomitant of achieving autonomy. Therefore, the start of minting activity in some of these cases might have resulted from the severing of the connection with the tribute system and the weakening of the minter's integration into the economic system of the *arkhē*, at least as much as to any need to sever symbolic ties with the Athenians. Those who revolted from Athens had to protect themselves from Athenian counterattacks and sometimes from subversion by Atticizers, while the Spartans were not always dependable allies during the Ionian War in terms of expeditiously

20 The single coin of Idyma in the Sakha hoard is argued to be a forgery or an insertion: J.P. Barron, *The Silver Coins of Samos* (London 1966) 31.

coming to the aid of those they induced to rebel. The subvention and fiscal supervision of an independent military establishment sometimes required a reliable local stock of money. Hence, an initiation of coining for military reasons need not follow revolt all that closely. And there were corresponding economic or fiscal stresses caused by the Peloponnesian War for states that remained loyal to their alliance with the Athenians. War expenditures took a greater share of a decreased production of Athenian coins. So a decreased flow of Attic money was entering some allied local economies. Finally, the termination of Attic hegemony disrupted the modes of economic cooperation and the circulation of coins in ways that cannot be distinguished from those changes influenced by allegiance under stress, embattled defection, and military exigencies. Accordingly, throughout this work the placement of alterations in minting practices during the Peloponnesian War, and especially in its Ionian or Decelean phase (and even in the immediate aftermath of Athens' defeat), must always be read as tentative. As series of coins tend more often to be lowered than raised in their dating, some late fifth-century coining activity, over which numismatists would have political historians puzzle concerning its ramifications for Aegean hegemony, may belong in the posthegemonic fourth century.

For one state among category II mints a judgment can be hazarded about the relationship of the initiation of minting and the city's allegience to Athens. Elaia has been considered a relatively early starter at coining compared to the other mints that were opened during the Attic hegemony. Its fractions are minted on the Attic standard and carry the head of Athena crowned with a garland of olive. Both features suggest an intention to produce a currency that was adapted to and complemented contemporary Attic issues, not one that hurled a gesture of defiance at Athenian hegemony. A local shortage of other coins and perhaps primarily Athenian silver is probably the cause for this initiation of coining. Unfortunately, the chronology for Elaian coinage is most obscure.

All these matters considered, it is unlikely that the initiation of coining by these category II allies has any relationship at all to the existence, implementation, or chronology of a Coinage Decree that prohibited minting silver. In this determination, the fact that these states began to coin in drachms and fractions is also significant. In the standing interpretation of the Coinage Decree, the common phenomenon among the allies of minting only coins of drachm and lighter weight is puzzling, as a legislated Attic monopoly over silver coins in the alliance must have been as valid for fractions as for staters. The traditional hypothesis then ought to raise a chronological question about the moment of the passage of the legislation to which is joined a political question about the adherence or resistance to it by the allies. Instead of these questions, the numismatic record of the category II cities prompts an investigation of the causes for an initiation of coining in drachms and fractions. That examination will quickly lead to the related exploration of why some mints ceased to coin except for drachms and fractions (cf. pp. 72–75).

Where coining only drachms and fractions is begun, some other currency must occupy the economic niche previously held by larger coins. That should normally be the same foreign currency utilized during the period of nonminting. The parallel switch from coining in a full range of denominations toward coining in drachms and fractions can be understood similarly, and is a process cognate with the gradual cessation of minting across the board (considered below).[21] When a community restricted its minting to lighter coins, where local stater-weight coins had previously been issued, the economic roles for those heavier coins were probably not then occupied by local lighter issues. Moreover, a pattern of interchange must have existed where local drachms or fractions were used in the division of larger coins or to provide change. The alternative that coexisting coin series were never permitted to interact appears less likely.

That Attic tetradrachms mainly served as the larger coins circulating in communities that stopped minting staters is suggested by a number of factors (to be discussed below), such as the prevalence of Attic tetradrachms and the scarcity of alternatives; the promotion of interaction with the Attic economy, the largest by far in the *arkhē*; and the facilitation of the payment of tribute. By analogy, the cities that began minting drachms and fractions only during the second half of the fifth century had previously recognized the validity of Attic tetradrachms. Once the decision had been made to begin minting smaller denominations, in principle no problem should have existed for the exchanges of monies necessitated by international trade or by the tribute system, since the larger denominations in local use were already in large part Attic coins.

The special case of Byzantion underwrites this conclusion: the coexistence of an allied mint restricting its output to lighter coins and the Athenian mint supplying heavier coins to the local economy has nothing to do intrinsically with the "right" or "prerogative" of minting in silver (the focus of previous scholarly investigation). Byzantion differs from the other category II economies by virtue of its size. None of the other states in this group ever paid more than 3T of *phoros*, while the Byzantines paid as much as 18T, 1,800 dr. Furthermore, Byzantion

[21] Cf. Gardner *JHS* (1913) 149, 181–82.

lies relatively far from Attica. As we discover below, similarly distant comparable economies were usually active minters. This anomaly could be partially explained by the fact that the Byzantines may have employed electrum coins, Cyzicene staters and Phocaic *hectae*, taking them in taxes from the traders passing through the Bosporus.[22]

Nevertheless, it is also likely that the famous iron money of Byzantion acted as a token currency in place of fractional silver.[23] The utilization of such coins uniquely at Byzantion was a product of special circumstances. Other *poleis* did not have the same ability to impose a relatively valueless medium of exchange on those resorting to their port and market without risking the diversion of business to alternative locales that conducted retail transactions in fractional silver. Byzantion had a unique, unsubstitutable location in transportation between the Propontis and Black Sea, so that its iron currency did not create a major economic disadvantage. Yet, the Byzantines did not differ from those minting lighter silver denominations in their probable use of foreign heavier coins. Consequently, the Byzantines began to mint drachms and fractions, not because some Attic legal restriction was ended or made irrelevant, but because the war had changed the flow of foreign coins to them in ways that increasing the supply of iron money could not redress by itself. For one thing, it is probable that the military catastrophes suffered by the Athenians in the Ionian War lowered the merchant traffic through the straits, causing Byzantine collection of taxes in foreign coins to diminish.

In our calculation of how much of the taxational activities (and the underlying economic activities) was conducted in terms of Attic and other panhellenic currencies, we can collapse category II, comprising initiators of drachm and fraction minting during the *arkhē*, into category I, the nonminting states (see Table 2.1, entry I + II). This amalgamation gives us another estimate of the scale of allied economic output susceptible to transactions in Athenian money.

CESSATION OF MINTING DURING THE *ARKHĒ*

The investigation why allied states stopped their minting activities during the lifetime of the *arkhē* is necessarily complex, as these influences can

[22] The fractional coinage of Kalkhedon, another Megarian colony across the straits in Asia, could have been used at Byzantion. Yet the coins appear too scanty to have had much of an impact on fiscal conditions, even if one could be sure that they were fifth-century.

[23] Arist. *Nubes* 249 with scholia 249a–c Holwerda; Strattis fr. 36 K = fr. 37, *PCG* 7.640; Plato Com. fr. 96 K = fr. 103, *PCG* 7.475–76 (from the *Peisandros*); Hesych. s.v. σιδάρεοι θεοί, σ 592 Latte; Ael. Aristid. 46.145.25; Pollux 7.105; 9.78. Contrast D.H. Crawford, "*Sidareoi* at Byzantium," *Athenaeum* 70 (1982) 276; see also M. Oeconomides, "'Iron Coins': A Numismatic Challenge," *RIN* 95 (1993) 75–78.

in principle be economic, fiscal, diplomatic, or hegemonic. That the monetary history of the Delian League must in large part be determined by the answers to this question is significant in itself. That far more cities ceased minting during the Athenian hegemony than initiated coining, as we have already seen, is an especially striking phenomenon, particularly since many relatively larger mints closed compared with the small mints that initiated activity. My working hypothesis will be that the attrition of allied minting activity during the Pentekontaeteia is to be attributed to several interrelated influences: an increasing dominance of Attic money among the allies; the metrological consolidation and economic integration that accompanied that dominance; and the creation of settled military conditions within an emergent large political entity.

In Table 2.3 (following this chapter, pp. 88–91 below), mints that went out of operation (category III) are divided into three subcategories: (A) those that ceased minting before 478; (B) those that ceased minting in 478–65; and (C) those that ceased minting in 465–45. The categories can be considered equivalent to (A) those states that ended their minting before the establishment of the Delian League; (B) those states that ceased minting either during the first assessments of the league and the first wave of commutations from the contribution of ships to payment of tribute or down to the aftermath of the battle of Eurymedon; and (C) those states that ceased tribute before a putative mid-century Coinage Decree or before the declaration of the Thirty Years Peace between Athens and the Peloponnesians in 446/5. As previously, the relevant citations on which these determinations are based are summarized in the Appendix.[24]

Early Fifth-Century Cessation of Minting

When we calculate the number of cities that were minting at various times, the early decades of the fifth century stands out as one peak of that activity. Notably, a number of cities that had minted in the late sixth or the early fifth century ceased coining by the time of Xerxes' expedition. There can have been no influence of Athenian legislation on their decision.[25] For this earliest group, some of whom may well have ceased minting even before the Persian invasion of the mainland, the logistics of minting may well have proved more trouble than the advantages conferred by more control over fiscal adminstration.[26] The potential profits of charging a minting

[24] Although her compilation deals with the inauguration of activity in coining by Greek *poleis*, see E. Schönert-Geiss, "Einige Bemerkungen zu präemonetären Geldformen und zu Anfängen der Münzprägung," *Klio* 69 (1987) 406–22. The material collected therein provides another useful bibliography on Greek mints.

[25] The evidence from hoards for the coins of this first group is summarized in the Appendix.

[26] Governments could not of course discharge their monetary responsibilities without sufficient coin. The springing into existence of many small mints in the late archaic period

fee might also have been counterbalanced by the difficulty of acquiring sufficient stocks of silver for a sizable striking. Any encouragement of civic pride through the existence of a local coinage would have been diluted by the circulation of more prevalent "international" coinages in the local economy. The coins of this first group are in any case rather meager issues (a conclusion underlined by some difficulties of attribution), so that it would have been difficult for the governments of their cities of issuance to impose an exclusivity for local coins even in the payment of taxes.[27]

Besides the influence of these factors in undercutting the advantages of coining, over time the intensified emissions of the larger mints in their regions may also have played a role in discouraging further minting activities. For example, the circulation of vast numbers of Aiginetan and Athenian coins (and to a lesser extent Corinthian coins) is probably implicated in the closing of insular mints. Similarly, the activities of the Rhodian mints may have been involved in the closing of Carian mints like those of Kalymna, Karpathos, Kaunos, and Khersonesos.

Observe also that numismatists have doubtless been using 480–79 as a convenient dividing line, and no one would be too surprised if some of these series did indeed extend into the 470s (if only with a light or residual use of dies cut before 480). Eretria might be an example of this phenomenon. Although the dislocations attendant on the Persian invasion undoubtedly played a role in the desuetude of so many series in categories IIIA and IIIB, it is equally likely that the initiation of payments of tribute in coin to Athens played a part in dampening any inclination toward a resumption of minting activity. A monetary watershed for the Aegean basin was marked by the shift from Persian hegemony to alliance with Athens, for the Persians exacted tribute in service, natural products, and (significantly for this study) weights of precious metals. Thus the Achaemenid system of taxation promoted the raising of taxes in silver by Greek cities, but, at the same time, created no impediments to the usage of local money. There were no exchange problems when transfers to satrapal treasuries were made in bullion. As we discover below, the requirement to pay the tribute to Athens in the form of Attic coins could create problems in exchanging currency. In contrast, no one would argue

---

perhaps reflects that coinage was not yet so prevalent that its availability for payment was not ensured without maintaining a capacity to strike coins as needed.

[27] A problematical attribution of coins to Anaphe exists: Imhoof-Blummer and Cox assign issues with an amphora obverse to the island; Robert is sceptical. Naxos is an alternative provenience. Varying assignments also exist for the coins of Andros (most significantly, to Karthaia on Keos). The existence of archaic mints at Kalymnos and Mylasa is also controversial. Note the relevant entries in the Appendix.

for so early a version of the Coinage Decree (as traditionally understood) that it could have mandated the closing of mints in 480–75.

We now return to our calculation of the number of cities that were not actively minting and the proportion of the allied tribute that they were contributing. Inasmuch as Athenian hegemonic *mandates* can in no way be implicated in the decision of these states to terminate independent coinages, it is appropriate that category IIIA also be combined with categories I and II, that is, (I) the allied states that never minted either before or during the existence of the alliance and (II) the allies who began minting smaller denominations (usually) rather late in the lifetime of the alliance. Approximately 70 percent of the cities that are attested to have paid tribute in each of our periods were not minting at the time of the foundation of the Delian League. In other words, the practice of using foreign currency in the local economy and taxational system must have been well established for a strong majority of the allied states at the moment of the league's conception. Because smaller states tended to discontinue coining comparatively earlier than their larger neighbors, the allies who never minted, those no longer minting by 478/7, or those not yet striking coins do not produce anything near the same percentage of the allied tribute (see entry I + II + IIIA in Table 2.1). The cities that ceased coining operations are, however, visibly larger in economic terms on average than the allied cities enumerated in our classes I and II.

Even if some of these series in category IIIA straggled a little further into the early years of the Delian League, they are surely to be classed with the next category of mints (IIIB). This class is composed of cities that stopped minting during the 470s and early 460s. It would again be imprudent to trace all or even many of these cessations of coining to legislation, although some decisions to leave off minting and accord a local validity to Attic money (and perhaps to other "panhellenic" coinages) may have been enshrined in bilateral agreements between individual cities and Athens (such diplomacy may lie behind Aristophanes' humor in the *Birds*: below pp. 213–16). In general, these closings of local mints are probably still better comprehended as political decisions concerning the costs and benefits of maintaining a local capacity to produce money.

Some of these cessations of minting activity were probably conditioned by the shift from ship-contributing to tributary status, as encouraged by main Athenian commander of Delian League forces, Kimon (Plut. *Cimon* 11.1–3). Commutations of previous service in person and through the contribution of ships enhanced the integration of the local economy with the Attic economy and intensified the demand for the Attic coins necessary (in the main) for tendering the required tribute (see below, pp. 267–71). The predominance of the Aiginetic and Euboeic/Attic standards among the insular mints, and indeed among early closers of their mints in general, may also have abetted the substitution of Attic and Aiginetan coins for local issues. Sixteen or seventeen out of twenty-eight mints in our categories IIIA and IIIB used the Euboeic/Attic or the Aiginetic standards. Here, where only a restricted number of local coins may ever have been in circulation, the economic role of the regional coinages would have been elevated from the beginnings of a monetary economy.

It has been a common observation of numismatists that the imposition of a putative ban on coining by the Athenians was most effective nearest Attica.[28] In contrast, the aforesaid prevalence of Athenian and Aiginetan alternative currencies among the islands can be thought to have achieved the same result without legislation. In fact, the very hypothesis of a variable effectiveness for the Coinage Decree over distance carries with it the seeds of the refutation of the traditional interpretation (a ban on allied minting), inasmuch as other stipulations of Attic imperial legislation are not ordinarily submitted to similar tests of efficacy by virtue of proximity. It is assumed, for instance, that when the Athenians made provision for the collection of tribute those rules were observed or were enforced by the Athenians, who used a show of military force or its actual application (in a last resort).[29] If the Athenians believed that the expenditure of military effort against recalcitrant (or difficult to protect) allies was disproportionate in cost to the advantages to be gained in exerting control, they dropped such states from their *arkhē* (as seen in the disappearance from the tribute lists of some Carian states during the late 440s and early 430s). A phenomenon like the level of continuity of coin production, which varied in intensity over geographical distance, looks more like the result of internal policy decisions by the allies than the effect of Attic legislation. Hence, the growing sway of Attic coinage over the Aegean islands, as evinced by the extinction of local mints, is the sort of differential result that cries out for an explanation other than an Athenian mandate.

[28] This point is most often made about the allies from the Cyclades, starting from the beginnings of the modern discussions of the Coinage Decree and fifth-century monetary history: for example, Weil *ZfN* (1910) 352; Gardner *JHS* (1913) 157–59, 181; E.S.G. Robinson, "Some Problems in the Later Fifth Century Coinage of Athens," *ANSMN* 9 (1960) 1–15, esp. 4, where effectiveness also varies with distance of mints from Athens.

[29] For instance, through the agency of the *argurologoi*, for which see *HCT* 2.202–203; Meiggs 254; Figueira, *Colonization* 174.

Special Circumstances Among the Insular Mints

In addition, the growing influence of Attic money and perhaps that of other "panhellenic" currencies is indicated by the experiences of several insular mints whose relationship to the Athenian government varied from that of the ordinary tributary. First of these states is Delos, which was never a tributary community, falling under a unique category of imperial administration that is hard to specify in the absence of direct testimony. The Delian mint does seem to cease about the time of the foundation of the Delian League, although probably not at the order of the Attic government.[30] One wonders why Delian coinage was not maintained, if only to provide a medium for the dedication of the *aparkhē* to Apollo out of the tribute of the early years of the alliance. The answer is probably economic: Delian coins had always been few and Attic and Aiginetan/Aiginetic coins were dominant in the Cyclades.

In the second instance are Skyros and Thera. Skyros was resistant to Attic hegemony and the Skyrians were expelled from their island, to be replaced by Athenian colonists in 476/5.[31] Thera was induced to join the Athenian alliance rather late (probably in the late 430s). Thera and Skyros are examples of insular mints that ended production prior to their affiliation with Athens. While there can be no causative role for an Athenian mandate, the Theran and Skyrian mints share the experience, alongside their neighbors within the *arkhē*, of a disinclination to continue minting their own coins.

A final comparative case is Melos, one insular mint that continued to strike coins. The coinage of Melos seems to betray hints of a prominence for the influence on coining of political symbolism. There may even have been a connection between coining and autonomy for the Melians. Melian coins of the second half of the fifth century are almost exclusively known from a hoard found on Melos itself (*IGCH* #27).[32] At least fourteen obverse dies and twenty-four reverse dies are attested in the hoard, so that a considerable output can be estimated; Kraay suggests an output of 76–150T from the known dies alone. Kraay preferred to date this whole issue to shortly before the fall of the island to the Athenians in

[30] T. Hackens, "Le monnayage de l'atelier de Délos à l'époque archaïque," *Études déliennes*, *BCH* Suppl. 1 (1973), 209–26; Hackens, "Les monnaies," in P. Bruneau and J. Ducat, *Guide de Délos* (Paris 1983) 107–11.

[31] For Skyros, it is not certain that the coins sometimes assigned to the island were truly issued there. Note *IGCH* #31, "Scyros" (fifth century); #1644, "Asyut" (ca. 475); cf. *IGCH* #87, "Cranidi" (ca. 325–300). See Price and Waggoner 49–50; cf. Erxleben *AfP* (1970) 120.

[32] Cf. *IGCH* #1790, "Malayer" (ca. 375). See C.M. Kraay, "The Melos Hoard of 1907 Re-examined," *NC*[7] (1964) 1–20. In general, see Kraay, *ACGC* 45–49.

416. Yet it is uncertain whether coins of a short-lived massive emission or a longer duration minting were less likely to be hoarded elsewhere. If massive strikings of Melian coins took place just before and during the Athenian siege, it is more likely that some of these coins would have been carried off by the besiegers or later discovered by the Athenian colonists sent to the island. If these coins fell into Athenian hands they would have had a better chance of being hoarded somewhere else.

Notwithstanding their die linkages, it is therefore possible that the issues of the Melian hoard may have been struck over the second half of the fifth century, with a starting date of 450–40.[33] The absence of discoveries outside the island may be owed to their lack of acceptability, and thereby circulation, outside Melos. The Melian use of the Milesian standard was in any case atypical for Cycladic mints and impaired the usefulness of their issues to persons abroad in an area where the Aiginetic and Euboeic/Attic standards predominated. Kraay also thought that his dating might entail a discontinuous operation for the mint when one compares the earlier Melian issues, those he dated to around mid-century.[34] With the discovery of one of the coins from the earlier issue in the "Elmali hoard" (*CH* 8.48: ca. 460), the earlier series must migrate upward at least a bit. The dies that make up the later coinage found in *IGCH* #27 might then constitute a resumption of minting. That determination might heighten an appreciation of their political or symbolic character. Other options would be a further spacing out of the later series or an elevation of the date of *IGCH* #27.

The intermittency or elongation of the series found in *IGCH* #27 may preclude that the Melians depended solely on these coins during the period 460–16. Nevertheless, they made sure that there were ample stocks of avowedly local money, minted consistently with the punning badge of their city, an "apple," on the obverse and often with an inscribed ethnic. The rich variety of reverse types is a particular feature of the last phase of this mint, having no precedent among earlier series. This circumstance may suggest that the attention lavished on these issues was a psychological investment by the ruling elite. That would be especially so if the dies (of which the die links suggest that more than one die was in simultaneous use) were not pushed to their limit of production in order to increase the range of types. In a region where economic and monetary consolidation was marked, the Melians made a decision to resist these

[33] Note Jeffrey, *LSAG*^{2} 321–22, who dates the coins to 450–40 on epigraphical grounds.

[34] *IGCH* #1483, "Massyaf" (ca. 425–400); #1644, "Asyut" (ca. 475); cf. #1830, "Kabul" (ca. 380); see also Kraay *NC* (1964) 19–20. Note Price and Waggoner 79.

trends that has the look of a gesture on behalf of autonomy.[35] Here was a steady commitment to the additional expenses to be borne in sustaining such varied issues to serve so small an economy. And the apparent lack of overseas circulation of Melian coins perhaps indicates that other practices were employed to sustain foreign commerce. Most of the neighbors of the Melians, whether contemporaneously affiliated with Athens or not (like the Therans), apparently did not judge the maintenence of a local mint at a level comparable to that of Melos to be an attractive proposition.

Monetary Circulation in the Mid-Fifth Century

As the foregoing discussion demonstrates, there was significant attrition of the active mints during the first half of the fifth century. While cessation of coining was not confined to these two areas, the closing of mints was most striking in the islands and in Thrace. Thus, proximity to Attica and the Saronic Gulf, and the consequent ease of intercommunication and travel by sea, were in all likelihood factors in the closure of allied mints. It is also possible that the degree of economic integration of the Aegean economies and the scale of trade had an impact on the extinction of such mints. The output of most of these mints was small, so that the proportion of transactions (even in the local economy) that were handled in nonlocal currency would have been large almost as soon as coins became the ordinary medium for the exchange of goods. Even a larger mint like Eretria still appears to have emitted an insignificant number of coins when compared (necessarily crudely) with the great mints of the Saronic Gulf region. After 450, very few coins from the mints in categories IIIA and IIIB were in circulation in the *arkhē* in any case. There is another reason why it is hardly surprising that the Island and Thraceward districts of the *arkhē* showed the greatest degree of monetary consolidation through mint closure. Evidence presented below shows that these two districts (along with Ionia) reveal the fewest irregularities in the assessment and the payment of tribute of the sort that can be connected with difficulties in exchanging non-Attic money for Athenian coins (pp. 285–87).

We can update our classification of the monetary status of the allied cities on the basis of categories IIIB–IIIC. While the allied states in category IIIB had all concluded their coining before the first tribute list,

[35] The richness of Melian minting paralleled practical efforts to assert autonomy during the Peloponnesian War. Note the aid given by the Melians to what appears to have been the expedition of the Spartan navarch Alkidas into the Aegean in 427 (Meiggs-Lewis #67, *Side* 1–7, 13–17; cf. Thuc. 3.29–32). See W.T. Loomis, *The Spartan War Fund: IG V, 1 and a New Fragment* (Stuttgart 1992) 62–66. The Athenian answer was a punitive expedition of Nikias in 426 (Thuc. 3.91.1–3). Melos was assessed in 425/4 (*IG* I^3 71.I.65).

the deployment of the evidence from category IIIC in Table 2.1 is a bit more problematical. I have naturally counted a mint as inactive only in the assessment periods after it ceased emitting silver coins. Consequently, as can easily be seen from the figures presented, by the time of the promulgation of the Thirty Years Peace of 446/5, a large proportion of the economic and financial assets of the Athenian allies was located in places where local minting had ended and processes of monetary consolidation (however dimly glimpsed) had had a significant impact.

By the end of this sequence of mint closures, over 80 percent of the Athenian allies were without local coinages that could compete with Attic money and the coinages of other international or regional mints (entry I + II + III in Table 2.1). Those that were not coining did not produce an amount of tribute or (presumably) reach an economic output commensurate with their numerical proportion among the body of the allies. The small size of the nonminters is the dominant factor in that disparity. It is worth observing that the approximately thirty-nine mints that ended their activities before 445 contributed an amount of tribute substantially greater than the more than one hundred allied states that never minted. Those who minted and stopped were on average larger than the never-minters. The fact should be emphasized that somewhat over one half the tribute actually attested in our various periods was already being paid by states that never or no longer minted their own coins. A great deal of the consolidation of the use of money that would occur during the existence of the *arkhē* had already taken place by what is conjectured to be the earliest date for the Coinage Decree.

Our review of numismatic scholarship suggests that category IIIC, those states that terminated their minting between 465 and 445, is not particularly impressive. That is true both absolutely and in comparison with categories IIIA and IIIB. And some of the mints in category IIIC may well have closed before 450–45, the earliest date suggested for a Coinage Decree that putatively prohibited minting of silver.

Erxleben has rightly called our attention to the absence of a dramatic threshold of mint closings around mid-century and the early 440s.[36] To him this observation undermines a mid-century chronology. An alternative hypothesis, to be developed below, can account for the absence of a dividing line in our evidence by arguing that the Coinage Decree did not prohibit the allies from minting silver nor did it demonetize non-Athenian coins within the *arkhē*. Thus a mid-century date need not be accepted at the cost of believing the decree was an aborted initiative,

[36] For example, Erxleben *AJP* (1970) 131.

as suggested by E.S.G. Robinson, "the measure as a whole never came near permanent success" and the "vast operation of recoinage never got under way."[37] It is wiser to see the decline of local coinage in the face of an expansion of the circulation of currencies with larger emissions, such as Attic money, as an organic development driven by the increasing integration of the Aegean economy and the nature of league finances (to be explored below).[38]

That fewer mints were terminated around mid-century in Erxleben's and our own reckoning than in that of Robinson, for example, should not contribute to chronological conclusions about Attic policy for another reason. Once the shibboleth of belief in a prohibition of allied minting is removed, we can begin to see that there was a parallel mode of monetary integration at work during the Pentekontaeteia. Before 460 *poleis* making adjustments to their systems of money often simply and absolutely ceased minting operations and presumably accepted some degree of local validity for foreign money. As time advanced, however, the phenomenon of ceasing the production of heavier coins, such as tetradrachms, staters, or didrachms, while continuing to strike drachms and fractions, becomes more notable.

SMALL-DENOMINATION COINERS

In category IV and especially in its IVC group, we find the first mints in our investigation that can be said to provide substantive evidence against the existence at any time of a prohibition on the minting of silver by the allies; in other words, the traditional interpretation of the Coinage Decree. In category IVC of the mints producing small-denomination silver coins that seem to have been in continuous production, there appear to be, for the most part (Kebren is a probable exception), mints with relatively sizable outputs.

Some of the states that concluded mint operations during the Attic hegemony moved toward a cessation by stages, first ending their production of heavier denominations and only later ending the production of lighter coins. Note as some possibilities Delos, Eretria, Lindos, Paros, Samothrace, and Skione, and almost all the states classified in category IVA (those that ended coining in 445–20). Most of the category IVA mints stopped minting heavier coins during the first half of the century, while coining of lighter issues continued after 445. We must be careful,

37 Robinson *ANSMN* (1960) 3.
38 Compare Babelon *RN* (1913) 462–66; Will, *Monde grec* 206–209.

however, not to make too much of the presence in category IVA of Poteidaia, which had a significant mint and had a relatively large economy.[39] With this exclusion, the other states in category IVA are in the main rather notable for the meagerness of their late fifth-century issues. Therefore the case for a coinage decree in the 420s or 410s is not really advanced by adducing this group. The Athenians would hardly have bothered to legislate on such a scale to bring to a close such insignificant emissions of coins. Rather, most of the states in category IVA ceased coin production in two stages, an earlier end to minting heavier coins and a later termination of limited issues of lighter coins.

In many cases, however, the cessation of production of larger coins was the only discernible stage of monetary adjustment that was actually undertaken (category IVC). In the standing interpretation of the Coinage Decree, this evolution is difficult to understand, inasmuch as the chief issue in understanding a legislated monopoly for Athenian coins must be when the ban, valid for fractions and drachms as much as for staters, came into force. Yet for a revisionist hypothesis regarding Attic monetary policy, the cessation of coining except for drachms and/or fractions could be connected with progressive monetary consolidation; second, it could be considered an aspect of cooperation with the Athenians (and not of recalcitrance); and finally, it could even represent part of a response to the demands of the tribute system. The switch from coining in a full range of denominations to coining in small denominations alone is a process cognate to the cessation of minting across the board.

As observed above, where only fractions and drachms continued to be coined, some other currency must have occupied the monetary niche previously held by larger local coins, and it is probable that Athenian tetradrachms served as the larger coins circulating in many of these allied communities. There is after all no evidence for so dramatic a change in market conditions that the economic and administrative roles previously performed by larger coins were no longer operative. Indeed, if the fifth-century Greeks experienced substantial inflation of prices, as appears likely, curtailing the production of heavier coins would have had an even greater impact. In some cases, to be sure, Attic tetradrachms were accompanied in circulation by the coins from mints of panhellenic

[39] The mint of Poteidaia was closed during the Peloponnesian War, but the city may have continued its minting down to its capture by Athenian forces. Poteidaia is not coincidentally the most productive mint in this group. Hence there may be no question of monetary consolidation or integration in the complete termination of Poteidaian minting activity. But for military and political disasters, Poteidaia might well have joined category IVC, the continuous minters of smaller denominations.

and regional significance. Once the decision had been made to limit minting to drachms and smaller denominations, no problem existed for any exchanges necessitated by the tribute system and by growing economic integration among the states of the *arkhē*, since the larger denominations in local use were already to some large degree Attic.

One class of mints issuing only fractions has already been touched on above, namely, those that started their minting during the Peloponnesian War (category II). Their decisions have been traced to changes in the output and the circulation of Athenian money caused by the tremendous costs of a war that also changed the mix of goods imported into Attica. Shortages in the local supply of Attic money could also have been triggered by increased public and private expenditure at Athens and to a reduced supply of silver from the mines at Laureion. No evidence in our possession demonstrates that they were in fact caused by any alteration in monetary policy or, specifically, by an attenuation in the force of a supposed prohibition on minting enjoined by the Coinage Decree. It is likely that a similar conclusion can be reached about the resumptions of the production of lighter coinage that is exhibited by the mints in category IVB. A monetary etiology is in most of these cases preferable to adducing disaffection from the Athenian cause, although that was sometimes also a factor.

Not only does the restriction of minting to smaller denominations (mostly self-imposed, it seems) show the accommodation of the local monetary systems of some of these cities to the dominance of Attic money within the *arkhē*, but the appearance of a head of Athena, sometimes crowned with olive, for the coins of some cities that minted only fractions has been taken to suggest loyalty to Attic leadership. Examples of this type are found in the late fifth century at Aineia, Assos, Dardanos, Elaia, and Ialysos.[40]

The record of the mints of the Rhodian cities of Ialysos, Kameiros, and Lindos may actually provide some direct confirmation for the hypothesis of consolidation driven by economic factors, for their issues involve still another process of monetary integration, an evolution entailing shifts in coin standard.[41] In the first half of the fifth century, Lindos and Ialysos minted staters and fractions on the Milesian standard. It is not at all hard to see how this arrangement might well confer economic advantages for islanders situated off the coast of southern Asia Minor. Lindos ceased

[40] Erxleben *AJP* (1970) 76–77, 91, 97, 104; cf. p. 80 on Klazomenai.

[41] See Erxleben *AJP* (1970) 90–91; J.H. Kagan, "The Decadrachm Hoard: Chronology and Consequences," in Carradice, *Coinage and Administration* 21–28, esp. 25–26.

minting staters around mid-century (a later silver fractional issue on the Euboeic/Attic standard cannot be certainly proven). In the third quarter of the century, Ialysos made a transition to minting only fractions, now on the Aiginetic standard.[42] That shift is also illustrative of the general influence of Aiginetic-weight money in interstate exchange (especially in the Cyclades). A third Rhodian city, Kameiros, had even earlier produced coins on the Aiginetic standard (from 500). All three Rhodian mints seem to have had small issues of Aiginetic fractions in electrum, probably as intermittent emissions.[43]

At a further stage, coins were struck on the Euboeic/Attic standard in the period from perhaps 430 (or a little later) at Kameiros and at Ialysos between 420 and 408 (according to Erxleben), after which the cities of Rhodes synoecized to form a single state. These few last coins are attested in single fractional denominations for each city, obols at Kameiros and diobols at Ialysos (where the attribution of the coins is not unquestioned, although the head of Athena on their reverse is significant). The two series might have been intended to complement each other. Both sorts of adjustments, the changes in standard to Aiginetic and to Euboeic/Attic and the restrictions in the weight of the denominations minted, worked in parallel. The progress of minting on Rhodes appears to indicate an intention to complement and facilitate exchanges with Aiginetic coinages and particularly with Attic money.

Because the period of Attic hegemony before the Peloponnesian War was relatively short, care must be exercised against establishing a false dichotomy between mints continuing with lighter coins and those mints closing. It is not inconceivable that some mints restricting their output to lighter coins were merely less far along (for a variety of local economic and political factors) in a general movement in the *arkhē* toward monetary or metrological consolidation. Thus a "snapshot" of these mints taken on the eve of the Peloponnesian War, to take a convenient vantage point, catches them in mid-evolution. Our classification of them as minters of fractions and drachms does not preclude that some of these allies might have closed their mints eventually, had (for starters) the Thirty Years Peace run out its term.

Although the Rhodian cities and Kolophon are well above the median size of tributary states, there are several smaller economies with, quite possibly, a low rate of coining among these cities (category IV). This

[42] See H.A. Cahn, *Knidos: Die Münzen des sechsten und fünften Jahrhunderts v. Chr.* (Berlin 1970) 180–85, 190. Cf. E. Schönert-Geiss, rev. in *Gnomon* 44 (1972) 270–74, who (additionally) is skeptical about the early date for the Coinage Decree.

[43] See Cahn, *Knidos* 90.

observation raises the possibility again that the size of the local economy affected decisions to continue minting. Scale seems to have had effects on the configuration of the *polis* economy and on its interaction with other economies that may have restricted the circulation of foreign money in certain places. The factor of distance also was at work: on the whole, those shifting to fractions are farther from Attica than those quitting their coining before 450. Yet we should recall that there were in any case few surviving allied mints near Attica or in the islands after 450.

INTERRUPTED MINTS

There are a number of instances where cities seem to have stopped their minting of smaller denominations and then resumed after an interval (category IVB). As observed above, some of these resumptions took place during the Peloponnesian War and probably have an etiology similar to the experiences of those cities that initiated drachmal and fractional minting in that period for the first time (category II). Some cases, however, deserve closer examination for their illumination of other trends in monetary policy and its reflection in numismatic data.[44]

Knidos

Hypothetical gaps in the continuity of coining placed around mid-century must be received with caution, inasmuch as earlier scholarly consensus on a mid-century date for the Coinage Decree cannot fail to have affected numismatic judgment (on the Thracian mints, compare Chapter 4 below). Let us take further the example of Knidos, which is classified based on scholarly consensus as a minter of lighter denomination coins that interrupted its production (category IVB). Here the painstaking scholarship of Cahn allows us to expose the reasoning behind the chronology for Knidian coins. Series II—its inception is dated by Cahn to 520—and subsequent stages of the mint involved the striking of Aiginetic standard coins. In series III and IV the mint struck almost exclusively drachms. There are many examples of a few die combinations of drachms in Cahn's series III, dated to 490–65 (for example, #56, #65, #66) and in series IV, dated to 465–49 (#71, #72, #77, ##82–83) by virtue of a massive hoard,

44 Skepsis is frankly a borderline and obscure case about which it is hard to believe in continuous minting instead of small, discrete, noncontinuous lighter issues spaced over the latest fifth century. Rather than being treated as an interrupted mint, the option that is chosen, it might be more appropriate to classify Skepsis with the intermittent mints, such as Ephesos and Ainos, that I have chosen to discuss under the active mints. I thank J H. Kagan, who was kind enough to review the fifth-century minting of Skepsis with me, using examples from his own collection.

IGCH #1186, "Bodrum," from the site of ancient Halikarnassos. This hoard, sometimes referred to as the "Huberfund" in the literature, contained ca. 2,000 Knidian coins, ending with series IV (it seems).[45] The hoard was dispersed in sales and there is no significant, detailed description of its contents or of the context for its discovery. This hoard allows us to focus on the critical question about the Knidian mint, the nature of the transition from series IV to V.

A first concern about the analysis of this hoard is an obvious matter in chronology. Since there are no known coins from other *poleis* to offer points of comparison, there can be little certainty that *IGCH* #1186 is correctly dated ca. 450 and does not belong to ca. 440 or even ca. 430. The effect of the appearance of Knidian series II coins in the Asyut Hoard is to bring the start of this emission down to 500. That redating certainly raises the possibility of connected redatings of the later series. Moreover, it is quite incongruous to suggest that the passage of the Coinage Decree was responsible for the demarcation in the product of this mint, which appears in this hoard as the lower boundary of series IV (as analyzed by Cahn), and then to follow by placing series V with its meager emissions in the period 449–11. Following the traditional interpretation of the decree, even that low level of output would be as objectionable to the Athenians as the more intense activity that preceded and followed.[46] Explaining scanty emissions as reflective of bouts of disaffection or resistance is hardly satisfactory, for the provision of a suitable money supply in the intervals between such emissions is hard to envisage. While one must sympathize with the tendency to look for external reference points in the subjective spacing out of coin series, a mid-century Coinage Decree does not really help for Knidos.

IGCH #1193, "Caria?, ca. 1966," is dated to ca. 410 in accordance with the supposition that its deposit is near to the time when Knidian minting resumed or reintensified. This hoard not only contains drachms from series VI, but examples from series V (supposedly from 449-11). Yet, once again, unless we associate rates of coining with political independence—a proposition for which there is even less evidence than for a conjunction of the bare fact of minting and autonomy—what would prohibit dating *IGCH* #1193 a few years earlier, before the mass defection of Athenian allies? Moreover, *IGCH* #1202, "Marmaris?," which is dated 390–80, includes earlier Knidian coins,

45 Cahn, *Knidos* 2–3.

46 Schönert-Geiss, review of Cahn, *Knidos*, *Gnomon* (1972) 271 and note 3.

now dated before 450.[47] Hence the succession and spacing of these issues (series IV–VI) cannot be known with certainty in the present state of our knowledge. Judgments on the interaction of coinage, politics, and diplomacy have had a pervasive influence. Knidos was a mint that emitted drachms on the Aiginetic standard that allowed it to exploit the large number of Aiginetic coins in circulation for transacting business. With the passage of time, its output diminished, a development that suggests further dependence on foreign coins. During the Peloponnesian War, coin production intensified, as it did elsewhere in the Attic *arkhē*. The Knidian mint should probably be classified with the continuous emitters of lighter denominations (category IVC), despite the misgivings springing from traditional numismatic treatments.

Interrupted Minting and Contexts

Categories IVB and V do, however, present some cases where the available scholarly commentary supports a mid-century interruption in minting. What this evidence for intervals in coining ought to tell us, however, is something quite different from a validation of the existence of a ban on the minting of silver in the mid-century period. Such intervals cannot be taken to prove the prohibition, unless one is also prepared to posit the existence of earlier bans that were responsible for the more numerous closings of mints earlier in the century. Why should anyone attribute different causations to cessations of minting larger denominations before 450 and to ceasing to mint lighter denominations after 450? Such cessations are better explained by the aforementioned progressive dominance of Attic money among the allied cities. Concomitantly, resumptions of coining seem to occur at widely varying moments; they reflect altered economic conditions, not legislative changes. Some cities found that an insufficient supply of Attic (and other?) coins were in local or regional circulation, usually lighter denominations, and responded by restarting their mints to remedy this deficiency, again usually by minting drachms and/or fractions.

The question arising from this observation is whether the Athenians took action to encourage the usage of their money. Even without a ban on the allied minting of silver, one can easily understand how Athenian encouragement of an ally's acceptance of the validity of Attic money might prompt certain allied states to suspend or curtail their own coining on the expectation that an exclusive or nearly exclusive use of Attic money in the local market was the optimal policy. This question cannot be

[47] Cf. Cahn, *Knidos* 214.

answered in the affirmative until all the literary and epigraphical material on money and the economy in the classical period is investigated below.

Suffice it to say here that such a fiscal explanation is in all probability preferable to sweeping hypotheses about the prosperity or poverty of allied states (based on macroeconomic speculation). This conclusion is sound, notwithstanding the charm of such analyses for those desirous of deterministic causations for political decisions. An example culled from these categories can help us to shun facile economic conclusions for changes in minting practices. Kolophon possessed a flourishing gold-working industry.[48] Yet that strength in the fabrication of precious metals did not necessarily militate in favor of keeping the local mint in continuous operation. Nor would the level of Kolophonian mint output lead us to any judgment about the health of such a related craft (for which we have independent testimony), let alone about the state of all craft industries or the whole economy.

Mints that may have resumed a fuller range of minting after an interval form a small category V. Methymna was nontributary and its record of punctuated striking of didrachms, tetrobols, and diobols may be connected with a lack of involvement in the tribute system. In the cases of both Thasos and Olynthos, political factors that transcend Attic monetary policies are implicated fairly clearly.

Some resumptions of coining fractions certainly had a political valence. The Olynthian mint parallels the experiences of the large number of establishments that ended their striking of coins with the retreat of the Persians or a little later. The main renewal of coining is of considerable political significance, although it bears more on the popularity and viability of Athenian hegemony than on the monetary affairs of the *arkhē*. The Olynthians minted tetrobols (with ΟΛΥΝ) some time after they revolted from Athens in 432. This decision was not merely (or perhaps chiefly) symbolic, given what must have been a straitened flow of Attic coins toward them during the Archidamian War.

Clement and Robinson had the Chalcidian League inaugurating its minting only a little later, commencing with fractions. The striking of larger coins might have started around 420 (as Gaebler believed), and would then have signified the shifting of the Chalcidian economy and finances to a peacetime mode after the establishment of the Peace of Nikias. One of the tantalizing (and unanswerable) questions concerning

[48] Kolophonian gold: Arist. fr. 352 K = fr. 366, *PCG* 3.2.206. Its quality was nothing short of proverbial: Zenob. 6.47 (= *CPG* 1.174); Apostol. 18.37 (= *CPG* 2.727); Macar. 5.27 (= *CPG* 2.181); Greg. Cyp. 3.38 (Leid. = *CPG* 2.41).

the interaction of coining and payment of tribute would be whether the Chalcidians were supposed to have paid their tribute to Athens after the Peace of Nikias in Attic tetradrachms or with their own money. The terms of the peace had placed them in the anomalous position both of being liable for only the Aristeidian assessments of tribute and of being conceded their autonomy, a condition usually irreconcilable with tributary status (cf. Thuc. 5.18.5).[49] If they were to pay in their own coin, that might be an indication that the Aristeidian or early tribute of the Delian League could have been paid in any coinage.

The virtual simultaneity of the inception of Olynthian and Chalcidian issues, however, constitutes a political anomaly that cries out for review and reformulation. Erxleben's response was to move the Olynthian tetrobols, which he considered to be on the Phoenician standard, to the 430s. Yet, we are better advised to follow the close study of Westermark, who argues that all the Chalcidian issues belong after 400. The Olynthian tetrobols were the only coinage minted by the Chalcidian rebels during the Peloponnesian War. They refrained in the fifth century from making a claim by coin type about their leadership of the Chalcidian League.

Thasos is quite comparable to some of the larger economies of the *arkhē*, such as Aigina, Chios, and Samos, that minted continuously during the hegemony of the Athenians. Thasos possessed not only the mines on the mainland over which it disputed with Athens but also others on the island itself. But for the dislocations of the siege of the city, the loss of mainland territories, and the financial stresses of repaying the Athenians for the cost of the war, one anticipates that the Thasian mint might well have remained in continuing operation (cf. Thuc. 1.101.3). The influence of Thasian money in the Thracian hinterland may indicate commercial interactions between Greeks and natives that militated in favor of the resumption of minting at a range of weights. The archaic minting of Thasos was customarily punctuated at the surrender of the city to Athenian forces under the command of Kimon in 463 and is held to have resumed in ca. 435 (the view argued by Robinson and accepted by Erxleben). That scenario may be compared with the more recent judgment of C.M. Kraay and O. Picard that the earlier series descended to mid-century and the Coinage Decree. Their view has drawn some support from the absence of the latest examples of this first phase from the "Decadrachm" or "Elmali Hoard" (*CH* 8.48: ca. 460), unless there was some retardation in the flow of Thasian money to the

49 See Figueira, *Excursions* 272–75.

hoarder of *CH* 8.48.[50] So any gap owed to the surrender of Thasos to Athens may have been of relatively short duration. Notwithstanding this determination, however, one suspects that the accumulation of Attic coins to repay an indemnity to the Athenians was probably the primary influence in Thasian fiscal policy down through the mid-century (cf. the increased assessment reflected in *IG* I^3 266.III.8; 268.III.15).

Note, however, that there are signs of monetary consolidation in the form that a later revival of coining took. When Thasian minting was resumed, the weight of coins was lightened so that a stater was equivalent to an Attic didrachm and some fractions would do equally for Attic pentobols and Abderite/Maroneian drachms, although caution is advisable because of the lack of literary evidence on equivalencies for exchange (see the citations to Picard in the Appendix). A further complication is the scanty output of the first stage of the fifth-century resumption. That could indicate Thasian use of foreign, especially Athenian, money. Nevertheless, it could also signify that the date of 435–30 for the resumption of minting (of Robinson and Kraay) is too early. Picard would place the total production of period 2 in 413–11. Thereupon, both the standard and standard units change again. In that case, it was only amid the distractions, alarms, and revolts of the Ionian War that Thasos restarted coining, just before the oligarchic government took Thasos away from the Attic camp (Thuc. 8.64.3–5). The question is by no means settled, and the numismatic data must be coordinated with the dating of the inscriptions mentioning fines in this coinage (for example, *IG* XII Suppl. 349).[51] A date after the outbreak of the Peloponnesian War for the resumption of minting may be the best option.

KOS AND THE CONSOLIDATION OF MINTING

Kos is a mint for which several patterns of minting have been postulated: a mid-century interruption, a mid-century closing of the mint, and continuous operations. The Koan mint, however, provides some indications that there are unappreciated aspects of monetary integration beyond those already identified, such as the cessation of minting, restriction of coin size, shift to the Attic standard, and Atticizing coin types. The record of Koan issues during the Pentekontaeteia may teach us that cities aimed their issues of coins at particular streams within the flow of circulation or even at niches within the economy. The question of termination of production then becomes a matter of secondary consequence.

[50] Price, *Coinage and Administration* 45.

[51] Duchêne, *Études thasiennes* 14, 86–87.

It has long been recognized that the *diskoboloi* of Kos have a connection with the cult of Triopian Apollo and its games, in which the cities of the Dorian *hexapolis* or *pentapolis* participated (Hdt. 1.144.1–3).[52] The coinage is outstanding for another characteristic as well. While neighbors stopped minting larger coins in favor of drachms and fractions, the Koans discontinued lighter coins in favor of a coin that has traditionally been understood as an Attic tetradrachm, but which Barron saw as a triple *siglos*. In contrast, the Koans minted a fuller range of coins both before and after the period of the *diskoboloi*.

The *diskoboloi* had what might be called a nonparochial or regional type on the obverse, depicting a competitor at the discus standing in front of a victor's tripod. Their reverse, however, bore the "national" badge of a crab that had been the obverse design of the archaic coin series. The latest crab coins, probably dating from the early 460s, were fractions that Kagan has analyzed as Persic third-staters.[53] Moreover, the obverse balances the inclusiveness that is seen in the type of the *diskobolos* with the political appropriation of an ethnic inscription (ΚΟΣ, ΚΩΣ, or ΚΩΙΟΝ). The later (fourth-century, it is usually assumed) coins had a head of Herakles, that, while it does not contain a specific allusion (to the best of our knowledge), makes no obvious gesture toward a wider entity such as the Dorian *pentapolis* or *hexapolis*.

For Barron, Persian *sigloi* functioned as a smaller denomination in the Koan economy. This supposition is not only problematic for the conclusion about politics to which it is joined—that is, that Kos was in rebellion from the Athenians during the 440s[54]—it also does not answer the question which coins played the role of fractional coinage on Kos in this period. An equally speculative but more likely sequence of values could have been: 1) heavy coin: *diskobolos*, which approximately equals the Attic tetradrachm, which is approximately equivalent to the triple

[52] See the references cited in Table 2.3 under Kos in category IIIC. The essential study is J.P. Barron, "The Fifth-Century Diskoboloi of Kos," in C.M. Kraay and G.K. Jenkins (eds.), *Essays in Greek Coinage Presented to Stanley Robinson* (Oxford 1968) 75–89. For citations on the significance of the type, see S.M. Sherwin-White, *Ancient Cos: An Historical Study from the Dorian Conquest to the Imperial Period* (Göttingen 1978) 22–23, 34–35, esp. note 34 (p. 35). That the type portrayed a contemporary sculpture is not an alternative that subverts my interpretation.

[53] J.H. Kagan, "IGCH 1185 Reconsidered," *RBN* 138 (1992) 1–24, esp. 12–13. Cf. S. Fried, "The Decadrachm Hoard: An Introduction," in Carradice, *Coinage and Administration* 1–9, for an example from *CH* 8.48, "Elmali."

[54] Barron, *Essays* 75–89; Sherwin-White, *Cos* 375–77. That *IG* I^3 1454.28–33 = *IG* XII.1 977 = Tod, *GHI* #110, which orders the Koans, Knidians, and Rhodians (the major commercial states in the area) to come to the aid of the Eteokarpathioi, is now dated 445–30 is an indicator against a period of disaffection of any length.

siglos; 2) middle weight coin: Attic drachm or *siglos*; 3) fractional coins: Attic fractions, Rhodian fractions (Aiginetic?), or Persic fractions.

To my mind, however, it is preferable to see the *diskoboloi* as a special series that was issued to celebrate the religious traditions of the Dorians of Asia Minor and the participation in them of the people of Kos. This purpose is commensurate with the size of the series; sixteen obverse dies were known to Barron (one more is known from *IGCH* #1644). How these coins were put into circulation to support this symbolism can only be a subject for further speculation, although the weight of the coins rules out small-scale transactions and minor expenditures by the state. One suggestion might be that Koan athletes in the Triopian games received stipends in cash from their government. Another hypothesis might be that the Koans paid cult dues to Triopian Apollo in the form of *diskoboloi*. A third scenario might involve a Koan version of theoric payments, either ones that allowed all Koans to attend the Triopian festival at government expense or a fund that made disbursements on the occasion of Koan victories.

At Knidos and on Rhodes (as we have already seen), minting during the later fifth century had the more practical role of providing smaller coins for the local economy. The Koans, however, may well have used Attic or regional coins in the local economy. Monetary consolidation at Kos need not have negated local autonomy or ideology through a mandating of the validity of Attic money. Rather, the process of monetary integration might have opened a specialized function for the *diskoboloi* as expressions of local pride in the religious traditions of the eastern Dorians.

If the foregoing suggestions are correct, several corollaries to Barron's conclusions on the mint of Kos may be in order. His appreciation of the date for the various versions of the *diskobolos* that is based on stylistic analogues from different media should perhaps be conditioned by the possible influence of conservatism for a series that may have its context in religious ritual. Thus, these coins may have continued later in the century than he has allowed. Second, a new sense of the rhythm of monetary output may be needed in which some series of coins that were not intended to be the sole means of exchange in their communities were issued periodically. Were the *diskoboloi* then struck annually, quadrennially, or in tune with some other cyclic rhythm, the import of which we cannot now even guess?

There was, however, perhaps not a total disinterest in religious and patriotic numismatic symbolism transcending Kos itself. Barron catalogues two coins in his series A (#11 and #12), which possess designs for the reverse (from two dies) that lack the Koan badge of the crab and seem to be minted on a different standard (Milesian, he suggests). They have the conventional obverse with the ethnic notation and one even shares an obverse die with a coin with the usual reverse (his A6). It is possible that these coins were minted by the Koans to permit the participation of some non-Koan group in the program that motivates the whole series (whatever that may have been).

TABLE 2.2 Monetary Activity of Allied Cities

The following abbreviations are used in the table: St. = staters, didrachms, tetradrachms, etc.; ~ L = large denominations; Dr. = drachms; Fr. = fractional silver; El. = electrum; brk. = break in minting; <“date” = terminal date for minting; “date”> = initial minting from specified date; * = continuous minting; B = Babelon; H = Head[2]; K = Kraay, *ACGC*; M = Mattingly (see appendix entries for citations to individual works); P = Price, *Coinage and Administration*; PW = Price and Waggoner, *Asyut Hoard.* The Appendix (pp. 563–98) summarizes the specific studies on which other determinations of chronology rest.

MINTS	*Robinson*	*Erxleben*	*Other Authorities*
Ionia			
Assos	Fr. 465–50	Fr. <430	Fr. *?
Chios	*	*	mid-century brk. (K)
Elaia		Fr. 450–400	
Ephesos	<450	*	*H; *B;
	420>		<450/412>K
Erythrai	<465	Dr. 470–50	St.<479B
		440–400	<450
		Fr. 450–40	
Gargara	Fr. 435>	Fr. 420>	420>H; 412>B
Klazomenai	L. <479	St. <450	St. <494H
	Fr. <450	Fr. 480–50	Fr. 494>H; <445
Kolophon	<450	Dr./Fr. >410;	Dr./Fr. 447–30 brk. (K);
	430–20>	389>	Dr./Fr. 476–394H;
			brk. after 450
Kyme	<479	<480	
Methymna	<479/435–20	<480/450>	<450/420>H; <460/450/40>
Miletos	Fr. *	Fr. *	St. <480
	or <450		
Mytilene	L. <465	St. <480	440>H; *B
	Fr. <427	Dr./Fr. <427	
	El. Fr. <427	El. Fr. <427	El. Fr. *H; El. Fr. 485>K
Phokaia	El. Fr. *		El. St. <500H
	Fr. <479		El. Fr. *
Pitane		Fr. 440>	end of fifth (H)
Samos	*	*	brk. 450–35 (K)
		(brk. 439)	
Teos	*	*	<449/412>K;
			interrupted in
			Peloponnesian War?
Hellespont			
Abydos	Fr. <450	St.? <480	480–50, 411–387H/B
	L. 411>	Dr./Fr. <430?	<449K
Antandros	L. <450	<450	
	Fr. 420>	Fr. 440>	

Astakos	L. 465–40	St. <480	Dr./Fr. *H
		Dr./Fr. 450–35	
Dardanos	Fr. 420>	Dr./Fr. 435>	St. <485
Kalkhedon	Fr. 479–50	Fr. 450>	Fr. <480/450>H
	435–20		Fr./Dr. 460–40?/412>B
Khersonesos		<480	<493H
Kebren	L. <479	Fr. 470–400	500–400H/B
	Fr. <420		bronze 430–12>
Kyzikos	El. *	El. *	
	L. <479		
	Fr. *	Fr. 480>	Fr. 480>B
Lamponeia		Dr./Fr. 425>	420>H; end of fifth (B)
Lampsakos	L. <479	Fr. <460	<450/394>H; *B;
			<490 Baldwin
	Fr. <450	430>	Dr./Fr. <450K
	420>		Dr./Fr. <470/400> Baldwin
	El. <450	El. *?	El. <394H; <500/460–50>
Neandreia	Fr. 420>	Fr. 425>	430>H; end of fifth (B)
Parion	Fr. <465	<465	<475P/W
Pordoselene	Fr. 427>	Dr. 420>	450>H; 400>B
Prokonnesos	Fr. 420>	Fr. 425>	400>H; 350>B
Selymbria	Fr. <450	Dr./Fr. <480	<450H/B; <465?
	411>	420>	<470/420>
Skepsis	L. <450	*	460–400H
	Fr. 411>		
Tenedos	<479	<465	
Thraceward			
Abdera	*	*	*H/B; <425/4M; Brk.
			439–37 (K); 15–20 yrs.
			later (PW); into third
			quarter of fifth century (P);*
Aineia	L. <479	St. <480	424>H/B
	Fr. 450–20	Fr. 450–20	Fr. <440–30?
Ainos	L. <450	St. <440	450>H; <425/4M;
	435>	425>	into 450–25P
		Fr. *	intermittent after 450
Akanthos	*	*	brk. 450–20 (K);
			<431 at earliest (PW);
			far into 450–25P;*
Aphytis	Fr. 440>	Fr. 440>	425>H; 440>B; 450–25>P
Argilos			<450–45
Bottiaioi		Fr. 432>	424H/B
Dikaia	L. <450	St. <450	
(Macedonia)	Fr. <450	Fr. <440	<425 or a little later
Dikaia	<465	<465	<475
(Thrace)			<475K; <465

(S)kapsa	<450	<465	
Maroneia	*	474>	<425/4M; brk. after 450 (K); into 450–25P; some punctuation and limitation after 450
Mende	brk. 450–40	St. <465 450> Fr. *	*H/B; St. <425/4M; brk. before 450 (K); into 450–25P/W; intermittent after 450?
Neapolis	L. <450 Fr. *	St. <435 Dr./Fr.*	<450K <480–65/425–24>
Olynthos	<479 432>	Ol. Fr. 430s> Chalcidian Fr. 432> Chalcidian St. 420>	<479; Ol. Fr. 430> Chalcidian St. 400> Chalcidian Fr. 400>
Peparethos	<479	<480	<490H
Poteidaia	L. <465 Fr. <450	St. <450 Fr. <429	
Samothrace	L. <479 Fr. <465	St. <476 Fr. <465	500–475K; Fr. <450
Sermylia	<465	<480	<480P/W
Skione	L. <479 Fr. <450 Fr. 435–24	St. <465 Fr. <421	 Fr. <450
Stageira	<450	<480–70	<475
Torone	L. <465 Fr. <450	St. <480 Fr. <455	St. <465–60 Fr. * or <421
Thasos	<464	<463 435>	
Tindaioi	<479	<480	
Tragilos		Fr. 450>	450>H; 400>B
Caria			
Aspendos		*	500–400H
Astypalaia	<465	<460	
Halikarnassos	<450	Dr. <450–40 Fr. 440–20	<480H/B, 400B
Idyma	425>	Dr./Fr. 425>	450>H/B
Kalymna	<479		
Karpathos	<479		<480P/W
Kaunos	<479?	<480	<480
Kelenderis	465>	465>	450>K; 465B
Khersonesos (Caria)	<479	<480	St. <465 Dr./Fr. <430
Knidos	<450	Dr. <460/450>	Dr./Fr. <480/412>H/B; Dr./Fr. <449/412/1>K

Kos	<479	St. 479–10	479–10B; <450–45K
	450–420		
Lykioi	*	*	
Mylasa	<465		
Oule			<440K
Phaselis	<450	St. <460	<466/400H
		Fr. <430	<440/420–11?>
Rhodes			
Ialysos	St. <465	St. <450	
	Fr. <450	Fr. <408	El. Fr. *?
Kameiros	St. <465	St. <430	St. <450
	Fr. <450	<408	El. Fr. *?
Lindos	St. <465	St. <465–60	<480K; <455
	Fr. <450	Fr. 450–40?>	El. Fr. *?
Termera	<479	<480	
Tymnes		<445	
Islands			
Aigina	<457	<431	<431
Anaphe		<480	
Andros	<479	<pre-500	<507
Chalkis	<479	<480	<490; <465K
Delos	<450	St. <480	<478
		Fr. <465	
Eretria	<465	St. <480	<490P/W; <early 470sK;
	411>	Fr. <465	<449??
		411>	
Iulis	<465	<465	<480/79H/B
(Keos)		Fr. 420>??	
Karthaia	<450	Dr. 480–65	
(Keos)			
Karystos	<465	<470–65	
Koressia	<450	<465	
(Keos)		Fr. 420>	
Naxos	<479	<480	<490P/W
Paros	St. <465	<480	<470?
	Fr. <450		
Seriphos	<479	<pre-490	
Siphnos	St. <465	St. <470–65	
	Fr. <450	Fr. <450	
		420>	
Tenos	<479	<480	
Thera	<479	<480	

TABLE 2.3 Initiation and Cessation of Allied Coining

(Roman numerals denote categories of Athenian allies)

The following abbreviations are used in the table: St.= staters, didrachms, tetradrachms, etc.; @ = probable cessation before first surviving tribute list; ~ L = large denominations; Dr. = drachms; Fr. = fractional silver; El. = electrum; brk. = break in minting; <"date" = terminal date for minting; "date"> = initial minting from specified date; * = continuous minting; B = Babelon; H = Head^2; K = Kraay, *ACGC*; M = Mattingly (see appendix entries for citations to individual works); P = Price, *Coinage and Administration*; PW = Price and Waggoner, *Asyut Hoard*. The Appendix (pp. 563–98) summarizes the specific studies on which other determinations of chronology rest.

II. STATES INITIATING MINTING DURING THE ATTIC HEGEMONY

MINTS	*Robinson*	*Erxleben*	*Other Authorities*
Aphytis	Fr. 440>	Fr. 440>	425>H; 440>B; 450–25>P
Bottiaioi		Fr. 432>	424>H/B
Byzantion		Dr./Fr. 404> 400>	400K; 416H/B; 411>
Elaia		Fr. 450>	<460H
Gargara	Fr. 435>	Fr. 420>	420>H; 412>B
Idyma	425>	Dr. 425>	450>H/B
Lamponeia		Dr./Fr. 425>	420>H; end of fifth (B)
Neandreia	Fr. 420>	Fr. 425>	430>H; end of fifth (B)
Pitane		Fr. 440>	end of fifth (H)
Pordoselene	Fr. 427>	Dr. 420>	450>H; 400>B
Prokonnesos	Fr. 420>	Fr. 425>	400>H; 350>B
Tragilos		Fr. 450>	450>H; 400>B

III. ALLIES CEASING MINTING DURING THE ATHENIAN HEGEMONY

MINTS	*Robinson*	*Erxleben*	*Other Authorities*
A. Allies Ceasing Minting before 478			
Anaphe		<480	
Andros	<479	<pre-500	<507
Kalymna	<479		
Karpathos	<479		<480P/W
Kaunos	<479?	<480	<480
Khersonesos (Thrace)		<480	<493H
Kyme	<479	<480	
Naxos	<479	<480	<490P/W
Peparethos	<479	<480	<490H
Seriphos	<479	<pre-490	
Tenos	<479	<480	
Termera	<479	<480	
Thera	<479	<480	
Tindaioi??	<479	<480	

B. Allied States Ceasing Minting in 478–65

Astypalaia	<465	<460	
Chalkis	<479	<480	<490; <465K
Delos	<450	St. <480	<478
		Fr. <465	
Dikaia (Thrace)	<465	<465	<475K; <465
Eretria	<465	St. <480	<490P/W; <early 470sK;
	411>	Fr. <465	<449??
		411>	
Karystos	<465	<470–65	
Iulis (Keos)	<465	<465	<480/79H/B
		Fr. 420>??	
Mylasa	<465		
Parion	Fr. <465	<465	<475P/W
Paros	St. <465	<480	<470?
	Fr. <450		
Selymbria	Fr. <450	Dr./Fr. <480	<450H/B; <465?
	411>	420>	<470/420>
Sermylia	<465	<480	<480P/W
Stageira	<450	<480–70	<475
Tenedos	<479	<465	

C. Allied States Ceasing Minting in 465–45

Abydos	Fr. <450	St.? <480	480–50, 411–387H/B
	L. 411>	Dr./Fr. <430?	<449K
Argilos			<450–45
Erythrai	<465	Dr. 470–50	St. <479B
		440–400	<450
		Fr. 450–40	
Karthaia (Keos)	<450	Dr. 480–65	@
Kos	<479	St. 479–10	479–10B; <450–45K
	450–420		
Lindos	St. <465	St. <465–60	<480K; <455
	Fr. <450	Fr. 450–40?>	El. Fr. *?
Oule			<440K
Samothrace	L. <479	St. <476	500–475K;
	Fr. <465	Fr. <465	Fr. <450
(S)kapsa	<450	<465	@
Skione	L. <479	St. <465	
	Fr. <450	Fr. <421	Fr. <450
	Fr. 435–24		
Tymnes		<445	

IV. FRACTIONAL MINTERS

MINTS	*Robinson*	*Erxleben*	*Other Authorities*
A. Allied States Ceasing Minting in 445–20			
Aineia	L. <479	St. <480	424>H/B
	Fr. 450—20	Fr. 450–20	Fr. <440–30?
Assos	Fr. 465–50	Fr. <430	
Astakos	L. 465–40	St. <480	Dr./Fr. *H
		Dr./Fr. 450–35	
Dikaia	L. <450	St. <450	Fr. <425 or a little later
(Macedonia)	Fr. <450	Fr. <440	
Halikarnasasos	<450	Dr. <450–40	<480H/B, 400B
		Fr. 440–20	
Khersonesos	<479	<480	St. <465
(Caria)			Dr./Fr. <430
Klazomenai	L. <479	St. <450	St. <494H
	Fr. <450	Fr. 480–50>	Fr. 494>H; <445
Phaselis	<450	St. <460	<466/400H
		Fr. <430	<440/420–11?>
Poteidaia	L. <465	St. <450	
	Fr. <450	Fr. <429	
B. Resuming Lighter Coinage			
Antandros	L. <450	<450	
	Fr. 420>	Fr. 440>	
Dardanos		Dr./Fr. 435>	St. <485
Knidos	<450	Dr. <460/450>	Dr./Fr. <480/412>H/B;
			Dr./Fr. <449/412/1>K
Kolophon	<450	Dr./Fr. >410;	Dr./Fr. 447–30 brk. (K);
	430–20>	389>	Dr./Fr. 476–394H;
			brk. after 450
Koressia	<450	<465	
(Keos)		Fr. 420>	
Neapolis	L. <450	St. <435	<450K
	Fr. *	Dr./Fr.*	<480–65/425–24>
Olynthos	<479	Ol. Fr. 430s>	<479; Ol. Fr. 430>
	432>	Chalcidian Fr. 432>	Chalcidian St. 400>
		Chalcidian St. 420>	Chalcidian Fr. 400>
Siphnos	St. <465	St. <470–65	
	Fr. <450	Fr. <450	
		420>	
Skepsis	L. <450	*	460–400H
	Fr. 411>		
C. Uninterrupted Series			
Ialysos	St. <465	St. <450	
	Fr. <450	Fr. <408	El. Fr. *?
Kalkhedon	Fr. 479–50	Fr. 450>	Fr. <480/450>H
	435–20		Fr./Dr. 460–40?/412>B

Kameiros	St. <465 Fr. <450	St. <430 Fr. <408	St. <450 El. Fr. *?
Kebren	L. <479 Fr. <420	Fr. 470–400	500–400H/B bronze 430–12>
Miletos	Fr. * or <450	Fr. *	St. <480
Torone	L. <465 Fr. <450	St. <480 Fr. <455	St. <465–60 Fr. * or <421

V. INTERRUPTED SERIES (INCLUDING HEAVIER DENOMINATIONS)

MINTS	*Robinson*	*Erxleben*	*Other Authorities*
Methymna	<479/435–20	<480/450>	<450/420>H; <460/450/40>
Thasos	<464	<463	

3

ELECTRUM MINTS

THE NEXT TOPIC in our investigation of minting activity and Attic monetary policy concerns the mints that produced electrum coins (see Table 3.1). Taking up these mints at this point is particularly appropriate because the *poleis* famous for their electrum issues also struck silver and the pattern of their minting of that metal generally parallels the activities of the coiners whom we have already considered, either those ceasing their production or limiting it to fractional issues. In addition, by their steady output of electrum coins several cities also resemble the "active" mints that will be discussed shortly. Two other matters condition an exploration of the electrum mints. The Coinage Decree obviously legislates about minting silver. Why that should be so makes an analysis of the usage of electrum coin particularly interesting. Second, one may rightly suspect based on our study of states that did not mint, ceased minting, or minted only fractions that electrum coins may have had a role in their economies.

When the electrum mints that were active during the Athenian hegemony are examined, a much depleted monetary phenomenon is seen. Electrum money preceded silver money by a margin of at least a generation and a large number of cities once produced issues in the alloy. Unfortunately, not all of these coins can actually be assigned unconditionally, owing to the lack of self-advertisement by some early electrum issuers. This alloy was adopted for coining for several reasons that unfortunately must be considered speculative owing to the absence of direct ancient testimony. Because they had a significant proportion of gold, electrum coins were a more compact medium for the storage and transportation of wealth than were silver coins or bullion. Electrum coins were also harder and thus more durable than gold coins, especially when we take into account the virtually universal practice of adding copper to the mixture.[1] Alloys of gold and silver were familiar to archaic metalworkers because of their previous use in the fabrication of jewelry, and it is possible that these workers' empirical understanding of the lower

[1] See F. Bodenstedt, *Phökaisches Elektron-Geld von 600–326 v. Chr.* (Mainz 1976) 12–16; see also Bodenstedt, *Die Elektronmünzen von Phokaia und Mytilene* (Tübingen 1981) 34–37.

TABLE 3.1 Category VI: Electrum Coiners

(See Table 2.2 [p. 84 above] for abbreviations used in this table)

Kyzikos	El. *	El. *	El. *
	L. <479		
	Fr. *	Fr. 480>	Fr. 480>B
Lampsakos	L. <479	Fr. <460	<450/394>H; *B; <490 Baldwin
	Fr. <450	430>	Dr./Fr. <450K;
	420>		Dr./Fr. <470/400> Baldwin
	El. <450	El. *?	El. <394H; <500/460–50>
Mytilene	L. <465	St. <480	440>H; *B
	Fr. <427	Dr./Fr. <427	
	El. Fr. <42 7	El. Fr. <427	El. Fr. *H; El. Fr. 485>K
Phokaia	El. Fr. *		El. St. <500H
	Fr. <479		El. fr. *

melting point of the alloys (again, particularly those containing copper) also encouraged the usage of electrum.

The retreat of electrum from general circulation and into circumscribed sectors of the classical economy was predictable.[2] Electrum coins assumed a token quality in that casual users lacked the ability to detect small disparities in the proportion of gold, and even moderate differences in the gold content created sizable discrepancies in the value of the coins as bullion.[3] Variations in color might betray differences

[2] Some late sixth-century Aiginetan silver coins (especially those with "union-jack" reverses) have a gold and tin content that may suggest that their silver was derived from electrum coins. It is unfortunately uncertain to what extent this effect is owed to a general supersession of earlier electrum issues by silver issues as monetary media and how much is to be attributed to the replacement of Ionian long-distance merchants by Aiginetans in key markets such as Etruria. See Figueira, *Aegina* 145–49 and Chapter 7, note 38 below.

[3] On chemical analysis of electrum, note the important review article of J.F. Healy, "Greek White Gold and Electrum Coin Series," *Metallurgy in Numismatics* 1 (1980) 194–215, esp. 204–13. Bodenstedt, *Elektron-Geld* 33–39, has the following extremes (lowest/highest) for the proportion of gold, silver, and copper for various periods. Phokaia, period I: Au 50.9/59.1, Ag 34.6/40.8, Cu 7.8/8.5; II: Au 43.3/47.7, Ag 43/46.7; Cu 9 2/10.2; III.1: 33.5/43.3, Ag 45.2/53.8, Cu 10.2/15.2; III.2: Au 31.9/44.4; Ag 45.2/55.8, Cu 10.4/15.3; III.3: Au 37.4/41.8, Ag 46.4/50.9, Cu 10/13.5; III.4: Au 35.4/43.1, Ag 45.7/51.7, Cu 10.4/13.3. Mytilene: period II: Au 42.5/48.7, Ag 41.8/46.8, Cu 9/10.7; III.1: Au 35.2/40.6, Ag 48.7/53, Cu 10/13; III.2: Au 34.2/41.2, Ag 48.5/53.4, Cu 9.7/12.4; III.3: Au 36.4/47.3, Ag 41.9/51.8, Cu 10.8/13.3; III.4: Au 37.4/41.4, Ag 47.1/50.8, Cu 11/13.7; III.5: Au 35.5/39.7, Ag 46.7/51.9, Cu 11.8/13.9; III.6: Au 38.4/40.4, Ag 46/51.4, Cu 10.3/13.7; III.7: Au 37.5/39.8, Ag 46.6/50.9, Cu 10.2/14; III.8: Au 35.8/40.3, Ag 47/49.7, Cu 11.8/14.5. There would be even greater ranges of proportions but for the decision of Bodenstedt to reclassify a certain few coins, from the classes based

in the proportions of gold, silver, and copper, but could not assist exact estimations of value.

Furthermore, different fifth-century electrum currencies seem to have been exchanged with Attic money at rates that superficially imply different relationships of value between gold and silver at the same time.[4] It is unlikely that significantly different value ratios for the two metals in fact coexisted. This indicates that factors other than the gold/silver value ratio affected the value of electrum coins for specific series when that value was expressed in terms of Attic drachms. The lack of a fixed ratio of value between silver coins and necessarily variable electrum coins meant that electrum coinages achieved their exchange rates against silver coinages (and exchange may have varied from coinage to coinage) through market forces. In the operation of these market forces the estimated bullion value of the gold and silver contained in the coins did not exercise exclusive sway. Thus, recipients of payment in electrum perforce accepted a guarantee of value from an issuing authority. Variations in the balance of precious metals in these coins may be contrasted with their regularity of weight (at least for the Cyzicenes).[5]

In addition, there seem to have been no systematic attempts to deceive the users of Phocaic electrum (about which Bodenstedt's analysis has told us more) by manipulating or lowering the gold content progressively or even cyclically, although an incremental lowering of gold content would be impossible for a layman to detect. The only ready explanation for fluctuations in the gold content of the coins may implicate marginal changes in the value ratio between gold and silver. Perhaps the required proportion of one metal for a batch of Phocaic *hectae* 'sixth-staters' was defined in terms of the market value of the other metal.[6] It is known

---

on stylistic and technical affinity to new classes based on their proportions of gold and silver. See also Bodenstedt, *Elektronmünzen* 333–58; Bodenstedt and P. Reimers, "Zerstörungsfreie Bestimmung der Legierungsbestandteile Gold, Silber und Kupfer von Elektronmünzen aus Phokaia und Mytilene," *JNG* 25 (1975) 17–31.

[4] Note Bodenstedt, *Elektron-Geld* 85, with the notable corrective remarks of J. Guépin in his review of this work in *JHS* 99 (1979) 217–18. See also R. Bogaert, "Le cours du statère de Cyzique aux Ve et IVe siècles avant J.-C.," *AC* 32 (1963) 85–119, esp. 109–10, 112–13.

[5] For Cyzicenes: H. von Fritze, "Die Elektronprägung von Kyzikos," *Nomisma* 7 (1912) 1–38, esp. 34; D. Rouvière, "Notes techniques sur les statères du Cyzique," *SNR* 38 (1957) 11–23, esp. 12.

[6] For example, let us take gold as the metal establishing the amount of silver. When gold appreciated in value relative to silver, that change raised the amount of silver that the same amount of gold could purchase. Conversely, when gold lost value in relation to silver, less silver could be acquired for the consignment of coins about to go into production. A similar mechanism has been suggested (rather speculatively) to account for the silver content

from the fourth-century monetary compact between Phokaia and Mytilene that the mixture was established by law (Tod, *GHI* 2.112.14–16; see below pp. 487–89). Although the *hectae* appear to vary significantly in their intrinsic value because of the varying proportions of gold that they contain, in the chronological context of their minting, *hectae* varied somewhat less in terms of the market value of the metals. This hypothetical balancing by ancient minters of the proportions of gold, silver, and copper in these coins would not affect the coins' later possession of a token value in a system of exchange wherein all Phocaic-standard *hectae* (and perhaps Cyzicenes as well) circulated in principle at parity.

In the earliest days of electrum coinage, before economies became significantly monetized, disbursements by the state were the largest component of all monetary transactions.[7] Such political exchange, or better, state-sponsored recirculation of assets, was not in truth noncoercive—the government could establish conventions of value for the transactions lying within its sphere of influence—but it did leave little room for the specific anxiety that arose over the evaluation of the different electrum coins in circulation that one might employ in individual deals.[8] Conversely, as the environment for transactions mediated by coins became more fluid, the use of silver coins whose content was more easily evaluated by a touchstone encompassed fewer ambiguities and anxieties.[9]

---

of the imperial Roman denarius, for which see E. Lo Cascio, "State and Coinage in the Late Republic and Early Empire," *JRS* 71 (1981) 76–86, esp. 80–81.

7 In the first decades of minting, the volume of coinage in circulation would have been insufficient to permit the majority of transactions to have been conducted using coins, even in the doubtful event that there would have been enough electrum fractions to handle most smaller transactions. It is after all improbable that mints can have issued in a year or two an adequate money supply, which they had no means of estimating, or, had they conceived such a project, that they would have had enough silver and gold in their possession to complete it.

8 The noncivic character of early electrum opens the possibility that some early issuers of coins had a quasi-governmental status (like certain Greeks in a Lydian elite or governmental context?), who were nonetheless sufficiently authoritative with the recipients of the coins to obviate any suspicion or objection over variable content. The famous Phanes issue may be relevant in this context, for which see, for example, L. Weidauer, *Probleme der frühen Elektronprägung* (Freiburg 1975) #39, pp. 18–19, 62–63. Yet, interpretation remains controversial: see, for example, P.R. Franke and R. Schmitt, "Φάνεος—Φάνος ἐμὶ σῆμα," *Chiron* 4 (1974) 1–4; M. Radnoti-Alföldi, "Phanes: Einige Gedanken zur Person," in S. Scheers (ed.), *Studia Paulo Naster Oblata*, I, *Numismatica Antiqua* (Leuven 1982) 1–6; E. Pászthory, "Die Legierung der Frankfurter Phanes-Stater," in *Studia Naster* 1.7–11; W. Kastner, "'Phanes' oder 'Phano'?" *SNR* 65 (1986) 5–10.

9 The issue was not merely the scale of transactions, although silver coins could be used with more ease and assurance for retail deals. Electrum fractions are fairly well attested in hoards. Let us note merely the western Anatolian pre-525 hoards in *IGCH* containing "twenty-fourths" (of the stater) or lighter coins: #1152–53, 1155–58, 1160–61. Cf. B. Holle,

A complicating factor in understanding the seventh- and early sixth-century use of electrum is the possibility that the ratio of value between gold and silver was inclined toward a higher valuation of silver, at least before 550–25.[10] If the volume of silver in circulation after 550–25 was more easily affected by improved mining and refining techniques and an intensification of mining activity, silver may have lost value relative to gold as the archaic period advanced. In that case, the mixture of the two alloys in electrum coins would have become increasingly problematical as economies became more monetized through the issuance of more silver coins (in the second half of the sixth century and in the early fifth century), since variations of the proportions of gold and silver had greater significance to the extent that the metals came to have more widely different values.

ELECTRUM IN THE FIFTH CENTURY

In the fifth century, electrum was a monetary medium for business conducted between Greeks and non-Greeks or between Mediterranean Greeks and colonial Greeks in the Black Sea region or in Hellespontine Asia Minor. In these settings, alternative participants in commerce were probably few. Many transactions may have been determined by conventions of pricing and of bargaining and were thereby stereotypical. Such interchanges were probably undertaken in the context of more encompassing relationships that may be crudely understood as a form of *xenia* 'guest-friendship' between Greek traders and local elites. These conditions dispelled some of the uncertainty that would prevail in more "advanced" markets, that is, markets with more variety, with a wider range of possible entrants, with more depersonalization of transactions, and with a greater number of alternative commercial partners. The social context of business conducted in electrum coins under these conditions can perhaps be thought to have raised to a deterrent level for the Greek merchant the disadvantages of exploiting the intrinsic variability of electrum coins in any *single* transaction.

Even so, the coiners of electrum were much reduced in number by the time of the foundation of the Delian League, with Methymna, the autonomous Athenian ally on Lesbos, as perhaps the last of the archaic

---

Historical Considerations on the Origin and Spread of Greek Coinage in the Archaic Age (Diss., University of Michigan 1978) 19–24.

[10] J.F. Healy, *Mining and Metallurgy in the Greek and Roman World* (London 1978) 52–53. Cf. M.J. Price, "Darius I and the Daric," in R. Descat (ed.), *L'or perse et l'histoire grecque*, *REA* 91 (1989) 9–14, esp. 12–13.

coiners of electrum to end its output. Methymna has been classified as an interrupted mint in my category V by virtue of the history of its silver issues. I also except the small electrum fractional coins that are attributed to the Rhodian cities (see the Appendix). During the period of the *arkhē*, Lampsakos and Kyzikos were alone in their issuing of electrum staters. Lampsakos ended its production of staters and possibly also its issues of fractions by 450. Baldwin's opinion was that a gap existed followed by a resumption and possibly another interval before the end of the century (see the entry in the Appendix). In any event, the emissions of Lampsakos were so modest in output that they do not compare with the production of the other remaining electrum mints (especially during the second half of the fifth century). Kyzikos also struck *hectae* 'sixth-staters,' 'twelfth-staters,' and 'twenty-fourth-staters' (the latter two denominations only in very small amounts).

Phokaia had long since stopped its production of staters, as attested by actual surviving coins, and concentrated on the minting of *hectae*. Mytilene also produced *hectae*, and it is known that, at the end of our period or a little later, Phokaia and Mytilene had agreed to coordinate their emissions and were to strike *hectae* in alternate years of minting (see below, pp. 487–89). The attraction of the denomination of the *hectē* may be owed to the ratio of value between Phocaic (and less probably Cyzicene) electrum coins and silver money. If the value of the notational Phocaic "stater" hovered around 24 Attic silver drachms (see below, pp. 276–78, 524–27), the electrum *hectae* were approximately equivalent to Attic silver tetradrachms. Although the relationship of the Lampsacene staters to the Phocaic-standard *hectae* is not absolutely clear, it is still quite possible that any Lampsacenes that remained in circulation were considered equivalent to 6 Phocaic *hectae*.

As we have seen from our discussion of the hoard evidence, electrum coins played a role in the monetary system of the *arkhē*, but we must be careful not to exaggerate their significance. Clearly they were occasionally received by the Athenians in payment of tribute as the postscript to the first tribute list indicates (cf. *IG* I[3] 259.postscript 9–12). That the tribute lists themselves betray the reception by the Athenians of tribute in the form of electrum coins must be continually held in the back of our minds while the fifth-century activity of those mints with traditions of coining electrum is discussed (see below, pp. 274–79). The use of electrum coins, however, as a medium of business in Attica and among the *poleis* of the *arkhē* is a more obscure matter.

Because Lampsacene staters do not appear in classical literary documents, our judgment about their utilization is entirely dependent on the archaeological context for their discovery and on their appearance on inscribed inventories. In contrast, Phocaic electrum coins are mentioned by Thucydides when he speaks of the ransom (2,000 st.) extracted by oligarchic Lesbian exiles from Rhoiteion after they had captured the town in summer 424 (Thuc. 4.52.2; cf. Pollux 9.93). A speech attributed to Demosthenes attests to the use of electrum coins in the same area: the Athenian Mantitheos boasts that he had recruited mercenaries by having collected from the Athenian *proxenos* at Mytilene 300 Phocaic staters ([Dem.] 40.36). A fragment of Callisthenes speaks of Φωκαΐδας, presumably Phocaic staters or *hectae*, at Atarneus and Mytilene (*FGH* 124 F 4). One may particularly note in this material the use of electrum coins as a means of subsidizing military operations and, behind this, their role as treasurized wealth.

If these references were taken literally, the issuance of actual Phocaic staters (of which numismatists now possess not a single example), would have to be assumed. Nevertheless, the staters in these testimonia could be considered to be merely units of accounting that were in reality composed of Mytilenean and Phokaian *hectae*. Strikingly, the *hectae* themselves are not mentioned in passages such as these. Furthermore, Mytilenean *hectae* are not distinguished from Phokaian *hectae*, although at the least one would have to guess that they comprised the donation of the Mytilenean *proxenos* to the Athenian Mantitheos. Thus the references just discussed might be understood to signify "a number of *hectae* of Phocaic standard equalling the specified number of staters."[11]

Cyzicene staters were apparently a more important currency than the Phocaic standard *hectae*, making a correspondingly greater impact on literary sources, just as they are more prominent in the evidence from the hoards (see Appendix).[12] Eupolis speaks humorously of the great supply of staters in Kyzikos (fr. 233 K = fr. 247, *PCG* 5.438–39: ἥδε Κύζικος πλέα στατήρων). A number of passages in the *Anabasis* of Xenophon, the geographical settings for which are in the Black Sea and Propontis regions, refer to Cyzicenes as military pay or allowances, such as the offers of support for the hoplites of the Ten Thousand at the rate of one Cyzicene per capita each month (Xen. *Anab.* 5.6.23; 7.2.36; 7.3.10) or a request for *sitēresion* 'subsistence allowance' made of Herakleia for 3,000 or 10,000 Cyzicenes (6.2.4–5). It is clear from the Demosthenic

[11] Tod, *GHI* 2.112 shows Mytilene and Phokaia coordinating their output of electrum *hectae*.

[12] The lexical and paroemiographical notices presumably reflect the number of references that have not survived: *Suda* s.v. Κυζικηνοὶ στατῆρες, κ 2627 Adler; Hesych. s.v. Κυζικηνοὶ στατῆρες, κ 4435 Latte; Diogen. 5.66 (= *CPG* 1.264); Apostol. 10.24 (= *CPG* 2.491).

corpus that Cyzicenes could comprise a loan for conducting business in the Black Sea (Dem. 34.23; [Dem.] 35.36), even for deals struck at Athens. There was then no apparent legal impediment to making such a contract. To others, such as Lysias, Cyzicenes were a means for hoarding wealth (Lys. 12.11), and even thirty of them could be a component of an inheritance worth mentioning, along with 20 *mnai* of silver (Lys. 32.6; cf. DH *Lys.* 25).

Athenian inscribed inventories and accounts contain entries that were composed of electrum coins. Before beginning a closer look at these official documents, it is important to note once again the troubling notation of "Phocaic staters," especially where *hectae* in the multiple of twelve that could be rounded to two staters, appear in a later entry (*IG* I^3 342.9–10, cf. 18–19). Either these staters have been missed from our numismatic record (as observed above) or there is a principle by which *hectae* either were bundled or were not combined that escapes us. In the latter case, inclusion of the dedicated staters in a vessel or their accompaniment by a dedicatory document might have affected the description of the item in question in the inventory.

We continue by outlining the evidence of the inscriptions, starting with the citations of Lampsacene staters. Here the evidence from epigraphy does not give a much more striking impression of their significance than the literary and hoard material. A cache of 74 Lampsacene staters is noted in the accounts of the *epistatai* of the Parthenon, where they were patiently transferred from one board to another without being utilized (traceable from 447/6 to 434/3).[13] These coins may constitute a pious gift intended to defray the cost of the construction connected with the Parthenon or a dedication. Their retention might also show that it was not easy to spend Lampsacenes in the 440s and 430s at Athens (without paying a prohibitive exchange charge). For whatever reason, the *epistatai* preferred to retain these staters on their "books" rather than expend them for their current costs.

As the needs of the Athenians became more pressing during the Peloponnesian War, such reserves were committed to expenditure to support military efforts. In a year that is uncertain but was possibly 409/8, the Treasurers of Athena made over to the Hellenotamiai various assets of the cults under their supervision, including a sizable amount (equivalent to more than 6T of silver) that can be restored to have been at least 1408 Lampsacenes and 4 *hectae* (*IG* I^3 376.95–96).

[13] *IG* I^3 436.31; 437.42, 60; 439.67, 109; 440.118; 441.166; 442.174, 199; 444.243, 280; 445.290; 446.318, 341; 447.348, 364; 449.381–82, 406–407.

The material for Phocaic electrum is similar, but richer in attestation. In both the fifth and fourth centuries, various Attic cults held small units of these coins on their "books" as demonstrated by their inscribed inventories.[14] Just as with the Lampsacenes, their fifth-century holdings were conveyed by their overseers to the Hellenotamiai, who used them for state expenditures during the Peloponnesian War, as an example from the accounts of the Treasurers of Athena indicates (*IG* I^{3} 380.34).

The material on the utilization of Cyzicenes is a little richer still, although it reveals much the same phenomena. For example, the inventory of the Treasurers of the Other Gods of 429/8 lists various holdings of Cyzicenes.[15] Among the other inventories with groups of Cyzicene staters and *hectae* were the Eleusinian cult[16] and the inventory of the Hecatompedon.[17] Moreover, the *epistatai* of the Parthenon carried a consignment of Cyzicenes on their accounts for a number of years (447/6–434/3) without transfer or sale, just like their treatment of the Lampsacenes, as noted above.[18] That the total amount of Cyzicenes held by Attic cults was superior to that held in the other electrum coinages is also shown by the greater number of notations that have survived in the accounts of the *logistai*, where transfers of Cyzicenes from the Treasurers of Athena to the Hellenotamiai are listed.[19]

As we have seen above in our discussion of the hoard material, electrum coins could be a component of personal reserves. They were a most convenient way to store gold and thereby constituted a compact medium for the storage and transportation of wealth. Hence, Lysias, who surely qualifies as an astute person in business and in personal affairs, has his cache of 400 Cyzicenes. It is no accident that they are grouped with 100 Darics. Nor is it surprising that Lysias offered to bribe Peison (whom

[14] In the Hecatompedon inventories: *IG* I^{3} 342.9–10, 19 = *IG* II^{2} 1382.8–9, 18 (405/4?); II^{2} 1384.5–6; 1386.14–15, 17; 1388.42, 44; 1389.4, 5; 1390.3, 5; 1393.23–25; 1400.19–21, 44 = *SEG* 34.116b (there is substantial continuity in the items described therein). In the inventories of the Treasurers of the Other Gods: *IG* I^{3} 383.19–20 (ca. 450). Some of the same pieces from the Hecatompedon inventories are also listed in the holdings of the Treasurers of Athena (and also of the combined boards of treasurers of the later fourth century): *IG* II^{2} 1408.7; 1409.15–16; 1414.10; 1455.32–33; 1457.5; 1459.II.6. In the Eleusinian inventories: *IG* I^{3} 384.5 (ca. 450); a group of *hectae* of unknown number: 386.I.50; 387.I.57; 388.7; 389.8. In the cult inventory of Asklepios: *IG* II^{2} 1533.46.

[15] *IG* I^{3} 383.I.15–16, 45–47, 55–56, 61–62, 80–81, 87–88, 108–109; II.160–62, 167–68.

[16] *IG* I^{3} 384.3–4; 386.I.10, 49; 387.9, 56; 388.6; 389.7; 390.3.

[17] *IG* I^{3} 341.11 (= *IG* II^{2} 1383); II^{2} 1405.6; *SEG* 34.116a.27–28 (= *IG* II^{2} 1401); 116b.43 (= *IG* II^{2} 1400).

[18] *IG* I^{3} 436.32; 437.43, 61; 439.68, 110; 440.119; 441.167; 442.175, 200; 443.234; 444.244, 281; 445.291; 446.319, 342; 447.349, 364; 449.383–84, 408–409.

[19] *IG* I^{3} 370.13 (418/7: 4,000+ st.), 57–58 (416/5), 64–65 (415/4: 248 st.); 376.101–103 (409/8?); 378.21, 24–25 (406/5?); 382.2–3, 13–14 (end of fifth century).

the Thirty had sent to arrest him), with silver coins and not with his Cyzicenes or Darics. Their usefulness to an Attic metic such as Lysias or to members of the elites of the allies was not only their possession of a monetary value that transcended their city of issue but also their validity beyond the borders of the *arkhē*.[20] Thus, like Aiginetan coins, electrum coins served as an emergency reserve that could be spent beyond the borders of the *arkhē* in predicaments of last resort. From private reserves, dedications of electrum currency were given to Attic cults. Finally they were melted down and spent during the Peloponnesian War.

Yet mentioning Cyzicenes in the company of Darics and Aiginetic staters prompts an exploration of another aspect of their circulation, their function as a product rather than as a medium for exchange. Hoarders possessed a number of alternatives to holding electrum coins, and Cyzicene staters and Phocaic *hectae* competed as media for hoarding assets. Because their token value appears to have often exceeded their value as specie and because their mints profited from monetary fees, it was also advantageous to the issuers that upper-class individuals throughout the *arkhē* hold resources in their electrum in preference to other currencies. Along with the need for such coins for commerce with non-Greeks, that profit from potential or actual hoarders may help explain the persistent and steady output of the mints of Kyzikos, Mytilene, and Phokaia.

Possibly a desire to enhance the attractiveness of the product encouraged electrum minters to include such a wide variety of designs, some incorporating motifs that were drawn either from the coins of allied states within the Delian League or from foreign cults.[21] Such motifs augmented the international, nonlocal associations of electrum money in general. Borrowed motifs may have been thought to increase the willingness to hold the coins in question among the citizens of those cities from whose coinages and symbolic traditions the motifs were derived. A notice of Hesychius seems to represent the status of Phocaic electrum in just such deliberations by possible consumers: Hesych. s.v. Φωκαεῖς: ὄνομα ἔθνους. καὶ τὸ κάκιστον χρυσίον 'Phokaians: the name of a people and the worst gold' (φ 1085 Latte). This notice reveals a more

[20] Hence the appearance of Darics in the hoards outlined above may be explained (Chapter 1, note 61) and their eventual (modest) infiltration of Attic official accounts. Note *IG* I³ 383.I.17–18; 43–44; 110–11; 386.I.48; 387.I.55; 388.5; 389.6. Cf. M.-F. Baslez, "La circulation et le rôle des dariques en Grèce d'Europe à la fin du Vᵉ et au IVᵉ siècles. Apport des inscriptions phéniciennes et grecques," *REA* 91 (1989) 237–46.

[21] For Cyzicenes (250+ types now known): von Fritze *Nomisma* (1912) 1–38; L. Mildenberg, "The Cyzicenes: A Reappraisal," *AJN*³ 5–6 (1993–1994) 1–12. For Phocaic *hectae* Bodenstedt, *Elektron-Geld* 76–78; *Elektronmünzen* 67–87.

essentially consumerist than monetary appreciation of the attractiveness of Phocaic electrum coins, as implicitly compared with other options, such as Cyzicenes and Darics.[22]

Kraay traces the supposed immunity of electrum money from Athenian interference not only to the critical economic role of the coins (about which more shortly) but also to an important difference in official status.[23] He argues from the disparate and nonadvertizing character of electrum coin types that these coinages were not the official coinages of their cities. They did not carry a stable official badge like the silver coinage that eventually appeared at Kyzikos with an ethnic abbreviation. Kraay concludes that "it is unlikely that official transactions at Cyzicus were conducted in electrum rather than in the silver which bore the city's name and its types which remained unchanged for long periods." Moreover, the indirect taxes that formed a part of the fiscal repertoire of the ordinary *polis* could best capture payments from retail transactions mediated through silver coins, unless we are mistaken about the meager number of electrum "forty-eighths" (roughly equivalent to a silver triobol) that were minted and about the absence of other even smaller denominations. Taxes on trade with partners outside the *arkhē*, however, were another matter (to which we will return just below).

Kraay has probably also overstated the role of locally minted silver in the internal finances of these cities. There were no indigenous heavier silver coins available in the cities minting electrum. Nor does their output of lighter silver denominations appear, from a modern vantage point, to be proportionate to the size of their economies, even if we could be sure that drachms and fractions were minted by Kyzikos, Phokaia, and Mytilene during the whole duration of the Athenian hegemony. In fact, Phokaia fairly certainly did not produce a fractional silver during the Pentekontaeteia. Therefore, if electrum coins were not the main medium for local taxes and expenditures in these cities, foreign silver and particularly Athenian owls, almost certainly circulated locally as valid coinage. Tetradrachms performed the functions of larger silver denominations in the local economies in almost any sensible scenario.

[22] Bodenstedt, *Elektron-Geld* 39–41, indicates that his small sample of late sixth- and fifth-century Cyzicenes that were submitted to chemical analysis had a significantly higher gold content than the Phocaic *hectae* minted during the Attic hegemony (Phokaia: Au 38.9; Mytilene: Au 38.5; Kyzikos: Au 51.4).

[23] Kraay, *ACGC* 261. The annually alternating production of *hectae* by Mytlilene and Phokaia attested in Tod, *GHI* 2.112, was doubtless aided by the noncivic character of the coins (see below, pp. 487–89).

Other Attic coins and local silver drachms and fractions probably served as smaller denominations.

Therefore, it is not surprising that only a single issue of Mytilenean electrum staters existed and that they uncharacteristically proclaim their civic affiliation with the legend ΜΥΤΙ.[24] The technically and stylistically corresponding *hectae* with dies cut by the same hand bear Μ or ΛΕ, with the latter designation amounting to a polemical claim by Mytilene to hegemony over the whole island of Lesbos. Both staters and *hectae* can be dated to the time of the rebellion from Athens in 428–27.[25] The poor quality of the stater indicates a lower than usual proportion of gold (and possibly a much higher amount of copper) and fits well with the exigencies of a crisis. It is likely that the issue of staters was intended for some large disbursements of funds by the Mytilenean government, either to pay mercenaries and suppliers (cf. Thuc. 3.2.1–2; 3.18.1) or to subvene the subsistence of poorer citizens who were under economic stress because of the Athenian military operations on the island (cf. Thuc. 3.27.3). Kraay observes that the reverse type is intended to emulate a Cyzicene stater. That may be the clinching detail that demonstrates that the coins were intended to pay for products or to enlist troops in the Black Sea region and Propontis, where Cyzicenes were a major medium of business.

The unparalleled nature of this issue may indicate that previously, during the long period of "imperial" peace, the Mytilenean government had conducted much of its business in foreign silver. The Mytilenean soldiers and sailors who had fought alongside their allies in so many operations of the Delian League had probably not been paid earlier in electrum staters. The Mytileneans had to do business with the same merchants as the Athenians. Such merchants were not only valuable logistical assets but they seem to have worked in an Attic monetary context (pp. 261–62 below). Whatever monies they had received, whether salaries or subsistence allowances, had probably been paid over in Attic silver, just as was the payment of the crews and marines of the Athenian ships serving with them. Attic silver would have been depleted as the Mytileneans made their preparations for revolt and paid some of their overseas suppliers in Attic coins, the main monetary medium of the

24 See J.F. Healy, "A New Light on the Unique Stater of Mytilene," *ANSMN* 8 (1958) 1–9; C.M. Kraay, "Greek Coinage and War," in W. Heckel and R. Sullivan (eds.), *Ancient Coins of the Graeco-Roman World: The Nickle Numismatic Papers* (Waterloo, Ontario 1984) 3–18, esp. 4; see also Bodenstedt, *Elektronmünzen* 240 with 62–64, and C.M. Kraay's review of this work in *Gnomon* 54 (1982) 499–500.

25 See also Robinson *Hesperia* Suppl. (1949) 332.

Aegean. Thus they may have reverted to an older pattern of military subsidy by using electrum thereafter, remembering that electrum coins had been used to support the military operations of the Ionian rebels.[26] The electrum *hectae* of this moment with their patriotic and chauvinist designations were also well suited to replace Attic tetradrachms in military subventions.

The cities that produced electrum issues show a pattern in the emission of silver issues that is congruent with the roles for silver and electrum in their local economies and taxational systems that have been outlined just above. Phokaia seems to have ceased all minting activities in silver early and so is comparable to the cities in class IIIA, as outlined above. There are a number of comparably sized economies in categories IIIA–IIIB. Lampsakos and Kyzikos shifted to an exclusive minting of drachms and fractions about the time of the origin of the Delian League. In addition, there is general agreement that the Lampsakenes interrupted or terminated their output of even these smaller denominations sometime around the middle of the century, comparably to a category IIIC mint. Judging from their assessments—before the Peloponnesian War, Kyzikos peaked at 9T and Lampsakos at 12T—both cities had relatively large economies, but fell well short of the major economies among the Athenian allies like Aigina, Chios, and Samos. They belonged to the second tier of economies and possibly to its lower register. Kyzikos would be found among the category IVC mints (minters of silver fractions and drachms), in the company of Erythrai (highest payment, 10T, 1100 dr.), Miletos (10T), and the Rhodian cities Ialysos (10T) and Kameiros (9T; and compare Lindos at 10T). Mytilene also shifted to an exclusive emission of fractions during the years of the Attic hegemony, although this city and its Lesbian neighbors (if they are to be seen as a single economic unit) belong among the largest allied economies.[27] Our examination of the silver issues of the mints specializing in electrum indicates that these cities were susceptible to the same influences, acting in favor of monetary consolidation, as the mints that coined silver exclusively. If one treats the electrum minters as minters of silver, the measure of monetary consolidation becomes entry I–VI in Table 2.1.

Another indication of monetary consolidation depends on the speculative explanation offered by Bodenstedt for a change in the gold content of Phocaic *hectae* in which the proportion of gold fell significantly between

[26] Note Kraay, *ACGC* 30. See also J. Dengate, "A Mint for the Coinage of the Ionian Revolt," *AJA* 72 (1968) 164.

[27] Cf. Figueira, *Colonization* 195–97.

his periods II and III at both Phokaia and Mytilene. Bodenstedt believes that this change brought the *hectae* into an easy exchange ratio with the Attic tetradrachm and that it took place in 478/7, at the formation of the Delian League.[28] The *hectae* became equivalent to Attic tetradrachms. There is the risk, however, of oversubscribing to a belief in rigid and stable exchange rates in this hypothesis. There is also another risk in hereby accepting a quasi-official function for Phocaic-standard coins in the fiscal affairs of the *arkhē* and positing the origin of that function at the very outset of the alliance.

Granting this diminution of the gold content of Phocaic-standard coins is correctly dated by Bodenstedt (and that is not certain), it might be preferable to advance an explanation implicating practical administration, since whatever amounts the Athenians were expending to support their fleets must have become an aspect of general knowledge among the allies, with some force as a precedent. Inasmuch as Phocaic electrum had a recognized role in the payment for the services of mercenaries, the minters of Phokaia and Mytilene might have acted to bring their coins into an equivalency with Attic coins in order that the payments made in *hectae* to military personnel and to suppliers could become equivalent to those made in silver by the Athenians. In this case, there would be no particular need to believe that the change in gold content exactly corresponded to the moment of the foundation of the alliance, for the desire to exclude discrepancies in the payment of military personnel could have grown with the success of the military operations of the league. Yet it may be that both these variations on the theme of the integration of Phocaic electrum with Attic silver are too labored. The simplest and preferable explanation for a lowered gold content for electrum coins is that the value ratio of gold and silver changed irreversibly so that the new coins were comparable to their predecessors according to some formula of the value ratio of the two metals.

THE STATUS OF ELECTRUM IN THE *ARKHĒ*

Our evidence falls well short of justification for seeing the Cyzicenes or Phocaic-standard *hectae* as a "reserve currency" of the Athenian *arkhē* in its totality, except when we understand this concept within carefully defined limits.[29] Nothing suggests a general utilization of electrum money in the internal trade or finance of the allied cities; as an everyday

[28] Bodenstedt, *Elektron-Geld* 48–50; 56–58.

[29] Cf. Bodenstedt, *Elektron-Geld* 57–58, 83–84.

feature of economic life (as far as we can tell) electrum was significant in northwestern Asia Minor, the (primarily Asian) Propontis, and parts of the Black Sea region, where it was used along with silver coins. Those trading with these regions could use electrum as money or make investments in terms of electrum coins.

For the rest of the economic life of the *arkhē*, it is more sensible to conclude that electrum coins were a repository of value used by individuals as one of the ways (among others like Darics, gold jewelry, utensils, or furniture) to hoard wealth, and not to invest it productively. While the Athenians undoubtedly preferred to receive the *phoros* from their allies in Attic coins, they did also accept payment in electrum on occasion (see below, pp. 274–79). Nonetheless, nothing just said precludes the conclusion that paying in electrum was truly preferable to payment in non-Athenian silver. Yet it was not simply the general currency of the Cyzicenes and *hectae* that promoted their use and acceptability, since other silver coins such as Aiginetan staters were at least as prevalent. It was rather that certain taxes, presumably those on maritime trade, may have been collected in electrum in the cities that were periodically allowed to tender tribute in electrum coins. The availability of those tax receipts in the form of electrum made payments in that medium a logical alternative when Attic silver coins were in insufficient supply for particular allied states.

Can we go further than this and assert that the tribute assessments themselves were calculated in Cyzicenes and Phocaic "staters" on the basis of the known yield of these maritime taxes and then translated into Attic drachms? In response, it is fairly safe to believe that tribute was not assessed in amounts resolvable into even numbers both of Cyzicenes or Phocaic-standard coins and of Attic tetradrachms for the express purpose of *promoting* the payment of *phoros* to Athens in electrum. What incentive did the Athenians have to amass electrum coins that they could not easily disburse through official channels, as the entries on the inventories of Attic treasuries reveal to us? The record of the tribute lists shows a slackening of electrum payments after the Thirty Years Peace. This judgment however, does not exclude that commercial taxes levied in electrum *hectae* and staters had some effect not only on the collection but also on the assessment of tribute. Declarations of yields from taxes in electrum may have had a role in the assessment process. Nonetheless, the persistence of unusual assessments and payments could be owed equally as well to conservative attitudes toward leadership that included a reluctance to raise allied assessments without substantial reasons (cf. pp. 285–88).

It has often been observed that the Coinage Decree deals only with silver and not with electrum, although that conclusion is weakened by the common restoration of τὸ χρυσίον 'gold' in the conclusion of the decree. After all, that term could denote some legislative action involving electrum coins, since they were denominated as "gold." Nevertheless, the restriction of the Coinage Decree to legislating about silver is doubtlessly correct insofar as the critical clause that was added to the oath of the *Boulē* mentions only coining in silver. Nevertheless, electrum may actually have been collected and dispatched to Athens in lieu of tribute payments in Attic money, if the hypothesis is correct that the decree was drawing in non-Athenian coins, perhaps in the place of the tetradrachms that ordinarily formed the bulk of the tribute. That supposition could be used to explain the restored reference to gold in the decree, but naturally there are other lines of interpretation along which the end of the decree can be reconstructed (see below, pp. 414–18).

Be that as it may, scholarly opinion has almost universally conceded that the electrum minting of Kyzikos, Mytilene, and Phokaia was not curtailed by this statute or by other imperial enactment. Credible reasoning is then introduced for such an exemption, which is based on the critical role of electrum coinage in the commerce of the Propontis and especially the Black Sea region (mainly Cyzicenes, but earlier perhaps also Lampsacenes) or on the part played by fractional coinage in electrum in the areas of northwest Asia Minor, where Darics also circulated (that is, the electrum *hectae* of Mytilene and Phokaia).[30] To this traditional view, the foregoing analysis has added rationales based on the function of electrum coins in taxation and on their complementary relationship with silver money in the economies and finances of electrum minters.

Earlier students of the decree were also eager to remind their readers that the replacement of electrum with silver tetradrachms would have had far-reaching disruptive effects, particularly for non-Greek customers. Nonetheless, the limitation of the exempting influence of such factors to electrum coinages is highly problematical in itself. Similar regional ascendencies can be hypothesized for silver coinages like those of the cities of the northern Aegean, many of whose trading partners would have been Thracians. We have already seen from the hoard evidence that the coins of certain northern mints, such as Thasos and Maroneia, had special roles in the economy of the Balkan peninsula. Like people living in the Troad, Hellespont, and the Black Sea region, these natives can be expected to

[30] See also Meiggs 167–68.

have been relatively less sophisticated in their knowledge of the conditions of trade and thus more dependent on traditional or stereotypical transactions that were denominated in familiar coins. As will be detailed shortly, it is hard to find any real interruption in minting by several important mints of the Thracian district.[31] Moreover, a similar case could even be made regarding some mints in Asia Minor.[32] Whenever a political causation is made to yield in one place to economic factors, however, it becomes odd that supervening economic forces worked only to preserve the prerogatives of electrum minters and not those of silver coiners (in the traditional understanding of the decree). Yet these concerns can be *raised* only from the numismatic evidence, while answering them will have to wait for a consideration of the fragments of the decree.

Once we part with (even hypothetically) an economic rationale for the exemption of electrum, it may be worth considering other political reasons why electrum was left alone in the crucial clause added to the oath of the councillors in the Coinage Decree. Surely the primary difference in fiscal terms between electrum money and silver money during the Athenian *arkhē* is that the tribute was assessed and usually paid in Attic silver. The currency of non-Athenian silver in allied cities meant that taxes would be collected in such coins and that in turn created exchange problems, if tetradrachms were the preferred medium for payment of tribute. Consequently, silver currency was a more legitimate, and thus more crucial subject for legislation than electrum.

This hypothesis may seem counterintuitive on the surface, for one might object that there is possibly as good, if not better, evidence for the Athenians being compelled to accept allied electrum in the tendering of the tribute than there is evidence for their acceptance of allied silver (see below pp. 274–79). If the Athenians vigorously preferred to receive their own silver (as will be suggested), why not legislate about the minting of electrum? In answering such a query, one must consider whether we are not in actuality testing the practical limits of classical political hegemony.

Where trade was transacted appreciably in electrum coins, there would necessarily be commercial taxes that were most easily collected in

[31] The difficulties of squaring a ban on silver coining with the apparent record of activity by the mints of the Thracian littoral has long been acknowledged: Babelon *RN* (1913) 477–78; Robinson *Hesperia* Suppl. (1949) 338. For recent discussions, see J.H. Kagan, "The Decadrachm Hoard: Chronology and Consequences," in Carradice, *Coinage and Administration* 21–28, esp. 23–26; Price in Carradice op. cit. 43–51. See below pp. 127–49.

[32] One might counter these possible economic parallels between Pontine and Propontine electrum and North Aegean silver by emphasizing the authoritarian and symbolic interpretation of the Coinage Decree. Thus it was legislation less hostile to electrum by virtue of the apolitical aura of electrum issues.

electrum. Since the Athenians were not prepared to create their own electrum coinage, it is hard to see how they could have ever imposed a simple prohibition on the employment of electrum money by others. The temptation or even the incentive for allies to pass electrum coins along to the Athenians would exist with equal urgency, regardless of attempts at restriction or prohibition. The Athenians were powerless to stop their allies from holding in the form of electrum money tax receipts, which were originally collected in electrum coins (that were necessarily non-Athenian), and yielding to the temptation to try to pass them along to the Athenians, either when they were short of Attic coins or when they were simply short of silver. Occasional shortages of Athenian silver for paying tribute on the part of the cities with receipts in electrum may have been tolerable, so long as the same cities recognized the validity of Athenian money. As I have already argued, it is likely that Attic money circulated regularly in the local economies of the cities coining electrum and was probably used for internal taxation and expenditure (along with other silver coins).

Thus, we can adapt the earlier hypothesis of an economic reason why the Athenians seem to have legislated about silver and not about electrum by introducing the vital fiscal and administrative considerations. In a revisionist interpretation of the Coinage Decree, the standing of Attic silver in these cities might be ensured by a provision that established the validity of Attic silver wherever allied silver was struck (as it was at Kyzikos, Lampsakos, and Mytilene). Concomitantly, there was no need for a provision stipulating that allied minters and users of electrum had to accept Athenian coins; in all probability, they were doing so already. But we are still very far from demonstrating the possibility of such a stipulation in Attic legislation, let alone in the Coinage Decree.

4

MINTS IN CONTINUOUS OPERATION

TO CONTINUE OUR SURVEY of allied mints, we turn in this chapter and the next to a consideration of those mints that seem to have manifested some degree of continuing, regular operation during the Attic hegemony and to have produced a range of denominations (Table 4.1). These mints are divided into category VIIA, composed of geographically scattered active mints, and category VIIB, those active mints of the northern Aegean region. Some alternative categories are also included in Table 4.1, and the classifications and chronologies summarized in Table 7.2 (pp. 191–92 below) may be helpful in reading this chapter.

GEOGRAPHICALLY SCATTERED ACTIVE MINTS

The mints in category VIIA divide into a few recognizable subclasses. These groupings do not reflect some legal or diplomatic status within the alliance but evoke different contexts for the economic activity of particular groups of allied states. It is perhaps easiest to start with a group of states whose distinctive circumstances will be disputed by few. Minting seems to have persisted along the southern littoral of Asia Minor. In the traditional viewpoint, one would have said that the Coinage Decree (however dated) had no effect in this region. A more accurate description would be to say that monetary consolidation was weaker in this region than in others under Athenian hegemony.

Lycia

We start with Lycia, although the special nature of the political organization of that region forbids our drawing any solid conclusions about Attic monetary policy. While some Lycians accepted Athenian hegemony (and a tribute payment of 10T shows the number was sizable at one time), there is no certainty that the Lycians who were minting throughout the second half of the fifth century were doing so while allied with Athens. Added complexity about the interaction of Athenian jurisdiction and minting derives also from the likelihood that dynasts with control or influence over civic mints issued coins through those mints. Thus there is no strong argument in either direction, if a review is confined to traditional questions such as the dating of a prohibition against minting silver or

Table 4.1 Category VII: Continuous Minters

(See Table 2.2 [p. 84 above] for abbreviations used in this table)

A. Miscellaneous Active Mints

Aigina (~ category IVA)	<457	<431	<431
Aspendos		*	500–400H
Ephesos (or category IVB or V)	<450 420>	*	*H; *B; 450/412>K
Kelenderis	465>	465>	450>K; 465B
Lykioi	*	*	
Teos (or category IVA)	*	*	<449/412>K; interrupted in Peloponnesian War?

B. Northern Aegean Mints

Abdera	*	*	*H/B; <425/4M; Brk. 439-37 (K); 15–20 yrs. later (PW); into third quarter of fifth century (P);*
Ainos (or category IVC)	L. <450 435>	St. <440 425> Fr. *	450>H; <425/4M; into 450–25P intermittent after 450
Akanthos	*	*	brk. 450–20 (K); <431 at earliest (PW); far into 450–25P;*
Maroneia	*	474>	<425/4M; brk. after 450 (K); into 450–25P; some punctuation and limitation after 450
Mende (or category IVB or IVC)	brk. 450–40	St. <465 450> Fr. *	*H/B; St. <425/4M; brk. before 450 (K); into 450–25P/W; intermittent after 450?

the degree of successful implementation of such a provision. The evidence of the hoards (examined above) shows that Lycia was a monetary "compartment" separate from the economic and monetary factors operative in the Aegean.[1]

[1] Kagan, *Coinage and Administration* 27.

From the perspective of the history of monetary consolidation during the *arkhē*, however, the prominence of what is called the "light Lycian" standard during the Athenian hegemony is more illuminating. It appears to be a local adaptation of the Euboeic/Attic standard, wherein the stater is intended to be equivalent to an Attic didrachm. Although the use of this standard was not universal, its currency is surely expressive of a desire to simplify exchange with those doing business (public or private) in Athenian coins and in other Euboeic/Attic currency. That the "light Lycian" standard was primarily employed in the valley of Xanthos and farther west is exactly what one would predict in a geographical estimation of the permeability of various areas of Lycia to Aegean economic influences. After the closure (ca. 460) of the "Decadrachm Hoard" (*CH* 8.48), there was a movement in Lycia toward the Attic standard that was well under way ca. 450.[2] Subsequently, coins with typological derivatives from Attic tetradrachms are to be dated to the beginning of the Peloponnesian War, at which time they indicate changing patterns in the outflow of Athenian coins.[3] Elsewhere this same phenomenon has been associated with a local replacement or supplementation of a reduced money stream of Athenian and Attic-standard money.

Pamphylia/Cilicia

The hoard evidence that suggests the dominance of coins on the Persic standard in the monetary circulation of southern Asia Minor has already been discussed in the treatment of the hoards found in that region (pp. 34–35). Two Greek *poleis* in the region, Aspendos in Pamphylia and Kelenderis in Cilicia, both minted Persic weight coins throughout the fifth century. Kraay thought that Aspendos might have had a gap in its issues between the series with a warrior with shield (obverse) and a *triskeles* (reverse) and the issue with a rider on the obverse and a boar on the reverse. If that is so, the interval would be in the late fifth century (420–410?). As so often in our categorization, intermittence of operation is hard to fix numismatically and thus to contextualize historically. These cities were too far from the Aegean basin for an appreciable number of the business transactions in which their residents participated to have been conducted with other allies of Athens who happened to use Athenian money. Business (and governmental dealings) conducted with non-Greeks in Persic-standard coins would have been a most important factor in encouraging the maintenance of local mints.

[2] See J. Spier, "Lycian Coins in the 'Decadrachm Hoard'" in Carradice, *Coinage and Administration* 29–41; also Kagan, *Coinage and Administration* 26.

[3] Kraay, *Coinage* 270–71.

The two cities are only known on the tribute lists in 425, so that any exchange problems attributable to acquiring sufficient Attic money for payment of tribute would not have affected minting until relatively late, if at all. One does suspect, however, that a rule that Attic money had to be accepted as legal tender—a revisionist reading of the crucial clause of the Coinage Decree—might actually have had a rationale regarding these cities, because it enhanced the accumulation of sufficient tetradrachms to pay the assessed tribute.

The local economies within such cities would not have been awash in Attic money and other allied coins, which justified their continued minting in addition to any arrangements made to use foreign coins. Like the northern Aegean mints that will be considered shortly, Aspendos and Kelenderis occupied coastal locations from which routes of communication and trade presumably radiated. The regional economy differed in that unlike Thrace one or two Greek coinages did not provide a monetary medium for the interior, but a variety of coins on the single, Persic standard.

Phaselis, the nearest to Athens of the allies of southern Anatolia, is comparable to Aspendos and Kelenderis in its participation in the commerce of this region, so strongly influenced by the Persic standard (at least on the basis of the hoard evidence). Phaselis, which had been an ally of Athens since the late 460s, does seem, however, to follow a more common profile for the cessation of minting (in the present state of the data). Coining seems to have extended down to ca. 440 (series 4), although the chronology for Phaselis may be too late because affected by the traditional interpretation and dating of the Coinage Decree.[4] The stater emissions (= double *sigloi*) comprising "emission 1" may have been greater in the period before accession to the Delian League and are, in any case, inferior to the strikings of tetrobols, "emission 2."[5] Heipp-Tamer places a resumption of minting in 411 with Series 5, dated by the revival of Persian influence over Phaselis (note Thuc. 8.99). This date is no more solid than the interruption date in the 440's. Phaselis may have seen a waning of striking and an emphasis on fractional coining during the 460s and 450s, with some anomalous issues mixed in with discontinuities

[4] See C. Heipp-Tamer, *Die Münzprägung der lykischen Stadt Phaselis in griechischer Zeit* (Saarbrücken 1993) 39–47 (< ca. 446/411>).

[5] These Series 4 staters share a die-linked coin with the larger late archaic issues (V25, R44), and only three obverse dies appear with seven reverse dies. For the tetrobols, however, nine obverse dies and ten reverse dies are known. A single pair of obol dies ("emission 3") is also attested.

("Unbestimmte Münzserien"), and a termination after 450. Any time during the Peloponnesian War will do as well for the resumption.

Ephesos and Teos

The pattern of minting practices in Ionia during the *arkhē* is complex. While the monetary consolidation that has been seen to be so prominent in the islands is significant in Ionia as well, the two regions differ in that insular mints closed (but compare Kyme in Aiolis or the silver issues of Phokaia), while the cities of the western coast of Asia Minor more often confined their minting to drachms and fractions. Erythrai and Kolophon seem to have restarted their mints over time with lighter issues, and Klazomenai and Miletos (especially) appear to have never ceased turning out fractions.

The two best candidates for mints that were continuously active across a range of denominations are Ephesos and Teos. Yet the earlier scholarship on Ephesos saw a gap in coining of several decades and more recently Kraay has argued for a sequence of intermittent issuances of coin. That is a particularly difficult phenomenon to document in the present state of our evidence. The historical reality of minting at Ephesos is quite obscure and the classification of Ephesos in this category is only one solution.

Teos was a mint that struck Aiginetic coins with the obverse of a right-facing griffin and an incuse square on the reverse. It is also now fairly clear that Teos did not cease minting around mid-century, as Balcer had suggested, and that the earlier view that the Teians were coining in the second half of the century ought to be revived. Accordingly, Balcer's chronology has been shown to be considerably higher than can now be sustained. A first blow was struck by the Teian staters in the Asyut hoard (ca. 475), not extending past Balcer group V, that led Price and Waggoner to lower the dates for Balcer's period I (ca. 510/505–495/90) by 10–15 years.[6] S. Hurter has presented a Teian overstrike of period II (comparable to Balcer group LIV) on a Tanagran coin that is placed 457–46, namely, during the period of Athenian dominance over Boiotia outside of Thebes, which included Tanagra.[7] She therefore judged that the end of period II could not precede 440 at the very earliest (and not Balcer's 449). In response, Mattingly put the beginning of period II after ca. 465.[8]

[6] Price and Waggoner 86–87.

[7] S. Hurter, "Teos over Tanagra," *Florilegium Numismaticum: Studia in honorem U. Westermark edita* (Stockholm 1992) = *NM* 38 (1992) 171–73.

[8] H.B. Mattingly, "A New Light on the Early Silver Coinage of Teos," *SNR* 73 (1994) 5–9.

Moreover, a Teian stater seeming to belong to period I, group VII, has now come to light overstruck on a reduced Abderite tetradrachm of the magistrate Hege– (May's period III, group XXXVI).[9] Although they are not the latest coins in *CH* 8.48, "Decadrachm Hoard" (ca. 465–60), coins of group XXXVI are attested in the hoard. Group VII cannot have been minted at Teos earlier than ca. 470–65. Hence a date for the termination of period I begins to drop further toward mid-century, if the order of classes in Balcer's pioneering study is respected, or toward 460, if group VII is moved (Mattingly suggests to after group XII). Mattingly would go even further, first by putting the Tanagran coin at the very end of its series so that the Teian overstrike is no earlier than ca. 445.[10] He would then argue that the owl in Balcer's group LI (period II) was copied ca. 440 from standardized Attic owls of the period after 450 (cf. pp. 180–82 below for an earlier chronology for the Attic mint). That would leave Balcer groups LII–LVIII of the period II staters still to be minted.

In general, since Balcer drew parallels between the representations of griffins on Teian coins and those on the coins of the Teian colony Abdera, a strong inclination toward downdating Teian issues flows out of downdating their Abderite counterparts (see pp. 134–38 below).[11] That tendency becomes especially strong if D. MacDonald is followed in his suggestion that Teos lagged behind Abdera stylistically. *CH* 8.47, containing staters through Balcer group LIV, #103, has a date of deposition of 445–35, according to MacDonald. Following Balcer's classification, there were some classes in period II still to be struck.[12] In the present state of our knowledge, whether the Teian mint closed or at what point the mint may have ceased operations cannot be discerned clearly nor can the length of any interval in coining be definitively determined. The date of 412 for the commencement of Balcer period III (groups LXXVI–LXXVIII) is also entirely arbitrary. Rebellion in Ionia might as easily serve as the lower boundary of period III as its beginning.

Teos was a source for Aiginetic-weight money in Ionia, which would have easily flowed into an international pattern of circulation. Although Ionia (in its broader sense) provides plenty of evidence against the existence of a prohibition on allied minting, it is also apparent that monetary consolidation, while not as advanced as in the islands, had been at work in this region. Cessation of minting, limitation of coining to lighter

9 D. MacDonald, "A Teos/Abdera Overstrike," *SM* 44 (1994) 37–40. See pp. 134–35 below.

10 Mattingly *SNR* (1994) 5–9.

11 Note J.M. Balcer, "The Early Silver Coinage of Teos," *SNR* 47 (1968) 5–50, esp. 10.

12 D. MacDonald, "A Note on *CH* VIII, No. 47: Ionia 1983," *NC* 155 (1995) 321–23.

denominations, and less continuous minting activities all appear fairly well attested in the area.

Aigina

The history of the mint on Aigina is the next obvious topic for exploration, inasmuch as there is every indication that the Aiginetan mint was active down to the expulsion of the Aiginetans from their island by the Athenians in 431. Thus, if one approached the classification of the mint of Aigina with an eye solely on the expulsion of the Aiginetans, one would place Aigina with mints such as Poteidaia. This, however, would be misleading, because the Aiginetan output of coins, unlike the other mints closed by Athenian military action, continued at a high level across a range of denominations until its termination. Discarding the possibility of a continuing coining by Aiginetan exiles, pseudo-Aiginetan coins and Aiginetic issues from other mints were inaugurated or augmented to supplement circulating coins, many of which were countermarked to sustain their validity. But for the political miscalculations of the Aiginetan oligarchs, their mint would have continued striking coins. Therefore, it would be wrong-headed to imagine that the main part of business transactions conducted in Aiginetan coins necessarily shifted to Attic money after 431.

Aiginetan issues are plentiful with a relatively static type of the obverse and a fitfully evolving reverse based on the pattern of indentations of the teeth of punch die that became stylized by stages. Classification and dating of issues is complex. The one clear line of demarcation is between the obverses bearing a turtle with a smooth carapace and those with animals with segmented shells called tortoises, although even here there are intricacies. We make a start on the complex history of the role of Aiginetan coins by making several observations about Attic atttitudes toward Aiginetan money (see pp. 255–56 below on the validity of Aiginetan coins).

Herodotus and Thucydides give ample testimony to the negative connotations that anything associated with the Aiginetan elite conjured up for ordinary Athenians during the Attic hegemony.[13] Indeed, there is even evidence to suggest that the hostility between Athenians and Aiginetans affected Attic perceptions of Aiginetan money, for Pollux tells us that the Athenians called the Aiginetan drachm the παχεῖαν δραχμήν 'fat drachm' out of hostility to the Aiginetans (9.76). Encapsulated in that epithet is perhaps a hint of Athenian polemics against the Aiginetan oligarchs.[14] I have also argued elsewhere that Atthidographic accounts

[13] Figueira, *Excursions* 44–51.
[14] Figueira, *Excursions* 76.

of the supposed monetary and metrological reforms of Solon are so pervaded by the spirit of the later political rivalry between Athens and Aigina that they reflected anachronistically the archaic traditions about the evolution of coinage, weights, and measures in early Attica (*Ath. Pol.* 10.1–2; Plutarch *Solon* 15.2–4 with Androtion *FGH* 324 F 34).[15]

Perceptions and psychological associations are one thing and actual economic practices are often quite another matter, for there is evidence that Aiginetan coins could be used even in Athens. First, the byname for the Aiginetan drachm that has just been noted would not have been necessary had Aiginetan coins not been in use within Attica. Concomitantly (as we shall see below, pp. 314–15), enough examples of Aiginetan weights (some publicly authorized) have been discovered at Athens to show that goods were packaged according to Aiginetic *stathma* 'weights.' A valuable testimonium derives from a later period. In the fragment of an unknown play, Diphilus can imagine a fishmonger asking for payment in Aiginetan obols after a price of 10 obols had been settled on with his customer (fr. 66 K = fr. 67, *PCG* 5.92). Not only did the fishmonger unilaterally increase the price of the purchase by this means, but he had the audacity to return change in lighter Attic obols.[16] Taste varies in the appreciation of ancient humor, but it is probably preferable to see a New Comic playwright as exploiting a possible situation.[17]

Aiginetan coins are inventoried in Attic accounts. We should remember, however, that there is no guarantee that notations like στατῆρες Αἰγιναῖοι were restricted to Aiginetan coins and did not occasionally connote other coins minted on the Aiginetic monetary standard as well. Although Athenian inscribed accounts do not give conclusive and detailed evidence on the penetration of Aiginetan coins into the *arkhē*—for one thing we have already considered the evidence from hoards from the Cyclades on the treasurization of Aiginetan coins—they do indicate holdings of Aiginetan or Aiginetic-standard silver by Attic cults that are presumably derived from dedications.[18] Just as the Treasurers of Athena

[15] Figueira, *Excursions* 61–86.

[16] Note L. Lacroix, "La monnaie grecque et les problèmes de la circulation monétaire," *BAB*[5] 55 (1969) 169–80, esp. 170–71.

[17] Another example of later interaction between the Aiginetan and the Athenian monetary systems may be glimpsed in the form of a bronze coin of uncertain provenience that bears two successive countermarks. The first is an owl, which suggests a currency for the coin in Attica, and the second countermark is a tortoise, which implies validity on Aigina after 457. See C. Gresham, "Aegina Countermark Torturous Enigma," *World Coins* 96 (1971) 1586–90.

[18] Note the inventories of the Treasurers of the Other Gods: *IG* I[3] 383.25–26, 89–90, II.180–81 (429/8); those of the *epistatai* at Eleusis: 386.6–8 (cf. 91–92: 408/7); 387.5–6 (407/6). Cf. for the Treasurers of Athena and the Other Gods: *IG* II[2] 1388.70 (398/7).

were making over to the *stratēgoi* stocks of electrum coins during the exigent days of the Ionian War, so too were they conveying their holdings in Aiginetan or Aiginetic coin to the same officials (as *IG* I^3 380.32–33 demonstrates).

In addition, the Athenians were compelled to take more direct cognizance of the Aiginetic monetary sphere whenever they dealt with mainland allies such as Argos and Mantineia for whom Aiginetic coinage constituted an established international monetary medium. The Athenian treaty with the Argives and Mantineians of 420 specifies that *sitēresion* 'subsistence allowance' in Aiginetan/Aiginetic money was to be given to each participant in an expeditionary force that was kept in the field for more than thirty days (*IG* I^3 83.23–24).

Nineteenth- and early twentieth-century discussion of the succession of Aiginetan issues wavered between widely varying dates for the major shift in type from a turtle with a smooth carapace—the type may well represent one of the large pelagic turtles—to a tortoise with a segmented carapace. Some scholars adopted the expedition of Xerxes as a line of demarcation. Others saw the hiatus in control of Aigina by an independent, indigenous government as marking the period of division between the turtles with their smooth carapaces (for the vast majority) and the tortoises with their segmented shells. Naturally, at this point in the evolution of scholarship on fifth-century monetary history, there as yet existed no justification in the Coinage Decree for positing a mid-century break in Aiginetan minting, so the emission of turtles (sometimes considered to be restricted to triobols and lighter weights) was thought in this case to continue until the expulsion of the bulk of the Aiginetans in 431. Under the impact of the redating of the Coinage Decree by virtue of the discovery of the Kos fragment, the possibility of an interruption before 431 received consideration. The aforesaid older view may then be contrasted with that of E.S.G. Robinson, who saw Aiginetan issues breaking off at 457 and resuming for the period 446–31.[19]

The hypothesis of a fifth-century resumption after an interruption had become necessary because of another independent discovery. While it had previously been thought by the majority of scholars that the first tortoises were to be placed in the fourth century, an overstrike of a tortoise by a fifth-century Cypriot king, Azbaal of Kition, had indicated that the

[19] E.S.G. Robinson, "A Hoard of Archaic Greek Coins from Anatolia," *NC*^{7} 1 (1961) 107–17, esp. 111–12; also R.R. Holloway, "An Archaic Hoard from Crete and the Early Aeginetan Coinage," *ANSMN* 17 (1971) 1–21, esp. 20–21.

first tortoises began to be minted in the fifth century.[20] That conjunction certified the impressions garnered from several other considerations. There are noticeable stylistic similarities between the latest "T-back" turtles and the first tortoises that do not equally prevail for the tortoise staters of the fourth century, such as the broad banded skew reverse, the height of relief of the shell, and the treatment of the carapace.[21] The low percentage of gold and a characteristic proportion of copper also link fifth-century tortoises to the last turtles.[22]

For the rationale for the type change, we enter an area of genuine speculation. At the start, however, it is doubtful that there was any symbolic gesture in the shift to what seems to be a land turtle. If a symbolic reason for the change is adopted in which the collapse of Aiginetan naval power was signaled, the revival of the same type in their fourth-century period of independence must appear an improbable act of masochism. At any event, an Athenian mandating of such a change would have been a pointless act of spite in any case (one uncharacteristic of the leadership of Perikles).[23] My own preferred explanation exploits the occasional earlier appearance of turtles with segmented shells (proto-tortoises) among the

[20] See S.P. Noe, "Countermarked and Overstruck Greek Coins at the American Numismatic Society," *ANSMN* 6 (1954) 85–93, esp. 89–90. Other overstrikes: *IGCH* #1820, "Balkh" (ca. 390–80); H.A. Troxell and W.F. Spengler, "A Hoard of Early Greek Coins from Afghanistan," *ANSMN* 15 (1969) 1–19, esp. 6, 11–12; *CH* 2.28, "Larnaca, Cyprus" (425); also C.M. Kraay, "Notes on the Mint of Side in the Fifth Century B.C.," *NC*[7] 9 (1969) 15–20, esp. 20. For hoard evidence on Azbaal, see, for example, *IGCH* #1254, "Selimiye" (ca. 400); #1255, "Cilicia" (ca. 400); #1483, "Massyaf" (ca. 425–20); #1820, "Balkh" (ca. 390–80); #1830, "Cabul" (ca. 380). See also Robinson *NC* (1961) 111–12; L. Cancio, "Citium y las estáteras de Égina," *GacNum* 62 (1981) 8–10.

[21] Robinson *NC* (1961) 111; R. Rago, "Il cambio di tartaruga ad Egina," *RIN* 65 (1963) 7–15; L. Beer, *The Coinage of Aegina: A Chronological Reappraisal Based on Hoards and Technical Studies* (Diss., Oxford University 1980) 195–98; D. Gerin, A. Kyrou, and P. Requier, "Une trouvaille de quatre fractions d'argent à Porto Heli," *SM* 149 (1988) 4–8, esp. note 4, pp. 5–6. Rago also notes that fifth-century tortoises are more often countermarked, a phenomenon that I would explain by noting that the recirculation of these coins during 431–404 would have been interrupted by the demise of the Aiginetan state that had created a primary space for their use as legal tender. With an Athenian colony on Aigina, relatively more early tortoises stayed in circulation away, not only from the island, but from the Peloponnesos and its other states on the Aiginetic standard. They were subjected to countermarking to reconfirm their validity.

[22] The observation was first made in C.M. Kraay and V.M. Emeleus, *The Composition of Greek Silver Coins: Analysis by Neutron Activation* (Oxford 1962) 12–14; note also Robinson *NC* (1961) 111–12; Rago *RIN* (1963) 9. More recently, a single tortoise from the fifth-century "Wells" hoard (belonging to L. Beer-Tobey) was subjected to chemical analysis that supports the same conclusion. See L. Beer, N.H. Gale, W. Gentner, G.A. Wagner, and J. Price, "Archaic Greek Coinage: Silver," *Metallurgy in Numismatics* 1 (1980) 1–54, esp. 18–21.

[23] Cf. Rago *RIN* (1963) 14–15.

turtles with smooth carapaces to suggest the existence of a second mint or minting facility that produced coins intermittently and perhaps at a very low rate.[24] This hypothesis is in good accordance with the Aiginetan provenience of proto-tortoises (cf. *CH* 1.12),[25] and with the considerable range of time over which they were issued.[26] The coins offer stylistic evolution in the treatment of the carapace of the "tortoise" and in the sophistication of the style of the reverse in an evolution paralleling the conventional turtles. A die with a conspicuous flaw that allows its products to be traced through a number of hoards (* in note 26) is associated with various styles of reverses ("union-jack"; "mill sail," "grouped triangles," "proto-skew"?).[27] If H. Nicolet-Pierre is correct that this single obverse die for a proto-tortoise was also used with a reverse die of the "small skew" variety, that observation would even further cement our conclusion of a long duration and intermittent output.[28] A stock of obverse dies of various ages, of which even the eldest was not necessarily beyond its usefulness, was mixed and matched with reverses for small issues over time in an operation kept separate (in some fashion) from the emissions of the main series of turtles.

If the main mint was connected with the provision and upkeep of the Aiginetan fleet, just as the Athenian *naukrariai* and *naukraroi* had important financial functions along with their equipping and supervising the pre-Themistoclean navy at Athens,[29] one might imagine that the second

[24] See Figueira, *Aegina* 115–21; Figueira, *Excursions* 290–92, cf. 163–68.

[25] For the proto-tortoises, see Holloway *ANSMN* (1971) 11–12, 17–21, who argues persuasively against the relegation of all these coins to the pseudaeginetica. See also Beer, *Coinage* 95, 101–102.

[26] Note the proto-tortoises of *IGCH* #6, "Cyclades?" (ca. 500); #11, "Isthmia" (ca. 480); #62*, "Myron" (ca. 350); #1177*, "Asia Minor" (ca. 480); #1644*, "Asyut" (ca. 475); #1645, "Zagazig" (ca. 470); *CH* 2.24, "Eirini, Paros" (ca. 470); *CH* 3.10* = 8.60, "Megalopolis, 1936" (ca. 430); *CH* 3.12*, "Myrina, Karditsa" (440); *CH* 8.35, "Selinunte" (ca. 490), for which see Arnold-Biucchi et al., *ANSMN* (1988) 17, 21–22; and *CH* 8.37*, for which see S. Gjongecaj, "Un trésor de statères éginètes trouvé à Hollm (Sud-est de l'Albanie)," in T. Hackens and G. Moucharte (eds.), *Proceedings of the XI International Numismatic Congress* 1 (Louvain-la-Neuve 1993) 107–12. The spread in their discovery also implies some considerable period of emission, from the earliest days of the active mint in the last quarter of the sixth century down to the production of proto-tortoises with trefoil collars as late as 480 and the early 470s (such as those in the "Asyut" hoard: see Price and Waggoner 76).

[27] See Beer, *Coinage* 181–83.

[28] "Remarques sur le monnayage d'Égine au VIe et au Ve siècle d'après la trouvaille de Mégalopolis de 1936," in V. Kondic (ed.), *Frappe et Ateliers monétaires dans l'antiquité et Moyen Age* (Belgrade 1976) 5–12, esp. 12; cf. Beer, *Coinage* 182, who notes a possibly inconsistent progression in the deterioration of the obverse die.

[29] See Figueira, *Excursions* 163–67.

minting authority differentiated itself allusively by adopting a land turtle as its badge. With the surrender of the Aiginetan fleet in the terms of the peace with Athens (Thuc. 1.108.4), the officials of the primary mint lost their raison d'être and the secondary mint came into its own. Moreover, the Aiginetan government may have exploited the type change to enact a demonetization of the earlier turtles for the purpose of paying taxes (on Aigina alone of course, the only place where such a directive would have had force).[30] That measure might have produced some additional income through minting fees at a time in which the Aiginetan oligarchy may well have been embarrassed for resources because of the great cost of the struggle with the Athenians (accompanied by a costly defeat at sea and the two-year siege of the city).

The lower limit for the emission of fifth-century tortoises is more firmly established in the year 431 than a date for their inception, 431 being the date at which the Aiginetans were expelled from their island by the Athenians. There are, however, some uncertainties even here. A significant proportion of the exiles driven from Aigina in 431 kept their cohesion and were settled by the Spartans in the Thyreatis (along Spartan borders with Argive territory: Thuc. 2.27.1–2).[31] These Aiginetans considered themselves to constitute the Aiginetan *polis* so that it is not impossible that they took some mint personnel and equipment into exile with them and continued to issue tortoise coinage (although it could not have been at previous levels of activity).

Let us pause a moment to contextualize this hypothetical minting, which remains a bare possibility as no evidence exists for a positive or negative judgment. Such assertion of political continuity by the exiles would be in concord with the literary and epigraphical evidence on their revanchist attitudes and anti-Athenian policies. If the Aiginetans in exile issued tortoises, their purpose was to expend funds in support of the Peloponnesian war effort in as orderly and accountable a fashion as they could.[32] Their motivation would not have been commercial; identifiable

[30] Figueira, *Aegina* 117–19. See also O. Picard, "La tortue de terre sur les monnaies d'Égine," *BSFN* 33 (1978) 330–33; cf. Beer, *Coinage* 195–96. Such demonetization was not an unknown device, as demonstrated by two passages in the [Aris.] *Oeconomica* 1347a8–11 (Hippias), 1349b28–34 (Dionysios I), and another testimonium in Polyaenus, *Strat.* 6.9.1 (Leukon of Bosporos), regardless of judgments on the historicity of the episodes in question. For a historical example dating from the Hellenistic period, see *IC* 4.162.5–6.

[31] See Figueira, *Excursions* 293–310 for full references and discussion.

[32] For Aiginetan military activities during the Peloponnesian War, see Figueira, *Excursions* 301–16, where, however, the supposition of further minting is not raised. Note there the

Aiginetan diehards would have done business in the *arkhē* during the Peloponnesian War only at considerable risk.[33] In their new homes on Spartan territory, the Aiginetans of the Thyreatis were both beyond the political influence of the Athenian alliance and also removed from the economic influences operating in the *arkhē* in favor of monetary consolidation. This divergence from the earlier integration of Aigina in the Aegean economy would have conditioned any effort to continue coining.

After the Aiginetans were expelled from their home island and ceased vigorous coining, various attempts were made to supplement the Aiginetan coinage in circulation, much as we can subsequently discern later attempts (as the Peloponnesian War wore on) in Egypt and even later in the Near East to add to what must have seemed an insufficient number of Attic tetradrachms that were traveling south and east (see below, pp. 528–35). Some of these pseudaeginetica had a respectable pedigree, since they appear to represent the first emissions of the mint at Kydonia, an Aiginetan colony on Crete.[34] The issue is limited to triobols that bore a crescent symbol in the field of the obverse, and their known findspots are overwhelmingly Cretan. Some later examples bear a monogram that is analyzable as KΥ, one assumes for Kydonia. Although some Aiginetans may have fled toward Crete as early as the 450s, the bulk of these coins, unless an exception is made for the possible staters of Robinson's group A (doubtful in my view), date after 431. Kydonia was probably another place of refuge for the Aiginetans expelled by the Athenians in 431.[35]

The decline of the Aiginetan economy and the slackening of mint activity just before and at the beginning of the Peloponnesian War seems to have stimulated the Cretan cities to begin their minting—the earliest mints are Gortyn and Phaistos between 450 and 425—for Crete had been an area in which Aiginetan and Aiginetic-weight coins had been the standard monetary medium.[36] The relatively common usage of earlier Aiginetan and Aiginetic coins as flans for overstrikes of Cretan

---

discussion of the new fragment of *IG* V.1, listing contributions to the Spartan war effort, for which see A.P. Matthaiou and G.A. Pikoulas, «Ἔδον τοῖς Λακεδαιμονίοις ποττὸν πόλεμον», *Horos* 7 (1989) 77–124; W.T. Loomis, *The Spartan War Fund: IG V 1,1 and a New Fragment* (Stuttgart 1992) 41–43.

33 Cf. Figueira, *Excursions* 302–303, 348–49.

34 E.S.G. Robinson, "Pseudaeginetica," *NC*[5] 8 (1928) 172–98; cf. Robinson *NC* (1961) 112–13. See also J.M. Jones, "Further Notes on the Delian Inscriptions," *ANSMN* 19 (1974) 1; cf. Jones, "Some Numismatic Problems in the Delian Inscriptions," *ANSMN* 17 (1971) 127–36, esp. 127–28.

35 See Figueira, *Excursions* 310–16, 322–23.

36 See Figueira, *Aegina* 133–36; see also Le Rider, *Monnaies* 161–74.

mints shows the Cretans attempting to refresh their money supply in the most expeditious fashion at hand.[37] It is also likely that the many mints of the mainland that were issuing Aiginetic-weight coins intensified their own coining activities after the termination of minting on Aigina.

Concerning the upper limit for the inception of the minting of tortoises, we are obviously dealing with a much more controversial matter. It is becoming increasingly clear that the fifth-century tortoises were issued in considerable numbers.[38] Even if the Aiginetan mint did not exceed its output during the 490s and 480s, it is still likely that the mint was the most active within the *arkhē* even after the subjection of Aigina to tributary status. Thus, a date before the Thirty Years Peace is probably necessary to accommodate the emission of the tortoises and one should prefer the hypothesis of a short hiatus between turtles and tortoises (a view consonant with the stylistic links between the two emissions).[39] An inception date of 457–56 appears the best alternative. In any event, there is no reason to introduce the supposed guarantee of Aiginetan autonomy that is mentioned by the Spartans on the eve of the Peloponnesian War. Any guarantee long preceded the period when the tortoises might have originated.[40] Hence the suggestion of Robinson, followed by Meiggs and Kraay, that Aigina was allowed to resume coining as a demonstration of an autonomy granted by the Thirty Years Peace is an unnecessary hypothesis, even if one were prepared to reject the paradigms for both political symbolism concerning autonomy and the end-purposes of Attic monetary legislation that will be proposed below.[41]

There is also evidence beyond the sheer size of the tortoise issues that indicates that an interval in coining of more than a short period is not likely, since the hypothesis of a longer interval during the 450s or, specifically, an interval of any duration around 450 fails to explain what we now have good justification for concluding from the numismatic data. There is reason to suppose that some tortoises in several hoards were accummulated prior to 450, such as *IGCH* #21, "Koumares" or "Koumades" (ca. 450), with its two T-back turtles with large skew

[37] Le Rider, *Monnaies* 54–55, 126–27, 140.

[38] Beer, *Coinage* 103–104, 112–13, noting particularly *CH* 3.10, "Megalopolis, 1936" and *CH* 3.12, "Myrina, Karditsa."

[39] See Rago *RIN* (1963) 13–14; Erxleben *AJP* (1970) esp. 68; Beer, *Coinage* 79–83, 112–13, 192–95; Gerin et al., *SM* (1988) 4–8.

[40] Thuc. 1.67.2; cf. DS 12.44.2; Plut. *Per.* 29.5. See Figueira, *Excursions* 255–92, where the preference is for a guarantee accorded at the entry of Athens and Aigina into the Hellenic League.

[41] Cf. Robinson *NC* (1961) 111–12; Holloway *ANSMN* (1971) 20–2; Meiggs, 183–84; Kraay, *Coins* 47.

reverses and one tortoise,[42] and *IGCH* #1647, "Naukratis" (450–25), with tortoises carrying a large skew reverse comparable to that of the last turtles (cf. *IGCH* #1483, "Massyaf" [ca. 425–400]).[43]

We may contrast these mixed turtle/tortoise hoards with their immediate predecessors, which illustrate the circulation of the turtle staters before the infiltration of tortoises into Peloponnesian and Cycladic hoards. Two such hoards are *IGCH* #15, "Olympia, 1958–60" (ca. 470) and *CH* 2.24, "Eirini, Paros."[44] *CH* 2.24, "Eirini, Paros" contains one proto-tortoise, and has received dates of ca. 470 and 460–50 (the latter according Grunauer-von Hoerschelmann). Another similar hoard is *IGCH* #28 "Charvari" (ca. 450–400), where there are no tortoises (but two early "T-back" turtles). *IGCH* #28, "Charvari" should be placed at the very upper end of the range of its dates, or very likely above that.[45] A final hoard in this group is *IGCH* #35, "Lappa," where a large Aiginetan component (40 st., 2 dr.), is deposited with 32 st., 17 dr., and 9 triob. (all Elean) with 1 Phocian triob.[46] The hoard contains turtles, some early (even sixth-century: #1–6) and some T-back with small skew reverses. The Elean coins are dated 475–52, and they appear fresher. The early tortoises had not yet reached this hoarder at the moment of the last opening of this hoard (ca. 455–50), unless the single tortoise drachm was his inclusion.

Important further evidence is provided by a series of hoards described more recently. Most significant in this regard is *CH* 3.12, "Myrina, Karditsa," in which the last classes of Aiginetan coins represented (out of 149) are "T-back" turtles with trefoil collars and tortoises, both with comparable large skew reverses.[47] The tortoises are die-linked, suggesting to Caramessini-Oeconomides a date near the beginning of the series, or ca. 440. Yet there is no particular reason to opt for a date that late, because there are also many turtles with thin collars and "union-jack"

[42] Cf. M. Caramessini-Oeconomides, "Deux trésors de statères éginètes du Cabinet des médailles d'Athènes," *SM* 30 (1980) 81–90, esp. 88–90.

[43] See Mattingly *JHS* (1981) 83, who, however, dates the hoard to the 430s.

[44] See S. Grunaeuer-von Hoerschelmann, "Zwei Schatzfunde archaischer Statere von Aigina," *Chiron* 5 (1975) 13–20, esp. 13–16, 16–20.

[45] M. Caramessini-Oeconomides, "The 1970 Myrina Hoard of Aeginetan Staters," *Greek Numismatics and Archaeology: Essays in Honor of Margaret Thompson* (Wetteren 1979) 231–39, esp. 232, 237; Caramessini-Oeconomides *SM* (1980) 82–88.

[46] See M. Oeconomides-Caramessini, "À propos du trésor de Lappa *IGCH* 35," *Kraay-Mørkholm Essays* 217–23, where 1 tortoise dr. is suggested as an intrusion. The refreshing of an earlier reserve would not, however, be impossible.

[47] See Caramessini-Oeconomides, *Thompson Festschrift* 231–39; Caramessini-Oeconomides, «ΕΙΔΗΣΕΙΣ ΕΚ ΤΗΣ ΝΟΜΙΣΜΑΤΙΚΗΣ ΣΥΛΛΟΓΗΣ ΑΘΗΝΩΝ», *AAA* 5 (1972) 176–82, esp. 180–82; Beer, *Coinage* 176–83, 184–86, 189, 198–200. Compare also *CH* 8.37, as described in Gjongecaj, *ICN* 11.

and "mill sail" incuse reverses, which ought to have preceded ca. 485 at the latest. Also deserving note is another hoard, *CH* 3.10, "Megalopolis, 1936," containing early tortoises and many developed T-back turtles with large skew reverses. There the earliest coins are late sixth-century turtles, so that our inclination toward seeing the received date of ca. 430 as too late should be encouraged.[48] We may compare the coins of these hoards with *IGCH* #62, "Myron." The greater variety (and possibly the fewer die links) of *IGCH* #62 probably indicate that further fifth-century mint activity followed the closure of *CH* 3.10 and 3.12.[49] Leslie Beer-Tobey would take the record of all these hoards as evidence for a short hiatus in minting activity on Aigina and add to the group the so-called "Wells Hoard" (*CH* 1.12).[50] The majority of its thirty-six coins are to be dated before 490. Yet there are two turtles with small skew reverses probably from the 480s, two "T-back" turtles with large skew reverses dating from the 470s, and a single early tortoise. We may have here an archaic hoard that was perhaps periodically refreshed or supplemented.

Countermarking is the affixing of a design by a punch on a coin in circulation and is commonly found on Aiginetan coins where it is indicative of their wide circulation.[51] Countermarks were used by money changers, by treasury officials, and by supervisors of the marketplace to validate coins about which there were doubts that might involve their quality, authenticity, or propriety in a particular interchange. Countermarks were individual to the countermarker, and thus identifiable. The scope of the validation that they implied was a function of the political authority and economic power of the countermarker. The permanence of countermarks extended the influence of their validation over distance and time; it allowed a retrospective appreciation or evaluation of the action of the countermarker, that was especially important in state scrutiny of coins.

Countermarking is a salient feature of *IGCH* #35, *CH* 3.10, *CH* 3.12, and *CH* 8.37 (and note also *CH* 2.24) and may indicate the turmoil in Aiginetan monetary affairs after the Athenian conquest.[52] Further

[48] Nicolet-Pierre, *Frappe et Ateliers* 5–12; Beer, *Coinage* 176–89, 200–202.

[49] Note Beer, *Coinage* 201–202.

[50] See Beer, *Coinage* 146–50. See also Mattingly *JHS* (1981) 83.

[51] G. Le Rider, "Contremarques et surfrappes dans l'antiquité grecque," in J.-M. Dentzer, P. Gauthier, and T. Hackens (eds.), *Numismatique antique: problèmes et méthodes, Annales de l'Est* 44 (Nancy-Louvain 1975) 27–56. Kraay, *ACGC* 15–16. See also Figueira, *Aegina* 136–39.

[52] See the illustrations in *SNG: France, Bibliothèque nationale: Cabinet des Médailles: Collection Jean et Marie Delepierre* (Paris 1983) #1550–1847, which collection houses the majority of *CH* 3.10. In *CH* 8.37, the later turtles are proportionately more often countermarked than the fifth-century tortoises.

support could be found in this phenomenon for the hypothesis that the turtle stater was demonetized for a time on Aigina itself. Not only did this development encourage the countermarking of earlier Aiginetan issues, but it also motivated some countermarking of more recent series like the tortoises. Such countermarking was a hedge against uncertainty over the future validity of Aiginetan coinage.[53] That anxiety could hardly be considered irrational in the light of one demonetization (if it truly occurred). The countermarkers sought to validate Aiginetan coins for special contexts when faced with some doubts over their general acceptability, a new experience in light of their former circulation and acceptance. A similar reception was accorded both turtles and tortoises after the Athenian occupation of Aigina. There was no longer a home market in which the coins stood as legal tender and to which they could be recirculated. That added another element of uncertainty to their evaluation for which countermarking attempted to compensate.

Aigina continued to mint coins during the Pentekontaeteia, striking turtles (mainly) during the period of its independence from Attic hegemony. The output of these coins was very substantial.[54] When the city was forced by Athens to enter its alliance as a tributary in the early 450s, there was a short interruption. Then the Aiginetans embarked on another sizable coinage, the fifth-century tortoises, which extended down to the date of 431, the expulsion of the Aiginetans from their island by the Athenians who founded their own colony in place of the previous polity.

The wide currency of Aiginetan and Aiginetic coinage gives a special character to hoards of the Pentenkontaeteia that contain these coins. There was nothing in principle to deny acceptance (let alone to invalidate) of archaic Aiginetan coins, if their weight had not fallen too greatly. Hence fifth-century hoards often comprise coins that were minted over a considerable period including staters with "union-jack" reverses that were struck in the last quarter of the sixth century. This phenomenon is well illustrated by *CH* 3.12, "Myrina, Karditsa," and *CH* 3.10, "Megalopolis, 1936." As noted, the practice of countermarking sustained the currency of such earlier issues. Accordingly, we not only lack any hiatus in the history of the Aiginetan mint that would support any date currently advanced for the Coinage Decree or for a prohibition of allied minting, but there is also no evidence to suggest that the circulation of Aiginetan money per se was a target for legislation by the Athenians beyond their

[53] Wear alone cannot be the primary rationale for countermarking of Aiginetan coins, as is shown by its limited showing among the worn coins of *CH* 1.8, "Greece, 1944" (ca. 480) or the "Ritter Hoard" as it is sometimes called. See Beer, *Coinage* 134–35.

[54] Cf. Figueira, *Aegina* 98–107.

taking initiatives toward monetary consolidation in their alliance. It has sometimes been imagined that Attic imperial legislation demonetized allied money or endeavored to exchange it en masse and that this action had some special relevance to Aiginetan coinage (see p. 254). Nothing in the hoard evidence or in the evidence of the coins themselves supports such a conclusion.

NORTHERN AEGEAN MINTS

We turn next to a separate classification of the mints that seem to continue to produce coins during the hegemony of the Athenians, namely, the Greek *poleis* of the Thracian littoral and the Chalcidice. It has already been demonstrated that this region was hardly immune to the influences motivating monetary consolidation. Some Attic allies in the northern Aegean ceased their minting and others reduced their coining to fractions. In the case of the Thasian mint, an allied city with a relatively large economy revived its minting in a manner showing an integration with Athenian money, after an interval that is agreed to have had a political causation. To the varied picture of the monetary situation of the region during the Penetekontaeteia, the early defection of allied states—with the revolt of the Chalcidians and Bottiaians indeed preceding the outbreak of general hostilities in the Peloponnesian War—and the welcome given to the Spartan expeditionary force under Brasidas from 424 add further political complications that warn against any facile assumption that minting patterns here need to have been driven predominantly by Attic legislation.

Mende

The city of Mende, lying on the Pallene peninsula of the Chalcidice, is perhaps the most marginal of the northern *poleis* that have been agreed to mint straight through the period of the Attic hegemony. The work of Noe on Mendean coinage still provides the basis for academic discussion. As we have seen elsewhere, the first topic for consideration is the possibility that minting activity was interrupted.

The addition of a new iconographical feature offers the obvious option for the break in emissions. It has been argued that an interruption took place between Noe's group I (Noe coins #1–19) and his group II, where a reclining figure of Dionysos is added to the back of the ithyphallic ass that is a permanent feature of fifth-century Mendean coinage. Yet the use of a Dionysiac coin from group II as a flan for a Geloan overstrike has been interpreted to point toward a pre-450 hiatus in minting.[55]

[55] G.K. Jenkins, *The Coinage of Gela* (Berlin 1970) 65–66.

Without questioning, for the moment, the accuracy of that chronology, it is worth stating that this dating would undercut any argument for a mid-century Coinage Decree on the basis of the mint at Mende. It does, however, leave open the possibility that Mende properly belongs in the category of interrupted mints that was discussed above (in either category IVB or category V). Moreover, my remarks on Ainos immediately below may help to sharpen our definition of the problem of the rhythm of production and its political ramifications among these "continuous" mints. Cessation and resumption of minting appears a complex phenomenon and there are no prima facie considerations that necessarily prompt the hypothesis of a special valence for stops and starts legislated by the Athenians. It is most difficult to hypothesize, let alone conclude, at which point a break in minting can be considered a termination, that is, a suspension of activity without the expectation of a resumption rather than a mere situational or vicissitudinous interruption.

Nonetheless, it is far from clear that the Geloan coin that used the Mendean coin as its flan really belongs before mid-century. Mattingly compares the overstrike with the Geloan coins found in *IGCH* #2082, "Villabate," which Jenkins dated to 450–45.[56] The overstrikes of Athenian coins in that hoard, however, probably demand that it be placed after the foundation of Thourioi by the Athenians and thus in the late 440s. Accordingly, Kraay has the Geloan overstrike dated to 440–35.[57] The reverse of the Mendean coin used as a flan at Gela had an incuse square that is surrounded by an ethnic, which is characteristic of the group II coins. The coin could happily be brought toward mid-century on the basis of the redatings of other northern mints that employ this feature of organization (Akanthos, Abdera, and Maroneia). That the incuse square on the reverse of these coins had already acquired an internal design in the form of a vine (from Noe #20), a feature that seems to have been inaugurated after mid-century elsewhere, underscores the later dating for the Geloan overstrike.[58]

Mattingly would break the series after Noe coin #66 (or #68), where there is an interruption of die linking (but not the only such), citing what he supposes were troubles in Thrace in 440–35. A mere break in die linkages, however, once the continuity of style in die cutting is

[56] Mattingly *Klio* (1977) 95–97; cf. Mattingly *Historia* (1961) note 164, pp. 186–87.

[57] Kraay, *Coins and History* 34–40 (with discussion of lower dates for Syracusan emissions); Kraay, "Fifth-Century Overstrikes at Rhegium and Messana," *La circolazione della moneta ateniese in Sicilia e in Magna Grecia, AIIN* Suppl. 12–14 (1969) 141–50, esp. 146–47.

[58] See M.J. Price, "The Coinages of the Northern Aegean," in Carradice, *Coinage and Administration* 43–47, esp. 46.

granted (as it must), cannot bear so heavy an interpretative burden. An intermittent mint with periodic gaps of a few years would satisfy the phenomena equally well. Mattingly would also see a resumption going down to a Coinage Decree in 425/4. Yet that is certainly too fine a distinction in chronology to be argued on the basis of current knowledge.

Moreover, as has been observed previously, our evidence is insufficiently detailed to allow us to distinguish intermittent mints from those with annual, continuous strikings. Thus, a leisurely rhythm of coining might actually be the historical reality at Mende, which would qualify this mint for classification as being in permanent operation. Mende was a mint that from the beginning of its coining used the Euboeic/Attic standard; thus it would have been exempt from any exchange problems with Athenian coinage and the interaction of the local economy with the regions of the *arkhē* employing the Euboeic/Attic standard would have been monetarily facilitated. It is probable that monetary concerns did not dominate decisions whether or not to mint at Mende, where Attic coins probably already circulated with acceptance.

The hoard evidence also suggests that coining in the late fifth century was confined to tetrobols (note Noe Pl. X, a–e), in which case Mende can also be imagined to follow the common pattern where a limitation to fractional coining took place during the history of the *arkhē*. Its neighbor, Poteidaia, was coining fractions when Athenian capture caused the termination of its minting. Aineia and Dikaia, lying to the northeast, were also minting fractions in the last stages of their coining activity.

This transition to fractional minting in the form of tetrobols was dated by Noe to the recapture of Mende by the Athenians in 423, when he thought production of tetradrachms ended (Thuc. 4.130.2–7).[59] Our decision on that question is linked to determining whether a shift in standard can have occurred during the Peloponnesian War (even as early as 423, as earlier scholarship maintained) or must be put after the war. As a rule, we ought to be skeptical about attributing numismatic changes to political events unless the changes call attention to their political context, and this chronology is faute de mieux. Therefore, the reduction to fractional minting could have antedated Athenian military operations at Mende. We could then envisage a hiatus before the inception of new

[59] Mattingly's suggestion (*Klio* [1977] 98–99) that a small issue of tetradrachms (see Noe Pl. X, D), dated by Noe dated to ca. 390, is in fact the revolt coinage of the city—so minting continued down to the revolt—depends heavily on his view of the stylistic affinities of these coins; few others would concede that there is much of a historical allusion to the rebellion in the conical "peltast's" helmet used as a symbol. Noe believed the coin to be of the Attic standard! Cf. S.P. Noe, *The Mende (Kaliandra) Hoard*, *NNM* 27 (New York 1926) 58–60.

issues with a changed standard. One may note here a tetradrachm with a profile head of Dionysos (Noe Pl. X, E) and a similar tetrobol (Pl. X, F) that Noe thought was struck on the Aiginetic standard. This shift would parallel other similiar adjustments in the northern Aegean mints toward the end of the century.

With the previous disclaimers kept in mind, it is still tempting to class Mende with the continuously active mints of the Thracian littoral.[60] In this case, however, it may be that the consolidation of standards and coinages that was so potent an influence on the monetary affairs of the alliance merely took a little longer to have its impact. It is probable that it is the adjustment to fractional coining, even if it had in part a political causation, to which our interest ought to be directed. There is no reason to believe that the Athenians legislated that change.[61]

Ainos

The history of the mint at Ainos also presents some problems of interpretation. The coins of Ainos have the obverse type of a head of Hermes and the reverse type of a goat, for the most part. The magisterial treatment is that of J.M.F. May, *Ainos: Its History and Coinage: 474–341 B.C.* (Oxford 1950). He correctly points out that there appears to be a discontinuity based on stylistic considerations that seems to separate the tetradrachms of his groups XV and XVI (with coins bearing the inscription of Antiadas), placed at the end of period I (with the diobols of group XVII), from the succeeding groups of period II, the latter best typified in their tetradrachm issues by groups XXVIII and following. For May, the upper boundary of this period of interruption is determined by nothing other than reference to the Coinage Decree. Coining was resumed in 435/4 by virtue of what amounts to special dispensation. Minting then continued for the remainder of the century.

Unfortunately, his determination of periodization as a whole is pervaded by dubious arguments that, for example, relate the ebb and flow of the striking of tetradrachms to the prosperity of the Ainian economy, or, in another instance, attribute low rates of mint output to economic recession. With equal logic one could argue the opposite: that scant resources had to be saved for minting tetradrachms to pay major expenditures such as military costs, so that tetradrachm issues mean impoverishment; or that military exigencies and ensuing economic difficulties demanded heavier minting.

[60] Price, *Coinage and Administration* 46.

[61] Cf. Mattingly *EMC* (1988) 328.

The rationale for the date of 435/4 for resumption of coining is that a reduction of assessment (if that indeed is what this is) to 4T (from 10T), first apparent (nota bene) in 436/5 (*IG* I³ 276.VI.28), and the absence of Ainos from later tribute lists signals a period when the city was garrisoned against the Odrysians. The subsequent issues of fractional coinage were to pay for the garrison. This explanation is completely ad hoc in nature. It is uncertain that Ainos did not pay tribute in some of these years; 431 and 429 being the only likely years of absence. Ainos seems to have been assessed in 425/4 (*IG* I³ 71.III.159). Any garrison under Attic military control would doubtless be paid in Athenian money, for which an official account would need to be kept. There is no reason to think that such troops would be paid in fractional coinage, inasmuch as it is unlikely that accounts would be settled on a daily basis (or even on a weekly basis).[62] In fact tetradrachms, the very coins that are not much struck in this period, would be the most likely medium for making such payments in local coin. It is equally disconcerting to observe that the same evidence that May adduces from the tribute lists have led others to a varied range of results about the status of Ainos.[63] Consequently, such arguments could only be probative if we were working from a strong probability, even a near certainty, of the validity of the traditional interpretation of the Coinage Decree, with its prohibition on allied minting and mid-century date. We should never work backward from chronologies for mints based on conjectural political history through numismatic extrapolations to further speculation about the history of Attic monetary legislation. The relations with the Odrysians were a feature of the political life of Ainos in this period, but the lack of evidence makes it presumptuous to guess at any reflection of these relations in the coinage.

At Ainos, the usually present symbols such as a vine, crescent, and club could mark mint runs or might be badges adopted by a sequence of officials at the local mint. Although May has these groups extending over two- or three-year spans in his periods I and II,[64] it is really more likely that any officials who supervised minting had an annual term, and that mint runs were themselves organized by years (even if the symbols were

[62] Note reviews of E.J.P. Raven in *NC*⁶ 10 (1950) 153–55; J. Babelon in *RN*⁵ 12 (1950) 224–25. See also the review of W. Schwabacher in *Gnomon* 23 (1951) 193–200, esp. 196–97.

[63] E. Meyer, *Geschichte des Altertums*⁵ (Stuttgart 1954) 4.1.720–23; *HCT* 1.276–78; Meiggs 249, 529. See most recently M. Tačeva, "Die Münzprägung von Abdera and Ainos im Verhältnis zum thrakischen Hinterlands," in T. Hackens and G. Moucharte (eds.), *Proceedings of the XI International Numismatic Congress* 1 (Louvain-la-Neuve 1993) 146–50.

[64] Cf. P. Naster in *RBN* 96 (1950) 231–33; Raven *NC* (1950) 154; G.K. Jenkins in *JHS* 72 (1952) 158.

not administrative badges). Extant examples probably do not comprise a complete series—there being seventeen groups in period I. Possibly, a few of the issues of the smallest magnitude were marked by symbols, examples of which have not survived. There will never be enough symbols, however, to cover the years annually between 474/3 and 449/8. Those limits are in any case entirely arbitrary; accordingly, twenty or so groups might actually have covered as many as forty-five to fifty years. The approximate parity of obverse and reverse dies could be taken to suggest that a generous allowance was made at the beginning of each coining run, when both sets of dies were probably prepared. Thus, usage of the more easily worn reverse dies was seldom pressed to the point of their discarding and a substitution with reserve or replacement punches. This scenario for Ainian mint operation suggests, at the least, that coining did not occur in every year.

The transition to period II is naturally problematical. Virtually all the issues at the beginning of period II are made up exclusively of diobols (groups XVIII–XX, XXII–XXIII, XXV–XXVII). Such a shift to fractional coinage is a common adaptation to the economic and fiscal conditions that prevailed during the *arkhē*, and there are quite a number of parallel cases, even in the Thraceward district of the alliance. These diobols do undeniably show stylistic similarities with the classes of tetradrachms that start with group XXVIII, though their much smaller scale of representation should be taken into account in esthetic judgments. Some tetradrachms, however, are associated with groups XXI (double-axe symbol)[65] and group XXIV (sapling) by their symbolism; each is represented by a single die pair.

An elaborate hypothesis is based by May on the "double-axe" symbol, arguing that it is an allusion to Odrysian hegemony, but that surely exceeds the limits of speculation.[66] Dissociating the tetradrachms from the diobols in the same series (and in group XXIV??) is tempting, and could have far-reaching results for the chronological ordering of the material. The tetradrachm obverses of groups XXI and XXIV have the unique characteristic of a head of Hermes facing left, and their reverses

65 See the comment in the review of Jenkins in *JHS* (1952) 158.

66 Tačeva, *ICN* 11, 149–50, cites the Thracian imitation of the tetradrachm with the "double-axe" on the reverse. This copying, however, does not establish any particularly Thracian resonance for the symbol, even if we admit that Thracian authorities are the likely emitters of these barbarous copies. Coins with other symbols (tetradrachms and tetrobols) are also imitated. Moreover, it is striking that the "double-axe" tetradrachm (group XXI) is by far the earliest coin imitated. Perhaps this is an indication that it should be lowered in date. Compare May, *Ainos* 279–80.

are less like the later tetradrachms. They may possess affinities with the tetradrachms of May's period I. Therefore, there is little reason to see a fourteen-year gap between their issue and the tetradrachms of period I.[67] So the two small tetradrachm issues could have been mixed in, after the mint went directly over to a concentration on diobols. Another hypothesis would make groups XXI and XXIV represent the last series of tetradrachms, which were followed by the groups limited to diobols.

An examination of a redating of class III of Abderite coinage appears below, but it is important to emphasize that any movement of that classification closer to mid-century has a ripple effect on Ainian coins. An Ainian coin from period I, group III (#9b), dated by May to 471/0–469/8, is overstruck on a period III, group XLII, Abderite tetradrachm.[68] That Abderite coin seems to follow the latest Abderite coins in the "Decadrachm Hoard" (*CH* 8.48: ca. 465–60). Hence, May's chronology for Ainian coinage is clearly too early by at least ten to fifteen years. That conclusion may well also entail the removal of any hiatus in Ainian mint activity. The aforementioned stylistic considerations encourage the same conclusion.[69] A suggestive result of downward adjustments of the chronology of Ainian minting is that the anomalous issue of Antiadas that introduces an incuse square on the reverse, with a design of a goat within the square, surrounded by an inscription is moved after 450 (see group XVI).

Therefore, Ainos may well provide a counterindication against the traditional dating of a ban against minting silver coins that was seen to have occurred around mid-century.[70] The categories established by the minting symbols seem to argue for a mint in continuous, but intermittent, production after the foundation of the Delian League for at least a generation or so (as earlier scholars such as von Fritze believed). In some years, the mint produced no output at all, while coins bearing a distinctive badge, sometimes in a range of denominations, were struck in others. Groups XVII to XXXVI of period II would then space out from the end of the 440s. At a moment, which was probably after mid-century, the Ainians followed the common practice of restricting their

[67] H. von Fritze, "Die autonomen Münzen von Ainos: Eine chronologische Studie," *Nomisma* 4 (1909) 16–32, esp. 21–22; von Fritze, "Die Chronologie der autonomen Münzen von Ainos," in M.L. Strack, *Die Antiken Münzen von Thrakien* 1.1 (Berlin 1912) 143–72, esp. 144–45. See also Mattingly, *Klio* (1977) 99–100, who would break after 425. Cf. Schwabacher *Gnomon* (1951) 195–96.

[68] Price, *Coinage and Administration* 46; Kagan, *Coinage and Administration* 25.

[69] Mattingly *EMC* (1988) 325–26.

[70] Price, *Coinage and Administration* 46, brings the coinage of Ainos well into the third quarter of the fifth century.

normal output to fractions. In their case, however, the characteristic symbols may allow us to place two small classes of tetradrachms in the midst of or at the head of the diobols, a classification that might well have been missed but for these symbols. These small issues of heavier coins (from the war years?) might have served some special practical or symbolic purpose, now irrecoverable by us. The next series, with the obverse type of a full-face Hermes, involved a standard change to Chian and appeared in the 400s or even after the war.

One or more interruptions may have broken into the continuity, but need not have been anything more than unusually long gaps in a traditionally intermittent production of coins. As such, they would not be of political significance unless minting ended with the intention, unlike in the past, that it would *not* be resumed. Insufficient information exists for any conclusion along those lines.[71] As we have seen elsewhere, an interruption of this nature is not without its parallels. Nonetheless, the resumption of coining of tetradrachms and not just fractions and the possibility of more than one interval may give Ainos a uniquely punctuated pattern of minting activity.

Abdera

Abdera offers a numismatic history with some striking similarities with Ainos and several salient differences. Abderite coins can be classified according to series that can be attributed to individual mint officials. Here, notably, there are not only symbols but letters of the names of mint authorities following EPI; subsequently, the presence of complete names clinches the interpretation (after a transitional period mixing entire and abbreviated names). Once again it is J.M.F. May's treatment of the mint that establishes a basis for discussion: *The Coinage of Abdera (540–345 B.C.)*, C.M. Kraay and G.K. Jenkins (eds.) (London 1966). Abderite coins bear a left-facing griffin on the obverse and an incuse square on the reverse. In May's periodization, there are too few minters to assign one to each year. Thus, an intermittent but regular cycle of minting might be suspected. Moreover, May ends his period IV (beginning about 473–70) at the supposed passage of the Coinage Decree in 449/8. The coinages of Ainos and Abdera are comparable in the number of surviving specimens, of die links, and of reverse dies, but differ in Abdera's use of noticeably more obverse dies (Ainos, 27 [with correction by Raven]; Abdera, 45, according to May). That probably adds up to significantly larger original runs of production. The issues of Abdera emphasized the

[71] Cf. Mattingly *Klio* (1970) 99–100.

production of tetradrachms, even after mid-century. That concentration meant that much more silver in weight was struck by Abdera than by Ainos for the same number of dies.

Here again, the arguments for an interval in coining and the extent of the hiatus must dominate our investigation of the Abderite mint. In a manner that was parallel to his interpretation of the minting of Ainos, May argued for a gap in minting between 448 and 439. Nevertheless, an observation of Jenkins placed a significant obstacle in the way of seeing such an interval, as he had drawn attention as early as 1955 to the fact that a coin of the magistrate Blousys is stylistically transitional between Strack's periods III and IV, spanning mid-century.[72] Further objections to May's chronology derive from more recent hoard evidence. These data, however, must be used conservatively, inasmuch as there is no assurance that the latest Abderite issues contained in distant hoards were the latest minted.

The Asyut hoard of ca. 475 contains coins from May's period II, which was probably still in progress when the hoard was deposited (*IGCH* #1644).[73] The "Decadrachm Hoard" (*CH* 8.48) of ca. 460—Kagan dates the latest non-Lycian elements to 465–62—shows the Abderites in the midst of May's period III (where only four magistratal names are mentioned), with the latest coins those of group XLI.[74] S. Fried links the two hoards by noting that the latest coin from Asyut (#143) shows an obverse die link with a coin from *CH* 8.48.[75] These indications clash with May's termination dates of 492 for period II and 473–70 for period III. Even with leeway given for an absence of the latest issues, our newer hoards (*IGCH* #1644 and *CH* 8.48) suggest ca. 475–70 for the end of period II and 455–50 for the end of period III, particularly since May felt that the so-called "B-type griffins" had to follow coins like those in *CH* 8.48, "Decadrachm Hoard" (groups XLIII–L).[76] The coin from group LII with the overstrike on the Ainian group III tetradrachm fits into such a revised chronology. The appearance of the name of the magistrate

[72] G.K. Jenkins, "Greek Coins Recently Acquired by the British Museum," *NC*[6] 15 (1955) 131–56, esp. 136–37.

[73] See Price and Waggoner 36–37. Mattingly *Klio* (1977) 92 also points to the fresh period II octadrachm (dated by May to 500) in *IGCH* #1177, "Asia Minor" (ca. 480); it is die-linked to the earliest octadrachm in the "Decadrachm Hoard" (*CH* 8.48: Fried, *Coinage and Administration* 3). Cf. Mattingly *EMC* (1988) 325. Schoenhammer 147–48 notes that *CH* 8.4 (ca. 475) contains a coin of period II, group VI.

[74] Fried, *Coinage and Administration* 3; Price, *Coinage and Administration* 45; Kagan, *Coinage and Administration* 25; Mattingly *EMC* (1988) 325.

[75] Fried, *Coinage and Administration* 3.

[76] See also the review of J.F. Healy in *Gnomon* 43 (1971) 100–101.

bordering an incuse square is inaugurated with the first coins of period IV; that feature might belong to mid-century or even somewhat later.

Group LV of period IV contains a series of coins under the magistracy of Nymphodoros, whom May would date implicitly to ca. 465. As Mattingly observes, this may well be the same man as the Abderite statesman who is known to us from the late 430s (Hdt. 7.137.3; Thuc. 2.29.1 4–7; cf. 2.67.1–3). It would be difficult putting Nymphodoros' magistracy (even if held early in his career) much before 450. Kleiner added art historical arguments to this historical conjunction and dated the coins of Nymphodoros to ca. 430.[77] The coins of Nymphodoros appear among the period IV coins that are included in *IGCH* #698, "Abdera" (ca. 460–50), along with coins as late as group LVI according to May and group LVIII according to Raven. The date of *IGCH* #698 should be revised downward. All these observations urge that the latter half of period IV (groups LIX–LXIX) begin in the 440s at the earliest.[78] Period IV should then start around mid-century (the moment of the supposed promulgation of a prohibition against minting silver?) and may even reach into the Archidamian War.

Without adducing the Coinage Decree, one will not find strong evidence in favor of creating an interval between May's periods IV and V. There is a reduction in the weight of the tetradrachm, but such a change does not necessarily warrant the hypothesis of a stoppage of minting activity, especially when Abderite minting was aligned with the standard of neighboring Maroneia. There are no strong stylistic clues pointing to a substantial hiatus lying between the two periods.[79] The innovation of a reverse with a square surrounded by the name of the relevant magistrate, in which a type has now replaced a simple incuse square, has its forerunner in group LXIX. Even May admitted significant continuity both with the cutters of late period III and early period IV dies and with the repetition of magistrates. Period V included nineteen known magistrates, and probably occupied the largest part of the war years.

It is also likely that the period VI coins follow on their predecessors fairly quickly.[80] Their novelty is a shift to what is usually considered

[77] G. Kleiner, "Zur Chronologie der Münzen von Abdera," *JNG* 2 (1950/51) 14–20.

[78] See Mattingly *Klio* (1977) 94–95 with the review of May by E.J.P. Raven in NC^7 7 (1967) 289–97, esp. 291–92.

[79] As J.P. Barron observed in his review in *CR* 18 (1968) 99–101, the stylistic grounds for a gap are not probative. Mattingly, *Klio* (1977) 94–95, has a good discussion of the transitional character of the issue of Deonysas (group LXVIII), bridging over to the style of period V.

[80] Characteristically, Mattingly, *Klio* (1977) 98, opts for a break that starts from the late 420s between period V and period VI. Yet the naked "peltast" on the reverse of a tetradrachm

an issue on the Aiginetic standard, and that modification is certainly reflective (but at what remove?) of the turmoil of the Ionian War. There is no particular need to place it as early as the revolt of Thasos in 411.[81] The rationale for the change in standard might have been the practical interoperability of Abderite officials and military forces with the Peloponnesians (after a hypothetical defection). Alternatively, period VI could even have occurred after the end of the Peloponnesian War, when an oligarchy might have taken power.

This change in standard could not have been of any appreciable symbolic significance because the Abderites had not indeed used and then abandoned the Attic monetary standard. Concomitantly, they did not relinquish the Aiginetic standard, once it was in place, although the Abderites veered back toward the Athenian camp at least once during the Ionian War (DS 13.72.2). That the alterations in standard Abdera undertook in this period were driven by fiscal and economic forces and not by political symbolism is indicated by the appearance of bronze coinage at Abdera at the end of the fifth century. That innovation should be understood as an effort to supplement an inadequate amount of fractional coinage in circulation.

Abdera appears to be a mint that sustained a considerable rate of production across a range of denominations for the whole period of its alliance with the Athenians.[82] There is no strong evidence for any interruptions. The simplest conclusion about the magistratal names is that they were officials holding office for a single year (as Kraay notes). That conclusion is particularly important toward the end of this chronology, for the nineteen names of period V give at least nineteen years for this series. Until we have firm proof showing that the number of names exceeds the number of years available for them in the fifth century, it is wisest to cleave to this easiest of explanations. Accordingly, there may have been rare short interruptions (a year or two) for special reasons, but

---

of the magistrate Nikostratos (group LXXIX) is hardly a sure allusion to Sitalkes' invading army of 431. The argument that the Demokritos of group LXXXVII is the philosopher, who cannot have been in Abdera after 425, is similarly adventurous. Kleiner, *JNG* (1950/51) 14–20, argues that the coins of Demokritos fit best typographically near the end of the century. Nor are the stylistic points in favor of an interval between period V and period VI very telling, although May's classification at the beginning of period VI does reveal problematical aspects. Cf. C. Peristeri-Otatzi, "Amphores et timbres amphoriques d'Abdère," in J.-Y. Empereur and Y. Garlan (eds.), *Recherches sur les amphores grecques*, *BCH* Suppl. 13 (Paris 1986) 491–96.

[81] I foreshadow here a discussion of a seemingly parallel change in standard that occurred a little earlier(?) at Maroneia where the hypothesis of an Atticizing adaptation has been suggested.

[82] Consider H. von Fritze, "Die Chronologie der autonomen Münzprägung von Abdera," in Strack, *Münzen von Thrakien* 1.1.19–127, esp. 22–23, 53–61.

acceding to their possible existence ought not to change our basic view of this mint.[83]

Akanthos

Another mint that seems to have coined continuously is Akanthos. That was the conclusion of the systematic study of the mint undertaken by J. Desneux, who, unfortunately, dealt exclusively with the tetradrachms, leaving aside the city's fractional coinage in tetrobols, diobols, and obols.[84] Desneux, however, saw 480 as an early moment of appreciable demarcation in the issues of Akanthos. In his view, the period before 480 was a much more active one for the mint. Desneux placed coins bearing the initial *alpha* (A) and the abbreviation AKAN before that date. Akanthian tetradrachms have a lion attacking a bull on the obverse. The pre-480 tetradrachms included those with justifiably archaic looking "mill sail" and swastika incuse style reverses. They also included, however, representatives of an evolution of the incuse square that culminated in neat squares with finely demarcated sides and divided by sharp right angled perpendiculars. A series placed by Desneux immediately following 480 had reverses that bore incuse squares with borders containing the inscription AKANΘION. In the other northern mints I have associated that feature with a mid-century context and perhaps even with the years following 450. O. Picard offered a different ordering of these coins in which the postures of the bull and lion are determinative, believing that the succession of attitudes followed a pattern.[85]

It is now likely, however, that the coins of Akanthos were dated too high according to Desneux's schema, judging from the more recent major finds in hoards. The Asyut hoard (*IGCH* #1644) contains coins exclusively from the early period of the activity of the mint (types B, C, E, and F). The one coin that bears a rosette symbol does not certainly belong to the hoard;[86] it is presumably comparable to the coins in Desneux's type G. No coins bearing an Θ or a A were found at Asyut. Thus the rosette series and the related issues bearing a *theta* symbol, which were more well represented in Desneux's catalogue (they start with his

[83] See also R.R. Holloway's review of May's monograph in *AJA* 71 (1967) 320–21.

[84] "Les tétradrachmes d'Akanthos," *RBN* 85 (1949) 5–122. One hopes that Shoenhammer will continue her promising work on Akanthian fractions, the first results of which are reported in Schoenhammer 105–106, 110–12, 114–16.

[85] O. Picard, "Le lion et le taureau sur les monnaies d'Acanthe," *Kraay-Mørkholm Essays* 225–31.

[86] See also Picard, *Kraay-Mørkholm Essays* 228 and note 7, where the appearance of the rosette-marked coins after the invasion of Xerxes is emphasized, as well as their stylistic affinity with the coins represented in the Asyut Hoard.

type F1B1), were not concluded ca. 480 (as he thought), but began around this time and extended into the 470s and even into the 460s.[87] This conclusion would be viable even if some allowance were made for a delay in the latest Akanthian coins reaching Egypt. Fried notes the latest Asyut coins as, respectively, Asyut #178–86: types E3, F1, F1A1; Asyut #173–77: types F2, F1A2; Asyut #188–89, type D.[88]

The "Decadrachm Hoard" (*CH* 8.48), buried around 465–60, offered much new documentation of the Akanthian mint. A variety of coins appear—the earliest Type C—predominantly *theta*-marked and rosette-marked coins, and some of the latter also marked with an *alpha* on the obverse.[89] Kagan describes the *alpha* coins as the next-to-last variety before the adoption of reverse inscriptions and notes the twenty new obverse dies in the hoard, a sign of the scale of the output for this series (and consequently for the coins marked with AKAN on their obverses that are not represented in *CH* 8.48). The "Antilebanon Hoard" (*CH* 8.45 = 6.4 [475]) contains a similar coin marked with a rosette.[90] This chronology would push the coins of period II with an inscription around a linear square toward the mid-century point and extending well into the third quarter of the century.[91] Style does not necessitate any gap between period I and period II, just as Desneux suggested.

Hence, Desneux's slackening of coin emission that was characteristic of period II was a phenomenon of the 450s and later. The issues of period II give the appearance of having been spaced out over time with punctuated emissions. During period II, a major iconographical change occurs in the posture of the animals on the obverse that is carried through into the next period. Desneux #93–102 eventually give way to issues that bear ΔI and ΔH on the obverse. On coins classified toward the end of period II, these abbreviations imply the aggregation

[87] Price and Waggoner 40–42; Price, *Coinage and Administration* 46. Observe also that May in his review of Desneux's monograph (*NC*[6] 10 [1950] 155–58) notes that period I may have ended a decade later than 480 and the shift to the Phoenician standard could have preceded 424. He does, however, also entertain with respect the hypothesis of an interruption of coining necessitated by the Coinage Decree. Desneux himself conceded a date of 470 for the inception of period II. See J. Desneux, "À propos de la chronologie du monnayage d'Akanthos," *RBN* 98 (1952) 113–15.

[88] Fried, *Coinage and Administration* 3.

[89] Fried, *Coinage and Administration* 3–4. Some type G coins also appear in this hoard.

[90] See S. Hurter and E. Pászthory, "Archaischer Silberfund aus dem Antilibanon," in A. Houghton, S. Hurter, P.E. Mottahedeh, and J.A. Scott (eds.), *Festschrift für Leo Mildenburg* (Wetteren 1984) 111–25, esp. #10, pp. 114, 123.

[91] Price, *Coinage and Administration* 46; Kagan, *Coinage and Administration* 23, 25. Kraay, "The Asyut Hoard: Some Comments on Chronology," *NC*[7] 17 (1977) 189–98, esp. 191–92, puts the introduction of the incuse square at Akanthos no earlier than ca. 465.

of the later coins of the period under two individuals who were probably annual magistrates.

In period III, coins that some have categorized as Phoenician standard and others as third Thraco-Macedonian follow the Euboeic/Attic tetradrachms and have been dated to the period of unrest triggered by the arrival of Peloponnesian forces in the area in 424.[92] May had noted the precedent of the adoption of the same standard by the Chalcidian League, with whose issues the Akanthian coins are quite analogous.[93] May then dated these coins to the 430s. Kraay, however, would opt for a date around 420 for their inception.[94] Yet a date for the Chalcidian League coins in the fourth century is probably preferable.[95] The appearance of abbreviations associated with officials on some of these coins is a sign of continuity with the preceding period. Moreover, the style of treatment of the obverse does not support an interval of significant duration between the last Euboeic/Attic and the first issues of different standard, although the divisions of the square on the reverse shows more granulation or stippling. There is no particular reason to posit a break, whether at mid-century after the manner of May and Kraay or at a later juncture. Regular small, intermittent issues may be the rule, unless we are missing many issues. Concomitantly, the change away from the Euboeic/Attic standard may not be as early as the 420s at Akanthos, and might well reflect the changed strategic and economic circumstances of the Ionian War in a manner comparable to the parallel changes in standard at Abdera and Maroneia.

Maroneia

The mint of Maroneia is another monetary operation for which the most fundamental chronological reconstruction was offered by J.M.F. May, who, as pointed out above, was a firm believer in the traditional interpretation of the Coinage Decree, for example, that it placed a prohibition on allied minting in silver around mid-century. For his work on the mints of the Thracian littoral, May used a date of ca. 450 for the Coinage Decree as the chief historical datum around which he reconstructed the sequence of issues in the Pentekontaeteia. E. Schönert-Geiss,

92 Desneux *RBN* (1949) 91.
93 May *NC* (1950) 157. Desneux conceded this view in *RBN* (1952) 114.
94 Kraay, *ACGC* 133–36.
95 See U. Westermark, "The Coinage of the Chalcidian League Reconsidered," *Studies in Ancient History and Numismatics Presented to Rudi Thomsen* (Aarhus 1988) 91–103, esp. 95.

who has studied the coinage of Maroneia more recently, followed May in general outline.[96]

Critical to our understanding of the mint is May's period III (the same terminology is adopted by Schönert-Geiss in her monograph), dated to 495/90–449/8. We start with the coins of didrachm weight. The output of didrachms in this period is relatively restricted. They were probably issued intermittently, with the dies possibly in use for some years. An early subseries bears the abbreviated ethnic on the obverse and has a quadripartite incuse square on the reverse with its quarters lightly dotted or stippled. One important group of didrachms are associated with an Arkhembrotos whose status and authority is unknown (they are inscribed ΕΠ ΑΡΧΕΜΒΡΟΤΟ).[97]

The other significant subgroup of staters of period III features on its reverse a small quadripartite square bordered by the full ethnic ΜΑΡΩΝΙΤΩΝ within a larger incuse square. Eventually, a vine stock will occupy the inner square. May and Schönert-Geiss date these didrachms just before the passage of the Coinage Decree, or just before 449/8. In contrast, on the basis of the "Decadrachm Hoard" (*CH* 8.48, "Elmali"), where the coins of Mende provide helpful parallel material, Price redates this style of reverse. For Price, this reverse signals a coinage extending into the third quarter of the century, as it seemingly parallels the evolution of design at other northern mints, where the introduction of this style of reverse belongs closer to 450.[98]

Much more common in period III are the issues of drachms (especially) and of fractional coinage. Nothing, however, prevents these coins from extending through the second quarter of the century. Here, there is considerable stylistic and organizational variety (such as right or left orientation) in the treatment not only of the horse protome of the obverse, but also in the ram's head design of the reverse. For example, sometimes the word ΜΑΡΩΝΟΣ appears in its entirety; on other drachms only the abbreviation ΜΑΡ is placed; and still other examples lack any ethnic reference. One reverse die (May's P. 22 = Schönert-Geiss III, R 2) bears

[96] J.M.F. May, "The Coinage of Maroneia: c. 520–449/8 B.C.," *NC*[7] 5 (1965) 27–56; E. Schönert-Geiss, *Grieschisches Münzwerk: Die Münzprägung von Maroneia* (Berlin 1970).

[97] Arkhembrotos could have been an eponymous archon or a mint official. His didrachms are agreed to be early in period III and on them his name has usurped that of the community. As an isolated proclaimer of his identity in a period of official anonymity, he was possibly not simply an annual official, but someone who held office for a span of years. Arkhembrotos could have been a Persian-sponsored "*arkhōn*" (that is, a tyrant) active at the time of Xerxes' expedition and in the early 470s, until the Athenians and the Delian League exerted efficient control over Maroneia.

[98] See Price, *Coinage and Administration* 46.

the abbreviation ΠΟΛ, while two reverse dies carry ΑΘΗ (May's P. 33, P. 34 = III, R 18, 19). To May, these were the abbreviated names of mint officials, a solution that is certainly one obvious alternative. Yet the intermittent appearance of that sort of reference would be troubling, as most reverse dies lack similar designations. In the succeeding periods, the magistrate's name, sometimes introduced by ΕΠΙ, becomes the rule and it appears only on the reverse surrounding the inner square of the design. These earlier denotations are thus anomalous in terms of the history of this mint.[99]

Accordingly, the mint of Maroneia exhibits the common pattern of cessation or curtailment of heavier coins in favor of drachms and fractions that is so prevalent during the Pentekontaeteia within the Athenian *arkhē*. That concentration on the minting of lighter coins elsewhere has been taken to mean that an attempt was being made to supplement a stock in circulation of heavier coins that was composed to a significant degree of Attic tetradrachms. The meager didrachm issues in May's period III resemble the activity of some mints that have been classified as intermittent. Whatever the role of local currency as compared to foreign money in the internal economy, it is apparent that there would not have been enough heavier local coins to contribute to a monetary stock anything like that provided by the earlier series, without the acceptance of foreign money as valid.

Schönert-Geiss develops systematically for Maroneia a line of historical reasoning analogous to that applied by May to Ainos and Abdera (and offered by him here also), in that an interval from 449/8 to 437/6 is posited for the operations of the local mint.[100] Period IV, with its didrachms, begins after 437/6. In this period IV, there are indeed certain modifications in the appearance of the coins. One should leave aside as lacking proof her dubious observations about the more modern or advanced character of the horse protome on the obverse of the coins minted after the assumed period of inactivity for the mint.[101] Nevertheless, the reverse has also been substantially rethought. The inner square now contains a vine stock and surrounding it, in the space within the

[99] If these are not the designations of minting officials, abbreviations might be considered like ΠΟΛ for πόλεος or πολιτικόν and ΑΘΗ for 'Αθηναίᾳ or 'Αθηναίων, although the historical context for this sort of identification would be unknown. I suggest below that the symbols on later Maroneian coins signaled the routing of funds for different purposes, some cultic and others secular. It is not impossible that these abbreviations mark the inception of the practice.

[100] Schönert-Geiss, *Maroneia* 17–19; see also Schönert-Geiss, "Zur Geschichte Maroneias von den Anfängen bis zum 4. Jh. u. Z.," *Klio* 61 (1979) 437–51, esp. 444–46.

[101] See Schoenhammer 203–204 for other critical esthetic appreciations.

outer border of the incuse square, the name of a magistrate also appears (starting with Poseidippos).[102]

It is questionable, however, whether this new design for the reverse, along with a slight reduction in the weight of the didrachms authorizes the conclusion that a twelve-year hiatus must have eventuated. There is a strong temptation to make more recent the coins of Abdera (period IV) that employ the same standard as the Maroneian coins with their reduced weights of periods IV and V. A slight (or, in reality, any) change in standard weight does not neccessitate that one posit a fresh start for the mint at Maroneia. There had, after all, been an apparent earlier reduction in the weight of the didrachms in period III. Nothing really forbids that the coins of May's (Schönert-Geiss's) period IV and period V do not immediately follow on the latest coins of period III. That had been the judgment of West in his review of the coinage of Maroneia, and it was accepted by Erxleben.

The situating of the earlier didrachms with the two incuse squares within each other after 450 urges the same conclusion. Mattingly argues for the succession of the first tetradrachms (of period V) on the preceding coins of period IV, while observing that their date must descend by a decade.[103] Therefore, among those who hold the view that there is no interval, opinion is then split between the earlier approach that the period IV coins began around 450 and those, working from some new material, who put the dividing line between 450 and 425.

One important feature of the output of periods IV and V at Maroneia is that the fractional issues that were earlier so prominent have now given way to a concentration on didrachms at first and then to tetradrachms. May and Schönert-Geiss assigned no lighter coins at all to these periods. It is this striking reversal in emphasis in minting activity that calls for explanation, a concern that will not change if some few fractional coins come to light in the future.

Decisions to cease the production of lighter coins are well attested in the *arkhē* during the third quarter of the fifth century, and we have already noted the Maroneian emphasis on the coining of fractions in May's period III. Rather then betokening some momentous economic or administrative revolution (devolution might perhaps be the more correct

[102] For the Mendean comparanda for these coins, see pp. 127–29 and note the comments of Schoenhammer 202–203.

[103] Mattingly *EMC* (1988) 326–27, who tellingly cites May's own comments on the backward character of the first Maroneian tetradrachms after his supposed interruption and his earlier placement of the same coins before mid-century (*NC* [1965] 48–49; cf. May *Abdera* 19–21, 23, 143, 147).

term), the disappearance of locally minted fractions and drachms is interpreted in this volume to imply a replacement of locally minted coins with foreign coins. Elsewhere this phenomenon usually meant that the local mint simply closed down. Exceptionally, at Maroneia, there was a revival of the minting of heavier coins, and the heavy coins themselves soon became heavier, with the tetradrachm supplanting the didrachm as the standard issue.

Clues to interpreting this anomaly can perhaps be found in two features of coins of periods IV and V at Maroneia, namely, the symbols on many of their obverses and the names of the magistrates that grace their reverses (the preposition ΕΠΙ sometimes appears). One name, Poseidippos, is known for the didrachms of May's period IV, and eight names are found on the tetradrachms of period V. The number of coins associated with these names varies greatly. So a hypothesis of equal terms for minting or eponymous officials is complicated by the widely discrepant outputs associated with the different names (although that detail would not necessarily be fatal against seeing the officials as annual). Moreover, there is an inadequate number of names to fill the years 437/6 to 412/11 on the assumption that the term of each official was one year. In addition, any removal of the gap in minting activity that was posited by May and Schönert-Geiss may intensify this problem, and the lack of such an interval is indeed probable.

A still further complication is created by the record of the symbols that appear on the obverses of the coins of period V. They are generic in nature and twelve different symbols appear in our data. Two officials have no symbols associated with them; four have one symbol; one has three symbols on coins bearing his name; and one official has *ten* symbols. Furthermore, the symbols do not appear to have been restricted to one name. The symbol of the *kantharos* is repeated for four names; the same two names share the owl(?), head of Apollo, and wheel.

Schönert-Geiss's solution to these puzzling details is to assign each combination of a symbol and a name to a single year, with the result that Metrodotos with his ten symbols holds office from 433/32 or 431/30 to 421/0 and Metrophon with three combinations presides(?) from 420/19 to 418/17.

This hypothesis can be faulted in two regards: first, the option of annual office-holding ought to prevail in the absence of solid counterindications. These years were, after all, the heyday of the Attic hegemony with its fostering of democracy. One might opt for a theory of multiyear terms. Yet I do not think that many students of this period would be comfortable with magistrates in an allied state occupying such *disparate* terms of office. If reelections are the solution, it cannot have been the case that officials were invariably reelected to consecutive terms and never had intervals in their strings of office. Once it is accepted that the all the years of Metrodotos and Metrophon ought not to be consecutive, Schönert-Geiss's stylistic ordering of series must be jettisoned, and there are problems accounting for die-linking between the two men. Extending the times of the emission of these coins with the names Metrodotos and Metrophon may make practical sense, but only if they were not conventional office-holders. But the specified ΕΠΙ with the names is then troubling. Second, the repetition of the symbols becomes intractable on the supposition that a combination of names and symbols marked years of issuance. Symbols that can repeat or indeed even be absent could never have constituted a notation for the identification of years of service and their monetary issues. Repetitive symbols (such as the kantharos), let alone absent symbols, are also poor candidates in any case for personal badges or notations.

The existence of a small group of eight extant names of officials that may cover a span of twenty-five years (or possibly the longer stretch of 440–404) implies that the mint did not emit coinage in every year. Even if we assume that the names connected with some smaller runs have been missed, there will never be enough names (even after guessing at the number of the undiscovered) to authorize us to assign one to each year. Nor are the combinations of symbols and names likely to have distinguished mint runs without some further specification being applied (like a letter), even if we reject the chronological aspect of the Schönert-Geiss hypothesis.

In understanding the symbols, however, we must remember that these issues cannot be the totality of the money in use in Maroneia in this period. Not only does the number of dies look inadequate (44 obverse; 59 reverse surviving) for an economy that could generate payments to the Athenians of 10T and 21T, but the stoppage of the production of drachms and fractions points to the utilization of external currency for the transactions formerly handled by these coins.

If we recognize that the traditional interpretations used by numismatists for the presence of symbols on classical coins do not work well for periods IV and V at Maroneia, another type of explanation may be essayed. This explanation will exploit our understanding that some coinings during the Attic hegemony injected coins into local economies where they circulated regularly alongside other coins of different appearance and provenience. The purpose in so minting can naturally have been the conversion of bullion into new coin or a supplementation of the local money supply. The raising of only this sort of motive, however, implies that all coins of a *polis* were disbursed indiscriminately without regard to the category of governmental expenditure. The elaboration and variety of numismatic iconography makes this unlikely prima facie as an absolute rule. As has already been seen with the *diskoboloi* of Kos, some supplementary emissions could memorialize specific thematics within local traditions. There a special context for the disbursement of the coins can be envisioned.[104] It is our new paradigm for the circulation of money in the Athenian *arkhē* that encourages us to explore the relevance of such hypotheses for decisions about coining.

The symbols on Maroneian coins of periods IV and V, which seem so inadequate as dating or accounting notations, actually work well as manifestations (or even advertisements) for the contexts in which the coins were to be used. In the wine-exporting city of Maroneia, that symbol repeatedly used, the *kantharos*, might connote some symposial or ritual setting for distribution of these coins; associated with four officials for four occasions on which the state undertook expenditures on behalf of communal celebration. For example, the government might have subsidized participation by citizens in a festival honoring Dionysos. Furthermore, it is not hard to see similar public or ritual contexts for Apollo's head, the wheel (which could stand for an agonistic setting), and what is assumed to be an owl (connoting Athena), all of which symbols repeat (recall the earlier coins with ΑΘΗ). Even the symbols appearing only once are susceptible to similar interpretations.[105] The targeting of these fifth-century series toward internal distributions would account for their scant impact on contemporary hoards, as compared with later issues that more truly reflect the intensity of the commercial interaction of Maroneia with the Thracian hinterland. This hypothesis of celebratory contexts might induce us to reinterpret the role of the individuals named on the coins so as to subsume liturgic duties in which they provided resources as well as supervision for governmental functions.

Obverse die links connect reverses of different officials, a detail that provides chronological links between magistrates in the Schönert-Geiss theory. Some reverse dies inscribed with the name of a single magistrate, authority, or liturgist are combined with obverses bearing several symbols. In the hypothesis citing special occasions for emission, this pattern of die linking would be comprehensible on the premise that the magistrate

[104] The former distinction between commemorative stamps and ordinary postage might strike an appropriate, similar note.

[105] The other symbols in this period are the star, crescent moon, cap, satyr's head, lyre, and laurel crown.

to whom it next fell to strike coins for the festival (if that is what the symbol truly means) symbolized by the *kantharos* started by making use of any obverse dies left over from the previous issuance of coins for the same purpose before proceeding to employ new dies (*kantharos*: linking Deonys and Deonytos; head of Apollo: Metrodotos and Metrophon). Concomitantly, if another series targeted for a different context was required of the same magistrate, authority, or liturgust, he naturally used any reverse dies left over from his previous striking that bore his name (as in the case of Metrodotos, one of whose reverses is paired with obverses with a satyr head and a head of Apollo).

The only pecularity that emerges from the foregoing reconstruction is that Metrodotos must be thought to have issued coins for ten special programs or purposes (as well as some that were not assigned to any category, as they lack any symbol). One ready hypothesis in the light of the aforesaid scenario would be that the year of Metrodotos was one of particular civic and religious emphasis for Maroneia. Yet, if the named individuals are visualized more as liturgists rather than simply as officials, spreading these occasions over different years would not have the same ideological coloration as long or repeated terms of office.[106]

Some issues appear without any symbol on the obverse, as do some of the coins bearing the name of Metrodotos and all the coins of the officials Athenes and Pythodoros. If the Schönert-Geiss dating according to stylistic criteria is correct, all these series belong in the second half of period V. That judgment puts them in all probability well into the Peloponnesian War. Schönert-Geiss places the earliest of the coins with no obverse symbols in 423/2. At that time, it might have been necessary to supplement the local money supply because of a lessened and inadequate flow of foreign (including Attic) money toward Maroneia. Other *poleis*, as indicated above, revived or initiated coining under the pressure of war conditions. The triobols of Aiginetic(?) weight produced in period VI of the mint (belonging to the end of the fifth century) probably arose from just such a need.

Period VI, when small issues of staters were struck, at first with the names of magistrates and later perhaps without (with some bearing symbols), has drawn attention for the sake of determining the standard that is employed. That determination has affected chronology. West argued that the standard was (Euboeic)/Attic, and the stater (quite

[106] The disparity in the number and size of issues would change its character. An official such as Metrodotos need not appear as the beneficiary of an improbably long incumbency or even as the presider over a concentration of occasions for disbursements, but rather as an unusually generous practitioner of democratic politics in the manner of a Kimon or Alkibiades.

variable in weight) that came to dominate emissions in period VI was equivalent to an Attic tridrachm. He saw the staters beginning after 430. This coinage bespoke stronger Attic influence on the Thracian coastlands and the Athenian alliance with the powerful Odrysian king Sitalkes. Putting aside the doubtful and partial argument from the macropolitical context, West also had a late date for the Coinage Decree in 415–14, so that an Atticizing coinage at neighboring Abdera could follow a short period of interruption owing to Attic legislation. At Maroneia, the shift to the Attic standard is somewhat earlier and the legislation of Klearkhos that was cited in the Coinage Decree could be made responsible for the change. West's dating for what was later called period VI, however, now looks distinctly too early. In further contrast, a shift among allies to the Attic standard hardly qualifies as an unusual phenomenon needing a specific political causation.

Schönert-Geiss took a very different position on the standard of late fifth-century Maroneian staters. She defended the suggestion advanced by some of the earliest observers that these staters are really Aiginetic didrachms. She also adduces as support the appearance of similar weight coins at Abdera.[107] Nothing is known of Maroneia during the Ionian War, but the isolation of the city and the propinquity of the Thracian hinterland could have been factors influencing a decision whether to remain loyal to the Athenians or to defect. It is fairly certain that no radical change of regime took place contemporaneously with the change in standard. Coins of the official (or authority or liturgist) Metrophon that bear the symbol of a four-spoked wheel are split between the two weight standards.

The coins of period VI carry on the tradition of period V in their denomination of officials on the reverse and their frequent use of symbols on the obverse. That there is a scanty issue of fractions in this period shows a slight break with the past (the Aiginetic triobols noted above). Period V produced no lighter denominations, but the change hardly amounts to a major fiscal or economic reorientation, since other states resumed minting drachms and fractions during the latter half of the Peloponnesian War. In other words, the unity of monetary circulation that had been the *arkhē* (or the vast majority of its territory) during the Pentekontaeteia possibly continued to include Maroneia at the outset of period VI. If the mint of Maroneia shifted to an emission of Aiginetic-weight coins during the Ionian War (perhaps an uncertain proposition

[107] Schoenhammer 209–10 opts for seeing Maroneia employing the standard of Abdera, which she considers local and anomalous.

in any case), an interest in the subsidization of and cooperation with Peloponnesian military forces may be implicated. There is no certain means of deciding when after 411 the government of Maroneia chose to make the change.[108] The coins of periods IV–VI probably succeeded each other without interruption. The first gold emission of the city is dated at the very end of the century.[109] While issuing coins in gold per se cannot be interpreted as a direct reflection of an effort to break away from the Athenian hegemony, it undoubtedly mirrors monetary adjustments to the gradual fraying and then shattering of the monetary unit that was the *arkhē*.

The persistence of mints in the northern Aegean coastal region is noteworthy. It may be that the existence of silver mining in the area lowered the administrative costs of minting even for those cities that did not have access to silver mines, such as Mende and Akanthos. Yet it may also be noted that both cities used the Euboeic/Attic coin standard. Moreover, the commercial interaction between cities of the Thracian littoral, such as Ainos, Abdera, and Maroneia, with the non-Greek interior may have created circumstances in which a termination of minting was disadvantageous for its disruptive possibilities.[110]

[108] *CH* 8.103, "Thrace?, c. 1986," ca. 350, contains significant new material from Maroneia period VI, indicating a number of hitherto unknown combinations of magistrates and symbols. There are also a larger number of coins from Abdera, although they mostly illustrate known dies and magistrates. Lorber believes that the hoard is from Abderite territory and has a date for the collection of the hoard of 376–65. That date might serve to lower the date for period VI at Maroneia. See C.C. Lorber, *Amphipolis: The Civic Coinage in Silver and Gold* (Los Angeles 1990) 176–83.

[109] See also E. Schönert-Geiss, "Maroneia und Die Thraker—Wechselbeziehungen zwischen Polis under Hinterland," *Eirene* 22 (1985) 39–53, esp. 52.

[110] The correspondences in standard between Abdera and Maroneia—regardless of how we choose to identify the standard—offer an indication that their coinages were intended to circulate together among certain groups of users.

5
THE MINTS OF THE AUTONOMOUS ALLIES

It has been recognized since the earliest work on the Coinage Decree that the coinages of the autonomous states, Samos, Chios, and the Lesbian cities represent special problems in analysis. Earlier commentary held that it was unlikely that these mints were covered by any supposed prohibition against allied minting of silver.[1] More recently, however, some scholars have argued in favor of the inclusion of these mints in a general prohibition, basing themselves on what they considered to be the unconditional phraseology that had been traditionally restored in the clause added to the oath of the *Boulē* in the Coinage Decree.[2]

Ignoring for the moment any judgments based on the numismatic and epigraphical material, it is indeed possible to support the earlier consensus on the basis of an exploration of the nature of autonomy during the fifth-century *arkhē*. Such a massive intervention in the internal affairs of the autonomous allies as a prohibition of coining silver (and even more so a demonetization of their coins) would make a mockery of the fastidiousness toward legalities that can otherwise be discerned in the evidence on Attic policy on autonomy.[3] Unfortunately, scholars have been unduly eager to believe that the inscribed evidence compelled an interpretation that admitted no exception for the autonomous allies, when we ought to have been warned against the conventional reading of that provision on the very grounds of its inclusivity of the autonomous.

The monetary policy of the autonomous allies on Lesbos has been addressed above in the chapter on mints producing electrum, for both Methymna and Mytilene had traditions of minting in that alloy. While

[1] Cavaignac *RN* (1953); Segre 172–73; cf. Gardner *JHS* (1913) 160–64 for qualifications.

[2] J.P. Barron, *The Silver Coins of Samos* (London 1966) 86–87; Meiggs 168; Meiggs-Lewis pp. 113, 115–17. Note also Barron, "Chios in the Athenian Empire," in J. Boardman and C.E. Vaphopoulou-Richardson (eds.), *Chios: A Conference at the Homereion in Chios* (Oxford 1986) 89–103, esp. 96: "no document demonstrates the ruthlessness of Pericles' determination more clearly than the decree, to be dated 448–446 on the ground of its letter-forms, which forbade the allied cities to strike *silver* coins of their own or to use any but Athenian weights, measures and coinage. . . . So fierce was this determination that the decree sets the penalty of death for anyone who even seeks to have the matter reconsidered."

[3] At least, that is, in terms of the Athenian understanding of autonomy. See Figueira, *Excursions* 255-92; note pp. 261–62, 272–74, and 285 on Chios; for Samos, see 261, 263–65, 274, 285.

Methymnian coining of electrum had ended in the early fifth century, for its silver coining Methymna was classed with the small group of allies that exhibited a pattern of interruption in their production of silver. The city appears to have been minting in the second half of the century after the assumed interruption. Granting the weakness of the hoard evidence about Methymnian coinage, one cannot accept received opinion with any degree of assurance, as the traditional interpretation of the Coinage Decree has perhaps clouded the issue. Methymna thus gives an unclear signal about the applicability of the Coinage Decree or Attic monetary legislation in general. In contrast, Mytilene was a mint whose striking of electrum *hectae* was its most conspicuous activity by virtue both of the literary or epigraphical testimonia and of the surviving examples of its coinage. Concerning its production of silver coins, there is agreement that Mytilene minted drachms and fractions down to its revolt in 427. Mytilene seems an exception to any prohibition on minting until that date.

Concerning Samos, it is unclear at first glance whether one would be justified in concluding that the Coinage Decree forbade allied minting of silver by the autonomous, even if the arguments of Barron and Kraay (to take two prominent recent scholars) on behalf of a gap in the operation of the Samian mint were totally convincing, because the interaction of allied status and monetary policy concerning Samos is complex. It is possible in principle to envisage all sorts of monetary ramifications from the subjugation of the island by Perikles and its resultant loss of autonomy in 440/39, without necessitating a result for the scope of the Coinage Decree.

In contrast, the case of Chios avoids the confusion of changes in autonomous status during the Athenian hegemony. Is Chios, then, our definitive litmus test on the general applicability of the Coinage Decree? Our answer will depend on whether it is possible to reverse the usual reasoning on the significance of hypothetical intervals in Chian minting (such as those suggested by Barron, Kraay, or Hardwick). If one agrees on the seriousness of Athenian respect for the autonomy of the ship-contributing allies, then any interval could also have had a nonhegemonic cause. Consequently, if the autonomous Chians, who ensured that their rights were respected carefully by the Athenians, could envisage suspensions of minting or even an abandonment of silver coining entirely, then economic factors would have to be carefully evaluated and *discarded* before proceeding to the supposition of Attic imperialism regarding other mints, even those of tributary allies. That caution would become especially prudent in the absence of contemporary comment on monetary legislation. In other words, one should be reluctant to reach a conclusion from the activities of the Chian mint that is divergent from his view on Chian autonomy, about which there is some direct evidence.

Furthermore, there is another reason why the minting activity of autonomous states makes the usual method of arguing over the nature of the Coinage Decree problematical. It is easy enough to understand how autonomy was associated with characteristics such as the possession of walls, the provision of ships for military service and the maintenance of a military establishment, and the absence of tribute. These aspects of a city's political situation affected the autonomous city alone, and their very existence served to accentuate the lack of freedom in policy-making for the nonautonomous. Once walls were begun, ships laid down, and tribute ceased, an important threshold of independence could be seen to have been overstepped for the *specific* allied state.

In the case of coining, however, we are faced with an aspect of political life with ramifications that were indeed not restricted to the autonomous city. If the Chians continued to coin, they not only rendered themselves theoretically able to evade an acceptance of Athenian coinage—assuming for the moment that any allied state desired to do so—but allowed any of their neighbors who could acquire Chian coinage in sufficient amounts, to refrain alike from using Athenian coins. In addition, insofar as these neighbors had already coined on the same standard as the Chians or Samians or on an easily convertible standard, their use of Chian or Samian coins would represent no distinct or conspicuous departure from past commercial and administrative practices. The same argument also has some force regarding mints outside the *arkhē* (on the Persic standard?) whose coins could be used by Attic tributary allies. The nonusage clause of the decree as traditionally interpreted might be understood to punish such employment of foreign money by individuals (nota bene), but that understanding seems to demand an elaborate and intrusive disciplinary apparatus for which there is no evidence.

This argument appears superficially to serve equally well as reasoning in favor of insisting that all allies of Athens must have been denied the right to coin. That particular conclusion will be hard to corroborate, as we will see momentarily. Therefore, after the numismatic evidence is presented below, the converse approach should become markedly more attractive. Forbidding coining among the subject allies was not sufficient—be there autonomous coinages or not—unless one also mandated that Attic coinage be the sole legal tender. Yet, once one mandates that Attic coins possess local validity universally in the *arkhē*, there will not turn out to be much reason to go further and forbid the minting of local coins as a supplement to Attic owls, unless the whole point of the exercise is a flaunting of hegemonic power.

CHIOS

Let us first consider in detail the case of Chios. It is worth noting at the outset that the earliest systematic treatments of Chian coinage by Mavrogordato and Baldwin, which were written before a mid-century date for the Coinage Decree became the majority view, found no internal grounds for placing a major interval in Chian fifth-century mint production. More recently, Erxleben has reviewed the evidence and reached the same conclusion. Baldwin assigned the latest didrachms from the mint to a transitional phase, dated 460–40, and the first tetradrachms to 440–20. She also specifically rejected a gap of ca. fifteen years starting from 425, in what may be considered a reaction to the early chronologies for the Coinage Decree. Until recently, there had been little advance beyond these rather vague chronological divisions. Now the research of N.M.M. Hardwick, working from an exhaustive survey of coins, must be taken into account.[4]

Mavrogordato placed what he called "the decree of Clearchus" in 431 (his shorthand for an indeterminable date 440–31), because he believed that the shift from the didrachm as the heaviest coin to the tetradrachm was a compromise that addressed the prohibition on non-Attic silver money, which the epigraphists had found in the inscriptional evidence. Why an adjustment of this nature would represent anything of worth (that is, a suitable item for establishing a compromise) for the Athenians in the course of a negotiation is left entirely unstated. Thereafter, J.P. Barron, followed by C.M. Kraay, provided the now prevailing interpretation, one that places the Coinage Decree at the center of the history of the fifth-century mint activity on Chios. More recently, however, Hardwick has challenged this consensus, arguing for a hiatus after 425 that would accommodate a decree in the late 420s.

There is general agreement that Chios minted didrachms and tetrobols, or *tritai* 'third-staters,' on an indigenous standard from the

[4] N.M.M. Hardwick, *The Coinage of Chios from the Sixth to the Fourth Century* B.C. (Diss. Oxford University 1991); Hardwick, "The Coinage of Chios from the VIth to the IVth Century B.C.," in T. Hackens and G. Moucharte (eds.), *Proceedings of the XI International Numismatics Congress* 1 (Louvain-la-Neuve 1993) 211–22.

late sixth well into the fifth century. The reason why the tetrobol is the smaller denomination of choice is presumably explained by the archaic convention, well attested in Ionia, of dividing the stater into thirds. The obverse type is a sphinx, gradually refined in its pictorial style, to which successively a wine amphora was added before the type, and then a bunch of grapes suspended above the amphora (itself a motif appearing in isolation earlier).

Hardwick believes that the mint was closed briefly after 493, with the defeat of the Ionian Revolt. He places the earlier series of staters with an amphora during the latest 490s and 480s by virtue of the hoard evidence. For instance, the Asyut Hoard of ca. 475 (*IGCH* #1644) contains early issues bearing the amphora.[5] He sensibly connects these emissions with the expenditures involved with rebuilding the Chian fleet for use in Xerxes' expedition. A later series of staters with a bulbous-necked amphora is witnessed in *CH* 8.48, the "Decadrachm Hoard" or "Elmali Hoard." The last phase of this period of minting activity saw the obverse design imposed upon a convex surface that has been compared to a shield. Hardwick notes a connected technical change, the inception of beveling of the teeth of the reverse punch. The lower end of this emission is more difficult to pin down. Hardwick has *CH* 8.48 and *IGCH* #1483, "Massyaf," as later hoards containing these coins. Rather than assigning a few dies to the mid-century period, it seems more prudent to raise the terminal date of the series from 435 toward 450.

The following series with a bunch of grapes before the sphinx represents Baldwin's "Transitional" series. Hardwick, who notes these coins' accentuation both of the rounded (or shield) effect on the obverse and of the beveling of the teeth of the reverse, opts for 435 for their inception, continuing well into the Peloponnesian War (ca. 425).[6] He cites *IGCH* #1191, "Phanae on Chios," as a characteristic hoard for this issue. The worn Chian coins in *IGCH* #1203, "Chalki" (ca. 380), appear with Samian and Rhodian coins of ca. 400, which might suggest the minting of these coins well before 400.

Earlier opinion had been unanimous that the shift from these last didrachms to the tetradrachm issues fell within this period. Kraay argued that the transition to this next phase of the mint was punctuated by an interval of inactivity engineered by the Coinage Decree. For him, the resumption of coining must have preceded the Peloponnesian War

[5] Hardwick, *Chios* 114–23, for his obverse dies A35–52; Hardwick, "The Solution to Thucydides VIII 101.1: The 'Chian Fortieths'," *NAC* 25 (1996) 59–69, esp. 63, citing unpublished hoard evidence.

[6] Hardwick, *Chios* 123–38, 149.

(see immediately below), but its rationale has been left rather mysterious. Perhaps we are to believe that the Coinage Decree was rescinded or that Chios belonged to a category of mints receiving special dispensation (for which idea, see below, pp. 177–79). This interpretation of Chian minting seems to force us back on the hypothesis of a transitory implementation for the supposed prohibition on minting silver. This turn of affairs can be seen to create its own complexities when confronted with both the reference to monetary legislation in Aristophanes' *Birds* and the discrepancies between the fragments of the decree themselves (see below, pp. 207–16, 455–63).

The new Chian coinage did not exhibit a change in standard but a different range of denominations was featured: tetradrachms, drachms, and triobols. The reverse had long remained a static feature, bearing an archaic-looking incuse square. Eventually, however, a more formalized (or stylized) version of the incuse square was begun with broad bands separating the quarters, the surfaces of which were now striated. The names of magistrates would eventually appear on the central horizontal band in this phase of minting (after 375, according to Hardwick). Naturally, the timing of the termination of the didrachms and the inception of the tetradrachm issues was crucial for the hypothesis of an interval in the continuity of minting. The Treasurers of the Other Gods at Athens offered an inventory in 429/8 that contained a total of 485 Chian dr. and 4 ob., a total that seems impossible with a currency that is solely composed of didrachms and tetrobols (*IG* I^3 383.27–28).[7] Consequently, the Treasurers were already accounting for holdings that included coins of the new silver series.

Chian coins have on them representations of Chian amphoras that were themselves in a process of stylistic and metrological evolution. The coordination of amphoras and coins is of capital importance for chronology. Barron has suggested that the bulbous-necked amphoras that are represented on the last of the didrachms and the electrum stater (to be discussed below) are dated ca. 450.[8] The bulbous-necked amphoras were replaced by straight-necked amphoras; they are depicted on the new tetradrachms. Mattingly has countered Barron by asserting that the bulbous-necked amphoras continued on well after mid-century, severing the connection between a transition ca. 431 and a mid-century

[7] Barron, *Silver Coins* 86–87; J. Boardman, "Excavations at Pindakas in Chios," *BSA* (1958–1959) 295–309, esp. 308, note 23; Mattingly *JHS* (1981) 80. Hardwick, *Chios* 28, 146–47, offers other solutions: coins in undocumented denominations, a survival of early half-staters, or a stater that had been cut in half. Cf. Hardwick *ICN* 11.215.

[8] Barron, *Silver Coins* 86–87; note also Kraay, *ACGC* 242–43.

decree.[9] Mattingly pointed to various archaeological contexts dating from the 430s where bulbous-necked amphoras were found, such as deposits in the Athenian Agora, the Punic Amphora Building at Corinth, and burials in the South Hill Cemetery in the Kerameikos at Athens. Barron then answered with a review of the six well-dated archaeological contexts in which late bulbous-necked amphoras and early straight-necked amphoras are found.[10] His emphasis on the aging of wine in the amphora and on reuse of amphoras is reasonable enough as an argument against Mattingly's assumption that the amphoras were necessarily contemporary with the latest painted pottery in the context. Yet, although Barron counters some of the arguments against radical redating, the transition to the straight-necked amphora may well have occurred ca. 440, or even somewhat later.

To put the matter briefly, the later the didrachms are thought to have continued, the less likely it will appear both that a mid-fifth-century Coinage Decree affected the transition from the didrachms to tetradrachms on Chios and that there was any interval at all in coining if *IG* I^3 383.27–28 truly shows the appearance of the tetradrachms.

There is another aspect of the archaeological record that complicates finding a role for Attic legislation in the metrological and numismatic changes on Chios. I refer to the alteration in amphora capacity that took place toward the end of the production of bulbous-necked pots in which the volume of these vessels could now be resolved into an even number of seven Attic *khoes*. While metrological consolidation will be discussed below, a few comments on the Chian situation are appropriate here.

The existence of "Atticizing" bulbous-necked amphoras (pictured on the didrachmns) suggests that metrological consolidation with Attic usage and the inauguration of the tetradrachms were not contemporary. Hence, the two changes were unlikely to have been the results of the same act of Athenian legislation. An objection that may be made to this point is that the existence of the controversial hiatus may obviate the need for a contemporaneity of the change in amphora capacity and the initiation of tetradrachms. Is it not the cessation of the didrachms that indicates the passage of the Coinage Decree? The bulbous-necked amphoras need not have reached the end of their period of production at the same time that the didrachms that pictured them ended; they merely changed size.

[9] Mattingly *JHS* (1981) 78–80.
[10] Barron, *Chios* 96–100.

At this juncture a matter noted by Mattingly becomes critical.[11] The stamps on the earliest straight-necked amphoras represented the didrachms that in turn had pictured the obsolete bulbous-necked amphoras. Therefore, there were three separate adjustments. Bulbous-necked amphoras were introduced containing a round number of seven Attic *khoes*, an adjustment to Attic standards on anyone's reckoning. Then straight-necked amphoras were substituted, still containing a round number of seven Attic *khoes*. Finally, the tetradrachm replaced the didrachm as the standard coin. Later still, the Chians may have offered some jars in eight Attic *khoes*.[12] That sequence of adjustments does not have the look of a mandated process, let alone the result of a single Coinage Decree.

A nuanced hypothesis for the changes in policy on Chios might run generally as follows: sometime after a Coinage Decree in the early 440s, the Chians adjusted the volume of their wine amphoras. Evidence is now lacking whether other *metra* were changed. The transportation of wine, however, would have been a most conspicuous context for the juxtaposition of Chian *metra* and Attic *metra*, given the scale of the Chian exports. Hence a specific concern about the capacities of these vessels is not impossible. The Chians may have acted under Athenian compulsion, but a voluntary adjustment by an autonomous *polis* is more likely, with or without diplomacy with the Athenians. A greater volume of trade and metrological consolidation abroad were incentives to package wine in containers whose volume could be reckoned both in Chian and in Attic measures. Unaffected by a Coinage Decree that forbade their minting—or anyone else's minting, as will be seen—the Chians continued to mint didrachms. Later, they considered a further alteration of their amphoras that was unmotivated by Athenian legislation. In changing the style of the neck of their wine amphoras, perhaps the Chians intended to guard against deception of their customers through reuse.[13] It is hard to determine the volume of amphoras of this size so that the temptation may have existed to shortchange buyers by refilling older, smaller containers. Finally, the Chians changed the denomination of their coins.

Hardwick offers a more radical interpretation in which changes in amphora capacity are even further decoupled from the introduction of these tetradrachms.[14] He argues that they began around 400,

[11] Mattingly *JHS* (1981) 78–79. See V.R. Grace, *Amphoras and the Ancient Wine Trade* (Princeton 1961) figs. 48, 49, with text.

[12] Mattingly *JHS* (1981) note 18 on pp. 80–81, reporting correspondence of Mabel Lang.

[13] Cf. M.B. Wallace, "Texts, Amphoras, Coins, Standards and Trade," *Ancient World* 10 (1984) 11–14, esp. 13, where the similar motivation of consumer resistance is cited.

[14] Hardwick, *Chios* 160–65; Hardwick *ICN* 11.215–19.

after a hiatus in the mint from the mid-420s until after 412. This interval is to be connected with the Coinage Decree.[15] We have already seen that the early metrological change creates complications for this hypothesis, as does the usual interpretation of *IG* I³ 383.27–28. Yet it must be conceded in Hardwick's favor that his theory has the advantage of accounting for the absence of early hoard evidence for the tetradrachms. Hardwick cites *CH* 5.17, "Ionia, 1977" (ca. 375), where Chian tetradrachms appear with worn ΣΥΝ tetradrachms (ca. 400) of Knidos, Rhodes, and Ephesos and tetradrachms of Hekatomnos of Caria. Nonetheless, this theory provokes some serious difficulties for understanding literary references to Chian money during the Ionian War, even if we choose to ignore its basis in an interpretation of the Coinage Decree that has been criticized elsewhere in this work. Since the Chian coins alleged to form part of *CH* 5.17 are not available for study, it is unknown how early one might place worn examples of the tetradrachms (as Hardwick suspects these to have been).

A consideration of this literary evidence may be coupled with the question why the Chians made this particular change in coin sizes from didrachms to tetradrachms. While the idea has been advanced that the mere fact of a shift to different standard sizes of coins is suggestive of a discontinuity in Chian minting activities, that supposition scarcely qualifies as the rationale for the new denominations themselves. Thus, it is worth considering whether the tetradrachm and its fellow coins might have an explanation in their own terms and not simply as tokens of change or unintended markers of a resumption in minting. Indeed, there are two contemporary passages that give valuable indications about the usage of Chian money in the relevant period.

In 8.101.1, Thucydides speaks of the Chian *tesserakostē* 'fortieth' when he describes how the Chian government gave each of the sailors of the Spartan navarch Mindaros three of these coins before his sailing in 411. It was generally agreed that the coins in question were three Chian tetradrachms per capita and that these "fortieths" had that appellation because they were equivalent to a fortieth of an Aiginetic coin *mna* (cf. ΣThuc. 8.101.1: ἀρχαῖα νομίσματα ἐπιχώρια).[16] A similar

[15] Hardwick, *Chios* 150–52. See also H.B. Mattingly, *The Athenian Empire Restored* (Ann Arbor 1996) 521.

[16] Head² 600; Gardner *JHS* (1913) 161–62; Gardner, *A History of Ancient Coinage: 700–300 B.C.* (Oxford 1918) 251–52; Gardner, "A Financial History of Ancient Chios," *JHS* 40 (1920) 160–73; J. Mavrogordato, "A Chronological Arrangement of the Coins of Chios; Part II," *NC*⁴ 15 (1915) 361–432, esp. 397; W.E. Thompson, "The Chian Coinage in Thucydides and Xenophon," *NC*⁷ 11 (1971) 323–24; cf. *HCT* 5.346–47. On the composition

reference comes from a slightly later context in the Ionian War, where the Spartan navarch Kallikratidas received a subsidy from Chios of a *pentedrakhmia* for each of his sailors in 406 (Xen. *HG* 1.6.12). Head has explained this term for a military subsidy by suggesting that two Chian tetradrachms had the same value as five Aiginetic drachms so that such a payment could be called familiarly a pentedrachm.[17] While no other suggestion has commanded the scholarly credence accorded to Head's suggestion, we cannot entirely exclude that the Chian subsidy for the men of Kallikratidas was merely 5 Chian drachms (a tetradrachm and a drachm coin), and that this payment had enough of a customary character to be casually called the *pentedrakhmia*. Counting against this hypothesis is the fact that the Chians referred to their large-denomination coins as staters.[18] Hence, the *pentedrakhmia* in a Chian context implies a reference to another currency, one customarily using drachms as the basic unit.

Hardwick must offer another explanation, because he would delay the introduction of the Chian tetradrachm.[19] The "fortieth" is the *tritē*, since forty of these "third-staters" would exchange with a gold Daric at a ratio of gold to silver of 1:12.45. One difficulty with this is that this value ratio of gold to silver looks a little elevated for 411 (pp. 521–22 below). And how could such a term achieve conventional status if it depended upon a changing value ratio of two metals for its applicability? Third, it is hard to see why anyone would be motivated before or during 411 to align the name of a Chian or Ionian military stipend with the Persian Daric. Moreover, this subsidy would be unimpressive at 3 *tritai* per capita, being unsatisfactory as advance pay for a month when only two days *sitos* had already been provided. Rather than comprising three Chian tetradrachms or ca. 46.8 g of silver, it now provides only 9.8 g. Instead of ten or more days of advance payment at a rate of an Attic drachm each day, it has dropped to two or more days forward pay.

of the Aiginetan *mna*, see Figueira, *Excursions* 74–75. This Thucydidean passage is further confirmation for the conclusion there.

[17] Thompson in *NC* (1971) comes to no firm conclusion; his discussion of likely amounts of tribute and these subsidies is not very fruitful, even if we ignore his insistence on seeing the Milesians as using a subsidy of Chian pentedrachms. W. Weiser, "Die Eulen von Kyros dem Jüngeren zu den ersten Münzporträts lebender Menschen," *ZPE* 76 (1989) 267–96, esp. 287 with note 97, has made a similar suggestion that draws in Attic coinage. He suggests that 3 Chian "fortieths" were worth 10 Attic dr., an exchange rate that slightly overvalues Attic coins and exceeds the usual 7:10 Aiginetic:Attic ratio. The *pentedrakhmia* was one half the military stipend of three "fortieths" and was equivalent to 6 Chian dr.

[18] M. Lang, "Numerical Notation on Greek Vases," *Hesperia* 25 (1956) 1–24, esp. #62 on p. 14.

[19] Hardwick, *Chios* 147–48; Hardwick *ICN* 11.215, 218 (note 46); Hardwick, *NAC* (1996) 64–65.

Finally, the *pentedrakhmia* mentioned in 406 can no longer involve Chian coinage, unless we can bring ourselves to believe that the *pentedrakhmia* could be an ordinary term for a payment of 15 *tritai*.

Therefore, if we return to the traditional explanation of the Chian "fortieth" and *pentedrakhmia*, a further point may be raised, that is, the casual character of their introduction into the texts of Thucydides and Xenophon. The *tesserakostē* and the *pentedrakhmia* must have been conventional terms for referring to Chian currency within a context where its value in terms of Aiginetan money was significant. Paying military personnel, and especially Peloponnesian soldiers, in terms of money on the Aiginetic standard was a well-established practice. The very dissidents from Chios who sympathized with the Spartan cause made a payment in Aiginetan staters for the Peloponnesian war effort, probably to Alkidas in 426 (Meiggs-Lewis 67.9–10; note pp. 121–22 with note 32 above).

One alternative would be to modify Hardwick's hypothesis of a later introduction of the tetradrachm to allow an inauguration before 411, premising their innovation on an intention to facilitate Chian cooperation with Peloponnesian military forces during the Ionian War. This conjecture would draw support from the pattern of mints changing over to the Aiginetic standard among Attic tributaries during the period of general rebellion from 412. Nevertheless, the term *tesserakostē* seems to have been familiar in 411, suggesting that the correlations between the Chian and Aiginetan monetary systems gained currency during the heyday of the *arkhē*. One may choose to return to a date just before 429/8 for the tetradrachms, thinking of *IG* I^3 383.27–28, but an introduction in 425–20 appears to be the lowest option to allow time for establishing the conventional character of the term *tesserakostē*.

The new order of denominations (tetradrachms, drachms, and triobols) initiated by the Chians may represent a more useful selection of coins of different sizes. As such, the new system may well be serving in response to shortages of local coin. Yet as a next step in our argument regarding the interaction of Chian and foreign coins, consider whether the choice of the tetradrachm as the largest coin was not in some part intended to create a coin suitable and acceptable for transfers of largish sums between those employing the Chian standard and users of the Aiginetic coin standard. Granted that amounts of 2 and 4 didrachms could have served equally well for the *tesserakostē* and the *pentedrakhmia*, there may also have been both practical and psychological reasons why a single coin that was equivalent to a fortieth of an Aiginetic *mna* might have had special utility. Outside of wages for personnel, a putative ease in coping with taxation or in calculating interest would merely head a list of possibilities. Under this hypothesis, the shift in the size of denominations at Chios would become another example of monetary consolidation during the mid-fifth century, although it is hardly so dramatic an example as ceasing minting or changing standard to the Euboeic/Attic metrological system.

This conjecture would then raise a further query. Why does Chios differ from its neighbors by its facilitation of exchange with the users of the Aiginetic standard, while other allies both symbolically and pragmatically make adjustments to bring themselves into a correlation with the Athenians and their Euboeic/Attic standard? The Chians as autonomous allies would not have been concerned about gathering sufficient Attic coinage to pay their tribute. Chios had a large economy by any standard for fifth-century *poleis*, including a comparison with other allied states. So a considerable amount of Attic coinage may have been carried to Chios only to be exchanged for local money and recirculated to Attica, regardless of the status of Athenian money on the island. Nonetheless, if the Chians acted to make exchange with some users of the Aiginetic standard easier, the simplest reason may be that they lacked comparable concerns over their monetary exchanges with those accepting the validity of Athenian money. That might be interpreted as a hint that Athenian coins were in regular use and had validity, if not official recognition, in the Chian domestic economy.

To assess this possibility, however, we must make a detour to consider the role of Chian coins among the Athenians. Here, interesting literary evidence is embedded in an anecdote that now survives in the form of glosses or scholia. The extant versions are the following:

> ΣGregorius Nazianzanus, *Or.* I, *Contra Iulianum* (*MPG* 36.1212d): κίβδηλον. οὐ νόθον, ἀλλὰ καθαρὰν κὰι γνησίαν. εἴρηται ἀπὸ ἱστορίας. οἱ Ἀθηναῖοι Χίους μισοῦντες ἐν τοῖς ἀδοκίμοις ἑαυτῶν νομίσμασι Χ ἐγχαράττοντες ἐκάλουν χίβδαλα: εἶτα πρὸς τὸ εὐφωνότερον μετεβάλον τὸ Χ εἰς Κ.

> ΣAristophanes *Birds* 158b (Holwerda): κίβδηλα ἐλέγετο νομίσματα τὰ ὑπὸ Χίων δεδηλημένα, ἤτοι βεβλαμμένα, κατὰ τροπὴν τοῦ χ εἰς k. Ἀθηναῖοι γὰρ καὶ Χῖοι πρὸς ἀλλήλους ἐμάχοντο, διὸ τὰ Χίων νομίσματα μετὰ του χ στοιχείου Ἀθηναῖοι ἐγχαράξαντες ἀπεστρέφοντο, καὶ ἐκάλουν αὐτὰ χίβδηλα ὡς διὰ τοῦ χ στοιχείου δῆλα ὄντα. παραλαβοῦσα δὲ ἡ συνήθεια τὴν φωνὴν τὸ δεδολωμένον νόμισμα κίβδηλον ὠνόμασεν, ἐναλλάξασα τὰ στοιχεῖα πρὸς τὸ εὐγλωττότερον.

> *Etymologicum Magnum*, s.v. κίβδηλον (512.44–48: Gaisford): ἀπὸ ἱστορίας οἱ γὰρ Ἀθηναιοι τῷ πρὸς τοὺς Χίους μίσει φερόμενοι, ἐν τοῖς ἀδοκίμοις ἑαυτῶν νομίσμασι τὸν τοῦ χ τύπου ἐγχαράττοντες,

ἀπερρίπτον βδελυσσόμενοι. κυρίως δὲ λέγεται κίβδηλον, τὸ ὑπόχαλκον χρυσίον.

The story follows a familiar form, the false etymology.[20] A word, in this case κίβδηλος, whose affinities were mysterious to its contemporary users, is connected with an explanation that traces its origin to an event in political history. It turns out that κίβδηλος was initially χίβδηλος and was changed for the purposes of euphonious pronunciation. This etymology is patently fanciful (κίβδηλος was in use in the sixth century), especially in its uniting of what were probably two separate factual observations. Counterfeit or fraudulent coins were truly denominated by the term κίβδηλος. And it may well also be true that coins that were invalidated or marked unsuitable for use were disfigured by chisel strokes in which the most efficient manner of demonetizing the coin was crossing cuts in the form of the letter *chi*.

The frame for the story is likewise interesting for it derives the application of the X not from some practical motivation, as just suggested, but from the first letter of the name Χῖοι. The action was supposedly taken when the Athenians were hostile to the Chians and were at war with them. The Athenians were better known for their friendship and admiration for the Chians as the chief members of their alliance. Aristophanes compliments them himself later in the *Birds* (879–880). Scholion 880b (Holwerda) provides other evidence, citing Eupolis, Hypereides, Theopompus, and Thrasymachus on the high standing of the Chians with the Athenians, which included the tendering of prayers on the Chian behalf. There were two notorious occasions when the two peoples were conducting hostilities with each other: during the Ionian War, when the Chians led the defection of the allies in 412, and during the Social War in the late 350s.

The glosses differ over the implication whether it was Athenian or Chian coins that were thus disfigured. It is uncertain whether these are true variants or one story is a simplification made by intermediaries who did not fully comprehend the tradition. Imagining that the coins were Athenian, we can make nothing more of the story, because the Athenians were merely adopting the initial letter of Χῖοι out of pure malice. The other story interests us more, namely, that the coins were Chian. It represents not only a mythographical *lectio difficilior*, less likely to be invented, but links the Chian identity of the Athenian enemy more integrally to the etymological derivation of the word κίβδηλος.

20 Cf. *Suda* s.v. κιβδηλία, κ 1573 Adler; κίβδηλον, κ 1575.

We need not concern ourselves with deciding whether it is likely that the Athenians actually invalidated Chian coins by intercrossing chisel cuts and made a play on words out of the resulting *chi* shapes (cf. p. 540 with note 4 below). That could be embellishment intended to make the etymology of κίβδηλος work or it could be the genuine dark humor of a military crisis. Rather, it is significant to note that the background to the anecdote takes for granted that Chian money was valid in Attica. The Chians had a leading and favorable status among Athenian allies. As we shall see from our discussion of Aristophanes *Birds* 1040–41, allied states sometimes recognized the validity of Attic coins by virtue of agreement. Unlike some subject or tributary allies, the Chians may have enjoyed reciprocity through their autonomous status. The contemporary hostility of the Chians to Athens naturally voided all diplomatic agreements between the two states, including any *symbolai* governing economic interaction (there being a prominent role for *symbolai* in governing relations with the autonomous). In our anecdote, valid Chian coins were reduced to the status of fraudulent coins by the affixing of a *chi*; Athenians would no longer be compelled to honor them.

The provenience of the anecdote is unknown, but a gloss appearing in a variety of settings could descend through Alexandrian scholarship from an Atthidographer. Note the introductory "signature" ἀπὸ ἱστορίας. A contextual detail like Chian coins moving from legality to invalidation might be historical, serving as a basis in fact for the etymological elaboration. It is not important to fix the chronology of an invalidation of Chian money, since any recognition of Chian money during the Second Confederacy of the fourth century (and invalidation amid the hostilities of the 350s) would in all likelihood be owed to a revival of agreements formulated during the *arkhē*. Such a recognition of the validity of Chian money did not mean that Chian coins were used much in Attica (despite *IG* I^3 383.27–28); no evidence suggests that they were. Market forces would have encouraged the Chians, as they did others, to use Athenian coins in Attica. The legal status of Chian coins was no guarantee of convenience of use. Finally, the validity of Chian coins in Attica, if this hypothesis is correct, would be balanced by the validity that has been suggested for Attic coins on Chios.

According to Barron and Kraay, bridging the two phases of Chian coining during the fifth century was a single issue of electrum staters (attested by a single coin) that is argued to possess affinities with both the didrachms and the tetradrachms. Baldwin, who surveyed the earlier chronologies that spanned the period from the Persian invasion and its aftermath into the early fourth century, established the "transitional" character of this coin. Barron points to the bulbous-necked amphora (in his view) portrayed on the coin and the lack of differentiation of the wing feathers of the sphinx as early features, while the physique of the sphinx with a column leg is reminiscent of the later tetradrachms. The wreath of vine surrounding the obverse is found on an early issue of tetradrachms. Yet the raising of the foreleg of the sphinx is a feature inherited from earlier series of electrum. This suggests a degree of traditionalism about this emission. In this issue on the Chian standard (allowing us to assign it to that mint), a fairly standard Chian obverse has been coupled with a "mill sail" style of incuse square for the reverse. That is an affinity with Cyzicene electrum staters. The Chian coin was found in a hoard with Cyzicenes. The weight of the coin is the same as that of Lampsacene electrum staters (Lampsakos long having used the same standard as Chios). This late electrum issue has been seen by Barron and Kraay as an attempt to preserve monetary independence by sidestepping the Coinage Decree through a shift in output of coinage into a metal not covered by the enactment.

Setting stylistic considerations aside for a moment, seeking a causation for this isolated electrum issue in the Coinage Decree is a curious hypothesis. Chios had produced earlier series of electrum coins, and there can be no suspicion that foreign relations, let alone an exercise of foreign hegemony, prompted their production. Why then should we seek a different background for the electrum issue during the Attic hegemony? Is it not more reasonable to assume that reasons similar to those motivating earlier issues of electrum were again implicated in the decision to coin in the alloy? For instance, the Chians seem to have issued an "alliance" coinage in electrum during the Ionian Revolt that was probably intended to subvene their contingent with the rebel fleet. The unique electrum stater issue of Mytilene is generally connected with the subsidization of military activity during the defection from Athens in the Archidamian War, and perhaps especially in the recruitment and support of mercenary troops raised in the Propontis and the Black Sea region. Both the Chian and the Mytilenaean staters have reverses that suggest efforts to give them currency in the area where Cyzicenes were a preferred medium for business. Finally, we have already seen that electrum coins were in general a medium of some prominence for the payment of military personnel.

Since the late issue in electrum shows affinities with the latest didrachms as well as the following tetradrachms, there is no reason prima facie why its time of minting cannot have coincided with either series, once the absolute sway of a prohibition of allied minting in silver, engineered by the Coinage Decree, is suspended during our investigation. It is fairly clear in any case that the prompting for the electrum issue, now represented by a single surviving coin, must be a single incident and not an effort to circumvent an Attic decision or policy. More traces would probably have been left by the necessarily *sustained* attempt to resist (albeit passively) the Coinage Decree by a shift away from minting silver. As will be seen, a revisionist reconstruction of the sense of the Coinage Decree could remove the necessity for the whole Chian exercise in resistance.

A military setting should be sought in which the Chians might have been motivated to defray the expenses of forces either enlisted at short notice or mobilized in unusual numbers.[21] It is possible that the time frame of 450–12 can be narrowed, especially if an observation of Hardwick is given its due weight. He observes that the amphora portrayed on the wreathed silver tetradrachm is in fact of the straight-necked variety and that the same type probably appeared on the related electrum stater.[22] In that case, the Egyptian expedition or the aftermath to its defeat look too early (in 454/3?) to qualify as the emergency when Chios had to take special action. The Samian revolt might possibly fit the bill, as the Chians are known to have assisted the Athenians in 441/0 at fairly short notice (Thuc. 1.116.1–2; DS 12.27.4; cf. Thuc. 1.117.2; DS 12.28.2). With the possibility that the didrachms might extend to the eve of the Peloponnesian War and with Hardwick urging their continuation down to 425, a special striking of coins with particular utility for the Chian military effort could be dated at any stage of the Archidamian War.[23] There is no strong reason to opt for the date of 425 just to allow for the imposition of a ban on minting silver through the Coinage Decree. Nor ought we to follow Hardwick in placing the electrum stater and the wreathed tetradrachm in 412, with the wreath as a celebration of the successful revolt. That symbol would be an unusually hybristic gesture for the prudent Chians (cf. Thuc. 8.24.2), given the vigor of the Athenian military reactions toward Chios in the Ionian War (Thuc. 8.15–24). One should still regard Chios as a continuously active mint, although its output may have slackened in the last third of the century, a common numismatic phenomenon for states allied with Athens.

[21] Cf. Figueira, *Aegina* 91–95.

[22] Hardwick, *Chios* 162–65, cf. 188–95; Hardwick *ICN* 11.216–18.

[23] Considerable controversy has enveloped the electrum issue as to its affinities with the emissions of other mints, especially Lampsakos and Kyzikos, a determination on which has also yielded a considerable range of dates. See also A. Baldwin, "The Electrum and Silver Coins of Chios," *AJN* 48 (1914) 1–60, esp. 44.

SAMOS

Samos is fittingly the last of the allied mints for our consideration. This *polis* possessed a rich numismatic tradition that accompanied a large economy, but a complex of political factors make a reconstruction of the Attic involvement with Samian minting difficult, although promising as a window onto imperial monetary history. The reigning interpretation is provided by the important monograph of Barron, although some of his conclusions have been controversial since his publication in 1966. Superficially, his reconstruction should be nonproblematical for the oldest interpretative tradition on the Coinage Decree, because he has autonomous Samos continue minting after a decree in the early 440s. Barron, however, believes in the applicability of the Coinage Decree (in its traditional interpretation) to Samos and the other autonomous allies. Hence his reconstruction of the sequence of Samian issues subsumes a striking anomaly.

At issue are Samian-weight tetradrachms that bear a lion's mask or scalp on the obverse. The starting point for this series is unclear; Barron assigns his class II to 482/1–478/7. Although Price and Waggoner suspect that Barron's gap between class I (which he dated to 494/3–490/89) and class II did not exist,[24] they observe that the material from the Asyut Hoard (*IGCH* #1644: ca. 475) confirms the initial date for class II, noting the interesting overstrike on an Aiginetan turtle stater with a small skew reverse. The cluster of Samian overstrikes on Aiginetan staters in the Asyut Hoard betray the conditions of the 480s. They number 2 out of 7 class I tetradrachms and 3 or 4 out of 11 class II coins. Huge expenditures were made on Aigina for defense preparations in response to an Attic attack on the island, probably in 488. There was a parallel spike in Samian spending (perhaps starting in mid-decade or a little later) to fulfill the military duties of a Persian subject state. Accordingly, some of the many Aiginetan staters in circulation were hurriedly restruck at Samos.

Barron's date for the inception of class III, ca. 477/6, looks correct. These coins carry a shoulder or protome of an ox on their reverse that is usually accompanied by a symbol (wheel, helmet, anchor). Sometimes, interestingly, the ethnic identifier ΣAM or ΣAMION appears in lieu of a symbol. The first subgroup of class III, issues ii–v, is die linked. Barron's analysis seems appropriate: this subgroup represents the earliest emissions of Samos in the Delian League.

[24] See also Hurter and Pászthory, *Festschrift Mildenberg* 119. J.P. Barron, "The Silver Coins of Samos Come of Age," *Kraay-Mørkholm Essays* 9–22, esp. 13–14, now dates class I to 500–485.

The next subgroup, class III, issues vi–x, is not die linked. That may indicate a situation where annual mintings were spaced out amid intervals of suspension. The olive branch of issue viii might symbolize the great victory of Kimon at Eurymedon and a spacing out of emissions could well bring these coins into the later 460s, a period of comparative peace for Samos. Barron, however, notes the appearance of class III coins, including issue viii, in the Decadrachm Hoard.[25] That might create a tight fit for this chronology. He prefers to see Eurymedon reflected in issue xiii, with its *aphlaston* symbol, but his date for the battle of 464 is too late.

The owl of issue x is placed by Barron in ca. 465/4, but might instead allude to Samian participation in the great Attic/Ionian victories over the Peloponnesians in 459 (with the coins celebrating an Athenian-sponsored distribution of booty?). Issue x is die linked both to a following issue marked by an *astragalos* 'knuckle-bone' on the reverse and to an anomalous issue (for this period) that bears no reverse symbol. This latter was apparently a large striking: Barron reports 9 coins, but 5 reverse dies. This intensity of minting, along with the tokens of carelessness and speed of production that Barron notices in the owl and the *astragalos* issues, might indicate a surge in military activity on Samos that was perhaps owed to a shouldering of more of the responsibility for allied efforts in Egypt, while the Athenians were heavily committed to combat in Greece against the Peloponnesians. If so, this was a brief flurry, as indicated by two smaller issues (xiii and xiv) that follow, with symbols, an *aphlaston* and a shield. The end of class III could be put in the middle to late 450s. Contrast Barron's dating for these coins in ca. 462/1 and 461/0. Mattingly achieves a similar result by comparing the sequence of Samian trihemiobols that picture amphoras to actual storage amphoras for oil, with the result that the middle of class III (vi–vii) comes down below 460.[26]

Class IV has stylistic affinities with the preceding coins (the incuse circle on the reverse and the lumpiness of the flan), but it also introduces an olive branch that will become a permanent feature of the succeeding classes. The symbols that marked the previous class of mint output disappear. The mint may have shifted into a more regular, possibly annual mode of striking and did without the symbols that had differentiated earlier separated issues. Class IV is linked with the larger succeeding class V

[25] *Kraay-Mørkholm Essays* 15.

[26] Mattingly, *BSA* (1981) 81–82. Cf. Barron, *Silver Coins* 71, 198. It is hard to speak conclusively about the trihemiobols because of their size. Moreover, we cannot be sure that Samian oil amphoras evolved consistently toward elongation and slimness of profile.

and it is even conceivable that these two groupings overlap chronologically. Class V introduces an incuse square and a fixed relationship of the dies, and class VI, where an olive branch begins as a continuing feature, is linked with class V. One artist is identified by Barron as beginning work in the latter part of class V, and his hand is seen in both succeeding classes.

If the olive branch here is a symbol of victory, then we must cast about for an occasion of suitable magnitude to render this motif a lasting feature of Samian coin design. Barron places these three classes of coins (IV–VI) in ca. 460/59–454/3, and it is highly unlikely that they can be any earlier; my previous suggestions would lower their dates five to ten years. In this period, an appropriate victory in which the Samians participated lies ready to hand: the important victory of the Delian League at Cypriot Salamis during Kimon's last expedition to the island, probably in 450/49 (Thuc. 1.112.2–4; [Simonides] *AP* 7.296; DS 12.3.1–4.6; Plut. *Cimon* 18.1–19.2; Nepos *Cimon* 3.4).

This chronology would entail rejecting Barron's suggestion that the ornamental collars worn by the oxen on the reverses of class VI allude to a hypothetical coup sprung by Samian oligarchs in 453 at the festival of Hera. Not only is it doubtful that Samos had a democracy to be overthrown at that time, but it is also improbable that the advertisement of such a sacrilegious act would be made in this way.[27] His association of the collars with the Heraia is, however, attractive. Do these coins allude to a particularly elaborate celebration of the festival (after the winding down of the war with the Persians?) or specifically to a special consignment of oxen sacrificed to the goddess? In any case, classes IV–VI may be seen as being minted in the 440s.[28]

Thus, we are brought to the crucial lettered class (class VII) that seems to number at least fourteen years from Β–Ξ (as marked in the bottom right-hand corner of the reverse). Barron begins this enumeration with 453/2 and ends it in 440/39 with the Samian revolt. There was never an "Α" year, and the first year of the sequence or the year just preceding the series—depending on how one interprets the political significance of this threshold—was occupied by a single year of class VI, carrying the reverses with oxen bearing ornamental collars. A die link connects class VI and the Β issue. I prefer a second possibility, however, which is raised by Barron himself, that a small "Α"

[27] Note the skepticism of H. Plommer in his review of Barron, *CR* 81 (1967) 212–14, seconded by Mattingly *BSA* (1970) 144–45.

[28] Mattingly's observations on the class VI tetradrachm found in *IGCH* #1647, "Naucratis," dating the coin to ca. 440 and the hoard to the 430s, are apposite (*BSA* [1970] 142–45; *JHS* [1981] 83–85). Compare pp. 123–24 above.

issue used the same obverse die (A 32) as the last class VI coins and the first of the "B" issue. After all, the surviving "Δ" issue is represented by a single coin in Barron's catalogue so that a small "A" issue may have left no surviving representative. That small change alone would throw off the neat chronology proposed by Barron.

Die links have led Barron to observe several interesting anomalies: coins with a panther's head in place of a letter seem to have been struck between the "I" and "H" issues, and a small group with no distinguishing mark could be placed between the "H" and "Θ" issues. Neither group has its own year in Barron's system. There are a number of explanations for their differentiation: either these coins (and perhaps those with an ivy leaf, discussed immediately below) were put into circulation via a different track from the lettered series; or they were targeted toward a specific constituency; or the coins were restricted to a particular and limited context. The evidence is lacking for a solid hypothesis, but these coins help us, nonetheless, with an important observation. The existence of the lettered coins should not convince us that such enumeration had an essentially constitutional valence, or the lettered series would not have been interrupted for (or disrupted by or intermingled with) these small issues.

There is, however, a further complication. A coin bearing an ivy leaf has been placed by Barron between the *lambda* and *mu* issues, in which the ivy leaf has usurped the position of the letter. This coin also carries a *rho* between the forelegs of the ox. Barron resists the easy conclusion that this coin is the scanty remnant of the last of the lettered series. Either the coins from the *omicron*, the *pi*, and the *koppa* issues have been lost or those letters marked years in which no minting was undertaken. He holds that the stylistic affinities put the coin (exhibiting a unique die pair) amid the "Λ" and "M" issues as the end of the "Λ" issue. These stylistic similarities are not probative, inasmuch as only a few years difference is at issue in any case.[29] The possibility of a suspension of minting (for the three years without extant examples) could have slowed stylistic evolution. Once again, an extension of the lettered series is a viable alternative (as Kraay has insisted). On the principle that the lettered series represents a single succession that was augmented by small series with different purposes and contexts marked by symbols, the format of the issue marked with an ivy leaf and with a *rho* may denote the intersecting of the main series and a "special-interest" emission (as defined above).

For Barron, the lettered series terminates with the revolt of the island, but had begun with an oligarchic coup that followed, during 453,

[29] Mattingly, *JHS* (1981) 82, supports Barron's reconstruction.

the Samian proposal to move the treasury of the Delian League from Delos to Athens (presumably in 454/3, but contrast below, pp. 267–269, 458–63). As he was a believer in a mid-century Coinage Decree, Barron's ordering of the lettered series requires that he hold that the Samians were in violation of the prohibition on minting silver down to their revolt. This supposition is certainly not impossible historically, and we would have no difficulty believing it, if (for example) Thucydides had vouched for it. Unfortunately, it is a conclusion that is forbidden to students of fifth-century history in the environment created by the survival of our data, as we must work back from an absence of effects toward an absence of (legislated) causes or simply leave off entirely any speculation about cause and effect in Attic hegemonic jurisdiction (and regarding the Coinage Decree in particular).[30]

Terminating the lettered series in 440/39 was not the received opinion before Barron's work: Head placed the lettered series between 421 and 409, Babelon after 431, and Gardner after 428. Robinson thought it began no later than 430, if not earlier. More recently, Kraay harmonized the view of the earlier scholarship that the lettered series belongs later in the century with the advances in stylistic understanding offered by Barron's monograph. Believing that, at a minimum, a seventeen-year series ([A]–Ξ + 2 years for special issues) and, more probably, a twenty-one-year series ([A]–P + 2 years) must be accommodated, Kraay placed the lettered tetradrachms ca. 435–15.[31] That left a short gap in the early 430s, right after the Samian revolt. Mattingly also places the lettered series (Barron's class VII) and its introductory group (class VI) after the suppression of the Samian revolt.[32]

For Kraay, the lettered series ended not long, if at all, before the Attic weight tetradrachms that most scholars (following, most notably, Robinson) have put after 412, in the period of close cooperation between the Samian democrats and the Athenian (antioligarchic) fleet based on the island. The views expressed above about the length of the lettered series and the correlations of earlier coins with external events fit better with this later chronology for the lettered coins. Among these correlations is the notable suggestion that the appearance of the olive branch ought

[30] The arguments ex silentio against this hypothetical defiance of Athens by the Samians can be elaborated at will; note H. Plommer in his review of Barron in *CR* 81 (1967) 212–14.

[31] Kraay, *ACGC* 240–42, 332–34. Cf. Kagan, *Coinage and Administration* 23–24. Kraay's further suggestion that the alternative usage of round and square incuse reverses are political indicators of oligarchy and democracy is improbable.

[32] Mattingly *JHS* (1981) 81–85.

to celebrate the last victories over the Persians or, for those inclined to believe in its historicity, the Peace of Kallias.

There is another noteworthy ramification of this view of the lettered series. Barron's class VIII.b has coins that carry the inscription ΕΠΙΒΑΤΙΟΣ on the top of the reverse, presumably to be understood as "in the magistracy of Batis." They should be linked with oligarchic Samians who established themselves at Anaia on the mainland. Although some oligarchs might have fled to the mainland as early as the aftermath of the great revolt, both Barron and Kraay note the stylistic link (in the modeling of the mane and forehead of the lion) of this issue with Samian Attic-standard tetradrachms, and place these exile coins just before 412. The coins were minted during the war years when the Samian exiles at Anaia are known to have been active (Thuc. 3.32.2; 4.75.1).

Morever, the other section of class VIII can be brought into the same pattern of explanation. Class VIII.a is linked by the aforesaid treatment of lion's face to both class VIII.b and class IX, the coins on the Attic standard. The single specimen of class VIII.a bears an "A" on the lower reverse that Barron would see as an abbreviation for 'Αναιΐτων. Yet the Samian aristocrats based at Anaia must have pretended to some claim to the legitimate leadership of the Samian government so that it is highly unlikely that they would have styled themselves without resorting to the ΣΑ (*vel sim.*) denotation of earlier coins, in a manner just like the pretensions of other groups of elite exiles. In addition, coming after the lettered series, of which examples would still have been in circulation (even if we accept Barron's early chronology), an *alpha* symbol would undoubtedly imply the first year of a new series.

Thus, three related developments may have occurred in close conjunction with the events of 412 and 411. When the Samian democrats rose against the oligarchs in 412 (Thuc. 8.21; cf. DS 13.34.2 for echoes of elite restiveness on Samos), they initiated a new lettered series, starting with an *alpha* to signify their new regime. It is quite possible that this was a deliberate disjuncture with the last issues of the prior lettered series, which had still been in progress during the years just preceding. Of the Samian exiles that fled in 412 (400 according to Thucydides), many will have fled to Anaia. Hence the issue of the Anaiitai (class VIII.b: the ΕΠΙ ΒΑΤΙΟΣ coins) copy contemporary Samian tetradrachms (class VIII.a). The next year, there occurred an attempt to overthrow the Samian government in conjunction with the oligarchic conspiracy at Athens that was suppressed through the combined efforts of Samian democrats and Athenian democrats serving in the fleet (Thuc. 8.63.3–4, 73.1–6). Thereafter, the Samians broke off their new series and commenced striking coins on the Attic standard.

The adoption of the Attic standard was not only expressive of the now closer solidarity between the Samian *dēmos* and the Athenian *dēmos*, but also reflected the economic situation. The Attic fleet had its main overseas base on Samos and its personnel was paid and spent wages in Attic coins. The Samians could more easily conduct their own renewed military activities (as a recently autonomous ally) in coins on the Attic standard, especially sharing in the procurement of supplies and in enlisting naval crews. If they were conducting their financial affairs on the Attic standard, the Samians could also more easily capture the spending of Attic military personnel through taxes, and then account for and handle that income. The Samian democrats obviated a fiscal situation that had the potential for a problem in the exchange of currency by a monetary consolidation. If the change in standard was additionally interpreted as an act of ideological solidarity with the Athenians, that reading was in keeping with Samian populist sympathies and marked a suitable response to the measures taken by the Athenians in favor of the Samian *dēmos*.

Thus, if we are forced to choose whether the lettered series (Barron's class VII) preceded or followed the Samian revolt, the foregoing discussion firmly supports placing them after the suppression of the revolt. That conclusion has important corollaries for Attic monetary policy. Samos gives no comfort for those who believe in a mid-century ban on allied coining of silver. By anyone's reckoning, the Samians were striking silver through the 440s. There are a number of responses to this situation. We may reinterpret the Coinage Decree to remove the prohibition on minting silver, as will be attempted below. Or we can redate the decree to the 420s, and deny a date to the lettered series in this period. Or we can deny that the decree was applicable to autonomous allies.

If the decree is redated to the 420s, that choice will not necessarily get us out of our problems about the Samian mint. Starting from 439/8, the fifteen to twenty-one years necessary for the lettered series would take us at least to the Peace of Nikias.[33] Moreover, no one would be very surprised if there was a gap in coining of a few years after 439, as Erxleben believes.[34] It would not be the result of the application of a

[33] Mattingly, *JHS* (1981) 85, makes the lettered series terminate neatly in 425/4, when the Coinage Decree was passed.

[34] See Erxleben *AfP* (1970) 82.

short-lived prohibition on minting silver. Just as in the case of Thasos, the dislocations attendant on a siege of the city and its surrender might be ample cause for an interval, but one that would not necessarily entail that coining was forbidden during this interruption.

This solution fits the phenomena rather well. It accommodates the lowered dates for classes III–VII that are probably needed. As the Samians paid their indemnity to defray the costs of their rebellion for the first few years after their surrender (*IG* I^3 68.21–25; 369.42–43; 370.18–20 [??]; 371.16–17; 375.34–37 [??]; cf. *IG* I^3 363), their need to focus on amassing Attic tetradrachms and to concentrate official energy on repairing the damage done to the Samian economy and revenues by their defeat were reflected in some years of no minting. Sometime later in the 430s, the Samians began to mint the lettered series. Those coins reached down into the period after the Peace of Nikias, when they may have faltered (or were not needed) in the years for which no lettered coins at all have come down to us. In any case, the last year of these coins was probably the *rho* issue that bore the ivy-leaf (in honor of Dionysos?). These coins did not precede by much Barron's classes VIII and IX that belong in 412–11 and following. In addition, this interpretation has the advantage of positing no substantial constitutional changes that are not supported by strong evidence, since the lettered series may be the coinage of the "oligarchic" regime that was overthrown in 412.[35]

Furthermore, even if we exempt the autonomous states from the force of a prohibition on minting silver, we are still not free of problems over Samos, because it lost its autonomy in 439. That change in status compels Barron's situating of the lettered series before 440 and a creation of something like his hypothesis of Samian defiance of a prohibition on minting. Besides its a priori improbability, that suggestion inevitably leads to circular reasoning. The Samians want to coin because autonomy and coining are tightly conjoined, but, in that case, why did the Athenians

[35] Caution is, however, required, since the distinction of Samian regimes as democracies and oligarchies, which is admittedly based on the ancient sources, probably does scant justice to the complexity of the political and social situation on the island, where factions may have ranged over a considerable spectrum in their views on the distribution of rights and access to decision making. Nor are we certain over the feelings of propriety invested in different categories of Samian coins by partisan groupings. Hence, a demonstration by some future discovery that one of Barron's categories (including the lettered series) spanned a constitutional change ought not to be held beyond possibility. For Samian government in this period, see most recently the overview of G. Shipley, *A History of Samos: 800–188 B.C.* (Oxford 1987) 113–22.

defy convention and apply the prohibition to the autonomous allies as well as to the tributaries?

The Samian mint should be seen to exhibit the familiar features of monetary consolidation that have been envisaged for other allies in the *arkhē*. The number of dies known for the Samian-standard coins of the Pentekontaeteia are probably insufficient to stock the complete money supply of an economy that was the size of the Samian economy. A mixture of other currencies probably was used on the island, including Attic coins, electrum coinage, and perhaps Aiginetan and Chian coins. The series with distinctive symbols may indicate some targeting of local issues toward certain particular channels of distribution. The shift to the Attic standard during the Ionian War is a dramatic example of monetary convergence with the Athenians.

6

WAS MINTING SILVER EVER PROHIBITED?

ALTHOUGH THE FINAL SECTION of this work will discuss the evolution of consolidation of monetary and metrological standards among the city-states of the Delian League and Athenian *arkhē*, it is useful to consider briefly here where the results of our numismatic investigations have left us concerning the traditional interpretations of the Coinage Decree.

In my category VII of continuous minters, I list thirteen states.[1] Let us consider these mints with regard to the hypothesis of a prohibition on the allied minting of silver either around mid-century or in the late 420s. The Aiginetan mint is strong evidence against a mid-century prohibition on allied minting of silver, but is of no help to us in deciding about a ban after the outbreak of the Peloponnesian War, because of the extinction of an independent Aigina. In addition, one might query the pertinence of several other mints for this review. Ephesos was a possible interrupted mint, and the Lycian minters may have lain outside the limits of Athenian influence. Ainos and Mende have been classed as continuous mints, but they have some affinities with our next group, states that minted coins below the weight of the stater, for there may have been intervals in the production of heavier coins by Ainos and Mende.

The cities that coined fractions throughout the period of the Attic hegemony, however, provide substantial weight against the theory of any forbidding of allied minting. There are six strong candidates for coining throughout the second half of the fifth century (category IVC).[2] Kyzikos, a mint better known for its electrum issues, also seems to have minted silver fractions continuously. There were several cities that seem to have stopped and resumed the striking of coins; some were coiners of small denominations, such as Kolophon (probably), Knidos, or Skepsis, where the minting of anything over the drachm weight is

[1] Abdera, Aigina, Ainos, Akanthos, Aspendos, Chios, Ephesos, Kelenderis, Lykioi, Maroneia, Mende, Samos, and Teos.

[2] Ialysos, Kalkhedon, Kameiros, Kebren, Miletos, and Torone. From these, Kebren might be subtracted for the meagerness of its issues and be considered an interrupted or intermittent mint. Kalkhedon might have started coining after a mid-century law or may represent another interrupted mint. The issues of the Rhodian mints are meager later in the century, and could be misplaced. Torone's coining may have ended with its capture in 424.

uncertain. Yet admittedly, there are attractions in attributing to these cities regularly intermittent sequences of output. The lack of refinement in present numismatic chronologies may have led to our "detection" of some intervals among the foregoing, while sparser data on other similar small mints make them appear to scholars as continuous.

Therefore, there were eleven mints that are strong counterindicators (in the present state of our knowledge) of the conclusion that any prohibition on minting silver ever existed.[3] Another eleven allies, while they do not give the appearance of copious, regular emissions, seem possible candidates for inclusion on a list of states unaffected by a legislated ban on minting.[4]

If we are evaluating a mid-century date for a prohibition on allied minting, the roster of mints unaffected by a ban on striking silver coins can be augmented. The great mint on Aigina is certainly to be reckoned as evidence against the ban. From the drachm/fractional minters summarized in category IVA, one can isolate a number of possibilities for unaffected mints: Aineia, Assos, Halikarnassos, Phaselis, Poteidaia, and possibly Astakos. Here also one might class the two Lesbian mints, Mytilene (certainly) and (quite possibly) Methymna. The better possibilities for exceptions to a conjectural mid-century prohibition should perhaps number twenty-four.[5] Other (less probative) evidence against a legislated ban is provided by seven allied mints.[6]

Sheer enumeration is thus a telling argument against the reigning line of interpretation on the Coinage Decree, namely, that it forbade the allies to mint silver at a point shortly after mid-century (consider Table 2.3 [pp. 88–91]), containing a synopsis of the scholarship on fifth-century minting, and the Appendix. The number of probable and possible mints that continue coining through the mid-century period exceeds the number of mints that may have ceased coining at that time by a count of over two to one on that reckoning (compare categories IIIC, IVA, and IVB). Even on the most liberal interpretation of the current evidence in favor of a prohibition, mints that remained active after 440 still exceeded all those terminating their coining between 455 and 440.

[3] Abdera, Ainos, Akanthos, Aspendos, Chios, Kelenderis, Kyzikos, Maroneia, Mende, Miletos, and Samos.

[4] Ephesos, Ialysos, Kalkhedon, Kameiros, Kebren, Knidos, Kolophon, Lykioi, Skepsis, Teos, and Torone. Teos and Torone are the group's strongest possibilities.

[5] Abdera, Aigina, Aineia, Ainos, Akanthos, Aspendos, Assos, Chios, Halikarnassos, Ialysos, Kameiros, Kalkhedon, Kebren, Kelenderis, Kyzikos, Maroneia, Mende, Miletos, Mytilene, Phaselis, Poteidaia, Samos, Teos, and Torone.

[6] Astakos, Ephesos, Knidos, Kolophon, Lykioi, Methymna, and Skepsis.

One more point deserves to be made on the quality of our evidence. The mints that appear to continue through 450 are generally better known than the mints that seem to end at that time. Hence, because of the additive nature of numismatic data, it is more probable that future discoveries will demonstrate some further activity for individual cities now classed as apparent terminators or interruptors than will prove that active mints had substantial intervals. A parallel quantitative argument has already been raised. The number of allied mints that close before 455 far outnumbers those mints that end striking between 455 and 440.

The foregoing observations on the states continuously minting during the fifth century ought to suffice for rejecting most of the other alternative dates for the Coinage Decree. There is no need to refute the hypothesis that a ban on minting silver promulgated ca. 435, for example, can be discerned in the archaeological record. That exercise would be tediously recapitulatory, a judgment standing equally for most of the other chronological options. We do, however, need to consider briefly a date in the late 420s, the chronology advanced by Mattingly and Erxleben (on epigraphical and political grounds).

Superficially, one might conclude from the synopses of minting activity presented above that the later the Coinage Decree is placed in the fifth century, the easier will be the task of demonstrating the possibility of its promulgation is made. The history of allied minting in the fifth century is admittedly the record of cities ending minting so that there are fewer active mints the later we cast our attention. Yet this observation accepts only one of the tests for the promulgation of a prohibition: the number of mints active after its supposed enactment. It neglects another test for a chronology of an enactment of the Coinage Decree, which is the number of mints that it terminated, for we must assume that there were mints that needed closing and indeed were terminated in order to argue that the Athenians would have gone to the trouble of legislating their closing in an act of general implication.

Placing aside the cases where cities stopped minting because of military operations in the Peloponnesian War (such as Poteidaia and Mytilene for silver), there are not many good examples of mints closed in the late 420s. Based on the foregoing discussion of minting activity (summarized in Tables 2.2 and 2.3 [pp. 84–91]), Aineia and Halikarnassos would be possible examples, with Phaselis a lesser possibility. We might also follow Mattingly in adding some northern mints such as Ainos or Mende, where emissions slackened, or the Samian mint, where, in contrast, intervals of a few years after 439/8 and during the period 420 to 412 seem to us the better option. Presumptive grounds for this classification would be that, once we bridge over hypothetical mid-century intervals, there are not enough series to fill out the century. Even then, we cannot create an impressive list of mints putatively closed by Attic legislation in 425–20

Moreover, another factor begins to influence our question once the perspective shifts to the end of the 420s. During the Peloponnesian War there was a revival of minting silver among allied cities, albeit usually a striking of drachms and fractions. That development can be traced to a variety of causes. Chief among them was the decline in the production of silver from Laureion. Also significant were the stresses on the Athenian economy and ensuing changes in patterns of expenditure by the Attic government, all of which were created by the scale of the hostilities (see below, pp. 496–521). Nonetheless, the allies who were beginning to mint smaller denominations constitute evidence against a traditionally interpreted Coinage Decree passed in the 420s.

The analysis of the previous chapters thus provides cold comfort for those wishing to date the Coinage Decree in the late 420s based on the numismatic data. Out of my roster of active minters either of larger denominations (category VII) or of smaller coins (category IVC), a number of possibilities can be identified for states both likely to be minting and probable members of the Attic sphere of control: Abdera, Ainos, Akanthos, Chios, Ephesos, Ialysos, Kalkhedon, possibly Kebren, Kyzikos, Maroneia, Mende, Miletos, Samos, Skepsis, Teos, and possibly Torone. To these, a group of allied states that seem to have had earlier interruptions in their production of coinage may be added. Numismatists have suggested that these allies resumed minting by 430: Antandros, Dardanos(?), Knidos, Kolophon, Methymna, Neapolis, and Thasos. One may also introduce some of the states in category II that might have initiated coining during the existence of the *arkhē* and before the late 420s: Aphytis, Elaia, Gargara, Pitane, and Tragilos. To these twenty-nine allies, one might group as possibly active mints not only Siphnos and Koressia, but the remaining states in category II (Gargara, Idyma, Lamponeia, Neandreia, Pordoselene, and Prokonnesos).

As more hoards are discovered and more mints are subjected to systematic review under the most advanced methodology, the picture of minting activity that is summarized above will evolve. The Appendix indicates the freshness of the present scholarship about the coining of individual cities. By comparing the entries there with Tables 2.2 and 2.3 summarizing the surveys of Robinson and Erxleben and other chronologies, the reader can judge the progress that has been made over the last twenty-five or fifty years and reach a prediction about the likely progress of scholarship in the *next* twenty-five or fifty years. To be sure, further evidence may encourage redatings that will break the continuity of some of these apparently active mints, but there is no real chance that the majority of them can ever be shown to have *all* ceased minting at one time, either in the early 440s or the late 420s (or at any other juncture that one would care to choose). Nor does it appear likely that we shall ever reduce the number of mints that continued to operate after some chosen moment, at which one dates the Coinage Decree, to the manageable handful that could be explained away by conjuring up specific reasons for excepting them from the force of the decree (revolts, special permission, and the like). We will never get the number of candidates for "defiance" of a supposed prohibition to be substantially outnumbered by the contemporary closings of mints.

However much one might be tempted to accede to the view that only a short break in coining will satisfy an understanding of the Coinage Decree as a prohibition of minting in silver—much skepticism has been devoted to this position above—it has to be rated improbable that enough breaks of this nature will ever be found among the exceptions to a ban on silver coining and especially among the continuous minters. The idea that these hypothetical breaks will all be coordinated with the interruptions of the other exceptions to the force of the decree beggars belief. If the "Decadrachm Hoard" (*CH* 8.48, "Elmali") turns out to be typical of the accessions to our knowledge that large newly discovered hoards can bring, then the future holds indications of more various fifth-century minting activity.

7

THE ATTIC MINT AND MONETARY OUTPUT

UNFORTUNATELY, we cannot approach the investigation of the monetary aspects of fifth-century Athenian political hegemony through an exhaustive review of the history of the Attic mint. The great number of surviving examples, scattered through the world's museums and private collections, and the stable or static character of the representational elements of Athenian coins render the exploration of the history of the mint at Athens a daunting prospect. A considerable range of minor variability is combined with a tremendous number of extant specimens, especially dating before 480 and after 460–50.[1]

THE ATHENIAN MINT IN THE PENTEKONTAETEIA

For the early part of the Attic hegemony, historians are, in contrast, fortunate to possess the short monograph of C.G. Starr that has also stimulated some important commentary in response.[2] The date for the termination of this period of early hegemonic coinage is controversial in a way that is significant for the history of Attic monetary affairs. Starr took the position, quite natural in the scholarly context in which he was writing, that the coin series of his study ended around mid-century and the massive issues of the succeeding period began in 449, the presumptive date for the passage of the Coinage Decree. He was reinforced in this view by his discussions with Kraay and Kraay's analysis of *IGCH* #1482, "Jordan" and #1645, "Zagazig."[3]

Nevertheless, the "Decadrachm Hoard" (*CH* 8.48, "Elmali") offers thirty-two (that is, a considerable number) of tetradrachms from Starr's group VA1, the inception of which was dated by Starr to 455 ("the last half of the 450s").[4] They were struck from thirteen obverse dies and twenty-five reverse dies, none of which were used for the specimens catalogued by Starr. Starr's dating would need to be adjusted if one accepts a date of

[1] Note, for example, J.H. Kroll, *The Greek Coins*, *The Athenian Agora* 26 (Princeton 1993) 4.

[2] C.G. Starr, *Athenian Coinage: 480-449* B.C. (Oxford 1970) as updated with Starr, "New Specimens of Athenian Coinage 480–449 B.C.," *NC* 142 (1982) 129–34.

[3] C.M. Kraay and P.R.S. Moorey, "Two Fifth Century Hoards from the Near East," *RN*[6] 10 (1968) 181–238, esp. 207–10.

[4] S. Fried, "The Decadrachm Hoard: An Introduction," in Carradice, *Coinage and Administration* 1–9, esp. 5–6.

465–60 for the "Decadrachm Hoard" on the basis of internal evidence. Kroll would bring the commencement of the massive issues into the 450s and associate them with the movement of the treasury to Attica in 454/3 (a particular conjunction that we may choose to condition: pp. 267–69, 458–63).[5] From the Agora material, he presents coin *8b*, a tetradrachm with an enlarged palmette and lettering on the reverse, discovered amid fill containing pottery down to the mid-century.[6] According to Kroll, on Starr's dating, such an example of the "slightly advanced stage of the standardized style" would be placed ca. 431. In light of its context, Kroll argues that *8b* was struck in the 440s and the earlier *8a* with more compact palmette and letters was minted in the 450s.[7]

The redating of the inception of increased minting in Attica stands against the theory of an absolute (or nearly absolute) prohibition on allied minting of silver just after the mid-century. The massive issues that supposedly responded to the passage of the Coinage Decree in fact preceded its earliest possible date. Rather, this higher chronology will prompt conjecture about Attic monetary history that is contributory to a revisionist interpretation in which no such prohibition was mandated. We start by noting that skepticism was quickly given, deservedly so, to the hypothesis of Starr that the lower monetary output prior to 449 (in his view) necessarily indicates Athenian impoverishment in the early years of the Delian League.[8] The magnitude of emissions of coins in major archaic and classical mints parallels the scale of governmental expenditures, especially when those expenditures are rising and reserves (public or private) are being converted to coin.[9] It does not necessarily reflect background economic vitality.

The 450s fit this paradigm, because they were a decade of combat for the Athenians, and there was fighting on two fronts, against both the Peloponnesians and the Persians. Moreover, most of the allies had shifted their contributions in the war efforts to the payment of tribute so that a larger proportion of the expenses of the Athenian/allied fleet

[5] Kroll, *Coins* 5–6, who notes that suspicion had been earlier directed against the date for the end of group V by H. Nicolet (briefly) in her review of Starr in *RPh*³ 48 (1974) 132–34 and by R.T. Williams, more forcefully, in his review in *Phoenix* 26 (1972) 411–12. Williams emphasizes the circularity of Kraay's dates for *IGCH* #1482, "Jordan" (ca. 445) and #1645, "Zagazig" (ca. 450).

[6] Note the catalogue entries and their notes in Kroll, *Coins* 17.

[7] Kroll compares *8a* with Starr 1′-3′ and *8b* with 4′-5′ (all illustrated on Starr, Pl. XXII), for which see Starr, *Coinage* 72–75.

[8] See the reviews of Starr, *Coinage* by C.M. Kraay, *NC*⁷ 12 (1972) 313–17; J.F. Healy, *CR* 23 (1973) 252–54.

[9] Note Figueira, *Aegina* 108–16.

were disbursed in Attic coin. By the late 450s, there was only the possibility that the Chians and the Samians might be handling the finances of their fleets in their own silver coin. The insular allies who are absent from the records of the first assessment period were probably conducting their military finances in terms of Attic money in any event (see also pp. 559–60 below),[10] and perhaps the same was true even for the Methymnians, whose mint was probably closed at this time. While the Mytileneans, who were no longer minting coins heavier than the drachm, might in principle have used electrum *hectae* for military allowances and pay, they could with equal probability have been employing Attic tetradrachms as the chief medium for the pay of their military personnel. Even the states with electrum mints probably dealt with most military expenses other than payments to personnel in Attic silver.

We might contrast the monetary and fiscal situation in the 460s. It was at that time that Athens was issuing decadrachms. Starr classifies these coins in his group IIC and reasonably associates them with Kimon's great victory at Eurymedon.[11] These striking coins with their distinctive reverses will not have been an emergency issue to support the mobilization of the league fleet, as there is no particular rationale in that case for the weight of the coins. Nor is the historical context suggestive of an emergency mobilization. Rather decadrachms were a means of allocating the booty from the campaign in which the large denomination of the coins was an advantage.[12] This coinage was a large one, as the eleven coins listed by Starr are all unique die pairs and, given the weight of the coins, each die would probably have struck much more silver in its useful life than the dies for tetradrachms. The "Decadrachm Hoard" has confirmed this impression by adding five new obverse dies. Fried has observed that the some of the decadrachm dies also have affinities with the group III tetradrachms that follow, which suggests (in her view) a "one-time commemorative minting." Thus Starr's group III probably belongs in the mid-460s, after Eurymedon.[13]

The standard coin for subsidizing military service before 460 (or possibly 462) was perhaps the didrachm (or it was at least as significant as the tetradrachm). The prominence of that denomination in active minting is unique to this period of the Attic mint within the fifth century.

[10] See, most recently, D.M. Lewis, "The Athenian Tribute-Quota Lists, 453–450 B.C.," *BSA* 89 (1994) 285–301.

[11] Starr, *Coinage* 38–42.

[12] For comparative instances, see C.C. Lorber, "Notes on West Greek Gold," *Nomismatika Khronika* 11 (1992) 11–17.

[13] Fried, *Coinage and Adminnistration* 5–6.

Didrachms continued to be struck from Starr's group IIA through his group IV, but were never again produced in Attic classical minting. After the Ephialtic reforms, payment of the sailors and other military personnel may have been raised or put on a regular basis so that the tetradrachm became the denomination through which the Athenians spent money to support the personnel of the fleet. Guaranteed salaries, the expectation of a sizable annual mobilization regardless of military needs, an increase in the daily rate of payment, and the regular enlistment of allied personnel are all developments that might be implicated in a decision to emphasize the production of tetradrachms. Some or all of these adjustments may well belong to the early and mid-450s.[14] Accordingly, the tetradrachm was minted to the exclusion of the decadrachm and the didrachm for the rest of the century.

In the 450s and thereafter, the tetradrachm had the added advantage over the didrachm as a medium for the payment for the expenses of the fleet in that any tetradrachms earned by the allies from their initial recipients in the normal course of business provided a most convenient means for paying tribute back to the Athenians. The presence of allied rowers in Attic service made such "captures" of tetradrachms a necessary and desirable feature of hegemonic finances.

The impact of these factors would be enhanced if a hypothesis about the monetary significance of the date 454/3 were true (discussed below on pp. 267–69, 458–63). If the treasury of the Delian League was moved

[14] Ulpianus, commentary on the pseudo-Demosthenic *On Organization* (13.160–61), assigns to Perikles what might be called a full-fledged system of pay, that is, one that includes the *dēmos* who served as rowers. See ΣDem. 13.169, in C. Müller (ed.), *Oratores Attici* (Paris 1857) 2.575. The professionalization of service in the fleet was an evolutionary process, starting from the subsidies made during the full mobilization against Xerxes (Plut. *Them.* 10.6–7 with Cleidemus *FGH* 323 F 21, also citing *Ath. Pol.* 23.1). The Atthidographic tradition reported Aristeides' efforts to provide *trophē* 'military subsistence' (*Ath. Pol.* 24.1–3) and perhaps a similar policy on the part of Kimon (Plut. *Cimon* 11.2; cf. 9.6). Doubtless, from the founding of the Delian League, Athenian commanders attempted to provide *trophē* to their Attic rowers and used federal revenues and booty to do so. There are, however, a number of open questions about these practices: the level of such payments, the extent to which the whole or a proportion of them was guaranteed, and the degree to which allied sailors and rowers were permitted to participate. By the period of the Peloponnesian War, the full system was obviously in place, as the narrative of Thucydides shows (cf. *Ath. Pol.* 27.2). Yet, it is unknown, for instance, when the rate of pay per diem reached a triobol or even a drachm for each sailor, even if the latter was an exceptional rate. Note Thuc. 3.17.4, cf. 6.31.3; the former being a passage whose authenticity and placement have been questioned (*HCT* 2.275–77). There are, however, indications from the 440s of the later mode of operation. Plutarch, in a passage reflecting Atthidography, states that Perikles kept sixty ships with paid sailors fully mobilized for eight months in peacetime (*Pericles* 11.4). The "Old Oligarch"—if his treatise belongs in the late 440s—complained of payments to the *dēmos* for service at sea ([Xen.] *Ath. Pol.* 1.13). See W.K. Pritchett, *The Greek State at War* 1 (Berkeley and Los Angeles 1971) 7–14.

to Attica during the lifetime of Aristeides, as the only surviving testimonia suggest, then the start of the inscribed lists of *aparkhai* might signal the imposition of new rules about the payment of tribute in tetradrachms, or, at least, about the payment of the *aparkhai* in Attic coin. The resulting greater demand among the allies for these coins might be reflected in the beginning of increased striking in the mint. Regardless of our feelings toward this hypothesis, the conversion of any reserves or booty whether in bullion or in non-Attic coin can be expected to have accelerated after 454/3. Significantly, the more intense emissions of tetradrachms are not the consequence of the Coinage Decree, even at its earliest possible date, but stand in its background. Was the increased outflow of Athenian money one of the necessary conditions for the enactment of any general monetary decree? Did it make the the imposition of the validity of Attic coinage (as the revisionist interpretation of the inscriptions will urge) increasingly viable?

In Chapter 9, the patterns of evolution in the Attic economy in this period that provide a backdrop to monetary legislation will be surveyed. Monetary policy and, consequently, the operations of the Athenian mint rested on the foundation of the mines at Laureion, which were at their height of productivity in the Pentekontaeteia. While it is unknown which percentages of silver were exported from Attica in bullion or coined form, the state, through its system of leases and through its other taxes, drew on the output of Laureion. The existence of the main tax on mining is betrayed by lexical notices on the procedure for punishing tax evasion, the *dikē agraphou metallou* (*Suda* s.v. ἀγράφου μετάλλου δίκη, α 345 Adler). The tax was a levy of one twenty-fourth (or 4.125 percent) on all output.

The estimates of C.E. Conophagos are naturally speculative but they do start from the amounts of waste products of ancient mining (such scoria and discarded ore) that have been processed in the nineteenth and twentieth centuries to reach an estimation of the amount of ore mined and processed in antiquity and thereby the yield in silver (ca. 3,500,000 kg).[15]

There is then left the necessarily arbitrary surmise that will assign different amounts of this total to various periods. The period of high production in the fifth century was estimated by Conophagos to reach 20 metric tons (or 736T) of silver per annum. As it is likely that much of this yield was never coined, going directly to workshops in Attica and abroad as bullion, a figure for the annual income to the state from the silver mines might be more indicative of the resources available for

[15] See C.E. Conophagos, *Le Laurium antique* (Athens 1980) 138–52, 341–54.

coining. Conophagos estimates an annual income of 100T (during the prime years of prewar production), but that is merely frail calculation from the supposed yield of the leases and leaves an extremely high profit margin for the industry.[16] The basic levy of one-twenty-fourth would have yielded ca. 30T by itself from the estimated total output. It is safer to conclude that 75–100T was a likely minimum for state income from all taxes that drew (even indirectly) from mine output and that ample supplies of bullion would have been available to sustain large programs of minting and monetary replacement by the Athenians. The other source of raw metal for Attic minting were the operations of the Delian League, where the conversion of booty into tetradrachms as well as the reminting of foreign money probably had a substantial role in the operations of the Athenian mint.

When we glimpse the Athenian reserves later in the century, they are being held in Attic coin. Hence the Kallias Decree can speak of a large sum of Athenian coin, τὰ τρισχίλια τάλαντ[α] . . . νομίσματος *h*εμεδαπõ '3,000 talents . . . of our coin' (*IG* I³ 52A.3–4). The accounts of the Treasurers of Athena from the Ionian War bear a similar notation: ἀργύριον ἐπίσεμον *h*εμεδαπὸν 'our coined silver' (*IG* I³ 372.2; 376.32, 38–39, 41, 52, 67–68, 82–83).[17]

MONETARY OUTPUT

The most important investigation of the Athenian rate of production of coins that can be presently undertaken is to gauge Athenian output against the indications of the intensity of production by allied mints. Placing aside the substantial lacunae in our evidence for the moment, it is additionally necessary to state another complexity within the problem, one that affects any assessment of the results. Based on the earlier chapters, no real evidence has been discovered for a general demonetization of allied coins during the duration of the *arkhē*, although individual allied cities may have chosen occasionally to invalidate earlier series of coins, presumably for fiscal reasons. These were local acts of policy, and nothing suggests that they either coincided with actions of or were mandated by the Athenians. Older coins continued in circulation; many of them may

[16] Conophagos, *Laurium* 352–54.

[17] These latter accounts show that this terminology has no value for determining the date of the Coinage Decree (see pp. 439–40 below). The Athenian references to "our money" throughout the last decades of the century do perhaps indicate that other series of coins held validity in the *arkhē* (as no general ban had ever existed). Why would it otherwise be necessary to specify the identity of the currency (see also *IG* I³ 383.I.98–99; cf. II.237–38)?

well have remained valid tender for paying local taxes and were usable in other settings. Those that were struck on standards of regional or international validity might even have been employable in places outside the political jurisdiction of their emission; many old coins were hoarded.[18]

Even if we could measure definitively the output of the active mints in the second half of the fifth century, our inability to calculate the number of surviving coins in circulation from defunct series would affect any estimates on their proportionate components of the money in circulation. A modern estimate of 2 percent for unaccountable loss from the coin supply per year is reached through many stages of assumption.[19] Intentional conversion, export outside the monetary economy of the Greeks, and hoarding appear to me to be underestimated in this calculation. Nevertheless, if modern analogies with the differential rates of loss between lighter denominations (such as silver dimes and quarters) and heavier denominations proved true for the fifth century, tetradrachms and other staters, which possessed considerable purchasing power, might have had a relatively low rate of annual loss. Even low rates of attrition (less than 2 percent), however, compounded over a decade or fifteen years draw down a money supply markedly if it is not refreshed with new issues. This phenomenon is clearly underrated because of our tendency to recreate the stock of money in circulation from hoards, where many coins appear precisely because they were less suitable for continued circulation. Coins from most of the mints that ended striking before 450 soon comprised a relatively small proportion of the money in circulation in allied states.

Of all the means of gauging the intensity of the activity of an individual mint from the surviving material, merely enunmerating the number of coins extant is the crudest of measures, as it leaves us prey to all manner

[18] Most of the mints classified in category III have not as yet been subjected to the level of systematic analysis that would allow us to reach any (even tentative) conclusions about the money supply of the allies in the first years of the Delian League. Generalizing from Tenos, where a thorough study of a small mint that ended its activity ca. 480 is available, one would conclude that these coinages ceased to be significant components of the local money supply not long after the closing of their mints. On Tenos, see L. Artemis-Gyselen, "Les monnaies archaïques de Ténos," *RBN* 123 (1977) 5–15.

[19] C.C. Patterson, "Silver Stocks and Losses in Ancient and Medieval Times," *EHR*² 25 (1972) 205–35. Note the sensible cautionary remarks on an annual attrition rate of 2 percent of T.V. Buttrey, "Calculating Ancient Coin Production: Facts and Fantasies," *NC* 153 (1993) 335–51, esp. 345–47. See also K. Hopkins, "Taxes and Trade in the Roman Empire (200 B.C.–A.D. 400)," *JRS* 70 (1980) 101–25, esp. 107–108; C.C. Patterson, "Dwindling Stocks of Silver and Their Relevance to Studies of the Metal Contents of Silver Coinage," in E.T. Hall and D.M. Metcalf (eds.), *Methods of Chemical and Metallurgical Investigation of Silver Coinage* (London 1972) 149–52. On wastage from all causes in the Roman imperial money supply, see R. Duncan-Jones, *Money and Government in the Roman Empire* (Cambridge 1994) 205–206, 212.

of vicissitudes, from the rate at which a particular issue was hoarded by contemporary users through the tastes of modern collectors. The chance find of a single large homogeneous hoard will have a disproportionate impact on the apparent size of the series of coins contained therein. More helpful is an enumeration of the obverse and reverse dies that are represented by the surviving coins, for here an estimate of the magnitude of the material that has not survived can be begun. Yet the classification of a mint by assignment of extant coins to obverse and reverse dies is a demanding exercise of scholarship. When we turn to quantifying the output of the mints among the allies of Athens we are stymied by a lack of specific studies that exhaustively present the extant coins with identifications of their obverse and reverse dies.[20]

Still better is the application of statistical techniques to estimate the total number of dies originally used in a particular series through an extrapolation either from die duplicates or die linkages among the surviving coins.[21] It has recently been argued that any one method of estimation may not be superior in a particular setting to the application of a group of formulas of which the results are averaged.[22] Nonetheless, it is uncertain, in the situation facing us regarding the evidence on fifth-century allied minting, whether such methods are warranted inasmuch as it is the relative intensity of production associated with different series that is of primary interest. Therefore I will use G.F. Carter's method, which

[20] On coin output, an excellent introduction is offered by T. Hackens, "Rythmes de la production monétaire: les monnayages archaïques et classiques de Grèce," in G. Depeyrot, T. Hackens, and G. Moucharte (eds.), *Rythmes de la production monétaire de l'antiquité à nos jours* (Louvain 1987) 1–13, which may be read with his, "La circulation monétaire, questions de méthode," *Études d'archéologie classique* 4 (1975) 213–22, *Annales de l'Est, Univ. de Nancy II*, #44. See also R.R. Holloway, "The Coinage Production of the Sicilian Greek Mints of the Sixth and Fifth Centuries B.C.," *Rythmes de la production* 11–20; T.R. Volk, "Mint Output and Coin Hoards," *Rythmes de la production* 141–221. Cf. K. Rutter, "Early Greek Coinage and the Influence of the Athenian State," in B. Cunliffe (ed.), *Coinage and Society in Britain and Gaul: Some Current Problems* (London 1981) 1–9.

[21] My own first efforts along these lines are found in *Aegina* 98–107, where two techniques of estimation are employed, one drawn from D.M. Metcalf's work on Anglo-Saxon coinage, "How Large was the Anglo-Saxon Currency?," *EHR*[2] 18 (1965) 475–82, esp. 476–77, using die duplicates, and the other from C.S.S. Lyon, "The Estimation of the Number of Dies Employed in a Coinage," *NCirc.* 73 (1965) 180–81, using die links. See also W.E. McGovern, "Missing Die Probabilities, Expected Die Production and the Index Figure," *ANSMN* 25 (1980) 209–23; W. Malkmus, "Note on a General Solution to the Missing Die Problem," *SAN* 17 (1986) 15–16, 18; Duncan-Jones, *Money* 144–50.

[22] F. de Callataÿ, "À propos du volume des émissions monétaires dans l'antiquité," *RBN* 130 (1984) 37–48. A detailed analysis of methods is offered by W.W. Esty, "Estimation of the Size of a Coinage: A Survey and Comparison of Methods," *NC* 146 (1986) 185–215.

has the advantage of also having been utilized by T. Hackens; thus the calculations below can in some cases be juxtaposed with his estimates.[23]

Let us start with the Attic mint as analyzed by Starr, limiting ourselves to the better attested tetradrachms. It should be remembered, however, that several major collections were overlooked in his monograph.[24] The additional material, however, in his article in *NC* (1982) can be used. The results are outlined in Table 7.1. When we add in the accessions to our knowledge of these early imperial owls that were gained from the "Decadrachm Hoard," the results are startling.[25] For each group, there are found a significant proportion of previously unknown dies, which suggests that a new study could refine (narrowing their range) the estimates that are offered in Table 7.1, but is unlikely to yield radically lower figures.

TABLE 7.1 The Production of the Athenian Mint

Group: Starr's date / This work	*Obv. / Est. obv.*	*Rev. / Est. rev.*
I: mid-470s/pre-475	12/110±89	11/57±33
IIA: late 470s/470s	8/31±19	9/66±60
IIB: early 460s/470s	6/12±5	8/31±19
IIC: mid-460s/pre-465	9/38±23	9/38±23
III: late 460s/mid-460s	9/38±23	11/65±52
IV: early 450s/late 460s	27/93±26	33/387±224
VA–B: late 450s/ late 460s-early 450s	64/389±107	68/687±250

Obviously, these calculations are not very satisfactory, because the small number of examples for each die combination means that the standard deviations in our outcomes are large. Thus the possible number of dies straggles over a considerable range. Yet the impressions with which we are left are not insubstantial. The output of Attic tetradrachms was great, even in this period before the massive issues of standardized

[23] G.F. Carter, "A Simplified Method for Calculating the Original Number of Dies from Die Link Statistics," *ANSMN* 28 (1983) 195–206. He offers three formulas in which n = number of known coins, d = number of known (different) dies, D = original number of dies.

1. $D = \frac{nd}{1.214n - 1.197d}$ when $n < 2d$
2. $D = \frac{nd}{1.124n - 1.016d}$ when $n = 2$ to $3d$
3. $D = \frac{nd}{1.069n - 0.843d}$ when $n > 3d$

See also Hackens, *Rythmes* 6–13.

[24] Nicolet *RPh* (1974) 132–34; Williams *Phoenix* (1972) 411–12.

[25] Fried, *Coinage* 5–6.

coins occurring later in the fifth century. Moreover, many talents of silver were coined as decadrachms, didrachms, and drachms. These emissions were considerably greater than the output of the other mints, which we are about to consider below. The "Decadrachm Hoard," with its many previously unknown dies, underlines this conclusion. While no one has as yet produced an exhaustive catalogue of these coins, the survival rate of Starr's groups I–III may be low, because the coins circulated in a comparatively limited geographical range compared both with groups IV–V (after 465) and with the standardized owls of the second half of the century. These latter coins served more truly as the money of the whole *arkhē*.

Second, early imperial coins (Starr's groups I–V) joined the pre-479 issues to provide a significant part of the currency circulating within the allied cities during the formative years of the Delian League. Half the economic activity of the allies was occurring in cities that were not minting by 445 and that about two thirds of allied output at that point belonged to cities not minting staters or tetradrachms (see Table 2.1, pp. 54–55 above). These substantial emissions of Attic tetradrachm "owls" of the early Pentekontaeteia indicate how that situation could be viable economically. An expanding level of economic activity could only be sustained because of the scale of coining achieved by the Athenian mint from 478 to 460.

Regarding levels of allied minting, there is not a wealth of examples to juxtapose with Attic minting activities. On the basis of numismatic data, the evidence of the tribute lists, and literary material, Chios, Samos, and Aigina possessed the largest economies and most significant traditions of minting among the states of the Delian League. Yet it is uncertain whether any of these mints could even to begin to serve as appropriate comparisons for the pre-450 Athenian mint. The output of the Chian mint is difficult to estimate, owing to the controversy over the existence of an interval in coining and the connected assignment of some issues to the fourth century that were previously believed to have belonged to the period of the *arkhē*. On the basis of recent work, however, the output of the Chian mint definitely appears much more modest than that of the Athenian mint.[26]

[26] N. Hardwick estimates thirty-seven obverse dies for his earlier series of post-480 didrachms (480–35); fifteen or sixteen obverse dies, perhaps nearly the whole series, for the later didrachms (435–25), with sixty-one dies for the related *tritai*. If one retains the earliest series of tetradrachms in the fifth century, the associated coinage would offer three obverse tetradrachm dies and seven obverse drachm dies. Hardwick would remove this issue from the fifth century. See Hardwick, "The Coinage of Chios from the VIth to the IVth Century B.C.," in T. Hackens and G. Moucharte (eds.), *Proceedings of the XI International Numismatics Congress* 1 (Louvain-la-Neuve 1993) 211–22, esp. 214–15; Hardwick, "The Solution to Thucydides VIII 101.1: The 'Chian Fortieths'," *NAC* 25 (1996) 59–69, esp. 61.

The Samian mint was comparable to the Chian mint in its output, as the estimated figures in Table 7.2 indicate. Both Chios and Samos saw their production of coins decrease as the century advanced, and Attic output increased. As for Aigina, while the later "T-back" turtles and the fifth-century tortoises were struck in considerable numbers, it is hard to believe that they could assume much of the contribution to circulation of the other coinages that were being terminated, if only because Aiginetan archaic issues had been so numerous.[27] It is uncertain whether enough post-478 coins were minted to replace the Aiginetan pre-480 coins in circulation one for one, let alone replace other coins from extinct series.

Unfortunately, the requisite studies are lacking for a comparison of the relative outputs of the Athenian mint and the majority of the mints of the subject allies. When one turns to the recent survey of the literature by Hackens, however, there were only four mints within the *arkhē* for which he deemed the research adequate to allow estimates on the basis of the assignments of coins to particular dies: Akanthos, Knidos, Abdera, and Ainos (with Side and Corinth, which, of course, lay outside Athenian hegemony).[28] To these mints, we can add Maroneia, based on the work of Schönert-Geiss, and Teos, from the research of Balcer. The Appendix may be consulted for the relevant citations of the specialist literature. I depart from the presentation of Hackens in my exclusion of coins below the tetradrachm or stater weight (except where noted).[29] The revised dates are offered following the discussions above.

It should also be noted that these estimates differ from those implied by the tables of Hackens through differences in counting and the assigning of dies to series. Moreover, the division of a series into separate issues that are distinguished by characteristic symbols (such as the coins of the Abderite and Maroneian mints) will have a substantial effect on estimates of output in a way that is impossible to correct in the present state of our knowledge. When the transition to the next symbol was made, it was not determined by the wear of the dies but rather by the reaching of some politically significant threshold. The estimated number of dies (especially obverse) in these series is probably too large.

While the Attic economy was larger than any single allied economy, it was not larger than all the allied economies taken together. Total state

[27] See pp. 122–26 above, and Figueira, *Aegina* 105–107.

[28] See Hackens, *Rythmes* 6–13.

[29] We could also add Dikaia to our list, again based on the work of Schönert-Geiss, but the tiny output of this early closing mint renders such an exercise pointless. Phaselis is another mint for which we have a die study (that of Heipp-Tamer), where the output is too small for inclusion.

Table 7.2 The Production of Selected Allied Mints

Abdera

Chronology: May|this work

	pre-520| pre-500	520–492| 500–475	492–70| 475–55/50	470–49| 450–30/25	439–10| 430–10/5	410–385
	(8dr./4dr.)	(8dr./4dr.)	4dr.	4dr.	4dr.	staters
Obv.	8/10	22/1	37	45+	24	33
Rev.	9/13	21/1	33	52	37	49
Est. obv.	23±11/17±3	60±15/1+?	66±8	58±3	33±3	62±9
Est. rev.	38±26/22±5	52±12/1+?	52±6	72±5	74±11	242±66

Ainos

Chronology: May|this work

	474–48|474–40/35	435–404|440/35–404			404–387
	(4dr.)	(4dr.)			(4dr.)
		435–425	425–417	417–405	Period III
Obv.	26	1	1	25	12
Rev.	44	1	1	28	23
Est. obv.	29±1	—	—	32±3	14±1
Est. rev.	60±4	—	—	51±5	39±6

Akanthos

Chronology: Desneux|this work

	530–480|–455 or 450	480–24|450–410	424–380|410–380
	(4dr.)		
Obv.	89	22	39
Rev.	82	21	44
Est. obv.	242±30	92±33	75±10
Est. rev.	189±21	74±24	103±16

Knidos

Chronology: Cahn|this work

	520–495|–490	490–65|–60	465–49|–40	449–11|440–11	411–394
	(dr.)	(dr.)	(dr.)	(dr.)	(dr.)
Obv.	16	6	4	5	3 + 10
Rev.	20	10	8	5	3 + 15
Est. obv.	16	6	4	8±2	3 + 11
Est. rev.	21	10	8	8±2	3 + 18

Maroneia

Chronology: May; Schöenert-Geiss|this work

	490s–449, 437–36|480–440/30 (2dr.)	436–411|440/30–411 (4dr.)	411–398 (stater)
Obv.	8	44	17
Rev.	10	59	17
Est. obv.	9±1	64±5?	52±17?
Est. rev.	15±2	113±12?	52±17?

Samos (tetradrachms)

Chronology: Barron|this work

	Class II/III ca. 480–461/0| ca. 480–455 or 450	Class IV/VI 460/59–454/3| 455/50–440	Class VII 453/2–440/39| 435–415
Obv.	19	8	11
Rev.	46	16	25
Est. obv.	23	9	12
Est. rev.	117	26	36

Teos

Chronology: Balcer|this work

	pre-495|pre-465/55 (staters)	478–449|465/55–430/25 (staters)	412–407|411 or 405? (staters)
Obv.	19	24	4
Rev.	27	31	5
Est. obv.	22±10	40±8	—
Est. rev.	80±38	75±21	—

income for Athens in 431 was ca. 1,000T (Xen. *Anab.* 7.1.27), of which 600T came from overseas (Thuc. 2.13.3). If the income from colonies is ignored, the 400–450T of income from the allies roughly equals domestic governmental revenue.[30] The allies, however, possessed their own public sectors at home that were supported by taxes raised locally. Therefore, the state income of all tributaries and the underlying economic output supporting it far exceeded the scale of the Attic economy. The large Chian, Samian, and Lesbian economies stood outside the tribute system, and must be added in to our calculation. Yet, Attic production of coins seems to exceed the output of all the allied mints combined, especially after 450. Therefore, a large proportion of the transactions undertaken between the citizens of allied cities took place through the mediation of Attic money.

[30] Figueira, *Colonization* 185–90.

It is also helpful to assign an output in coins to each die in order to grasp the scale of the monetary phenomena under study. Here, however, we have advanced significantly further into the realm of speculation, as T.V. Buttrey has recently argued, since many factors differentiated the operation of one mint from another and thereby affected the output for each estimated die.[31] It turns out that there are two lines of approach that offer perspectives on the actual number of coins that could be expected to have been struck on average from each die in a series. One depends on empirical research that duplicated the ancient methods of coining in an effort to estimate the practical life of dies. The experiments of D.G. Sellwood yielded expected die lives of 4,000 for the more vulnerable reverse dies (as they took the force of the hammer directly) and 8,000 for the obverse dies.[32]

The other approach exploits our ability to investigate the Amphictyonic coinage of Delphi during 336–34 (on the Aiginetic standard), by juxtaposing the amount of silver consigned to these issues with an estimate of the number of obverse dies used for the series. A complicating factor, however, is the uncertainty surrounding the percentage of these coins that staters comprised (as against fractions). E.J.P. Raven thought that 122–200T were struck, and four-sevenths of the bullion became staters. Accordingly, 10,000–30,000 was the most likely range for the output of the average obverse die.[33]

A more recent study by P. Kinns has attempted refinements of these conclusions on the basis of further evidence and some advances in methodology.[34] Kinns estimates that each of the Amphictyonic obverse dies was responsible for 23,333–47,250 coins. In my view, the higher reaches of this range were not feasible on average, although Kinns' points about the relatively high relief of the staters and about the lack of visible

[31] Buttrey *NC* (1993) 335–51; Buttrey, "Calculating Ancient Coin Production II: Why It Cannot be Done," *NC* 154 (1994) 341–52.

[32] D.G. Sellwood, "Some Experiments in Greek Minting," *NC*[7] 3 (1963) 217–231. Sellwood's experiments were continued by L. Beer in detailed simulations of the Aiginetan mint, for whose work see L. Beer, "Results of Coin Striking to Simulate the Mint of Aegina," in T. Hackens and R. Weiler (eds.), *Proceedings of the 9th International Congress of Numismatics: Berne, September 1979* (Louvain-la-Neuve 1982) 47–51; L. Beer Tobey and A.G. Tobey, "Experiments to Simulate Ancient Greek Coins," *Metallurgy in Numismatics* 3 (1993) 28–33. Unfortunately the fullest account (L. Beer, *The Coinage of Aegina: A Chronological Reappraisal Based on Hoards and Technical Studies* [Diss., Oxford University 1980] 265–88, 295–97) is inaccessible to most scholars. See also C. Conophagos, H. Badecca, and C. Tsaimou, "La technique athénienne de la frappe des monnaies à l'époque classique," *Nomismatika Khronika* 4 (1976) 4–33.

[33] E.J.P. Raven, "The Amphictionic Coinage of Delphi: 336–334 B.C.," *NC*[6] 10 (1950) 1–22, esp. 11–15. For other estimates, see Duncan-Jones, *Money* 163–67.

[34] P. Kinns, "The Amphictionic Coinage Reconsidered," *NC* 143 (1983) 1–22.

wear on the dies used for extant coins ought to be especially noted. Our evolving understanding of die usage may then well lead us to raise rather than lower our estimates both of mint output and of the size of the money supply in most *poleis* during the Classical period.

The data are not yet sufficiently copious and usefully organized to answer what are perhaps the central questions. What were the effects of the monetary consolidation of the first years of the *arkhē* on the output both of allied mints and of the Attic mint? What were the ramifications of the passage of the Coinage Decree (whenever one might date it) on the level of allied and Attic minting during the second half of the century? In the first instance, it is notable that the Attic mint appears much larger than those allied mints for which output can be estimated. Nevertheless, it may be even more significant that it seems to be the Athenian mint alone that reacts to the monetary integration undertaken by the allied states, at least if the mints surveyed above were typical (and there is no reason to believe that they were not). These allied mints do not seem to have compensated for the termination of local monies elsewhere in the empire by expanding their own production. In other words, any expanded circulation of nonlocal money to serve allied economies that were now no longer provided with indigenous coins came in the form of more copious Attic currency. For example, even if the neighbors of Abdera recognized the validity of Abderite coins when they closed their mints, there would not have been sufficiently more Abderite coins—if there were any more at all reaching them that could be spared from local use—to serve their established (or historical) monetary needs.

Against this background of high estimated rates of output for Attic tetradrachms, only a pitiably small sample of Athenian coins have been subjected to any chemical evaluation. This would include analyses of trace elements and especially neutron activation analysis of their trace composition of lead that would allow a hypothetical determination of the geographical origin of their silver. Yet those coins that have been analyzed do form a strikingly homogeneous body (on the basis of our current knowledge) that does not betray a massive infusion of silver from sources other than Laureion.[35] And some indication of silver from other

[35] I.L. Barnes, W.R. Shields, T.J. Murphy, and R.H. Brill, "Isotopic Analysis of Laurion Lead Ores," in C.W. Beck (ed.) *Archaeological Chemistry, Advances in Chemistry Series* 138 (Washington, D.C. 1974) 1–10; V.E. Chamberlain and N.H. Gale, "The Isotopic Composition of Lead in Greek Coins and in Galena from Greece and Turkey," in E.A. Slater and J.O. Tate (eds.), *Proceedings of the 16th International Symposium on Archaeometry and Archaeological Prospection, Edinburgh, 1976* (Edinburgh 1976) 164–76; W. Gentner, O. Müller, G.A. Wagner, and N.H. Gale, "Silver Sources of Archaic Greek Coinage," *Naturwissenschaften* 65 (1978) 273–84, esp.

proveniences would have been expected from the demonetization and conversion of all the coinage of allied states postulated in traditional interpretations of the Coinage Decree. That supposition would be particularly true on the customary view that many mints were still in operation and were ordered to be closed. Analyses through neutron activation of the characteristic ratios between the isotopes of lead in a cross section of Attic coins fall within the "field" that researchers have established by analyses of samples taken from the Laureion region itself. The results for Athenian coins may be contrasted with those achieved for Aiginetan coins (mainly specimens from the Asyut Hoard collected by L. Beer-Tobey), where the impression is one of marked heterogeneity of origin for the silver and the mixing of silver from different sources.[36] In the fifth century, the district of Laureion was perhaps increasingly prominent among Aiginetan silver sources, along with Siphnos, Mt. Pangaion, the Pactolos watershed, and even Spain as other possibilities (all but Siphnos being unconfirmed).[37] Since the Aiginetan government acquired its silver through taxes that drew directly or indirectly on commercial activity, that result fulfills expectation.[38]

276–80; N.H. Gale, "Lead Isotopes and Aegean Metallurgy," in *Thera and the Aegean World* (London 1978) 1.529–45; N.H. Gale, "Some Aspects of Lead and Silver Mining in the Aegean," *MIGRA* 2 (1979) 9–60, esp. 19–26; L. Beer, N.H. Gale, W. Gentner, G.A. Wagner, and (M.)J. Price, "Archaic Greek Silver Coinage," *Metallurgy in Numismatics* 1 (1980) 1–54, esp. 12–21, 29–33. For further background on methodology, see R.H. Brill and W.R. Shields, "Lead Isotopes in Ancient Coins," in Hall and Metcalf, *Methods* 279–301. See also P.A. Schubiger and O. Müller, "Trace Elements in Ancient Silver Coins by Neutron Activation and Solvent Extraction with Bismuth Diethyldithiocarbamate," *Radiochem. Radioanal. Letters* 24 (1976) 353–62; P.A. Schubiger, O. Müller, and W. Gentner, "Neutron Activation Analysis on Ancient Silver Coins and Related Materials," *Journal of Radioanalytical Chemistry* 39 (1977) 99–112.

36 Chamberlain and Gale, *16th International Symposium*; Gentner et al. *Naturwissenschaften* (1978) 279–82; O. Müller and W. Gentner, "On the Composition and Silver Sources of Aeginetan Coins from the Asyut Hoard," in *Proceedings of the 18th International Symposium on Archaeometry and Archaeological Prospection, Bonn, 1978, Archaeo-physika* 10 (1979) 176–93; N.H. Gale, "Lead Isotopes and Archaic Greek Silver Silver Coins," *Archaeo-physika* 10 (1979) 194–208, esp. 201–206; Beer et al. *Metallurgy in Numismatics* (1980) 18–21, 28, 33–43. See also P.A. Schubiger, O. Müller, and W. Gentner, "Chemical Studies of Greek Silver Coins from the Asyut Hoard," in *16th International Symposium* 164–76.

37 Cf. Beer et al. *Metallurgy in Numismatics* (1980) 36.

38 An important result of these analyses was that some earlier Aiginetan coins (described as having "union-jack" reverses) are rich in gold and tin, leading to speculation of the derivation of their metal from electrum coins (with an original alluvial source in the Pactolos valley of Lydia). That would not only confirm that a transfer of silver (and incidentally of gold, not reused monetarily) into Aiginetan hands took place through commerce in the Aegean basin but would also illustrate the way in which sixth-century Aiginetan merchants succeeded Ionian merchants in many markets. See Gentner et al. *Naturwissenschaften* (1978) 281–82; Gale *Archaeo-physika* (1979) 204; Müller and Gentner *Archaeo-physika* (1979) 181–82; cf. Beer et al. *Metallurgy in Numismatics* (1980) 23 for reservations.

The results of chemical analyses can hardly be described as conclusive, but they best fit a scenario in which the great output of the Laureion mines allowed Attic coins to be consistently and substantially Attic in the provenience of their silver (although the paucity of analyzed coins probably obscures some variation). If the allies paid their tribute mainly in Attic tetradrachms and there were no enormous demonetizations and conversions of allied coins, no mechanism existed for silver of disparate origin contained in foreign coins to infiltrate the Athenian money supply. Coins with silver from sources abroad were not acquired by the Athenian government to be reminted in a manner comparable to the pattern exhibited by the Aiginetan mint.

We are still painfully far from being able to discuss the money supply of the Athenian *arkhē* in quantitative terms, but we can isolate some likely determining factors. A large output of silver from Laureion, which is especially significant in the light of the region's historical silver production before 485 and after 400, accompanied an accelerating amount of production from the Attic mint. Contemporaneously, allied mints made a smaller contribution to the money in circulation in the *arkhē* through their closure and through their restriction of output to smaller denominations (and through other similar limitings of the emissions of staters). In this environment for the utilization of silver coins, even modest rates of attrition (<2 percent) of the silver money in circulation would quickly have had a marked effect on the ratio of Attic coins to the non-Attic silver regularly used in transactions within the *arkhē*. That effect would be accentuated, if economic output in toto and per capita was indeed rising during the Pentekontaeteia (as every indicator suggests).

That result would not have been predicted from an analysis of the contents of the hoards alone and deserves particular emphasis. It may be that the hoards tend to understate the preponderance of Attic money in the local market. Not only are hoarders biased toward heavier coins, but they are innately conservers who must envisage emergency contexts for expenditure that differ from current, everyday economic behavior. Although we depend greatly on hoards for reconstructing the mix of coins in circulation, the coins in hoards stand in an ambiguous relation to the money supply. Although they may join that supply at the option of the hoarder, by the very fact of hoarding they are not regularly used for daily transactions.

The question of what means were available to ancient political authorities for affecting the volume and composition of the stock of coins in circulation is a vexed one, with doubts having been expressed over the existence or possibility of any significant governmental intervention at all.[39] The activity of the Athenian government in our period should satisfy the objections of even the strongest skeptic, since the archaeological record manifests support of an increased output of coins for two reasons. The Athenians were striking many coins to sustain military expenditures (first and foremost), and to support the Periclean building program (secondarily). Before the emission of bronze coins, Athens, like other contemporary *poleis*, lacked any ability to augment directly an insufficient supply of its own coins in circulation by means that did not involve additional spending. This solution could put political leaders at a disadvantage when they are compared with the politicians of states employing token money.

The Athenians, however, did possess the ability to affect the money supply indirectly by altering the terms under which their mint accepted old coins and bullion for restriking. When we consider the conversion process that is set in train in the Coinage Decree, these conditions will definitely bear recalling. It will not be necessary to envisage that only a massive call-in and demonetization of allied monies could have a significant impact on the money supply in the third quarter of the fifth century. The transformation of an amount of non-Athenian money equivalent to the tribute of one year, for example, would necessarily stand as an important stage in the shifting of the proportions of Athenian and non-Athenian money in daily usage.

[39] For a useful survey, see C.J. Howgego, "Why did Ancient States Strike Coins?" *NC* 150 (1990) 1–25. The debate has been preoccupied by better-attested Roman monetary practices, with the position skeptical of intervention except for military expenditures well represented by M. Crawford, "Money and Exchange in the Roman World," *JRS* 60 (1970) 40–48, and the position accepting more sophisticated policies exemplified by E. Lo Cascio, "State and Coinage in the Late Republic and Early Empire," *JRS* 71 (1981) 76–86.

PART II

LITERARY EVIDENCE FOR MONETARY POLICY

8

THE LITERARY EVIDENCE

THE ONLY LITERARY ALLUSION to Athenian monetary legislation is provided by Aristophanes' *Birds*. Note that the expression "monetary legislation" is used here and not "Coinage Decree" because it is not certain at this point whether Aristophanes is referring directly to the piece of legislation that we find attested epigraphically.

THE SOUNDS OF SILENCE

The absence of other references to the Coinage Decree is in itself significant. The silence of our sources, however fragmentary they may be, is odd for an important act of Athenian aggrandizement such as the declaration of an Attic monopoly over the minting of silver coins that, according to the traditional interpretation, is assumed to have been consummated in the Coinage Decree. Moreover, if the Athenians intruded on allied autonomy or exploited the allies economically, it is surprising that there is not some discernible allusion within extant literature.

Some absences are particularly telltale. No hostile speaker or Athenian apologist in Thucydides thinks to mention the Coinage Decree or any other piece of Attic monetary legislation. As we shall soon see, Thucydides never even juxtaposes coining with autonomy (see below, pp. 248–50). Thucydides does refer to the fastidiousness of the Athenians in exacting required services from their allies/subjects (Thuc. 1.99.1–3), but he never adverts to Athenian interference with allied monetary independence, although payments in non-Athenian currency would clearly impinge on the collection of the tribute. No Thucydidean allusion is ever made to any enforcement necessary to suppress allied metrological practices that were at variance with Attic norms. In contrast, the Athenians are made to defend the concentration at Athens of adjudication involving allied litigation that some might consider a similar manifestation of a tendency toward centralization (cf. Thuc. 1.76–77 with [Xen.] *Ath. Pol.* 1.16–18; Isoc. 4.113; 12.63, 66). As far as can be gathered from Thucydides, allied aristocrats objected to the *arkhē* both because they found subordination to the Athenian *dēmos* psychologically unacceptable and because they felt themselves inhibited from exercising their superiority over other societal groups in their home cities. The strictures of the

"Old Oligarch" reflect the same attitudes. Yet no oligarch in the surviving documentation ever seems to have protested the Coinage Decree or any other step in the evolution of Athenian monetary policy.

Another aspect of the absence of allusion to Attic monetary legislation concerns retrospective views on the fifth-century *arkhē*. Naturally, since Athens was defeated in the Peloponnesian War, intense attention was directed in the fourth century and later toward any problematical or sensitive facet of fifth-century Attic policy, such as colonization or the expulsions and executions of rebellious and hostile populations. Subsequent practical statesmen and commentators, however, are alike disinterested in the monetary dimension of earlier Athenian hegemony. The supposed invalidation of allied metrological and monetary traditions and laws never appears in the criticisms and apologies of Andocides and Isocrates (to take just two prominent examples).[1] Nor is there even a hint of any existence of an Atthidographic treatment of the matter in the remaining fragments, in anonymous lexical glosses and scholia, or in those frequent utilizers of Atthidography, Plutarch and Aelius Aristides.

As Thomas R. Martin observes, one would also expect the issue of monetary interference to have been addressed in the Decree of Aristoteles, the so-called "charter" of the fourth-century confederation (*IG* II[2] 43). We would look for it among the powers forsworn by the Athenians, such as ownership of land in allied states (*IG* II[2] 43.25–31 = Tod, *GHI* #123).[2] The impulse to seek such protection was amply justified by subsequent Athenian behavior, since objectionable features of the fifth-century Attic hegemony were revived to the eventual discredit and weakening of Athenian claims to leadership (including exactions, garrisons, and colonial irredentism). The supposed monopoly over coinage, weights, and measures was ignored by the allies as a precedent for future intrusions on their autonomy that needed to be guarded against. Strikingly, it was also to be the one abuse to which the Athenians had no further recourse. A traditionalist on the Coinage Decree might well counter this observation by asserting that the Athenians were to be congratulated for sparing themselves unpopularity in this one important regard. Nonetheless, inasmuch as the Athenians were not unwilling to earn obloquy

[1] See J.T. Chambers, "The Fourth-Century Athenians' View of Their Fifth-Century Empire," *PP* 30 (1975) 177–91; E. Lévy, *Athènes devant la défaite de 404: Histoire d'une crise idéologique* (Paris 1976) 57–79. See also Figueira, *Colonization* 240–42.

[2] Martin, *Sovereignty* 206–207.

concerning more objectionable aspects of their fifth-century leadership,[3] one is left to explain what turned out to be an atypical capacity for forbearance in this one case.[4]

This problem of absence of criticism of the supposedly imperialistic Coinage Decree and other Athenian monetary legislation intensifies the later we place the Coinage Decree in the Pentekontaeteia. Moreover, the total silence of Thucydides also becomes an ever greater concern when the legislation is placed during the war years (or even during the prelude to hostilities). From that perspective it begins to appear not only that Athenian monetary legislation was not significantly objectionable to the allies of Athens, but also that it was not judged to be threatening by the Peloponnesians. The traditional view of the Coinage Decree sees it as establishing a complete monopoly for Attic coinage over a vast sweep of the Hellenic world. Could Sparta's allies have looked with equanimity on the deliberate creation of a vast economic and monetary unit to which they stood as outsiders? As shall soon be seen, however, the evidence for a legislated monopoly is not telling. Furthermore, the incremental progression of Athenian monetary policy will be found to have lacked a negative impact of sufficient scope to trouble the Peloponnesians, that is, one significantly beyond the changes in economic patterns necessarily wrought by the establishment of the Delian League and the great augmentation of Athenian economic strength and military power thereafter.[5]

ARISTOPHANES

Let us then turn to our important literary *testimonium* on monetary policy toward the allies. Aristophanes has Pisthetairos and Euelpides, his two disenchanted émigrés from war-torn Athens, entertain a succession of public nuisances in the *Birds*, once they have founded their *polis* of

[3] Contrast, for example, the injudicious handling of the Samian cleruchy, which amounted to nothing less than a public relations disaster (cf., for example, Douris *FGH* 76 F 96; Craterus *FGH* 342 F 21). See Figueira, *Colonization* 27–30, 52, 242–48 for full references.

[4] There is indeed an explanation for the apparent "forebearance" of the fourth-century Athenians from general monetary legislation and it concerns the distinction between *phoros*, the "tribute" of the fifth-century *arkhē*, and *syntaxis*, the "contribution" of the fourth-century alliance (see below, pp. 474–76, 558–60). That explanation is, however, discordant with the traditional understanding of the Coinage Decree.

[5] During the Pentekontaeteia Aiginetan coinage continued to be struck in considerable amounts. Aiginetan staters had a currency not only in the Peloponnesos but within the boundaries of the *arkhē*, a situation that had the effect of mitigating any legislation promoting the validity of Athenian coinage within the Attic alliance. Note pp. 36–41 above.

the birds. Right after the *episkopos* 'supervisor of the allies,' a ψηφισματοπώλης 'decree-seller' makes an appearance. The comedy is sustained throughout these episodes by bringing the two jaded Athenians into contact with the very evils of the politicized life that they had endeavored to leave behind in Attica (1035–57).

Ψη: «'Εὰν δ' ὁ Νεφελοκοκκυγιεὺς τὸν 'Αθηναῖον αδικῇ»
Πι. Τουτὶ τί ἔστιν αὖ κακόν, τὸ βιβλίον;
Ψη. Ψηφισματοπώλης εἰμὶ καὶ νόμους νέους
ἥκω παρ' ὑμᾶς δεῦρο πωλήσων.
Πι. Τὸ τί;
Ψη. «Χρῆσθαι Νεφελοκοκκυγιᾶς τοῖσδε τοῖς μέτροισι καὶ
σταθμοῖσι καὶ ψηφίσμασι καθάπερ 'Ολοφύξιοι.»
Πι. Σὺ δὲ γ' οἱσίπερ 'Ωτοτύξιοι χρήσει τάχα.
Ψη. Οὗτος, τί πάσχεις;
Πι. Οὐκ ἀποίσεις τοὺς νόμους;
Πικροὺς ἐγώ σοι τήμερον δείξω νόμους.
Επ. Καλοῦμαι Πισθέταιρον ὕβρεως εἰς τὸν Μουνιχιῶνα μῆνα.
Πι. Ἄληθες, οὗτος; Ἔτι γὰρ ἐνταῦθ' ἦσθα σύ;
Ψη. «'Εὰν δέ τις ἐξελαύνῃ τοὺς ἄρχοντας καὶ μὴ δέχηται
κατὰ τὴν στήλην—»
Πι. Οἴμοι κακοδαίμων, καὶ σὺ γὰρ ἐνταῦθ' ἦσθ' ἔτι;
Επ. 'Απολῶ σε καὶ γράψω σε μυρίας δραχμάς—
Πι. 'Εγὼ δὲ σοῦ γε τὼ κάδω διασκεδῶ.
Ψη. Μέμνησ' ὅτε τῆς στήλης κατετίλας ἑσπέρας;
Πι. Αἰβοῖ· λαβέτω τις αὐτόν. Οὗτος, οὐ μένεις;
'Απίωμεν ἡμεῖς ὡς τάχιστ' ἐντευθενὶ
θύσοντες εἴσω τοῖς θεοῖσι τὸν τράγον.

DS: "If a citzen of Cloudcuckooland should harm an Athenian . . ."
Pi: What is this nuisance now; what is this writing?
DS: I am a Decree-seller and I have come here among you to sell new laws.
Pi: What's your point?
DS: "The citizens of Cloudcuckooland are to use these measures and weights and decrees just like the Olophyxians."
Pi: You will quickly use the very ones which the Ototyxians ["Groanlanders" or "Men of Wails"] use.
DS: Who is this man? Why are you behaving this way?
Pi: Will you not take away these laws? I shall display bitter laws for you this very day.
Ep: I am summoning Pisthetairos on a charge of *hybris* 'outrage' in the month of Mounykhion.
Pi: Is this guy really here? Are you still here?
DS: "If someone should drive out the *arkhontes* 'administrators' and does not receive according to the stele . . ."

Pi: Alas, I am cursed, are you really still here?
Ep: I shall destroy you and charge you with the penalty of
 10,000 drachmas . . .
Pi: And I shall scatter your two (voting) jars.
DS: Do you remember when you used to befoul the stele at night?
Pi: Ugh. Let someone grab him. [To the Priest] My good man, are you not staying?
 Let us depart from here as quickly as possible to sacrifice a goat to the gods inside.

Any prudent discussion of the text must start from the extraordinarily influential comments of Wilamowitz, for he has been considered to have intuited from this passage the existence of legislation directing that the allies utilize Athenian weights, measures, and coins. He is even held to have predicted the Coinage Decree, the fragments of which epigraphists duly began to identify thereafter.[6] In 1880, Wilamowitz made the following observations:[7]

> Der staat selbst gab natürlich nur attisches geld aus, und es leuchtet ein dass durch die fortwährende umprägung eine ganz unverhältnissmassige masse attischer münze in umlauf kam, die denn auch weit über die grenzen der civilisirten welt cursierte, zumal es an einem hinweis nicht fehlt dass der vorort auch auf einheit in mass gewicht und münze bei den stadten hinarbeitete,[56] und es ist artig zu hören, wie die würdigen staatsmänner Spartas, der sittenstrengen stadt, die überhaupt die wertmetalle als teufelswerk verbannt, ihre bestechungen in den laureotischen eulen einstreichen.[57] [This note is not important for this discussion.]
>
> Note 56: Belegen kann ich das nur mit dem gesetzesfragment bei Aristoph. Vög. 1040 χρῆσθαι Νεφελοκοκκυγιᾶς τοῖςδε τοῖς μέτροισι καὶ σταθμοῖσι καὶ νομίσμασι καθάπερ 'Ολοφύξιοι . . ., wo νομίσμασι, wie ich sehe, schon Bergk aus ψηφίσμασι verbessert hat. es ist dringendes bedürfniss dass ein ordentlicher philologe eigens darum numismatik lerne, dass er die münzen des fünften jahrhunderts geschichtlich verarbeite.
>
> The government itself naturally disbursed only Attic money, and it is clear that through the continuous minting an entirely disproportionate mass of Attic coins came into circulation which then also traveled far beyond the boundaries of the civilized world, especially since a hint is not lacking that the government also strove toward unity in measures,

[6] For example, A. Wilhelm, "Zu jüngsten Veröffentlichungen griechischer Inschriften," *AAWW* 61 (1924) 149–62, esp. 158; *IG* I^2, p. 285; Tod, *GHI* 1.165; Erxleben *AfP* (1969) 91.

[7] U. von Wilamowitz-Moellendorff, *Aus Kydathen* (Berlin 1880), *Philol. Untersuchungen* 1, 30–31 with note 56.

weights, and coins among the cities,[56] and it is nice to hear how the estimable statesmen of Sparta, of the puritanical city which completely prohibited precious metals as the work of the devil, earned the wages of their acts of corruption in the owls of Laureion.[57] [This note is not important for our discussion.]

Note 56: I can only show this with the fragment of a law in Aristophanes *Birds* 1040 . . . where, in my view, Bergk has already made the improvement νομίσμασι from ψηφίσμασι. There is an urgent need that a proper philologist learn numismatics expressly in order that he work over historically the coins of the fifth century.

In his *Reden und Vorträge*, Wilamowitz repeated the same sentence, changing only the text of the note in light of his knowledge of the existence of what he considered epigraphical support:[8] "Ich konnte diese Vermutung nur mit einer schwachen Stütze versehen und wurde verlacht; jetzt kenne ich eine noch veröffentliche Urkunde von einer der Inseln, die den Beweis voll erbringt."[9] I find it noteworthy that Wilamowitz no longer felt it necessary to refer to *Birds* 1040 in *Reden und Vorträge* and that he himself claimed the Siphnos and Syme fragments (eventually) as corroboration for his earlier conjecture.

It stands as no reproach to the great erudition of Wilamowitz to observe that his remarks stand in an improbably modernizing overall appraisal of the Attic economy. To Wilamowitz, Athens was a great commercial and industrial power (after Solon managed a crisis in credit) and the wide diffusion of Athenian coins paralleled Attic economic hegemony. Even the appearance of Attic coins beyond the Greek world was expressive of trade relations, as though the Near Eastern importers of Greek silver were themselves operating in a fully monetized economy. That silver coins served in an important sense as a medium for exporting silver was a notion simply not envisaged when Wilamowitz wrote. Scholars conflated determinations of the origin of goods traded, of the identity of the merchants trafficking in these products, and of the provenience of the currency used as a medium for any transactions. This background

[8] I cite from *Reden und Vorträge* (Berlin 1901) 52 with note 1. The second edition of Berlin 1902, offered the same note. The third edition of Berlin, 1913, presented a slightly different note to represent the knowledge of more than one fragment: "Ich konnte diese Vermutung nur mit einer schwachen Stütze versehen und wurde verlacht; jetzt haben mehrere Urkunden von den Inseln den Beweis voll erbracht." The fourth edition of Berlin, 1926 is radically revised and has no corresponding discussion.

[9] "I could provide this conjecture only with a weak support and was opened to ridicule now I know of a still unpublished inscription from one of the islands which fully proves the conclusion."

unsurprisingly conditioned Wilamowitz' glancing appreciation of the passage in the *Birds*.

Rather like some early twentieth-century commentators on Attic monetary policy, Wilamowitz seemed to assume that the dominance of Athenian currency was to a considerable extent incrementally realized through nonlegislative influences. Therefore, in his first thoughts, the fragmentary law in the *Birds* was merely a legislative concomitant to a basically economic and fiscal evolution. There is no suggestion then that Wilamowitz envisaged a general ban on allied minting or a consolidation of local weights and measures. Rather he implied the existence of laws affecting individual communities like the Olophyxians. Thus, Wilamowitz did not predict the actual decree, which survives in the fragments, as it is traditionally interpreted, despite his eventual implication that it proved his original conjecture.

If we start by examining the text of *Birds* 1040–41 in its most basic terms, Aristophanes' allusion simply vouches for the existence of Athenian *psēphismata*, which order individual allied cities to adopt a monetary and metrological regime comparable to the utilization of measures, weights, and coins by some other state. Naturally, it has not been a large extrapolation for scholars to aver further that this other state must invariably have been Athens during the lifetime of the Delian League, but that conclusion may not be as untroubled as it appears on first glance.

Nevertheless, there is no evidence in the *Birds* for the specific type of legislation that is attested by the inscriptions, where the Athenians seem to have legislated for all the allies at once (in the traditional view, for the creation of a monopoly for Attic measures, weights, and coins). The specificity of the law comedically adapted in *Birds* 1040–41 was well appreciated by those commenting on these lines before Wilamowitz. These earlier scholars had made fairly good sense of the material in this passage by supposing that Cloudcuckooland could be expected to use Athenian measures, weights, and laws, because, as a *polis* founded by two Athenians, it could be considered an Athenian colony that would normally use the institutions of its founding city.[10] Given the conflation of the concepts of colony and tributary ally during the *arkhē*, this observation is not without considerable value.[11]

[10] Here is a sample of the early modern commentaries that adopt this interpretation: C.D. Beck, *Aristophanis Aves* (Leipzig 1782) 109; I. Bekker, *Aristophanis Aves* (London 1829) 206; W. Dindorf, *Aristophanis Aves*[3] (Oxford 1837) 631; F.H. Blaydes, *Aristophanis Aves* (Oxford 1842) 73–74; C.C. Felton, *The Birds of Aristophanes with Notes* (Cambridge, MA, 1849).

[11] See Figueira, *Colonization* 230–32.

Making sense of the historical context for Aristophanes' humor here entails a careful dissection of several levels of misdirection and distorted referentiality.[12] In such discussions, the length to which individual insights may be pressed is particularly problematical and exploring the boundary between implied or tacit humorous details and repressed, submerged, or subconscious resonances is alike delicate.

The Decree-seller attempts to sell imperial decrees to the founders of the new city (hence "new laws" in one sense). Essentially, he is hawking a selection of legislation that would establish in general terms the relations between the hegemonic state and any new community that fell for the first time under the shadow of its military and political power. They are all in prose, which heightens the effect of the character of the Decree-seller.[13] Almost all the commentators have seen him as providing an illegal service. He is not just selling copies of decrees—that is inconceivable as they are not inscriptions—but proposing that he gain their passage.[14] On one level, the Decree-seller can be viewed as a demagogue who has temporarily made his way overseas, to the discomfiture of the Athenian émigrés.[15]

The first psephism is clearly a bit from a decree establishing the penalty if a citizen of Cloudcuckooland harms an Athenian citizen (1035). A little later (1050), the Decree-seller will try to cite an enactment that looked out against expulsions of Athenian *arkhontes* and the failure to receive other officials "according to the stele" (which is presumably a shorthand way to refer to inscribed copies both of treaties with Athens and of oaths to be taken in their support).[16] In both these cases, the specific decrees on offer are also useful in their dramatic context. The first is a little precaution against an unfavorable reaction from the potential customers and the second is meant to inhibit Pisthetairos' propensity to vent his

[12] On his allusions to monetary issues, see L. Burelli, "Metaphore monetali e provvedimenti finanziari in Aristophane," *ASNP*[3] 3 (1973) 767–86. Aristophanic reflections of monetary changes of the late fifth and early fourth century will be treated below (pp. 500–502).

[13] A.H. Sommerstein, *Birds* (Warminster 1987) 269.

[14] Cf. B.B. Rogers, *The Birds of Aristophanes* (London 1906) 142; Sommerstein, *Birds* 269; note also N. Dunbar, *Aristophanes Birds* (Oxford 1995) 567–68, who compares the "instant odes" of 904–53 and the "instant oracles" of 962–91.

[15] Accordingly, I am resistant toward the suggestion of J.M. Balcer, "Imperial Magistrates in the Athenian Empire," *Historia* 25 (1976) 257–87, esp. 267, 269–71, that conflates the Decree-seller with a herald sent to announce Athenian legislation to allied cities such as we see in the Coinage Decree section ix (see pp. 380–88 below). Nor were *kērukes* to be considered *arkhontes* like those established during the *arkhē* in allied cities, as their function was communication and not the exercise of authority (compare pp. 391–92).

[16] Dunbar, *Birds* 572, makes the case for giving 1046–47 to the Decree-seller and 1049–50 to the Episkopos.

annoyance by physical abuse. At that point, if the Decree-seller cannot make a sale to Pisthetairos, perhaps he can sell the Episkopos a psephism that will either deter Pisthetairos or permit the Episkopos, who is, after all, just such an Athenian official, legal recourse (grounded locally) for future retaliation. The Episkopos will attempt to enlist the Decree-seller in lines 1046–47. Obviously, the nature of legal coinage in Cloudcuckooland and the validity of local metrological standards fits the moment of the establishment of a new *polis*, and we shall see that the word ψηφίσμασι makes the law an especially apt choice in the immediate context.

The three laws cited are particularly appropriate for acts of political corruption because they are tried and true examples of hegemonic adminstration. To this extent, Pouilloux is correct that there is a joke concealed in the expression "new" of νόμους νέους 'new laws' (1037).[17] The humor, however, does not reside in the point that these are old or obsolete laws, as he suggests in an attempt to make a chronological argument about the date of the initial promulgation of the Coinage Decree and its period of validity.[18] Rather the Decree-seller is not offering to sell anything that will demand much propaganda and special pleading before the *Ekklēsia* 'Assembly' before passage. Their triteness may ensure that no one will question their proposal about an allied *polis* of which no Athenian had ever heard. This earns the placement of these particular laws in his stock: any self-respecting demagogue ought to be able to guarantee their passage and get away with taking a bribe to do so.

While there are undoubtedly examples of cruel humor in Aristophanes—witness the interview between Dikaiopolis and the Megarian in *Acharnians* 729–835 or the wisecrack about a Melian famine in *Birds* 186—nothing here suggests that the legislation at issue represented a painful topic for the audience. The activism of the Decree-seller constitutes a political vice, amply worth condemnation and ridicule, but the way in which it is introduced into this comic indictment of Athens in no way argues for its place in a more serious list of charges.[19] We must not forget that on the most basic level of reception the Decree-seller is offering these three laws for purchase by Pisthetairos as the oecist of a new city-state or colony of Athens, as though they would be so attractive to the birds that they should be eager to buy them.

[17] J. Pouilloux, *Recherches sur l'histoire et cultes de Thasos, Études Thasiennes* 3, 5 (Paris 1954–1958) 1.118, note 3; cf. Pouilloux, "Des rapports actuels de l'épigraphie et de l'histoire grecques," *AC* 22 (1953) 32–49, esp. 38–39 with note 5 on p. 39. Cf. Meiggs 587.

[18] His point was anticipated and answered by Segre 166.

[19] Dunbar, *Birds* 570, recognizes the tone.

Naturally, the presumption that Cloudcuckooland's first priority ought to be the achievement of the status of tributary ally of Athens pokes fun at Athenian self-centeredness and helps to point up the deliciously megalomaniacal project of Pisthetairos that Cloudcuckooland itself should become the hegemonic power of the cosmos. Yet there may also be additional humor embedded in the character of the psephisms themselves, inasmuch as they present at first glance rather poor candidates for *sale* to an ally: this "coinage decree" is at the least prescriptive and the other two laws seem to meet the listeners head on with their punitive aspect. Nonetheless, it is a fine point whether there is enough stated here to lead the audience past the triteness and Athenocentrism of the laws to appreciate further their humorous incongruity. If they are thought to have crossed that threshold, there is no reason not to inquire whether the additional step was taken in which the very unattractiveness of the three psephisms embodied a second (but not last) stratum of comic signification.

The first law handled hostile action against an Athenian much as the oath imposed on the Chalcidians of Euboia in 446/5 tried to forestall such hostile acts against the Athenian *dēmos*.[20] In a parallel fashion, the Athenians made provision for similar protection of individual allied communities (*IG* I³ 75.15–16; 101.52–53). Actually, in the surviving documentation, protection against *adikia* 'injury' is most often charged to Athenian officials on behalf of allied *euergētai* 'benefactors' and *proxenoi* 'diplomatic intercessors.'[21] In the case of the offense of killing the particular individual, the punishment is explicitly the same as for an Athenian (*IG* I³ 19.11–13 [restored]; 161.2–6; 162.9–12 [restored]). There is, however, no example of a decree ordering adjudication and punishments in the apparent manner of the snippet of the Decree-seller. Yet, consider the implication of *IG* I³ 164.23–27, where binding and arrest are coupled with killing as eventualities that trigger punishment on behalf of the honorands like the protection afforded an Athenian. The first decree might have gone on to establish a punishment for *adikia* of an Athenian like that which the honorific decrees reference. Nonetheless, there is also some possibility that such a decree might have then continued to introduce other protected classes (including Attic

[20] *IG* I³ 40. 27–32: καὶ χσύμμαχος ἔσομα|ι *h*οῖος ἂν δύνομαι ἄριστος καὶ δικαιότ|ατος καὶ τõι δέμοι τõι 'Αθεναίον βοεθέσ|ο καί ἀμυνõ, ἐάν τις ἀδικε̃ι τὸν δε̃μον τὸν | 'Αθεναίον, καὶ πείσομαι τõι δε̃μοι τõι 'Αθ|εναιον...

[21] *IG* I³ 19.2–7, 9–11; 24.6–9; 72.11; 91.20–24; 156.1–2; cf. 102.33–34; 110.16.

proxenoi in Cloudcuckooland; Pisthetairos and Euelpides perhaps?) in the spirit of the individually focused attempts in the surviving inscriptions.[22]

A similar conclusion can be drawn about the provision for respecting Athenian *arkhontes*, who are known to have been dispatched to allied cities, not only from the Decree of Kleinias, and from the Coinage Decree itself, that mention them as a class (*IG* I^3 34.6–7: τὸς ἄρχ[οντας ἐν] τε͂σι πόλεσι; see also below, pp. 341–52), but also from specific cases.[23] We can possibly glimpse imperial *arkhontes* most clearly in a group of five officials active at Miletos after its revolt (*IG* I^3 21.61–62), who appear amid regulations that have their purpose in large part in protecting the Milesians (a garrison also appears) from the plots of the Medizing oligarchs who had previously held power in the city. Against this background of ambiguity over whose interests these two decrees serve, it becomes an open question whether the decree mentioned in the *Birds* on the metrological usages of Cloudcuckooland is meant to seem *absolutely* authoritarian.

It is ironic that a single pair of lines that has been said to make so unconditional a reference to an Attic decree that is represented by surviving fragments has been emended without warrant from the manuscripts at no fewer than three loci. Our further investigation can be usefully organized around a discussion of the suggested emendations. Cloudcuckooland's metrological decree mandates that its citizens are to use a specific set of weights and measures, with our and the audience's expectation being that coins will follow as the third term.[24] We get instead ψηφίσμασι 'decrees.' That substitution makes fine dramatic sense, because the Decree-seller is naturally looking to make sales. If Cloudcuckooland is to use Attic psephisms, he is just the man to supply them.

Self-interested substitution may not, however, exhaust the humor inherent in ψηφίσμασι. Even if one adopts the interpretation of the Coinage Decree and of other lost measures of monetary legislation that view them as exploitative or imperialist devices, such jurisdiction would still fall far short of the vast aggrandizement implied by the substitution of the term "decrees." Using the same decrees as the citizens of another state implies nothing less than adopting their polity and entire way of life.

[22] Dunbar, *Birds* 568, also suggests tentatively a slightly different approach, envisaging a *symbola* in which two states protected each other's citizens from molestation.

[23] See Meiggs 213–14, 586. For citations, note *IG* I^3 62.5–6; 72.11–12 [restored]; 101.54–55; 110.19–20; 122.5–6; cf. 135.4?; 114.9, 11??.

[24] That formula much transcends Attic monetary legislation. See also Figueira, *Excursions* 68–69.

We are reminded again that Cloudcuckooland is in a sense a colony of Athens over which Attic hegemony is natural and in which the adoption of Athenian laws is de rigueur. As played for laughs, the Decree-seller no sooner sets foot in Cloudcuckooland than he stakes a vast claim for Attic hegemony.

If one accepts that such an interpretation is legitimately humorous, we should be prepared to accept the manuscript reading and should not be willing to emend the text so as to read νομίσμασιν.[25] That change implies, in my judgment, a sort of cruder referentiality that falls considerably short of Aristophanic subtlety here. It cheats us of a humorous subversion of our expectation in a sequence of terms having the status of a cliché. Thus most editors have rejected the need to emend.[26] A final factor telling against Bergk's suggestion is that the scholia gloss ψηφίσμασι with ἀντι τοῦ νόμοις, showing that any change of the text—and the emendation is creating a *lectio facilior* in any case—is ancient (note Σ1041, Holwerda).

Further analysis also depends on whether to retain the phrase setting up μέτροισι in this line or to emend. The manuscripts read just as I have printed: τοῖσδε τοῖς μέτροισι. . . .[27] We could envisage that the Decree-seller is imagined to have some samples of "standards" just as he presumably came equipped with a scroll bearing the decrees.[28] Like hucksters and con men of other periods he is determined to convince his customers that the products he happens to have with him are just the ones they really need. If the manuscript reading is maintained, not only does the unanticipated member of the series, ψηφίσμασι, bear the comic emphasis, but the very paraphernalia of the Decree-seller could have been exploited for laughter in a way hard to specify from the text alone. Alternatively, the demonstrative could be covered by assuming that the *biblion* containing the decrees also contained a specification of the *metra* and *stathma*.

25 None of the earlier commentators (see note 10 above) opted to emend. Bergk described νομίσμασι (in his edition of 1857) as an expectation. The emendation has been accepted by J. van Leeuwen, *Aristophanis Aves* (Leiden 1902) 162; it is printed in the Loeb edition of B.B. Rogers, *Aristophanes* 2 (London 1937) 230 and also in his edition of 1906 (*Birds* 142), but Rogers rightfully registered strong doubts (*Birds* 284–85). He corrected himself with ψηφίσμασι in the *corrigenda* of his edition of 1930 (p. xcii).

26 One may add F.W. Hall and W.M. Geldart, *Aristophanis Comoediae*[2] (Oxford 1906); V. Coulon and H. van Daele, *Aristophane*[2] 3 (Paris 1967) 74; Sommerstein, *Birds* 126; Dunbar, *Birds* 571.

27 The manuscript reading has been kept by Hall and Geldart (1906); Dunbar, *Birds* 560.

28 Cf. Dunbar, *Birds* 570.

There is, however, a common emendation, which various commentators attribute to Boissonade, Hamaker, or Cobet: τοῖς αὐτοῖς μέτροισι 'the same measures. . . .'[29] If this emendation is accepted, we might have an example of Aristophanes refusing to settle for a single gambit in creating verbal humor. He is compounding the effect by confounding expectation. The reference to the "same measures . . ." increases the momentary anticipation that the Athenian Decree-seller must say 'Ἀθηναῖοι, but he, in fact, says 'Ὀλοφύξιοι, introducing the inhabitants of a minor, partially barbarian city in Thrace.[30] Thus his divergence could be meant to amplify our sense of unreality and intensify the mood of arbitrariness pervading the actions of the Decree-seller. His decrees represent a bad bargain in that they enjoin impossible, arbitrary, or incredibly disruptive conditions.

Nevertheless, Rogers, who has now been seconded by Sommerstein, observed that one should expect οἷσ(περ), if Aristophanes truly meant to say "the same measures and weights and decrees as the Olophyxians."[31] Consequently, that we have καθάπερ militates against the emendation τοῖς αὐτοῖς. This same line of reasoning stimulated Sommerstein to emend to τοῖς ἡμεδαποῖς μέτροισι . . . 'our measures and weights and decrees, just like the Olophyxians.'

Notice how Sommerstein's emendation subtly, but significantly, changes the sense of the line. With τοῖς αὐτοῖς . . . emphasis falls on the homogenization of the practices of Cloudcuckooland with those of the Olophyxians in the dramatic context. Yet, it is still possible that the noncomic, real-life decree envisaged by the audience in response to the joke conveyed the idea of homogenization with the practices of the Athenians. In contrast, with Sommerstein's emendation that idea is now conveyed by the main clause and cannot be implied by the phrase καθάπερ 'Ὀλοφύξιοι. That phrase now serves the single, albeit necessary, purpose of setting up the next joke: Pisthetairos' threatening invocation of the Ototyxians.[32] Sommerstein's emendation does also have the interesting effect of emphasizing the existence of an arrangement with an individual ally that uses the relationship with another ally as a paradigm.

[29] The emendation is accepted in the editions of van Leeuwen (*Aves* 162); Coulon and van Daele (*Aristophane* 3.74); and R. Cantarella (*Aristophane: Le commedie* 4 [Milan 1949] 158).

[30] Thuc. 4.109.3–4; for example, *IG* I³ 259.II.25–26, 262.I.26.

[31] Rogers, *Birds* 284–85; Sommerstein, *Birds* 269. Dunbar, *Birds* 570–71, admits this slight irregularity for its status as "decree-formula."

[32] Commentators have usually noted that the fabricated ethnic Ototyxioi is derived from the verb ὀτοτύζω 'wail aloud' (that is, make the cry ὀτοτοῖ).

Yet, to my mind, the humor of the sentence has been weakened. Although equality with the insignificant Olophyxians still highlights the minimization of both the autonomy and importance of Cloudcuckooland in Sommerstein's version, Aristophanes must be thought to have diverged markedly from any original model for this law. It is improbable that an Athenian law can ever have said τοῖς ἡμεδαποῖς μέτροισι . . . καθάπερ (ethnic name), because the last phrase is redundant for a psephism. What would be the significance of noting that another allied state had also been directed to use Athenian standards? Moreover, it is indeed true that the adjective ἡμεδαπός is unobjectionable in general, as it is attested in Attic epigraphy as referring to Athenian money.[33] It is, however, never used prescriptively, but only descriptively to qualify Athenian monetary holdings. Aristophanes strove for verisimilitude regarding his three psephisms for this scene. That makes this divergence from any conceivable official phraseology unlikely and helps to condemn the emendation τοῖς ἡμεδαποῖς μέτροισι.

We must return to the valence of the phrase καθάπερ 'Ολοφύξιοι 'just like the Olophyxians' to make the right judgment on whether or what to emend. The pertinent parallel is provided by the Phaselis decree of ca. 460–50, where the conduct of *dikai* between Phaselites and Athenians in the court of the polemarch is to occur καθάπερ Χ[ίοις 'just as for the Chians' (*IG* I^3 10.10–11).[34] Here the context is clearly one of reciprocal agreements (lines 11–14: . . . τῶ|[ν δὲ ἄλλω]ν ἀπὸ ξυμβολῶν κατ|[ὰ τὰς ὅσας] ξυμβολὰς πρὸς Φα|[σηλίτας] τὰς δίκας ἐν[α]ι). The phrase is the formula for equating the rights and privileges of one allied city with another or with the Athenians themselves, as this and other examples of καθάπερ with ethnics demonstrate amply.[35] The language as it stands unemended belongs to a paradigm for an abbreviated explanation of the details associated with the orders of the decree: the citizens of Cloudcuckooland were to implement a set of metrological practices

[33] *IG* I^3 52A.4; 372.2; 376.32, 39?, 41, 52, 68–69?, 82–83; 383.I.98–99, II.238; cf. 104.30–31.

[34] *IG* I^3 10.6–11: . . . ὅ τι ἂμ μὲ[ν] 'Αθ|[ήνησι ξ]υ[μβ]όλαιον γένηται | [πρὸς Φ]ασηλιτ[ῶ]ν τινα, 'Αθή[ν]η|[σι τὰς δ]ίκας γίγνεσθαι παρ|[ὰ τῶι πο]λεμάρχωι, καθάπερ Χ|[ίοις. . . . See P. Gauthier, *Symbola: Les étrangers et la justice dans les cités grecques* (Nancy 1972) 177–82; S. Cataldi, *Symbolai e relazione tra le città greche nel v secolo a.C.* (Pisa 1983) 99–143. See Figuerira, *Excursions* 161–62 for some of my views on the Phaselis decree and its date.

[35] *IG* I^3 40.42: (oath for the Chalcidians) καθάπερ 'Ερετριεῦσι; 40.72–73: (*euthunai* at Chalcis) καθάπερ 'Αθένεσιν 'Αθεναίοις; 127.22: (peace with Sparta on same terms): [κ]αθάπερ 'Αθηναίοις, καὶ τοῖς νῦν οἰκõσιν Σάμον. Cf. *IG* I^3 9.5–6; 62.4–5: (cost of grain at Aphytis): καθάπερ Με]θωναίοις; 70.11: . . . καθάπερ Χίω[ν τοῖς ἥκοσι(?); 71.58: (ox and panoply to Panathenaia) [καθάπερ ἄποι]κ[οι(?); 164.26-27: (punishment for those harming an Athenian *euergetes*): κ[αθάπερ 'Αθεναίοις. Note also *IG* I^3 8.24: . . . καθά]περ Σουνιεῦσι.

and legislation (with monetary practices in the back of the audience's mind) corresponding to those already in use between Athens and a third community, the Olophyxioi. The use of the older forms of the dative may direct attention toward a piece of model legislation much earlier than the 410s.[36] These standards are understood as set forth in the βιβλίον; hence the expression τοῖσδε τοῖς μέτροισι.... When Pisthetairos comes to threaten the Decree-Seller with the laws οἰσίπερ or οἶσπερ (Dindorf's emendation) ὠτοτύξιοι, the syntax changes, because he has no prop to which to point.[37]

The unemended text implies the existence of a decree enjoining the usage (χρῆσθαι) of metrological standards that were in fact current in an allied city. There is nothing here of a prohibition of minting or even of an exclusive use of Athenian standards, although, if the analogy were pressed, Cloudcuckooland, as a newly founded *polis* without previous monetary or metrological practices, is somewhat anomalous in this setting.[38] And the intersecting paradigm, wherein Cloudcuckooland is an Attic colony, also influences the context. Based on Aristophanes, we cannot specify the details and style of the practices enjoined on the citizens of Cloudcuckooland. The humorous introduction of the Olophyxians in the Decree-seller's *psephism* has not extruded the Athenians from their rightful place, but the Olophyxians stand in place of the name of a more prominent Athenian ally. That extrusion helps to make the *psephism* on offer by the Decree-seller such a comically bad deal for Cloudcuckooland—just as did the substitution ψηφίσμασι 'decrees' for νομίσμασι 'coins.'

This conclusion would suggest in turn that the Athenians may have gradually encouraged the usage of their standards and money, employing a paradigmatic arrangement with an unknown allied city or a set of such paradigms. When states entered the Attic alliance or at points when their status was reviewed (such as after Athenian interventions), some pattern of metrological and monetary activity was implemented following an established model. Although a role for Attic money and standards

[36] Dunbar, *Birds* 571, who also cautions that shorter datives might have been altered by a copyist determined to create a trimeter here. See also Koch, *Volksbeschlüsse* 371.

[37] J. Tzetzes glossed οἷσιπερ, ἐκείνοις τοῖς μέτροις (Σ1043, Koster).

[38] Nor must the emendation τοῖς αὐτοῖς..., of which I remain most skeptical in any case, compel us to believe that the law underlying the joke made for the *exclusive* use of Athenian measures, weights, and coins. Treaties mandating that allies have the same friends and enemies as a *hēgemōn* do not forbid that ally having other friends and enemies, so long as the other friends were not enemies of the *hēgemōn*, and the other enemies, his friends. One might object that using Athenian standards and coins inevitably entails not using anyone else's, including one's own. Yet, if that is so, it is surprising that we are never told so explicitly.

probably was prominent in the paradigm(s), Aristophanes *Birds* 1040–41 does not provide support for Athenian imposition of a monopoly of their money and metrological usages. There is no certainty that the provision for measures, weights, and coins καθάπερ 'Ολοφύξιοι 'just like the Olophyxians' (or its real-world counterpart[s]) did not subsume a usage of other coins and standards. Those who have found a citation from *symbolai* 'reciprocal trade agreements' a plausible restoration in the Coinage Decree (section ii: see pp. 336–37) will take encouragement from the realization that the paradigm for adoption of Athenian standards and money might have been a model, consensual agreement made between relative equals (such as the Athenians and the Chians or another autonomous ally). We see in the *Birds* an allusion to unknown Athenian monetary legislation and not to the Coinage Decree—certainly as it is customarily interpreted. Here one senses the extent of the legislation and diplomacy that has been lost from our sight.

PART III

MONETARY POLICY IN HISTORICAL CONTEXT

9

CONTEXTS FOR MONETARY POLICY

I DO NOT PROPOSE in this chapter to essay the considerable task of writing a summary history of imperial Athens, although it would take little less than that effort to exhaust all the political and economic assumptions underlying the traditional views on the Coinage Decree. Even eschewing that vast project, a reconstruction of fifth-century Athenian monetary policy is severely hampered by the absence of official documents from the first years of the Delian League. Rather, the following discussion intends to touch on only those features of Athenian institutional history that were assumed to be fundamental in earlier interpretations of the nature of the Coinage Decree, namely, basic suppositions about the Athenian economy, interstate trade, and allied autonomy. It will be seen that much that provides a basis for confident assertions about the functioning of monetary legislation is actually highly problematical. Based on the foregoing investigation of the numismatic and literary evidence, some leads toward a less ad hoc portrait of monetary conditions can be presented.

The best available method for proceeding is a re-creation based on a commonsense ordering of the source material. I shall state at the start that the "common sense" being applied here is that of a non-Marxist ancient historian whose own views on economics were formed from youthful reading of various "neo-orthodox," market-oriented economists, chiefly those belonging to the Austrian and Chicago schools.[1] Such modern work cannot provide an exact road map for ancient economic contexts, but it inevitably informs the perspectives of this scholar and so deserves to be noted at the outset. The degree of persuasiveness of the resulting analysis should be the criterion for appraisal, not the citation of an intellectual pedigree or an abstracted "demonstration" that a particular model is superior (be it Marxist, monetarist, or whatever).

[1] For example, note works such as F. von Hayek, *The Road to Serfdom* (Chicago 1942); von Hayek, *Studies in Philosophy, Politics, and Economics* (Chicago 1967); L. von Mises, *Human Action: A Treatise on Economics* (New Haven 1949); M. Friedman, *Capitalism and Freedom* (Chicago 1962).

THE ECONOMIC CONTEXT

Let us begin by considering what the Athenians could have gained had they imposed their own weights, measures, and coins on their allies. As already noted, Segre described the Coinage Decree as an act of commercial imperialism, and he has not been alone in that judgment, as the general accounts surveyed above indicate. Nevertheless, evaluating this supposition turns out to be harder than one anticipates at first glance since there are so many assumptions undergirding a conclusion of economic imperialism that will need to be uncovered.

The Archaic Attic Economy

First of all, this hypothesis is presumably dependent on the view that Athens was a great commercial state from an early date (an ancient Venice or Holland).[2] The exaggeration of the scale of archaic Athenian trade is chiefly owed to a misreading of the widespread finds of Attic pottery, and it is surely adventurous to insist that such craft goods were necessarily carried by Attic merchants. I have argued elsewhere for the conclusion that Ionian and subsequently Aiginetan traders were the leading agents in the conveyance of Athenian craft goods during the archaic period.[3] The Dark Age and early archaic economy of Athens was predominantly agrarian, with a political and social elite made up of wealthy landowners. The earliest evidence is mythological inasmuch as the Athenians laid claim to the inauguration under divine instruction of the triad of essential foodstuffs: grain, olives, and wine.[4] The encapsulation of some of these traditions in the *Homeric Hymn to Demeter*, in a poetic tradition shaped by aristocratic patronage, shows their structural status in the formation of elite identity. The term *pentakosiomedimnos* 'of five hundred bushels' that was later to denominate the highest Solonian census class probably served as one epithet for describing this wealthy Attic agricultural upper

[2] A. French, *The Growth of the Athenian Economy* (New York 1964) esp. 43–46, which may be taken as exemplary of the tendency.

[3] Figueira, *Aegina* 264–80; Figueira, *Excursions* 58–59.

[4] Grain cultivation: Isoc. 4.28–31; Xen. *HG* 6.3.6; *Suda*, s.v. προηροσίαι, π 2420 Adler (~ Lyc. fr. 14.4 Conomis); cf. *IG* II^2 1134.22–24 = *SIG*^{3} 704E.16–18; see also *Homeric Hymn* 4.470–82; Apollod. 3.191. Cultivated olive trees: Hdt. 8.55; Apollod. 3.178–79; Hyg. *Fab.* 164; Augustine *CD* 18.9; cf. Hdt. 5.82.1–3. Production of wine: Nonnus, *Dionys.* 47.34–35; Apollod. 3.191–92; Hyg. *Fab.* 130; Servius, *In Georg.* 2.389.

class.[5] The terracotta models of granaries, found in Geometric tombs, contribute to the same conclusion.[6]

The agrarian character of the Attic economy as late as the first half of the sixth century is indicated by the Solonian census system, with its thresholds for assignment to census class calculated solely in agricultural production (*Ath. Pol.* 7.3–4; Plut. *Solon* 18.1–2).[7] That the elite was primarily drawn from landowners as late as the 560s and 550s is shown by the existence of regional parties consisting of blocs of farmers, although the separation of the Paralia as a region suggests that coastal Attica was drawing on nonagricultural sources of income.[8] The term *naukraros* means ship's captain and was used in Attica for those individuals who assisted in the provision of ships for the navy.[9] They were persons with ties in private life to seafaring, some of whom will have been merchants, along with pirates, fishermen, and even some exporting landowners. Yet the system of *naukrariai* within which the *naukraroi* were organized were subdivisions of Attic tribes (*Ath. Pol.* 8.3; Poll. 8.108; Cleidemus *FGH* 323 F 8); hence they mobilized the largely agricultural population of Attica for naval service.

Agricultural goods comprised a significant component of Athenian exports in the archaic period. The regional role of Attic food exports including the tiding of neighboring communities over dearths can be seen in the Attic affinities of the Saronic Gulf cults of Damia and Auxesia, goddesses of agricultural fertility (inter alia).[10] Dependent labor played a role in the viability of this trade, and, in the acute stage of the Solonian crisis, dependent laborers themselves were exported as slaves. A sizable export trade in olive oil is shown by the use of a

[5] The description of *Ath. Pol.* 7.3 that Solon τιμήματι διεῖλεν εἰς τέτταρα τέλη, καθάπερ διῄρητο καὶ πρότερον 'divided into four classes according to assessment of property, just as they were also divided previously' is not strictly correct. The names for the census classes probably existed as important social markers, not as legal terms. Cf. Rhodes, *CAAP* 137–38.

[6] Regardless of whether one decides that the impressive funerary chest bearing five models of granaries (from an EG II grave ca. 850 from the north slope of the Acropolis) affirms the pre-Solonian currency of *pentakosiomedimnos*, it is an eloquent social document. See E.B. Smithson, "The Tomb of a Rich Athenian Lady, ca. 850 B.C.," *Hesperia* 37 (1968) 77–116, esp. 83, 92–97; J.N. Coldstream, "The Rich Lady of the Areiopagos and Her Contemporaries: A Tribute in Memory of Evelyn Lord Smithson," *Hesperia* 64 (1995) 391–403, esp. 395–98, who provides a review, as well as the most recent comparative material.

[7] For references, see A. Martina, *Solon* (Rome 1968) ##344–49, pp. 170–73.

[8] *Ath. Pol.* 13.5: εἶχον δ' ἕκαστοι τὰς ἐπωνυμίας ἀπὸ τῶν τόπων ἐν οἷς ἐγεώργουν 'each faction took its title from the district in which they farmed.'

[9] Figueira, *Excursions* 163–67 for full references.

[10] Figueira, *Excursions* 50–53, 57–58, 78–80.

characteristic type of amphora, the "SOS" amphora (from ca. 760–50), of which the majority has been shown to be Attic by a predominance of the findspots and by chemical analysis.[11] Notwithstanding the wide dissemination of these pots, nothing urges that Athenian merchants even participated in, let alone dominated, the conveyance of Attic oil to foreign markets.[12] Indeed their very standardization (as compared to containers of succeeding periods) may suggest that those exporting olive oil had no assurance that they could communicate the provenience and quality of their product save by using a standard vessel in a manner unlike the product differentiation that marks the more export-conscious late archaic pottery industry. After Solon forbade the exportation of grain, exports of olive oil would have received greater attention in the early sixth century (Plut. *Solon* 24.1).[13]

Economic conditions changed after 600, with the Solonian legislative program having a major effect.[14] The craft industry in Attica strengthened during the sixth century, helped by Solonian encouragement of skilled immigrants (Plut. *Solon* 24.4). The checking of the aristocratic presumption of the Eupatrids (the later Pedion faction) will have helped Attica to retain its craftsmen.[15] Hence the artistic advances of Attic

[11] A. Johnston and R.E. Jones, "The 'SOS' Amphora," *BSA* 73 (1978) 103–41. For their common subjection to graffiti, see A.W. Johnston, *Trademarks on Greek Vases* (Warminster 1979) 1–2, 48–50. See also B.B. Shefton, "Greeks and Greek Imports in the South of the Iberian Peninsula: The Archaeological Evidence," in H.G. Niemeyer (ed.), *Phönizier im Westen* (Mainz 1982) 337–70, esp. 338–42. Examples from ca. 600 are preserved in the Odessa Museum, probably from Olbia (*Archaeological Reports for 1983–84*, p. 79).

[12] Note J. de Hoz Bravo, "Un grafito griego de Toscanos y la exportación de aceite ateniense en el siglo VII," *Madrider Mitteilungen* 11 (1970) 102–109, on examples exported to southern Spain.

[13] The "SOS" amphoras paradoxically disappear ca. 580–70, just after the time at which Solon was limiting agricultural exports to oil. See Johnston and Jones *BSA* (1978) 140–41. The lower boundary may be caused by a shift in the paths by which Attic oil was sold abroad, as well as by Italian olive production. The Euboians are prime candidates as the chief carriers of "SOS" amphoras, when one considers the findspots (with the Phoenicians as secondary traders?). Chalcis and perhaps even Pithekoussai may be alternative sites for production. See the comment of A. Johnston on G. Vallet, "Les cités chalcidiennes du détroit et de Sicile," in *Gli Eubei in Occidente: Atti del diciottesimo convegno di studi sulla Magna Grecia* (Taranto 1979) 147. The decline of the pot type is perhaps connected with assumption of the export of Attic goods by Ionians and Aiginetans who practiced a more sophisticated commercial intermediation. Cf. G. Vallet, "L'introduction de l'olivier en Italie centrale," *Hommages à Albert Grenier* (Brussels 1962) 3.1554–1563, esp. 1159–60; M. Gras, "Amphores commerciales et histoire archaïque," *DialArch* 5 (1987) 41–50.

[14] Cf. Figueira, *Excursions* 80–84

[15] Figueira, *Excursions* 58–59, 82–83, tried to trace the establishment of middle proto-Attic potters of the "black and white" style on Aigina to the social crisis of the seventh century.

black-figure artists and potters had the social context in which to flourish, with their products feeding international markets. It has been fashionable to minimize the significance of the pottery industry, but such judgments are quite simplistic, as they ignore the number of ancillary workers supported by the active participants and (more importantly) miss the multiplier effect for jobs of a craft producing finished products.[16] Potters occupied buildings, burned fuel, and consumed other goods, all of which raised employment and stimulated output in these other areas of the economy. Moreover, the pottery craft leaves eminently visible remains, while other industries, the products of which were less durable and thus are more poorly known to us, may alike have had some place in the emergence into social significance of Attic crafts. In particular, the coloration, decoration, and iconography of Attic painted pottery may hint at the vitality of the contemporary Athenian metallurgical industry, of which the products have not survived.[17]

In this same period, the first political impact of wealth from manufacturing is seen in the creation of the board of ten magistrates that replaced the eponymous archon during the civil strife of the late 580s and early 570s (*Ath. Pol.* 13.1–2). Here is a political role for the *dēmiourgoi* 'craftsmen' alongside the Eupatrids and the farmers, but even this secondary political participation is likely to have been a reflection of changes in social relations of the *asty* 'urban center' alone.[18]

The tradition that Solon became a merchant when he decided to leave Athens after his reforms is (I believe) of sixth-century provenience (*Ath. Pol.* 11.1; Plut. *Solon* 25.6; cf. Hdt. 1.29). The removal of the *nomothetēs* 'lawgiver' from the scene after his legislation is a conventional theme, and is unlikely to portray the historical reality of Solon's later life (a period notoriously elaborated in Attic tradition). That this *topos* of distancing the lawgiver from his *polis* takes the form here of converting Solon into a trader implies that a merchant *based* in Attica was a rarity for some time after Solon's archonship in 594/3. Otherwise, a member of the Athenian merchant community would be expected to carry on his trade between points abroad and Attica. For the story to work in conventional

16 Cf. R.M. Cook, "Die Bedeutung der bemalten Keramik für den griechischen Handel," *JdI* 74 (1959) 114–23, who estimates 400–500 workers at any one time in the sixth century.

17 See M. Vickers, "Artful Crafts: The Influence of Metal Work on Athenian Painted Pottery," *JHS* 105 (1985) 108–28.

18 T.J. Figueira, "The Ten *Archontes* of 579/8 at Athens," *Hesperia* 53 (1984) 447–73, esp. 469–71.

terms, becoming a merchant must be tantamount to keeping away from Athenian territory entirely.[19]

At the end of the sixth century and in the first decades of the fifth, another significant change in the Attic economy occurred, the development of mining at Laureion. It must be noted, however, that silver mining was a primary extractive industry and would not necessarily have stimulated a large expansion in Attic commerce.[20] It would, however, have promoted the craft industry providing silver plate and utensils. The availability to the community of income from all craft production and later from silver mining sustained imports of grain and permitted a further shift of the farming sector of the economy away from grain production and toward the production of olive oil, the surplus of which could also be exported. The Athenian economy was thus transformed during the sixth century: a grain-exporting economy (ca. 600) probably with a net outflow of population through the export of Athenians as slaves and the departure of emigrants, became a grain-importing economy with a strong inflow of immigrants and especially of slaves (ca. 500).[21]

The early sixth-century economy at Athens had exported craft products, but the late sixth- and early fifth-century economy probably had more dynamic exports of finished products, along with olive oil and above all silver. Nevertheless, Athenian colonial policy down through the lifetime of Perikles, be it manifested through *apoikiai* 'colonies' or *klēroukhiai* 'cleruchies,' shows the continuing predominance of the primary, agrarian and extractive, sectors of the Athenian economy.[22] Athenian colonization did not seek to create *emporia* 'commercial ports' per se although an imperial colony like Amphipolis (founded in 437/6) was a center for regional exchange, but rather replicas of the traditional Attic economy of the early fifth century.

While agriculture vied with mining as the largest sector of that economy, silver must have constituted the largest component of exports and

[19] Figueira, *Excursions* 84–85. An alternative ostensible purpose for his travels, *theōria* 'sightseeing,' is equally conventional. See M. Manfredini and L. Piccirilli, *Plutarco: la vita di Solone* (Milan 1977) 263–64 for other references and discussion. A relevant parallel is the tradition on Lycurgus, where the motif of the departure of the lawgiver in order to protect his reforms appears in its stronger manifestation, namely, his suicide (Plut. *Lyc.* 29.2–5; Nic. Dam. *FGH* 90 F 56.1; *Suda* s.v. Λυκοῦργος, λ 824 Adler, with a likely derivation from Ephorus, cf. *FGH* 70 F 175). For discussion, see Manfredini and Piccirilli, *Le vite di Licurgo e di Numa* (Milan 1980) 284–85.

[20] See E. Ardaillon, *Les mines du Laurion dans l'antiquité* (Paris 1897) 134–36; R.J. Hopper, "The Laurion Mines: A Reconsideration," *BSA* 63 (1968) 293–326, esp. 303–304.

[21] Cf. Figueira, *Excursions* 80–86.

[22] See Figueira, *Colonization* 181–85, 234–36.

probably exceeded the total of other export goods in value. Attic silver coins became a primary medium for the export of silver from Laureion. Attic coinage began after 550 with the issues of Wappenmünzen 'heraldic coins'; the first owls were minted between 525 and 510, and Attic coins probably did not begin to become prevalent until after 510.[23] The plentiful late archaic Attic coinage reflected both the output of the silver mines and metallurgical skills on a high level that had earlier made some Athenian followers of Peisistratos welcome in the development of the mines of Mt. Pangaion in Thrace ca. 560–50 (cf. *Ath. Pol.* 15.2). The wide dissemination of Attic tetradrachms (as indicated by the hoard evidence outlined in Chapter 1 above) shows that they were used to pay for imports in amounts that surpassed any recirculatory flow back to Attica. Hence Attic coins comprised a significant proportion of the bullion transferred from Greece to Egypt and the Near East.

The Themistoclean naval law (482) suggests that the maritime sector of the economy had also grown; otherwise the capacity to build so many new triremes would not have existed.[24] The growth of crafts may have provided workers able to act as auxiliaries to the shipwrights, joining the latter when the annual production of triremes increased markedly. Thus the ability to mount a "crash" program of construction may reflect the growth in all industries and not necessarily only the expansion of shipbuilding capacity. Nevertheless, the necessity of allocating the windfall in state revenues from the mines to shipbuilding and the need to assign administrative and financial responsibility to a cross section of upper-class Athenians[25] may imply that the simplest expedient, ordering Athenian *naukraroi* (including merchant ship captains) to supervise the building of more ships, was not feasible even with the subsidization (*Ath. Pol.* 22.7, Polyaen. *Strat.* 1.30.6; cf. Hdt. 7.144.1–2; Plut. *Them.* 4.1–3).

The Classical Athenian Economy

Considering the commercial activity attested by the growth of the Peiraieus during the Pentekontaeteia, it is remarkable how little evidence there is for merchant endeavors by Athenian citizens.[26] Mining continued to be a vital sector of the economy, as the silver production

[23] Figueira, *Excursions* 62–66, cites recent scholarship in detail.

[24] The most complete review of the literary evidence remains J. Labarbe, *La Loi Navale de Thémistocle* (Liege 1957) esp. 10–17. For some thoughts of my own, see *Excursions* 163–72.

[25] Rhodes *CAAP* 278, citing A.R. Burn, *Persia and the Greeks* (New York 1962) 292 (with note 36).

[26] A good collection of the evidence, which is fragmentary and quite skewed by the chances of survival, is C.M. Reed, *Maritime Traders in the Greek World of the Archaic and Classical Periods* (Diss., Oxford University 1981).

at Laureion reached its historic heights (see pp. 184–85 above). Not only were wealthy politicians, such as Kallias Lakkoploutos, Nikias, and Kallias's son Hipponikos, who are attested individually,[27] indicative of this phenomenon, but Aeschylus in his *Persai* of 472 dramatizes the importance of the yield of the mines, both retrospectively and prospectively (lines 237–38): Queen Atossa: "What else is there in addition to these things? Is there sufficing wealth at home?"; Chorus: "Some fountain of silver there is for them, a subterranean treasury."

Capital expenditure after the Battle of Plataia in 479 did not only go to rehabilitate the devastated properties of the Athenians (as Thucydides observes in 2.16.1). The procurement of slaves was the other major area of capital deployment. Since most manumitted slaves did not repatriate themselves, the acquisition of slaves acted as a coercive form of immigration. Attic slavery concentrated the manpower needed to sustain an expansion of silver mining and to provide replacement laborers in workshops or farmsteads, thus freeing Athenians to exploit political and military sources of income.

After the Persian Wars, the main new ingredient in the economy was the influx of resources into Attica because of the Delian League and the war against Persia, be it from tribute, from the acquisition of booty and slaves from military campaigns, or from the visits to Attica (for military service or for other political business) of many citizens of the allied states (cf. [Xen.] *Ath. Pol.* 1.16–18). Attica became not only the largest concentration of consumers within the states of the league, but perhaps also the greatest productive center, for in near-subsistence economies, concentrations of population will perforce be centers of output. And the Athenians had the good fortune to possess a considerable base in craft industries and in mining which had been built without the assistance of hegemonic influence. As the "Old Oligarch" noted, a greater variety and supply of goods were to be found in the Peiraieus than anywhere else, so that the port became a place ever more visited during the Attic hegemony ([Xen.] *Ath. Pol.* 2.7–8, cf. 11–12).

The bulk of this commerce seems to have been in the hands of metics (resident aliens) and *xenoi* 'foreigners.' Indeed the ethnic identity of many of the agents of commercial life in the *arkhē* may not have changed all that radically after 480. Attica had merely drawn to itself trade that heretofore had been dispersed among other sites (and particularly among the smaller cities) of the Aegean basin. Traders relocating to

[27] Xen. *Poroi* 4.14–15; Plut. *Nic.* 4.2; Nepos *Cimon* 1.3. See also J.K. Davies, *Wealth and the Power of Wealth in Classical Athens* (New York 1981) 79.

Attica attracted metic craftsmen and organized workshops themselves, as is shown by the example of the family of Lysias at the top end of this class of metic entrepreneurs (Lys. 12.4, 8, 18–19; fr. 1.6 Albini). In some trades, such as grain provision, the wholesalers (so-called *sitopōlai*) appear to have been exclusively metics (note Lys. 22.5; cf. 22.16, 21).[28]

ECONOMIC RATIONALES FOR THE COINAGE DECREE

How would the passage of the Coinage Decree or other monetary legislation have affected these economic circumstances? We can make a start toward an answer by considering the largest nongovernmental item of the fifth-century Athenian balance of trade, silver exports. Here we need to pose the question whether the supposed prohibition on allied coining would have affected the utilization of Athenian silver.

The Silver Supply and the Value of Silver

Although Athens continued as a major producer of silver in this period, the mandating of a monopoly for Attic coins could not increase the demand for Attic silver in and of itself. Silver was not used only for coining. The scale of artistic production and the rate of religious dedication were potent factors in establishing the demand for the metal. In turn, these factors were conditioned by many other forces, such as the status of incomes and perceptions of international security (to name only two). The demand for silver to be used specifically for coining was a function of the nature of the money supply. The money supply was in its turn affected by assets held in bankers' accounts, by the amount of silver passing between coins and other forms, by the number of coins in active circulation as compared to those hoarded, and by the velocity of the circulation of Attic money at home and abroad.[29]

Still another circumstance affecting the demand for silver was the role of silver in a series of relevant balances of payments: the one between Athens and the *arkhē*, that between the *arkhē* and the rest of the Greeks, and finally that between the *arkhē* and its non-Greek neighbors. Indeed we would especially need to determine this last balance, specifically in regard to which rate bullion and coins within the Attic alliance, paying for imports, were passing outside the alliance or even entirely outside the Greek world. We do know from the hoards that coins themselves acted as

[28] See T.J. Figueira, "*Sitopolai* and *Sitophulakes* in Lysias' Oration 'Against the Graindealers,'" *Phoenix* 40 (1986) 149–71.

[29] On the issue of the money supply, compare K. Hopkins, "Taxes and Trade in the Roman Empire (200 B.C. to A.D. 400)," *JRS* 70 (1980) 101–25, esp. 108–10.

a medium (alongside bullion and jewelry) for the export of silver, even to the (quasi-monetized?) economies of the Near East and Egypt.[30] Anyone, however, with even a passing knowledge of the ancient evidence on the economy of the fifth century will also recognize that impossible demands have been placed on the data by merely noting the aforesaid conditions for discussing the demand for silver. Thus, the following remarks must cleave to generalities.

No interpretation of the Coinage Decree has explained how a ban on allied minting would have altered the total supply of silver in the *arkhē* or the size of the money supply. Even if we accept the decree as ordering a massive conversion process by which all allied silver was called in and replaced with Attic coinage (something that I very much doubt: see below, pp. 332, 353–54), Athenian owls would merely be replacing other series of coins in silver, and the raw material for the reminting will have been the silver in allied coin that was summoned to Attica to be recoined. That process would not raise the demand for silver.

A best estimate is that Attica and the *arkhē* experienced a growth in population and in output, both communally and per capita, during the Pentekontaeteia (cf. Thuc. 1.1.1; 2.16.1; cf. 2.31.2).[31] Although the Athenians might have been absorbing a greater percentage of the output of the allied cities than ever before when they increased tribute assessments in 425 (although the contention is unproven), that such increases were possible at all suggests a growth in the aggregate wealth of the allies.[32] There are no countervailing factors—at least that come easily to my mind—that would urge a belief that silver was a good that was, exceptionally, experiencing a fall in demand during the Pentekontaeteia, be that silver Athenian or of any other origin. The impression given from the archaeology of the Laureion district is that this was a period of expansion.[33]

Furthermore, some significant literary indications are also available. Thucydides recounts that one of the devastating results of the establishment of a Peloponnesian base at Dekeleia in 413 was the defection of 20,000 Athenian slaves, many of whom were skilled craftsmen,

[30] Note C.M. Kraay, "Hoards, Small Change and the Origin of Coinage," *JHS* 84 (1964) 76–91, esp. 80–82.

[31] Some of my own thoughts appeared in Figueira, *Colonization* 185–93, 201–15.

[32] See Meiggs 322–32 for an overview. Cf. L. Kallet-Marx, *Money, Expense, and Naval Power in Thucydides' History 1–5.24* (Berkeley and Los Angeles 1993) 164–67.

[33] C.E. Conophagos, *Le Laurium antique* (Athens 1980) 96–105. Another recent overview is offered by J.E. Jones, "The Laurion Silver Mines: A Review of Recent Researches and Results," *G&R* 29 (1982) 169–83.

n.b. χειροτέχναι (7.27.5). Skilled workers were the most able to make their way as free men, and among the *kheirotekhnai* well situated for escape were probably mine workers (cf. Thuc. 6.91.7; Xen. *Por.* 4.25).[34] Any appreciable number of slave workers in the mines must have been built up after 480–79, when Attic slaves were diverted for military service and then freed. An incremental buildup would have been offset by deaths, manumissions, and superannuations, the peculiar difficulties of concentrating labor in a slave industry. I doubt that Attic slave numbers could have grown so great unless there had been a reasonable, continuing expectation that all the silver that could be produced would be sold.

That is the impression also garnered from the *Poroi* of Xenophon, written ca. 355/4. He states that Laureion had always been able to satisfy those wishing to add workers in the region (4.3–6), and the chief current problem to be obviated is the absence of slaves to work the mines on the level of intensity that had been reached in the fifth century (4.13–18).[35] Contrasting gold to silver, Xenophon notes that increases in the supply of gold lead to a fall in its price and in its value relative to silver (4.10). Silver, however, has maintained price stability: οὔτε τοῦ ἀργυρίου ἀτίμου ποτὲ ἐσομένου 'nor will silver ever become devalued' (4.11).[36] The late fifth-century evidence may bear him out, as it shows gold losing value relative to silver (pp. 511–17, 521–27). Although there is much to criticize in his grasp of supply and demand in specific regard to the supply of silver, Xenophon is quite candid on the elasticity of the demand for silver (contrasted with consumer goods like household furnishings: *Poroi* 4.7–10):[37]

> ἀργύριον δὲ οὐδεὶς πω οὕτω πολὺ ἐκτήσατο ὥστε μηκέτι προσδεῖσθαι: ἀλλ' ἤν τισι γένηται παμπληθές, τὸ περιττεῦον κατορύττοντες οὐδὲν ἧττον ἥδονται ἢ χρώμενοι αὐτῷ. καὶ μὴν ὅταν γε εὖ πράττωσιν αἱ πόλεις, ἰσχυρῶς οἱ ἄνθρωποι ἀργυρίου δέονται. [Examples of public and private consumption during prosperous times follow.] ὅταν τε

[34] S. Lauffer, *Die Bergwerkssklaven von Laureion*² (Wiesbaden 1979) 141, 281; P. Gauthier, *Un commentaire historique des* Poroi *de Xénophon* (Geneva/Paris 1976) 157–59. See also W.L. Westermann, *The Slave Systems of Greek and Roman Antiquity* (Philadelphia 1955) 7–8. Conophagos, *Laurium* 105–106, 341–49, estimates 11,000 slaves directly employed in mine preparation, silver extraction, and refining, but his estimates must depend on back calculations using modern analogies from his estimates of silver output. Cf. V.D. Hanson, "Thucydides and the Desertion of Attic Slaves during the Decelean War," *CA* 11 (1992) 210–28, who prefers to see the 20,000 as primarily agricultural workers, but even after his often rather tortured/tortuous arguments there is still ample room for a large defection (10,000+) of skilled mine personnel.

[35] Gauthier, *Poroi* 116–23, 136–44.

[36] See S. Lauffer, "Das Bergbauprogramm in Xenophons Poroi," *MIGRA* 1 (1975) 171–205, esp. 172–73, 176–77.

[37] See Gauthier, *Poroi* 123–34.

αὖ νοσήσωσιν ⟨αἱ⟩ πόλεις ἢ ἀφορίαις καρπῶν ἢ πόλεμῳ, ἔτι καὶ πολὺ μᾶλλον, ἀργοῦ τῆς γῆς γιγνομένης, καὶ εἰς ἐπιτήδεια καὶ εἰς ἐπικούρους νομίσματος δέονται. [There is next a comparison with gold, the market for which Xenophon claims can be saturated, leading to a fall in value.]

No one yet has acquired so much silver that he no longer had further need for it. If there is a very great supply for any persons, burying the surplus they take no less pleasure than if they were using it. Admittedly, whenever cities are prospering, men have a strong need for money. . . . And whenever cities are in distress either from crop failures or from war, they have still greater need of money both for necessities and for mercenaries, while their land is idle.

The underlying assumption is that buyers could be found for, if not an infinite amount of silver, at least an output significantly greater than that prevailing in the mid-fourth century and approximating the historic levels attained at the height of the late fifth-century industry (cf. 4.11–12). Xenophon's answer is to urge large-scale state purchases of slaves to be leased as mine workers, starting with 1,200 and later reaching 10,000 (4.18–27).[38]

Athenian monetary legislation was not therefore predicated on manipulating the demand for Attic silver. There was no way to increase the value of Attic silver except by increasing demand or restricting supply outside Attica.[39] Demand was probably increasing anyway and no simple means existed to accelerate demand other than by increasing the general prosperity of the allies and other Greeks. There is no reason to think that limiting other sources of metal was feasible, let alone contemplated. Uncoined silver is a fungible good, so that the output of Athenian mines simply added to a common stock from which consumers drew their supplies, without any significance attaching to the origin of the silver being utilized. The chemical analysis of Athenian coins substantiates this contention (pp. 194–96 above). The only likely impact of the existence of the mining industry at Laureion on Athenian monetary legislation is that the presence of a reliable source of the metal may have encouraged the Athenians to think that they could emit enough tetradrachms to sustain an ever larger economic and fiscal role for their currency in the *arkhē*.

Hence, we must always look coldly on elaborate theses about monetary (as opposed to fiscal) manipulations, especially those that posit

[38] On fourth-century mines and the Athenian economy, compare H. Montgomery, "Silver, Coins and the Wealth of a City-state," *OpAth* 15 (1984) 123–33, esp. 128–31.

[39] Cf., for example, P. Gardner, "Coinage of the Athenian Empire," *JHS* 33 (1913) 147–88, esp. 153.

elaborate bimetallic monetary systems at fixed rates of conversion.[40] No one has ever suggested a plausible reason for the Athenians to have been concerned about the value of Attic tetradrachms relative to gold or electrum coins, when their revenues and public expenditures were mainly in silver and their own silver coins at that. The value ratio of silver to gold was governed by the market conditions affecting the two metals (as noted immediately above for silver; cf. Xen. *Por.* 4.10) and by the monetary conditions for the circulation of the metals in minted form. No one has ever suggested how the Athenians could affect such ratios, unless they minted and spent more or less silver and/or gold, and the only time during which they are known to have done so, they acted under the pressure of the Peloponnesian War. The Coinage Decree did not legislate about electrum coinage so that it could scarcely aspire to alter the value ratio between coined electrum and silver, even as an unrealistic goal of policy.

Although one might suppose that silver depreciated in relation to gold when treasures of Greece began to be melted down and expended to underwrite the hostilities of the Archidamian War, traces of such a development cannot be discerned in the evidence. What is found is the opposite, a depreciation of gold relative to silver in Attica during the Peloponnesian War. Initially, this may in part be owed to a refusal of buyers to accept payment in anything save the most easily used silver denominations at a time of very unsettled political conditions. Additionally, the curtailment of supplies of silver from Laureion and the eventual diminution of Athenian income also had a substantial effect. Finally, another contributing influence was exerted toward the end of the war by the emission of the first gold coins (see pp. 517–21 below).

Attic Commerce

Turning to the commercial ramifications of an imposition of Athenian coins and standards, we shall find little possibility for narrow economic advantage. Before we consider in detail the plausibility of the idea

[40] Note, for example, J. Johnston, "An International Managed Currency in the Fifth Century," *Hermathena* 47 (1932) 132–57, esp. 148–50; J.P. Guépin, "Greek Coinage and Persian Bimetallism," *Jaarboek voor Munt- en Penningkunde* 49 (1962) 1–19, esp. 11–12. On bimetallism note M.D. Bordo, "Bimetallism," in J. Eatwell, M. Milgate, and P. Newman (eds.), *The New Palgrave: A Dictionary of Economics* (London 1987) 1.243–45; on modern bimetallism see A.S. Milward, "The Origins of the Gold Standard," in J. Braga de Macedo, B. Eichengreen, and J. Reis, *Currency Convertability* (London 1996) 87–101, esp. 92–101. Cf. R. Bogaert, "Le cours du statère de Cyzique aux Ve et IV siècles avant J.-C.," *AC* 32 (1963) 85–119, esp. 108–109. See also M.R. Cataudella, "Aspetti e strumenti della politica monetaria ateniese fra V e IV secolo," *Sileno* 12 (1986) 111–35, for some cautious speculation on bimetallism.

that merchants based in Attica prospered in some special way from a prohibition on allied coining in silver, it is worth recalling what such an opinion compels us to assume: namely, that the Athenians were willing to legislate in order to give a particular subset of the members of their community a parochial advantage not as consumers but as providers of services.[41] While there is ample evidence to show that the Athenian *dēmos* acted to procure a plentiful and cheap supply of grain[42] —to take the most prominent example of legislation to benefit Attic consumers—no one has cited a parallel case in which the Athenians sought to convey such an advantage to businessmen. Merchants may at times have profited from Athenian consumer-oriented laws,[43] but the commentators who see commercial imperialism in the Coinage Decree implicitly demand something of a more specific and activist nature.[44] It is likely that the majority of the merchants will have been metics or *xenoi*, and that the major proportion of commerce was in their hands. Thus the mere imputation of such motivation to the Athenian *dēmos* is disconcerting. We may compare the tough going anticipated by Xenophon for his modest suggestions to attract more metics, as outlined in his *Poroi* (2.1–7).

Also, assuming such a motivation begs the question of precisely how the prohibition on using non-Athenian coins conferred the benefit at issue. Athenian producers of goods, providers of services, and their intermediaries gained no competitive edge by the mandating of Athenian weights, measures, and coins, for there is no indication in anyone's interpretation of the decree that anything was created by imposing or encouraging the usage of Attic standards except a level playing field where both Athenians and allies competed on equal terms. In a culture without elaborate equipment that assisted in production, the costs in

[41] It is a very different thing to favor consumers through price-fixing or monopoly (as wrong-headed as those policies often are, in the long run) and to legislate an advantage for producers and merchants. Ignoring that distinction vitiates the force of a parallel such as that of Gardner *JHS* (1913) 152–53, who notes Tod *GHI* #162 (2.181–85), an inscription reaffirming the status of Athens as the sole recipient of Kean *miltos* 'ruddle.'

[42] See Figueira *Phoenix* (1986); P. Garnsey, *Famine and Food Supply in the Graeco-Roman World* (Cambridge 1988) 139–42.

[43] See Figueira *Phoenix* (1986) 161–67.

[44] Gardner, *JHS* (1913) 152, offers this formulation, which may appear in our current sensibility concerning ancient economic conditions perilously close to a non sequitur: "It seems very likely that in this fashion the Athenians meant to gain a commercial advantage. We know from the facts of modern commerce that trade is facilitated when the trading countries have the same monetary standard and measures. And, of course, the Athenians may have estimated this advantage at a higher rate than actual experience would justify." Note the hint of a misguided imperialism in the last sentence. The same thinking lies behind Mattingly's observation that "commercial advantage and imperial pride were the main motives behind the Coinage Decree" (Mattingly *Historia* [1961] 184; cf. p. 7 above).

"retooling" would have been minimal. One could imagine that a slight cost might be incurred for replacing molds used for casting vessels, to take an obvious example, if Athenian *metra* were exclusively mandated, but such costs could never constitute more than a tiny one-time portion of the cost of the production of goods.

Without an economic intermediation that was dependent either on advanced financial mechanisms or on sophisticated media of communication,[45] the monetary, metrological, or organizational terms in which commerce was conducted were alike on an equal footing. In contrast, one may consider the elaborate strategies of mercantilist politicians and theorists from the fifteenth through the eighteenth centuries that were aimed at achieving an excess of exports over imports balanced by an inflow of precious metals.[46] Without entering into a discussion of the imprudence of such measures, the absence of parallel policies from the fifth century B.C. deserves noting.

The creation of the *phoros* 'tribute' system had the (possibly unanticipated) effect of changing the rules of any game of economic imperialism that we might fancy to have existed during the fifth-century *arkhē*. Now the Athenian government not only levied taxes on its own citizens but allied states taxed their citizens to pay *phoros* to Athens, making their economic well-being lie within the best interests of the Athenians. Although governments obviously make grievous errors of policy all the time that undermine the ability of their constituents to draw on resources for taxes at the same or a higher level, it would be unusual for a regime to intend deliberately to weaken the ability of its taxpayers to contribute, in this case the tributaries.[47] One could assume that the Athenians were prepared to decrease the allied tax base in order to enjoy an increase in economic output within Attica. They would not, however, have done so to increase their internal tax receipts because it was scarcely easier to raise money in Attica (through *eisphorai*?) than to raise the level of the *phoros* abroad. These considerations, however, find no echo in our sources. Instead we must confront squarely the lack of any explanation in the traditional interpretation of the Coinage Decree how such differential economic harms were to be worked upon the allies.

[45] See Figueira, review of E. Cohen, *Athenian Economy and Society: A Banking Perspective* (Princeton 1992), *Bryn Mawr Classical Review* 5.2 (1994) 109–13.

[46] For general surveys, see W.R. Allen, "Mercantilism," in *The New Palgrave* 3.445–49; J. Viner, "Economic Thought: II. Mercantilist Thought," in D.I. Sills (ed.), *International Encyclopedia of the Social Sciences* (New York 1968) 4.435–43.

[47] Cf. Erxleben *AfP* (1971) 162.

Nonetheless, it has happened that scholars have exploited the "consumerism" of Attic economic legislation in order to conclude that the Coinage Decree was predicated on a desire to bring more goods and business to the Peiraieus. Monetary legislation as a mechanism to enhance the commercial dominance of the Peiraieus appeared in the citations from the work of Russell Meiggs that were noted in my introduction (see above, pp. 8–9). The views of A. French are quite similar, but are more fully described:[48]

> The effect of the measure was to compel the allies to pay their tribute to Athens each year in Athenian coined silver, since no other coinage was recognized as valid. But to obtain this coinage the allies obviously had to buy it directly or indirectly from Athens. To do this they were forced to sell their surplus products either to Athens or to states which sold to her. The result was a pattern of trade in which the Peiraieus provided a centre to which the allies exported their rural products in competition with each other.

We could in truth write a similar vignette in which the situation of the Athenians was lamented since they had to trade their precious silver to foreigners in return for the food that they needed to survive. But such a scenario would be equally fallacious. Indeed, the passage of the Coinage Decree (as usually understood) would have obviated the exploitative situation sketched by French because it would have made Attic coins the medium of exchange throughout the *arkhē*, removing the need for travel to Attica through the standardization of coins, weights, and measures supposedly engineered by the decree.

Nothing forced the allies to exchange goods for Attic silver coinage, save their desire to acquire silver, a fact so eloquently exploited by Xenophon in the *Poroi*. He observes that the advantage of the Peiraieus was that it always offered importers a return cargo in silver (money) even when other exports, which were generally abundant there, were in default (3.2). He also implies that silver was plentiful and less expensive in Attica than elsewhere.[49]

> ἀλλὰ μὴν καὶ τοῖς ἐμπόροις ἐν μὲν ταῖς πλείσταις τῶν πόλεων ἀντιφορτίζεσθαί τι ἀνάγκη: νομίσμασι γὰρ οὐ χρησίμοις ἔξω χρῶνται· ἐν δὲ ταῖς Ἀθήναις πλεῖστα μὲν ἔστιν ἀντεξάγειν ὧν ἂν δέωνται ἄνθρωποι, ἢν δὲ μὴ βούλωνται ἀντιφορτίζεσθαι, καὶ [οἱ] ἀργύριον ἐξάγοντες καλὴν ἐμπορίαν ἐξάγουσιν. ὅπου γὰρ ἂν πωλῶσιν αὐτό, πανταχοῦ πλέον τοῦ ἀρχαίου λαμβάνουσιν.

48 French, *Athenian Economy* 121.
49 Note Gauthier, *Poroi* 76–80.

> Moreover, it is necessary for merchants in the majority of cities to ship some return cargo, since they do not use money that is useful abroad. Yet, in Athens, it is possible to export as a return cargo the greatest number of the goods that men need, and if they do not wish to ship a return cargo, even exporting silver money, they export an excellent product for commerce, for wherever they sell it, everywhere they receive a return greater than their buying capital.

In addition, Xenophon's description of the status of the Peiraieus prevailed in the mid-fourth century after the Social War, when the Athenians had forfeited any major advantage exerted by political and military hegemony over the *leading* commercial states of the Aegean. There was no monetary legislation in place like the Coinage Decree (as far as we know) that was required to create favorable terms for the export of silver or for the Peiraieus as an entrepot in general.

Another item in this series of economic considerations is the effect on pricing of mandating a monopoly for Attic money. We have already seen the issue of pricing shaping the suggestion that Attic monetary legislation favored the availability and low price of goods in the Peiraieus. One supposes that claims of this nature lie embedded in judgments like that of Sutherland that "the first Athenian steps to control world-coinage occurred perhaps in 449" (citing Segre's publication of the Kos fragment of the Coinage Decree).[50] Such an enactment could not, however, equalize prices throughout the *arkhē* because the market for many goods was fragmented. Yet it would obviously simplify the evaluation of goods and thereby prices by the establishment of a common monetary medium. It is indeed possible to protest that archaeological evidence has forced us to concentrate unduly on the decree as a regularization of coining, while standardization of measures and weights also affected daily life significantly. However, the impact of a consolidation of weights and measures on reaching and evaluating prices underlines that, especially in the present state of our knowledge, coins are likely to remain rightfully at the center of inquiries into the nature of this legislation. The use of weights and measures is necessarily intermeshed with the status of the monetary medium (although it is possible to envisage changes in coinage that need not affect the other standards since coin weights may vary in their divergence from stathmic weights). Yet evaluating goods in terms of Athenian money was always easier when the goods were offered for sale

[50] C.H.V. Sutherland, "Corn and Coin: A Note on Greek Commercial Monopolies," *AJP* 64 (1943) 129–47, esp. 142–43.

in weights and measures that were compatible with the Attic system of *stathma* and *metra*.

Just as the Athenians could not manipulate the demand for or the value of their silver by monetary legislation, there was also no manifest way that they (or for that matter anyone else) could specify prices of goods in terms of some artificial value for their coins and reasonably expect to sustain their commerce.[51] The record of price controls, ancient or modern, is not a very happy one, inasmuch as they invariably create dislocations of supplies. The Coinage Decree as it is usually envisaged looks like a misplaced weapon in an arsenal of price control in any case. In the first place, the Athenians would have been concerned to set prices in their own market and port and not in the *arkhē* as a whole—there would have been no differential advantage in doing the latter in any event—and there is no reason to think that a general monopoly over weights, measures, and coins helped in even a wrong-headed fixing of prices. If the Coinage Decree had effected the administrative control of prices, any unfair price-fixing in Attica would have become more overt through a standardization of coins, weights, and measures.

The Simplification of Use of Money

The chief result of a standardization of weights, measures, and coins would have been to simplify the terms of trade. The advantages in a single coinage for pricing and the evaluation of prices have already been noted. Furthermore, there might well have occurred a movement toward a standardization of goods exchanged by virtue of a common set of weights and measures (see Chapter 11 below). That regularization would have opened more markets to goods from a greater number of sources, certainly widening choice, probably improving quality, and quite possibly lowering some prices. The mental manipulation of a variety of *metra* 'measures' and *stathma* 'weights' was not without psychological costs, including the possibility of expensive errors, so that any simplification through the acceptance of a single standard expedited commerce and lowered the threshold of expertise required for entry to particular levels of trading.

[51] Compare M.I. Finley, "Classical Greece," *Deuxième Conférence internationale d'histoire économique: Aix-en Provence 1962* (Paris 1965) 11–35, esp. 22–23. Note especially: "Unless Athens stopped all trade outside the Empire and unless she controlled all sources of raw silver, she could not 'trade away' Athenian money 'at Athenian valuation' in the sense in which that phrasing has been used. After all, the need is not on all one side. Athens had few surpluses, other than silver, and many shortages. Before she could manipulate coin-values to substantial advantage, she would have to exercise a compulsion on the exchange of goods in the Aegean far beyond anything proposed or even dreamed of. How, for example, could she have compelled others to bring in corn and slaves for her to purchase with over-priced drachmas, and at the same time have compelled others to buy Athenian vases, olive oil, or wine with the same coins but at a different coin-value?" (p. 23).

Because of the acceptance of a single coinage everywhere, exchange problems that created costs through fees and delays would have been greatly mitigated.[52] A single form of money obviates that common problem of foreign trade: timely acquisition of enough money in the currency of a trading partner so that a sale can be consummated at the optimal time of choice for both parties. Without the costs of exchange within the *arkhē*, resources previously allocated to that purpose could now be directed toward other uses. In a society with only the most primitive instruments of credit, the general validity of Athenian coinage was in that case commercially advantageous, but the benefits accrued to everyone.[53] That the government of a *polis* could be aware of and act to ameliorate inconveniences of exchange may be demonstrated with particular force by a curious series of fractional coins at Croton that facilitated exchange by virtue of an unusual degree of state intervention.[54]

Our emphasis on alleviation of costs of exchange assumes that classical Greeks preferred to treat their coins as having a conventional value. While based on their content of silver, that value transcended mere metallic worth by drawing on the validation inherent in authorization of coinage by the state. There is not drawn together in any one place in this work all the evidence for this view, which many scholars take for granted. Indeed, much in its support has emerged in the course of the investigations of Part I.[55] Indeed, the pattern of curtailment of allied minting that has been traced there seems to show a monetary validity for foreign and Attic coins in the *arkhē*, and not only their treatment as mere bullion.

52 Virtually alone among the early students of the decree, E. Cavaignac, *Études sur l'histoire financière d'Athènes au Vᵉ siècle* (Paris 1908) 184, appreciated this situation, especially relative to state finances. Note also L. Lacroix, "La monnaie grecque et les problèmes de la circulation monétaire," *BAB*⁵ 55 (1969) 169–80, esp. 173; E. Will, *Le monde grec et l'orient* (Paris 1972) 208, who, however, also speaks of "les monnaies mauvaises et médiocres." Cf. Mattingly *Historia* (1961) 184. See also Gardner *JHS* (1913) 153–54, who, however, confuses the issue with the commercial and symbolic rationales, and J. Hasebroek, *Staat und Handel im alten Griechenland* (Tübingen 1928) 170–71, who speaks of a "Wechselmonopol."

53 A. Giovannini, basing himself on the inclusion of weights and measures in the decree, is rare in his willingness to accept both a commercial motivation and that it could be unselfish. See his *Rome et la circulation monétaire en Grèce au IIᵉ siècle avant Jésus-Christ* (Basel 1978) 75–76; also Hasebroek, *Staat und Handel* 170; C.G. Starr, *Athenian Coinage: 480–449 B.C.* (Oxford 1970) 69–70.

54 Their reverses are drawn from the numismatic iconography of other cites (Corinth, Akragas, and Messana, certainly; possibly Syracuse, Athens, Himera, and Taras). According to C.M. Kraay the coins made up the difference between Crotoniate coins and a major denomination of the city whose badge is pictured on the reverse. See Kraay, "À propos de monnaies divisionaires de Croton," *SM* 8 (1958) 99–102; *ACGC* 181–82.

55 In general see pp. 56–58 above; see above pp. 36–38, 125–27 and below 255–56 on Aiginetan coinage in mainland Greece; pp. 105–109 above on electrum coinage; pp. 161–63 above on Chian coinage; pp. 483–84 below on Aiginetic coins in Attica; and pp. 497–511 below on bronze money.

This concept may be held to pervade the very semantics of fifth-century coinage, about which a recent study has emphasized the centrality of the "isonomic criterion of a silver fiduciary money," especially in contrast with Greek appreciations of the Asiatic/Persian use of coins.[56]

In a "universe" of small political units, an exclusively token money had great difficulties in becoming predominant because of the competitive disadvantage in international trade at which it put its users in contrast with those using good silver. Nevertheless, once economic conditions compelled the recourse to bronze money in the late fifth century and afterward to sustain an anticipated money supply and the current scale of transactions, money whose intrinsic value was a fraction of its market value moved into assiduous use.[57]

Consequently, the economic ramifications of a single monetary system should have been beneficial, but the benefits will have gone to both Athenians and non-Athenians indiscriminately. There is no differential *economic* impact that would render the Coinage Decree (as it is usually interpreted) a piece of imperialistic, as opposed to merely hegemonic, government.[58] Therefore we seem to have generated a "revisionist" hypothesis on the political resonances of the Coinage Decree, in which this legislation takes on an altruistic aura as an enactment acting to the advantage of all the citizens of the states of the alliance.[59]

[56] M. Caccamo Caltabiano and P. Radici Colace, "Darico persiano e nomisma greco: differenze strutturalli, ideologiche e funzionali alla luce del lessico greco," *REA* 91 (1989) 213–226; see also Caccamo Caltabiano and Radici Colace, "Lessico monetale greco," in M. Caccamo Caltabiano and P. Radici Colace (eds.), *Atti del I Seminario di Studi sui Lessici tecnici greci e latini* (Messina 1991) 139–222. Herodotus reveals a cognate Lydian/Persian dichotomy surrounding the social thematics of gold, as shown by M. Lombardo, "Oro lidio e oro persiano nelle *Storie* di Erodoto," *REA* 91 (1989) 197–212. See also pp. 545–46 below.

[57] A Hellenistic inscription (ca. 250–221) from Gortyn mandated the use of bronze obols in place of silver obols (which it demonetizes) under penalty of fine (*IC* 4.162 = *SIG*³ 525).

[58] One means out of this dilemma demands the acceptance of a date for this legislation in the 420s in order to suppose that the Athenians were marking off their *arkhē* from the Peloponnesian area of monetary circulation, with its basis in Aiginetic metrology (cf. Erxleben *AfP* [1971] 161). In light of the practical measures taken against Peloponnesian shipping in the Archidamian War, for which see Figueira, *Excursions* 326–35, as potentially disruptive a measure as the Coinage Decree in the traditional view seems a needless provocation of the allies. The Athenians had ample punitive means to curtail Peloponnesian and allied commerce with each other. The intrinsic difficulty of irreparably damaging the more or less autarkic economies of Sparta and many of its allies was eventually to recommend the Sicilian expedition. As it was, the destruction applied to Sparta's agricultural base by the establishment of Athenian positions at Pylos and Kythera was substantial. The Athenians, however, lacked the patience to wait on the slow working of not only the direct injuries to Spartan *klēroi*, but also the more subtle effects of the curtailment of the supply of Helot labor. See T.J. Figueira, "Population Patterns in late Archaic and Classical Sparta," *TAPA* 116 (1986) 165–213, esp. 187–99. Compared to direct methods, the Coinage Decree does not appear to be an effective technique for economic warfare during active hostilities.

[59] M.I. Finley came close at times to such a conclusion on the economic ramifications of the decree (although he saw it as imperialistic for its enfringement of autonomy). See *The Ancient*

Altruism, however, appears at first glance, a fragile thread of egress from the maze of interpretative approaches to the Coinage Decree, inasmuch as benevolent intervention in trade practices may be no less hard for some to accept than exploitative intervention. Moreover, before we assent to such a rethinking, we shall need to recall the punitive aspects of the application of the decree as it is traditionally interpreted. Would the Athenians have had to hedge lawmaking that was perceived as advantageous by their subjects with threats of punishment for noncompliance? Is there then a discord between our appreciation of the benefits of the Coinage Decree and that of fifth-century Greeks? Are we missing its negative impact because of an improper modernization of ancient economic experience?[60] If standardization of metrological standards was reciprocally beneficial, why did the allies not regularize weights, measures, and coins spontaneously? The last question has already begun to be answered in Part I: the allied cities did curtail their minting, limit the local denominations available, and make changes of standard and standard coin in order to use Attic money (and possibly other coinages) in their local economies. We shall see below that the punitive aspects of the decree themselves deserve revision.

THE DECREE AS A MEASURE FOR GENERATING REVENUE

Based on the foregoing discussion, the Coinage Decree (or any other enactment in service of monetary consolidation) seems benign legislation when one adopts a broad perspective on its costs and benefits, one based on its economic effects. There is, however, a way to envisage the Coinage Decree as a self-aggrandizing legislative act because it had a rationale in raising Athenian public income. This approach need not deny the effects of improving exchange and the evaluation of goods throughout the *arkhē*; it merely suggests that the Athenians were not directly motivated by such less immediate and less concrete intentions but were moved by an

---

Economy (Berkeley and Los Angeles 1973) 169 (cf. "Classical Greece" 23), where he puts the issue in these terms: "It has been held that there was a commercial motive, a desire to give Athenian merchants an advantage over others. The logic escapes me. Everyone had been equally the victim of a profusion of mints; had the Athenians been able to enforce their decree for a sufficient number of years, everyone in the empire would have benefited slightly but equally, the Athenians no more than others, questions of pride and patriotism apart. Only the money-changers would have been losers, and no one has yet suggested that such a powerful decree was passed just to hurt them." I am not sure of even his final conclusion, inasmuch as the general increase in trade and prosperity during the Pentekontaeteia may have left money changers with plenty of other business, and many coinages were still in existence outside the *arkhē*. It was also open to money changers to diversify into banking functions. See also Finley, "The Athenian Empire: A Balance Sheet," in *Economy and Society in Ancient Greece* (New York 1978) 41–61, esp. 56 with note 46 (p. 257).

[60] Cf. Cataudella *Sileno* (1986) 118–29.

urgency to raise revenues in one particular political context, be it in the 440s or 420s.[61] This is an approach recently urged by Thomas R. Martin, who offers it as a positive explanation for the causation of the law, after his useful arguments against the Coinage Decree as an act of symbolic imperialism (see below, pp. 250–51).[62] Before we discuss this hypothesis, one weakness needs to be confronted directly: conjecturing taxation as the decree's purpose leaves us totally at sea about Athenian motivations for imposing metrological changes.

The only available technique for the Athenians to make money from the extant sections of this legislation would be the levy on each *mna* of silver conveyed to the mint that appears in section v of the composite decree. I print the text of *IG* I³ 1453.

v. [ἐν δὲ τῶ]ι ἀργυροκοπίωι τὸ ἀργύ[ριον ....20.........
.....μὴ ἔ̆λ]αττον ἢ ἥμυσυ καὶ α[.............29..............
.....]ι αἱ πόλεις πραττ[............28...............
δραχμὰς ἀπὸ τῆς μν[ᾶς: ....23...........
κατ]άλλαττεν ἢ ἐνόχο[υς ἔ̆ναι κατὰ τὸν νόμον]·

In previewing my discussion of this section below (pp. 353–62), it is fairly clear that some operation is to be conducted, probably coining, on a stock of silver in the mint. The further appearance of a form of πράττω, one of whose meanings is 'exact payment,' followed by the expression δραχμὰς ἀπὸ τῆς μν[ᾶς 'drachms from the *mna*,' has been taken to suggest the exaction of a minting charge. The likely supplements for the missing numeral before the word δραχμὰς are three (the majority view) or five, if we accept that something approximating the extant completions for line v.3 must have appeared.

Affecting the character to be assigned to this fee are a series of further conclusions that were drawn by the early commentators on the Kos and Aphytis fragments. They need not in fact be true or even probable. There has been seen in this section of the decree provision for allied states—with further opportunity perhaps granted to private citizens in section xiii—to surrender silver (bullion and coins?) to the mint. It was also customary in earlier scholarship to suppose that the supervisors of the Athenian mint received these resources and returned new tetradrachms to allied governments (and perhaps to individuals, on the basis, again, of section xiii).

61 Note Sutherland *AJP* (1943) 143.

62 See Martin, *Sovereignty* 197–202, working from the received epigraphical reconstructions of my sections v–vii.

This operation has often been viewed as a vast program of monetary conversion in which large consignments of allied money were brought to Athens for reminting. We have already seen that the hoard evidence shows no support for this program of conversion (note especially the hoards containing Aiginetan coins). A number of *poleis* have already been identified that continued some form of operation in the second half of the fifth century. They utilized stocks of silver or worn coins available for reminting that cannot have been converted by the Athenian mint at any time. In contrast, chemical analysis of Attic coins does not betray an assimilation of silver from non-Attic sources that had composed allied coins.

The surviving epigraphical evidence does not in point of fact compel such a hypothesis. In my discussion below, another procedure will be proposed for a limited conversion of foreign funds to Attic coins wherein the allied states were credited for the value of the silver contributed in their own coinage, while the mint proceeded with coining some of its own reserve. The Attic coins minted were thereafter injected into the ordinary stream of revenues. I shall reargue below on grounds of administrative feasibility the same conclusion that has been reached above on the basis of numismatic evidence, namely, that a thoroughgoing demonetization of allied silver and its replacement with Attic coin was not attempted. If the epigraphical reconstruction presented below were indeed correct, it would become improbable that the process of levying the minting charge on a more restricted pool of contributions or exactions could yield significant revenue.

I shall also suggest there that it is an amount comparable to the annual allied tribute that is the most probable stock of funds for reminting. If we take the largest estimate available in this hypothesis such as 1,000 talents, a 3 percent or 5 percent fee does not deliver a large payoff to the Athenian treasury, only 30T or 50T. And then there is the issue of the character of this levy as a one-time expedient, since allied coins cannot of course have been invalidated on an annual basis.

To make the exaction in section v of the Coinage Decree a substantial augmentation of Athenian revenues, it would be necessary both to return to the doubtful hypothesis of a general conversion of monies and to hypothesize the highest possible rate of taxation. Even a 5 percent or 10 percent levy on 10,000T, a sum probably exceeding the highest level of federal reserves, would only yield 500T or 1,000T.[63] That amount is

[63] This particular point also affects the issue of a Coinage Decree that called in all non-Athenian silver in allied official holdings. Cf. Martin, *Sovereignty* 200 with note 11, who construes the expression "... no less than half" in section v to refer to official holdings. Admittedly, no one has as yet suggested a supplementation of the text that would offer that sense. Nonetheless, this supposition would force us to guess at the total public reserves. This process, I suspect, will yield for most students of the Delian League estimated aggregates well

comparable to collecting the tribute of a period not exceeding two and a half extra years (depending on when we date the decree). Before becoming enamored of the estimates toward the higher end of this range, one should note the high levels that they imply about allied mint output from 479 to 449 (which are not likely to have actually occurred: see pp. 189–94). Admittedly, we lack the ability to say much about total mint output by decades, and are even less qualified to speak about the life expectancy of different issues and denominations in the money supply. Nevertheless, the record of incremental cessation of allied minting by some *poleis* and the continuation of coining by others militates against tremendous holdings by governments in allied coinages that were available for a call-in at any one time.

One further factor deserves emphasis here against the theory of a massive demonetization and conversion. As the Athenian material indicates, some classical treasuries or, shall we say, monetary authorities evolved from bodies administering funds held by cults. The treasurers of Athena, to take one example, *loaned* monies to the Athenians, as their holdings did not simply constitute another component of public funds but fell within the penumbra of the goddess's influence. Insofar as some allied stocks of non-Athenian money shared the same nature, their exaction for transformation into Athenian tetradrachms may well have excited religious concerns. How would the Athenians have combated a charge of *hierosylia* 'robbery of cult property'? Could the Athenians have levied a minting charge for reminting coins that had been dedicated to Hera of Samos, for example, and bore types inspired by the iconography of her cult?

The discussion to this point has been deliberately vague on exactly how and where in the process of minting the exaction mentioned in section v was implemented. Most commentators have envisaged it as a minting charge levied on converted allied coins. In other words, it is likely that the original condition of the coins and wastage were not factors. When Greeks wanted to *exchange* coins, they resorted to money changers and not to mint officials, who presumably did not credit the depositor for some token or exchange value of the coins delivered. Rather, mint personnel merely weighed the coins and bullion consigned to them. They then credited the depositor with the amount of coin customarily returned from that weight, as *stathmic* (or "weight") *mnai* always exceeded coin or

---

below the total of federal reserves, although the lack of real evidence forbids anyone making very much of the argument. The difficulties surrounding the extraction of monies under cultic protection would probably have been intractable, as will be noted momentarily.

numismatic *mnai* in their actual weight (5 percent in fifth-century Athens), while allowing for wastage (cf. *IG* II² 1013, lines 29–32, for example).[64] On some occasions, perhaps, if the consignment(s) was large enough, mints simply delivered whatever amount remained after what was wasted as the "batch" was minted.

The phrase ". . . drachms from the *mna*" is thus likely to refer to the exaction of a number of new drachms from the *mnai* just minted. Thus it was a levy at the end of the process, after the condition of the coins and wastage were already taken into account. What needed defraying at that time were the expenses of the mint itself. In that case, only a part of the fee could be considered a net gain, because there were clearly costs in the minting process that needed to be offset. Thus any windfall in revenue is only the excess over those costs, not the whole 3–5 percent.[65] A 3–5 percent minting charge has struck most scholars as a rather modest charge.[66]

It is also important that emphasis is laid on the diverse functions of the 5 percent differential between the stathmic *mnai* and the coin or numismatic *mnai* and the possible 5 percent levy that some scholars restore in section v of the Coinage Decree. On occasion, the two have been wrongly conflated.[67] On a fundamental economic level, the existence of the *stathmic*/numismatic differential (irrespective of its magnitude) was owed to a recognition that coins assumed a token value over raw silver through their issue by the state. Coins were more valuable than an equivalent weight of bullion. Such a premium for coins also encouraged their employment in preference to bullion and that was advantageous to governments that found it easier to raise revenue and spend in the form of coins. The scale of this differential was connected with the practical

64 M. Lang and M. Crosby, *Weights, Measures, and Tokens*, *The Athenian Agora* 10 (Princeton 1964) 15–17; see also Figueira, *Excursions* 73–76.

65 There is no discriminatory (hence imperialist) intent in the decree, once a mass demonetization and recoining is rejected. For one thing, the minting fee seems low enough so that one can scarcely imagine that a lower rate was charged individual Athenians bringing silver and old coins to the mint.

66 See Finley, "Classical Greece" 22–23: "The possibility ought not be ignored—as it seems to be by everyone writing on the subject—that the treasury actually lost on the operation." See also Martin, *Sovereignty* 201 with note 13, for the recognition that the minting charge was moderate (based on fees in other periods). Cf. E.J.P. Raven, "The Amphictyonic Coinage of Delphi: 336–334 B.C.," *NC*⁶ 10 (1950) 1–22, esp. 6–9.

67 See, for example, O. Mørkholm, "Some Reflections on the Production and Use of Coinage in Ancient Greece," *Historia* 31 (1982) 290–305, esp. 290–96. While the *agio* 'exchange fee' charged by money changers is not unrelated to *stathmic*/numismatic differential, it is also conditioned by other factors affecting the utility of the currency under exchange.

operation of the mint.[68] It also had to be large enough to exceed wastage or pure loss in the conversion of bullion to coin.[69] Furthermore, it needed to be large enough to cover the discrepancies in measuring that inevitably take place at every stage of such a process (especially with the balance scales then available). Mint officials could not reasonably be made responsible for the phantom amounts of silver introduced into the procedures of the mint through crude or erroneous measurements. The *stathmic*/numismatic differential gave them a cushion against such technological and administrative inefficiencies. In contrast, a 3–5 percent minting charge was a user fee or tax. It might have been applied at a rate that was required to satisfy real costs of the mint; or its level could have been adjusted to provide additional income for other budgetary purposes; or it could have been waived for intragovernmental transfers.

Moreover, if the allies were allowed to contribute their non-Athenian coins in lieu of tribute (in one hypothesis presented below), there is considerable likelihood that these coins, many of which may have already circulated for a long time, would have had to be reminted in any event somewhere else, probably sooner rather than much later. On the hypothesis that the minting charge was paid by the allies, the only loss for them would be the premium that the Attic mint could charge over other mints for conversion, but it does not appear probable that the fees of other mints were much, if at all, lower than 3–5 percent.

Nonetheless, hesitation is proper before we come to the conclusion that this levy was raised from the allies, as several other patterns of implementation are possible. I shall suggest below that a central aspect of the Coinage Decree was permitting the allies a year in which they contributed an amount equivalent to their tribute in whatever coin that they chose. In that eventuality, any minting fees during conversion were not charged to the allies but exacted by the *epistatai* of the mint from the money in the mint that was provided to Athenian officials in lieu of the tribute. The foreign coin may well have been coined subsequently, with the *epistatai* being permitted to charge the minting fee at that time. Each of the rounds of levies would have been internal to Athenian accounts and would not have affected allied expenses during the process, if the correct assumption is that the allies got credited for what they contributed whatever its form.

68 The fourth-century material from Delphi suggests that the weight of old coins surrendered to a mint for recoining was discounted by individual batch, and not by standard charge. See O. Picard, "Les monnaies des comptes de Delphes à '*apousia*,' " in D. Knoepfler (ed.), *Comptes et inventaires* (Neuchatel/Geneva 1988) 91–101.

69 An isolated *exemplum* noted by Aristotle illustrates the collection of waste silver by cleaners in the mint (*Problems* 936b23–28).

Once again it is the assumption that the coinage in circulation in the allied states was in process of replacement en masse that drives the conjecture that the silver ordered to be coined in the beginning of section v derived from the resources of the allies outside of their tribute payments.[70]

In conclusion, it is the lack of solid evidence that the Athenians were levying the fee of section v.4 on the *allies* that discourages hypotheses aimed at justifying the Coinage Decree as a device for taxation. To be sure, had the Athenians been able to extract all the non-Athenian silver coinage in the whole *arkhē* in one blow, a sum of some magnitude could have been exacted. After they had paid their considerable minting and administrative expenses, they might have been left with what amounted to a capital levy of a few percent on the money supply of the allies that was held at that time in non-Athenian coins. Such a vast demonetization has no basis in firm literary, epigraphical, or archaeological evidence, even if we could bring ourselves to believe it was feasible. As we have seen above, a considerable percentage of the economic activity of the allies was already being conducted in Attic money by ca. 450 and that would have limited markedly the yield of any general demonetization. Furthermore, the majority of the mints operative in the early 440s continued to operate. When the latitude accorded the Athenians as the *hēgemones* of the Delian League in assessing allied tribute is remembered, the use of a minting fee for a single revenue enhancement appears cumbrous and unnecessarily indirect.

THE COINAGE DECREE AND POLITICAL SYMBOLISM

Even if signs of economic or commercial imperialism are hard to discover in the Coinage Decree, it might be objected that the foregoing sections of this chapter reflect a sensibility that is essentially modernizing and "capitalist." The Athenians and their subjects did not calculate—and may even have lacked the means to calculate—the costs and benefits of policy decisions in such a way as to appreciate the economic value of monetary consolidation or metrological integration. My previous discussion would thereby impose on ancient appraisals of politics a value

[70] Less need be said about the provision that is often restored in section xiii of the decree allowing individuals to convert foreign silver at the mint (see below, pp. 411–14). Whatever originally stood in this section would not have affected the status of this legislation as revenue enhancement. The majority of persons using Athenian coinage customarily got their coins through ordinary business practices, including exchange. Therefore, the mint would have been a source of last resort for those who could not otherwise acquire a sufficient amount of Athenian money for their needs. Furthermore, there are other restorations for that section with quite different senses.

system and a set of reactions that are foreign to them. It may then become a historical irony of the first order that we can discover considerable merit in an Attic consolidation of money and standards, whereas the allies of Athens perceived only an encroachment on their lives of great symbolic impact. The substitution of hegemonic practices for traditional procedures proclaimed unabashedly the sovereignty and superiority of the Athenian *dēmos*, as the authorities discussed in my introduction suggest (for example, Bury-Meiggs; Fine; *World of Athens*; Rhodes; Mattingly; Lewis in *CAH*²; Meiggs).[71]

In its turn, this riposte to my comments above is itself open to the overarching counterargument that the understanding of the behavior of the market (or even of the *agora* or marketplace) assumed in these explanations above is not a particularly technical one.[72] Rather, Greeks involved in business would have had a sound intuitive appreciation of the costs intrinsic to problems of exchange of currency as well as of difficulties of evaluation of costs or of prices in the face of many currency systems. They were confronted with these circumstances on a regular basis. Such purposive economic behavior can indeed be paralleled from the classical period.[73] Behind the record of allied cessation of minting and alteration of monetary processes, one may freely suspect that economic common sense of this type predominated. My counterargument might also be buttressed by a critique of Marxist (and other ideological) characterizations of analyses of optimizing patterns of behavior as "capitalist" interpretation, a critique arguing that such patterns are not only widely evidenced in other cultures but specifically attested among classical Greeks.[74]

[71] Note also Gardner *JHS* (1913) 153: "We may suggest that after all it was mainly a matter of national pride. Athens was fond of dictating to the subject allies whenever she could. . . . And it is well known how strong motives pride and love of dominance were at Athens"; Mattingly *Historia* (1961) 185: "For many of the 'better folk' the prohibition of coinage will have seemed the last intolerable encroachment on their city's rights"; Finley "Classical Greece" 24: "the psychological benefits of such an unprecedented demonstration of power and humbling of her allies"; Finley, *Ancient Economy* 169: "Athens was now able and willing to demonstrate who was master within the empire by denying the subject-states the traditional symbol of autonomy, their own coins." See also A.M. Andreades, *A History of Greek Public Finance* 1 (Cambridge, MA 1933) 310 with note 5; Finley, *Economy and Society* 56; Will, *Monde grec* 209–10; Cataudella *Sileno* (1986) 111.

[72] Cf. Will, *Monde grec* 210: "Si l'on peut voir en lui le témoignage d'un pressentiment empirique des avantages que pouvait présenter une unification rationelle des systèmes monétaires, il reste que l'époque n'était pas capable de maîtriser des mécanismes dont l'analyse n'avait pas été abordée."

[73] For examples, see my discussions in "Karl Polanyi and Ancient Greek Trade: The Port of Trade," *Ancient World* 10 (1984) 15–30 and *Phoenix* (1986) 149–71.

[74] For some general remarks, see T.J. Figueira, "A Typology of Social Conflict in Greek Poleis," in A. Molho, K. Raaflaub, and J. Emlen (eds.), *City States in Classical Antiquity and Medieval Italy* (Stuttgart 1991) 289–307.

It is also worth observing that an interpretation of the decree that sees it as having a psychological impact for its hegemonic symbolism is weaker in isolation than in conjunction with practical instances of exploitation like those explored and rejected above.[75] We can never be certain in the absence of explicit ancient commentary to the contrary that the economic benefits arising from a single coinage and unified metrological standards were not appreciated by allied political elites. Any appreciation of shared profit from the Coinage Decree conditions whatever authoritarian aura with which modern scholars would choose to surround this legislation. In the virtual absence of ancient references (save for Aristophanes' *Birds*?), we could face a fifth-century political environment that was perhaps typified by several levels of political signification, possessing contradictory moral and expedient construals.[76]

Coinage and Autonomy

One way in which Attic legislation that restricted allied minting or imposed Attic metrological and monetary standards might have been construed as imperialism would be through its violating allied autonomy or its signifying that the allies had been deprived of their autonomy. The idea that the Coinage Decree was a deliberate attack on autonomy possesses an extraordinary tenacity, even in the face of a comprehension of the complexity of the conditions that underlay minting. Let us consider Erxleben's treatment. He begins from the supposedly strong association of minting and autonomy.[77] But he goes on to note that many cities had curtailed their minting of their own accord, although even this is attributed to a sinister sounding influence: "durch politisches und wirtschaftliches Überwicht." Thereupon, this partial "achievement" of a monopoly by the Athenians, on the benefits of which and rationale for which we are left virtually in the dark, had to be completed by legislation.

[75] Compare my discussion of attributions of "exploitation" to ancient socioeconomic contexts in *City States* 303–305.

[76] Although I do not believe that it is as plausible a reconstruction as that to be offered below, it is not impossible to account for the absence of ancient references to the decree in the following manner. The Athenians might have cloaked a gambit of symbolic hegemonism with a profession of shared advantages, because they knew that their allies would thereby become disarmed in their resistance. By their consciousness of this impotence in resistance, the elites of the allied cities would then be demoralized by the monetary and metrological symbols of nearly absolute Athenian power. Like other successful *turannoi*, the Athenians would have demonstrated their power while seeming not to have acted in a self-centered fashion and the shared repressed recognition of that situation would be more dehumanizing than a blatant imposition. This solution, however, lacks the explanatory power of the alternative investigated in the next chapters.

[77] Erxleben *AfP* (1971) 162.

A refutation of this linkage of autonomy and minting is not restricted to the aforesaid general objection that it fails to give due weight to ancient perceptions of economic advantage. First of all, no one has ever explained in any reasonable manner why the less politically sensitive weights and measures were included in the mandated conversion of standards established by the decree, if the valence of the legislation in terms of power politics rested in an ideological or symbolic connection between coinage and autonomy.[78] For what propagandistic or symbolic purpose was it necessary to legislate over weights and measures? Furthermore, there is considerable doubt whether coinage was used to certify the presence or absence of hegemony or autonomy, or, even granting a symbolic valence for coinage, whether the Athenians actually deployed this weapon in their arsenal of tools of domination.

My own views on autonomy were initially formulated in conjunction with the raising of the issue of autonomy by the Aiginetans and Spartans on the eve of the Peloponnesian War, a crux in the evolution of the concept on anyone's reckoning (Thuc. 1.67.2, 139.1, 3, 144.2).[79] In answer to these political attacks on Athenian authority over their allies, Perikles protested (justifiably, I believe) that the Spartans could not trace their demands for autonomy to international agreements that were held as currently valid by both themselves and the Athenians (for example, the Thirty Years Peace). Specific to the issue of coinage, there appears to have been no special grant of autonomy to Aigina in the Thirty Years Peace by virtue of which the Aiginetans had resumed coining (the tortoise staters).[80] Despite later Aiginetan protestations, their city could not be considered autonomous during its subjection to Athens (as will be seen shortly).

As our investigation of this mint has established, the Aiginetans probably restarted their minting soon after their subjugation by Athens (and almost a decade before the Thirty Years Peace). Motivated by economic factors, this resumption preceded the earliest date for the Coinage Decree and continued during any period of the enforcement of a mid-century decree. The plentiful tortoises may have had a primary circulation both on Aigina and outside the *arkhē*, where Aiginetans and others traded using Aiginetan/Aiginetic coins. The continued importance of Aiginetan coinage demonstrates an intractability of Greek economic circumstances to the dictates of hypothetical policies whose primary purpose lay in symbolic gestures.

[78] Giovannini, *Circulation monétaire* 75–76; Martin, *Sovereignty* 198–99.

[79] Figueira, "*Autonomoi kata tas spondas* (Thucydides 1.67.2)," *BICS* 37 (1990) 63–88, which also appears in an augmented version in *Excursions* 255–92.

[80] Cf. Meiggs 183–84; see Figueira, *Excursions* 274 and pp. 123–25 above.

Furthermore, some general conclusions and corollaries of an analysis of autonomy on the eve of the Peloponnesian War are pertinent to our exploration of the genesis of the Coinage Decree.

Inasmuch as the Spartans had no silver coinage themselves, the connotation of *autonomia* current among the Peloponnesians—they seem to have equated autonomy with *eleutheria* 'freedom' almost unconditionally—will probably not have had a specifically monetary dimension. As has been seen, the majority of Spartan allies used coins on the Aiginetic standard and the hoard evidence suggests that those coining on this standard may have accorded Aiginetan money (if not other Aiginetic coins) customary or statutory recognition in their economies. Clients and dependencies of Corinth used the Corinthian standard in series that sometimes imitated Corinthian issues. These practices do not corroborate an employment of coinage to establish autonomy among the Peloponnesians, although the relations of Corinth and its dependencies show that numismatic iconography could signal political affiliation, as it were, a converse of complete independence.

In Athenian usage as reflected in Thucydides, autonomy language is juxtaposed with the absence of tribute and the maintenance of an independent military establishment, including the possession of walls and the contribution of ships to allied forces (Thuc. 1.117.3; 3.10.5, cf. 3.11.1; 3.39.2; 6.85.2, cf. 6.84.3; 7.57.4–5; 8.91.3; cf. Andoc. 3.14). These two characteristics were joined together in practice during the *arkhē* and are significantly more prominent than the core meaning of autonomy suggested by etymology, namely, that autonomy is using one's own laws (cf., for example, *Suda* s.v. αὐτονομουμένη πόλις, α 4512 Adler). There is no parallel collocation with coinage, in particular the minting of a characteristic series of coins with the badge of the state. While the epigraphical evidence from Attic diplomatic usage cannot be qualified as conclusive, here again any mention of coinage is absent from the grants of autonomy to Mytilene (*IG* I^3 66, cf. Thuc. 3.50.1–3; *IG* I^3 67) and Samos (*IG* I^3 127; cf. *IG* I^3 96; Thuc. 7.57.4, 8.21).[81]

In the Attic ideology of hegemony, self-administration and self-legislation (which constitute the implied aspects of autonomy) depend on the presence of a defensive capacity.[82] Autonomous states can negotiate international legal and economic agreements like *symbolai* (cf. *IG* I^3 127.17–18), even though they are constrained by a military alliance with

[81] Other grants of autonomy may have been made to the *koinon* of the Eteokarpathioi (*IG* I^3 1454.11–12 = Tod, *GHI* #110, 2.28–30) and Selymbria (*IG* I^3 118.10–11). For discussion, see Figueira, *Excursions* 264 with note 34.

[82] See Figueira, *Excursions* 260–66, 284–88; cf. 217–21.

Athens. In Athenian grants of autonomy, Athens bestowed rights of self-government and established a foundation for cooperation in foreign affairs that included allied remilitarization. No evidence indicates that they ever provided for the resumption of coining or the reestablishment of local metrological standards when they accorded autonomy. An enjoining of Athenian coins and standards (like that arguably found in the Coinage Decree) showed that allied cities were not autonomous, not because they lacked a local coinage that symbolized autonomy but because autonomy by its nature was a substantial freedom from enfringement of the prerogatives of local government by Athenian legislation—as opposed to merely being subject to Athenian military orders.

We have already partially explored a final confusing element in our interpretation of the Coinage Decree and the nature of autonomy in the fifth century, namely, its ramifications for autonomous allies. The numismatic evidence supports continuous minting for Mytilene (down to 427), Samos, and Chios during the period of Attic hegemony. This result is concordant with a judgment that the line between the autonomous and the tributary was sharply drawn so that grants of autonomy possess all the signs of legislation representing significant ameliorations of status. While this appraisal of the numismatic data is not fatal to a belief that the Coinage Decree constituted exploitative imperialism, it does confute the view that a prohibition on minting silver was in all likelihood extended (in the prevailing view of scholars) to the autonomous states with the same rigor that it exercised over the tributary allies. As noted earlier, the general application of the Coinage Decree has been used to prove its authoritarian character.

The numismatic evidence does have a further impact in revealing an absence of dichotomy or distinctiveness in the histories of minting during the *arkhē* as experienced by autonomous and nonautonomous cities of similar size and socioeconomic institutions (see above, pp. 52–53; below pp. 481–82). This observation cuts both ways: indiscriminate application of the decree is either a proof of repression of both classes of ally or a hint that neither the tributaries nor the autonomous were exploited by the decree. Accordingly, the attested history of the terminology concerning autonomy is not only at variance with the traditional explanation of the decree but seems to belong essentially to a completely different system of political discourse.

The fifth-century Athenian evidence on coining and autonomy can be supplemented by material from later periods, some of which is discussed by T.R. Martin in his monograph *Sovereignty and Coinage in Classical Greece* (Princeton 1985). Martin's main purpose is to refute those who argued that the desuetude of the coinages of Thessaly (and other states falling under Macedonian control in the fourth century) is to be attributed to a Macedonian intervention that removed coined symbols of autonomy.[83] Yet, the demonstration of the motivations behind cessation of the activities of civic mints under Macedonian control has only a tangential impact on determining Athenian hegemonic practice. Martin does make the valuable point that regularizing weights and measures should not be explained by positing a role for them as symbols of autonomy;[84] this argument homes in on the weakness of the Coinage Decree as symbolism about sovereignty that I have noted above. His further point that the same consideration affects the decree's failure to prohibit electrum is vitiated by the lack of a self-advertising quality in electrum issues (see above, pp. 101–102).[85]

The other major extant examples of monetary legislation also show no preoccupation with the issue of autonomy.[86] The fragmentary inscription in which Mytilene and Phokaia plan to coordinate their minting of electrum *hectae* 'sixths' (of the stater) stands without as much as a sideward glance in its surviving portion toward the necessity for legal reservations to protect the appearance of the independence of the two cities (Tod, *GHI* #112, 2.34–36).[87] There was a natural tendency of cities to establish their currency as legal tender for reasons of facilitating administrative supervision and taxation. The two extant epigraphical exhibits bracketing our period are a law of Eretria from ca. 550–25 (*IG* XII.9 1273/1274) and a fourth-century decree from Olbia (*SIG*^{3} 218), where the validity of Cyzicene staters is also conceded.[88] Neither document suggests that a local monopoly for official coinage of the state was promulgated as a demonstration of autonomy. As the numismatic evidence implies in cases

83 Martin, *Sovereignty* 54–59, 153–65, 219–48; cf. 21–33.

84 Martin, *Sovereignty* 196–99.

85 Martin's suggestion that the decree was intended to raise money (*Sovereignty* 199–201) has been discussed above; linkage with the system for tribute collection will be explored below.

86 An early overview was offered by T. Reinach, "L'anarchie monétaire et ses remèdes chez les anciens Grecs," *Mém. Acad. Ins. et Belles-Lettres* 38 (1911) 351–64.

87 A recent discussion was offered by H. Engelmann, "Wege griechischer Geldpolitik," *ZPE* 60 (1985) 165–76, esp. 166–70, who strongly links coining and sovereignty/autonomy. Even if we could be sure that the law does not create joint jurisdiction for the two cities in trying a malfeasant "mixer" of the alloy (the critical stage of this minting process)—a judgment that should be resisted in any case—I doubt that an arrangement for exclusive jurisdiction over one's own mixer would establish the existence of a concern over a possible alienation of sovereignty.

88 F. Cairns, "ΧΡΕΜΑΤΑ ΔΟΚΙΜΑ: *IG* XII,9,1273 and 1274 and the Early Coinage of Eretria," *ZPE* 54 (1984) 145–55, would deny that the inscription even refers to coinage, a conclusion of which I remain doubtful (for which see below, pp. 398–99). On Olbia, cf. Cataudella *Sileno* (1986) 124–25.

like Melos and Kos, the most that can be asserted is that minting one's own coins, bearing a civic badge, could be a source of pride and an advertisement of local tradition, but the literary and epigraphical material does not justify our believing that coining was necessary to demonstrate or substantiate autonomous status.

Coinage and Political Symbolism

Once we necessarily turn to more general issues regarding the issuance of coins by a city and political symbolism, categorical answers become more difficult to reach. The iconography of coins celebrated local traditions and enhanced communalism in doing so.[89] The explicit evidence postdates the classical period; there archaizing, patriotic attitudes are indulged, but balanced with practical considerations.[90] We are forced to speculate about the perceptions belonging to fifth-century coiners. When cities like Kos and Maroneia retained limited series of heavier coins, we may suspect not only that they channelized the dissemination of these coins (as discussed above: pp. 80–83, 143–49) but that they appreciated their character as communicative gestures. Occasionally, an independent *polis* like Melos may have lavished resources on its coins beyond the norm in order to strike an independent pose. Some former allies of Athens may have revived coining after their break with the alliance to celebrate a recreation of a *patrios politeia* 'traditional constitution' in which earlier coining had played a role. Practical concerns, however, in maintaining independence and economic viability are more usually at work in such situations (pp. 58–61).

[89] There are many mythological etiologies that explain coin types, whose historicity need not concern us here. Note Poll. 9.84 for Mytilene, Chios, Iasos, Dardanos, Aspendos, Rhegion, Kephallania, Thasos, and Argos. For specific cases, note Athens: *Suda* s.v. βοῦς ἐπὶ γλώττης, β 460 Adler; Plut. *Thes.* 25.3; ΣArist. *Birds* 1106; Corinth: Poll. 9.75–76; Iasos: Ael. *De nat. animal.* 6.15; Plut. *Mor.* 984E–F; Kyrene: Hesych. s.v. βάττου σίλφιον, β 350 Latte; Phot. s.v., β 99 Th.; *Suda* s.v., β 186 Adler; Miletos: *SEG* 1.425; Mytilene: Hesych. s.v. κυζικηνοὶ στατῆρες, κ 4435 Latte; Phot. s.v.; Rhegion: Poll. 5.75; Tenedos: Steph. Byz. s.v. Τένεδος (*Eth.* 616); Troizen: Plut. *Thes.* 6.1.

[90] The most striking piece of non-Attic evidence is a much later (133–20) inscription of Sestos (Michel, *Recueil* #327 = *OGIS* #339 = *ISestos* #1) that speaks of the decision of the *dēmos* to use local bronze coinage (lines 43–44: νομίσματι χαλκίνῳ χρῆσθαι ἰδίωι), with one stated reason being that the civic badge appear on the coins (lines 44–45: χάριν τοῦ νομειτεύεσθαι μὲν τὸν τῆς πόλεως χαρακτῆρα). Yet even here the motivation of drawing revenue is prominent (lines 45–46: τὸ δὲ λυσιτελὲς τὸ περιγεινόμενον ἐκ τῆς προσόδου λαμβάνειν). A matter of civic pride and not autonomy, however, is at issue, since Sestos continued to lie within Attalid hegemony during the period spanning its use of Attalid coinage and its own coins. Note L. Robert, "Les monétaires et un décret de Sestos," *RN*[6] 15 (1973) 43–53, esp. 49–50; H. von Fritze, "Sestos: Die Menas-Inschrift und das Münzwesen der Stadt," *Nomisma* 1 (1907) 1–13.

An essential question is whether the Athenians felt it necessary to spoil such expressions of local pride, even if their enjoyment, as has been explained, carried no particular claim either to independence from Attic hegemony or to autonomous status within the Athenian alliance. One piece of evidence directly bears on the Athenian attitude toward the symbolism of allied coin types, but it is a telling one. If effacing local coinages was political symbolism of any great impact, it would be hard to understand why the Athenians themselves utilized the civic badges of their allies in federal administration, as they seem to have done with a provision of the Kleinias Decree (*IG* I³ 34.11–18: χσύμβολα δὲ π[οιέσα]σθαι π|ρὸς τὰς πόλες, *h*ό[πος ἄ]ν μὲ ἐχσ||[ε̃ι ἀδικε̃ν τοῖς ἀ[πάγοσι τὸμ φ|όρον. γράφσασα δ[ὲ *h*ε] πόλις ἐς | γραμματεῖον τὸ[μ φό]ρον, *h*όντιν' ἂν ἀποπέμπει, σεμε|ναμένε τõι συμβ[όλο]ι ἀποπεμπέτο 'Αθέναζε· τὸς δὲ ἀ|πάγοντας ἀποδõ[ναι] τὸ γραμματεῖον ἐν τε̃ι βολε̃ι ἀ|ναγνõναι *h*όταμ[πε]ρ̣ τὸμ φόρον ἀποδιδõσι . . . [make *symbola* for the cities in order that it will not be possible for those conveying the tribute to act wrongly. The city, having inscribed the tribute, whichever it is sending, on an accounting tablet and having coded it with a symbol, sends the tablet to Athens. The ones conveying the tribute are to hand over the tablet before the Boulē, for review whenever they hand over the tribute]).

One might imagine the Athenians to have provided these *symbola*,[91] but even that scenario would raise the question whether this was the first instance of such a practice and whether allied preferences had been canvassed in the creation of a stock of *symbola* previously. D.M. Lewis, however, views this function as a reciprocal one in which allied city and Athenians cooperated in the creation of their *symbolon*.[92] Thus it is likely that the cities themselves might have suggested the civic badges that they used to seal the *grammateion*. Each city needed a unique symbol, which it kept in its own possession. Such a provision would certainly help forestall allied excuses in the case of a dispute. Why should the Athenians open themselves to the charge that a *symbolon* they had provided had been duplicated before its conveyance to the allied city? For cities that had, at some time or other, minted coins, there is considerable likelihood that the ally (or even, for that matter, the Athenians) would normally opt for using the same *kharaktēr* 'type' as that impressed on the local coins. In any event, the casual way in which this legislation refers to the utilization of such

[91] See B.H. Hill and B.D. Meritt, "An Early Decree Concerning Tribute," *Hesperia* 13 (1944) 1–15, esp. 11.

[92] D.M. Lewis, "The Public Seal of Athens," *Phoenix* 9 (1955) 32–34, with a note by W.P. Wallace; cf. W.P. Wallace, "The Public Seal of Athens," *Phoenix* 3 (1949) 70–73. See also P. Gauthier, *Symbola: Les étrangers et la justice dans les cités grecques* (Nancy 1972) 82–85.

symbola in the control of the dealings of Athens and its subjects indicates that advertisements of local identity were not necessarily objectionable to the Athenians (compare p. 505 below).

A discussion of a special version of the theory seeing the Coinage Decree as representing political symbolism can conclude this section. C.H.V. Sutherland and E.S.G. Robinson (apparently independently) suggested that the Athenians did not so much desire the presence of their coinage throughout the *arkhē* as they wanted to remove the circulation of Aiginetan coins.[93] After the subjugation of Aigina the continuing utilization of its coinage by the allies was an unacceptable reminder of Aiginetan naval rivalry and of the long resistance of the island to Athenian dictates. A number of considerations stands against this hypothesis, many of which have already been presented in my general remarks on autonomy and coinage. Moreover, we now know that the coinage of Aigina that bears the obverse image of a segmented turtle or tortoise must have begun in the fifth century.[94] The tortoises were in production in great numbers during the supposed force of the Coinage Decree, if the decree is to be dated at mid-century. Naturally, a date in the 420s for the Coinage Decree would necessitate our restating the Athenian motivation as a sort of *damnatio memoriae*, undertaken after the expulsion of the Aiginetans from their island in 431. In any event, the evidence from the hoards indicates a continuing role for Aiginetan coinage even in the Aegean, if not as the primary monetary medium, at the very least as a means for holding funds in reserve. There is no sign from the hoard evidence either within or without the *arkhē* of a call-in and demonetization of the tortoise staters by the Athenians. As we have seen, the Athenians had to deal with the real influence of Aiginetan and Aiginetic coinage, despite their feelings of antipathy toward the Aiginetans themselves.

The Costs and Benefits of Numismatic Symbolism

The chief reason for the lack of a closer tie between coinage and autonomy was probably the difficulties that most polities confronted in sustaining an abundant local currency. There were easier ways both within symbolic behavior (like religious activity at panhellenic sanctuaries) and practical methods (such as fortifications) toward establishing a claim to

[93] Sutherland *AJP* (1943) 143: "its purpose was certainly to call in the coins of Aegina—now subject—at a profit." E.S.G. Robinson, "The Athenian Currency Decree and the Coinages of the Allies," *Hesperia* Suppl. 8 (1949) 324–40, esp. 325: "The mass of Aiginetan money still circulating was a continual reminder of Aegina's recent greatness, a continual irritation to Athens, and perhaps a considerable factor in promoting the decree." See also Mattingly *Historia* (1961) 184; Finley, "Classical Greece" 24.

[94] See Figueira, *Excursions* 288–92 and pp. 118–25 above.

independent standing. Many cities did not coin (for Athenian allies, see above, pp. 52–56), including Megara, a *polis* that was always defending its particularly embattled sovereignty against those copious producers of coinage, Athens and Corinth.[95] Others ceased minting during the first half of the fifth century. There were also mints during the heyday of the *arkhē* where local small change or drachma-weight coins supplemented Attic tetradrachms (see above, pp. 71–75). Other mints seem to exhibit a limited state currency, mainly in the output of a few dies, sometimes in only stater or tetradrachm weights, that circulated in the local economy alongside foreign monies.

Therefore, mixed monetary regimes came into existence in which coinages of different proveniences interacted synergistically in offering coins of various weights and standards and in supplying a disparate but appropriate medium for various types and sizes of transactions.[96] This paradigm for a mixed monetary regime was possibly established by or inherited from the pattern of circulation of the first silver coinage of international significance, the Aiginetan coins that bore the image of a turtle.[97] These coins were involved in the introduction of a primitive monetary economy to many areas of homeland Greece, where from the earliest the turtles were a dominant component in hoards, accompanied by other Aiginetic currency (pp. 36–38, 125–27). The turtles were indeed called the "coin of the Peloponnesus" (Poll. 9.74; Eupolis fr. 141 K = fr. 150, *PCG* 5.378; Apostolius fr. 12.31b (= *CPG* 2.550); Hesych. s.v. χελώνη, χ 343 Latte; cf. καλλιχέλονος, κ 495).

The wide adoption of the Aiginetic standard presumably overlies an equal or even wider acceptance of Aiginetan staters as valid coins or legal tender in many jurisdictions.[98] When local coinages were initiated on the Aiginetic standard, their output was in many cases insufficient to handle the majority of transactions within the community. In some cases, fractional coins were in default, leaving a wide base to

[95] T.J. Figueira, "Chronological Table: Archaic Megara, 800–500 B.C.," in T.J. Figueira and G. Nagy (eds.), *Theognis of Megara* (Baltimore 1985) esp. 262–73, 277–78, 288–302.

[96] For various legally recognized coinages on Hellenistic Amorgos at Arkesine, see Chapter 2, note 19 above.

[97] Figueira, *Aegina* 71–78, 80–88.

[98] The direct Classical and Hellenistic evidence for the official or quasi-official standing of Aiginetan coinage is fairly plentiful: Athens (Diphilos fr. 66 K = fr. 67, *PCG* 5.92 *apud* Athen. 6.6.225B); Crete (Dosiadas *FGH* 458 F 2 *apud* Athen. 4.22.143B); Delos (for example, *ID* 7.101 from 372–67); Epidauros (for example, *IG* IV.1 102 from 400–350); Argos (*IG* IV 617, post 323); Delphi (for example, *FD* 3.1 294 from 425–375). See also P. Marchetti, "Les cours de l'attique et de l'éginétique et les reapports or-argent dans les comptes de Delphes," in D. Knoepfler (ed.), *Comptes et inventaires dans la cité grecque* (Neuchatel/Geneva 1988) 103–10. See also pp. 483–84 below.

the pyramid of transactions that could not be serviced in the official state coinage. Furthermore, Aiginetan or Aiginetic money appears as an official medium for payment in treaties involving Peloponnesian states (*IG* I^3 83.22–24; Thuc. 5.47.6–7; Xen. *HG* 5.2.21).[99] In more agrarian, autarkic economies, Aiginetan turtles (in a range of weights) introduced through interstate exchanges blended with coins of local provenience that were struck on the Aiginetic coin standard.[100]

The utilization of archaic Aiginetan coinage suggests a more complex attitude toward the possession of a state coinage than either of the two alternatives in terms of which the debate on coinage and autonomy has been heretofore stated, that is, disinterest in coining as political self-assertion or an insistence on the issuance of coinage as a token of autonomy. The states that began coining on the Aiginetic standard in the late sixth and early fifth centuries probably felt pride in the issuance of money with the civic badges of their states. After all, there is no good reason why they cannot be thought to have experienced some modest degree of the same satisfaction that Aristophanes expressed over the quality and beauty of Attic, Laureotic tetradrachms (*Frogs* 718–26). Sometimes the publicizing of shared images was an important motivation, where coining was not necessary to supplement Aiginetan and Aiginetic coins in local circulation; in other words, where governments could have used other coins on the Aiginetic standard in collecting taxes.

Nevertheless, the continued local, valid circulation of one or more international coinages demonstrates the practical limits even on a profession of civic pride through minting. If Aiginetan or Aiginetic and eventually Athenian coins were used in much the same way as local money, it was probably impractical for the state to refuse to accept them as well in taxation. Thus it is difficult to see how the government of a *polis* could separate a subset of prestigious transactions in which coins bearing the civic symbol held an exclusive or privileged position, unless the government was itself disbursing funds. Certain payments by the state such as subventions for political or ritual activity, two areas closely enmeshed

[99] A treaty of Attalos I and the people of Malla in Crete dating from the end of third century contains a clause providing for payment of one Aiginetic drachm (presumably any coin[s] of the standard) per day for each soldier sent by the king to aid his Cretan allies (lines 22–23). See P. Ducrey and H. van Effenterre, "Traités attalides avec cités crétoises," *Kretika Khronika* 21 (1969) 277–30, esp. #2, pp. 281–300; also P. Ducrey, "Nouvelles remarques sur deux traités attalides des cités crétoises," *BCH* 94 (1970) 637–59.

[100] The references to Aiginetan weights and measures at Sparta, where there was no silver coinage in legal use, helps to show both the pervasiveness of Aiginetic metrology and the role of Aiginetan or Aiginetic money as an international medium of exchange. Note Athen. 4.19.121C, Plut. *Mor.* 226D; cf. Plut. *Lyc.* 12.2.

with communal identity, might have been reserved for money bearing the emblem of the community. Yet it is important to stress that any such reservations for the use of local coinage lay in the area of expenditure and not in the delimitation of a class of transactions undertaken by private individuals. This distinction will turn out to have important ramifications for Athenian monetary legislation.

Inhibiting Expressions of Numismatic Symbolism

The hegemony of the Athenians over their tributary allies was demonstrated by the very existence of the system for collecting the tribute and by the promulgation of interventionist legislation. Without a strong conjunction between coining and the possession of autonomy, the Coinage Decree cannot be taken to have furthered that demonstration in and of itself. What it may have done (in the traditional interpretation) was to deprive the allies of some opportunities to make public display of their official coinage and its attendant symbolism. Rather than having a panhellenic impact as a proof of Attic hegemony, the Coinage Decree would in that eventuality have had a series of restricted, local impacts as the occasions for the special deployments of local money recurred through the religiopolitical calendar. At these junctures, the dissemination of local coins could no longer occur as it had in the past. Our willingness to accept the importance for the Athenians of curtailing such situations is largely predicated on our evaluation of the degree to which Athenian hegemony (was the decree enacted under Perikles or Kleon or Nikias?) strove for gratuitous exercises in power politics.

How many other examples are there of Athens misusing its prerogatives merely to prove the extent of Athenian power to control the conditions of everyday life or the very vestments of communal identity? Before answering this question, it is important to note the extent to which superficially relevant parallels in fact differ in their sensibility. One may criticize the Athenian attempt to integrate their *arkhē* by promoting the idea that their allies were their colonists who owed allegiance to their mother city by virtue of that colonial derivation.[101] Naturally, some allied cities with their own rich mytho-historical traditions were bound to resist on some level such a reordering of their past. But that does not alter the fact that the promotion of this symbolism was meant to be unifying and was intended to indicate the existence of *reciprocal* ties, subsuming both duties and responsibilities, not merely Athenian superiority.

[101] See Figueira, *Colonization* 230–33.

Much the same could be said about Athenian claims to the origination of various aspects of agriculture or the effort to achieve a cultural preeminence through the Periclean building program or through the elaboration of religious celebrations that included magnificent poetic and musical performances. At the worst, such policies were misguided efforts at "winning the hearts and minds" of the allies. They did not seek to highlight Athenian domination by demonstrating its irresistibility.

The use of the Coinage Decree as a symbol both of the termination of the status of Athens as primus inter pares and of its emergence as an imperial state seems particularly poorly chosen for inclusion in the supposed policies of the Athenians of the Periclean period. In the traditional interpretation, the Coinage Decree did not symbolize Athenian hegemony, but blurred the distinction between the autonomous and the tributaries in a manner inconsistent with other Athenian policies on autonomy. If there was any room for communal pride in the possession of a local coinage, the existence of preserves for the deployment of local money (and local money alone) did not impede the achievement of the utilitarian purposes of monetary and metrological consolidation. No obvious gain, whether symbolic or propagandistic, seems to justify the intrusion on these preserves, or to make it worthwhile that the allies be affronted. It will, however, take an exploration of the area of administration in which disunity of currencies and standards was most felt by Attic politicians to understand the linkage between the economic advantages of monetary and metrological consolidation and administrative expediencies.

10

TRIBUTE AND MONETARY POLICY

IN THE PRECEDING DISCUSSION, two areas of particular difficulty emerged in our investigation of earlier interpretations of the Coinage Decree. One problematical area involved envisaging the decree as economic imperialism or even as a device for expropriating resources or levying a tax on the allies. Nonetheless, when a beneficial economic effect both for Athenians and for allies is conjectured in response, the apparently punitive aspects of the decree remained troubling. Thus the implementing of monetary and metrological consolidation through the injunctions of an Athenian *psēphisma* (instead of through a series of acts of uniformity by the allies themselves or through reciprocal agreements with the Athenians) caused theoretical problems, after already appearing improbable on the basis of the numismatic data.

Second, the history of the concept of *autonomia* during the *arkhē* is ill-matched with the traditional reconstruction of the Coinage Decree. If the decree violated the autonomy of the allies, its trespassing was most obvious in the area where the Athenians would have wanted it least, namely, concerning the autonomous allies with their active commerce and long monetary histories. Here scholarly appreciations of the unconditional language of the decree seemed to clash with the numismatic evidence for continuous minting on Chios, minting at Mytilene down to its subjugation after rebellion in 427, and virtually continuous minting on Samos (save perhaps for a politically motivated gap in the early 430s).

Both areas of concern are alleviated when we turn to a final set of rationales for the issuance of the decree, namely, fiscal or administrative efficiency. The pitfalls and uncertainties of an exploration of the economic psychology of the Greeks of the Athenian *arkhē* can hereby be reduced to more manageable proportions, because an administrative motivation for the decree can be reconstructed that bridges the realm of economic intuitions and that of practical state policy. It will turn out that fiscal policy, in the form specifically of decisions concerning confederate revenue, serves as the vital intermediate link between the economic behavior of individuals and the policies of each allied government and of the hegemonic state.

THE LOGISTICS OF ATTIC HEGEMONY

Before such a hypothesis can be advanced with any confidence, however, we must try to specify precisely which aspects of the administration of the Delian League affected monetary legislation and policy about metrological standards. The comments of M.I. Finley on the Coinage Decree in 1967 helped to direct scholarly attention toward the connections between the decree (as traditionally interpreted) and imperial administration.[1] He noted the possible facilitation of the activities of Athenian commanders in the field. The general use of Athenian money would make it easier to procure supplies and conduct business with the subject allies. As the allies themselves would also be using Attic weights and measures, that single standard being in use for procurement would greatly simplify logistical management and subsequently governmental supervision of the activities of the forces of the league.

In this shift in focus, albeit quite helpful, Finley characteristically downplays the part played by economic (as opposed to more narrowly defined administrative) thinking in the background of Attic monetary legislation. As so often, his criticism is aimed at what he perceived as modernizing analyses, but which are better understood in this instance as statist interpretations. Thus his polemics were best targeted at those who attributed to ancient governments elaborate manipulations of economic conditions that were aimed at achieving specific advantages (like the speculation about the Athenian creation of a bimetallic monetary system, noted in the previous chapter). These policies disturbingly appeared to be based (if only implicitly) on sophisticated collection of data, record-keeping, and quantitative evaluation. We may agree with Finley most readily wherever such modern explanations depend on a conceptual apparatus that cannot be rendered into attested fifth-century political terminology.

Before we assent, however, to Finley's hypothesis that simplification of logistics was a primary motivation for the Coinage Decree, we should remember that Athens as a hegemonic state probably held a privileged position as a customer during most of the fifth century. This special status is not only an outgrowth of military and political leadership but a simple reflection of a situation where a well-provided consumer, such as the fleet of the Delian League, may have been able to dictate its terms of business regardless of the local monetary situation in which it found

[1] "Classical Greece" 23–24; Finley, *Ancient Economy* 168–69; seconded by D.M. Lewis, "The Athenian Coinage Decree," in Carradice, *Coinage and Administration* 53–63, esp. 61–62; see also Erxleben *AJP* (1971) 161.

itself. As shall be seen shortly, the only prudent assumption is that league and Athenian forces endeavored to conduct their business and to disburse funds through the medium of Attic coins, especially tetradrachms.

The main capital expenses for building ships, outfitting them, and constructing ship-sheds and other support facilities were incurred in Attica, where the aforesaid conclusion is patently true.[2] Nothing, however, suggests that it was not also true abroad, especially where Athenian or federal naval forces had a permanent or continual presence. Insofar as Athenian colonies provided a setting for the basing of such forces, much as Eion did during the Amphipolis campaign (Thuc. 4.104.5, 106.3–107.2, 108.1; cf. 4.102.3; 5.6.1–3), their commanders could once again easily have used Attic money.[3]

As naval or amphibious units, the forces of the alliance probably had the advantage of largely using Athenian money to make purchases of supplies in any case. Supplies shipped from Attica were perforce purchased with Attic money. Squadrons of triremes and transports often carried with them only modest amounts of consumable supplies, but they were also shadowed by merchant ships. Sailors were expected to procure their own food either out of their salaries or from allowances provided for that purpose (cf., for example, [Arist]. *Oec.* 1350a23–30).[4] Accompanying merchants carried perishable supplies to satisfy these needs, and also purchased slaves and booty from the forces at sea. Naval personnel received their pay in Athenian money so that the attendant merchants would have had to handle transactions in this medium. One suspects that this arrangement was quite in their own interests as well, because it simplified later conversion.

The well-documented first expedition against Syracuse provides some interesting evidence, although it must be recalled that this was an extreme manifestation of the projection of classical Greek naval power. The expedition included the triremes, 30 *olkades* 'transports'

[2] Regular construction of triremes in Attic yards: DS 11.43.2 (under 477/6); *PStrasbourg* 84 = *ATL* 1 T9, 2 D13 = Anonymous Argentinensis 9–11 (variously restored and dated); ΣDem. 22.13–14; Andoc. 3.5–9; Aesch. 2.172–75. For the role of the board of τριηροποιοί, see *IG* I³ 117.4–9; 153.4; 182.8–13; 366.13; 439.77. For a useful survey, see D. Blackman, "The Athenian Navy and Allied Naval Contributions in the Pentekontaeteia," *GRBS* 10 (1969) 179–216. I take the notice that Kimon was accepting money and empty ships (Plut. *Cimon* 11.2: λαμβάνων . . . ναῦς κενάς) from allies unwilling to go on campaign as rhetorical and operational: rhetorical, because a variety of undermanning was probably the point of historical reference; operational, because Kimon was manning the ships with paid rowers and crediting the ally with having supplied its contingent. I do not think that many usable old allied triremes passed into Attic hands.

[3] See Figueira, *Colonization* 172–76 for assorted examples.

[4] See W.K. Pritchett, *The Greek State at War* (Berkeley and Los Angeles 1971–1991) 1.41–52.

not only carrying grain, but bakers, stone workers, carpenters, and siege supplies, and 100 *ploia* 'boats' that were requisitioned to sail with the *olkades* (Thuc. 6.44.1; cf. 6.22). Many other *ploia* and *olkades* sailed along voluntarily (ἑκούσιοι) for the sake of commerce (ἐμπορίας ἕνεκα). Of the cities solicited to provide shelter for the expedition, Rhegion and Messane refused to receive the expeditionary force within their walls but did provide an extramural market, while Naxos and eventually Katane received them within (Thuc. 6.44.2–3, 50.1–51.2). The Attic forces seem to have conducted business in west Greece in Athenian money, not only with the floating "*agora*" accompanying them, but also with those cities willing to shelter them, although they doubtless also expended any allied contributions in foreign currency that came in during the course of operations (cf. Thuc. 6.46.1, 88.4). It comes as no surprise that when Plemmyrion was captured by the Syracusans in 413, much property belonging to the *emporoi* 'merchants' conducting business with the army was taken and that this was a major blow to the prospects for success of the expedition (Thuc. 7.24.2). A component of the logistical "life-support" system of fifth-century Attic fleets was this supply flotilla of private ships.

Over the winter of 415–14, the Athenians sent a ship back to request *khrēmata* 'money' and cavalry (Thuc. 6.93.4). Strikingly, when Thucydides describes the Athenian compliance with this request, he substitutes the word *trophē* 'subsistence' for *khrēmata* (6.93.4: οἱ Ἀθηναῖοι ἀκούσαντες ἐψηφίσαντο τήν τε τροφὴν πέμπειν τῇ στρατιᾷ καὶ τοὺς ἱππέας). The second expedition led by Demosthenes and Eurymedon also brought *khrēmata* along with other supplies (DS 13.11.2; cf. Thuc. 7.42.1: τὴν ἄλλην παρασκευὴν ἱκανήν). The Athenian coins attested in Sicilian hoards laid down during the late fifth century seem to have been brought into the region by Athenians who were present in these expeditionary forces.[5]

Since this elaborate provision for transport and skilled support personnel was exceptional, the foregoing portrait applies a fortiori to the normal operations of the forces of the Delian League mounted in the Aegean basin (and to an extent in the rest of the eastern Mediterranean). This suggests that the monetary or exchange aspects of imperial logistics could not have been a sufficient stimulus toward monetary reform in themselves.

[5] See Chapter 1, note 14. The governments of Rhegion and Messane overstruck Attic tetradrachms that they seemed to have acquired through direct payment or taxation as the least expensive means for reusing coins inconvenient for their own expenditure. Cf. S. Garaffo, *Le riconiazioni in Magna Grecia e in la Sicilia*, *Studi e Materiali di Archeologia Greca* 2 (Catania 1984) 126–27.

Let us turn now to the issue of local *metra* and the conduct of Athenian operations. We have already noted that regularization of the sizing or packaging of goods would simplify sales; such standardization falls within the ambit of the economic benefits of metrological consolidation. It is doubtful, however, that we are justified in offering facility of procurement by Athenian commanders as sufficient motivation for an imposition of standards. Athenian military forces were the best subsidized and most privileged buyers during the period suggested for the legislation (450 to 420 or 415, at the latest). When dealing with merchants who accompanied military forces, Athenian officers probably operated within an environment already typified by Attic standards and money. With local sellers, they would ordinarily have made rough and ready conversions into Attic terms of those goods they intended to purchase and made bids or requisitions on that basis. Admittedly, there were mistakes inherent in this sort of calculation, but the hegemonic authority and sheer economic clout of Athenian officers, who bought with ready cash, probably kept the Athenian treasury from being victimized. In any case, most of the money expended on campaign would have been spent by naval personnel who procured their own food and sold booty in terms of Attic money.

The facilitation of commerce through monetary and metrological consolidation (as discussed above) subsumes the experiences of Athenian officials in procuring supplies. If military procurement has any relevance for the study of the Coinage Decree, its impact could lie in the paradigmatic functioning of the supply train of merchants accompanying Athenian expeditions. Here was a microcosm of the economy of the whole *arkhē* that operated, it would appear, mainly in terms of Athenian money, although it may have also been able, if the Syracusan campaign is indicative, to cope with inputs of other civic currencies. There might have been a few Athenians who, working within the more autarkic sectors of the Attic economy, were so insulated from interaction with nonresidents that they were unaware of the negative effects of the multiplicity of standards existing within the *arkhē*. If such persons existed, the almost universal experience of military service abroad would have helped them to understand the benefits of the general acceptance of a single version of the standards. Consider the passages from comedy that show humorous experiences with foreign money by Athenian soldiers abroad: Eupolis fr. 233 K = fr. 247, *PCG* 5.438–39; Strattis fr. 36 K = fr. 37, *PCG* 7.640.

Hence David Lewis's remark, "I am not suggesting that anyone responsible for Athenian legislation knew or cared what length of foot the builders used on Samos," construes the impact of metrological divergence too narrowly.[6] In point of fact, there is some evidence that the Samians or the government of another neighboring ally cared enough about the disparity of their *metra* and Attic *metra* to legislate an integration of the two systems (see below, pp. 307–11). Furthermore, Lewis focuses on what appeared to him as a relatively obscure aspect of the existence of local standards, rather like judging the impact of the adoption of the metric system by noting the size of the screws within a washing machine motor. In doing so, he unnecessarily yields too much ground to a primitivist vision of classical economic life. If we chose the example of the differential content of a shipment of wine and what tax its carrier should pay, would a disparity of *metra* still appear a matter of abstruse awareness? Any confusion in correspondence between different monetary and metrological standards impeded interstate exchanges. Once it is admitted that legislation consolidating metrological standards could aid the participants in all transactions across monetary and metrological boundaries, it hardly seems justifiable to segregrate any one group of participants, like Athenian officers procuring supplies in the *arkhē*, as precipitators of this legislation (at least, without direct ancient testimony).

Although the implication has never to my knowledge been made explicit, one possible motivation in seeing an expediting of military administration as a causative factor in the promulgation of the Coinage Decree is that the presumed punitive and authoritarian features of the traditional interpretation can thus be understood. That connotation, however, embodies the commitment of both Athenians and allies to the efficiency of league operations. The facility with which Athenian commanders procured supplies that were paid for by allied tribute, used by allied naval personnel and metics of allied origin, and acquired from allied vendors would scarcely have been a subject of an only parochial interest, one confined to the Athenians alone and excluding the allies themselves.

Another related aspect of the fiscal administration of the Delian League is fortunately available for an amplification on the scope of the question of causation for the decree. Finley's characteristic focus is on the arrangement of economic activity to the benefit of an administering authority, which is disbursing funds, but this perspective is one-sided by virtue of its neglect of the income side of administrative policy. We cannot begin to appreciate Athenian legislation about money until we have reconsidered the process by which the largest single annual transfers of resources occurred in the fifth century, through the collection of *phoros*

6 *Coinage and Administration* 61.

'tribute' from Athens' subject allies. If allied economies were operating on a local level in terms of their own indigenous currencies and standards (to whatever degree) and the Athenian government conducted all its business in terms of Attic money and standards, that great transfer of resources had to occur across monetary and metrological boundaries.

Hence, if we return to the two areas of difficulty noted at the beginning of this chapter, fifth-century economic sensibility, on the one hand, and appreciation of autonomy and sovereignty, on the other, we may now view them from a changed perspective. If the Athenian government necessarily presided over large monetary conversions in the course of the collection of the tribute, then the official appreciation of the value of monetary and metrological consolidation would closely parallel that of the individual economic agent who crossed metrological and monetary boundaries to conduct business in everyday experience. Second, we can begin to envision why monetary and metrological policy is not explicitly correlated with the concept of autonomy. If Athenian monetary policy was largely conditioned by the collection of tribute, it would have been obvious that those directly affected by that policy were already nonautonomous by virtue of their being tributary. It was the nonautonomous status of a payer of *phoros* on which our sources focus because that responsibility necessarily entailed other Athenian intrusions into local administration in order to ensure a smooth flow of payments. Notwithstanding this appraisal, an enduring mystery resides in the conflict between our perception of the benefits of monetary and metrological consolidation and the status of the Coinage Decree as a supposed act of aggrandizing imperialism.

THE TRIBUTE SYSTEM AND THE MONEY OF THE *ARKHĒ*

We turn then to taxation as an aspect of Athenian fiscal administration serving as a cause for the enactment of Athenian monetary legislation, especially taxation of the allies in the form of *phoros* 'tribute.' Although the possibilities of this perspective have not been fully worked out, it is noteworthy that there have been some suggestions that the tribute system was somehow involved in the genesis of the Coinage Decree.[7] In particular, the requirement that the tribute be paid in Attic currency has been offered as a motivation for the decree. The appearance in

[7] See E. Cavaignac, "Le Décret dit de Kléarkhos," *RN*[5] 15 (1953) 1–7, esp. 5. Compare Starr, *Coinage* 68–70, who offers the following formulation: "but a much more likely reason for this remarkable ordinance was the desire of Athenian treasurers for a uniform currency." See also Will, *Monde grec* 208; Schuller, *Herrschaft* 216; Martin, *Sovereignty* 201–203.

section ii of the composite decree of the Hellenotamiai, the "Treasurers of the Greeks," who were responsible for the oversight of collection and administration of the tribute, offers a strong indicator. While it has been suggested that the purpose of the Coinage Decree was to mandate that the tribute be paid in Attic tetradrachms,[8] it is improbable that such a roundabout way of ordering this simple result would have been chosen.[9] Rather, one might hypothesize that the Coinage Decree was meant to aid allied efforts at paying their assessed tribute in Athenian money and discouraging both allied and Athenian divergences from this requirement, after the policy for payment in Attic money had existed for some time.[10]

By the time at which the tribute lists exist as testimony, the tribute was largely paid in Attic coins. There is no doubt that reserve funds insofar as they later existed were also held in Attic tetradrachms. Consider the 3,000T νομίσματος *h*εμεδαπõ 'of our money' that are noted in the first finanical decree of Kallias, usually dated to 434/3 (*IG* I³ 52A.3–4). There are thus two alternatives when a requirement to pay in Attic coin was established: at the foundation of the alliance or when the league treasury was moved to Athens.

Earlier scholars, who assumed that there was a series of Athenian laws on allied monetary affairs, posited an early imposition of Attic coin as the medium for payment.[11] That a formal requirement had prevailed since the foundation of the Delian League is an alternative that still seems to be at least marginally preferable. In other words, *phoros* by its very nature meant funds paid in the medium used or mandated by a *hēgemōn*. Practical concerns, even at the start, compelled this provision. The league's capital

[8] See Cavaignac *RN* (1953) 5; French, *Athenian Economy* 121–22; S.K. Eddy, "Some Irregular Amounts of Athenian Tribute," *AJP* 94 (1973) 47–70, esp. 47–48; Martin, *Sovereignty* 201–202.

[9] Martin recognized the difficulty and went on to cite the profit motive in recoining (*Sovereignty* 203).

[10] A recent exception to this view is U. Wartenberg, *After Marathon: War, Society and Money in Fifth-Century Greece* (London 1995) 24.

[11] See E. Babelon, "La politique monétaire d'Athènes au Vᵉ siècle avant notre ère," *RN*⁴ 17 (1913) 457–85, esp. 462–66; cf. Will, *Monde grec* 208. Basing himself on an appreciation of the natural dominance of Attic coinage by virtue both of the tribute system and of Athenian direction of federal military activities, Babelon stated a striking hypothesis. It is still worth noting, although the maturation of epigraphical and numismatic evidence has rendered it unsustainable. To Babelon, the Coinage Decree represented the extreme manifestation during the Peloponnesian War of a long-standing Athenian policy to enjoin exclusive use of Attic money. The decree of Klearkhos, which is cited in our section xii, had contained the same prescriptions as the extant decree. The tone of the decree is to be explained by Athenian impatience in face of allied restiveness during the war. See also Babelon *RN* (1913) 466–69, 480–81; Cavaignac, *Études* 184–85.

expenditures were dominated by procurement of ships and their basic equipment. Such outlays were made primarily at the Peiraieus and with Attic coinage. Ongoing costs will have had as their largest component the provision of *trophē* 'subsistence' to ships' companies, and, once again, payment was in the form of Athenian money.[12]

Indeed, the assessments, starting from the establishment of the system by Aristeides, must have been in terms of Athenian money.[13] Our confidence in this assertion follows from a consideration of Aristeides' likely procedure in his famously just evaluation of the ability of the allies to pay for their own defense. As the Athenians were to spend the tribute, Aristeides must have conceptualized the cost of military forces of various sizes in terms of the Attic money with which he had worked as an Athenian *stratēgos*. He would also have received reports from the allies about the present and historical size of their forces, resources, revenues, and, where applicable, earlier payments to the Great King. His proverbial justice may have resided in the first instance in the skill with which he elicited accurate information from allied leaders, so that he will have succeeded in handling good information in a manner that withstood criticism from other members of the league. Second, Aristeides must have been reputed just for his responsiveness and evenhandedness in using allied declarations for the purposes of assessment. The individual assessments were translated into Attic money; otherwise they could scarcely have been compared and disputes adjudicated.

In contrast, some scholars have posited the second of our alternatives, that a shift from allowing payments in local money to requiring Athenian money was mandated at the time of the beginning of the tribute lists in 454/3.[14] That year has also been considered to be the moment at which the treasury was transferred from Delos to Athens. This other alternative does deserve consideration, because it prompts some interesting speculations. For one thing, once the inauguration of the tribute lists in 454/3 is justified by an imposition of a requirement to pay in Attic coin or by some other watershed in monetary history(!), there is no further need to explain the inception of the lists by the movement

[12] Note Cavaignac, *Études* 184; Babelon *RN* (1913) 462–64, 480. Hence the occasional arguments that are made in favor of a mid-century date for the Coinage Decree based on the conduct of Athenian finances and their accounting exclusively in terms of Attic money are not really probative. Contrast B.D. Meritt, "Perikles, the Athenian Mint, and the Hephaisteion," *PAPS* 119 (1975) 267–74, esp. 268–69.

[13] Cf. Plut. *Arist.* 24.1–4, cf. 25.3; DS 11.47.2; also Aesch. 3.258; Andoc. 4.11.

[14] See R. Weil, "Das Münzrecht der ΞΥΜΜΑΧΟΙ im ersten attischen Seebund," *ZfN* 28 (1910) 351–64, esp. 354–56; see also Segre 174; Cavaignac *RN* (1953) 5. Cf. Babelon *RN* (1913) 468–69.

of the treasury. In other words, there is no necessity to cite both the movement of treasury *and* another requirement like the payment in Attic coin to account for the beginning of the lists; either rationale is sufficient.

Accordingly, if the year 454/3 and the beginning of the inscribed *stelai* bearing records of the *aparkhai* signal the passage of a monetary threshold, the transfer of the treasury of the Delian League to Athens can be dated earlier.[15] The charm of this dissociation is that the only surviving chronological pointers bearing on the transfer of the treasury (at the proposal of the Samians) place it during the lifetime of Aristeides (Plut. *Arist.* 25.3) or following on the break with the Spartans over the dismissal of Kimon and his men from Ithome (Just. 3.6.4). These testimonia direct us toward the late 460s.[16] Nonetheless four important innovations in the tribute system could still be linked and placed in 454/3: the stipulation that payment be made in Attic coinage; the dedication of the *aparkhai* to Athena; the provision that the *aparkhai* be tendered to the Treasurers of Athena in Attic coins; and the commencement of inscribing the payment of the *aparkhai*. The shift in treatment of the *aparkhai* could even be understood as an act of religious propriety: the Athenians could scarcely be expected to dedicate their own coins bearing the head of their patron Athena to any deity—remembering Delian Apollo (cf. Thuc. 1.96.2)—other than Athena herself. In this hypothesis, the cult of Delian Apollo had received the *aparkhai* and had accepted a variety of coinages in the period from 478/7 down to 454/3, in other words not only while the treasury was on Delos but even after the treasury was transferred to Athens in the 460s.

Despite the attractiveness of some elements of this theory, one should prefer the conclusion that the allies were always required to pay in Attic coin, however often exceptions may have been tolerated in the early years. That does not, however, remove the innovations about the nature of the *aparkhai* as a rationale for the inception of the lists (as will be explored below, pp. 457–63). Whether or not we are

[15] For the consensus view accepting a transfer in 454/3, see, for example, *ATL* 3.262–64; Meiggs 47–48; Schuller, *Herrschaft* 169–70. Cf. W.K. Pritchett, "The Transfer of the Delian Treasury," *Historia* 18 (1969) 17–21. The latest discussion of the transfer of the treasury is that of N.D. Robertson, "The True Nature of the 'Delian League' 478–61 B.C.," *AJAH* 5 (1980) 64–96, 110–33, esp. 112–19, 124–30, which departs from the consensus of 454/3 in favor of 462/1. I am not completely persuaded by his presentation, but note the intensifying effect of its acceptance for this argument.

[16] The other evidence is consistent with this conclusion, although the prominence of Perikles in the *dēmos* would have to be held as exaggerated. Compare DS 12.38.2, 40.1 = Ephorus *FGH* 70 F 196; DS 12.54.3, 13.21.3; Plut. *Per.* 12.1; Nepos *Arist.* 3.1; Aristod. *FGH* 104 F 1.7.

prepared to believe that the requirement for tendering the tribute in Attic coin preceded the transfer of the league treasury to Athens, that movement may have had a financial impact.[17]

Both these alternatives make Attic coin required during some time prior to the earliest suggested date for the Coinage Decree. Therefore, if the issue was not permission for or prohibition of the allies paying tribute in foreign money that was the problematical factor in motivating the Coinage Decree, what was it about the system for the collection of the tribute that could have affected monetary arrangements? Let us answer with the difficulty of exchanging non-Attic money and Attic coins.

Troubles could arise at both ends of this process of taxation and expenditure. From the outset of the alliance, the income of many allied cities, out of which they paid their assessed tribute each year to the Hellenotamiai, was presumably composed of local money except where other currencies were traditionally accepted as valid either through interstate agreement or by local concession (note our categories I–II and possibly members of category IIIA). The allies then had the task of exchanging a portion of their income, received in non-Athenian coin, into Attic tetradrachms to render their assessed *phoros*. We can recall our discussion above of the number of allied cities still minting a range of denominations in the early 470s to appreciate this point.

Presumably, these cities acquired Athenian money through private or governmental monetary exchange. Conceivably, this process could have its costs. Just as today, those who exchange money charge a fee for their services. If local exchange was handled through a state bank,

[17] Delos had been a traditional place of resort for the Ionians of the islands and the mainland of Asia, and a place situated amid cities using different coinages and standards. Money changing might have been comparatively well evolved there. It is possible that the business of exchange was somewhat less developed in less commercial Attica (regarding the number and resources of money changers?) in the years around mid-century, so that late exchanges for the purpose of acquiring the required amount of Athenian money—if they were indeed permitted—might have been a more difficult task. It is exactly in the context of the mid-century (at the earliest) that the activities of money changers and bankers are first attested in Athens, but that impression might be a mirage caused by the survival of the data. See R. Bogaert, *Banques et banquiers dans les cités grecques* (Leiden 1968) 61–63, who collects the evidence for fifth-century money changing and banking at Athens: a reference to a χρυσαμοιβός 'gold-changer' (Aes. *Ag.* 438); the meetings of the sophist Hippias with students and others at the tables of the money changers, so before 411 (Plato *Apol.* 17C; *Hipp. Min.* 368B); the bankers Antisthenes and Arkhestratos, who passed (before 395) their bank in the Peiraieus to their freedman Pasion (Dem. 36.43, 48; Isoc. 17.43); and their contemporary Sokrates who, like Pasion, inherited his bank from his masters (Dem. 36.28). As for Delos, the only evidence involves the loans of the cult treasury of Apollo, starting from 434/3, 433/2 (Meiggs-Lewis #62 = *IG* I³ 402). See Bogaert, *Banques* 126–27. See also F. Bourriot, "Une famille de banquiers athénien celle d'Antimachos, Vᵉ–IVᵉ s.," *ZPE* 70 (1987) 229–34.

then the allied government had to bear the expense for administration of the bank and for its continuation and assume responsibility for its solvency, probity, and efficiency. If Athenian money was in short supply either locally or regionally, or if their own money was in little demand beyond their borders, allied governments would have had to pay an added premium over the token value of their coinage or perhaps even over its value by weight. Moreover, each year a number of cities either regionally or in the *arkhē* as a whole may have been seeking Attic money at about the same time to make up for shortfalls in governmental stocks. That situation may have caused special pressures on exchange. Nor would other governments have been the only competitors for Attic tetradrachms. Governments would have to have bid against everyone else in the Aegean basin who wanted tetradrachms for the purposes of ordinary business, to trade at the Peiraieus, for travel to Attica, or as a hedge against political or personal insecurity.

If problems were not surmounted in acquiring the requisite amounts of Attic coins before the official delegation left home to tender its tribute in Athens, the allied embassies might still cope with their difficulties in Attica. Exchanges were probably possible in Athens, if allied officials could find money changers interested in acquiring their own specific foreign currency (or currencies). Such relatively late exchanges of currency will naturally have had their costs: Athenian money changers would be able both to demand a high price for tetradrachms and to charge a comparatively higher fee for access to their services.[18] The final option for allied ambassadors in converting from a local currency to tetradrachms would have been for the allied government to surrender coins to the mint in Athens, where they would presumably be treated as bullion (regardless of their form). That imposed on the ally the minting charge levied by the Athenians and the loss of any premium their own currency possessed over raw bullion in local, regional, or international circulation. If the mint pressed its advantage toward those who needed to handle larger consignments or to get money back quickly, a surcharge might be tacked on. That might only represent a "petty cash" profit for the mint, but could represent a greater embarassment when the allied ambassadors had to present their accounts at home. Nevertheless, these late opportunities may not even have been available if the Athenians were always rigorous

[18] It was in the interest of both parties to avoid a situation like that experienced by the Carthaginians who were paying an installment of their indemnity in 199 (Livy 32.2.1–2; cf. 30.44.4). The coins were found to be highly adulterated (25 percent in the tests of the quaestors), so that the ambassadors had to borrow the deficit at Rome.

in limiting their receipt of tribute to only those amounts appearing on the inventories provided by the ally and created at home (*IG* I³ 34.14–18).

The potential difficulties that surrounded the payment of the tribute in Attic tetradrachms by allies whose tax receipts may often have been in local money did not end with the revenue phase of the process of taxation and expenditure. Money was circulated from the allies through the Athenian government to those who received payment for their service in and to the league's fleet. The clearest example (and quite possibly the most significant) involved allied sailors serving for pay in the fleet. As the allies stopped contributing ships, their political institutions were demilitarized, but many of their citizens would still have found service in the Athenian fleet, and these persons will have been paid in Attic coin.

Thus, a second problematic boundary of exchange was created. A large part of what would now be called the "defense sector" of the allied economies was shifted "offshore," but allied citizens still participated. Consequently, not only did local currency have to be transformed into Athenian money for the payment of tribute, but conversion back into local money was also necessary, if civilian spending by allied military personnel was to occur in places where local money was still predominent and Attic money scarce or invalid. This second series of exchanges was an influence on allied monetary policy whenever allied sailors did not sever their ties with their home cities.[19] It was in the interest of allied states that these individuals be able to spend their wages expeditiously at home so that taxes on this spending could contribute to the revenue stream in their "mother" cities. Otherwise, allied military personnel would not return even a part of their wages (paid out of tribute) to their home communities and subsequently to their governments. Just like its effect on simplifying the aggregation of tetradrachms to pay the tribute, monetary consolidation obviated these difficulties in exchange concerning allied business and allied revenue.

Moreover, insofar as the allies were trading partners of the Athenians, they faced the same predicament when tapping the expenditures of

[19] The degree of identification with Athens of allied sailors can be placed on a spectrum of degrees, and the intensity of loyalty to Athens and commitment to Athenian service may not have been classifiable by the difference between the categories metic and *xenos*. Would a fervently democratic sailor from one of the nearby Cyclades have needed to become a metic? See Thuc. 1.121.3 (*xenoi*) with 1.143.1–2 (*politai*, metics, and *xenoi*); 7.63.3–4 with scholia (metics and possibly democratic *xenoi*); Isoc. 8.48 (*xenoi*, *douloi*) with 8.79. See also Meiggs 439–41. A much altered situation in the Ionian War is illustrated by *IG* I³ 1032 = *IG* II² 1951+, where the number of slaves, both those purchased by the state and those serving with their masters, has become elevated because of the personnel shortages experienced by the Athenians. See Figueira, *Aegina* 59–60, note 30; P. Funke, "Konons Ruckkehr nach Athen im Spiegel epigraphischer Zeugnisse," *ZPE* 53 (1983) 149–89, esp. 164–69.

various recipients of Athenian military and political outlays as they had encountered in coping with spending by their own citizens in Athenian service.[20] The phenomenon clearly lacks the dramatic possiblities for disruption that might be envisioned for the failure of allied cities to find the requisite amounts of Attic coinage for contributing their tribute. Yet the degree to which allied military personnel participated in Athenian forces and the extent to which allied governments recaptured some of the outlays made by the Athenians out of their tribute would have affected the allied appreciation of the process of the commutation of the provision of ships to the payment of *phoros*. And the satisfaction of the allies with this process conditioned their appreciation of Athenian hegemony. Commutation was also responsible for a good deal of the increase in Athenian military power during the Pentekontaeteia. Evidence is lacking, as so often, about rationales for decision making, but resultant situations can be deciphered. The decision to pay tribute rather than to contribute ships, the service of allied sailors in the Athenian navy, the professionalization of that service, and the decisions by allies to curtail coining can be viewed as complementary historical processes.

The foregoing analysis may now be juxtaposed with the numismatic record of the retreat of allied coining before coinages in wider use, such as Athenian money. Until the effects of the Peloponnesian War made themselves felt, numerous allied cities either ended their coining or restricted minting to smaller denominations, and thus created a context for the local circulation of Attic tetradrachms and other stater-weight coins. Our cautious review of monetary output above indicates that the majority of the coins entering newly vacated niches for circulation would have been Attic coins. Disregarding their individual motivations, these allied cities had acted with the actual result that they were shielded from exchange problems. When the mints that curtailed coining were organized into categories in Part I, three points of demarcation were used as separators: 478, 465, and 445. The date of 478 has been discussed above for its significance in the retreat of the Persians and the foundation of the Delian League. The period leading up to 465 has been equated with the years of Kimonian military activities, and 445 with the aftermath of the Thirty Years Peace. Let us now observe how monetary exchange could have evolved as more and more cities ceased contributing in ships. The competition for Attic money might have become more constraining, especially inasmuch as the supply of tetradrachms could be uneven regionally. Since Attic money was circulated through payments

20 For a short survey of the classical Attic economy, see pp. 220–27 above.

for the imports by Athenians or through the expenditures by Athenian officials and military personnel overseas, there were bound to be areas of relative abundance and dearth that shifted as league operations changed locale and eventually moved out from the Aegean basin. The period 465–45 saw the professionalization of service in the Athenian fleet.

TRIBUTE PAYMENT IN NON-ATTIC COINAGE

The foregoing discussion has presented a context for Attic monetary legislation, but it is now fair to inquire whether there is any positive epigraphical evidence for problems in paying the tribute in Attic coins.

Before doing so, however, the status of the historical and literary sources must be squarely confronted. The reference to a consolidation of standards in the *Birds* of Aristophanes may well be an offhand allusion to a common diplomatic demarche in establishing such integrated metrological practices. One such remark, however, does not equal a series of contemporary comments. Nonetheless, monetary legislation should be seen as an ongoing Athenian preoccupation, as suggested by the existence of the Coinage Decree, by the law represented by the fragmentary *IG* I^3 90 (below pp. 424–30), and by the law of Klearkhos, noted in section xii of the Coinage Decree itself. In that case, the historical record will not reveal manifestations of a crisis to which the Coinage Decree responded. While the functioning of the tribute system will be shown to be imperfect, its relatively high efficiency was probably owed to the periodic intervention of monetary legislation that worked to mitigate problems in the exchange of local coins for Attic money. Neither perfect nor crying out for drastic intervention, the collection of tribute remained an administrative procedure forever in the background during the height of the Attic hegemony.

Thus, it becomes important to make a careful evaluation of the evidence that does exist on irregularities in the payment of tribute. Here a debt is owed to S.K. Eddy, who first argued systematically that certain patterns of payment on the tribute lists arose out of an impingement on that system of non-Athenian currencies.[21] Combining Eddy's observations with other suggestions, we can propose four relevant patterns that are attested on the tribute lists: the presence of electrum in the total of the *aparkhē* 'one-sixtieth dedication' in 454/3; atypical amounts in the payment of Hellespontine *aparkhai*; anomalies in the Carian *aparkhai*; and unusual payments of tribute.

[21] Eddy *AJP* (1973) 47–70.

The *Aparkhē* of 454/3

The notation of the Logistai on the total of the *aparkhē* on tribute list 1 of 454/3—if the postscript of the list has been correctly interpreted (*IG* I[3] 259.VI.Postscript, 6–12)—indicates that those officials received Cyzicene electrum staters, presumably in place of silver coins.[22] The *aparkhē* was 56, 66 (the reading of *IG* I[3]), or 96 staters, which accordingly delivers an amount of tribute of 3,360, 3,960, or 5,760 staters respectively. For accounting purposes, payments of electrum were denominated as χρυσίον 'gold' in the summation, but interestingly no special notation was made for individual entries (as far as we know) to represent any variation in the medium of payment.[23] Strikingly, Phocaic electrum coinage makes no appearance here. The year 454/3 was, however, the only occasion on which the *aparkhai* are known to have been tendered in anything other than Attic silver (a development discussed below on pp. 457–63).

For the purposes of the tribute system an exchange rate for Phocaic electrum coins of one *hectē* 'sixth-stater' equaling an Attic tetradrachm may be adopted for the moment (for other rates, see below pp. 524–27). If a Lampsacene stater was equivalent to six Phocaic *hectae*, it too was worth 24 Attic drachms. So also was the notional Phocaic "stater," which seems to have been an accounting denomination and not an actual coin (see above, pp. 99–100). When oligarchic Lesbian exiles extracted 2,000 Phocaic staters from Rhoiteion in summer 424 (Thuc. 4.52.2; cf. Pollux 9.93), that amount is presumably explained by the current assessment of 8T for the town in 425/4 (*IG* I[3] 71.III.126): 2,000 staters equal 8T of Attic silver at an exchange rate of 1:24. There is, however, considerable controversy over whether both Cyzicene staters and the Phocaic standard sixth-staters of Phokaia and Mytilene were exchanged with Attic money at the same rate, owing to the heavier weight of the Cyzicenes and their higher gold content (see below, p. 526). Various exchange rates have been argued for Cyzicenes up to one equaling 27 drachms. We are hampered in reaching a conclusion by the fact that our other data indicate the silver valuation at which Cyzicenes were valued in Attic accounts. The exchange rate at which the Athenians

[22] M.F. McGregor, "The Postscript of the First Attic Quota-List," *GRBS* 8 (1967) 103–12; B.D. Meritt, "The Tribute Quota of 454/3 B.C.," *Hesperia* 41 (1972) 403–17, esp. 416–17; Meiggs-Lewis 87–88. Cf. *ATL* 3.274, note 21.

[23] The failure of the tribute lists to make such distinctions is probably another sign that all payments were to be assumed to have been paid in Attic coin.

were prepared to receive them in payment of the tribute might in fact have been lower.[24]

At a rate of conversion of 1 Cyzicene stater to 24 Attic drachms, an amount equivalent to 13T, 2,640 dr., 15.5040, or 23.0240 in silver drachms is reached for the tribute received in electrum of 454/3. When an exchange rate of 1:27 is used, silver equivalents of 15.0720, 17.4920, or 25.5520 can be estimated. This was a considerable sum on any reckoning.

Anomalous Payments of *Aparkhai* in the Hellespont

The existence of payments of tribute in electrum may be further betrayed in the individual entries on the lists of *aparkhai* by the appearance of odd amounts in the tribute of certain Hellespontine cities: Alopekonnessos, Dardanos, Elaious, Kyzikos, Lampsakos, Madytos, and Tenedos. Some implied figures for tribute that are stated on the inscriptions in terms of Attic drachms are resolvable, as Eddy has noted, into electrum coins at a rate of exchange of one stater equaling 24 Attic drachms.[25] To reaffirm the special character of these payments, it is helpful to compare the record of collection from the island district. Here virtually all the payments are full talent amounts or in common fractions of talents, which are either multiples of 100 or 1,000 drachms or the amounts of the $\frac{1}{4}$ talent (1,500 dr.) or the $\frac{1}{5}$ talent (1,200 dr.).[26]

A complete list based on Eddy's discussion is given in Table 10.1, in which the sums have been supplemented and altered as necessary. Nothing suggests that those paying in electrum were held to be culpable or were subjected to punishment. Rather, the Athenian attempts to reconcile the reality of receipts in electrum with the general rule of payment in Attic silver suggest that special permission had been granted by the Athenians themselves. Therefore, some allied cities had received the dispensation of paying tribute in their own money or in money that had long circulated legally in their local economy and was received in taxes.

24 Note S.K. Eddy, "The Value of the Cyzicene Stater at Athens in the Fifth Century," *ANSMN* 16 (1970) 13–22, esp. 21–22.

25 See Eddy *AJP* (1973) 50–54.

26 One exception from the islands may be probative of the general thesis. The split payment of the Hephaisties of Lemnos in 446, 2,160 + 1.4640, does not equal that community's usual whole assessment of 3T. That fact is less interesting to us than the observation that the first part payment suggests payment in electrum coins by its divisibility into 24 (*IG* I³ 265.I.96, II.113). That would not particularly surprise us, because Lemnos lies near the mouth of the Hellespont on the trade route to Attica. Although there is no geographical explanation that comes easily to mind, the island of Ios twice shows payments of 840 dr., an amount consistent with payment in electrum staters at a rate of 1:24 (*IG* I³ 263.IV.23 [449]; 264.IV.15 [447]).

Table 10.1 Some Unconventional Assessments and Payments in Hellespontine Tribute

Heavily restored amounts are underlined; composite payments are joined by (+). Target payments of tribute in conventional amounts are supplied in square brackets [ ]. Degrees of conjecture are marked by question marks. All epigraphical references are to *IG* I^3.

Alopekonnessos
3,240 [3,600 or 3,000??]: 263.V.14 (449)
300? + 1,560? [2,000]: 281.III.32, 53 (429)
80 + 1,920 [2,000]: 282.III.55, I.21, (428)

Dardanos
2,760 [3,000?]: 263.III.33 (449); 264.IV.17 (447)
1 + 3,240 [1.4000 or 1.3000?]: 265.I.74, 99 (446)
4,080 + 1,920 [1]: 281.III.31, 52 (429)

Elaious
1,080 + 1,920 [3,000]: 281.III.15, 47 (429); 282.III.56–57, I.9 (428)

Kyzikos
4,320 [?]: 265.I.95 (446)
8.3500 + 1,920 [9]: 281.III.9, 45 (429)
8.1680 + 4,320 [9]: 282.III.31, I.10 (428)

Lampsakos
? + 3,600 [12]: 265.I.90, II.59 (446)

Madytos
80 + 1,920 [2,000?]: 281.III.30, 51 (429); 282.III.57, I.8 (428)

Tenedos
2.5020 [3]: 272.II.27 (439)
2.5280 + 1.3720 [4.3000]: 263.III.39; V.15 (449)
2.5280 + 3,240 + 2,160 + 2,160 [4.3000]: 265.I.5, 102; II.108–9 (446)
2.5280 [3]: 269.II.8 (442); 270.II.5 (441); 271.II.24 (440); 277.IV.24 (434); 279.II.10 (432); 281.III.12 (429); 282.III.30 (428)

Bodenstedt reviewed Eddy's findings in his important monograph on the electrum coinages of Phokaia and Mytilene.[27] He would admit that the following states from the foregoing list were candidates for payment in electrum coins, specifically of the Phocaic standard: Alopekonnesos, Dardanos, and Elaious. It may also be noted that the remaining payments of these states, not particularly unusual in themselves, can also be translated into Phocaic *hectae* at the exchange rate of 24 Attic drachms per

[27] F. Bodenstedt, *Phökaisches Elektron-Geld von 600–326 v. Chr.* (Mainz 1976) 64–73.

"stater" (a denomination existing for accounting purposes only). He also accepts for this category Lampsakos, an ally for which the majority of the oddities of payment of tribute do not permit so neat a resolution—they are listed in Table 10.3 below (pp. 286–87).[28]

Beyond these determinations, however, Bodenstedt has noted a number of tributary states whose implied tribute payments can be resolved into Phocaic "staters" on an exchange rate of 1:24: Aineia, Ainos, Aphytis, Argilos, Assera, Galepsos, Maroneia, Samothrace, Skione, and Thyssos. These suggestions are indeed speculative, inasmuch as there are no real peculiarities in the amounts of tribute that these allies paid. Thus, only the bare possibility of payment in Phocaic *hectae* exists, while our working assumption must always be that payment was made in Attic coins. Bodenstedt also includes Abydos, a city that does in truth present some oddities in its payment of tribute, as one may note in Table 10.3. Yet the odd payments of the Abydenes (notably) are not readily convertible into Phocaic staters at the rate of 1 st. to 24 silver dr.; rather, only the more conventional Abydene payments are amenable to such conversion.

Bodenstedt characterizes Kyzikos and Tenedos as cities whose unconventional payments of tribute are to be explained by their payment in Cyzicenes that exchanged with Attic drachms at a rate of 1 to 27. As we shall see below this exchange rate for the Cyzicene stater is not without its positive arguments. From this category, one must exclude the part payment of 1,920 dr. that Kyzikos made in 429, as it is not divisible by 27 but only by 24, while the 8.3500 payment also made in 429 is not evenly divisible either by 24 or by 27. The other atypical payments of the two cities are reconcilable with an exchange rate of 1:27; also appropriate for an exchange rate of 1:27 are the more conventional and well-attested payments of 9T for Kyzikos[29] and 4.3000 for Tenedos, the total also reached by the partial payments of 449.[30] Nevertheless, both the conventional and the unusual tribute payments of these cities that will work with an exchange rate of 1:27 will also translate evenly into round numbers of staters at a rate of 1:24. To choose between the two options, there is only the slight indication that the totals of staters for the 1:27 exchange rate look "more convincing," as Meiggs puts it.[31]

[28] Strikingly, the irregular payments of the Thracian tributary Berge (also noted in Table 10.3) can also be resolved into whole (relatively round) numbers of Phocaic "staters."

[29] *IG* I³ 269.II.23; 270.II.19; 271.I.32; 273.II.19; 277.IV.30 (restored); 279.II.30; 280.II.34.

[30] *IG* I³ 261.I.4 (restored); 267.I.29; 268.II.3 (restored).

[31] Meiggs 442–43. Note also R. Bogaert, "Le cours du statère de Cyzique à Athènes aux Vᵉ et IVᵉ siècles avant J.-C.: état de la question," *RBN* 123 (1977) 17–39, esp. 24–25.

Despite its appearance of "fudging," or having it both ways, the most sensible conclusion may indeed be that payers in electrum could sometimes get the Athenians to accept Cyzicenes at a ratio of 1 to 27 Attic dr. On other occasions, the Athenians may have considered it enough of a concession to receive electrum coins at all, and decided to take the Cyzicenes at the same rate as Phocaic electrum coins, although the former were intrinsically more valuable than the latter.[32]

It is striking that some of the evidence for payments in electrum staters is revealed only by the occurrence of multiple payments. In other words, had a single payment been made by Madytos in 429, for example, the round 2,000 dr. would have betrayed no variation from a "normal" type of assessment—in this case a third of a talent—that is well documented in our lists. Thus the dossier of such anomalies is made thinner not only through the fragmentary state of the evidence but also through an unavoidable missing of instances because of their happening to equal round-number assessments. There are also the part payments in which one element cannot be rendered into an equal number of staters at the same rate as the other payments or the total in the same year, such as the payment of 8.3500 of Kyzikos itself in 429 and Alopekonnesos with its 1,500 in the same year. This pattern seems to betray that in at least some of these cases a combination of payments of tribute in more than one currency had occurred.

Once such installments not equaling conventional assessments are seen to admit interpretation as indications of the mixing of different currencies, we should probably also consider that some of the other odd numbers from the Hellespontine region show the effects of the same underlying forces (see Table 10.3 below). Unusual payments may reflect a rendering in Attic money of payments of tribute wholly or partially in non-Athenian coin, although they do not yield to the interpretation of a homogeneous payment in electrum coins. The clustering both of tribute payments that we suspect to have been made in electrum and of other odd amounts in the same years in the collection of the Hellespontine tribute suggests an analogous causation for both phenomena.

As Eddy observes, these anomalies tend to cluster in two groups chronologically, one in the early 440s and the second in the early 420s. The first group lies readily open to our interpretation of difficulties in exchanging non-Athenian coin into Athenian money. While it would

[32] Bodenstedt, *Elektron-Geld* 65–69, presents Koressia (on Keos), Lemnos, and Paros as possible payers in Cyzicenes at the rate of 1:27, but, once more, no aberrations in the amount of payment mark them out as extraordinary.

be tempting to attribute all the anomalies from the early 420s to a resumption of exchange problems under the influence of the economic dislocations caused by the Archidamian War, it is also important to note first the explicit information provided by the lists themselves. On the list of 429, a heading is restored over the (mostly) smaller partial payments of the Hellespontine cities: [μισθὸν ἐτέ]λ̣εσαν *h*αίδε ἀ̣[πὸ] τõ | [*h*ε]λλ[εσποντί]ο φόρο (*IG* I³ 281.III.42–43).[33] In the next year, 428, a similar group of cities is listed with no other rubric inscribed above than *h*ελ]λεσπόντ[ιος (282.I.1–10). The next rubric, however, is [π]όλες αἳ[δ]ε ἀρχαῖς | [ἔδ]οσαν τὸμ φόρον (282.I.11–12).

Both sets of these payments, some of which appear to have been made in electrum staters, probably went to supply Athenian forces in service in the region with *misthos* 'pay.' There would have been no difficulty either for Athenian commanders or for ordinary military personnel in purchasing supplies in this coinage, since electrum coins were in general use in this region. In these years, the assignment of payments of tribute to local use preempted procedures by which the revenues of some Hellespontine states were delivered to the Athenians in Attic money. The allowance of provision of electrum staters balanced the inconvenience of having to pay tribute earlier than usual. This instance was exceptional and is not evidence on the question of the payment of tribute in electrum in Attica in the early 420s.

The fragmentary character of the tribute lists forbids our accomplishing very much by juxtaposing the possible total amounts for the electrum received from the allies in 454/3 and what individual payments seem to imply about the cities that were paying tribute partially or completely in staters and *hectae*. If one adds up the highest payment for each of the states noted in Table 10.1, the result will fall within the range of possible totals for the entire amount of Cyzicenes received in 454/3, as noted in the postscript of that year's list. In fact, however, the likelihood of the mixture of different coinages in the payment or payments of single cities renders this exercise of little profit, especially since there may be at least two types of electrum coins paid over in other years, something that is not reflected in the postscript of 454/3.

Anomalous Payments of the *Aparkhai* in Caria

The Carian district of the empire may offer some further traces of non-Attic payments of tribute, in this case in several silver coinages (see Table 10.2). Eddy has pointed out the possibility that some Carian

[33] See *ATL* 1.449–50, 453–54.

Table 10.2 Some Unconventional Assessments and Payments in Carian Tribute

Heavily restored amounts are underlined; composite payments are joined by (+). Target payments of tribute in conventional amounts are supplied in square brackets [ ]. Degrees of conjecture are marked by question marks. All epigraphical references are to *IG* I^3.

Amynanda
3,050 [3,000]: 260.I.15 (452)

Bolbai
1,030 [1,000?]: 260.I.12 (452)

Erines
4,130 [4,000 or 4,500??]: 260.I.14 (452)
3,240 [3,000 or 3,600??]: 263.V.11 (449)

Euromos
2,500 [2,500]: 263.V.30 (449); 265.II.83, 106 (446); 267.V.21 (444); 269.IV.31 (442); 270.IV.31 (441); 272.II.71
5,000: 271.II.80 (440)

Halikarnassos
1.4840 [1.4000]: 271.I.78 (440)

Hyblissos
1,030 [1,000]: 260.I.7 (452)
1,060 [1,000]: 262.V.26 (450)

Idyme (Paktys)
1.0890 [1 or 1.2000??]: 260.I.16 (452)
5,200 [1?]: 264.I.25 (447)

Kasolaba
2,500 [2,500]: 259.IV.27 (453); 260.VIII.15 (452); 261.IV.24 (451); 262.I.12 (450); 263.II.32 (449); 264.IV.32 (447); 265.I.44 (446)

Khalketor
2,100 [2,000?]: 263.II.38 (449); 264.II.24 (447); 265.II.14 (446); 267.V.30 (444); 269.IV.30 (442); 270.IV.30 (441); 271.I.82 (440); 272.II.75 (439)

Lepsimandos
1,030 [1,000?]: 260.I.13 (452: a part payment juxtaposed with a payment in a lost amount: 260.VIII.14)

Mylasa
5,200 [5,200 or 1?]: 266.V.10 (445); 267.V.31 (444); 269.IV.34 (442); 270.IV.33 (441); 271.II.82 (440); 272.II.76 (439)

Oula
1,030 [?]: 260.I.18 (452)

Ouranion
1,030 [?]: 260.I.17 (452)

Sambaktys
1.0400 [?]: 259.II.27 (453)

Tarbana
1,030 [?]: 260.I.19 (452)

tributaries made payment to Athens in Persian *sigloi* or equivalent coins, with 4 *sigloi* exchanged for 5 Attic drachms (note Xen. *Anab.* 1.5.6).[34] He assigns the towns of Euromos and Kasolaba and the dynast Sambaktys to this category, where unusual assessments become round numbers when expressed in *sigloi.*

Eddy's other suggestions concerning odd amounts among the payments of tribute by Carian states are less compelling, inasmuch as we do not have direct ancient evidence on exchange rates and must extrapolate from the weights of surviving coins, a risky procedure.

Eddy notes the 5,200-dr. payments by Mylasa, which he suggests closely approximate the value of 2,000 Mylasian staters.[35] Yet the attribution to Mylasa of these archaic (n.b. ca. 500) coins is hypothetical and the original identification of the coins by E.S.G. Robinson brings with it an added conclusion, namely, that the Mylasian stater was a double *siglos.*[36] Using the exchange rate of 1 *siglos* = 1.25 Attic dr., 5,200 dr. paid in Mylasian staters will not translate into a conventional assessment even in terms of the local money. The other Carian ally that paid tribute of 5,200 dr. is Idyme in 447, but Paktyes of Idyme contributed 6,890 dr. in 452 and this other figure significantly clouds the issue.

One might also distinguish Mylasa, which had an earlier conventional payment of 1T (cf. *IG* I^3 263.I.12 [449]; 265.II.82 [446]), from the states that are considered next, with their aberrant assessments on their *first* appearance among the surviving entries of the lists. Furthermore,

34 Note Eddy *AJP* (1973) 54–55. See, however, note 66 below.

35 Cf. Eddy *AJP* (1973) 55–56.

36 See E.S.G. Robinson, "A Hoard of Archaic Greek Coins from Anatolia," *NC*^{7} 1 (1961) 107–17, esp. 114–15.

even if the assessment of 5,200 dr. was made in 445 to accommodate a payment in local money, that supposition does not entail that similar payments in non-Attic coin were made in every subsequent year in which the same sum is recorded. The assessment of 5,200 dr. is not only an unconventional assessment, but it is also quite a bit lower than the earlier requirement of 1T, and this reduction would have needed its own rationale. Hence, the Mylasians may have tried to defend the propriety of their lowered tribute to the Athenians—despite its unconventionality—even after they had begun to pay an abnormal amount entirely in Attic tetradrachms. But all this speculation depends on the supposition that there were enough Mylasian staters available even to consider tendering them to the Athenians. This particular instance does not stand up very well to scrutiny.

Eddy also introduces the tribute payments of 1030 dr. that were made by a number of Carian states (Bolbai, Oula, Ouranion, Lepsimandos, and Tarbana).[37] These amounts are restricted to 453/2 and, where we have later information, these allies are seen to pay conventional amounts.[38] The partial payment of Lepsimandos in 452 is telltale in the manner of the multiple payments of the Hellespontine cities that we considered earlier, since the second payment of that state may have raised its contribution to a round, conventional figure. Hence there could be other comparanda hidden in the round numbers of the Carian tribute of 452.

Eddy further adduces Amynanda, with its payment of 3,050 dr., and Erines, with its 4,130 dr. in the same year, noting that the former slightly misses being three times 1,030 dr. and the latter just misses quadruple that amount. Both tribute payers eventually settled down to conventional payments (3,000 dr. for Amynanda is attested in 443: *IG* I³ 268.IV.26), but Erines paid 3,240 dr. in 449 before reaching the conventional 1,000 dr. (266.III.24 [445]; 268.IV.34 [443]). Eddy also traces the 6,890-dr. payment by Paktyes of Idyme to the underlying phenomenon of payment in the unknown currency that exchanges with Attic money in units and fractions of 1,030 dr.

If simple exchange parities were at issue, however, a near miss, as in the cases of Amynanda and Erines, could be considered quite damning. Nevertheless, it cannot be excluded that mixing of payments in different coinages might also be at work and its uncertain impact necessarily

[37] Eddy *AJP* (1973) 56–59. See also Mattingly *Klio* (1977) 90–92.

[38] Lepsimandos, 1,500 dr.: *IG* I³ 261.IV.25 (451); 262.I.13 (450); 264.IV.31 (restored: 447); 265.I.42 (restored: 446); 1,000 dr.: 266.III.17 (restored: 445); 267.III.28 (444); 268.IV.28 (443). Ouranion, 500 dr.: 262.V.27 (450).

complicates any analysis. Strikingly, Erines has already been seen to share a payment of 3,240 dr. in 449 with Alopekonnessos, Dardanos, and Tenedos among our presumptive payers in electrum staters. Conceivably, Amynanda and Erines might have been able to pay over some Athenian or more convertible coins, and so Eddy's near misses are partially misleading, as they might cloak a payment in mixed coinages. The same conclusion about mixed currencies might include Hyblissos, inasmuch as one should be reluctant to follow Eddy in seeing this Carian town, probably lying inland but of uncertain specific location, as paying in Chian staters.[39]

Although we should prefer to have some earlier evidence on the amounts of tribute payments, if any, by these states before framing a hypothesis, I would suggest that the odd payments of 452 might reflect collections by Athenian forces or officials in the field. The editors of *ATL* suggested such an intervention to account for the very appearance of the roster of Carian states heading list 2 of 453/2 (*IG* I³ 260.I.3–19).[40] There is no particular reason, however, to see compulsion at work (as in the version of *ATL*) rather than payments reflecting an Athenian vindication of allied independence from Persian or Medizing interference. The idea that the Carians would be more concerned at this date about Athenian aggrandizement, for which the exactions of tribute in these amounts offer no corroboration, is in any case particularly gratuitous. The odd drachma amounts like 1030 need not be fines for noncompliance or *epiphorai*, as the authors of *ATL* held them to be.[41] As Eddy noted, there are no separate rubrics or notations of payment in these cases, nor are all the unconventional amounts in fact conventionalized by this hypothesis, for later *epiphorai* are reckoned by sixtieths.[42]

By the same token, Eddy's implication that some geographic ordering or common monetary situation is at work here is probably wrong-headed, since these tributaries seem to have been scattered throughout Caria. Thus there is no good reason to see economic or administrative pressures forcing these and just these states to pay in non-Athenian money, while neighbors were capable of coming up with the required Attic coin.

39 It is the payment of Hyblissos of 1,060 dr. in 450 (*IG* I³ 262.V.26) that Eddy, *AJP* (1973) 56, explains by positing a payment in Chian staters. If the restoration of a payment of 1,030 dr. in 452 were correct (*IG* I³ 260.I.7), Hyblissos would be another case in the class of the payers of that amount and its multiples. Its later assessment, 2,000+ dr., attested in *IG* I³ 71 II.108 of 425/4, may have been more conventional, as we might anticipate.

40 *ATL* 3.7–8, 266; Eddy *AJP* (1973) 66–68.

41 *ATL* 1.453, 3.7; Meiggs 194–95, 432–33; cf. S. Hornblower, *Mausolus* (Oxford 1982) 26–28 for the period.

42 Eddy *AJP* (1973) 63–64; see also Mattingly *Klio* (1977) 90 with note 39.

One suggestion might be that the record of the odd amounts on the tribute lists of 452 does not reflect some quirk in the methods of an assessment that was made by the Athenians, nor is it a mere exaction of the tribute owed the Persians, as Eddy suggested (cf. Plut. *Cim.* 12.3–4), but instead an Athenian recognition of some independent administrative situation. For example, how would the Athenians have reacted if their forces had intervened in Caria while Persian tax collection was in progress? They could scarcely extract another round of payments—although such levies were sanctioned by previous assessment at home—from those ready to resist Persia who had already paid. In contrast, they must have done more than simply excuse those demonstrating the fact of having made payments to the Persians, for these *aparkhai*, as genuine offerings to Athena, are unlikely to have been provided out of contributions that were totally excused. To take one example, did the Athenians perhaps draw off a portion of the booty taken in operations to be treated as *phoros*, next credit their allies for their tribute already paid to the king, and then tender the *aparkhai* to Athena? Whether this particular scenario is correct or not, it is likely that some such administrative manipulation is responsible for the spotty incidence of odd assessments in Caria in 452 and their disappearance thereafter.

Eddy explains the amounts of these Carian assessments on the basis of payments on the Phoenician standard. He adduces in support the small number of coins known to him from Idyma, which he judged to be struck on a drachm of 3.7 g.[43] For example, the 6,890-dr. payment by Paktyes of Idyma would equal 8,007.33 Phoenician dr. and the 1,030-dr. contributions would equal 1,197 Phoenician dr. These are close enough to the round figures of 8,000 dr. and 1,200 dr. to be acceptable to Eddy's mind.[44] Nevertheless, there is considerable uncertainty whether the Phoenician standard can have been so dominant in Caria around mid-century.[45] Further doubts involve the uncertainty that there would have been enough indigenous coins in circulation to make this provision for payment in local (Phoenician-standard) currency feasible. In addition, as soon as we move away from the scanty ancient data on actual exchange, we are

[43] Cf. Eddy *AJP* (1973) 52–54. The support would be the coins of Idyme, for which see B.V. Head, *Catalogue of Greek Coins of Caria, Cos, Rhodes, & C.* (London 1897) 127, ##1–5; *SNG: Germany, Sammlung von Aulock* ##2559–62; *SNG: Danish National Museum* #419; Babelon 2.2.997–99. One might, however, describe the standard as Rhodian/Chian. The nominal upper limit for these coins of 450 is probably a generation too early in any case.

[44] Eddy *AJP* (1973) 57–58.

[45] Issues on the Aiginetic standard predominated. See E.S.G. Robinson, "A Find of Archaic Coins from South-West Asia Minor," *NC*[5] 16 (1936) 265–80; M. Thompson, "Some Noteworthy Greek Accessions," *ANSMN* 12 (1966) 1–18, esp. 8–9.

at the mercy of calculations from the averages or means of the weights of the surviving coins, without knowing the discounts or premiums that different coinages experienced under historical trading conditions.

Therefore, considerably greater credence is owed to the general suggestion that a situation involving a correspondance between standards accounts for this series of unconventional tribute payments of 452 than to the specific hypothesis that Carian money on the Phoenician standard was involved. In line with the hypothesis stated above on the spottiness of the incidence of these payments, I suggest that tribute paid to the Persians in bullion was being converted into Athenian money for the purposes of crediting these states for their outlays. The Athenians may then have withdrawn from their booty coins, starting with their own, in sufficient number to balance the credit.

The same cautionary note is valid when we consider the possibility of tribute payments in Persian *sigloi*, an option for the allied cities that is not improbable in principle. Some odd tribute amounts can be resolved into totals of *sigloi*, but these calculations not only demand shifting exchange rates for the *siglos* (even if the sometimes slight disparities fall within ranges established from surviving coins) but also require equivalencies unattested in the literary evidence.[46]

Unusual Payments of Tribute

Scattered on the tribute lists, various other anomalies appear that approximate those which we have already seen in association with instances that may be interpreted as indicating payment in non-Attic coinage. These are presented on Table 10.3.

Some are thoroughly anomalous and resist speculation in the present state of our evidence. One thinks first of odd amounts, especially when they repeat. A number of cities have unconventional assessments for which no plausible explanation has as yet been offered, for example Aigantioi, Berge, Gargara, Othoros, Phegetos, and Thrambaioi.[47] We have already seen the assessments featured by Berge as typical of those allied states paying in electrum. For these cities, it is relevant to recall again that assessments initially set for facilitating a payment in

[46] M. Vickers, "Fifth Century Chronology and the Coinage Decree," *JHS* 116 (1996) 171–74, suggests the following possibilities: Abydos (444, 429); Byzantion (429, 428); Kos (431); Kyzikos (429, 428). Eddy, *AJP* 1973, 54, had already suggested Sambaktys in 453.

[47] Mattingly, *Klio* (1977) 90, has noted that the Aigantioi and the Thrambaioi play one twelfth more than their normal tribute, possibly as a punishment. He is 5 dr. off for the Aigantioi.

Table 10.3 Other Unconventional Assessments and Payments

Heavily restored amounts are underlined; composite payments are joined by (+). Target payments of tribute in conventional amounts are supplied in square brackets [ ]. Degrees of conjecture are marked by question marks. All epigraphical references are to *IG* I^3.

IONIAN DISTRICT

Gargara
4,660 [4,500 or 4,800?]: 269.I.26 (442); 270.I.34 (441); 273.I.20 (438)

HELLESPONTINE DISTRICT

Abydos
4.2260 [4.3000?]: 259.II.29 (453)
4.0315 [4?]: 267.II.3 (444)
1,345 + [4?]: 269.II.12 (442)
5.3260 + 2,740 [6]: 281.III.17, 48 (429)

Byzantion
? + 4.4800 + 3.5840 [15.4300?]: 265.I.79, 103, 104 (446)
15.4300 [15.4300]: 269.II.26 (442), 270.II.22 (441)
15.0460 [15.4300?]: 271.I.37 (440)
18.1800 [18?]: 279.II.32 (432)
21.4740 + 8.940 [30?]: 281.III. 18, 49 (429)
13.600? + 16.90 [30?]: 282.III.59, I.5 (428)

Kalkhedon
7.3010 [?]: 261.V.19 (451)
5.5100 + 900 [6]: 281.III.6, 44 (429); 282.III.33, I.2 (428)

Kebren
1.2700 [1.3000?]: 263.II.33 (449)

Khersonesitai
13.4840 [18??]: 263.V.12 (449)

Lampsakos
11.3075 (or 6.3075) [12]: 279.II.31 (432)
10.2700 + 1.2820 (or 1.2770) [12]: 281.III.13, 46 (429)
1.2160 + 10.2100 [12]: 282.III.35, I.4 (428)
13.4800+ [?]: 283.III.37 (427)

Parion
2,100 + 3,784? [1]: 281.III.24, 50 (429)
2,220 + 3,780 [1?]: 282.III.51, I.7 (428)

Perinthos
3.4930 + 6.1070 [10]: 263.III.37, V.10 (449)
6.1515??: 280.II.19 (431)

Sigeion
760 [1,000?]: 264.III.36 (447)
1,000 + 240 [1,000 or 1,200??]: 265.I.70, 101 (446)

THRACEWARD DISTRICT

Aigantioi
3,250 [?]: 281.II.26 (429)

Ainos
? + 1.2555 [12?]: 265.I.39, 106 (446)

Berge
2,880 [3,000??]: 261.IV.29 (451)
3,240 [3,200??]: 265.I.93 (446)
3,120 [3,200??]: 277.VI.30 (434); 279.II.51 (432); 280.II.43 (431)

Othoros
700 [700]: 270.III.26 (441); 271.II.55 (440); 276.V.28 (435); 277.VI.24 (434)
500: 278.VI.33 (433)

Phegetos
1,600 [1,800]: 263.III.18 (449); 264.IV.33 (447); 265.I.47 (446)

Sermylie
7.4320 [8??]: 259.V.9 (453)
5.5500 [6??]: 262.II.28 (450)

Thasos
2.2760 [3]: 264.IV.9 (447)
3,240 + ? + ? [3?]: 265.I.94, 107, II.66 (446)

Thrambaioi
1,085 [1,000??]: 281.II.25 (429)

Torone
7.5440 [8?]: 264.IV.16 (447)
12T + 4.0560 [16??]: 265.II.71, 101 (446)

CARIAN DISTRICT

Kos
3.3360 + 1.2640 [5]: 263.I.7, V.40 (449)
3.3360 [5?]: 264.III.10 (447)
? + 3.3360 + 2160 [5?]: 265.I.92, II.37, II.102 (446)
3.4465 [5?]: 280.I.36 (431)

ISLAND DISTRICT

Aigina
26.1200 [30]: 263.IV.39 (449)

non-Athenian currency may have continued at the same level through administrative conservatism or inertia.

Another sign of a role for non-Athenian money may be multiple partial payments, and once again repetition heightens their singularity. Arguably, a single divided payment might be caused by an attempt to pay as much as possible in a first installment, regardless of the odd amount. The historical reasons behind these divisions of payment need not delay us; for example, note the list of states paying the arrears of the previous year that opens list 8 of 446 (*IG* I^3 265). It is the quantitative nature of a repeated divided payment rather than its rationale that interests us.

Because the figures repeat themselves, payments by Kalkhedon in 429 and 428 are to be classed among the multiple payments of possible significance, while those of Perinthos in 449 and 431 would represent a much slighter possibility. Kos provides a more complicated picture. Its normal assessment was 5T. The amount of 3.3360 repeats itself, in a partial payment filling out the full assessment in 449, in another partial payment that probably reached the assessed amount in 446, and in a single payment widely missing the assessment in 447. Another substantial miss of assessment also occurred in 431.[48]

There are naturally other possible explanations for this phenomenon. A multiple payment that repeats at the same dividing point could be owed to a patterning within the flow of revenues of an allied city. The repeated partial payment of the same or almost the same amount occurred because a tax or a set of taxes supporting the payment of tribute had been farmed out to yield a particular amount that unsurprisingly remained the same over the short term. In that case, the etiology of the partial payments and their amounts are probably irrecoverable. Exchange of non-Athenian coins remains one possibility.

Another explanation was *apotaxis*, that is, the division of cities previously grouped together in the assessment of their *phoros*. The newly divided polities would consequently pay the unconventional amounts that had been their previous contribution to the sundered unity. This is almost surely the reason why the Lindians of Rhodes paid the odd amount of 8.2700 and the Oiatai, qualified as 'of the Lindians,' paid 3,300 dr. in 454/3 and 452/1 (note *IG* I^3 259.III.26, IV.6; 261.III.28, IV.14).

The opposite process of *syntely* produces similar oddities on the tribute lists, as in the example of Mekyberna in 453, when it paid 2.1880 with Stolon and Polikhne (*IG* I^3 259.V.10–12). Another instance is perhaps

[48] Cf. *IG* I^3 271.II.67 (440); 279.I.54 (432); also the restorations in 262.IV.15 (450); 269.IV.15 (442); 270.IV.15 (441); 272.I.79 (439).

Erythrai.[49] One suspects that there are similar factors behind the complementarity of 1,800-dr. payments by Syme[50] and the 2.4200 of the Carian Khersonesioi.[51] While these two allies cannot be seen to pay complementary sums simultaneously, the situation revealed in the lists may have been created by their taking of partisan positions on the issue of their grouping as a single unit. Syme paid under a series of special rubrics, as *idiotai*,[52] or as assessed by the *Boulē* and a dikasteric court of 1,500.[53] Perhaps the people of Syme convinced the Athenians to allow them to pay their former syntelic assessment. The Khersonesioi may have continued to pay for Syme to substantiate a claim about the constitutional relationship of the two polities.

Another more significant class of payment worth particular attention in this regard involves the near misses of the assessed amount of tribute.[54] They may cloak either the existence of payments in non-Athenian money or a background of difficulties in exchanging foreign specie for Attic tetradrachms. To come a little short in so crucial a responsibility as paying the tribute seems a ludicrous error to make, and a real but limited deficit could probably always be made up with a loan from Athenian friends such as the *proxenoi* of the allied community. It is preferable to conclude that allied embassies sometimes arrived in Athens with a sum of money including foreign money that seemed equivalent prima facie to their assessed tribute. They could not achieve an exchange, however, that yielded this required total under prevailing market conditions. Accordingly, they may have petitioned the Athenians to pay with their original assets, including foreign money, or they may have paid over whatever their exchange yielded and the Athenians accounted that amount as full payment in a partial dispensation from the assessment. Concessions may have been granted on the grounds that the ally had made a good faith effort by bringing a payment that might have approximated the value

[49] 8T, 3,300 dr.: *IG* I³ 263.V.13 (449); 10.0900: 279.I.48 (432); 10.1100: 280.I.40 (431).

[50] *IG* I³ 278.VI.28 (433); 279.II.96 (432); 280.II.82 (431); cf. the restorations in 281.III.63 (429); 282.II.45 (428).

[51] *IG* I³ 268.IV.20 (443); 271.I.79 (440); cf. the restorations in 269.III.35 (442); 270.III.38 (441); 272.II.72 (439).

[52] *IG* I³ 278.VI.18–21 (433); 279.II.89–92 (432); 280.II.76–79 (431).

[53] *IG* I³ 281.III.60–61 (429); 282.II.43–44 (428).

[54] Thus near misses differ qualitatively from other fluctuations that are proportionately more subtantial. As exemplary of the latter category, the changes in payments made by cities of the Thracian littoral might be noted that have been traced to variations in their relations with the Odrysians (cf. Thuc. 2.97.3 on the income in tribute of the Odrysians). See Meiggs 249, 253; B. Isaac, *The Greek Settlements in Thrace until the Macedonian Conquest* (Leiden 1986) 98; Figueira, *Colonization* 190 with note 73; A.J. Graham, "Abdera and Teos," *JHS* 112 (1992) 44–73, esp. 62.

of the actual amount assessed under more favorable terms of exchange. Similarly, the rare cases of overshooting the assessment may be owed to the Athenian acceptance of the foreign currency delivered by allies without compelling them to exchange at all, but taking the excess as a defraying of the costs of their inconvenience.

Among the straightforward near misses, these cases are noteworthy. In 449 Aigina paid 26.1200 or 88 percent of 30T.[55] Thasos paid 2.2760 (82 percent) in 447 when its assessment was probably 3T.[56] Another instance may be Torone, when, in 447, it paid 7.5440 or 99 percent of a possible assessment of 8T.[57] Lampsakos seems to have made two payments adding up to 11.5520 (or 11.5470) in 429, while its traditional assessment had been 12T.[58] That would be a slight deficit, less than 1 percent, and similar situations seem to have occurred in 432 and 428 (for payments of 96 percent and 97 percent). The payment by Lampsakos for 427 is also likely to have fallen short of a raised assessment. Parion paid 5,884 dr. (98 percent) in 429 out of a 1T assessment.[59] A miss by somewhat a wider margin would be attested for the Khersonesitai, who paid 13.4840 in 449 or 77 percent, at least, if their assessment was still 18T.[60] Ainos in 446, Kebren in 449, Kalkhedon in 451, Perinthos in 431 (a wider miss), and Sigeion in 447 are possible cases.

A similar group is composed of cities that seem to miss closely the moving target of a changing assessment. Sermylie, which paid 7.4320 in 453 of what appears to be an 8T assessment—thus 97 percent—and then 5.5500 in 450 out of an uncertain assessment that may have been 6T belongs in this group.[61] The very confused record of payment for Byzantion may betray a similar pattern.

Abydos may be the rare instance of an ally that paid in foreign money exceeding its assessment in 444 (*IG* I^3 267.II.3), as its assessment was 4T in 441.[62] Torone's payment of 16.0560 was either a

[55] *IG* I^3 263.IV.39 (449); cf. *IG* I^3 259.VI.18 (453); 260.IV.17 (452); 261.V.5 (451).

[56] *IG* I^3 264.IV.9; cf. 259.V.14 (453); 261.V.20 (451); 262.IV.4 (450).

[57] *IG* I^3 264.IV.16; cf. 259.II.15 (453); 260.VIII.10 (452).

[58] *IG* I^3 281.III.13, 46; cf. 270.II.6 (441); restored in 271.I.29 (440).

[59] *IG* I^3 281.III.24, 50; cf. 277.V.4 (434); 279.II.27 (432). Cf. also 280.II.26 (431).

[60] *IG* I^3 263.V.12. Cf. 259.II.28 (453); 260.X.6 (452); 261.II.31 (451). Inasmuch as Athenian colonists or cleruchs (accompanied by Athenian military forces: Plut. *Per.* 11.5) may have been dispatched to the Chersonese at this time and the civic character of some of the communities there may even have changed, it is not difficult to hypothesize several reasons for a reassessment or a remission of a part of the tribute of 449. See Figueira, *Colonization* 218, 221–22, 260–62.

[61] *IG* I^3 259.V.9 (453); 262.II.28 (450); cf. 260.III.2; IX.6 (452).

[62] *IG* I^3 270.II.8 (441); cf. 263.V.3 (449). Yet, the payment of 4.2,260 in 453 (*IG* I^3 259.II.29) might suggest an assessment of 4.3,000 for both years, 453 and 444.

similar overpayment or a deficit payment for a higher assessment (*IG* I^3 265.II.71, 101). Some other possibilities are Sigeion (446), Berge (446), and the Thrambaioi (429).

Another characteristic of the anomalies that have been collected here deserves to be noted. The half-obol symbol is quite rare among the records of the *aparkhai*. One special class of notation where it does appear are the *epiphorai* 'additional payments' or 'punitive payments.'[63] The fixed ratios for the *epiphorai* demanded the half-obol notation in order to render that additional amount. Among states that were not cited for the *epiphorai* are some that have been suggested to have nearly missed their assessment: Ainos in 446, Lampsakos in 432, and Abydos in 444. In the case of Abydos, a half obol also appears in the fragmentary payment of 442 that almost certainly missed the assessed tribute (*IG* I^3 269.II.12). Other irregularities have led us to note Kos in 431 and Perinthos in that same year, and the Thrambaioi in 429. Leros also paid a sum including a half obol in 427, but there is no point of comparison for this payment, since the island contributes through the *syntely* of the Carian Khersonesioi on all the other extant lists (*IG* I^3 283.III.34). In these situations, it may be the case that Attic equivalencies of foreign currencies are at issue and the half-obol symbol was perforce called into duty to express the sums paid over to the Hellenotamiai.

More Comments on Tribute Payments in Non-Attic Coins

Some further comments are in order about the evidence for payments of tribute in non-Attic coinage by allied states.

I. Our most direct evidence, which is provided by the postscript to the first tribute list and by the unconventional assessments from the Hellespont discussed above, involves payment in electrum. Not only do the characteristic assessments identified by Eddy as resolvable into Cyzicene staters and perhaps into Phocaic *hectae* appear in the Hellespontine district, where one would expect them, but the same numbers appear elsewhere at places scattered through the *arkhē*. It is likely that this pattern is owed to an order of Athenian preferences in collection of the tribute. When they could not receive payment in their first choice, their own money, the Athenians next opted to take payment in an electrum money, an international currency, rather than in allied silver, since electrum staters and *hectae* could probably be spent more easily by Attic officials abroad than many types of non-Athenian silver.

[63] Notion: *IG* I^3 272.I.25 (439); Stageira, 277.VI.18 (434); Pitane, 279.I.57 (432); Khalkeatai, 280.I.55 (431).

They were in any case probably a medium for the flourishing Propontine and Black Sea trade in natural products, much of which went to the Peiraieus. Because of their high value and portability, electrum coins were also a preferred form to pay military personnel. If the Athenians received electrum coins in tribute, such coins might have been easier to spend on campaign than some alternative silver monies.

II. The chronological incidence of irregularities in the payment of tribute shows two clusters, one in the late 450s and early 440s and another in the late 430s and early 420s, although other scattered anomalies exist. The earlier group of abnormalities and unconventionalities is the larger one. As has been recognized since Eddy's article, the chronology of these irregularities would accommodate a Coinage Decree issued in the early 440s, such as in 449–446.[64]

The tribute lists derive for the most part from the period after the promulgation of a mid-century decree. It is therefore impossible to gauge with finality the magnitude of any problems faced by allied cities in conversion of their tax receipts into Attic coin for tribute payment during a good part of the period when we might expect problems to have been more acute. These are all the years in the 460s and 450s in the midst of conflict with the Persians and the Peloponnesians leading up to the first tribute list. On the hypothesis, however, that the Coinage Decree did not forbid allied minting in silver, but imposed only the validity of Attic money alongside local money (see below, pp. 495–500), no dramatic threshold should be expected in the presence or absence of evidence for payments in non-Athenian money. Rather, the evidence would match reasonable expectations based on that hypothesis: irregularities are more common in the earliest lists, which may precede the legislation, and revive when the exigencies of war create financial pressures on allied cities once more. The role of the decree of Klearkhos mentioned in section xii of the Coinage Decree is also to be remembered, for it probably preceded the Coinage Decree.

That the Peloponnesian War led to intensified exchange difficulties would be unsurprising based on the paradigm presented earlier in this chapter. Hostilities depressed maritime trade, and with this dampening may have come a retarding of the flow of foreign currencies in general and an altered direction to the movement of tetradrachms in the *arkhē*. State expenditures were higher and more was also being spent by military

[64] Eddy, *AJP* (1973) 48, 59, saw a decree dated to 446, while Meritt, *PAPS* (1975) 269–70, suggests that the Coinage Decree was legislation that followed on a moratorium of the collection of tribute in 449/8.

personnel on campaign. The end result may then have been occasional shortages of Athenian coins with which to pay tribute assessments, where there had been no problems for several decades. Many assessments increased after the outbreak of the war and that would have intensified the governmental demand for Attic coins as well as sapping allied economic vitality through a diversion of resources. Shortages in the local supply of Attic money have already been suggested as the cause for the initiations and resumptions of coining by various allies (starting from the farther reaches of the *arkhē*) after the outbreak of the Archidamian War.

III. Both Lewis and Mattingly have gone on record about their uncompleted research that sought to explain a wide range of anomalies on the tribute lists in terms of other currencies.[65] In contrast, I have interpreted the payments that narrowly miss the assessment assigned a particular tributary state as signifying a breakdown of a more indeterminate nature in the provision of the requisite amount of *Athenian* coins. The near misses may hide a spectrum of Athenian concessions, ranging from simply settling for the whole payment in non-Attic coin through payments in mixed currencies to an acceptance of whatever amount an exchange of foreign money yielded in Attic coin regardless of its slight deficit. These anomalies help us to understand that resolutions of all odd tribute payments through formulas based on the bullion values (or even market values, if we had them) of various non-Athenian coinages are unlikely to be feasible.[66] Non-Athenian coins might well have been employed to supplement Athenian tetradrachms in individual payments in quite irretrievable proportions.

Furthermore, I suspect that the payment of the *aparkhē* in Attic tetradrachms bearing Athena's head was more rigorously enforced than the payment of the whole tribute in owls, and that any such rigor was exercised more consistently against civic silver coinages than against the more "international" electrum monies and especially against theophoric or cultic silver currency. If there was a more stringent rule to pay the *aparkhē* in Attic silver, especially after the first list, that propensity may open an interesting possibility for the dating of the Coinage Decree (see below, pp. 459–62). In addition, it is also likely that the acceptance of payment in foreign coins always remained a dispensation granted by Athenians, who may well have stipulated a rate of equivalency on the basis of their own, sometimes parochial, appreciation of the relevant

[65] Mattingly, *Coinage and Administration* 65; Lewis, *Coinage and Administration* 62–63.

[66] For example, the exchange rate for even a silver currency like the *siglos* could vary: Xen. *Anab.* 1.5.6: *siglos* = 7.5 Attic ob.; Hesych. s.v. σίγλον, ς 585 Latte = 8 Attic ob.; Phot. s.v. σίκλος = 8 Attic ob.

economic factors. They were after all acting as money changers of last resort in such situations.

CONCLUSION

Tribute collection promoted the use of Athenian money. Since the status of Attic coins in each city was the most significant factor in determining the availability of Athenian tetradrachms for paying tribute, an allied government could minimize its exchange difficulties and ease its payment of tribute by increasing its income in the medium of Athenian coins. It could do this only by establishing Attic coins as a legal means for the payment of taxes. By recognizing Athenian money as locally valid, allied communities could draw on the large reservoir of Attic coins generated by the payments of the Athenian government. No more effective measure could be taken by the allies to demonstrate to the Athenians their readiness to provide payment in Attic silver than to recognize Attic coins as legal tender locally. That demonstration provided a hedge for them against any contingeny that impeded rendering the tribute in Attic money.

The conditions militating in favor of the acceptance of Athenian money as legal tender among the subject allies also promoted the replacement or a supplementation of local currency by Attic coins. A growing recognition of Athenian money as the normal medium for transactions marked the monetary history of the Pentekontaeteia. The numismatic evidence suggests that this growing acceptance of foreign currency was an incremental process revealing no single, dramatic watershed. The pervasive usage of Attic coins was mainly an outgrowth of decisions made by the allies themselves or by the allies in conjunction with the Athenians. This latter possibility is the model implied by Aristophanes' *Birds* 1040–41.

If the anomalies presented above show Athenian acceptance of allied tribute payments in non-Athenian coins, the Athenians seem to have adopted a stance of flexibility toward allied difficulties involving exchanging currencies. It appears that intractable *and* therefore tolerated exchange problems may have resulted from political and specifically military stresses on exchange and on tax collection. In the fiscal context just suggested, certain questions emerge, with which the epigraphical evidence on the Coinage Decree will need to be confronted.

If the major issue in imperial monetary history was expediting a cycle of taxation and expenditure, in which allied cities acquired sufficient Athenian money to fulfill their responsibilities, was it necessary to prohibit entirely operation by allied mints? Could this same aim not be served satisfactorily by improving allied access to an appropriate amount of Athenian money? As has been seen, the Athenians seem to have been flexible to the degree that they sometimes received foreign currency in payment of tribute. Can an impact from these "dispensations" be observed in the tenor of Attic monetary legislation? How does this flexibility square with our perceptions about the punitive aspects of the Coinage Decree?

11

METROLOGICAL CONSOLIDATION

WE HAVE ALREADY SEEN how other interpretations of the Coinage Decree, both the economic exploitation hypothesis and the symbolism/autonomy theory, founder on our inability to incorporate the enactment of a consolidation of weights and measures. Indeed, the only explanation of that imposition that has received any credit above (despite its unfashionable aura of altruism) has been the obvious one. The consolidation of the standards for weights and measures simplified the conditions of interstate commerce and thereby benefited both the Athenians and the allies. That chastening experience must prompt us to essay a consideration of the issue of the connection of the supposed imposition of Attic standards and the difficulties involving the levying of tribute that have just been suggested as the rationale for Athenian monetary legislation.

METROLOGY AND THE COINAGE DECREE

One relevant comment, with which our discussion begins, was made by T.R. Martin.[1] The Athenians were seeking to simplify collection of taxes by regularizing the forms and containers in which goods arrived in the Peiraieus. This seems to strike the requisite note, calling our attention to the *administrative* aspects of Athenian metrological legislation.

Nonetheless, it is likely that one can rule out this particular regularization of standards as an effort to obviate time-consuming investigations of cargoes in order to avoid cheating by merchants. Based on the wide latitude generally adopted by ancient tax officials, the assumption should be that tax collectors in Attica and in the ports of the *arkhē* imposed their estimation of the value of shipments, erring on the side of protecting the interests of their own government and the Attic treasury. Foreign merchants had to live with such judgments or adopt the alternative of appealing to superior officials or further to a *dikasterion* 'popular court' in Athens and to the relevant authorities elsewhere as necessary parts of the cost of doing business with the Athenians. Moreover, Martin's suggestion begs the question of whether some of those shipping to Attica

[1] Martin, *Sovereignty* 203–205; see also Lewis, *CAH*^{2} 5.131.

were not already using Attic measures or were not bound legally to make sales in the Peiraieus, if not in Attic weights and measures, at least, in a way compatible with an evaluation in terms of either Attic weights and measures or some recognized panhellenic standard.[2]

There is not much classical information on the office of the *metronomoi*, whom we know from the *Athenaion Politeia* to have supervised the usage of weights and measures in Attica: κληροῦνται δὲ καὶ μετρόνομοι ⟨ῖ⟩, πέντε μὲν εἰς ἄστυ, ε̄ δὲ εἰς Πειραιέα: καὶ οὗτοι τῶν μέτρων καὶ τῶν σταθμῶν ἐπιμελοῦνται πάντων, ὅπως οἱ πωλοῦντες χρήσονται δικαίοις (*Ath. Pol.* 51.2; cf. Harp. s.v. μετρόνομοι). An inscription from the end of the second century shows the *metronomoi* being ordered to exercise their supervisory powers in a fashion that must be in its general lines traditional (*IG* II² 1013).[3] The tight control they are seen to be exercising over the measures used for retail sales (1013.18–29) may well have had its corollary in a policing of the form in which foreign goods were offered for sale. Certainly, such legislation constituted a more effective means for supervising trade and raising an appropriate revenue than a regulation of all allied metrological practices.

Even if the Athenians had wanted to expedite the collection of commercial taxes in the Peiraieus, why was it necessary to impose Attic weights and measures on the whole *arkhē*? Surely, they would have avoided the intrusion on local jurisdiction abroad by simply ordering that the sale of goods within *Attica* itself had to conform to Attic weights and measures, if that provision did not already exist.[4] And what of all the goods that flowed into the Peiraieus from outside the *arkhē*, such as wheat from the Crimea and Egypt and naval stores from Macedonia? This trade was hardly simplified by imposing Attic weights and measures on the allies, but not imposing metrological homogeneity for "exotic" goods coming to the Peiraieus.

2 The evidence for such equivalencies is presented below.

3 See also H.W. Pleket, *Epigraphica* 1 (Leiden 1964) #14, pp. 22–27.

4 Martin's citation of the provision of "first fruits" to the Eleusinian cult as another place where metrological consolidation would be beneficial can also be construed against a connection with the Coinage Decree (Meiggs-Lewis #73 = *IG* I³ 78). There is no specification of Attic measures in the decree (78.5–7). This absence, however, should not be thought to indicate that such stipulation was otiose because the Coinage Decree had already banned non-Attic *metra*. *IG* I³ 78 contains a provision inviting nonallied Greeks to tender *aparkhai* to Eleusis. The same proportion prevailed regardless of the size of the *medimnos* (a *hekteus* for each 100 *medimnoi* of barley and *hemiekteon* of wheat). There is no indication in the decree that the Athenians intended to enforce the exaction administratively. On the allowances to Methone and Aphytis to import grain from the Hellespont (*IG* I³ 61, 63), cf. pp. 311–12 and Chapter 14, note 29 below.

If we are not to be satisfied solely with a causation that depends exclusively on the general economic benefits of metrological consolidation—although these benefits can never slip far into the background—we must seek an intermediate rationale that is grounded in a more direct concern of hegemonic administration. Then we may opt for a hypothesis that will allow us to connect the consolidation of weights and (dry/liquid) measures in the *arkhē* with the system for the levying of tribute. This hypothesis should parallel the explanation how difficulties in exchange that were attendant on tendering the tribute in Attic tetradrachms might be implicated in a decision to impose on the allies the utilization of Athenian money. Nonnumismatic metrology affected imperial finances because all allied cities would have depended to some degree—one suspects that it was always significant—on indirect taxes for their revenues.

The protection of consumers doubtless motivated the establishment of boards of magistrates like the Athenian *metronomoi*, and it is easy to understand why they guarded against the use of illegal weights or the adulteration of foodstuffs. Nevertheless, some of the enforcement of the employment of specific weights and measures in the marketplace was also owed to a desire to supervise standardized sales to facilitate tax collection. Hence the well-known Thasian law of the end of the fifth century (ca. 425–400) demonstrates that consumers were protected from the watering of wine (lines II.10–11, 14–15), and shows that Thasian producers were protected from competition in which their merchant marine would carry foreign wine (II.8–11).[5] Provisions that only stamped containers be used in wine sales by *pithoi* (I.4–6) and that wine be sold only in larger containers and not dispensed in smaller units are more comprehensible as administrative conveniences than as true consumer protection.[6] The stipulation that wine and grapes on the vine could not be sold before the new moon of the month Plynterion may have a similar rationale, although that is less certain (lines 1–2), as protection against speculation and hoarding might play a role here.

Compatibility between metrological systems allowed different regimes of taxation to be easily comparable. That effect grew as such compatibilities were made manifest in the actual modes by which goods were offered for individual sale. Thus the Athenians could evaluate the justice of allied representations about their ability to pay various levels of assessment because the real incidence of the commercial taxes of the allies

5 *IG* XII Suppl. 347 = H.W. Pleket, *Epigraphica* 1 (Leiden 1964) #2, pp. 8–9.

6 Note J. Pouilloux, *Recherches sur l'histoire et les cultes de Thasos* (Paris 1954), *Études Thasiennes* 3, 1.129–34.

could be readily judged.[7] The transparency of allied finances fostered by even a partial convergence of metrological standards would not only promote facility of administration, an obvious concern of the Athenians, but would also enhance allied ability to judge for themselves whether Athens had assessed their own city's tribute fairly and commensurably with the assessments of others. Reciprocal policing of assessments by different allied governments helped to create equitable treatment as well as the perception that all the allies bore a proportionate burden.

THE ARCHAEOLOGY OF CLASSICAL METROLOGY

Archaeological data exist on the usage of measures among the Athenian allies that are parallel to the evidence from coins, chiefly ancient amphoras that indicate what standards of capacity were in use in allied cities. Study of this subject is still evolving, as many programs of measurement of amphoras have not achieved final publication. Frustratingly, historical analysis can only offer a snapshot based on published data, which may well be misleading. Nevertheless, available scholarship suggests that during the fifth century, transport (and storage) vessels experienced an evolution toward a consolidation or integration of metrological practice in which Attic measures of volume became increasingly influential. The study of these commercial amphoras has attracted less attention than that of coins. As observed above, silver coins exercise a particular fascination by virtue of their beauty, their evocation of historical occurrences, and their continuing value that mundane vessels for transport and storage can never hope to rival.

Amphora Capacities

The study of commercial pottery is also intrinsically more difficult than numismatic inquiry, given its imposition of more travel to the Mediterranean, its objects of study being more difficult to handle and measure, and the high threshold of expertise required even to begin to make scholarly judgments (deterring less than totally committed inquiry).[8] Hence

[7] Such representations are a poorly attested subject save for the existence of fragments of two speeches of Antiphon: "On the Tribute of the Lindians" (fr. IX.25–33 B/T) and "On the Tribute of the Samothrakians" (fr. XV.49–56). Antiphon's activism in this area was probably substantial, perhaps helping to establish him as a patron of the allies (cf. Thuc. 8.68.1; [Plut.] *Mor.* 832F), but constitutes only a small part of a large hegemonic phenomenon.

[8] See M.B. Wallace, "Progress in Measuring Amphora Capacities," in J.-Y. Empereur and Y. Garlan (eds.), *Recherches sur les amphores grecques*, *BCH* Suppl. 13 (Paris 1986) 87–94. See also J.B. Brashinsky (= I.B. Brašinskij), "Standards of Rhodian Amphoras," *KSIA* 156 (1978) 11–16.

any aspiration to balance the extended discussion of monetary integration that was undertaken above with a history (however sketchy) of metrological consolidation is unrealistic. The picture presented below remains suggestive of the underlying economic history, but cannot pretend to be exhaustive.[9] Rather, our focus to start must be on the few series of amphoras on which some of the necessary preliminary archaelogical work has begun: those from Chios and Thasos, first and foremost, and, to a lesser extent, the sequence of amphoras from Samos and the amphoras from Mende.[10] In this discussion, the research of Virginia Grace holds an important place.[11] Grace believed that the effects of the Coinage Decree could be detected in the amphora series of Chios, Thasos, and Mende.[12]

Moreover, here, once more, H.B. Mattingly has been a diligent proponent of the relevance of dates of acts of metrological consolidation for the issue of the dating of the Coinage Decree.[13] One must, however, be careful about attributing causation when allied cities strove for a common utilization for their containers with those of the Athenians and other allies, for convenience in trade acted as an incentive toward coordination of size

[9] On transport/storage amphoras and economic history, see J.-Y. Empereur, "Les anses d'amphores timbées et les amphores: aspects quantitifs," *BCH* 106 (1982) 219–33; Y. Garlan, "Greek Amphoras and Trade," in P. Garnsey, K. Hopkins, and C.R. Whittaker (eds.), *Trade in the Ancient Economy* (London 1983) 27–35 with notes, 183–86. On their use, see V. Grace, *Amphoras and the Ancient Wine Trade* (Princeton 1961); C.G. Koehler, "Handling of Greek Transport Amphoras," *Amphores grecques* 49–67. See also I.K. Whitbread, *Greek Transport Amphorae: A Petrological and Archaeological Study* (London 1995) 9–50. The subject of the economic background to metrological consolidation has been relatively neglected.

[10] The "gray" amphora type that was used for the transport of wine and for storage and has been associated with Lesbos would constitute another body of material for the investigation of metrological consolidation. J.B. Brashinsky reports some measurements in *Metody issledovania antichnoi torgovli: na primere Severnogo Prichernomor'ia* (Leningrad 1984) 176, but the capacities do not appear on superficial review to be Attic. In general, see B.G. Clinkenbeard, "Lesbian Wine and Storage Amphoras: A Progress Report on Identification," *Hesperia* 51 (1982) 248–67; M.L. Lawall, *Transport Amphoras and Trademarks: Imports to Athens and Economic Diversity in the Fifth Century* B.C. (Diss. University of Michigan 1995) 196–217.

[11] See V. Grace, "Early Thasian Stamped Amphoras," *AJA* 50 (1946) 31–38, esp. 31; Grace, "Standard Pottery Containers of the Ancient Greek World," *Hesperia* Suppl. 8 (1949) 175–89, esp. 182; Grace, *Amphoras*; V. Grace and M. Savvatianou-Petropoulakou, "Les timbres amphoriques grecs," *Exploration archéologique de Délos* 27 (1970) 277–382; Grace, "Exceptional Amphora Stamps," in G. Kopcke and M.B. Moore (eds.), *Studies in Classical Art and Archaeology* (Locust Valley, NY 1979) 117–27.

[12] On Mende, see V. Grace in P.E. Corbett, "Attic Pottery of the Later Fifth Century from the Athenian Agora," *Hesperia* 18 (1949) 298–345, esp. 337. Concerted research has not yet reached final publication in the West (as far as I am able to determine). Brashinsky lists volumes in *Metody* 177–79; see also Brashinsky, "New Data on the Greek Imports on the Lower Don," *KSIA* 124 (1970) 12–18 (in Russian); Brashinsky, "Notes on the Trade of the Elizavetouskoye Settlement on the Don," *KSIA* 145 (1976) 68–71 (in Russian).

[13] See Mattingly, *Coinage and Administration* 65; Mattingly *JHS* (1981) 78–86.

in such vessels.[14] Attica was a huge market in and of itself, before one takes into account allied cities employing Euboeic/Attic measures or similar commercial practices (naturally an enumeration of these cities is infeasible). Greek commercial law tended to specify the weights and volumes in which goods could be sold as a protection to consumers (cf. *Ath. Pol.* 51.2). In some markets, Attic *metra* were probably not only recommended by their local usage but mandated by law. This extended market was best exploited by those selling in conformation with Attic measures of capacity. Among the pertinent (and nonpolitical) motivations for an accommodation with Athenian metrology would have been an ease in paying taxes and a desire to provide oil and wine in containers that were as familiar as possible in capacity to their customers (whether intermediary or final).[15]

Furthermore, it is significant that our best evidence concerns containers for Chian and (secondarily) Thasian wine, the two preeminent varieties of quality in the fifth century.[16] To modern scholars, fifth-century Athens has been viewed primarily as a hegemonic power, and Chios and Thasos are seen as its allies, differing in their duties and privileges vis-à-vis the Athenians. From the standpoint of the commerce in wine, however, Attica represented the largest single market, and Chios and Thasos (and perhaps Mende) were the large-scale producers of the highest quality product. Although detailed quantitative reports on the number of surviving amphoras are not available, impressions garnered from the literature suggest a major (if not predominant) use of Chian and Thasian amphoras during the *arkhē* that presumably transported, at least initially, their respective wines.[17] To the best of our knowledge, the important secondary role for these vessels in the general storage of goods was shaped by their primary employment in the shipping of their original contents, wine. Thus a considerable proportion of the value of cargoes of wine shipped each year in the *arkhē* resided in Chian

[14] Gauging the force of this influence is, however, a sensitive process, as an interpretation of the range of variation in Hellenistic Rhodian amphora capacity shows. See P.M. Wallace Matheson and M.B. Wallace, "Some Rhodian Amphora Capacities," *Hesperia* 51 (1982) 293–320, esp. 298–302; also Lawall, *Transport Amphoras* 298–99.

[15] For an overview of the archaeological evidence on Athenian liquid measures, see M. Lang, "Liquid Measures," in M. Lang and M. Crosby, *Weights, Measures and Tokens, The Athenian Agora* 10 (Princeton 1964) 56–64.

[16] Note Hermippos fr. 82K. See F. Salviat, "Le vin de Thasos: amphores, vin et sources écrites," *Amphores grecques* 145–200; see also C. Seltman, *Wine in the Ancient World* (London 1957) 72–77; J.B. Barron, "Chios in the Athenian Empire," in J. Boardman and C.E. Vaphopoulou-Richardson (eds.), *Chios: A Conference at the Homereion in Chios* (Oxford 1986) 89–103, esp. 94–95.

[17] See Lawall, *Transport Amphoras* 278–92, 395–405.

and Thasian (and perhaps Mendean) vintages. Even if we ignore the possibility of Athenian hegemonic legislation, it is not at all surprising merely in economic terms that the best evidence for metrological consolidation may involve adjustments in containers for wine, a high-value and high-volume agricultural product, made by the two leading producing states, which aligned their practices with the usage of the largest international market.[18]

There is, however, another feature of our evidence that has not received its due emphasis. The traditional interpretation of the Coinage Decree contends that Attic coins and metrological standards were imposed on the allies and the use of non-Athenian coins and standards was prohibited. Although such a monopoly for Athenian money can be thoroughly questioned, it is relatively easy to envision in principle the operation of such a displacement of allied coins. Determining whether a community was or was not using Attic coins exclusively would have been a straightforward exercise for Athenian officials. The situation could even be evaluated by modern scholars, if we could by wishing summon forth the required data. In contrast, standards for weights and measures are not embodied in physical objects in the same way as a numismatic standard is in coins. The use of certain coins might be prohibited and substitutions might be mandated. Notwithstanding actual standard weights and containers, standards for weights and measures are more truly abstractions used in classifying and manipulating objects.

While it is surely feasible in principle to determine whether a particular container conforms to Attic standards of *metra*, the Attic character of that vessel need not preclude its conformity to other standards as well.[19] Thus, we ought not to expect and do not surely find (as far as our present knowledge goes) the Attic standard for volume replacing other standards, but distinguish the existence of containers that seem to fit equally well into the Attic system or into the local standard for volume. Consequently, the attested metrological phenomena do not accommodate the traditional interpretation of the Coinage Decree. Rather they are reconcilable with the hypotheses to be presented in the commentary below on the decree that held that this legislation merely mandated the *validity* of Attic measures in allied cities. Would an invocation of Attic measures have necessarily entailed anything more elaborate in some cases than (to take

[18] Plut. *Mor.* 470F: Chian wine for 100 dr. per *metrētēs*! For other prices, see W.K. Pritchett, "The Attic Stelai: Part II," *Hesperia* 25 (1956) 178–328, esp. 184, 196–203.

[19] Although a coin could share the same standard as Athenian coins, it does not thereby become an Athenian coin in the way that a foreign amphora could contain an Attic *metrētēs* of wine, since a vessel and its contents are easily separated or altered.

one possibility) chalking on a *pithos* or amphora, designed according to traditional rules, its capacity in Attic *khoes*?[20]

Yet, before elaborating any further on these basic observations, a brief treatment of the state of present scholarship is in order. Let us start with Chian transport amphoras (about which also see above, pp. 155-58). At some point ca. 450–40, the prevailing style of bulbous-necked amphoras that were used in the wine trade expanded in their capacity and became equivalent to 7 Attic *khoes* (as shown from the numerical notations on surviving pots found in Attica).[21] Although the accommodation to Attic *metra* is undoubted, it is uncertain whether these resized amphoras were still consistent with Chian *metra* to a whole number of *khoes*. One view, adopting a 7:8 ratio for the relationship of Chian to Attic *metra*, affirms continued consistency wherein the amphoras had increased from 7 to 8 Chian *khoes*.[22] Another view works from coin weights to posit an 8:9 ratio of Attic to Chian liquid *metra*.[23] In that case, continued equivalence in *both* systems of *metra* could only be achieved at the level of a consignment of amphoras.[24] The conceptual nature of metrological integration, however, means that equivalence could have been expressed in some other, notational or symbolic, manner. We lack the documentary evidence to reconstruct a fifth-century appreciation of compatibility in liquid measures.

A confirming datum for the general chronology may be the picturing of an amphora from just before the transition on a gemstone (a jasper

[20] M.B. Wallace notes, however, that such notations might reach a point (for example, "7 *khoes*, 5 *kotylai*") where the usage of Attic *metra* could appear rather "attenuated" (personal communication, 8/7/97). Evidence on actual marking is not sufficiently copious or reported to permit definitive conclusions on this question. See Lawall, *Transport Amphoras* 340–50.

[21] See Grace, *Exploration archéologique* 359–60; Grace, *Studies* 120–22; cf. C. Boulter, "Pottery of the Mid-Fifth Century from a Well in the Athenian Agora," *Hesperia* 22 (1953) 59–115, esp. 104–105, which draws on the research of Grace. See also Brashinsky, *Metody* 172–73; Brashinsky, "Méthode pour l'étude de la capacité déterminée des amphores grecques," *Soviet Archaeology* (1976) 3.87–102 (résumé in French). Lawall, *Transport Amphoras* 98–104, argues for overlapping periods of production of bulbous-necked and straight-necked amphoras between 440 and 430/25.

[22] For the metrological relationship, see M. Lang, "Numerical Notation on Greek Vases," *Hesperia* 25 (1956) 1–24; M.B. Wallace, "Texts, Amphoras, Coins, Standards and Trade," *Ancient World* 10 (1984) 11–14, esp. 12–13. There is later confirmation in the form of a Chian *sēkōma* 'wine measure' for which see W.G. Forrest, "A Chian Wine Measure," *BSA* 51 (1956) 63–67, with its measurements corrected in Forrest, "The Inscriptions of Southeast Chios, II," *BSA* 59 (1964) 32–38, esp. 37–38.

[23] See Wallace, *Amphoras grecques* 88–89; Barron, *Chios* 98; Lawall, *Transport Amphoras* 296.

[24] M.B. Wallace suggests the example of a batch of 27 amphoras holding 18 Chian or 16 Attic *metrētai* (personal communication, 8/7/97). He goes on to make the interesting observation that a consignment of 12 larger amphoras would carry 8 Chian or 5 Aiginetic *metrētai*, while barely missing an equivalency of Chian and Attic measures.

scaraboid) that has been assigned to the Chian master, Dexamenos, and can be placed in the third quarter of the century.[25] Then sometime later, straight-necked Chian amphoras replaced these vessels, although they retained their commonality with Attic *metra* through continuing the capacity of 7 Attic *khoes*. Grace suggests that the change was made to emphasize the adjustment to the Attic standard, and was accompanied by the addition of the stamped state badge. I have suggested above that isolating reuse of older vessels may have specifically been a motivation.[26]

To reiterate, it is difficult it is to pin down these two transitions exactly. The most likely date of the accommodation of Attic *metra* is perhaps within the decade 450–40, while the inception of the straight-necked amphora probably belongs in the 440–30 and the initiation of the Chian tetradrachm coinage somewhere between the late 430s and ca. 400. Naturally, these developments should not necessarily be linked with the same decision or with each other. Notably, the transition to the larger containers does not seem to coincide with any significant dividing line in Chian coin emissions, nor does it appear probable that there was a break between the Attic capacity bulbous-necked amphoras and the Attic capacity straight-necked amphoras. Grace points to bulbous-necked and straight-necked amphoras found in the same context.[27]

Let us turn next to Thasian amphoras.[28] Grace was again the first to offer that their evolution might have been connected with the Coinage Decree.[29] The adjustment to Attic *metra* appears similar to the Chian pattern, although less has been done on the subject in the West. Jars

[25] Grace, *Classical Art* 120–22. For Dexamenos, see J. Boardman, *Greek Gems and Finger Rings* (New York 1970) 194–97.

[26] It is possible that a further step in the evolution of Chian amphoras saw some late fifth-century vessels produced with a capacity of 8 Attic *khoes*. See Mattingly *JHS* (1981), note 18, pp. 80–81, citing a letter of M. Lang. See also Brashinsky *Soviet Archaeology* (1976) 100. Naturally, deciding on the compatibility of such amphoras with both Attic and/or Chian metrology would depend upon the adoption of one of the aforesaid ratios of equivalence.

[27] See Grace, *Amphoras* with its discussion of pictures #44–45; Grace, *Exploration archéologique* 359–60. The vases pictured in *Amphoras* #44–45 are a bulbous-necked and a straight-necked amphora of a volume consistent with Attic *metra* that derive from the same deposit. See L. Talcott, "Attic Black-Glazed Stamped Ware and Other Pottery from a Fifth Century Well," *Hesperia* 4 (1935) 476–523, esp. 495–97, 514–16, dating to ca. 430; cf. Grace, "Stamped Amphora Handles Found in 1931–1932," *Hesperia* 3 (1934) 197–310, esp. 296–97, 303–304.

[28] On Thasian amphoras, see A.-M. Bon, and A. Bon with V. Grace, *Les timbres amphoriques de Thasos*, *Études thasiennnes* 4 (Paris 1957) 9–26; also M. Debidour, "Réflexions sur les timbres amphoriques Thasiens," *Thasiaca*, *BCH* Suppl. 5 (1979) 269–314, esp. 271–75, 304–307; Y. Garlan, "Les timbres amphoriques thasiens: bilan et perspectives de recherche," *Annales* 37 (1982) 837–46.

[29] Grace *AJA* (1946) 31, although her first concern was to deny a connection between the inception of stamped handles and the enactment of the Coinage Decree.

earlier in the century might have been designed solely on the Thasian standard that related to the Attic by a ratio of 10:9, although our evidence is weak.[30] An amphora described as belonging to the third quarter of the century had the capacity of 8 Attic *khoes*. It is uncertain what standing such a jar could still have had within the contemporary local Thasian metrological system. Before seeing the intervention of Attic legislation in this conjectured adjustments, it is worth observing that it may not have coincided with the parallel changes that took place in the Chian series of amphoras. That outcome would underline the role of economic forces in such alterations.

The same conclusion could also be reached if another hypothesis about Lesbian container amphoras turned out to be correct.[31] The full-scale vessels are gray in color and possess characteristic handles and profiles. A second group of smaller pots, considered to be fractional containers, are similar in shape, but their color is red. The discovery on Thasos of a defective example of the latter, apparently discarded before use, suggests that these fractional containers for Lesbian wine were produced on Thasos. These red fractional amphoras begin in the late sixth century and so the cooperation that led to their creation was not the result of political dictation. It would be interesting to determine whether this cooperation between the businesses of the two islands extended to metrological convergence or integration. Another series of red clay containers may belong to Thasos or another of the northern Aegean islands, working on the same system of *metra*. These also seem to show a metrological adjustment toward Attic *metra*.[32] It is, however, most uncertain that the alteration was meant to accommodate the Attic standard.

In the case of Thasos, it is fortunate that there is some epigraphical evidence that may supplement the conclusions built on an examination of the material remains. A Thasian inscription that has been dated to 425–400 has been analyzed by M. Lang to provide support for the hypothesis of the creation of an interoperability of local and Attic *metra*

[30] Mattingly *JHS* (1981) 83–84, citing J.B. Brashinsky, "A Thasian Amphora from Nymphaeum and Questions of Ancient Metrology," *VDI* 144 (1978) 135–43 (in Russian with English summary on pp. 142–43). Cf. Brashinsky, *Metody* 179–83.

[31] B.G. Clinkenbeard, "Lesbian and Thasian Wine Amphoras: Questions Concerning Collaboration," in Empereur and Garlan, *Amphores grecques* 353–62. Lawall, *Transport Amphoras* 210–12, is skeptical.

[32] Mattingly *JHS* (1981) 86, citing the information of M. Lang (through personal communication) on the volume of three pots from this series (one from 470–60; two from 460–40). For the type of the amphoras, see Boulter *Hesperia* (1953) 105–106.

on the island.[33] She translates the inscription: "the [approved] measure of vessels: | 55: 60: | 44: 22," and interprets these notations as the specifications for a *pithos* 'storage jar' with a depth of 55–60 "fingers" and a maximum diameter of 44 and a minimum of 22 "fingers." We know from another inscription that the characteristics of the *pithos* are likely to have been legally defined (note *IG* XII Suppl. 347.II.13: . . . μηδ' ἐκ ψευδοπίθο . . .). It is not a coincidence, Lang argues, that the volume of such a vessel according to ancient formulas is the minimum volume at which a round number of dry measures, in this case 6 *medimnoi*, and a round number of liquid measures, 8 *metrētai*, can be accommodated in the same container.

Moreover, an approximately round number of cubic feet in two metrological systems may be accommodated in the same vessel: 12 ft^3, where the foot equals 0.296 m and 9 ft^3, where the foot equals 0.326 m.[34] Lang opted for seeing the short foot as an Ionic foot, which was part of the traditional metrology of Thasos, and the longer foot as an Attic foot. Attractive though this hypothesis might be, caution must be our watchword. As shall be seen shortly in our discussion of the Oxford metrological relief, this short foot can also be envisaged as an "Attic" foot (or even a Solonian foot). Thus it may be safest to note the convergence of two metrological systems without forcing a conclusion on the political affinity of either length foot. Consequently, the inscription sanctions and perhaps directs the usage of a multipurpose container for dry and wet goods that could be used with equal acceptence by those using two systems of *metra*. Hypothetically, Attic measures have not dislodged local *metra* here but have instead been reconciled to them by the nearest practical approximation.

This conjectured reconciliation of Attic and Thasian measures in the same containers might account for the fact that the Attic Stelai (the record of the sale of the goods of the Hermokopidai), referring to the estate of Adeimantos on Thasos, mention *pithoi* and an amount of wine in amphoras and *khoes* without specifying the system of measures (*IG* I^3 426.45–51).[35] The goods sold were scarcely repackaged; giving the Attic equivalent of a consignment of Thasian wine appears nonproblematical.

[33] M. Lang, "A New Inscription from Thasos: Specifications for a Measure," *BCH* 76 (1952) 18–31; cf. Salviat, *Amphores grecques* 176–77.

[34] Based on W.B. Dinsmoor, "The Basis of Greek Temple Design: Asia Minor, Greece, Italy," *Atti del settimo congresso internazionale di Archeologia Classica* 1 (Rome 1961) 355–368, esp. 357–60. Dinsmoor identifies a short foot as Ionic (0.294 m) and notes a Doric foot or 0.326 m, also used for buildings in Attica.

[35] W.K. Pritchett, "The Attic Stelai, Part I," *Hesperia* 22 (1953) 225–99, esp. 270–79; D.A. Amyx, "The Attic Stelai, Part III," *Hesperia* 27 (1958) 163–254, esp. 168–70; Salviat, *Amphores grecques* 150–51.

Samian transport amphoras are believed to have been used for the conveyance of olive oil.[36] They represent a significant series about which Grace has established a succession of types that exploits in part the relationship of the stamps on the amphoras to Samian coin types. It is indeed possible that some of the changes in the shapes of fifth-century Samian amphoras about which Grace speculates are owed to the influence of metrological integration (whether or not we imagine it to have been legislated). Yet again the capacity studies are in default, so that even a hypothesis on the subject cannot be offered. Mende appears to have used the Attic standard during the *arkhē* much as the city used the Euboeic/Attic standard in coinage.[37] Hence it is illustrative of metrological integration, although the absence of an earlier stage during which local *metra* prevailed makes its case not contributory to conclusions about the general status of metrological consolidation in the *arkhē*, and it is uncertain whether Attic *metra* were used exclusively for Mendean amphoras.

The Oxford Metrological Relief

It is also appropriate to discuss right after Samian amphoras a metrological relief now in Oxford.[38] Its specific provenience is unknown, but the non-Attic appearance of the marble and a suspected affinity with the stone of mainland Ionia and its offshore islands have been observed.[39] Contributing to the same conclusion is the collection of the stone for the Earl of Arundel, whose agent, W. Petty, was active in Ionia.[40] Experts on sculpture have pronounced this work to have affinities in style with the Parian or the Samian school.[41] B.S. Ridgway notes that the gabled tomb

36 On Samian amphoras used for the export of olive oil, see V. Grace, "Samian Amphoras," *Hesperia* 40 (1971) 52–95; Grace, *Studies* 118–20, especially important for the summary of the scholarship in Russian of J.B. Brashinsky in note 12 (p. 119), including: "New Data on Olbian Trade with Samos," *KSIA* 109 (1967) 23–26 and "Research of the Elizavetouskoye Mound Site in 1966," *KSIA* 116 (1969) 111–17. See also Brashinsky, *Metody* 176. Cf. Mattingly *JHS* (1981) 85.

37 Lang *Hesperia* (1953) 10 (#44), 12 (#57); Mattingly *JHS* (1981) 85 (esp. note 51) with B. Schlörb-Vierneisel, "Eridanos-Nekropole: I. Gräber und Opferstellen hS 1-204," *AM* 81 (1966) 4–111, esp. 35 (#62). Other jars, whether dating later or sold to different customers, were not an even number of Attic *khoes*. See also Brashinsky, *Metody* 177–79; C.J. Eiseman and B.S. Ridgway, *The Porticello Shipwreck* (College Station 1987) 51–53.

38 A. Michaelis, "The Metrological Relief at Oxford," *JHS* 4 (1883) 335–50; Grace *Hesperia* (1971) 86 with note 89 (pp. 86–87); B. Wesenberg, "Zum metrologischen Relief in Oxford," *Marburger Winckelmann-Programm* (1975–1976 [1976]) 15–22; B.S. Ridgway, *Fifth Century Styles in Greek Sculpture* (Princeton 1981) 65; E. Fernie, "The Greek Metrological Relief in Oxford," *AntJ* 61 (1981) 255–63.

39 Michaelis *JHS* (1883) 337–38.

40 D.E. Haynes, "The Arundel Marbles," *Archaeology* 21 (1968) 85–91, 206–11.

41 Paros: E. Langlotz, *Frühgriechische Bildhauerschulen* (Nuremberg 1927) 132–36; Parian or Samian: G. Lippold, *Die griechische Plastik, Handbuch der Archäologie* 3.1 (Munich 1950) 176.

was relatively common in Asia Minor. A. Michaelis argued that the ratio of 6:7 (represented by the two systems of linear measurement pictured on the sculpture) prevails for the relationship of Attic to Egyptian measures (but see immediately below).[42] Among Greek communities, Samos then becomes a logical candidate for him for the provenience of the sculpture. Herodotus informs us that the Egyptian *pēkhus* 'cubit' was equivalent to the Samian *pēkhus* (Hdt. 2.168.1–2). That testimony, however, does not exclude the use of the same *metra* by other Ionian communities. The material is lacking to reach a solid conclusion about the origin of the stone. Suffice it to observe that the relief probably derived from an Ionian city that was (presumptively) under Athenian hegemony in the fifth century, be it Paros, Samos or one of its dependencies, or another city on the same system of *metra*.

In a pedimental configuration, the relief depicts a man from the mid-chest upward with outstretched arms (head in profile to our right) that are parallel to the ground. Above his shoulder on our left is a footprint. The distance from fingertip to fingertip should constitute an *orguia* 'fathom' that should be six times the length of the foot, but it is in fact seven times the length of the foot pictured here. This sculpture thus illustrates two different standards of linear measurement. The two standards so pictured were probably currently employed in the city where the monument was erected. The more important system was exemplified by the dominant figure in the relief. Therefore, it is possible that not only the *orguia* 'fathom' is to scale but possibly the *daktyloi* 'fingers' (Wesenberg concurs only for the fingers) and the *palastai* 'palms' are proportionately correct, and the *orguia* may be divided into four *pugmai* 'ells' or 'short cubits.'[43] The secondary system of *metra* is merely represented by the measure of its foot.

The relief illustrates the existence of two metrological standards in the same location in a manner suggestive of the metrological consolidation exemplified by contemporary amphoras.[44] Michaelis argued that the foot is Attic (0.296 m), with the span of the figure exemplifying the local

---

Ridgway, *Styles* 65, cites the discussion of A. Kostoglu-Despinis, *Problemata des Parianes Plastikes tou 5ou aiona p.Ch.* (Diss., Thessaloniki 1979) 159–60, Pl. 52, and note 472–74, who accepts a Parian derivation.

[42] Michaelis *JHS* (1883) 338–39. Note H.J. Kienast, *Die Wasserleitung des Eupalinos auf Samos*, *Samos* 19 (Bonn 1995), 172–74.

[43] For further suggestions on the proportionality of secondary features of the relief, see E. Lorenzen, *Technical Studies in Ancient Metrology* (Copenhagen 1966) 58–72; H. Ben-Menahem and N.S Hecht, "A Modest Addendum to 'The Greek Metrological Relief in Oxford,'" *AntJ* 65 (1985) 139–40, 142, with pl. xxxviii.

[44] For this reason, one must reject the suggestion of Fernie (*AntJ* [1981] 257), despite its relevance on the basis of traditional interpretations of the Coinage Decree, that the visual program of the relief dates it to the period before the mandating of a single set of *metra*.

standard (which is Ionic).[45] Wesenberg has come to a slightly different conclusion: for him it is the whole breadth of the relief that represents the *orguia*, illustrating a relationship of 27:32 with the Attic foot.[46] This judgment does not alter the metrological conclusion that two systems are being harmonized. While there has been much controversy over the relationship and the exact dimensions of feet in various fifth-century measurement systems, the appearance of the Attic foot on this monument has been generally conceded.[47] The fact is, however, that the specific identity and area of usage for the foot is far from assured.

The choice of the Attic foot and the local *orguia* for primary illustration was perhaps based on the fact that *orguia* probably represented a round number multiple of the Attic foot and was thereby a point of intersection between the two systems. In this interpretation the relief appears to represent metrological integration along the same lines as has been suspected in the changes in Chian transport amphoras; not a substitution so much as a consolidation.[48]

It is possible to adduce a similar, more recently discovered sculpture in support of our interpretation of the Oxford relief. A fragmentary metrological relief was found on Salamis in 1985.[49] Only part of the head of the figure has survived, along with a shoulder and arm outstretched to the right (incised in limestone). A forearm, hand-span, rule, and foot are disposed in incision in the field around the forearm of the figure. This relief also illustrates two metrological systems: one for the rule, fathom, forearm, and hand-span and another for the foot. The length of the foot (0.301 m) is consistent with the so-called "Hellenistic foot," identified by Broneer.[50] That might give a late fourth-century date for the sculpture, which is too worn and fragmentary to date by other means. Thus, the Salamis relief does not attest to the status of fifth-century metrological conditions. Yet it is valuable for understanding the Oxford relief in several

45 Michaelis *JHS* (1883) 337.

46 Wesenberg *Marburger Winckelmann-Programm* (1975–1976 [1976]) 18–19, which is strongly supported by Fernie *AntJ* (1981) 257–58.

47 Wesenberg *Marburger Winckelmann-Programm* (1975–1976 [1976]) 15–18, esp. with note 4, pp. 15–17, containing copious citation of previous scholarship. G. Gruben ("Naxos und Paros," *AA* [1972] 323–79, esp. 325–26) believes that this foot was the "Solonian foot."

48 The assertion, unlikely on inspection, that the Attic foot is a later addition to the monument (or to its design, an over fine distinction in any case) confuses this issue to a certain degree, but could itself be driven by the theory that the Coinage Decree must have abolished non-Attic measures at some point. See Fernie *AntJ* (1981) 256. Cf. Michaelis *JHS* (1883) 350; Wesenberg *Winckelmann-Programm* (1975–1976 [1976]) 21–22.

49 I. Dekoulakou-Sideris, "A Metrological Relief from Salamis," *AJA* 94 (1990) 445–51; E. Burger, B. Müller-Huber, and L. Thommen, *Der Entwurf des Künstlers: Bildhauerkanon in der Antike und Neuzeit* (Basel 1992) 25–31.

50 O. Broneer, *Temple of Poseidon* (*Isthmia* 1) (Princeton 1971) 174–81.

ways. First, it shows that the coexistence of two systems of *metra* could be noncontroversial, even in Attica itself. Second, the currency of the two metrological systems portrayed on the Salamis relief is unlikely to have been created by hegemonic legislation, in which the usage of a secondary system, perhaps illustrated by the foot, was imposed for some ulterior political motive. Finally, the coming into prominence of a new system of *metra* did not in this instance—any more than during the fifth-century *arkhē*, we have argued—necessitate a termination of the usage of an earlier system of *metra*. Rather, at the very least, a period of overlapping usage is indicated. This array of measures was meant for use, and the block probably formed a part of a building.

In contrast, it is clear that the Oxford relief was not meant to provide a practical guide to the use of the two systems of *metra*, as it is impossible to consult or use the exempla illustrated on the stone in any conventional sense.[51] The relief could have topped a votive offering, although what would constitute an appropriate ex voto for it to accompany is rather mysterious.[52] The crowning member of a funerary monument is another surmise, with the tomb of an architect, sculptor, or philosopher as special suggestions. In my view, those professions might be considered to be ordered here in descending probability. The tomb of an official charged with supervision of the marketplace or a monument for a statesmen involved in metrological reform might be added to this list. Another suggestion is that the most common use for a block of this shape is as a lintel above a doorway that was meant to be seen from below.[53] In that case, the building might have housed the headquarters of a board of *agoranomoi* or *metronomoi* (or some other officials associated with the supervision of the market). The last major line of recent interpretation is to suggest that the cornice topped an inscribed law regulating *metra*, perhaps even the Coinage Decree itself. This attractive hypothesis can be neither supported nor refuted at the present time.[54] A similar conjecture, conceived in a more pragmatic vein, might see the sculpture atop a detailed and eye-level illustration in stone or through other materials and objects clamped to stone of a prevailing system of measures.

The date of the sculpture is contested, and suggestions in favor of the subsequent addition of the foot (unlikely to my mind) complicate the

[51] Cf. M. Robertson, *A History of Greek Art* (Cambridge 1975) 1.199, with note 77 (2.650). This problem is only partially obviated by Wesenberg's suggestion that the whole breadth of the relief marked the local *orguia*.

[52] For this and the other suggestions, see Ridgway, *Styles* 65.

[53] See Fernie *AntJ* (1981) 259–60.

[54] Wesenberg *Winckelmann-Programm* (1975–1976 [1976]) 21–22. Note also Kostoglu-Despinis, *Problemata* 159–60, as cited by Ridgway, *Styles* 65.

issue. Michaelis put the sculpture in the decade before 450 (a placement also followed by Haynes and Kostoglou-Despinis).[55] Boardman opts for a date around mid-century, and Wesenberg will accept a latest date only somewhat thereafter.[56] Lippold, at least by implication, would allow a date as late as 430.[57] Ridgway makes the interesting comment that "an Ionic provenience would explain the Lingering Severe style of the carving and accord with a date around 440–430."[58] It is uncertain whether these datings represent completely independent esthetic judgments or whether they have been at least subconsciously influenced by an extrapolation from the prevailing dates for the Coinage Decree. Nonetheless, it is striking that the relief may well precede the earliest epigraphical date for the fragments of the decree.

CONCLUSION

The evidence on changes in the metrological practices of Athenian allies seems to reveal an integration in which Attic measures were accorded validity and currency in allied economies. These developments are parallel to monetary history, where Attic coinage became increasingly dominant. In many places, where local coinage still continued to be struck, Athenian coins also circulated as legal tender. It is unclear which range of behavior the Coinage Decree, either in its traditional sense or in a revisionist interpretation, would have forbidden or tolerated regarding the usage of weights and measures. At a minimum, products packaged in Attic weights and measures were probably expected to be accepted in all states still coining silver.

It is true that the decree for Methone (*IG* I^3 61.34–41 [426/5]) and the decree for Aphytis (*IG* I^3 62.1–5 [428/7]) lack specification of the type of *medimnoi* of the grain the two states are permitted to import from the Hellespont.[59] Our problem is being sure that this assumption of the validity of Attic measures is a result of the passage of legislation like the

[55] Michaelis *JHS* (1883) 342–44; Haynes *Archaeology* (1968) 209; Kostoglu-Despinis, *Problemata* 159–60.

[56] J. Boardman in Boardman, J. Dörig, W. Fuchs, and M. Hirmer, *Greek Art and Architecture* (New York 1967) 12 with Pl. 42; Wesenberg *Winckelmann-Programm* (1975–1976 [1976]) 22.

[57] Lippold, *Plastik* 176.

[58] Ridgway, *Styles* 65.

[59] Lewis, *Coinage and Administration* 61–66. A further point is made about the specification of Euboian talents in *IG* I^3 435.69–71 (cf. 101–105 for a similar restoration); the accounts for the statue of Athena Promachos (from ca. 450), while parallel notation lacking later in *IG* I^3 472.139–45 (from 421–416/5). It is possible, however, that the Athenians wanted to specify Euboeic weights in the earlier context because the Euboeic and Attic weight systems had diverged in the late archaic period, while the coin standards had not.

Coinage Decree and not of an Athenian expectation that those asking them for concessions like the two states in question were expected to work in the metrological framework of Attic officials, Attic *metra*, in any case. That expectation probably prevailed at all times.

As suggested above, it may also have been necessary for those doing business in allied markets to declare in some way the Attic capacities and weights of all goods for sale, much as commercial convention and ease of selling often now urge that products in English measurements also receive metric denotations. Consolidation of *metra* has been shown from the archaeological evidence to be sometimes a matter of using containers of capacities that were valid both in the local and the Attic systems. Yet the exploitation of points of equivalence between the two systems might not have led in every case to the sort of gross changes that are now easily decipherable. It is unknown whether it ever became compulsory to *replace* local *metra* in their totality with Attic *metra* where the two systems could not in some way be reconciled in the actual packaging and presentation of goods for sale. Here, in addressing this major question, we are bedeviled by the absence of chronological specificity in the limited manifestations of the metrological consolidation that can now be discerned.

Metrological consolidation in the current state of the scholarship seems to straggle over a considerable duration. The metrological relief from Oxford might indicate the existence of integration in some places as early as 460. The Chian adjustment to Attic *metra* in their transport amphoras looks best in the period 450–30. Thasian adjustments could be as early as 450, but might better be placed after 435 and the revival of Thasian coining (if that is its correct date). The Thasian metrological inscription (as interpreted by Lang) is even later. It may eventually turn out that the disparate chronology of the various signs of metrological consolidation will group themselves into one or more restricted temporal contexts, after another generation or two of research. The progress of scholarship in monetary consolidation, however, may be a better indicator of the future. A more complex evolution might gradually unfold, one that is even less open to explanation as an outgrowth of Attic legislation. The Coinage Decree may well turn out to be a threshold, but one merely marking a single stage in a long metrological development.

In the traditional interpretation of the Coinage Decree, the application of a currency or a validity for Attic *metra* and *stathma* has always seemed less amenable to an imperialistic interpretation than an imposition of Athenian coins. The symbolic impact of ensuring that the allies used Attic weights and measures seemed somewhat feeble, especially when it was juxtaposed with the cost of enforcement. The rationale in the revisionist reconstruction is that the resolution of all goods sold into a harmony with Attic monetary and metrological standards created a transparency for the operation of allied systems of taxation on local economic activity. Contentions made by allied states about their ability to pay various levels of assessment of tribute would have to be accompanied by explanations about their tax receipts. If taxes were levied on products in weights and measures that were conforming to Attic standards, the incidence and yield of those taxes could be reviewed by the *Boulē*, by dikasteric courts, and the Assembly with ease. It was by virtue of the more thorough monetization of its economy and administration that the Attic *arkhē* differed from other ancient "empires." That factor makes it difficult to compare the forces militating in favor of metrological convergence in the Attic sphere of influence with other hegemonic contexts.

In the midst of a welter of assertions, the Athenians presumably preferred to hear that the tax for grain importation at Miletos, for example, was 5 Attic obols for 5 Attic *medimnoi* of wheat (to make up figures for illustration) than to hear that it was 6 Milesian obols for 6 local *medimnoi*. That may have been because they wanted expeditiously to compare a tax at Teos that was 3 Aiginetic obols for $3\frac{1}{2}$ Aiginetic *medimnoi* and their own tariff of one Attic drachm for 5 Attic *medimnoi* (to provide still more exemplary numbers). In this example it can be seen why the Athenian government was especially anxious to see that those still minting their own silver used Attic metrological standards, inasmuch as comparing revenue in different metrological *and* monetary systems is much more difficult than adjusting for *either* a metrological *or* a monetary disparity of standards.[60] This is exactly the end toward which our interpretation of the decree will point.

If this motivation for including rules about *stathma* and *metra* in the Coinage Decree seems insufficient in its motivating force, it is worth remembering that interoperability and simplification of metrological standards was advantageous economically. The same sort of influence of the Attic economy on foreign producers may be indicated by an upsurge in markings ca. 430–25 found on Chian and Mendean amphoras.[61] It is likely that some of the changes that brought goods in different communities into containers that were easily usable in other political jurisdictions were taken spontaneously or through reciprocal diplomacy. Therefore, if the Athenians ordered that their allies conduct business using Attic standards in some sense (as well as any local standards in use), they probably

[60] See my discussion below in Chapter 18.
[61] Lawall, *Transport Amphoras* 303–306.

anticipated not only that results of such an instruction would be mutually beneficial, but that the mandate was generally conformable with actions that were already being taken by some allied cities and individuals.

One final observation closes this section of our investigation. It is noteworthy that the process of integration did not work merely in one direction, that is, from the hegemonic power to its allies and tributaries. The Salamis metrological relief attests the influence in fourth-century or Hellenistic Attica of metrological consolidation. For our period, a similar situation may be exposed by the role played by Aiginetic weights in Attica. For all their disdain and hatred for the Aiginetans, their political rivals and later subjects, the Athenians could not and did not ignore the influential Aiginetic system of weights and measures in the conduct of their business affairs. Fifth-century weights have been found at Athens marked with either a turtle or tortoise, the two political badges that are successively found on Aiginetan coins.[62]

Smaller denominations are accordingly marked with the half-turtle and quarter-turtle and the half-tortoise. These weights seem to mark points of significance or correlation and conversion between the Attic system of weights and the Aiginetic *stathma*. The turtles, half-turtles, and quarter-turtles marked (respectively) one-sixth, one-twelfth, and one twenty-fourth of an important standard weight, the Aiginetic stater (not to be confused with the much lighter stater coin, a didrachm). The tortoises and half-tortoises represented one fourth and one eighth of an Aiginetic weight stater, but not necessarily the same one. The weights indicate some variation so that some adjustments may also have occurred by design within the two subsystems (the "turtle" weights and the "tortoise" weights).

The variation between points at which the turtles and tortoises correlated with the Attic system of weights and the different weights of the actual *stathma* within each series may indicate that both the Attic and the Aiginetic weight systems were evolving independently of each other during the late archaic and classical periods, down through the subjection of the island by the Athenians. When the systems of weights changed, points of intersection between the two systems seem to have been adjusted accordingly. The Athenians adopted a more contemporary symbol found on Aiginetan coins, when they chose to illustrate a more recent system of weights in use by the Aiginetans. The number of the surviving weights—Pernice listed 120 in his now dated conspectus—

62 See Lang, *Weights* 5, 8–11; E. Pernice, *Griechische Gewichte* (Berlin 1894) 100–15; Figueira, *Excursions* 68.

indicates that the cross-calculations that rendered the weights of products in terms of the other system were frequent. It may well be that the "turtle" and the "tortoise" weights were in simultaneous use, as one group of users of Aiginetic weights employed an earlier system ("turtle" weights), while others (the Aiginetans themselves perhaps) shifted to the "tortoise" system.

Yet it is inconceivable that any Athenian politician proposed on philosophical or ideological grounds that Attic merchants and craftsmen be mandated to work in accordance with the Aiginetic weight system along with their own Attic system of weights. Rather, economic factors were sufficiently determinant for this mode of metrological integration. Hence there are examples of Attic weights bearing turtles and tortoises that are marked ΔΕΜΟ or ΔΗΜΟ for δημόσιον 'public.' That appellation meant not only that they were officially recognized as valid, but also that some of them were probably utilized by public officials.[63]

[63] *IG* II² 1013, of the end of the second century, shows an Attic *emporikos mna* being adjusted away from an alignment with Aiginetic *stathma* into a relation with Roman weights.

PART IV

EPIGRAPHICAL EVIDENCE FOR MONETARY POLICY

12

THE COINAGE DECREE: PART I

THE DISCUSSION in the preceding chapters, working from the numismatic data and from the literary evidence for Athenian monetary legislation, has subjected the earlier interpretations of the Coinage Decree to thorough criticism for their implications about the financial and economic history of the Athenian *arkhē*. So far we have found intractable difficulties in contextualizing such legislation as economic self-aggrandizement, and, in addition, have questioned the symbolic significance of creating a monopoly for Attic silver coinage, measures, and weights. A consideration of the costs and benefits to Athens of any putative demonstration of hegemony in monetary and metrological matters has also made such "imperialism" appear counterintuitive. Finally, we have come to doubt whether any advantage accrued to the Athenians in monetary or metrological consolidation by prohibiting allied cities from minting coins per se, as compared to other actions, mainly undertaken by the allies themselves, that might serve the same ends and are well attested in the archaeological record. Not only do initiatives like changes in standard and standard coin help to disprove that there was ever a total ban on allied minting but the variety of modes of adjustment to the local circulation of foreign money call into question the necessity for the Coinage Decree as usually reconstructed.

This exploration has instead pointed toward the subject of administrative efficiency in the sphere of tribute collection as one likely context for the more immediate motivation(s) behind any Athenian legislative act about money. Once again, however, the hypothetical imperatives emerging from tribute collection do not superficially offer a good "fit" with the traditional interpretation of the Coinage Decree, for a prohibition on allied minting seems disproportionate to the goals sought. The actual treatment of non-Athenian coins in the receipt of the tribute suggests an "evil" that was tolerated, an experience hardly in keeping with the usual portrait of the punitive aspects of the decree. Expediting tribute collection, moreover, is only the most governmentally conspicuous payoff from unifying weights, measures, and coins, out of a series of the reciprocal economic benefits, which renders problematic the almost universal appreciation that the decree was unwelcome Attic hegemonism.

Accordingly, we consider now whether the epigraphical evidence can be interpreted in such a way that it contributes to an emerging revisionist reconstruction of monetary legislation during the fifth-century Attic hegemony or whether the data from epigraphy must remain enigmatically counterindicative.

THE FRAGMENTS OF THE COINAGE DECREE

We begin with a description of the inscriptions that have traditionally been assigned to the Attic Coinage Decree,[1] as it is usually called. We shall continue to use the same designation, despite the eminently sensible calls for a title more descriptive of its references to weights and measures. For the moment, we shall hold in abeyance the question of whether these documents represent portions of the same, single legal text rather than texts drawn from an (albeit) coherent body of law but constituting separate enactments.[2]

The fragmentary copies of the Coinage Decree and their major treatments in earlier scholarship may be summarized as follows:[3]

1. A short, nonstoichedon fragment in Ionic lettering derives from the island of Syme (*IG* I³ 1453A).[4] The stone appeared to the first editor, Chabiaras, to be local limestone. The stone has since been lost.

[1] *IG* I³ 1453 may be consulted for the standard apparatus.

[2] Minor disagreements of other editions with the texts of *IG* I³ 1453, such as those concerning the dotting of letters that are preserved in other fragments, shall not be treated here, except where they touch on explication of content.

[3] For an overview, see *IG* I³ 1453, 2.893–99; *ATL* 2.61–68, D14 (except for the fragment from Odessa). *Composite texts*: E. Ziebarth, *Beiträge zur Geschichte des Seeraubs und Seehandels in alten Griechenland* (Hamburg 1929) "Anhang II," #74, p. 135 (Smyrna, Siphnos, larger Syme fragments); Tod *GHI* #67, pp. 1.163–64 (Smyrna, Siphnos, both Syme fragments); *ATL* 1.579 (T69), 2.67–68 (without Odessa); G.F. Hill (revised by R. Meiggs and A. Andrewes), *Sources for Greek History between the Persian and Peloponnesian Wars*² (Oxford 1951) B39, pp. 295–96 (without Odessa); H.W. Pleket, *Epigraphica* 1 (Leiden 1964) #3, pp. 9–11; Meiggs-Lewis² #45, pp. 111–17; Erxleben *AfP* (1969) 136–139, cf. 131–36 for another *apparatus criticus* for each fragment; Koch, *Volksbeschlüsse* 374–78. *English translations*: N. Lewis, *The Fifth Century* B.C.: *Greek Historical Documents* (Toronto 1971) 11–12; M.M. Austin and P. Vidal-Naquet, *Economic and Social History of Ancient Greece: An Introduction* (Berkeley and Los Angeles 1977) #101, pp. 326–28; S. Hornblower and M.C. Greenstock, *The Athenian Empire*³ (London 1986) = London Association of Classical Teachers, *Lactor* #1, AE #157, pp. 131–133; C.W. Fornara, *Archaic Times to the End of Peloponnesian War*² (Cambridge 1983) #97, pp. 105–109; M.F. McGregor, *The Athenians and Their Empire* (Vancouver 1987) 76–77 (partial); For additional bibliography, note *SEG* 3.713; 10.25; 12.12; 18.3; 19.7; 21.18; 22.5; 23.8; 24.2; 26.6; 28.2; 29.7; 31.7; 34.11; 35.4; 36.6; 37.6. D.M. Lewis was kind enough to offer me a part of his description of the line length before the publication of fascicle 2 of *IG* I³ (per litteras, 12/9/93).

[4] N. Chabiaras, «Σποράδων ἐπιγραφαί», *AE* (1922) 39–52, esp. 39 (with photograph). Chabiaras, who did not recognize the context for the Syme fragments, dated them to the third century. See also *IG* XII Suppl., p. 215 (F. Hiller von Gaertringen); *ATL* 2.62 (with photograph). I have not enumerated the physical details of the fragments, as they are not controversial, except for noting characteristics that affect issues of interpretation.

2. A marble inscription from Kos, edited by Segre, in Attic lettering using three-barred *sigmas* was responsible for the redating of the law to the mid-fifth century (*IG* I^3 1453B).[5]

3. Another fragmentary Ionic stoichedon text in limestone was found at Aphytis in the Chalcidice during the excavations at Olynthos led by the Johns Hopkins University. It was published by D.M. Robinson (1453C).[6]

4. The longer Ionic fragment from Syme played an important role in initial reconstruction of the general contents of the law (1453D).[7] It was recognized independently by Hiller von Gaertringen and Wilhelm to belong to the "Coinage Decree," the fragment of which from Siphnos was collated by Wilhelm. It has also been lost.

5. An Ionic, nonstoichedon marble inscription from Siphnos was recognized as belonging to the Coinage Decree by Wilhelm, and encouraged the retrospective assignment to the same law of the fragment

[5] Editio princeps: M. Segre, "La legge ateniese sull' unificazione della moneta," *ClRh* 9 (1938) 149 (151)–78 (with photograph). This discovery was noted in many short references: Segre, "Nuove iscrizioni di Coo," *Aevum* 9 (1935) 254–55; M. Guarducci, "Il trattato tra Filippo e i Calcidesi," *RFIC* 63 (1935) 497–507, esp. 497; *AJA* 39 (1935) 392; M.N. Tod, "The Progress of Greek Epigraphy, 1935–1936," *JHS* 57 (1937) 160–218, esp. 198; Tod, "The Progress of Greek Epigraphy, 1937–1938," *JHS* 59 (1939) 241–81, esp. 251–52. More substantial treatments can be found in *IG* XII Suppl., p. 215; *ATL* 2.63–64 (with photograph); E.S.G. Robinson, "The Athenian Currency Decree and the Coinages of the Allies," in *Hesperia* Suppl. 8 (Princeton 1949) 324–40; A. Georgiadès and W.K. Pritchett, "The Koan Fragment of the Monetary Decree," *BCH* 89 (1965) 400–41 (with photographs); Erxleben *AfP* (1969) 96–106. See, most recently, M. Segre, *Iscrizioni di Cos* (Rome 1993) #1, 1.11 (with photograph: tav. 1, vol. 2).

[6] *Editio princeps*: D.M. Robinson, "A New Fragment of the Athenian Decree on Coinage," *AJP* 56 (1935) 149–54 (with photograph: Plate I). Short notices include P.F. Hofer, "Ein athenisches Münzdekret des 5. Jahrhunderts," *SNR* 26 (1934) 195–96; *AJA* 39 (1935) 392; Guarducci *RFIC* (1935) 497; L. Robert, *BE* "Chalcidique," *REG* 49 (1936) 370; Tod *JHS* (1937) 160–218, esp. 192; R.P. Austin, *The Stoichedon Style in Greek Inscriptions* (Oxford 1938) 99; *SEG* 10.25. For more interpretive comment, see also Segre 153–63 (with photograph); *IG* XII Suppl., pp. 215–16; *ATL* 2.63–64 (with photograph); Erxleben *AfP* (1969) 107–18; R.S. Stroud, "Three Attic Decrees," *CSCA* 7 (1974) 279–98, esp. 280–81 (with photograph). On a redating, which was inspired by the announcement of the Kos fragment, see D.M. Robinson and P.A. Clement, *Excavations at Olynthus: Part IX, The Chalcidic Mint and the Excavation Coins found in 1928–1934* (Baltimore 1938) xxviii, cf. 272–74; also D.M. Robinson, "Inscriptions from Macedonia, 1938," *TAPA* 69 (1938) 43–76, esp. 43.

[7] A first description was offered by Chabiaras in *AE* (1922) 40–41 (with photograph), but the identity of its contents was recognized by F. Hiller (von Gaertringen), « Ἀττικὸς νομισματικὸς νόμος ἐκ Σύμης», *AE* (1923) 116–17 and A. Wilhelm, "Zu jüngsten Veröffentlichungen griechischer Inschriften," *AAWW* 61 (1924) 149–62, esp. 157–62. Thus the discussion of Chabiaras, although not lacking in insights into the nature of the text, was quickly made obsolete. Hiller also reported restorations and interpretations of G. Klaffenbach and (to a minor extent) of U. von Wilamowitz-Moellendorff. Early important treatments were made by F. Hiller von Gaertringen and G. Klaffenbach, "Das Münzgesetz des ersten athenischen Seebundes," *ZfN* 35 (1924–25) 217–21; Wilhelm *AAWW* (1924) 157–62. For other restoration and commentary, note *SEG* 3.713; Tod, *GHI* #67, pp. 1.163–66; *IG* XII Suppl., p. 216; *ATL* 2.64–65 (with photograph); Erxleben *AfP* (1969) 118–20.

from Smyrna (1453E).[8] Discovery is attributed to L. Pollak with Hiller von Gaertringen. This inscription has also been lost. This Siphnian inscription played an important part in the early studies.

6. The fragment most lately discovered is an Ionic stoichedon text deriving from the Archaeological Museum at Odessa (1453F).[9] It was catalogued in February 18, 1933 (#251). P.O. Karyshkovsky, its first Russian editor, believed that its origin was Olbia (Parutin), where it was acquired (by S.S. Dlozhevsky). The date of this acquisition is, however, controversial and may have preceded 1930 (the death of Dlozhevsky), although arguments from what normal procedures might have been are probably useless for that time and place (especially when the memory of events in the 1930s was probed in the 1950s). This provenience at Olbia was questioned by Brashinsky, who noted that the timing of the cataloguing of the piece stood against an Olbian origin. Notable is its absence from parallel lists of finds at Olbia compiled and preserved at the then Institute of Archaeology of the U.S.S.R. Academy of Sciences in Moscow. D.M. Lewis suggests that the marble ("finely granulated bluish") is not typical of Olbian inscriptions. Since the Odessa Archaeological Museum seems to contain antiquities from disparate sources (Bulgaria, the Aegean, even Alexandria), in point of fact an origin in the Aegean is a good possibility.[10] The inscription is said to have been misplaced in 1959, after having been moved to the archaeological collection of the museum of the University of Odessa.

7. An Ionic text from Smyrna in marble that has been lost suffers a similar uncertainty of provenience, as Smyrna was never listed among Athenian tributaries. Although discovered first, it awaited Wilhelm's

[8] A. Wilhelm, *AAWW* 34 (1897) 178–88, esp. 180; Wilhelm, "Epigraphischer Bericht aus Griechenland," *JOAI* 1 (1898), "Beiblatt," cols. 41–50, esp. col. 43; Wilhelm, in *IG* XII.5 480 (its first substantial editing in 1903); cf. the notice in M.N. Tod, "The Progress of Greek Epigraphy, 1941–45," *JHS* 65 (1945) 58–99, esp. 87. See also *SIG*^{3} 87; Michel, *Recueil* #1439; *IG* I^2, p. 295; Tod, *GHI* #67, pp. 1.163–66; *ATL* 2.65 (with photograph of squeeze); Erxleben *AfP* (1969) 120–21.

[9] Its text is best consulted in *IG* I^3 1453F or in *SEG* 21.18, pp. 5–6, where the Ukrainian and Russian discussions are summarized, including the Russian *editio princeps* of P.O. Karyshkovsky in *Materialy po arkheologii Severnogo Pricheromor'ia, Odessa* 3 (1961) 64–70, and J.B. Brashinsky (= I. B. Brašinskij), *Afiny i Severnoe Prichernomor'e* (Moscow 1963) 74–75, with note 72. See also Erxleben *AfP* (1969) 121–23 for a clear and relatively accessible overview.

[10] See B.D. Meritt, "The Second Athenian Assessment Period," *GRBS* (1967) 121–32, esp. 128; Meritt, "Perikles, The Athenian Mint, and the Hephaisteion," *PAPS* 119 (1975) 267–74, esp. 267; Lewis, *Coinage and Administration* 56. Meritt cites B. Latischew, "Die in Russland befindlichen Griechischen Inschriften," *AM* 10 (1885) 113–30, esp. 114, which reports the arrival at Odessa in 1827 of a ship from the Aegean that bore inscribed stones as ballast; they were later added to the collection of the Museum of Odessa. Cf. H.B. Mattingly, "New Light on the Athenian Standards Decree (ATL II, D 14)," *Klio* 75 (1993) 99–102, esp. 100–101.

work for its identification (1453G).[11] This inscription is also cited as the "exemplar Arundelianum" because it was shown to Baumeister by a member of the entourage of Lord Arundel after his death as a part of his latest acquisitions. Hiller supposed that it perhaps was to be placed in the same collection, deriving from Paros, to which the *Marmor Parium* (containing the famous chronological work) belonged (*IG* XII Suppl., p. 216). Gardner contested this possibility, which Hiller himself noted had been doubted by Wilhelm.[12]

8. The supposed fragment from Hamaxitos (*IG* I^3 1454*ter* = *SEG* 38.1251) will be discussed below as becomes necessary. It cannot be assigned to the Coinage Decree in the present state of our understanding.

Before beginning a substantive exploration of the surviving fragments, it is useful to try to visualize the contributions made by the various inscriptions. On the following two pages I reproduce a text that is based essentially on the composite text of *IG* I^3 1453. A few obvious emendations have been left in place. The following printing conventions have been observed: the fragment from Kos is in boldface; Aphytis, in underline; Syme, in italics; Siphnos, in double underline; Odessa, in shadow; Smyrna, in strike-through; and restored letters are in reduced type. Curly brackets are used to denote places where the order of the text differs between fragments. Note that the format of these texts as inscribed is greatly discrepant. Thus one cannot easily work back from the interwoven contributions of the different fragments in this text to envisage the layout of the originals. Where it becomes necessary, the extant sections of the separate inscriptions will be reproduced.

The fragments from Aphytis and Kos dominate the beginning of the surviving text. The inscription from Aphytis has significant correspondences with the Syme fragment, not only in section ix where the heralds are despatched—that could be considered a coincidence caused by the common possession of a formula—but also in the more particular clause on punishment in section viii (see below, pp. 375–79). The remains of the Syme fragment play a critical role in bridging over to the second half of the decree, reconstituted with help from the fragments from Siphnos, Smyrna, and Odessa, to a degree because the impact of the preservation

[11] A. Baumeister #22 in *Bericht über die Verhandlungen der Königl. Preuss. Akad. der Wissenschaften* (Berlin 1855) 186–99, esp. 196–97, recognized by A. Wilhelm, *AAWW* (1897) 180, and published in *IG* XII.5 480. See, for substantive reconstruction and comment, *IG* XII Suppl., p. 216; *ATL* 2.66; Erxleben *AfP* (1969) 123–28; also *SIG*^{3} 87; Michel, *Recueil* #1439; *IG* I^2, p. 295.

[12] P. Gardner, "Coinage of the Athenian Empire," *JHS* 33 (1913) 147–88, esp. note 7, p. 150.

i. [..........29?..............]**αι τὰ γ**[..........31-32.............. I.1
... π]**όλεσι ἢ αρ**[.........27-28..............]

ii. [οἱ] **δὲ ἑλληνοταμ**[ίαι......24-26................ II.1
ἀ]**ναγραφόντων· ἐὰ**[ν........24-25............π]**όλεων**
τινος ἐσα[γ.........23-24..........ἐς τ]**ὴν ἡλιαίαν τὴν**
τῶ[ν θεσμοθετῶν....12-13....ο] **ἱ δὲ θεσμοθέ**[τ]**αι**
πε[...8-10...]ντων [....11-13....]**ασι**
ἕκαστον.

iii. **ἐὰν δὲ** [...8-9... τ]ῶν ἀρχόν[των ἐν τ]**ῆσι πόλεσι μὴ** III.1
ποιῆι κα[τὰ ...8-9...]μένα ἢ τῶν [πολι]**τῶν ἢ τῶν ξένων**,
[ἄτ]**ιμ**[ος ἔστω καὶ τὰ χρή]ματα δη**μόσια** [ἔσ]**τω καὶ**
τῆς θεοῦ τ[ὸ ἐπιδέκατον].

iv. [καὶ εἰ μ]ή εἰσι **ἄρχοντες ᾿Αθηναίων ἐ**[πι.....13-14.... IV.1
ἐν τῶι] **ψηφίσματι οἱ ἄρχοντε**[ς οἱ ἑκάστης πόλεως· καὶ]
ἐὰμ μὴ ποιῶσι κατὰ τ[ὰ ....23-24..........]**όντων**
τούτων πέρι ἀτ[.......18-19.......].

v. [ἐν δὲ τῶ]**ι ἀργυροκοπίω**ι τὸ ἀργύ[ριον.....15-20..... V.1
... μὴ ἔλ]**αττον** ἢ ἥμισυ καὶ α[............29.........
.....]ι αἱ πόλεις πραττ[............28.............]
δλραχμὰς ἀπὸ τῆς μν[ας·..........23..........
κατ]αλλάττεν ἢ ἐνοχο[υς ....16.......]

vi. [ὅ δὲ ἂν περιγ]ίγνεται ἀργυρίο[..........27........ VI.1
........]σθαι ἢ τοῖς στρατ[ηγοῖς ἢ ....19........]

vii. [ἐπε]ιδὰν δὲ ἀποδοθῆι, [............28........... VII.1
....]αι καὶ ῾Ηφαισ[τ ......13......].

viii. [καὶ ἐάν τ]*ις εἴπ*[ηι ἢ] ἐπιψηφίσηι περ[ὶ VIII.1
....21....... ἐς ἄλλο] τι χρῆσθ*αι ἢ δανε*[ίζεσθαι ....
....22......]ς τοὺς ἕνδεκα· οἱ δ[ὲ ἕνδεκα θαν]*άτωι*
ζ[ημιωσάντων· ἐὰν] δὲ ἀμφισβητῆι ἐσ[αγαγόντων ἐς τὸ
δικαστήρ]*ιον*.

ix. κήρυκας δὲ ἑλέσθαι τὸ[ν δῆμον ....22 or 31.....
.......]ένα, ἕνα μὲν ἐπὶ Νή[σους, ἕνα δὲ ἐπὶ 'Ιωνίαν,
ἕνα δὲ ἐφ' 'Ελλήσπο]ντον, ἕν[α] δὲ ἐ[πὶ τὰ ἐπ] ὶ Θράικης·
το[ύτοις δὲ ....ca. 40..................ἀ
ἀπ]οστειλάντ[ων .....ca. 16.... εὐθυ]νέσθω μυρία[ισι
δραχμῆσι]. IX.1

x. [ἀναγ]ράψαι δὲ τὸ ψήφισμα τ[όδε τὸς ἄ]ρχοντα[ς τ]ὸ[ς ἐ]ν
ταῖσι πόλεσιν [καὶ θεῖναι ἐν στή]ληι λιθίνηι ἐν τῆι ἀγοραι
{Sym., Od.: ἑκάστης} τῆ[ς πό]λεως {Sm.: ἑκάστης} καὶ τὸς
ἐπιστ[άτας ἔμπροσθεν] τô
ἀργυροκοπίο· ταῦτα δὲ ἐπ[ι ......15...... ἐ]ὰμ μὴ αὐτοὶ
βόλωνται. X.1

xi. δεηθῆναι δὲ αὐτῶν τὸγ κήρυκα τὸν ἰοντα ὅσα
[κ]ελεύο[σιν] 'Αθηναῖοι. XI.1

xii. προσγράψαι δὲ πρὸς τὸν ὅρκον [τ]ὸν τῆς βολῆς τὸν
γραμματέα τὸν τῆς [βολῆς τα]δί· ἐάν τις κόπτηι νόμισ[μα]
ἀργυρίο ἐν τῆσι πό[λεσι] καὶ μὴ χρῆται νομ[ίσμασιν τοῖς]
'Αθη[να]ίων ἢ σταθμοῖς ἢ μέτ[ροις .....12..... νομίσμασι]ν
καὶ σταθμοῖς καὶ μέτροῖς[.........21.......... κατὰ τὸ
πρότε]ρον ψήφισμα ὅ Κλέαρχ[ος ἕιπεν]. XII.1

xiii. [...........c. 30...........]αι τὸ ξενικὸν ἀργύριον[..ca. 30
.... ὅ]ταμ βόληται· τὴν δὲ πό[λιν ....ca. 28
............] αὐτὸν δὲ τὰ [ἑ]αυτο ἕκαστ[ον ....ca. 23
.... τὸ ἀργυ]ροκόπιον. XIII.1

xiv. ο[ἱ δ'] ἐπιστάτ[αι ....ca. 31..............
ἀναγ]ράψαντες κατα[θέντων ......ca. 12..... ἔμπροσθεν το
ἀργυροκο]πίο σκοπεν τῶι βο[λομένωι ....ca. 33.............
ξύμπαν τὸ ἀργύριον τὸ] ξενικὸν χω[ρὶς ....ca. 41
..................]ν ἀργύρι [ο ....ca. 24.......... XIV.1

of the phrase ἐυθυ]νόσθω μυρία[ισι in the Siphnos fragment is somewhat ambiguous (see below, pp. 385–89). On the one hand, one might argue that the overlap of elements of the Aphytis and Syme fragments culminating in this phrase from the Siphnian inscription indicates a single decree. On the other hand, the uncertain syntax of ἐυθυ]νόσθω μυρία[ισι, as the clause has traditionally been reconstructed, might indicate that (at the least) some divergence was possible in the versions of the decree represented by the different examples. This particular discrepancy, however, can be removed by restoring differently.

The Syme, Siphnos, Smyrna, and Odessa fragments are interwoven in sections x–xii. The pattern of correspondences demonstrates that the inscriptions do not simply share "boiler plate" formulas, which were used in a variety of documents. The contributions of the different exempla to the significant phrases τõ ἀργυροκοπίο (x.3–4) and ἐαν τις κόπτηι νόμισ[μα] (section xii.2) indicate that a piece of monetary legislation is at issue. The common contributions to the clause added to the oath of the *Boulē* in section xii also seem to transcend the commonality that might be expected of monetary laws within the same tradition to suggest exempla sharing whole or specific components.

In the earlier parts of the decree, the divergences between the Kos and Aphytis fragments vary significantly with the credence one places in a line not longer than 40 letters for the Kos version (following the text of *IG* I^3 1453A). The Aphytis fragment is markedly shorter in its line 23 (section ix.1–2 of the composite decree: . . . τὸ]|[ν δῆμον . . . . ca. 31 (Aph.: 22) . . . .]ένα, ἕνα μὲν ἐπὶ Νή|[σους . . .). Moreover, the Smyrna fragment differs slightly in its word order at several points. In x.3, τῆ[ς πόλεως ἐκάστης may be restored, while the Odessa and Siphnos fragments appear to vouch for ἐκάστης τῆς πόλεως. In line xii.2, the phrase τὸν τῆς βουλῆς is immediately followed by τάδε in the Siphnos and Odessa fragments, while the Smyrna decree had a longer introduction to or inception of the clause added to the oath of the *Boulē*; ἐς τὸ λοιπόν is a popular restoration. Here the Smyrna version may agree with the Syme decree. Some might concede that these discrepancies are inconsequential, although the lacunae in the Syme and Smyrna inscriptions forbid a firm conclusion. It must be remembered, however, that the Smyrna decree is the only one to provide any indication of further clauses after the clause added to the oath of the *Boulē*.

Table 12.1 provides a list of noteworthy variants. Of those admitted by Lewis, there are several that I would exclude. For the supposed omission of the ἦ (attested in Aphytis line 3) on Kos line 10, see the discussion of section iii below. The plus (+) and minus (–) signs denote the difference in length between the line in question and the corresponding line or lines. As a convention, the Aphytis version has been placed in the left column and the Syme version on the right.

TABLE 12.1 Epigraphical Variants

iii.3: Aph. 4: –2 or 3 letters	Kos 11: +2 or 3 letters
v.1–2: Aph. 10: +5 letters	Kos 17: –5 letters
ix.1–2: Aph. 23: –ca. 9 letters	Sy. 4: + ca. 9 letters
x.1: Si. 2–3: +3	Sy. 8: –3 letters
x.2–3: Si. 4–5: ἑκάστης τῆς πό]λεως	Sm. 3: τῆ[ς πόλεως ἑκάστης
Od. 2: ἑκάστης] τῆ[ς πόλεως	
xii.2: Si. 10–11: τὸν γραμμα[τέα τὸν τῆς βολῆς ταδί]	Sm. 6: τὸν γρα]μματέα τὸν τῆς [βολῆς. . . .ca. 10. . . . ταδί]
Od. 5–6: [τὸν γραμματέα τὸν τῆς βολῆς ταδί]	Sy. 12: [τὸν γραμματέα τὸν τῆς βολῆς. . . .ca. 10. . . . ταδί]
xii.5: Si. 14–15: καὶ σ[ταθμοῖς καὶ μέτροις	Sm. 9: καὶ μ]έτροις καὶ σταθμοῖς
Od. 8–9: καὶ σταθμοῖ]ς κα[ὶ μέτροις	

We may question whether even minor differences do not suggest that the written texts from which stonecutters worked differed from each other rather than merely showing omissions and variations that the inscribers may have allowed themselves. If there existed more than one "edition" of the Coinage Decree, one must inquire whether that could be a function simply of the wide dissemination of the law or must imply validity over a span of time. The existence of different exemplars of even a single decree could either be proof of a continuing authority or an indication of a punctuated validity wherein a piece of legislation that was negated or had fallen into desuetude was revived, reissued, or repromulgated.

There are no strong internal grounds for dividing fragments of the Coinage Decree between two laws, but, equally, this possibility cannot be absolutely disproven. The hypothesis of two coinage decrees represented by these fragments will remain an option for some scholars; it would a means to address the chronological and administrative problems that emerge from attempts to integrate the epigraphical evidence, not only with the rest of the data on Athenian interference with the local affairs of their allies/subjects, but also with paradigms for organization of the Athenian empire.

An investigation of this possibility will absorb our attention below (pp. 407–408, 411, 418). Yet a few words are necessary here, for positing two laws entails an interesting extrapolation. It would force us to admit that Athenian monetary legislation was a much larger phenomenon than the surviving testimonia suggest at first scrutiny, because the next most likely alternative to all the fragments representing a single law is that monetary and metrological legislation was sufficiently formulaic that the remains of more than one enactment create for us the impression of identity when only similarity exists. Thus the existence of terminology and formulas specific to such legislation necessitates a succession of enactments on money, exchange, and metrological standards that drew on a set of clauses to use as components and these laws may have cited from each other. That conclusion in turn would make it difficult to correlate legislation attested by surviving inscriptions and the monetary, administrative, and economic changes that are believed to be discernible during the history of the Athenian *arkhē*. Lost enactments that may have acted with similar or equivalent force confuse the issue.

The inscription may be conveniently discussed using text sections comparable to those of the composite text of *IG* I^3, and based on *ATL* 2.67–68. The discussion below divides the Coinage Decree into four parts. To avoid the repetition of short notes referring to the same passages in modern scholarship, editions have sometimes been referenced in the following discussion by the names of the editors (except where clarity demanded a fuller notation). The reader is urged to consult the notes on the various fragments for all authors and editions that are used here.

We can begin our investigation by exploring the shorter Syme fragment (*IG* I^3 1453A) which may illustrate the lost parts of the psephism that perhaps preceded section i. The meaning of this short text is particularly problematical, with the difficulty being increased by its disappearance.

Chabiaras	*IG* I^3 1453A
- - - - - - - - - - - - - - - - - -	- - - - - - - - ολε - - - - - - - - - - - -]
- - - - - - - - - - - - - -]ολε[- - - -	[- - - - - - - - ἀρχ]οντες - - - - - -]
- - - - - - - - - - - χ]οντε[ς- - - -	[- - - - - - ἐ]λληνο[ταμι- - - - - -]
- - - - - - - - - - - - ʽΕ]λλήν[ων- -	
- - - - - - - - - - - - - - - - - -	

These lines could come from the beginning of the law, as attested by the other fragments, but that entails doubting Chabiaras on his belief that a sure trace of the *omega* of ʽΕλλήνων was visible on the stone. The editors of *ATL* express their doubts on the basis of the photograph. Segre had already suggested ʽΕλλην[οταμίαι, but he also thought that an *omega* was more likely on the basis of the photograph.[13] Hiller in *IG* XII suggested:

[13] Segre 164, note 1.

ἄρχοντες ἐν τῆσι π]όλε[σι--
--ἀρχ]οντε[ς Ἀθηναίων
-----Ἑλλην[οταμίαι

That would correspond with lines 2–3 of the Kos fragment (sections i and ii.1 of the composite decree). *ATL* objects that this reconstruction assumes a line that is too short on the basis of the ca. sixty-letter line length of the longer fragment from Syme (citing D.M. Robinson).[14] *ATL* then offers a restoration of the small Syme fragment with a line length of ca. fifty-five. The underlined letters appear in the Kos fragment.[15]

[----------]όλε[------------ca. 27------------αι]
[τὰ γ.........ca. 19......... ἄρχ]οντε[ς ἐν τηϭι πόλεϭι ἢ ἀρχοντες Ἀθη]-
[ναίων........ca. 14........ οἱ δὲ ἑ]λληνο[ταμίαι----------]

Yet this small fragment might with some likelihood derive from an otherwise unattested section of the decree that may have preceded the surviving parts as witnessed by the other inscriptions (as Robinson implied and Erxleben suggested). Nor is it to be ruled out entirely that this fragment could represent a piece of another Attic law of relevance to Syme, although Chabiaras (followed by subsequent commentators) asserted that both Syme fragments belonged to the same stele. The chief conclusion to be drawn is that, at the very best, the small fragment from Syme allows us (in the reconstruction of *ATL*) to add a few letters that precede the surviving portion of the Kos fragment.[16]

SECTION I[17]

i. [--------]αι τὰ γ[.............31–32............. I.1
...π]όλεσι ἢ αρ[............27–28............]

It is necessary to note at the outset that there has been considerable disagreement over the line lengths of the stoichedon Kos fragment. Segre restored lines 1–8 and 11 with forty letters, with lines 9–10 and 12–17 as

[14] "A New Fragment of the Athenian Decree on Coinage," *AJP* 56 (1935) 149–54, esp. 149 with note 3 (pp. 149–50).

[15] Erxleben *AfP* (1969) 101–102 rejects this hypothesis on the basis of the implied difference in line length for the two Syme fragments (ca. 55 for the short fragment; 56–62 for the major fragment). H.B. Mattingly, "The Second Athenian Coinage Decree," *Klio* 59 (1977) 83–100, esp. note 11, pp. 85–86 counters by suggesting that . . . *hοι* ἄρχοντες οἱ ἐν τε͂σι π]όλεσι . . . be restored in line 2 of the Kos fragment. He concedes that he must move -ολε- back a little.

[16] As we shall note below, the putative fragment from Hamaxitos (*IG* I[3] 1454*ter*), if accepted, would force the smaller Syme fragment to a still earlier *locus* in the decree.

[17] My initial texts at the outset of each section will use the composite text of *IG* I[3] as a point of departure.

including forty-one letters. The editors of *ATL* restore a strict stoichedon order of forty-one letters throughout the Kos fragment. On reexamination of the Kos fragment, Meritt later reaffirmed his belief in a consistent forty-one-letter line length, but changed his views on the preservation of the edges of the stone. He asserted that the right edge of the stone is preserved (as Segre had initially observed).[18] Thus there is room for one letter less to the right of the surviving text and the lost left part of the stone should be held to be a letter longer. Erxleben suggested forty letters for 1–7 and forty-one for 8–17, because from line 8 he agrees with *ATL* in positing room for another letter along the right margin of the stone.[19]

The text of D.M. Lewis in *IG* I³ 1453A not only adopts Meritt's narrowing of the lacunae to the right of the preserved text, but also opts for the shortest estimates for the lacunae to the left of what remains. Lewis writes that "vv. 40 litt. cum magna haesitione praetulimus. aliorum supplementa cum perpendes, fluctuationem hanc in mente certe retinebis."[20] Lewis also observes that a length of forty-one letters does seem required both in line 10, unless ἒ was omitted after ἐφσεφισμένα by the stonecutter, and possibly in line 11, for the expression τὰ δε χρέματα is unsound usage (see below, pp. 345–46). It is a singular feature of the Kos fragment in comparison with the Aphytis fragment that its Attic lettering, with signs for aspiration, is not only not longer (especially in the version of the *IG* I³) than the Ionic Aphytis fragment (without aspiration and using compound letters) but very often shorter. A forty-letter line length for the Kos fragment considerably complicates the problem of harmonizing the Kos and Aphytis texts. I give a conjectural text of the Kos fragment following the line lengths of *IG* I³ on pp. 362–63 below.

For this reason, the calculation of Mattingly that intends to discover the extent of the missing opening of the decree cannot be received with assurance.[21] Mattingly observed that the *iota* that is restored at the head of Aphytis line 2 is equivalent to line 8, space 25 in the Kos fragment, and the *delta* that *ATL* restored to head line 12 of the Aphytis inscription matches Kos 19.4. Ten lines of the Aphytis text occupy ten lines, twenty spaces of the Kos text. At the initial point of line 2 of the Aphytis

[18] Meritt *GRBS* (1967) 127–128; see also Mattingly *Klio* (1977) note 9, p. 85.

[19] Erxleben *AfP* (1969) 96–97. In an additional note on p. 212, Erxleben expresses doubts on Meritt's position on the basis of Segre's photograph, while conceding that Meritt has the advantage of autopsy.

[20] *IG* I³, p. 894 (also personal communication, 12/9/93).

[21] Mattingly *Klio* (1977) 85. Cf. Mattingly *Klio* (1993) 99–102, esp. note 3, p. 100, for adjustments made on the basis of the "Hamaxitos fragment" (to be discussed shortly).

inscription the Kos inscription is already at space 25 of its respective line. Therefore twelve lines are needed before line 2 of the Aphytis inscription in order to permit the Kos inscription to get twenty-four spaces ahead of the Aphytis inscription. More recently, Mattingly has corrected to six prior lines.

Even if these alignments could be trusted, the lack of verbatim correspondence between the two inscriptions spoils this calculation. There are other complicating factors. For one thing, the Kos fragment may have needed ten lines and twenty-one spaces to match the ten lines of the Aphytis copy and may have been only twenty-three letters ahead at the start of the corresponding line 2 of the Aphytis fragment (according to the *IG* I^3 and Erxleben). Second, the Kos fragment might have been two or even three letters shorter in its lost opening lines and that discrepancy spoils any extrapolation from the observation of the surviving overlapping portions of the two fragments.

The beginning of the extant material thus cannot be reconstructed with any certainty. The phrase ἄρχοντες ἐν τε͂σι π]όλεσι ἢ ἄρ[χοντες 'Αθεναίον has been suggested on the basis of iii.1 and iv.1 (Wilhelm, accepted by *ATL*).[22] It is not without considerable justification that Erxleben objects that both phrases describe Athenian officials (without distinguishing the categories!).[23] One would rather expect a juxtaposition of Athenian and allied officials, inasmuch as the other likely contrast, one between officials stationed in allied cities and those on Athenian territory proper, would be difficult to account for in this context. The phrase ἄρχοντες το͂ν χσυμμάχον would be a possibility, as it is the clearest way to distinguish and link Attic and local officials in the cities.[24] Such juxtapositions of Athenians and allies appear in imperial decrees.[25] Phrases

[22] Cf. *IG* I^3 34.5–11: ... Κλενί[ας εἶπε· τὲ]μ β|ολὲν καὶ τὸς ἄρχ[οντας ἐν] τε͂σ|ι πόλεσι καὶ τὸς [ἐπισκό]πος ἐ|πιμέλεσθαι *h*ό[πος ἂν χσ]υλλέ|γεται *h*ο φόρος κ[ατὰ τὸ ἔ]τος *h*|έκαστον καὶ ἀπά[γεται] 'Αθένα|ζε·

[23] Erxleben *AfP* (1969) 97–98. See also Mattingly *Historia* (1961) note 50, p. 158, who offers ἢ ἀρ[γύριον (cf. *SEG* 19.7).

[24] The formula ἄρ[χοντες το͂ν χσυμμάχον το͂ν 'Αθηναίον, which would be an attractive supplement, cannot be accommodated in the space for 27 or 28 letters that is available. Did it appear earlier in a lost part of the inscription? A similar approach has been taken toward the restoration of *IG* I^3 72.11–12 by Meritt: ὅπος δ' ἂμ με ἀ[δικε͂τ]αι μ[εδεὶς μέτε ὑπ' ἰδιότο μέτε ὑπ' ἄρχοντος 'Αθεναίον ἒ το͂ν χσυμμάχον | τ]ο͂[ν 'Αθε]ναίον.... See B.D. Meritt, "Attic Inscriptions of the Fifth Century," *Hesperia* 14 (1945) 61–133, esp. 111–14; D.W. Bradeen and M.F. McGregor, *Studies in Fifth-Century Epigraphy* (Norman 1973) 89, 91.

[25] *IG* I^3 34.34–35: ... το͂ι β]ολομένο[ι 'Αθενα]|ίον καὶ το͂ν χσ[υμμάχον·; 55.5: ... ἢ 'Αθηναίω]ν τις ἢ τῶν ξυμμάχ[ων; 64.11: 'Α]θεναί[ον] καὶ το͂ν χσυμ[μάχον. For

with τῆσι πόλεσι, however, are common in fifth-century inscriptions (cf., for example, *IG* I^3 61.43, 51–52).

Hiller's suggestion of καταλλαττόντον 'let them exchange'—the verb is itself unobjectionable, see section v.5 below and *IG* I^3 90.14—depends to a large extent on the hypothesis that the decree enacted an exchange of allied monies in this section. Erxleben restores freely to reach this conclusion: ἀδόκιμα ἔν]αι τὰ γ[εγραμμ|ένα νομίσματα ἐν *h*απάσεσι τε͂σι π]όλεσι ἒ ἄρ[χοντας | 'Αθεναίον παραδέχσασθαι, which I think is doubtful on the basis of terminology as well as content.[26] The phrase τὰ γεγραμμ|ένα νομίσματα seems an ad hoc construction, and the assumption of the presence of Athenian archons in all allied cities is unsupported. Attempts to posit that a demonetization of allied coinages was enacted in these lines, however, find no evidence for support or refutation in the surviving text. Moreover, we have already seen that numismatic evidence cannot be marshaled in support of this proposition. That such a massive project of monetary transformation was ever contemplated is doubtful in terms of practical administration, as is presented elsewhere (see pp. 242, 353–54). The groundlessness of efforts to state otherwise was recognized as early as the work of Cavaignac.[27] Once we have made allied officials share the subject of the clause, the restoration of καταλλαττόντον is no longer viable. The further suggestion νομίσματα is in turn rendered doubtful.

One might speculate instead that this clause contained a provenience for the information registered in section ii. As for further restoration, it must work from the reading of i.1 that is printed above (line 2 of the Kos fragment). Pritchett's reading of ΑΙΙΑΓ leads to no easy alternatives.[28] The neuter plural term in i.1 that begins with a *gamma* is quite possibly τὰ γραμματεῖα 'registers,' which appears in *IG* I^3 52A.11 in a similar context

other references to the "Athenians" and the "allies of the Athenians," cf. also *IG* I^3 48.19–20; 63.10–11; 75.10; 91.20–21.

[26] Erxleben *AJP* (1969) 98–99. Many other objections could be raised. The phrase τὰ γεγραμμένα νομίσματα is vague here compared with other usage of the participle (see *IG* I^3 36.7; also 106.21–22; 131.18; note the restoration in 58.14). On these comparisons, the phrase τὰ γεγραμμένα νομίσματα should refer to entries inscribed elsewhere and not refer to another part of the same document. The expression ἐν *h*απάσεσι τε͂σι πόλεσι would not be correct terminology for the cities of the *arkhē* (note *IG* I^3 61.59–60 [restored]; 71.55–56) and its correct attribution is to a measure of panhellenic scope (*IG* I^3 78.30–31: . . . τε͂σι ἄλλεσι πόλεσιν [τ]ε͂[σι] *h*ε|[λ]λενικε͂σιν ἁπάσεσι; cf. 83.25–26). The role of the Athenian *arkhontes* 'officials' is unclear in the restoration, and παραδέχσασθαι 'to receive an item in an inventory' looks out of place here. See also Robinson 325 for a similar suggestion without a proposal for restoration.

[27] Cavaignac *Études* 186; *Id.*, "Le décret dit de Kléarchos," *RN* 15 (1953) 1–7, esp. 4–5.

[28] Pritchett *BCH* (1965) 440.

involving accounting for funds.[29] To go further would perhaps be to indulge in tendentious restoration, but πεμπόντον would be possible for an imperative ending the clause (cf. *IG* I^3 61.25; 71.57). In the suggested restorations at the end of each section, I have shifted into Ionic script for consistency, and used changes in point size to distinguish restored from surviving text.

i. [– – – – – – – –]αι τά γ[ραμματεῖα . . . .⁸. . . . ἢ ἄρχοντες ἐν I.1
τῆσι π]όλεσι ἢ ἄρ[χοντες τῶν συμμάχων πεμπόντων]

i. . . . the registers . . . either officials in the cities or officials of the allies are to send.

SECTION II

ii. [οἱ] δὲ ἑλληνοταμ[ίαι . . . . .24–26. . . . . II.1
ἀ]ναγραφόντων· ἐὰ[ν . . . . .24–25. . . . . π]όλεών
τινος, ἐσα[γ . . . . .23–24. . . . . ἐς τ]ὴν ἡλιαίαν τὴν
τῶ[ν θεσμοθετῶν . . . . .12–13. . . . . ο]ἱ δὲ θεσμοθέ[τ]αι
πε[. . . .8–10. . . .]ντον {[–]ντων?} [. . . . .11–13. . . . .]ασι
ἕκαστον

Here are introduced the Hellenotamiai, whose presence may be taken as an indication that the collection of the tribute was intimately involved with this decree.[30] That situation would hardly be surprising if the fiscal motivations, particularly those involving revenue, for such legislation were accepted (as outlined above, pp. 264–73). The appearance of the Hellenotamiai also calls our attention to the Athenian focus for the implementation of the surviving portions of the decree, as the *stratēgoi* and the *epistatai* of the mint are mentioned too (vi.2; x.3, xiv.1). For a decree that is thought to supervise allied affairs highhandedly, it is surprising that orders to the allies and to allied authorities are not more in evidence (cf. οἱ ἄρχοντε[ς οἱ ἑκάστης τῆς πόλεως . . .] in section iv.2).

Some group, probably the Hellenotamiai, are registering something or someone. The great majority of the uses of ἀναγράφω in fifth-century Attic inscriptions specify the transfer of a document (usually a *psēphisma*) to permanent record (almost always a stone stele). Another smaller (but still well-represented) class are the registrations of the names of *euergetai* and *proxenoi*, which sometimes also entail the recording on a stone stele for

[29] *IG* I^3 52A.10–12: ἐχσαλειφόντον ἐπει|[δὰν] ἀποδὸσιν, ζετέσαντες τά τε πινάκια καὶ τὰ γραμματεῖα καὶ ἐὰμ π|[ο ἄλ]λοθι ἐ̃ι γεγραμμένα.

[30] Cf. Schuller, *Herrschaft* 36–37 with note 185.

permanent commemoration. It is hard to envisage how these passages can possibly stand as true analogues for the bureaucratic activities likely to be found here. Only a few documents seem to help with specifics. The Kleonymos Decree has . . . ἀναγ[ραφόντον δὲ *h*οι ἑλ]λ̣ενοτα̣||[μ]ίαι ἐς σανίδι τὰς [πόλες τὰς ἐλλιπό]σας τõ φό||[ρ]ο . . . (*IG* I³ 68.18–20). The Kleinias Decree may have a similar formulation, although much is owed to restoration: τὸς δὲ [*h*ελλεν]||ο[ταμίας ἀναγράφσαντας ἐ]ς πινάκιον λελ[ευκομέν|ον ἀποφαίνεν καὶ τὲν τάχσι]ν τõ φόρο καὶ̣ [τὰς πόλες| *h*όσαι ἂν ἀποδõσιν ἐντελε̃ κα]ὶ ἀπογ̣[ράφεν . . . 7 . . .] (*IG* I³ 34.43–46). The First Kallias Decree has the *tamiai* of Athena registering sacred monies in a number of instances (cf. *IG* I³ 133.17).[31] The first fruits for Eleusis from Greek cities are to be handled similarly.[32]

It is no surprise then that suggested restorations for section ii.1–3 envision the creation of a roster of cities or a list of the monies tendered by particular cities. The editors of *ATL* have suggested *h*οι] δὲ *h*ελλενοταμ[ίαι τὰ ἀργυροκόπια ἐν τε̃σι πόλεσι ἀ]ναγραφόντον.[33] The trouble with this suggestion is that it is far from clear that τὰ ἀργυροκόπια can mean 'mints' as governmental institutions rather than strictly 'mints' in the sense of physical contexts for minting, as the other appearances of the word in Attic inscriptions indicate. If, despite this concern, τὰ ἀργυροκόπια is the correct restoration, we must make a critical alteration in its connotation here. As the numismatic record suggests (see pp. 175–79 above), if a list of mints existed here or elsewhere in the decree, it could only have been a roster of the mints which remained active.[34] A list

31 *IG* I³ 52A.21–30 has a series of parallel formulation: καὶ παραδεχσάσθον *h*οι ταμίαι *h*οι λαχόντες παρὰ τõν νῦ[ν] | ἀρχόντον καὶ ἐν στέλει ἀναγραφσάντον μ̣ιᾶι ἅπαντα καθ' ἕκαστόν τε | τõν θεõν τὰ χρέματα *h*οπόσα ἐστὶν ἑκάστοι καὶ συμπάντον κεφάλαιο|ν, χορὶς τό τε ἀργύριον καὶ τὸ χρύσιον. καὶ τὸ λοιπὸν ἀναγραφόντον *h*|οι αἰεὶ ταμίαι ἐς στέλεν καὶ λόγον διδόντον τõν τε ὄντον χρεμάτον | καὶ τõν προσιόντον τοῖς θεοῖς καὶ ἐάν τι ἀ[π]αναλίσκεται κατὰ τὸν ἐ|νιαυτόν, πρὸς τὸς λογιστάς, καὶ εὐθύνας διδόντον. καὶ ἐκ Παναθεναί|ον ἐς Παναθέναια τὸλ λόγον διδόντον, καθάπερ *h*οι τὰ τε̃ς 'Αθεναίας τ||[α]μιεύοντες. τὰς δὲ στέλας, ἐν αἷς ἂν ἀναγράφσοσι τὰ χρέματα τὰ *h*ιερ||[ά, θέ]ντον ἐμ πόλει *h*οι ταμίαι.

32 *IG* I³ 78.26–30: ἀναγράφσαντες δὲ ἐ[μ] | πινακίοι τὸ μέτρον τõ καρπõ τõ τε παρὰ τὸν δεμάρχον κατὰ τὸ[ν δ|ε̃]μον *h*έκαστον καὶ τõ παρὰ τõν πόλεον κατὰ τὲν πόλιν *h*εκάσ[τεν]|| [κ]αταθέντον ἐν τε τõι 'Ελευσινίοι 'Ελευσῖνι καὶ ἐν τõι βολ[ευτ]ε||[ρ]ίοι.

33 For the spelling ἀργυροκόπιον, note *IG* II² 1013.30; *SEG* 10.394.1–2, 395.2–3; *SEG* 21.667.1. The variant ἀργυροκοπεῖον was the dominant literary form: Aesch. *apud* Poll. 7.103; Andoc. fr. 3.5 (ΣArist. *Wasps* 1007b); Aris. *Prob.* 936b26; Harp. s.v.; J. Chrys. *MPG* 58.508.40, 61.193.1–2; Lib. *Or.* 25.22, 28.20, 31.12; *Decl.* 26.8. Yet there has undoubtedly been orthographic regularizing both by copyists and eventually by editors; note Polyb. 26.1.2 (cf. Athen. 5.21.193D).

34 Cf. G. Klaffenbach, review of *ATL* 2, *DL* 71 (1950) 33–37, esp. col. 35, who assumed that allied mints that existed in all the more important cities undertake the exchange of local

of closed mints would be otiose if all mints were to be closed, as the traditional interpretation of the decree expounds.[35] The information that Aigina or Miletos, for example, had previously struck coins served no purpose—even in the unlikely event that it needed to be listed here—if all minting activity in silver was now to cease.

IG XII Suppl., accepted by Erxleben, offers *hoι*] δὲ *h*ελλενοταμ[ίαι τάς τε πόλεις καὶ τὸ ἀργύριον ἀ]ναγραφόντον. That falls a letter short according to the more strictly stoichedon reconstruction of *ATL*. The parallel usage of ἀναγράφω for a register of cities for a financial purpose in the Kleinias and Kallias decrees stands in favor of this suggestion, insofar as a list of monies tendered in a process of conversion could be at issue. If that were the case, the role of the Hellenotamiai would indicate that the conversion of currencies was taking place as a part of (or analogously with) the process for payment and disposition of tribute over which the Hellenotamiai presided.[36]

Concomitantly, we would expect the *stratēgoi* to be named here if a large demonetization and replacement of allied money were afoot, as the chief military officials of the alliance would make more logical supervisors of a vast circulation of money to Athens in a general invalidation of allied currencies (improbable though that may be, in my opinion).[37] The spirit of this restoration should be preserved, but there need be no strong allegiance to its literal wording. Similar freely composed alternatives, would be *h*oι] δὲ *h*ελλενοταμ[ίαι τὰ χρέματα (or τὰ ἀργύρια) ἐκ πόλεος (*h*)ἐκάστες ἀ]ναγραφόντον or *h*oι] δὲ *h*ελλενοταμ[ίαι τά τεταγμένα ἐκ τõν χσυμμάχον ἀ]ναγραφόντον. There would need to be a further manipulation to reduce the first restoration by one letter to fit a line length of forty (like *IG* I^3).

The next clause (ii.2–6) introduces the punishment of the Hellenotamiai, if they have been derelict, as it seems, in the process of registration. Note that on almost any likely reading of this provision, it is a stipulation whose intent was protective of the allies, for the phrase τõν π]όλεόν τινος implies some error in responding to their actions. The creation of the register was to preserve an accurate record of their tendering of monies

currencies (citing the shipment of large sums during war). The suggestion still fails to address either the objection stated in my text or the unlikelihood of a large-scale demonetization and conversion of currencies.

35 Against a list of mints, see Erxleben *AJP* (1969) 99; cf. Robinson 325.

36 Thuc. 1.96.1–2; cf. *Ath. Pol.* 30.2. On the functions of the Hellenotamiai, see Meiggs 44, 236–38, 244–46.

37 Contrast Mattingly *Klio* (1977) 86, who connects sections i and ii with the responsibilities of the Athenian archons in the cities.

or, less likely, to protect their right to mint. Moreover, with the latter alternative, the provision for punishment would once more suggest that any list of mints could not possibly involve those to be closed. In a law forbidding any minting, no one would imagine that omission from the record of mints that were closing authorized a continuation of coining. Hence the Hellenotamiai must have been threatened with punishment for an error leading to a significant injury (probably to allied interests). In constructing the restoration, the assumption is that the operative word of the previous clause might repeat; hence ἀναγράφοσι or ἀναγραφε͂ι. Restorations vary according to different line lengths. Segre, followed by Lewis in *IG* I³, offers ἐὰ[ν δὲ μὲ ὀρθο͂ς ἀναγράφοσι τὸ το͂ν π]όλεόν τινος. *ATL* suggests ἐὰ[ν δὲ μὲ ὀρθο͂ς ἀναγραφε͂ι τὸ ἐκ το͂ν π]όλεόν τινος.[38] As for μὲ ὀρθῶς, the nearest fifth-century parallel is *IG* I³ 71.39–40: ἐ]ὰμ μὲ ὀ[ρθο͂ς] δοκο͂σ[ι διακο]νε͂[ν, and surely that cannot convince us of its proximity to the wording here, although the sense of the clause as restored is quite likely.

As for the legal procedure that is at work here, the presumptive restoration for the verb in the beginning of ii.3 is a form of ἐσάγω (εἰσάγω).[39] The same verb probably appears in section viii.4. For the end of the line, we must note the parallel legal language in the Chalcis Decree (*IG* I³ 40.75–76: . . . ἐς τὲν ἐλιαίαν τὲν το͂ν θεσμοθετο͂ν κατὰ τὸ φσέφισμα το͂ δέμο). It is the phrase in the middle of ii.3 that is more contested in its restoration. In order to complete the legal procedure started in ii.2, Segre offered (followed by *IG* XII Suppl.) ἐσα[γέσθο μὲν δίκε ἀπὸ χσυμβολο͂ν ἐς τ]ὲν ἐλιαίαν . . . , citing *Ath. Pol.* 59.6. That has been questioned by Hopper because of his doubt over the validity of *symbolai* 'reciprocal treaties,' where disputes could be initiated as private

[38] If the fragmentary decree from Hamaxitos (*SEG* 38.1251) is accepted as another copy of the Coinage Decree, almost its sole contribution to the text would fall in this clause. Schoenhammer 9–10 suggests ἐ]ὰν δὲ τις ἀμ[φισβετε͂ι . . . , adopting the restoration of *IG* I³ 1454*ter* for the Coinage Decree. See also D.M. Lewis, review of H.W. Pleket and R.S. Stroud (eds.), *SEG* 38 (Leiden 1988), *CR* 43 (1993) 208; Lewis does not, however, accept *IG* I³ 1454*ter* as a copy of the Coinage Decree. The appearance of this verb is not impossible, as section viii advises (note *IG* I³ 6A.33–34; 58.14–15; 118.25–26; cf. 34.61–62, 69; also 41.19–20). This restoration, however, leaves virtually no room for the predicate of the clause. It also necessitates that the Hellenotamiai not be the implied complement of τις, and that is improbable. The term ἀμφισβετέω should mean that someone is disputing his guilt over some act. At a great stretch here, the word could mean that someone was disputing an action of the Hellenotamiai, but how that led to an *esagōgē* to the Heliaia is hard to envisage. The restoration leaves the target of the procedure unexplained.

[39] Note Koch, *Volksbeschlüsse* 382–85.

cases, for the adjudication of a charge involving hegemonic jurisdiction.[40] However, if *symbolai* played any role in this provision there are two points that need to be made.[41] The first is that Erxleben should not be followed in deriving from their appearance an argument against a mid-century date for the initial promulgation of the decree.[42] Second, the appearance of *symbolai* in this clause would stand as another instance of the consensual nature of the rules enjoined here and remind us of the reciprocal agreements on monetary and metrological matters implied in Aristophanes' *Birds* (see above, pp. 207–16). With the reciprocity that may be seen represented throughout the decree, one might be less troubled about this point.

More telling against Segre's suggestion is that εἰσάγω is almost always used in the active or middle voices where imperial decrees order the introduction of such prosecutions, with those responsible for prosecuting usually specifically named in the examples where our context is sufficiently complete for us to judge.[43] It is also the lack of clarity over who is to prosecute that weakens Hopper's otherwise attractive hypothesis of ἐσα[γόντον μὲν περὶ τούτο 'Αθέναζε ἐς τ]ὲν ἐλαίαν τὲν τõ[ν θεςμοθετõν κατὰ τὸν νόμον. . . .].

The editors of *ATL* suggest a restoration with a more likely deployment of εἰσάγω: ἐσα[γέτο *ho* βολόμενος αὔτικα μάλα ἐς τ]ὲν ἐλιαίαν τὲν τõ[ν θεσμοθετõν τὸς ἐδικεκότας. This is clearly a possible supplement. The expression *ho* βολόμενος does appear in judicial contexts but construed with γράφω and not εἰσάγω, although there are no examples

[40] R.J. Hopper, "Interstate Juridical Agreements in the Athenian Empire," *JHS* 63 (1943) 35–51, esp. "Note," p. 51.

[41] *Symbolai* specified the treatment in law of disputes between the citizens (or a citizen and foreign government), none of the extant examples of or references to which establish monetary or metrological protocols. Note *IG* I³ 6A.40–43; 10.7, 11–14; 41.108–109; 66.14–16; 113.23; 118.22–26; 127.17–18; 222.1. In general, see Thuc. 1.77.1–3 with *HCT* 1.236–44, which provides further citations. For later instances, note *IG* II² 144+ = *SEG* 17.18, for which see M.B. Walbank, "Athens and Stymphalos: *IG* II², 144+," *Hesperia* 55 (1986) 319–54; *IG* II² 179 for Athens and Naxos; *SEG* 17.17 (= *IG* II² 46+) for Athens and Troizen; *SEG* 17.19? for Athens and Siphnos; *SEG* 17.20 for separate agreements with Knossos and another city. This flurry of diplomacy may have been triggered by the foundation of the Second Confederacy. See also P. Gauthier, *Symbola: Les étrangers et la justice dans les cités grecques* (Nancy 1972) 157–205; S. Cataldi, *Symbolai e relazioni tra le città greche nel V secolo A.C.* (Pisa 1983) 231–50.

[42] For the arguments on the chronological significance of the role of the Heliaia here vis-à-vis the polemarch, see Erxleben *AfP* (1969) 102–104, (1971) 160, countered by Schuller, *Herrschaft* 214.

[43] *IG* I³ 21.50; 33.4–5; 34.28–29, 35–36, 70–71; 41.88–90, 115; 55.6–10, 21–22; 58.15; 68.47–48; 71.27–28, 44, 49–50; 82.28; 236.6–11.

of the nominative.[44] The phrase αὔτικα μάλα is common enough not to raise strong objections, but it is noteworthy that it is never used of a judicial procedure elsewhere in imperial lawmaking, barring our acceptance of its restoration below in section viii.3 of the Coinage Decree (a conclusion not to be encouraged). The phrase τὸς ἐδικεκότας appears inapposite in a legal context, as its only other appearance in an Attic decree is in a rhetorical passage in Khremonides' decree of 266/5 (*IG* II^2 687.32). Here it may have the added disadvantage of implying that these malefactors might be drawn from outside the ranks of the Hellenotamiai. Perfect participles are rare in Attic decrees of the fifth century (cf. *IG* I^3 476.177), although their use gradually becomes more common thereafter.

I suggest a different approach toward restoration, one based on the recognition that there is too little space here for a full outlining of or even complete reference to any legal procedure (note also the absence of any time reference). That may indicate that the procedure cited here had already been described in an earlier, lost section of the decree. A likely form of the verb is ἐσα[γόντον, since it is so well attested (*IG* I^3 21.50; 34.35, 70; 41.115; 82.28; restored in 41.90; 58.15; 68.47–48; 71.49; 117.14; 236.6). Moreover, the restoration ἐσ[αγαγόντων is widely accepted in section viii.4 of the decree, and acceptance of that restoration strengthens the case for reading the related term here. Various boards are possible for the officials directed to bring these cases, but I opt for a board of ἐσαγογε͂ς. Note that these would not be the *Eisagōgeis* known from the fourth century, who do not appear to have had any direct continuity with their fifth-century predecessors (cf. *Ath. Pol.* 52.2; Pollux 8.101; Dem. 37.33–34).[45]

Rather their kinship would lie with the *Eisagōgeis* that are known from the decree organizing reassessment of the allies in 425/4 (*IG* I^3 71). In line 7, provision seems to be made for empaneling thirty *Eisagōgeis*: κυαμεῦσαι δὲ ἐ]σαγογέα[ς τριάκοντα. These men are to oversee adjudication of cases concerning tribute: τõν δὲ διαδικασιõν *h*οι] ἐ̣σ̣[α]γ[ογε͂ς ἐπ]ι̣μ̣ε̣[λεθέντον τõ φόρο καθάπερ ἂν φσε]|φίσεται *h*ο [δε͂μος: ἐσαγογέον δὲ *h*ο λα]χὸ̣ν κα[ὶ *h*]ο πολέμαρ[χος ἀνακρινάντον τὰς δίκας ἐν τ]|ε͂ι ἐλιαίαι [καθάπερ τὰς δίκας τὰς ἄλ]λας τõ[ν ἐ]λιαστõν (12–14). A comparable jurisdiction has been suggested for a similar board which a restoration (accepted by the editors of *ATL*, Meiggs-Lewis, and *IG* I^3) posited for

44 For τõι βολομένοι: *IG* I^3 34.34–35; the context is lost in 14.8; τὸν βολόμενον: *IG* I^3 64.5–6; 68.45–47 (restored). The use of *ho* βουλόμε[νος in *IG* I^3 41.61, where the context is lost, may not be judicial.

45 See, in general, Rhodes, *CAAP* 582–83.

the Kleinias Decree: ἐσαγόντον δὲ *h*οι | [ἐσαγογε̃ς ἐς τὲν ἑλιαίαν τὸς 'Αθε]ναίοις τὸμ φόρον | [ὀφέλοντας *h*εχσε̃ς κατὰ τὸμ πίνα]κα τε̃ς μενύσεος (*IG* I^3 34.70–72). For the predicate of the verb, the phrase τὰς δίκας or τὲν δίκεν might be conjectured, as they seem to assume that role elsewhere.[46]

If this hypothesis is correct, the appointment of Eisagōgeis along with the appearance of the Hellenotamiai would indicate that the process outlined in these sections of the Coinage Decree was akin to or associated with tribute system. The Eisagōgeis would probably have had other duties in prosecuting improprieties earlier in the process of collection of these monies; it might not have been worthwhile to create them merely to watch over registration practices.

The punishment on conviction of the Hellenotamiai by the Thesmothetai then follows. Segre and *IG* Suppl. XII give us ο]ἱ δὲ θεσμοθέ[τ]αι πε[ριζεμιοσά]ντον [μυρίασι (or χιλίασι) δραχμ]ᾶ⟨ι⟩σι *h*έκαστον.[47] An obvious problem here entails the misspelling of δραχμ]α⟨ῖ⟩σι or δραχμ]ε̃σι, which is complicated by the Aphytis fragment, making its first contribution, seeming to be at least a letter longer in both the lacunae here, if we follow the shorter line of *IG* I^3. In reaction, Erxleben offers the restoration ο]ἱ δὲ θεσμοθέ[τ]αι πε[ριζεμιοσά]ντον [φυγεῖ καὶ χρέμ]ασι ἕκαστον, where χρέμασι is hard to justify on account of its vagueness.[48] Segre raised the possibility of δραχμε̃σι μυρίασι (or χιλίασι), which he then rejected for its reversal of what he took to be a formula. Working from the restoration in *IG* I^3 59.45: . . . δραχμε̃σι χιλί]ασι *h*έκα̣[στος . . . , however, we cannot exclude a reversed order for the formula.

Yet this really does not get us out of difficulties, because the verb remains a *hapax legomenon* and verbs compounded with περι- are in any case rare in Attic official language. Moreover, we seem to be a letter too short for the Aphytis fragment (with a forty-one-letter line for the Kos fragment). The editors of *ATL* restore ο]ἱ δὲ θεσμοθέ[τ]αι πε[νθ' ἐμερο̃ν δό]ντον [δίκας τοῖς φέν]ασι *h*έκαστον, an alternative with considerable attraction if only because so many words beginning with πε- in Attic

[46] *IG* I^3 41.90–91: ἐσαγόντον τὲν δίκε]ν το̃ι αὐτο̃ι μενὶ *h*οι ναυτοδ[ί|και; 71.49: . . . περὶ] τ[ο]ύτο α̣[ἰεὶ δίκ]α̣ς [ἐσαγόντον . . .

[47] The problematical reading πε- in line 7 of the Kos fragment was supported by J. Hondius (see Segre 165 with note 1).

[48] Cf. Erxleben *AfP* (1969) 101–102, where the parallel of literary texts such as Thuc. 2.65.3, Plato *Laws* 721B, that intentionally simplify, is not probative, while *IG* I^3 96.7 with δέμευσιν χρέμ[άτον is not parallel, even if we accept the restoration. Erxleben would admit πρ- as a possible reading at the end of Kos line 7. He also raises, only to reject, προσζεμιοσάντον, noting Isoc. 1.33; Plato *Gorg.* 516D. The connotation 'add as punishment' or 'punish in addition' seems to invalidate that suggestion in any case.

inscriptions are in fact numerals. The term φένασι is paralleled by *IG* I^3 46.7 (*ho* φένας ē *ho* γραφσάμενος), but if this entails that *hέκαστον* be the direct object of φένασι and cannot be construed adverbially, the parallel is less alluring. This would an early example of elision of a numeral, and perhaps that may be taken as an argument against the restoration of *ATL*.[49] The supplement *h*ελλενοταμί]ασι (dative of reference or [dis]advantage?) would demand considerable reformulation. I could print here either the restoration of Segre or that of *ATL*, but not with confidence that there is not a better alternative.

ii. [οἱ] δὲ ἑλληνοταμ[ίαι τὰς τε πόλεις καὶ τὸ ἀργύριον II.1
ἀ]ναγραφόντων· ἐὰ[ν δὲ μὴ ὀρθῶς ἀναγράφωσι τὸ τῶν
π]όλεων
τινος, ἐσα[γόντων *h*οι ἐσαγογε͂ς τὰς δίκας ἐς τ]ὴν
ἡλιαίαν τὴν
τῶ[ν θεσμοθετῶν κατὰ τὸν νόμον· ο]ἱ δὲ θεσμοθέ[τ]αι
πε[νθ' ἡμερῶν δό]ντων [δίκας τοῖς φήν]ασι
ἕκαστον.

ii. The Hellenotamiai are to register both the cities and the money. If they should not register correctly the entry of any of the cities, let the *Eisagōgeis* introduce the cases to the Heliaia of the Thesmothetai in accordance with the law, and the Thesmothetai should conduct the cases in five days for those informing in each instance.

SECTION III

iii. ἐὰν δὲ [. . . .8–9. . . . τ]ῶν ἀρχόν[των ἐν τ]ῆσι πόλεσι μὴ III.1
ποιῆι κα[τὰ [. . . .8–9. . . .]μένα ἢ τῶν [πολι]τῶν ἢ τῶν ξένων,
[ἄτ]ιμ[ος ἔστω καὶ τὰ χρή]ματα δημόσια [ἔσ]τω καὶ
τῆς θεοῦ τ[ὸ ἐπιδέκατον].

The remaining content of this part of the decree suggests a widening of the enforcement of the psephism. Notice that with the restoration of the previous section by the editors of *ATL*, one should expect some idea of the penalities at this point. Substantial restoration goes back to Segre. Moreover, it is also possible that earlier, entirely lost, provisions of this legislation are protected against enfringement here; Segre compared

[49] See A.S. Henry, "The Dating of Fifth-Century Attic Inscriptions," *CSCA* 11 (1978) 75–108, esp. 93, 100–101.

a movement from specific magistrates to generalization in *IG* I^3 71.31–33.[50] Nevertheless, τῶν πολιτῶν and τῶν ξένων do not appear to be workable partitive genitives with τῶν ἀρχόντων, with the word order presenting a first problem. Significantly, ἄρχοντες . . . τῶν πολιτῶν cannot be an equivalent for ἄρχοντες (τῶν) Ἀθηναίων (cf. *IG* II^2 374.7–8; 502.17; *SEG* 16.60.7), nor could ξένων qualify allied officials, where . . . τῶν συμμάχων would be expected (as restored in *IG* I^3 72.11–12).[51] Seven letter substitutes for πολι]τῶν that could be plausibly juxtaposed with ξένων do not spring readily to mind, even after scanning electronically the 2,500+ appearances of -των and -τον in *IG* I^3, fascicle 1.

These observations force us back on difficult recourses like Erxleben's introduction of ἒ (ἤ) before τõν ἀρχόντον.[52] Yet the separation of the other two genitives is made still more unpalatable by this device. Moreover, the need to drop the same conjunction to fit the emendation into the lacuna of the Aphytis fragment trivializes the restoration. Another suggestion is *ATL*'s idiosyncratic insertion of ἔχσο (without τις: ἄλλος ἔχσο τõν ἀρχόντον). A third possibility is Mattingly's ἐὰν δὲ [τίς πο πλὲν], which is also unparalleled, but not quite as farfetched as *ATL*'s suggestion.[53] That wording, however, would imply that the archons in the cities were themselves authorized to act against the decreed provisions, because πλήν is only used in official terminology to denote a category of behavior that is genuinely excluded from the authorized activities or jurisdiction of another group; in other words, it is not merely utilized to describe another group of individuals without defining a real distinction in their authority.[54] Both these options seem to damage

[50] *IG* I^3 71.31–33: καὶ] ἐάν τις ἄλλος δι[δõι φσε̃φον τε̃]ṣι [πόλεσι μ]ὲ ἔναι τ|[ὰς] τάχσ[ες κατὰ Π]ạ[ναθένα]ια τὰ ṃ[εγάλα] ἐπὶ ṭε̃ς πρυτανεί[ας *h*έτις ἂν πρ]ότẹ [πρυ-τα]νεύει ἄτ|[ι]μος ἔσ[το καὶ] τὰ χ[ρέματα] αὐτõ δ[εμόσι]α ἔσ[τ]ο καὶ τε̃ς θεõ [τὸ ἐπιδέκατ]ọν·.

[51] *IG* I^3 72.11–12: ὅπος δ' ἂμ μὲ ἀ[δικε̃τ]αι ṃ[εδεὶς μέτε ὑπ' ἰδιότο μέτε ὑπ' ἄρχοντος Ἀθεναίον ἒ τõν χσυμμάχον] | [τ]õ[ν Ἀθε]ναίον . . . The usage of ξένος in surviving inscriptions amplifies the point: they are never foreigners in their role as allies. Note *IG* I^3 40.52–54: τὸς δ|ὲ χσένος τὸς ἐν Χαλκίδι, *h*όσοι οἰκõντες | μὲ τελõσιν Ἀθέναζε . . ., for which see Figueira, *Colonization* 258; also *IG* I^3 58.23–24: μὲ δέχεσθαι δὲ μεδέν]α χσένον ἐχσέστο ἐ[ς τὰς ο|ἰκίας μέτε *h*ικέτεν μεδένα μέτε αὐτό]μολον ἒ ἐνέχεσ[θαι . . .; and *IG* I^3 138.3–4: τὸς τοχσότας τός τε ἀστ[ὸς καὶ τὸς χσένος τρ]|ε̃ς ὀβο⟨λ⟩ὸς τõ ἐνια[υτ]õ ἀπὸ τõ[ν καθ' ἑκάστος μισθõν]. Cf. *IG* I^3 47B.16.

[52] Erxleben *AfP* (1969) 104–105. The comparison from *FD* 3.2 139.3–5 is inapposite: ἐὰν | δέ τις τῶν ἐν ταῖς πόλεσιν οἰκούντ[ων], ἢ ξένος ἢ πολίτης ἢ δοῦλος, ἀνὴρ | ἢ γυνή. . . . The incongruous juxtaposition of Athenian *arkhontes* with foreign citizens and noncitizens is not hereby obviated.

[53] Mattingly *Klio* (1977) 86.

[54] The following fifth-century example is typical: *IG* I^3 6C.24–26: [ἀτελε̃ μ]ύστεμ μὲ ἐν[εῖναι μυε̃|ν μεδέ]νạ π̣λὲν τõ ἀφ' [ἑστίας μυ|ομέν]ο. . . See also *IG* I^3 40.71–74:

the phraseological parallelism between this clause and the beginning of section iv that is based on a juxtaposition of Athenian *arkhontes* and allied *arkhontes*. That parallel permits the framer to abbreviate the punishment procedure in section iv.3–4, while another abbreviation is possible in the phrase with κατὰ. . . .

One could always opt for seeing τῶν πολιτῶν ἢ τῶν ξένων as parallel genitives, adding additional categories out of which transgressors might come, although this makes for a rather paratactic phrasing. The "archons in the cities" might need to be understood as local (not hegemonic) officials, although that creates complications for the next section.[55] Still, while the genitives could remain partitive in function, their separation from τις is still marked. Moreover, if we must have a reference here to private citizens, one would really expect ἰδιωτῶν. The absence of this concept is troubling.[56]

The length of the respective lacunae in the Kos and Aphytis inscriptions is another disturbing factor. Aphytis has room for eight letters, but the Kos fragment has room for eight or nine letters, depending on whether we restore a line length for Kos line 8 of forty letters (a consistent feature of *IG* I^3) as Segre originally held, or forty-one letters (the view of the editors of *ATL*). If the variable length lacunae must be conceded, then the restoration would have to become something like *h*οστισοῦν 'anyone whatsoever' for the Kos fragment and ὁστισοῦν for the Aphytis fragment. Although the word is not attested in Athenian official terminology, its usage in the Lysian corpus advises us that it is, at least, a possibility here.[57] The employment of the term in Plato is also helpful in providing some passages where ὁστισοῦν appears in the protasis of conditional sentences. *Laws* 869E gives us an instance that indicates its use in a legal context: ἐὰν ὁστισοῦν ὁτῳοῦν ἀφιῇ τοῦτο ἑκών, ὡς ἀκουσίου

. . . τὰς δὲ εὐθύνας Χαλκιδεῦσι κατ|ὰ σφõν αὐτõν ἔναι ἐν Χαλκίδι καθάπερ Ἀθ|ένεσιν Ἀθεναίοις πλὲν φυγε̃ς καὶ θανάτ|ο καὶ ἀτιμίας.

55 Cf. H. Leppin, "Die ΑΡΧΟΝΤΕΣ ΕΝ ΤΑΙΣ ΠΟΛΕΣΙ des delisch-attischen Seebundes," *Historia* 41 (1992) 257–71, who argues that the *arkhontes* here and in *IG* I^3 34 are local officials.

56 *IG* I^3 40.5–7: οὐδὲ τὲν πόλιν ἀνά|στατον ποέσο οὐδὲ ἰδιότεν οὐδένα ἀτιμ|όσο οὐδε φυγε̃ι ζεμίοσο . . .; 40.11–12: οὐτὲ κατὰ τõ κοινõ οὐτὲ κατὰ ἰδιότο οὐδ|ὲ ἑνός . . .; 101.52–53: [κα]ὶ *h*όπος ἂμ μ[ὲ ἀδικõνται μεδὲν μέτ]|ε ὑπὸ ἰδιότο μέτε ὑπὸ κοινõ πόλεος . . .; 118.22–25: ὅσα δὲ ἄ]λλα χσυμβόλαια πρὸ τõ ἐν τοῖς ἰ|[διόταις πρ]ὸς τὸς ἰδιότας ἒ ἰδιώτει πρὸς τὸ κ|[οινὸν ἒ κο]ινõι πρὸς ἰδιότεν *vacat* ἒ ἐάν τι ἄλλο γίγ|[νεται, δια]λ̣υεμ π[ρ]ὸς ἀλλέλος. . . . Cf., for other examples, *IG* I^3 102.47; 210.2; 236.7. As is so often the case, the restoration of another document can point up our predicament. Note *IG* I^3 63.1–3 as restored: ἐὰν δέ τις] | [ἒ] ἄρχ[ον ἒ ἰδιότες εἴπει ἒ ἐπιφσεφίσει παρὰ τ]|όδε τὸ φ[σέφισμ]α . . .; cf. 72.11–12.

57 Lys. 4.19; 19.13, 42; 31.19.

γεγονότος τοῦ φόνου, οἵ τε καθαρμοὶ γιγνέσθωσαν τῷ δράσαντι καὶ ἐνιαυτὸς εἷς ἔστω τῆς ἐκδημίας ἐν νομῷ.[58] Nonetheless, the very fact that the indefinite pronoun ὁστισοῦν would be followed in the restoration by a genitive that defines the group out of which "no one at all" is noted could be said to constitute a contradiction in terms. As much as the general sense of the reference of this clause to Athenian officials might be conceded, certainty in the exact wording eludes us, unless we accept the shorter line of the *IG* I³ for the Kos fragment. The costs of that option, however, are felt elsewhere in the restoration of the decree.

Moreover, there is a problem in perspective here that the previous discussions such as those of Segre and *ATL* have not confronted. If there is truly a juxtaposition of *politai* and *xenoi*, then the two categories cannot be equated with Athenians and allies.[59] Rather *politai* and *xenoi* must be understood from the vantage point of an Athenian legislator looking at an allied city from outside, from Attica. In that case, *politai* become the citizens of the allied state in which the *arkhontes* are resident and the word *xenoi* becomes a denomination for the citizens of still other states.[60] They could, however, scarcely be Athenians. Although *politai* and *xenoi* would be unusual in this usage, we must inquire what the framer's practical alternatives could have been. Clearly, *summakhoi* would not be an appropriate designation for the officials or citizens of an allied government interacting (for want of a more precise word) with other individuals or another state on its own behalf, for it is possible that the *xenoi* with whom they were dealing were also *summakhoi* themselves from the perspective of the hegemonic government in Attica. Thus, one conclusion would remain that the officials of allied cities and any foreign officials are hereby barred from contravening the terms of the decree. Another option would be that the *politai* and *xenoi* are separate categories, two classes of nonofficials.

Nonetheless, it would be preferable to have section iii refer through some formulation to Athenian imperial officials, allowing a contrast with the content of section iv.[61] An alternative that helps us toward that

[58] See also *Laws* 935C: ἐὰν δέ τις ἐν ἄλλοις τόποις λοιδορίας ἄρχων ἢ ἀμυνόμενος ὁστισοῦν μὴ ἀπέχηται τῶν τοιούτων λόγων. . . . Cf. *Euthyph.* 5E; *Charm.* 170E; *Hipp. Ma.* 298D; *Rep.* 350A.

[59] Cf. P. Gauthier, "Les XENOI dans les textes athéniens de la seconde moitié du Ve siècle av. J.-C.," *REG* 84 (1971) 44–79, esp. 55–56.

[60] Note D. Whitehead, "*IG* I² 39: 'Aliens' in Chalcis and Athenian Imperialism," *ZPE* 21 (1976) 251–59, esp. 254, 258.

[61] Cf. *IG* I³ 34.6–7: . . . ἄρχ[οντας ἐν] τε͂σ|ι πόλεσι καὶ τὸς [ἐπισκό]πος. . . . Contrast also *IG* I³ 76.10–11: . . . 'Αθεναίον μὲν τὲν βο[λὲν καὶ τὸς στρατεγὸς] κα[ὶ τὸς λοιπὸς ἄρ]|χοντας τὸς ἐ[ν ταῖς πόλεσι ταῖς Βοτ]τια[ίον. Note also *IG* I³ 156.5–8: ἐν δὲ

result would be to construe the genitives with the participle -μενα, which makes discovering a valid parallel rather more difficult. This would entail jettisoning the commonly accepted ἐψηφισμένα. The term appears on fifth-century inscriptions, but the associated phraseology is not precisely parallel (cf., for example, *IG* I[3] 10.20–21; 84.18). That ἐψηφισμένα could be construed with the following genitives seems impossible on almost any understanding. Furthermore, the use of ἐψηφισμένα and possibly ὅσα ἐν τõι] φσεφίσματι in close proximity to convey exactly the same idea is also a little disconcerting. There is in addition the problem that the forty-letter line of *IG* I[3] forces Lewis to suggest hesitantly that the ἔ after -μενα in the Aphytis fragment must have been left out (accidently?) in the Kos fragment. Some device like that must be found for line 10 of the Kos fragment, if the inscription is forty-letter stoichedon throughout. Another option would be to accept ἐψηφισμένα in line 10 with ὅσα ἐν τõι] φσεφίσματι in line 13, allowing nearby discrepancies in the treatment of the *psi*.

The participial phrase τὰ χσυγκείμενα/ξυγκείμενα/συγκείμενα 'compacts' or 'agreements' might be preferable to τὰ ἐφσεφισμένα, since it can also be paralleled from fifth-century documents.[62] The phrase κατὰ τὰ ξυγκείμενα appears in Thucydides and Xenophon in diplomatic language for shorthand references to the terms established by previous, valid interstate agreements.[63] Unfortunately, neither in official epigraphy nor in fifth-century literary documents are there parallels where one speaks of not acting κατὰ 'in accordance with' τὰ συγκείμενα any more than anyone ποιεῖ 'acts' not concordantly with τὰ ἐψηφισμένα in extant contexts (cf., however, *IG* I[3] 40.49). An interesting parallel, however, is offered by Thuc. 5.25.2: καὶ ἅμα καὶ τοῖς 'Αθηναίοις οἱ Λακεδαιμόνιοι προϊόντος τοῦ χρόνου ὕποπτοι ἐγένοντο, ἔστιν ἐν οἷς οὐ ποιοῦντες

τε̃σι ἄλλεσι πόλεσι *h*ο|ίτινες 'Αθεναίον ἄρχοσι ἐν τ|ε̃ι *h*υπερορίαι *h*ό τι ἂν *h*έκασ|τοι δυνατοὶ ὄ̃σιν. . . . See also *IG* I[3] 21.4–6 (res.): *h*αιρε̃σθαι δ]ὲ πέντε ἄν[δρας τὸν δε̃μον ἐχς *h*απ|άντον α]ὐτίκα μάλα ὑ̔πὲρ πεντέκοντα ἔτε] γεγονότ[ας, ἐχσομοσίαν δὲ μὲ ἔ̃να|ι αὐτοῖς μ]εδὲ ἀνθ⟨α⟩ι[ρεσιν, τούτος δὲ ἄρ]χεν . . .; line 31: . . . πρὸς [τὸς ἄρχοντας . . .; line 45: . . . *h*]οι ἄρχοντες *h*οι 'Αθενα[ίον . . .; *IG* I[3] 62.5–8. Note also Thuc. 1.115.5; [Xen.] *Ath. Pol.* 1.19, cf. 1.14. An overview is provided by J.M. Balcer, "Imperial Officials in the Athenian Empire," *Historia* 25 (1976) 257–87. See also pp. 388–90 below.

[62] Note *IG* I[3] 38.5: χσυνκείμε[να . . .; 75.27–30: ὄ̃μ[οσ|αν δ'] αὐτοῖς 'Α[θεναίον *h*ε βολὲ καὶ *h*οι σ]τ̣ρατεγοὶ ἐμμε|[νε̃ν ἐ]ν ταῖς χσυνθ[έ]χ̣[αις *h*ὰς χσυνέθεντ]ο πρὸς *h*αλιᾶς | [*h*οι ἐπ]ὶ τὰ χσυγκε[ίμενα; 76.12–15: ἀμυνõ τοῖς] Βοττι[αίοις τοῖς] | χσυντιθεμέ[νοι]ς [τὲν χσυμμαχίαν, κ]αὶ τὲν χσ[υμμαχία]|ν πιστõς καὶ [ἀδ]όλο[ς φυλάχσο Βοττι]αίοις προ[θυμόμε|ν]ος κατὰ τὰ χ[συ]νκε[ίμενα; cf. *IG* I[3] 12.2–4: 'Αθεναίοις | καὶ *h*αλι]κυαίοις 'Ελ[ύμοις φιλίαν καὶ χσυμμαχίαν εἶναι κατὰ τὰ χσυ|γκείμεν]α τὰ πρὸς 'Αθ[εναίος *h*ὰ 'Εγεσταίοις ἐστίν.

[63] Thuc. 3.70.2; 5.47.8; 8.58.5; cf. 4.68.5; Xen. *Anab.* 7.2.7.

ἐκ τῶν ξυγκειμένων ἃ εἴρητο. The option of χσυγκείμενα, however, cannot avoid a certain clumsiness in understanding the succeeding genitives, which we would have to stretch to interpret as subjective genitives, with the passive σύγκειμαι understood to imply necessarily the active συντίθημι (see the references in note 62 above). Another attraction of this approach is that it strengthens the parallelism of sections iii and iv, while avoiding the difficulty of having the Athenians threaten severe punishment of *xenoi* so unconditionally, some of whom might have been nonallies. To accommodate the shorter (forty-letter) line of *IG* I³ one would need to restore συγκείμενα, but that is no worse than the other alternatives at the very least.

Such a reconstruction would interestingly imply that the actions of Athenian officials *in individual allied cities* were to be in accord with prior agreements, whether they be of allies with Athenians, or of allies with third parties (that is, *xenoi* for the purposes here), or perhaps even of *xenoi* with the Athenians. It is open then to envisage that the exchange of monies and consolidation of standards mandated by the decree could impinge on the conditions of the local administration and the local economy in ways about which it was impossible to generalize. While the Athenians were determined to have the provisions of the decree implemented, they refused to hand a carte blanche to their officials to supersede other agreements. If we see the Coinage Decree as necessarily intrusive, this clause may enjoin upon Athenian administrators that they attempt to apply it conservatively.

The stringent punishments are straightforward and can be readily paralleled: *atimia* and confiscation of property with a tithe (probably) to Athena.[64] If this clause of the law could be restricted to Athenian officials, another feature would be added to the portrayal of the decree as primarily focused on policing Athenian officeholders. The varying available space, however, in the Kos and Aphytis fragments should also be observed. The Kos fragment has room for two or three extra letters in the phrases ἄτιμος ἔστω καὶ τὰ χρή]ματα δημόσι[α ἔστω, a problem that Segre solved by providing τὰ δὲ χρέματα αὐτõ δε]μόσια [ἔσ]το. The word αὐτõ in this formula creates no difficulty as it is attested more often than not, as in *IG* I³ 14.33, 21.28, 40.34, and 71.33, but δὲ rather than καὶ runs quite

[64] Note Koch, *Volksbeschlüsse* 385–89. For the tithe, note Robinson *AJP* (1935) 152. Cf. *IG* I³ 40.32–36: ὀμόσαι δὲ Χαλκιδέον τὸς *h*εβõντ|ας *h*άπαντας· *h*ὸς δ' ἂμ μὲ ὀμόσει, ἄτιμον αὐτ|ὸν ἔναι καὶ τὰ χρέματα αὐτõ δεμόσια καὶ | τõ Διὸς τõ 'Ολυμπίο τὸ ἐπιδέκατον *h*ιερὸ|ν ἔστο τõν χρέματον; 71.32–33: ἄτ|[ι]μος ἔσ[το καὶ] τὰ χ[ρέματα] αὐτõ δ[εμόσι]α ἔσ[τ]ο καὶ τε̃ς θεõ [τὸ ἐπιδέκατ]ọν . . .; cf. 14.33; 21.27–28; 46.27–29; 89.54.

counter to our expectation on the linkage of clauses.[65] Mattingly suggests καὶ τὰ χρέματα αὐτõ δε]μόσια [ἔσ]το, in which -αι of καὶ occupies a single *stoichos*.[66] Lewis in *IG* I^3 suggests the phrase καὶ χρέματα αὐτõ δε]μόσια . . . appeared on the stone as an error in inscribing. Another alternative, which would lack a good comparandum—perforce, given the lack of parallel Attic and Ionic texts—would be to add a particle to the Kos restoration that might have been absent on the Aphytis fragment, like καὶ τὰ μὲν χρέματα δε]μόσια [ἔσ]το (cf. *IG* I^3 40.58; 89.16).

It is important to observe that the appearance of Athenian *arkhontes* in the allied cities here ought not to stimulate overgeneralization.[67] It is clear that such officials must have existed in some numbers so as to make such an instruction necessary in our decree. That would be consonant with *Ath. Pol.* 24.3 with its ἀρχαὶ . . . ὑπερόριοι δ' εἰς ἑπτακόσιους.[68] Given the number of allied cities and the tendency of the Athenians to appoint panels to discharge supervisory functions that were in principle dischargeable by a single person, a total of seven hundred would not allow an *arkhon* in every city. There is no certainty, moreover, that all those included as archons in the count of seven hundred will have been "governors,"[69] since it is possible to envisage that any Athenian official, a *phrourarkhos* or an *episkopos*, for example, might be included in a general category such as *arkhontes*.[70]

The brunt of local administration by Athenians might be carried by *arkhontes* established relatively permanently in some allied cities, but it is possible that *stratēgoi* and *episkopoi*, who would not have been local fixtures, needed to be envisaged here as well. The previous section is after all involved with the specific and perhaps most obvious delict of the Hellenotamiai in their failure to carry through the registration properly, and that leaves a wealth of other contingencies about the collection and the conveyance of foreign money to be covered in general terms here. It will also be argued shortly that the Athenian *arkhontes* in this section are balanced by local *arkhontes* in section iv. The conclusion that most

[65] *IG* I^3, p. 894.

[66] See Mattingly *Klio* (1977) 86, who also notes correctly the status of the phrase as the regular formula. The fourteen-letter lacuna of *IG* I^3 would suggest a two-letter word as a minor difference between the Kos and Aphytis fragments.

[67] Note Meiggs 223; Schuller, *Herrschaft* 45–48; cf. Leppin *Historia* (1992) 269–71.

[68] The number is questionable and was possibly repeated from the number of officials at home that are noted immediately before. See Rhodes *CAAP* 305.

[69] That is, *arkhontes* who exercised executive and judicial functions in place of, along with, or advisory to local officials.

[70] Compare Erxleben *AJP* (1969) 105–106.

allied cities had Athenians in residence serving as *arkhontes* exceeds the evidence contained in this clause of the Coinage Decree.[71]

A more recent discovery can also be introduced at this point in our investigation, namely, an inscription found in the excavation of sanctuary of Apollo Smintheios at Gülpinar that mentions the community of Hamaxitos, the Hellenotamiai, and Thesmothetai (*SEG* 38.1251 = *IG* I^3 1454*ter*).[72]

[.]χ̣ο̣ι̣▨ε̣[---
οἱ δὲ ἑλλε̣[νοταμίαι-------------. ε-]
ὰν δὲ τις Ἁμ̣[αξιτῶν----------οἱ ἑλλ-]
ε̣νοταμ̣ί̣α̣ι̣ [--------------------]
[.]η θεσμ̣οθέτ̣[αι-----------------]
[.] δὲ τις τον ἀ[λλον?-------------]
[.] δὲ [τις] τον [-----------------]
[.] δε [-----------------------]
[. . . . . .]νο[--------------------]

Some features reveal the inscription as bearing legislation of the fifth-century *arkhē*, either an agreement between Hamaxitos and Athens, an Attic instruction for that ally, or a general imperial decree.[73] The Hellenotamiai appear along with the Thesmothetai who are probably expected to see to the adjudication of charges that may envisaged in the protasis of lines 2–3 and perhaps in the indefinite subject τις that may stand in an alternative protasis in line 6.

The first editor, E. Schwertheim, noted the similarity of the appearance of these items to their instance in the Coinage Decree (for him the "Klearchos Dekret"). On this basis, H.B. Mattingly has identified this inscription as another fragment of the Coinage Decree.[74] He notes that if one gives the Hamaxitos Decree a line length of 53 letters, Kos lines 4–10 matches up with Hamaxitos 2–9 in their surviving letters. Naturally, this result is the product of an arbitrary assignment of line length and a function of the fragmentary character of the two inscriptions. Moreover, we are confronted with a choice whether to aim for incorporating the

[71] See *HCT* 1.380–84. Cf. Schuller, *Herrschaft* 45–46. We ought also not generalize from this provision to erect the theory of the subsidiary character of allied officials. Naturally, the first priority of the Athenians is to order their own officials before resorting to injunctions for allied magistrates. Cf. Schuller, *Herrschaft* 127.

[72] E. Schwertheim, "Ein Dekretfragment aus dem 5. Jh. v. Chr. aus Hamaxitus," *Araştirma Sonuçlari Toplantisi* 6 (1988) 283–85. For the sanctuary and Hamaxitos, see J.M. Cook, *The Troad: An Archaeological and Topographical Study* (Oxford 1973) 226–35.

[73] See Lewis *CR* (1993) 208.

[74] Mattingly *Klio* (1993) 99–100; Vickers *JHS* (1996) 171–74, esp. 172.

smaller Syme fragment at the beginning of the Kos fragment or to employ this document in the same role. The options are irreconcilable.

The two documents begin diverging in section iii.1 where the Hamaxitos protasis is shorter; the Hamaxitos decree line 7 seems to offer still another protasis that must come long before the next conditional clause in the composite decree that opens section iv.1. As previous editors (including the earlier work of Mattingly) have restored section ii, it is some deficiency of the Hellenotamiai that is the issue. In the Hamaxitos decree, as the first editor suggested, it is likely that an improper act by a citizen of this allied state is provided against (Ἀμαξιτῶν, *pace* Hermann in *SEG* 38.1251). Given the findspot of the document, the ethnic here is prima facie likely as anything else. While we could perhaps bring ourselves to believe that subsequent versions of the Coinage Decree might have individualized its provisions for new allies, this specific change in perspective is much harder to justify. Unless some further evidence appears, this inscription should not be classed with the fragments of the Coinage Decree.

Hamaxitos was one of the Aktaian cities that had been dependencies of Mytilene but had been removed from Lesbian control after the suppression of the great revolt of 427 (Thuc. 3.50.3). Hence the city appears in the assessments of 425 (4T: *IG* I[3] 71.III.129), and of 421 (*IG* I[3] 77.IV.18). Since the erection of this inscription should therefore date after 427, it can be of no help in a chronology for the Coinage Decree, despite its four-barred *sigma*. The stipulation that allies were to erect copies of the Coinage Decree in their marketplace might have urged inscription of the decree after the Mytilenean hegemony, if we could be comfortable with the discovery of this inscription in a sanctuary of Apollo. Hamaxitos was a very poor candidate during the 420s for violating the prohibition on minting silver or any other stipulation of Attic monetary legislation. In the unlikely event that the document turns out to be another fragment of the Coinage Decree, it would speak to the continued validity of this legislation and not its initial promulgation.

iii. ἐὰν δέ [τις ἄλλος τ]ῶν ἀρχόν[των ἐν τ]ῆσι πόλεσι μὴ III.1
ποιῆι κα[τὰ τὰ συγκεί]μενα ἢ τῶν [πολι]τῶν ἢ τῶν ξένων,
[ἄτ]ιμ[ος ἔστω καὶ τὰ χρή]ματα δημόσια [ἔσ]τω καὶ
τῆς θεõ τ[ὸ ἐπιδέκατον].

iii. If some other one of the archons in the cities not act in accordance with the engagements either with the citizens or with the foreigners, let him be deprived of civic rights and let his property be exappropriated and a tithe belong to the goddess.

SECTION IV

iv. [καὶ εἰ μ]ὴ εἰσι ἄρχοντες Ἀθηναίων, ἐ[πι . . . . . 13–14 . . . . . IV.1
ἐν τῶι] ψηφίσματι οἱ ἄρχοντε[ς οἱ ἑκάστης τῆς πόλεως· καὶ]
ἐὰμ μὴ ποιῶσι κατὰ τ[ὰ . . . . 23–24 . . . .]όντων
τούτων περὶ ἀτ[. . . . . . . 18–19 . . . .

This section presents the subsequent provision for enforcement, containing in line 1 a provision establishing responsibility in the absence of Athenian officers. Segre suggested (to general acceptance) ἐ]πιτελεσάντον *h*όσα ἐν τõι φσε]φίσματι for the Kos fragment in its line 13 and ἐπιτελεσάντων ὅσα ἐν τῶι] ψηφίσματι for the Aphytis fragment in its line 6 (lines 1–2 in our composite) as a description of the action of the allied magistrates. The restoration of the Kos fragment here exceeds the restoration of Aphytis by a letter. Segre included the extra letter while opting for lengths of forty-one letters for Kos lines 13 and 14. Yet, the *IG* I^3 has forty letters for 13 and 14.

The Kos fragment according to Segre:

. . . ἄτ]ι̣μ̣[ος ἔ] 11
[στο . . . . . . 15 . . . . . . δε]μόσια [ἔσ]το καὶ τε͂ς θεõ τ[ὸ]
[ἐπιδέκατον καὶ εἰ μή εἰσι] ἄρχοντες Ἀθεναίον, ἐ[πιτ]-
[. . . . . 13 . . . . . ἐν τõι φσε]φ̣ί̣σ̣ματι *h*οι ἄρχοντε[ς *ho*]-
[ι *h*εκάστες τε͂ς πόλεος· . . . 15

The Kos fragment according to *ATL*:

. . . ἄτ]ι̣μ̣[ος ἔ] 11
[στο . . . . . . 15 . . . . . . δε]μόσια [ἔσ]το καὶ τε͂ς θεõ τ[ὸ ἐ]-
[πιδέκατον καὶ εἰ μή εἰσιν] ἄρχοντες Ἀθεναίον, ἐ[πιτ]-
[. . . . . 13 . . . . . ἐν τõι φσε]φ̣ί̣σ̣ματι *h*οι ἄρχοντε[ς *ho*]-
[ι *h*εκάστες τε͂ς πόλεος· . . . 15

The Kos fragment according to *IG* I^3:

[ἔστο . . . . . . 14 . . . . . . δε]μόσια [ἔσ]το καὶ τε͂ς θεõ τ[ὸ] 11
[ἐπιδέκατον καὶ εἰ μή εἰσι] ἄρχοντες Ἀθεναίον, ἐ[πι]-
[. . . . . 13 . . . . . ἐν τõι φσε]φ̣ί̣σ̣ματι *h*οι ἄρχοντε[ς *h*]-
[οι ἑκάστες τε͂ς πόλεος· . . . 14

The Aphytis fragment:

[τῆς θεοῦ τὸ ἐπιδέκατον· καὶ εἰ μ]ὴ εἰσι ἄρχον[τες ᾿Αθην]- 5
[αίων, ἐπι ......13...... ἐν τωῖ] ψηφίσματι οἱ [ἄρχοντ]-
[ες οἱ ἑκάστης τῆς πόλεως·... 7

Notice how the editors of *ATL* have maintained forty-one letters in line 13 of the Kos fragment by adding a moveable *nu* to εἰσι, while Segre restored forty.

Nevertheless, there are doubts that can be raised concerning ἐπιτελέω in contexts such as these (see pp. 389–90 below). Attic officials are more often enjoined to "take care of" or "take management over" (ἐπιμελέομαι). The Aphytis fragment could be restored: ἐ[πιμελήθεντων τῶν ἐν τῶι] ψηφίσματι 'shall take care of the provisions of the decree' (also noted by Lewis in his apparatus).[75] The longer fourteen-letter lacuna of the Kos fragment, according to Segre and *ATL* provides a problem in restoration. Simple reformulations appear infeasible, so that some major change must be contemplated, like ἐπιμελόσθον τὸν ἐν τõιδε φσε]φίσματι or ἐ[πιμελέθεντον *h*όσον ἐν τõι ψε]φίσματι.[76]

The shorter line of *IG* I^3 has the direct result of making the lacunae in the Kos and Aphytis fragments the same length, suggesting the absence of compound letters or of an aspirate as in *h*όσα, unless the text diverges from its practice. The result of accepting the forty-letter length for lines 12–13 is that we could adopt essentially the same reading as first suggested for the Aphytis fragment: ἐ[πιμελέθεντον τõν ἐν τõι φσε]φίσματι 'should care of the provisions in the decree.'

It is noteworthy that the officials who were "archons in the cities" in the previous section, when they are implicitly differentiated from Athenian officeholders operating within Attica, become "archons of the Athenians" when seemingly juxtaposed with the "archons of each city" (if that restoration is indeed correct).[77] A slight variation between the treatment of the conjunction must also be posited: Kos line 14 (1453B): καὶ] ἐὰμ μὲ ποιõσι; Aphytis line 7 ἐὰν δὲ μ]ὴ ποιῶσι; but I do not believe that this variation is objectionable here. Line 3 of section iv could contain the same formula after κατὰ, which is represented in the previous section.

[75] This imperative is attested, either with the genitive, with ὅπως, or with both, on imperial inscriptions: *IG* I^3 37.22; 58.35; 71.12; 73.28. Note also *IG* II^2 2801.5 (if correctly restored): ... ἐπιμεληθέντων τῶν] κατὰ τὸ ψήφισμα [κεχειρο]τονημένων.

[76] The imperative ἐπιμελόσθον is common and unproblematical: *IG* I^3 21.42, 74; 39.6; 40.19–20, 44; 64.19–20; 72.12; 82.25; restorations in 71.45; 72.30; 82.41; 159.18; 173.4

[77] *IG* I^3 1453B reads ἑκάστες in line 14 of the Kos fragment, while Segre and the *ATL* printed an aspirate as elsewhere in the inscription. The absent aspirate allows *IG* I^3 to maintain the same emendation.

Note that most editors can restore the Kos and the Aphytis fragments in the same way through the variant spellings of ἐφσεφισμένα (Kos) and ἐψηφισμένα (Aphytis). The text of *IG* I^3 has a thirteen-letter restoration after the participle in the Kos fragment (line 15) and a fourteen-letter restoration in Aphytis line 8, unless we relinquish ἐψηφισμένα in favor of a word of the same length for both Kos and Aphytis fragments.

Segre's conjecture for lines iv.3–4 was ἔστο κατὰ τõν ἀρχ[οντον τούτον περὶ ἀτιμίας δίοχσις 'Αθένεσι. Once again, it is likely that we should supplement περὶ ἀτ[ιμίας in line 4 in order to restore a punishment of the loss of civil rights.[78] The phrase περὶ ἀτ[ιμίας δίοχσις 'Αθένεσι is framed on the analogy of the action against local officials in the Erythrai Decree (*IG* I^3 14.11–12: δίοχσιν δ' ἔναι [κατ|ὰ τ]õ[ν] ἐλεχθέν[τ]ο[ν].[79] These restorations were accepted by the editors of *ATL* and by Hiller in *IG* XII Suppl., p. 215. In the traditional view, the Ionic Aphytis inscription is a letter shorter here than the Attic Kos fragment, a fact that could be explained by their necessarily different treatments of the word δίοχσις/δίωξις.[80] Disregarding the merits of the precise wording, the placement of a disciplinary process here is fairly apparent. Notice that as these are probably allied officials, the specification of their trial at Athens was necessary.

iv. [καὶ εἰ μ]ή εἰσι ἄρχοντες 'Αθηναίων, ἐ[πιμελήθεντων τῶν IV.1
ἐν τῶι] ψηφίσματι οἱ ἄρχοντε[ς οἱ ἑκάστης τῆς πόλεως· καὶ]
ἐὰμ μὴ ποιῶσι κατὰ τ[ὰ ξυγκείμενα?, ἔστω κατὰ τῶν ἀρχ]όντων
τούτων περὶ ἀτ[ιμίας δίοξις 'Αθήνησι·

iv. And if there are no officials of the Athenians, let the officials of each city take care for the provisions of the decree; and if they do not act in accordance with the engagements?,

[78] Robinson *AJP* (1935) 152, however, read the Aphytis text as . . . τούτομ περὶ ἅς . . . but most have followed Segre's reading (p. 158). See Schuller, *Herrschaft* 49, for the place of this provision among the testimonia attesting to the superior jurisdiction of Athenian courts.

[79] Koch, *Volksbeschlüsse* 389–91, suggests . . .]οντων τούτων περὶ ἄτ[ιμοι ὄντων καθ' ἑαυτοῦ. That may have the advantage of putting the threat of punishment in the imperative. Yet, . . . τούτων περὶ. . . seems rather unlikely in an official document.

[80] It is, once again, a corollary of the forty-letter line adopted by the *IG* I^3 that the lacunae in the Aphytis and Kos fragments become the same length. That seems to rule out anything like δίωξις that will have different Attic and Ionic lengths. An alternative restoration, having much the same import, would be as follows: . . . ἔναι κατὰ τῶν ἀρχ[όντων τούτων περὶ ἀτ[ιμίας γραφὰς 'Αθήνησι. See *IG* I^3 34.42–43; *SEG* 17.19.4–6; cf. *IG* I^3 19.11–12.

> let there be a prosecution against these officials at Athens involving loss of civil rights.

What I have chosen to dub Part I of the decree seems to outline a process in which registers were to be conveyed to Athens and the Hellenotamiai were to receive and register something, presumably funds received from the allies. In the surviving evidence we enter on only the tail end of this movement of funds. Sections ii–iv deal with the enforcement of this process, starting with a measure aimed at ensuring that the Hellenotamiai carry out their registration properly. Then there is a shift designed to cover eventualities where other phases of the process have not been conducted appropriately. I argue that the change in focus back to the allied cities is significant, because it gives us a glimpse into an earlier stage of the movement of funds, when the activity was taking place in allied cities and there was a danger that other conditions of administration and trade might be affected by the collection of the funds. At this stage of the decree, the Athenians were establishing the maximum penalty for malfeasance by their *arkhontes*, although in my view it is unclear whether only the stipulations of the decree or a wider range of agreements were being protected. Secondary responsibility falls to allied officials who are also to submit to punishment if they fail.

13
THE COINAGE DECREE: PART II

SECTION V

v. [ἐν δὲ τῶ]ι ἀργυροκοπίωι τό ἀργύ[ριον ....15–20......... V.1
.....μὴ ἔλ]αττον ἢ ἥμυσυ κὰι α[.............29.............
.....]ι αἱ πόλεις πρατт[..............28..............
δραχμὰς ἀπὸ τῆς μν[ᾶς·...........23...........
κατ]αλλάττεν ἢ ἐνόχο[υς ἔναι κατὰ τὸν νόμον]·

The part of the decree starting with section v shifts to a new subject, the coining of money by the Athenian mint and its conversion. Yet there is a bit of a surprise lurking for us here, inasmuch as our expectation that monies received from the allies are about to be minted is confounded. Arrangements are clearly being made about silver in the mint (v.1) and the proportion of not less than half is mentioned. There are two possible approaches to understanding this situation: either the money already collected must be received at the mint or the stock of bullion already at the mint is to be used.

How we shall proceed is conditioned by our basic assumptions about the conversion of assets under way here. If we judge that this operation, since it is localized in the mint—manifestly the Athenian mint—would probably draw on the silver stock of the mint (see immediately below), it will be most unlikely that any truly massive demonetization and conversion of currency is envisaged. In this view, the Athenians could not have made a massive replacement without drawing heavily on their and the alliance's reserves, and there is no evidence (within or without) to suggest that was done.[1] The amount of silver available in the mint could not possibly equal the money supply of any significant portion of the *arkhē*,[2] and the whole stock of the mint would not necessarily have been available based on this provision. Such a supply of metal could act

[1] For suggestions of a massive call-in of allied coins, contrast Finley, "Classical Greece" 22; L. Lacroix, "La monnaie grecque et les problèmes de la circulation monétaire," *BAB*[5] 55 (1969) 169–80, esp. 172–73; Starr, *Coinage* 69; Schuller, *Herrschaft* 46; Martin, *Sovereignty* 200–201.

[2] This conclusion is probably true even though our discussion above indicated considerable monetary consolidation. That is because the infiltration of Attic tetradrachms and drachms into allied stocks of coinage was balanced by large stocks of non-Attic drachms and fractions. See above, pp. 71–75.

only as an equivalent or a replacement for an amount comparable to the annual tribute (at the most). The estimate above for the annual income from the mines that was available for coining was 75–100T. The issue of a general invalidation of allied coinages and their collection and dispatch to Athens for conversion shall be discussed again below. Two reasons for disbelieving in a demonetization (which will be fleshed out in comments below) can be advanced here: (1) it would have been extraordinarily difficult to move beyond public stocks of silver and money so as to commandeer, if only temporarily, wealth hoarded in private hands; (2) the disruptions attendant on reducing the money supply were considerable.[3] We have already noted the religious complications above (p. 242). Finally, while the calculus of risks differed for governments, something of the same inhibition against hazarding large sums of money at sea must also have prevailed for public decision-makers (cf. Isoc. 17. 35–36; [Dem.] 50.28).

A significant problem in reconstruction is the different lengths of the lacunae in the Kos and Aphytis fragments. If we discount the words almost universally restored, Segre and the *ATL* have a sixteen-letter lacuna in the Kos fragment, while *IG* I[3] has fifteen letters. The Aphytis fragment is agreed to have a twenty-letter gap.

Detailed restoration goes back to Segre who offered for the Aphytis fragment: ἐν δὲ τῶ]ι ἀργυροκοπίωι τὸ ἀργύ[ριον τὸ νῦν ὑπάρχον κόψασθαι μὴ ἔλ]αττον ἢ ἥμισυ καὶ ἀ]πὸ τούτου ὅσον οἱ ἄρχοντες καὶ αὐτα]ὶ αἱ πόλεις πράττ[ωσι καταλλάτεν, δίδοντας ἑκατὸν δραχμὰς ἀπὸ τῆς μν[ᾶς· τοὺς ἐπιστάτας τὸ ἀργύριον κατ]αλλάτεν ἢ ἐνόχο[υς ἔναι κατὰ τὸν νόμον. The Kos fragment must have a shorter text of the first part of this restoration: ἐν δὲ τõ]ι ἀργυροκο[πίοι τὸ ἀργύριον τὸ νῦν ὂν κοφσάσθαι μὲ ἔλ]αττον ἒ *h*έμυσυ. . . . Lewis has called doubt upon the use of the middle voice for the infinitive in these restorations. Erxleben suggested ἐν δὲ τῶι ἀργυρο]κοπίωι τὸ ἀργύ[ριον τὸ ξενικὸν αὐτίκα κόψαι μὴ ἔλ]αττον ἢ ἥμισυ καὶ ἀ]πὸ τούτου ὅσον οἱ ἄρχοντες καὶ αὐτα]ὶ αἱ πόλεις πράττ[ουσιν, καταλλάτεν, λαβόντας τρε̃ς δραχμὰς ἀπὸ τῆς μν[ᾶς.[4] In the Kos fragment, line 17, the word *αὐτίκα* is to be dropped according to Erxleben.

More influential, however, has been a text of *ATL* derived from E.S.G. Robinson. Its Aphytis version is the following: ἐν δὲ τῶι ἀργυρο]κοπίωι

[3] See Erxleben *AJP* (1969) 107–109, whose suggestions of multiple consignments of foreign money and newly minted Athenian coin would partially obviate this objection. Such a mechanism, however, lies quite outside the clauses as conventionally restored.

[4] Erxleben *AJP* (1969) 109–10.

τὸ ἀργύ[ριον δεξάμενους εὐθὺς κόψαι μὴ ἔλ]αττον ἢ ἥμισυ (also accepted by Meiggs-Lewis) καὶ ἀ]ποδόσθαι ὡς ἂν νόμισμα ἱκανὸν ἔχωσ]ι αἱ πόλεις· πράττ[εσθαι δὲ ἀεὶ τοὺς ἐπιστάτας τρεῖς] δραχμὰς ἀπὸ τῆς μν[ᾶς· τὸ δὲ ἄλλο ἥμισυ (also Meiggs-Lewis) πέντε μηνῶν κατ]αλλάτεν ἢ ἐνόχο[υς ἔναι κατὰ τὸν νόμον. The Kos fragment would be restored: ἐν δὲ τõ]ι ἀργυροκοπ[ίοι τὸ ἀργύριον δεχσάμενους κόφσαι μὲ ἔλ]αττον ἒ ἕμυσυ καὶ ἀ]ποδόσθαι. . . . Mattingly, who does not offer an extended argument in favor of a particular restoration, suggests that αὐτοῦ, governed by ἔλαττον and with τὸ ἀργύριον as its antecedent, appeared in the Aphytis copy and was dropped in the Kos fragment.[5]

Since there are no true epigraphical parallels, restoration in this section can only be a free composition based on the surviving words. A number of objections may be raised to these and related restorations, which may be taken successively.

1. While the phrase ἐν δὲ τῶι ἀργυρ]κοπίωι is emphatic, signaling a change in context for the administrative mandates, it is disturbing that the officials charged with undertaking the required actions do not appear until the third injunction. A shift has taken place from the imperative mood to infinitives, the absence or postponement of the subjects of which is not reassuring in these versions.

2. The restoration ἐν δὲ τῶ]ι ἀργυρκοπίωι τὸ ἀργύ[ριον τὸ νῦν ὑπάρχον could be correct, for it explains why it is necessary to locate the required activity in the mint: that the silver to be minted is already there (note the parallel in *IG* II^2 244.21 and the similar restorations in *IG* I^3 86.16; 96.3). The phrase τὸ ἀργύριον τὸ νῦν ὂν in Segre's reconstruction of the Kos fragment cannot be directly paralleled, but there are similar participial phrases such as *IG* I^3 52A.5–6: ἐφσεφισμ||[έ]να, τά τε παρὰ τοῖς ἐλλενοταμίαις ὄντα νῦν . . . (cf. 52B.12–13).[6] Note also the restoration in *IG* II^2 12.12–13: τὸ ψήφισμα τ[ὸ καὶ πρότερον ὂν α]ὐτῶι. It is not then that either of this pair of restorations is impossible on its own terms, but that the replacement of one by the other seems problematical. We do not have other enactments in different versions that would allow a decision in favor of the appearance of such variation.

3. The antecedent of the participle δεξάμενους is unclear for some time. With the participle the incongruity of the phrase "in the mint" is increased, for where else would the reception of silver for minting take place?

[5] Mattingly *Klio* (1977) 86. He also prefers ἀ[ποδίδοναι or ἀ[ποδõναι (note 10, p. 85).

[6] See also *IG* II^2 35.11–12: καὶ τὰς συνθ]ή[κ]α[ς τ]ὰς νῦ[ν] ὃ||[σας . . .; 1044.14: . . . τὸν δ]ὲ νῦν ὄντα . . .; 1055.7: . . . οἱ δ]ὲ θεσμοθέται οἵ τε νῦν ὄν[τες . . .; 1180.16–17: (τὴν ἀγορὰν) . . . ἐπειδὴ ἡ νῦν οὖσα συν|ωικοδόμηται.

4. One trouble with restorations like those of Robinson, Erxleben, and some texts to be offered below is that it would be preferable to have had something along the lines of the more usual τὸ ἀργύριον τὸ ἐν τῶι ἀργυροκοπίωι, if the silver in the mint was to be minted. A participle (as in Segre's suggestions) is a partial palliative.

5. Erxleben observes that the infinitive ἀποδόσθαι (usually restored in section vi.2) will lack its logical object under the suggestions of Robinson and *ATL*.[7]

6. Our understanding of this section of the decree has been affected by the improbable view that the aforesaid demonetization or, at least, a vast replacement of prevailing currencies is in train. Hence one restores the unlikely clause "in order that the cities have sufficient money," which too conveniently provides the historical commentary that the early editors sought for supporting their own interpretation of the decree. Would the framer of the decree, however, have stood back in just this one place to provide the wider political and economic context for what is mandated by the enactment?

7. In addition, the restoration τὸ δὲ ἄλλο ἥμυσυ is troubling, because the next section is read as beginning ὃ δὲ ἂν περιγ]ίγνεται ἀργυρίο (from De Sanctis through Segre). That looks like a reference to the remaining silver (money?), either the remaining amount in the mint or what remains after the minting charge was extracted by the *epistatai* of the mint. Other interpretations of this restored phrase, where it refers to the yield of the minting fee (see immediately below), give deployments of περιγίγνομαι, which are much less vivid and less appropriate. Here also the phrase τὸ δὲ ἄλλο ἡμύσυ cannot be correct since the previous order was to mint "no less than half"; thus no one could be assured that there was another "half" about which dispositions were to be made.

8. Some may also have difficulty with the introduction of a time limit, a feature directly attested nowhere else in the decree for the implementation of a particular stipulation. In contrast, section ii.5 was reluctantly restored above so that it contained an order that a judicial procedure had to be initiated within a specified number of days. That restoration does not closely parallel the use of the time limit that is proposed here.

9. The instruction to mint at least one half the silver in the mint could be considered surprisingly inexact. Could the *epistatai* have interpreted this instruction to mean that they could coin all the silver in the mint or all the silver received from the allies? If the silver received from the allies

[7] Erxleben *AJP* (1969) 110.

was a mass of disparate currency and bullion handed over by the allies, the inexactitude of this stipulation has an increased impact. Instead, we would prefer that the amount of silver at issue was limited by reference to some other sum of money, the size of which could already be known to the proposer and later to the *epistatai*. That would probably have been the money that had been received from the allies in sections i–ii of the decree, be it the annual tribute or some other tax or exaction, and not simply monies handed over for conversion.

10. Erxleben's restoration is not unacceptable prima facie, although it is hard to understand why the Athenians will have distinguished between foreign money, unusable Athenian coins, and bullion in identifying the raw material to be used for coining. The mint was not a bank exchanging money and it probably treated any silver in terms of its weight in the process of minting. Clearly, the restoration cannot command a commitment to his idea of a conversion of the coinage of the allies through a succession of consignments for reminting, as that process would be mandated in a part of the decree that does not survive. Finally, the word αὐτίκα is uncommon without μάλα in imperial legislation (cf. *IG* I^{3} 61.5).

There are then two likely alternatives: either the *epistatai* were replacing the monies registered in the beginning of the Kos fragment under the proviso that they had to coin at least half the holdings of the mint, regardless of the amount of the registered monies; or, if a participle like δεξάμενους is restored, the minting of half the silver was predicated on the known amount received from the allies. One objection to thinking that the decree ordered the *epistatai* to commence by minting half the silver in the mint is that it was not likely that the mint ordinarily had that much silver on hand. Accordingly, there was not enough silver to equal even an appreciable proportion of the allied tribute to provide the *stratēgoi* with a consignment of funds in the form of fresh tetradrachms. Answering this objection, rates of tetradrachm production, even in the period 478–50, were sufficiently robust that considerable amounts of material for coining must always have been on hand for use in the mint (see above, pp. 185–89, 196–97).

Consequently, I am inclined to hypothesize here a sequence in which an order is given to the *epistatai* to begin striking no less than half the mint's stock of silver into coin; silver (money) is then received from the allies; the previously coined batch of money is later put into the pattern of normal expenditure with the money from the allies replenishing the supply in the mint. This understanding calls for three ideas in the first lacuna: the *epistatai*, a word or phrase placing the silver in the mint or specifying the silver in the mint (as Erxleben offers), and an infinitive form of κόπτω 'strike into coin.' Unfortunately, however, there appears to be room for only two of these ideas.

Furthermore, any such formulation runs up against the constraints of space in the Kos fragment, where there is space for four letters less according to Segre and the *ATL* and five letters less space according to *IG* I^3. The shorter wording of the Attic-script Kos fragment is particularly disconcerting, since the resolution of compound consonants demands more space. Thus, we are forced to employ the devices of removing small words without changing the meaning, of positing orthographical variants that shorten the text, or of hypothesizing that simple words replaced compound words through an excision of their prefixes. These suggestions will mitigate some of the difficulties that have been seen above for the earlier restorations. They all, however, carry us into epigraphical terra incognita.

The following restoration of the Aphytis fragment line 11 would strike the right note, avoiding most of the problems stated above: ἐν δὲ τῶ]ι ἀργυροκοπίωι τõ ἀργυ[ρίο τοὺς ἐπιστάτας ἐπικόψαι μὴ ἔλ]αττον ἢ ἥμισυ.[8] Note that the accusative has had to become a partitive genitive with ἥμισυ. We are still left with the problem of working out a solution that is practical for the shorter lacuna in the Kos fragment line 17. It could be restored ἐν δὲ τõ]ι ἀργυροκοπίοι τõ ἀργυ[ρίο τὸς ἐπιστάτας κόψαι μὲ ἔλ]αττον ἒ *h*έμυσυ. . . . Unfortunately, a combination of ψ and φς in the same inscription may also have been established, if the restorations that have previously been offered are valid. *IG* I^3 84 indicates that a combination of ψ and φς would not be unparalleled (see line 22 with lines 7, 18, 24, and 26 *bis*). Nonetheless, the possibilities of this approach are limited by the considerable space occupied by the unit τοὺς ἐπιστάτας. The shorter line of *IG* I^3, which makes available a lacuna of fifteen letter spaces, out of a line of forty letters, is particularly intractable.

Another alternative approach attempts to knit the phrases ἐν δὲ τῶ]ι ἀργυρκοπίωι and τὸ ἀργύ[ριον more closely together by adopting Segre's suggestion with the proviso of a compound verb: ἐν δὲ τῶ]ι ἀργυροκοπίωι τὸ ἀργύ[ριον τὸ νῦν ὑπάρχον ἐπικόψαι. . . . Line 17 of the Kos fragment can be generated from this restoration through simple reduction and respelling: ἐν δὲ τõ]ι ἀργυροκοπίοι τὸ ἀργύ[ριον τὸ *h*υπάρχον κόφσαι. If we accept the shorter forty-letter line of *IG* I^3 which leaves us only fifteen letters with which to restore, the Kos fragment could become ἐν δὲ τõι ἀργυροκοπίοι τὸ ἀργύ[ριον τὸ *h*υπάρχον κόψαι . . . or . . . τὸ ἀργύ[ριον τὸ νῦν ὂν ἐκκόπσαι.

[8] For the verb, see Arist. *Oec.* 1349b31.

As for the next clause, the objections have already been registered toward Robinson's self-conscious clause giving an administrative rationale for the order to mint. Segre, followed by Erxleben, connects the order to exchange in section v.5 (Aphytis lines 13–14) with the notion of exaction or taxation implied by πραττ[in section v.3 (Aphytis line 11). The drawbacks of this restoration are twofold: we never get a satisfactory subject for the infinitives, though we expect the *epistatai* to get the order, and the minting fee, so attractively posited by Robinson, must be relinquished. Segre replaces the minting fee with an improbable specification of the size of the *mna.*[9] Erxleben gives us a fee for making an exchange or *agio*, quite a different levy from a minting fee. One might suggest instead a restoration that is consistent with the vision of the whole decree that has been presented above: καὶ ἀ[πολαβε̃ν τὸ ἀργύριον ὅσον ἐσφέρουσ]ι αἱ πόλεις or ἀ[πολαμβάνεν τὰ χρήματα ἃ ἐσφέροντα[ι αἱ πόλεις. Naturally, there are many similar combinations. Another possiblility would establish the tribute as the source for replacing the silver that the mint has struck: καὶ ἀ[πολαμβάνεν ὁπόσον ἂν το̃ φόρο φέρωσ]ι.

Most editors of the Kos and Aphytis fragments have sought to connect πρατ- with the exaction of the minting charge, the application of which is suggested by the phrase δραχμὰς ἀπὸ τη̃ς μν[ᾶς, as Robinson first argued.[10] He then suggested both τοὺς ἐπιστάτας and ἐπικαταλλαγήν.[11] Economy of presentation argues for the restoration of τοὺς ἐπιστάτας here, if we do not restore the same phrase in line 1 of section v or in section v.4. If we do restore τοὺς ἐπιστάτας in v.1 and/or v.4, ἐπικαταλλαγήν may be restored here (on the basis of its usage in Theophrast. *Char.* 30.15). Hence, Robinson's possibilities are πράττ[εσθαι δὲ ἀεὶ τοὺς ἐπιστάτας τρει̃ς] δραχμὰς ἀπὸ τη̃ς μν[ᾶς and πράττ[εσθαι δὲ αἰεὶ ἐπικαταλλαγὴν τρε̃ς] δραχμὰς ἀπὸ τη̃ς μν[ᾶς. The spellings of ἀεὶ/αἰεὶ and τρει̃ς/τρε̃ς cannot be pinned down. Moreover, the word ἀεὶ/αἰεὶ is hardly certain, inasmuch as its chief usage in imperial phraseology is to denote the status of annual boards (like the *stratēgoi*) with changing memberships. The general sense of this restoration is certainly attractive, so that most commentators have put a full stop after πόλεις. As I have implied above, it cannot be entirely ruled out, however, that a stipulation was made here

[9] Segre 160; this seems an unnecessary precaution against a confusion over the number of drachms in the *mna*. That was an impossible eventuality in an Athenian official document, where no one would look for an Aiginetic *mna*. See Figueira, *Excursions* 70–72.

[10] Robinson 327.

[11] Cf. Cataudella *Sileno* (1986) 112 with note 8, who supports Robinson.

about an exchange of money so that the cities could exact taxes; thus, αἱ πόλεις and πρατт- could be construed in a single clause.[12]

A restoration can be predicated on an appearance of a source for the minting fee, but only if we have restored τοὺς ἐπιστάτας above in v.1 or will restore it in v.4: (for example) πράττ[εσθαι δὲ ἐκ τούτο νομίσματος τρε̃ς] δραχμὰς ἀπὸ τῆς μν[ᾶς.[13] Alternative restorations would be: ... ἀπὸ τοῦ νομίσματος τρεῖς] δραχμὰς ...; ... ἀπὸ τοῦ κεκομμένου τρεῖς] δραχμὰς ...; ... ἀπὸ τούτο κεκομμένο τρε̃ς] δραχμὰς ...; or ... ἐκ τούτου ἀργυρίου τρεῖς δραχμὰς.... This would satisfy any perceived necessity to specify that the minting fee is being drawn from the "silver ... no less than half" of section v.1–2. If the *epistatai* are not restored above or below, then we must have them here by adopting an approximation of Robinson's suggestion.

As for the minting charge, most commentators have agreed with the earlier editors in opting for three drachms on the *mna*, although five would be possible, πέντε] δραχμὰς ἀπὸ τῆς μν[ᾶς. Meiggs-Lewis sensibly objects that that seems to be too high a fee.[14] It ought also to be emphasized that in my reconstruction of this section of the decree, the levy for minting is not borne by the allies but by the Athenians (see also above, pp. 239–45). The Athenians have already accepted payment of funds from the allies—my preference is to consider this money as received in lieu of tribute—and the newly minted Athenian tetradrachms are not going back to the allies; they are to join the normal stream of revenue in this view (see below, pp. 365–68). It is only in the eventuality that a large-scale conversion of currencies is taking place that the allies would bear the cost of the minting fee.

The content of the next provision is surely signaled by the probable restoration κατ]άλλατεν 'to exchange' in Aphytis line 13. One may compare *IG* I^3 90.14–16, where, in a very fragmentary setting, καταλλάττεν is followed in the next line by νομίσμ[ατι. A number of suggestions have been offered: *ATL*: τὸ δὲ ἄλλο ἥμισυ πέντε μηνω̃ν κατ]άλλαττεν; Segre:

[12] As noted above, an approach similar syntactically but differing in import was taken by Segre, 159, followed by Erxleben (1969) 110, who offers ἀ[πὸ τούτου ὅσον οἱ ἄρχοντες καὶ αὐτα]ὶ αἱ πόλεις πράττ[ουσιν.

[13] Erxleben *AfP* (1969) 110–11 achieves a similar result with ... λαβόντας τρε̃ς] δραχμὰς ἀπὸ τῆς μν[ᾶς.

[14] Meiggs-Lewis 113. O. Mørkholm, "Some Reflections on the Production and Use of Coinage in Ancient Greece," *Historia* 31 (1982) 290–305, esp. 290–92, opts for the higher levy of five dr. for each *mna*, resting his conclusion on the 5 percent disparity between the weight and coin *stathma* during the fifth century. The history of the relationship of weights and coin weights indicates greater complexity than one would want to explain on the basis of variations in minting fees. See above, pp. 243–44.

τοὺς ἐπιστάτας τὸ ἀργύριον κατ]αλλάττεν. It is doubtful whether the former suggestion makes sense, even in its own terms, since the exchanging would have to be thought to subsume the act of reminting. There no particular reason to believe that it did. Moreover, it deserves emphasis that there is also no cause to introduce at this point the other half of the money (either in the mint or delivered by the allies to the mint) and to set a time limit, unless we are unalterably committed to a massive demonetization and replacement of currencies. As observed above, the phrase "the other half" is inapposite. The rather more banal supplement of Segre is probably preferable, or else something like (for example) τοὺς δ' ἐπιστάτας τὰ χρήματα κατ]αλλάττεν. This suggestion has the advantage of avoiding an asyndeton by inserting δέ (cf. xiv.1 below).

Nevertheless, it is also worth noting that the verb καταλλάσσω is regularly used in a variety of constructions, with accusative and dative, with accusative and genitive, and with accusatives and prepositions like ἐπί and πρός, in order to describe the exchange of products, money, and even states of mind for each other. A frankly tendentious example of how such a construction would work in this context might be represented by τὸ δὲ ἀργύριον ἐπὶ τῶι φόρωι κατ]αλλάττεν. Once again, this restoration probably requires the phrase τοὺς ἐπιστάτας to have appeared earlier in this section. This section probably involved a crossing of paths between the monies mentioned as registered at the beginning of the surviving decree and the money ordered to be minted here.

The word ἐνόχο[υς establishes the liability of the magistrates who fail to implement this provision. If κατὰ τὸν νόμον is correct, we may get a glimpse of other legislation that regulated the operation of the mint. It is true, however, that the term ἔνοχος is not customarily used with the preposition κατά, but with a dative, as *IG* I^3 93.44 seems to suggest: . . . ἐ]νόχον ἔναι ζεμία[ι. . . . The other inscribed examples of the construction are unfortunately much later.[15] Nonetheless, literary *comparanda* are quite common, with a construction with the genitive running a distant second among contemporary writers.[16] D.M. Robinson offers ἢ ἐνόχο[υς ἔστω τῆι αὐτῆι ζημίαι. We might compare *IG* I^3 157.15: . . . ἒ τε͂]ι αὐτε͂ι ζ[εμίαι ἐνεχέσθον . . . ; or the more heavily restored *IG* I^3 71.11–12: ἒ ὀφέλετο *h*έκαστος τὲ]|ν αὐτὲν ζεμ[ίαν.[17] Along the same line of reasoning, C. Koch suggests κατ]αλλάττεν ἢ

[15] *IG* II^2 1013.58, 1328.18–19; *SEG* 21.494.41; 22.114.6 = 25.139; 24.147.10.

[16] Let us limit citation to early Attic orators: Andoc. 1.82; Antiph. 1.11; 4.1.4, 6; 4.2.3, 7; 5.9, 68, 85, 87; 6.4, 5; Lys. 3.4; 7.37; 10.22; 13.85; 14.7, 9, 47; 23.12. See also Xen. *HG* 7.3.8; *Mem.* 1.2.64.

[17] Robinson, *AJP* (1935) 152.

ἐνόχο[υς ἔναι τῆι προδοσίαι.[18] That reading is possible, but to consider failing to make a monetary exchange the equivalent of treason exceeds the warrant offered by the extant portions of the decree.

v. [ἐν δὲ τῶ]ι ἀργυροκοπίωι τὸ ἀργύ[ριον τὸ νῦν ὑπάρχον V.1
ἐπικόψαι μὴ ἔλ]αττον ἢ ἥμυσυ καὶ ἀ[πολαβἔν τὸ
ἀργύριον ὅσον
ἐσφέρουσ]ι αἱ πόλεις· πράττ[εσθαι δὲ ἐκ τούτο
νομίσματος τρἔς]
δραχμὰς ἀπὸ τῆς μν[ᾶς· τοὺς δ' ἐπιστάτας τὰ χρήματα
κατ]αλλάττεν ἢ ἐνόχο[υς ἔναι κατὰ τὸν νόμον]·

v. Coin no less than half the silver now present in the mint and take in return the silver [money] so much as the cities contribute; out of this silver levy three drachms from the *mna*; the *epistatai* are to exchange the money or be liable in accordance with the law.

In our reconstruction of this section, the activities ordered by the decree are straightforward: the Athenians were either altering the method of collection of the tribute in a manner comparable to their occasional reception of payments from individual cities in non-Athenian currency or were arranging the reception and processing of some other exaction. They could have received all the tribute in the form of whatever currency the cities chose to pay, or, perhaps, combined such an exaction with a call-in of some non-Athenian money of the allies. Instead of going from the Hellenotamiai into the normal stream of revenue, this money went first to the mint, where it offset at least half of the supply of bullion that had already been converted to coin.

Inasmuch as the contribution to a composite text of the Kos fragment ends with this section, it may be useful to offer a version of the fragment following the forty-letter line length of *IG* I^3, taking over some suggestions made by the editor, Lewis. It remains doubtful, however, in my view whether a consistent line length of forty is a viable option when we compare the Aphytis fragment. Adjustment to the shorter lacunae has necessitated using some restorations that were not preferential choices in the discussion above.

[. . . . . .29. . . . .]αι τὰ γ[ράμματ-]
[εῖα . . . . 8. . . . ἒ ἄρχοντες ἐν τῆσι π]όλεσι ἒ ἄρ[χοντε-]
[ς τὂν χσυμμάχον πεμπόντον. *h*οι] δὲ *h*ελλενοταμ[ίαι]

[18] Koch, *Volksbeschlüsse* 390–91.

[τάς τε πόλεις καὶ τὸ ἀργύριον ἀ]ναγραφόντον. ἐὰ[ν δ-]
[ὲ μὲ ὀρθο̃ς ἀναγράφο̃σι τὸ το̃ν π]όλεον τινος, ἐσα[γέσ-]
[θο μὲν δίκε ἀπὸ χσυμβολο̃ν ἐς τ]ὲν ἐλιαίαν τὲν το̃[ν θ-]
[εσμοθετο̃ν κατὰ τὸν νόμον· *ho*]ι δὲ θεσμοθέ[τ]αι πε[ρι-]
[ζεμιοσά]ντον [δραχμε̃σι χιλί]ασι *h*έκαστον. ἐὰν δέ [τ-]
[ις ἄλλος το̃ν ἀρχόντο̃ν ἐν τ]ε̃σι πόλεσι μὲ ποιε̃ι κα[τ-]
[ὰ τὰ χσυγκείμενα το̃ν πολι]το̃ν ε̃ το̃ν χσένον, [ἄτ]ιμ[ος]
[ἔστο, καὶ χρέματα αὐτο̃ (sic) δε]μόσια [ἔσ]το κὰι τε̃ς θεο̃ τ[ὸ]
[ἐπιδέκατον καὶ εἰ μέ εἰσι] ἄρχοντες Ἀθεναίον, ἐ[πι-]
[μελέθεντον το̃ν ἐν το̃ι φσε]φίσματι *ho*ι ἄρχοντε[ς *h*-]
[οι ἑκάστες τε̃ς πόλεως· κὰι] ἐὰμ μὲ ποιο̃σι κατὰ τ[ὰ συ-]
[γκείμενα, ε̃ναι κατὰ το̃ν ἀρχ]όντων τούτον περὶ ἀτ[ι-]
[μίας γραφὰς Ἀθένεσι· ἐν δὲ το̃]ι ἀργυροκοπίοι τὸ ἀρ-]
[γύριον τὸ νῦν ὂν ἐκκόπσαι μὲ ἔλ]αττο[ν ε̃ ἔμισυ καὶ . . .

SECTION VI

vi. [ὃ δὲ ἂν περίγ]ιγνηται ἀργυρίο [. . . . . .27. . . . . VI.1
. . . .]σθαι ἢ τοῖς στρατ[ηγοῖς ἢ . . . . .19. . . . .]

This clause seems to legislate about a residuum [n.b.] of silver or silver money. A choice appears necessary among three possibilities. The remaining silver—if that is the correct restoration—could be the amount accrued from the exaction of the minting fee. Alternatively, it could be what was left after the minting fee was levied. In the third option it could be the remaining stock of bullion and coins in the mint, either from the original stock or from what was withdrawn from circulation or levied from the allies. It would thus also be what was still on hand in the mint after the *epistatai* had implemented the order given to them earlier in the decree to coin at least half the silver in the mint. It is especially easy in the present state of the evidence to waver between concluding that the next step was a (re)coining of the rest of the available silver in the mint or seeing merely a conveyance of some or all of the minted or exchanged money to the *stratēgoi*. Yet, the comparative evidence, while not exactly parallel, militates in favor of our second option (note Xen. *HG* 2.3.8).[19]

In considering possible restorations, let us start by noting that some form of the verb ἀποδίδωμι is strongly suggested for]σθαι by the phrase ἐπε]ιδὰν δὲ ἀποδοθῆι in section vii.1 (Aphytis line 16). Segre suggested:

[19] The verb is attested in the meaning 'to carry a sum over': *IG* I^3 435.1, 7, 33, 39, 60, 66, 84, 91, 98, 117, 123; 436.30; 437.59; 439.108; 441.165; 444.279; 446.316, 340; 447.347, 362; 449.378, 404; 450.419–20. See Koch, *Volksbeschlüsse* 617.

ὃ δὲ ἂν περιγ]ίγνεται ἀργυρίο[υ κόψασθαι μὲν αὐτίκα καὶ ἀποδιδό]σθαι ἢ τοῖς στρατηγοῖς ἢ τοῖς ἀποδέκταις εὐθύς. The first batch of silver has already been exchanged with the Athenian *arkhontes* and the allied cities. Under this understanding, the remaining stock of silver is to be minted and sent into the revenue/expenditure stream.[20] If we adopt a reading like this, one could still envisage that, after coining the first half of the silver in the mint, the law went on to establish that the first consignment was to be offset by allied money before specifying the treatment of the second part of the bullion originally in the mint (as Segre restores). In other words, the restoration of section v presented above need not be disqualified.

Nevertheless, the weakness of Segre's restoration of this section is that it is difficult to explain why any silver at all was to be sent on to the generals in this way. Practical considerations complicate the picture. First, if the silver in the mint included a large amount of superseded allied coins, might not the coining the rest of the silver and its conveyance to Attic officials constitute a massive appropriation of allied money by the Athenians? Moreover, the sum forwarded cannot in any eventuality have comprised an amount that exceeded what the *stratēgoi* were likely to spend in the normal course of their annual duties. No evidence argues in favor of the *stratēgoi* being permitted to accrue assets significantly surpassing their short-term requirements.[21] The approach to restoring this section ought to be one in which the *stratēgoi* are not sent an amount of money exceeding their normal needs. Whatever that is thought to have been, it would not have been equivalent to all the non-Attic coins in circulation or even the public allied holdings of non-Athenian money.

E.S.G. Robinson and the editors of *ATL* would have us read: ὃ δὲ ἂν περιγ]ίγνεται ἀργυρίο[υ τοῦ πεπραγμένου κόψαι καὶ ἀποδό]σθαι ἢ τοῖς στρατηγοῖς ἢ τοῖς ἀποδέκταις εὐθύς. Here the silver that was to be minted as per the instruction of the previous section has been received from the allies; it was not the stock of silver already held in the mint. That first consignment of newly coined money, at least half the amount received, has already been returned to the allies. The second component of the holdings of the mint has also been ordered

[20] Seeing the *stratēgoi* in their expected role of recipients of funds for their usual expenditures is more palatable than positing broader financial or economic responsiblities such as the traditional interpretation would appear to indicate (cf. Schuller, *Herrschaft* 39).

[21] We could, of course, lessen the incongruity of a large sum being sent on to the *stratēgoi* by restricting the order to mint: ὃ δὲ ἂν περιγ]ίγνεται ἀργυρίο[υ τοῦ ξενικοῦ κόπτειν καὶ ἀποδιδό]σθαι. . . . Only the foreign coins were to be reminted, leaving the remainder of the bullion in reserve in the mint.

"exchanged," presumably minted (although that stage is disturbingly left unstated) and again sent back to the allies. Now a third consignment (the income from the 3-dr. levy for each *mna*) is to be minted and added to the revenue stream flowing to the *stratēgoi* and possibly to the *apodektai*.

A number of observations are in order that are specific to this restoration of *ATL*. First of all, it is likely that any fee was exacted *after* the minting process had occurred, that is, after any losses in handling and processing had already taken place (see also above pp. 244–45). The levy would be most easily reckoned on the assumption that the requisite fee of three or five drachms from each *mna* was subtracted from the newly minted coins. There is, after all, no suggestion that weight drachms rather than coin drachms are at issue (or are being juxtaposed with each other), as they would necessarily have been for a fee levied at some stage before minting was completed. So the 3-dr. levy would already have been in coined form. Moreover, one would rather surmise that any minting charge was customarily retained by the *epistatai* to underwrite the normal operation of the mint. Thus, any funds levied in this way by the decree should not have been available for an addition to the (customary?) stream of revenue made over to the *stratēgoi*. Nor, on this understanding, would it be necessary to detail by a clause in the decree the fate of a levy on the conversion of silver into coin.

Another ramification of the restoration proposed by the editors of *ATL* is that it forces us to have already opted for their hypothesis that the bulk of the silver from the mint, now coined by the *epistatai*, was to be exchanged for money surrendered by the allies in a large operation of conversion, the traces of which they restore in section v.2–3. We have already doubted the feasibility and questioned the prudence of such an operation (see above, pp. 242, 353–54). Accordingly, in *ATL*'s interpretation, section vi must simply account for the money raised by the "3-dr." fee. There is, to repeat, considerable doubt whether the Athenians would have provided so specifically for the money from such a minting charge.[22]

Furthermore, a skeptical reader might well object to the restorations both of Segre and of *ATL* by noting that the hypothesis of two or three

[22] Erxleben *AJP* (1969) 111–12 replaces τοῦ πεπραγμένου with ἐκ τῆς ἐπαλλαγῆς, which affects the meaning of the section by changing the minting fee into an exchange fee. For ἐπαλλαγή, see *BGU* 6.1375.6–7 (248); *PCair.Zen* 1.59022.2, 4, 7, 13, 15, 17 (late 250s); 4.59567.3 (ca. 250); *PTebt* 3.2.866.33 (237), 1063.2 (third century). In context, however, my criticisms focusing on the large exchanges of *ATL* do not extend to his treatment, as the amount from the allies that is exchanged is of unknown magnitude. His reading may, however, be faulted for its view on the utilization of the minting fee.

rounds of coining of silver in the mint by its *epistatai* and thereby two or three consignments of silver about which dispositions need to be made in so few lines is unduly complex and essentially gratuitous. For both Segre and *ATL*, assuming that their restorations of section v.4–5 are correct, the word καταλλάττεν in section v.5 necessarily bears a heavy explanatory burden. For Segre, this term is sufficient to account for the utilization of a first round of minting for the purpose of the recirculation of Attic coins back to the allies in order to compensate them for the monies supposedly levied from them earlier in the decree. This surmise, however, begs a central question, namely, why another amount of silver needed to be coined and provided to the *stratēgoi* (in section vi). Why were the Athenians giving the *stratēgoi* an additional infusion of resources, unless the assets on which they had usually counted were no longer available?

A similar problem is encountered on the acceptance of the restoration of *ATL* where the activity implied by the infinitive καταλλάττεν must subsume minting (for example, like the restoration κόψαι in v.2) and return to the allies (for example, like ἀποδόσθαι also in their v.2). In my interpretation καταλλάττεν merely describes how the *epistatai* replace their original stock of silver with an amount of disparate silver received from the allies; in other words it connotes the simple act of exchange of two categories of money, Attic and non-Attic.

A simpler, minimalist approach is to be preferred. A principle of economy of assumption has already been asserted in our investigation of the beginning of the extant parts of the decree. If the Hellenotamiai received anything from the allies, it will have been in all likelihood (quasi-)tribute payments (or payments in lieu of tribute), since those are the only allied funds with which they are surely known to have dealt. Concomitantly, if the *stratēgoi* were receiving money, it is likely that it constituted the resources normally channeled to them over the year to conduct the military activities of the Delian League. Ordinarily, that allotment of funds had its origin in tribute. Nor is it necessary on the basis of this section to believe that the Athenians were diverging from their ordinary behavior in the providing of money to the generals. There is no reason why these monies were not made over to the *stratēgoi* in the customary manner of disbursing funds as they were needed for particular operations, rather than in one great donation.

Consequently, while a division of monies would be implicit in a phrase like ὃ δὲ ἂν περιγ]ίγνεται ἀργυρίο[υ, that fact does not compel two sequences of coining. If it does seem implicitly to divide the silver of the mint into two amounts with different fates, the simplest hypothesis is that these two components were respectively the levy exacted by the minting fee (its relegation to the *epistatai* and to the mint needing no specification) and the remainder and majority of the silver ordered to be struck into coin in section v.1–2. Section vi might be restored to explain the fate of the money coined in section v.1–3, after the minting fee was exacted. I would suggest *exempli gratia*: ὃ δὲ ἂν περιγ]ίγνεται ἀργυρίο[υ τοῦ κεκομμένου σύμπαντος ἀποδό]σθαι.

A reference to the *apodektai* is next restored, that is, the officials who received state monies. The presence of the filler word εὐθύς warns that the phrase ἢ τοῖς ἀποδέκταις εὐθύς ought to be received with no great enthusiasm.[23] That consideration does not, however, alter the fact that the *apodektai* are reasonable co-recipients with the *stratēgoi*, since they received revenue of all types (cf. *Ath. Pol.* 48.1).[24] Nonetheless, one substantial difficulty does spring to mind. The casual ambiguity is disturbing about the destination of what on any extant interpretation was probably a fairly large consignment of funds. There is no room here for a designation of an amount (that is, an unknown number of talents or *mnai*) or of a fraction (like ἥμισυ 'half'). I would remove the uncertainty of the destination of the money by adding a more palatable uncertainty over the timing of an act (or acts) of consignment. The transfer did indeed have to occur after a number of other stages of the process mandated by the decree were completed: ἢ τοῖς στρατ[ηγοῖς ἢ τοῖς νέοις στρατηγοῖς 'to the Generals or to the next board of Generals' (cf. *IG* I³ 387.2; 433.39, 49; 465.137).

It is further possible that some prevailing regime for the regular transfer of funds to the *stratēgoi* was being altered vis-à-vis the source of the transfers. The *epistatai* were perhaps taking the place of the Hellenotamiai. It was envisaged that this new pattern might extend into the next official year. Whether the recipients are to be *stratēgoi* and *apodektai* or *stratēgoi* alone, my interpretation is once again prompted by

[23] Unsurprisingly, the word εὐθύς (for which see Segre 161) is less attested (note *IG* I³ 61.54) than restored on imperial documents (34.29, 39; 66.8; 71.45; 85.10; 104.37). Note Meritt's comment, "otiose," in *PAPS* (1975) 271. His own solution is to have these lines refer to the instructions for the building of the Hephaisteion: ἢ τοῖς ἔργων ἐπιστάταις. While this does not by any means represent an impossible formulation, *epistatai* are usually either identifiable from context, or, if their identity needs to be specified, are described more completely: *IG* I³ 459.3–4: ἀγάλματος ἐπισ|τάτεσι, cf. *IG* I³ 457.3–5: ἐπ]|ιστάτεσι ἀ[γαλμά]|τος; 462.2: ἐπιστάτ]αι π[ρο]πυλαίο ἐργασ[ίας]; 474.1–2: [ἐ]πιστάται τõ νεὸ τõ ἐμ πόλει ἐν *h*õι τὸ | ἀρχαῖον ἄγαλμα.

[24] Note, for example, *IG* I³ 84.15–18: κ|αταβαλλέτο τὸ ἀργύριον ἐπὶ τε̃ς ἐνάτες πρυτανείας τοῖς ἀποδέκ|ται[ς], οἱ δὲ ἀποδέκται τοῖς ταμίαισι τõν ἄλλον θεõν παραδιδόντον | [κ]ατὰ τὸν νόμον; *IG* I³ 117.4–7: ἐς τ]ὲν πο[ίε]σιν τõν [νε|õν δανεῖσαι τὸς στρα]τεγὸς τ[ὸ]ς μετὰ Π[ε|ρικλέος ἀργύριον παρ]ὰ τὸν {τ[õ]ν} ὄντον ἀ|[ποδεκτõν τοῖς ναυπεγ]οῖς. Cf. Segre 161.

the assumption that revenue from the allies, perhaps in the form of or in lieu of tribute, was being diverted and steps were taken being for the rerouting to the generals of a comparable sum of money.

The specific restorations that are being explored in these sections of the decree were prompted by a hypothesis of a special enactment for the conversion of non-Athenian money into Attic coins during the payment of the tribute in one year. The Athenians effected a special minting of half the silver in the mint in order to allow the allied states to undertake a significant conversion of the non-Athenian currency in their civic treasuries while tendering their required *phoros*. Tribute received in a variety of coinages and perhaps as bullion went to replenish the stock of silver held by the mint. By the diversion of the tribute to the mint, the Attic policy of encouraging that tribute be tendered in Attic money appears to have been reversed for this year.[25] Thereafter, the newly coined money from the mint seems to have been given to the *stratēgoi* and perhaps to some other board of officials. The only mechanism for the circulation of Attic money into allied hands, as enacted in these sections of the Coinage Decree, worked through the customary expenditures of funds by the generals and other Athenian officials. In this way, the Athenians injected some additional Attic money into the Aegean economy. Whether any similar mechanism ever existed to allow the allies to acquire Attic coins at times of need depends on our interpretation of later sections of the decree.

vi. [ὃ δὲ ἂν περιγ]ίγνηται ἀργυρίο[ῦ τοῦ κεχομμένου σύμπαντος VI.1
αποδό]σθαι ἢ τοῖς στρατ[ηγοῖς ἢ τοῖς νέοις στρατηγοῖς.

vi. Whatever remains of all the silver that has been coined is to be handed over either to the *stratēgoi* or to the new board of *stratēgoi*.

SECTION VII

vii. [ἐπε]ιδὰν δὲ ἀποδοθῆι, [. . . . . .28. . . . . VII.1
. . . .]α̣αι καὶ τῶι Ἡφαισ[τ. . . . . .13. . . . . .]

[25] One might suppose that the *aparkhē* was paid by the Athenians on behalf of the allies in Attic coin, crediting them as though they had paid in Athenian money. That would merely be a general application of the conversion to Attic money of the more occasional payments in non-Attic coins (outlined above, pp. 273–95). Yet, as will be seen, it is also possible that a special *aparkhē* was paid out of these monies whose treatment is described in sections vii–viii. In that case, the year of the Coinage Decree might be the year lacking a record of the *aparkhai*. See below, pp. 457–63.

The earlier interpretations of the next two sections of the decree constitute a graphic example of how tendentious restoration can drive the analysis of an epigraphical document in unfruitful directions. One key to an interpretation here is offered by the phrase ἐπειδὰν δὲ ἀποδοθῆι, which provides a link to the previous section, if ἀποδό]σθαι (*vel sim.*) is correctly restored in section vi.2. A naive anticipation would be that the *stratēgoi* are here ordered to undertake some action with the money after it has been supplied to them.

Earlier scholarship, however, took a different line of approach from this expected one. The interpretation of these lines and the following section has been built around what appeared to be a reference to the gods Athena *and* Hephaistos in section vii.2. In particular, therefore, one notion dominating commentary on the decree has been that of the repayment of debts to Hephaistos and Athena. Note Segre's reconstruction: [ψηφίσασθαι καὶ περὶ τῶν τῆι 'Αθηναί]αι καὶ τῶι 'Ηφαίσ[τωι ὀφειλομένων.[26] Vying with this hypothesis about debt repayment was an idea, somewhat less favored, of the institution of a "tithe," as in the formulation of D.M. Robinson: [τὸ ἀργύριον διδόσθω καὶ τῆι 'Αθηναί]αι καὶ τῶι 'Ηφαίσ[τῶι τὸ ἐπιδέκατον].[27] Such restorations were rendered plausible by the undoubted record of holdings and loans involving the treasury of Hephaistos (*IG* I^3 369.85 [423/2]; 383.I.57 [429/8]).

Various conclusions for the chronology of the decree were derived from these restorations. While noting the absence of explicit connections between minting and Athena and Hephaistos, David Robinson remarked on the presence of the shops of metalworkers in the vicinity of the Hephaisteion (cf. Andoc. 1.40). He also introduced the issue of the erection of the Hephaisteion, observing that it must precede the inception of the accounts of the cult statues of the two deities in 421/0 (*IG* I^3 472; cf. *IG* I^3 82). Dinsmoor integrated these insights with his investigation of the art historical and archaeological data for dating the Hephaisteion, and pronounced in favor of a mid-century date (October 17, 449, to be exact) for the inauguration of the festival of Hephaistos.[28]

Other ancillary conclusions were also derived from these restorations. It was possible to speculate on the most likely dates for loans to

[26] Segre 162-63; followed by *IG* XII Suppl. p. 217; *ATL* 2.64.

[27] See Robinson *AJP* (1935) 153, who first remarked on the importance of the pairing of the two deities for interpretation.

[28] Cf. W.B. Dinsmoor, *Observations on the Hephaisteion*, *Hesperia* Suppl. 5 (Princeton 1941), esp. 152. Erxleben, *AfP* (1971), argues for a date in the late 420s; cf. H.B. Mattingly, "Periclean Imperialism," in E. Badian (ed.), *Ancient Society and Institutions* (New York 1967) 193–223, esp. 203.

Hephaistos to be repaid, with Segre opting for a date after the Peace of Kallias but before 446.[29] Another corollary concluded that the Coinage Decree must antedate the creation of the Treasurers of the Other Gods. If we see their foundation in the second of Kallias' decrees and date that legislation to 434/3, the Coinage Decree accordingly comes before that enactment (cf. *IG* I^3 52A.8, 16, 21–24, 30-31; 52B.19–29).[30] If a later date is preferable for the second decree of Kallias, the Coinage Decree could then also be dated later, after the manner of Mattingly's redatings.[31]

Stroud's reexamination of the Aphytis fragment, however, revealed traces of a triangular letter before -αι, apparently excluding 'Αθηναί]αι.[32] Instead we must read either an *alpha* or a *lambda*, rendering -]ααι or the combination -]λαι on the stone. Meritt defended 'Αθην]άαι as a likely restoration on the basis of the appearance of this and similar spellings in dedications.[33] *IG* I^3 prints τῆι 'Αθην]ạ́αι. . . .

Stroud's own suggestion is that 'Ηφαίσ[- provides a reference to the Hephaistikon ἀπὸ Λαυρείου that is alluded to in a number of imperial inscriptions as a source for the funding of public works.[34] Following a suggestion of M. Crosby that this is the name of a mine at Laureion called the Hephaistikon, Stroud offers . . . καὶ τῶι 'Ηφαισ[τικῶι ἀπὸ Λαυρέου.

[29] Segre 169–70, placing emphasis on the expression . . . νομίσματος *h*εμεδαπõ . . . (*IG* I^3 52A.4) as a sign that the original order to pay back debts to the other gods closely followed the Coinage Decree. Cf. H. Schaefer, "Beiträge zur Geschichte der attischen Symmachie," *Hermes* 74 (1939) 225–264, esp. 253–57; also Erxleben *AJP* (1969) 113–15.

[30] Segre 162–63.

[31] H.B. Mattingly, "The Financial Decrees of Kallias (IG i^2 91/2)," *PACA* 7 (1964) 35–53, dating to 422; also, Mattingly, "Athenian Finance in the Peloponnesian War," *BCH* 92 (1968) 450–85, esp. 458–60. Cf. Meritt *GRBS* (1967) 129–31.

[32] R.S. Stroud, "Three Attic Decrees," *CSCA* 7 (1974) 279–98, esp. 280–81. Stroud's reading (printed by *IG* I^3) incidentally refutes Mattingly's argument that the decree established a fund to Hephaistos and Athena, which he finds also in *IG* I^3 82.14–17 of 421/0.

[33] Stroud *CSCA* (1974) 298 reports a communication of B.D. Meritt that reads 'Αθην]άαι on the basis of a new examination of the photograph. Meritt cites the forms 'Αθηνάας in *SEG* 15.84 (sic; cf. 16.42.32) and 'Αθενάαι in *IG* I^3 809. The spelling 'Αθηνάας appears in *IG* I^3 1082; II^2 1388.2; 1412.13; 2344.1; *SEG* 21.527.10, cf. 44, 52; 651.2; and in a *horos* reported in G. Gruben, "Die Ausgrabungen im Kerameikos," *AA* (1964) 384–467, esp. col. 414, and is restored in a number of stoichedon inscriptions containing the same phrasing as *IG* II^2 1388.2–3: οἱ ταμίαι τῶν ἱερῶ]ν χρημάτων τῆς 'Αθηνάας καὶ τῶν ἄ[λλων θεῶν (1375.1–3; 1377.1–2; 1378.1–2; 1392.2–3). The word 'Αθενάαι used in dedications is also quite common: *IG* I^3 534; 559; 621; 688; 740; 779; 809; 810; 899; *SEG* 16.42.32 (cf. *IG* II^2 17); restorations are *IG* I^3 99.9; 240.11, 12.

[34] *IG* I^3 465.126: [παρὰ ταμ]ιõν *h*εφα[ισ]τικõ ἀπὸ Λ[αυ]ρ̣[είο]; note the parallel restorations in 444.249: [παρὰ ταμιõν *h*εφαιστικõ] ἀπὸ Λαυρε[ίο]; 445.294: [παρὰ ταμιõν *h*εφαι]στικ[õ ἀπὸ Λαυρείο]; 464.103: [παρὰ ταμιõν *h*εφαιστικõ ἀπὸ Λαυρείο]. See M. Crosby, "The Leases of the Laurion Mines," *Hesperia* 19 (1950) 189–212, esp. note 4, 190–91, who suggested that the Hephaistikon was a mine, but (n.b.) also admitted the possibility that it was a sanctuary.

This mine may have had particular significance—by virtue of its direct control by the government—for public finances, that distinguished it from the vast majority of the mines which were leased to contractors, as Segre first suggested in connection with the Coinage Decree. Stroud also raises the possibility that money borrowed for building the Parthenon and Propylaia—their accounts provide the other epigraphical evidence for the Hephaistikon—was being repaid in the Coinage Decree.

Let us first consider the possibility of a reference to the Hephaistikon mine, following Stroud's suggestion. The qualification ἀπὸ Λαυρεῖο 'from Laureion' is somewhat troubling as a specification for a mine and could as well denominate a treasury dedicated to Hephaistos that was supplied by a ritual levy from the mines at Laureion. But theophoric names for mines existed, and there may have been characteristic rituals celebrated in connection with them.[35] Another problem here is that the *tamiai* of the Hephaistikon always appear in conjunction with usage of the funds derived thence. While it is certainly possible to create a scenario in which they would not be missed here, one would be much more comfortable were they to appear in the decree.

Moreover, the reading -λαι would suggest either an aorist participle or a feminine dative. An infinitive, something like ἀποστεῖλαι, would entail that another infinitive should in all likelihood follow Ἡφαισ[τ- and so deprive us of the space needed for specifying the name of the mine. Assuming one is limited to words that are actually known to appear on Attic inscriptions, no dative restorations come readily to mind. Otherwise, the realm of free composition is entered. As has already been seen, Ἀθην]άαι is possible, but probably only if a dedication is at issue.[36] In other words, Athena and Hephaistos are more likely to be paired as recipients and there can be no easy allusion to the Hephaistikon mine.

It now appears that the ideas both of repayments to cults and of tithes to cults, as previously conceptualized, must be discarded. D.M. Lewis has shown that the conditional clause in our section viii is an "entrenchment

[35] Crosby *Hesperia* (1950) 193, 306–308. For ritual, note J.E. Jones, "Another Eleusinian Kernos from Laureion," *BSA* 77 (1982) 191–99, esp. 197.

[36] Meritt *PAPS* (1974) 270–71, restores as follows: . . . καὶ ἀποδόσθαι ἢ τοῖς στρατ[ηγοῖς ἢ τοῖς ἔργων ἐπιστάταις· [ἐπε]ιδὰν δὲ ἀποδοθῆι, | [οἰκοδομῆσαι ἐπὶ Κολωνοῦ τῆι Ἀθην]άαι καὶ τῶι Ἡφαίσ[τωι νεὼν καὶ βωμόν. Yet the insertion here of the funding of the Hephaisteion is abrupt and incongruous on the basis of the rest of the decree. Can the overseers of the building of the temple merely have been the "*epistatai* of works" without some further specification? The use of funds derived from the allies, through a minting fee (as Meritt believes), seems imprudent. We are admittedly in the realm of speculation, but the "entrenchment" of monies (in section viii) allocated to a building project does seem rather unnecessary. Cf. Rhodes, *Empire* note 6 on p. 4.

clause," in which resources are protected for a special purpose.[37] An important clue to this reconstruction is supplied by δανε[ίζεσθαι (to be preferred to δανε[ίζεν) in section viii.2. This verb, as it is juxtaposed with χρῆσθαι, indicates that the creation of a fund is at issue, for it would be absurd to add the additional specification that no one was to borrow non-Athenian money after its very use was forbidden. Why single out this one manner of utilization out of so many possibilities for specific prohibition?

Any restoration that aspires to any probability of being close to the original ought to address several concerns.

1. Phrasing needs to be found for separating the funds, which will then be protected in section viii. One hint to the appropriate terminology is provided by the description of the 1,000T fund set aside at the beginning of the Peloponnesian War for dealing with a naval attack on the city: Thuc. 2.24.1: καὶ χίλια τάλαντα ἀπὸ τῶν ἐν ἀκροπόλει χρημάτων ἔδοξεν αὐτοῖς ἐξαίρετα ποιησαμένοις χωρὶς θέσθαι καὶ μὴ ἀναλοῦν. In *IG* I³ 93.47–50, in connection with the first Syracusan expeditionary force, we see a similar usage of a word containing the element ἐξαιρ-:[38]

[– – – – ἐ]π' ἄλλο ἔργον με[δ' ἐπ' ἄλλεν σ]τρατιὰν
[– – – – – τ]ρισχιλίον· ἐ[ὰν δέ τις εἴπει] ἒ ἐπιψσ-
[εφίσει – – – – – – –]ς ἐχσαιρ[. . . . . . 14 . . . . . .]ον μ̣[.]
[– – – – – – – – – – – – – –]ογ̣ι̣τ̣[. . . . . 20 . . . .]

The main verbal form of this clause is quite possibly an infinitive or an imperative of ἐξαιρέω. Another extant fifth-century Attic decree on fiscal affairs, the fragmentary *IG* I³ 82, the "Hephaisteia Decree," contains in lines 15–16 . . . τõ *h*ε[φα]ίστο καὶ τε̃ς 'Αθεναίας̣. . . . . 26 . . . . |. . . . 9 . . . .] 'Αθεναίο[ι]ς̣ *h*όθεν χρὲ ἐχσαιρε̃⟨ν⟩ ἀργύ̣[ριον. . . . Here the appearance of Hephaistos and Athena in close proximity again is striking, although the reference to μοσιχε̃ς in line 14 and the Hieropoioi of line 17 suggests that the context

[37] D.M. Lewis, "Entrenchment-Clauses in Attic Decrees," in D.W. Bradeen and M.F. McGregor (eds.), ΦΟΡΟΣ: *Tribute to Benjamin Dean Meritt* (Locust Valley, N.Y. 1974) 81–89, esp. 83–85. He compares the second Kallias Decree (*IG* I³ 52B.17–19); the reservation of 1,000T and 100 triremes at the beginning of the Peloponnesian War (Thuc. 2.24; 8.15.1); and a presently irretrievable provision in *IG* I³ 93.47–50. Other decrees not dealing with the protection of funds also contain similar entrenchment clauses: *IG* I³ 46.20–29; 63.1–5; 71.31–33; 89.52–54; cf. *IG* II² 43.51–63. See also M.N. Tod, review of *ATL*² in *JHS* 69 (1949) 104–105.

[38] Lines 45–47 seem to relate to a situation where monies reserved for the Sicilian expedition are protected or the 1,000T reserve established by Perikles early in the war is being protected once again by an entrenchment clause. See Meiggs-Lewis #78, pp. 236–40; *HCT* 4.224–27.

may be sacral.[39] In *IG* I³ 101.63, the infinitive ἐχσαιρε͂[σθαι is a likely restoration, while *IG* I³ 139.12 seems to attest a finite verb form (... ἐπ]ειδὰν ἐχσα[ιρ ...).[40]

2. If we retain the spelling 'Αθην]άαι, then that spelling is likely to be a result of the influence of dedications. Naturally, there is little room for a full formula of dedication here, but the phrase ἀπαρχὴν 'Αθην]άαι is attested (*IG* I³ 547; 680; cf. 859*bis*) and its familiar archaism would account for the spelling.[41] Such wording would dovetail nicely with the formulations built around ἐξαιρ- that were surveyed in paragraph 1 immediately above. Note the restoration printed in *IG* I³ 101.63–64: τε͂ι δὲ Παρθένοι ἐχσαιρε͂[σθαι τὲν ἀπαρχὲν κα|θ*h*άπερ τὸ πρότερον *h*ὲν ἂν Νεοπολιτο͂ν *h*ο δ]ε͂μος ε[ὔ]χσεται.[42] The reader will have noticed that some such restoration will fit well within the reconstruction suggested above in which the allies were contributing non-Attic money to the Hellenotamiai in place of the customary tribute, with a part of the contributions initially replaced by a minting of (at least) half the silver available in the mint. That newly minted coin took the place of the allied payments that were sent to the mint to make up deplenished stocks. Rather than the treasurers of Athena receiving the *aparkhē* as was established practice, a fund of Athena and Hephaistos held in the Hephaisteion and perhaps conveniently accessible to the mint got an *aparkhē*.

3. It is not only on the aforesaid interpretations but on general grounds that the protected fund cannot have been the whole sum of

[39] Mattingly, *AJP* (1974) 281–82, believes that the same protected fund is involved in *IG* I³ 82. Noting its archon date of 421/0, he argues that it is unlikely that the Coinage Decree can be dated in the 440s; that gives too long a period for the fierce protection of this reserve. This lapse of time, however, would be almost exactly equivalent to the period during which the Periklean reserve was protected in the Peloponnesian War. Moreover, it is far from certain that a reserve established in the Coinage Decree was protected from any use rather than merely from any use other (ἐς ἄλλο] τι) than the one specified (be that in a lost portion of the decree or elsewhere). The funds reserved could then have experienced a considerable turnover. W.E. Thompson, "The Protected Fund of Athena and Hephaistos," *AJP* 98 (1977) 249–51, is also skeptical.

[40] Some later examples solidify the technical valence of ἐξαιρέω and its relatives: *IG* II² 1443.12–13: [ἀσή]μου ἀργυρίου τοῦ εἰς τὰ στρατιωτικὰ ἐξαιρεθέντ||[ος] ...; 1613.240–43: ... σκεύη | [κρεμ]αστὰ ἐπὶ τὰς ἐξαιρέ||[τους τ]ριήρεις ἐν τῆι σκευο|[θήκηι] ...; *SEG* 2.9.8–9: ἑλέσθαι δὲ τρεῖς ἄνδρας, οἵτινες λα|βόντες τὸ ἐξαιρεθὲν ἀργύριον ἀναθήσουσι εἰς τὸ ἱερὸν στήλη[ν] ...; *SEG* 21.233.30–31 (= *IG* II² 47): ἀπὸ τοῦ ἀργυρίο το͂ ἐκ το͂ λιθοτομε̣[ί]ο [ἐκτ]ὸ[ς] [τ]ο͂ ἐξαιρομένο. ...

[41] For the more common τὴν ἀπαρχὴν τῆι 'Αθηναίαι or τἀθηναίαι: for example, *IG* I³ 559; 699; 702; 740; 920; 921; 926–30; 935.

[42] B.D. Meritt and A. Andrewes, "Athens and Neapolis," *BSA* 46 (1951) 200–209, esp. 206–207. However, it is the *aparkhē* to Athena of Athens that is at issue, with any other monetary obligations of the people of Neapolis to the Athenians having been remitted. See Tod, *GHI* #84, 1.210; Meiggs-Lewis #89, p. 275; cf. *ATL* 1.525–26, 3.xii.

money conveyed to the *stratēgoi*. Even without considering large amounts, such as a minting fee levied on all the non-Athenian coinage of the allies in one traditional view, or half the bullion in the mint, now newly coined, the fact that the reserve established at the beginning of the Peloponnesian War to be used in the most dire emergency was not larger than 1,000T indicates that the money reserved here was probably a much more modest amount. There would also have been no reason to make the funds over to the *stratēgoi* only to have the same money pass right away into the protected fund. The question then arises whether the manner of the partition of money originally consigned to the *stratēgoi* is subsumed in the act itself of assigning an *aparkhē*.

In light of these concerns, restorations for this section of the decree might well start with phrasing that conveyed the following sense: [ἐπε]ιδὰν δὲ ἀποδοθῆι, [οὗτοι ἐξαιρῶσι τὴν ἀπαρχὴν τάθην]ᾳαι καὶ τῶι ῾Ηφαίσ[τωι.... Another possibility might be [ἐπε]ιδὰν δὲ ἀποδοθῆι, [ἐξαιρεῖν τὴν ἀπαρχὴν τὴν τῆι ᾿Αθην]ᾳαι καὶ τῶι Ηφαίσ[τωι.... What might then follow is shaped by the question whether one can assume that the *aparkhē* here is the sixtieth customarily due Athena from the tribute. Indeed we cannot exclude that a term such as δεκάτην should be restored. Another method for delimiting the size of the *aparkhē* would have been to set a ceiling for its size. Thus it may be possible that the largest sum of money that could be reserved was specified by a phrase like, for example, ἐς ΔΙΙ τάλαντα 'up to 12 talents.'

If, however, no proportion or amount needed to be specified, the rationale or purpose for the protected fund might have been noted. Although congruence with the rest of our interpretation must replace a true historical argument here, for which contextual and comparative material are lacking, that the reserve was to be used later in exchanges is attractive. A possible restoration would be ἐς καταλλαγήν 'for exchange.'[43] The fund was protected to allow its use in ongoing conversions of currency by the allies so that they could pay their tribute in Attic coin. The Coinage Decree may have otherwise intended to minimize the necessity for such exchanges, but it might also have provided for some residual conversions. Nevertheless, this is all admittedly speculative, with the range of possible restorations being quite formidable.

Although section vii seems to create a protected fund of monies, despite our best efforts it is uncertain to what end this action was taken. The strong punitive mechanism established in section viii seems to indicate

[43] The next clause will now no longer be restored καὶ ἐάν τ]ις εἴπ[ηι ..., but ἐὰν δέ τ]ις εἴπ[ηι, so as to create a space of fourteen letters to accommodate this restoration.

that the role of these monies was an important one, but perhaps the full story of their employment is not set out in section vii. There may not be enough room for such a set of orders. Thus the monies under protection in section viii could merely be equated with another fund in section vii, the purpose of which was provided in other legislation. That other fund might either have been composed of the silver produced by the Hephaistikon and possibly another mine (a less likely alternative to my mind), or a preexisting temple fund under the protection of Athena and Hephaistos and associated with the Hephaisteion.

vii. [ἐπε]ιδὰν δὲ ἀποδοθῆι, [οὗτοι ἐξαιρῶσι τὴν ἀπαρχὴν VII.1
τάθην]άαι καὶ τῶι Ἡφαίσ[τωι . . .

vii. Whenever it has been handed over, they should reserve the *aparkhē* to Athena and to Hephaistos . . .

SECTION VIII

viii. καὶ ἐάν τ]ις εἴπ[ηι ἢ] ἐπιψηφίσηι περ[ὶ τούτων VIII.1
. . . . . . .15. . . . . . ἐς ἄλλο] τι χρῆσθαι ἢ δανε[ίζεσθαι, ἀπαγέσθω
αὐτίκα μάλα πρὸς] τοὺς ἕνδεκα· οἱ δ[ὲ ἕνδεκα θαν]άτωι
ζ[ημιωσάντων· ἐὰν] δὲ ἀμφισβητῆι, ἐσ[αγαγόντων ἐς τὸ
δικαστήρ]ιον.

Section viii establishes the mechanism for some form of summary punishment before the Eleven.[44] In earlier reconstructions based on the restoration of D.M. Robinson (followed by Segre and *ATL*), an abrupt shift back to the general provisions of the decree was envisaged: καὶ ἐάν τις εἴπηι ἢ] ἐπιψηφίσηι περ[ὶ τούτων ὅτι ἔστι ξενικῶι νομίσμα]τι χρῆσθαι ἢ δαν[είζεν, ἀπογραφέσθω αὐτίκα μάλα πρὸς] τοὺς ἕνδεκα. The rest of the text just above, which is derived from the *IG* I^3, follows Robinson's original restoration. Much of it is not held to be controversial and only the contested details will be emphasized below.[45]

M.N. Tod in his review of *ATL* 2 recognized the problematical character of ὅτι ἔστι . . . (a doubt now fully warranted).[46] He went on to note that an infinitive or ὡς δεῖ should follow ἐπιψηφίσηι (cf. *IG* II^2

[44] See Robinson *AJP* (1935) 153–54.

[45] For the use of ἀμφισβητέω, compare *IG* I^3 6A.32–33; 34.61–62 (res.), 68–69 (res.); 41.19–20; 58.14–15; 118.25–26. For the phrase ἐσ[αγαγόντων ἐς τὸ δικαστήρ]ιον, compare *IG* I^3 82.28: ἐσαγọ́γ̣[τον ἐς τὸ δικασ]τ̣έρι̣[ο]ν τὸ τõ ἀρχοντος; 117.11–12: ἐσαγό[σθον προδοσίας ἐς τὸ δ]ικαστέριον (cf. *SEG* 23.21); for restored passages, note *IG* I^3 68.47–48; 236.6, 11; *SEG* 31.6.42–43 (*IG* I^3 21).

[46] *JHS* 69 (1949) 104–105.

411.26–27, 30–31; *SEG* 28.103.36–38; restored in *IG* I^3 63.2–3; 114.12–13), and suggested ἐξεῖναι or ὡς δεῖ ἀλλοδαπῶι νομίσμα]τι.[47] The rationale for all these restorations in viii.1–2 is undermined by Lewis's argument about the role of the protected fund here. Moreover, as has been remarked, the idea of forbidding loans after having outlawed any use of non-Athenian money is nonsensical. The phrase περ[ὶ τούτων cannot bring us back to the general content of the earlier sections of this decree; rather it is more likely that this expression is a reference to the preceding clause.[48] That makes good sense in the hypothesis of the creation of a protected fund (explored just above).

A hypothetical reconstruction can draw credibility from its degree of parallelism to Thucydides 2.24.1 on the creation of the reserve at the beginning of the Peloponnesian War. I have placed in curly brackets the extant syntactical and semantic similarities and in double curly brackets the posited *comparanda*: καὶ χίλια τάλαντα ἀπὸ τῶν ἐν τῇ ἀκροπόλει χρημάτων ἔδοξεν αὐτοῖς {{ἐξαίρετα}} ποιησαμένοις χωρὶς θέσθαι καὶ μὴ {{ἀναλοῦν}}, ἀλλ' ἀπὸ τῶν ἄλλων πολεμεῖν· ἢν δέ {τις εἴπῃ ἢ ἐπιψηφίσῃ} κινεῖν τὰ χρήματα ταῦτα {{ἐς ἄλλο}} {τι}, . . . {θάνατον ζημίαν} ἐπέθεντο.[49] Lewis is right that the phrase ἐς ἄλλο] τι takes on considerable probability from Thucydides. If the infinitives χρῆσθαι and δανείζεσθαι (note *IG* I^3 52B.13–14) depend directly on the main verbs of this clause, then there would be viable restorations like περὶ τῶν ἐξαιρέτων ἀναλῶσαι ἢ ἐς ἄλλο] τι χρῆσθαι ἢ δανε[ίζεσθαι . . . or . . . ἢ ἀναλοῦν ἢ ἐς ἄλλο] τι χρῆσθαι ἢ δανε[ίζεσθαι (note also *IG* II^2 1091.9; 1611.106, 157, 185).[50]

Attempts to tamper with the protected fund are agreed to have made the perpetrator liable to summary measures. While some earlier commentators opted for seeing an ἀπογραφή here (following D.M. Robinson), Lewis strongly objects, because of the role of the Eleven and because the penalty is summary execution. He cites *Ath. Pol.* 52.1: καθιστᾶσι δὲ καὶ τοὺς ἕνδεκα κλήρῳ, τοὺς ἐπιμελησομένους τῶν ἐν τῷ

[47] Klaffenbach suggested περ[ὶ τὸ ἐξε͂ναι ἅπασι ξενικῶι νομίσμα]τι χρῆσθαι. . . .

[48] Previous difficulties over the referent of περὶ τούτων, for which see Erxleben *AfP* (1969) 116–17, would be neatly avoided by this approach to restoration.

[49] "and they decided, while making 1,000T from the monies on the Acropolis a reserve, to set them apart and not to spend them, but to make war from other resources; and if anyone spoke or put to a vote to (mis)allocate these funds for some other purpose . . . they established death as the penalty."

[50] Compare also *IG* II^2 1243.5–9: μὴ [ἐ]ξεῖ[να]ι δὲ αὐτῶν μη[θενὶ τὰ χρήματα ταῦτα]| [εἰς ἄλ]λο τι μετε[νε]γκεῖν ἢ καταχ[ρήσασθαι ἢ ἀναλῶ|σαι ἐ]κ τῶν καταλ[ει]πομένων, ἀλ[λὰ πάντα ἀκίνητα ἔστω· εἰ| δὲ μ]ή, ὅ τε εἶπ[ας καὶ] ἐπερωτήσ[ας καὶ ἐπιψηφίσας ὀφειλ]|[όν]των ἑκατὸν [δραχμ]ὰς ἱερὰς [τῶι Διονύσωι. . . .

δεσμωτηρίῳ, καὶ τοὺς ἀπαγομένους κλέπτας καὶ τοὺς ἀνδραποδιστὰς καὶ τοὺς λωποδύτας, ἂν μὲν ὁμολογῶσι, θανάτῳ ζημιώσοντας, ἂν δ' ἀμφισβητῶσιν, εἰσάξοντας εἰς τὸ δικαστήριον, κἂν μὲν ἀποφύγωσιν, ἀφήσοντας, εἰ δὲ μή, τότε θανατώσοντας. . . .[51] Robinson, while he had maintained this restoration, had also recognized in his commentary on these lines the relevance of the procedure of ἀπαγωγή before the Eleven.[52] Although ἔνδειξις plays a part in summary action (note *Ath. Pol.* 29.4 and Plato *Apol.* 32B–C), Lewis emphasizes the expeditious character of the *apagōgē* procedure.[53] He posited ἀπαγωγὴν αὐτοῦ εἶναι πρὸς] τοὺς ἕνδεκα. While no directly matching passage is extant, at least the term ἀπαγωγή appears in a fragmentary setting that might be comparable (*IG* II² 128.14–17).

This suggestion is at least as attractive as the text of *IG* I³ that uses Mattingly's conjecture: ἀπαγέσθω | αὐτίκα μάλα πρὸς] τοὺς ἕνδεκα.[54] It has already been noted that the phrase αὐτίκα μάλα is not otherwise attached to judicial procedures in extant imperial inscriptions (see pp. 337–38 above). The supplement θαν]άτωι | ζ[ημιωσάντων appears virtually inevitable. We should resist, however, this restoration being used as a chronological indication.[55] A lack of data forbids our concluding that the death penalty as a deterrent against misusing the reserve fund established in 431, our earliest surviving evidence, was innovative rather than merely a traditional deterrent.

Therefore, with this reinterpretation of section viii, there falls one of the chief props for the hypothesis of the Coinage Decree as an imperialistic enactment that reflected the growing authoritarianism of the Athenian style of leadership.[56] It is most improbable that this clause punished

[51] "They also appoint the Eleven by sortition, who are to supervise those in prison and arrest thieves, slavers, and muggers, and if they admit their guilt, they punish them with death, and if they dispute their guilt, haling them before a dicasteric court, and if they are acquitted, they release those arrested, but if not, they then execute them. . . ."

[52] Robinson *AJP* (1935) 154; see also Erxleben *AfP* (1969) 117; Koch, *Volksbeschlüsse* 392–97.

[53] Lewis, ΦΟΡΟΣ 83–84.

[54] Cf. Koch, *Volksbeschlüsse* 394–95.

[55] Lewis, ΦΟΡΟΣ 89.

[56] Cf., for example, Meiggs-Lewis p. 114. Note the interesting juxtaposition of mechanisms for external and internal control in Meiggs 404–406:

> The strong language of the Coinage Decree, the Decrees of Clinias and Cleonymus providing for the tightening up of tribute collection, and the Assessment Decree of 425 is the language of ruler to subjects. There is no suggestion in any of these decrees that the Athenians are concerned with the interests of anyone save Athens. The Coinage Decree prescribes that . . . [the traditional restorations and interpretations of sections iv, x, and xi follow] . . . The firm tone used toward allies in the imperial decrees to which we have referred is used also towards the Athenian

the emission or usage of non-Athenian money as was once thought. The Athenians were not steeling themselves against giving the allies any special latitude for coining their own silver, as earlier commentary on this portion of the decree implied. Rather they were protecting a fund designed to serve some other purpose, whether my hypothesis of a reserve to assist future monetary exchange is accepted or not. While the allies were possible sources for the money coined or perhaps had contributed monies to replace the silver minted, it is fairly clear that this protected fund was extracted from funds normally under Athenian control and under the authority of the *stratēgoi*. Like so much else in this law, the emphasis here falls on what the Athenians intended to do to control their own political behavior and not to lay down conditions to the allies. Consequently, it is the initiatives of Athenians acting in the Council and Assembly that are circumscribed by section viii of the Coinage Decree.

viii. καὶ ἐάν τ]ις εἴπ[ηι ἢ] ἐπιψηφίσηι περ[ὶ τῶν ἐξαιρέτων VIII.1
ἀναλῶσαι ἢ ἐς ἄλλο] τι χρῆσθαι ἢ δανε[ίζεσθαι, ἀπαγωγὴν
αὐτοῦ εἶναι πρὸς] τοὺς ἕνδεκα· οἱ δ[ὲ ἕνδεκα θαν]άτωι
ζ[ημιωσάντων· ἐὰν] δὲ ἀμφισβητῆι, ἐσ[αγαγόντων ἐς τὸ
δικαστήρ]ιον.

viii. and if anyone speaks or moves a vote concerning the reserved monies to expend, or to use for any other purpose, or to loan, let there be a summary arrest of this person before the Eleven; the Eleven should punish him with death; but if he disputes his guilt, they are to bring him before a dicasteric court.

Part I of the decree, as I have chosen to call it, seems to provide for a movement of money from the allies toward Athens, and includes the protection of the integrity of this process. In Part II, focus shifts to the Athenian mint, where a stock of silver is to be coined. Most students of the Coinage Decree have believed that allied money and silver in the Attic mint intersect in Part II of the decree. I have argued for an order to mint at least half the previous stock of silver and then for the

---

> executive. It would seem that obstruction and evasion is anticipated not only from the allies but also from Athenian magistrates. The Coinage Decree contains a clause safeguarding the decree against amendment and repeal. . . .

In our interpretation this anticipation of Athenian uncooperativeness is an important indicator of the character of Attic hegemony.

replacement of the minted money by allied monies (perhaps tribute). We may recall the actual phenomenon of tendering tribute in the form of non-Athenian coin as attested by the tribute lists, where the receipt of electrum coins occurred. If the Athenians were accepting electrum coins from the allies in the process that is implemented in this decree, it is understandable why they could not simply order that the funds registered by the Hellenotamiai be converted to Attic coin in the mint. The *epistatai* would need to manage the separation of the gold from the silver within the electrum coins and/or to make some commercial arrangement to exchange the coins or their gold component in return for silver. Hence, the term καταλλάττεν (v.5) might even have its ordinary meaning here of 'exchange through money changing.'

The minted silver, comprising one consignment of coin in our view, was subjected to a minting charge of three drachms for each *mna*. That levy remained in the hands of the *epistatai*. The larger remainder was next to go to the *stratēgoi*, with a provision made that the process might extend into the next official year. From these funds the *stratēgoi* were to contribute to a fund, protected by an "entrenchment" clause. Any attempt to divert this fund was deterred by the strongest sanctions. Our suggestion for the use of this fund was to allow the allies to undertake the conversion of non-Athenian money into Attic coinage in future years. Regardless of the credence owed to the specifics of this last aspect of the hypothesis, it is relatively clear that a massive call-in of non-Attic coins cannot have been mandated in this part of the decree.

14

THE COINAGE DECREE: PART III

SECTION IX

ix. κήρυκας δὲ ἑλέσθαι τὸ[ν δῆμον . . . . Sy.: ca. 31/Aph.: 22 . . . . .
. . . .]ένα, ἕνα μὲν ἐπὶ Νή[σους, ἕνα δὲ ἐπὶ 'Ιωνίαν,
ἕνα δὲ ἐφ' 'Ελλήσπο]ντον, ἕν[α] δὲ ἐ[πὶ τὰ ἐπ]ὶ Θράικης·
τό[υτοις δὲ . . . . Sy.: ca. 40 . . . .
ἀπ]οστειλάντ[ων . . . . Sy.: ca. 16 . . . . . εὐθυ]νόσθω μυρία[ισι
δραχμῆσι].

By its subject matter, the next part of the decree signals that the psephism is moving toward culmination (as originally suggested by Hiller von Gaertringen and Klaffenbach). The contributions of the Aphytis and Syme fragments reduce the uncertainities to more manageable proportions, with the Siphnos fragment soon joining in.[1] To aid our discussion, I reproduce the restorations printed in *IG* I^3, much of which has an ancestry in earlier commentary.

ix. κήρυκας δὲ ἑλέσθαι τὸ[ν δῆμον {Sy.: καὶ πέμψαι} ἀπαγγελοῦντας
τὰ ἐψηφισμ]ένα, ἕνα μὲν ἐπὶ Νή[σους, ἕνα δὲ ἐπὶ 'Ιωνίαν,
ἕνα δὲ ἐφ' 'Ελλήσπο]ντον, ἕν[α] δὲ ἐ[πὶ τὰ ἐπ]ὶ Θράικης·
το[ύτοις δὲ τὴν πορείαν ἑκάστωι συγγράψαντες οἱ στρατηγοὶ
ἀπ]οστειλάντων αὐτίκα μάλα· εἰ δὲ μή, εὐθυ]νόσθω μυρία[ισι
δραχμησι].

In section ix there is a provision for the dispatch of heralds to different parts of the alliance in order to inform the allies of the terms of this decree. Here the formulation ἀπαγγελοῦντας τὰ ἐψηφισμ]ένα, suggested by Tod (cf. *ATL*: καὶ πέμψαι {Sy.: ἐς τὰς πόλες} κατὰ τὰ ἐψηφισ]μένα), takes on greater likelihood than the similar restoration of the prepositional phrase in section iii, for the participial phrase can be paralleled in this case from a likely restoration (see above, pp. 343–45).[2] The Syme fragment is a little longer in its nonstoichedon line 4, and that is usually explained by positing a minor discrepancy such as κήρυκα[ς δὲ ἑλέσθαι τὸν δῆμον

[1] The contributions of the Aphytis fragment render the earlier reconstructions of this section of interest only for the history of the study of the decree. Cf., for example, Hiller and Klaffenbach *ZfN* (1924–25).

[2] Note also *IG* I^3 64.8–9: . . . ἀπ[αγγέλαντες πρὸς]| τ[ὸ]ς ἐπ[ι]στάτας. . . .

καὶ πέμψαι ἐς τὰς πόλες κατὰ τὰ ἐψηφισ]μένα (*ATL*); ... τὸν δῆμον αὐτίκα μάλα ἀπαγγελοῦντας τὰ ἐψηφισμ]ένα (Tod); or ... καὶ πέμψαι ἀπαγγελῶντας τὰ νῦν ἐψηφισμ]ένα (Segre).

The practice of sending heralds is itself paralleled in the Kleonymos Decree (*IG* I³ 68) and in greater detail in the assessment of 425/4, where an itinerary is also specified (*IG* I³ 71).[3] Messengers appear also in the Kleinias Decree without their being specified as *kērukes*; *IG* I³ 34.22–28: 'Αθ]εναίος δὲ *h*ελομέ|νος ἄνδρας τέττ[αρας ἀποπέμπεν ἐπὶ] τὰς πόλες ἀντ|ιγραφσομένος τ[ὸμ φόρον τὸν ἀποδοθέντα κα]ὶ ἀπαι|τέσοντας τὸμ μὲ [ἀποδοθέντα παρὰ τõν ἐλλιποσ]õν, τ|ὸ μὲν δύο πλε̃ν ἐπ[ὶ τὰς ἐπὶ Νέσον καὶ ἐπ' 'Ιονίας ἐπὶ] τ|ριέρος ταχείας, [τὸ δὲ δύο ἐπὶ τὰς ἐφ' 'Ελλεσπόντο κα]|ὶ ἐπὶ Θράικες.

This passage is cited in part because the similarity of the number of districts and their order of listing to that found in the Coinage Decree will become significant momentarily. It is certainly no accident that these analogues belong to legislation about the processes for exaction of the tribute. As argued above, the Coinage Decree probably belongs to the sphere of Athenian administration that included tribute collection. Whether chronological conclusions from the itineraries of the heralds are also to be drawn is a controversial issue.

The use of the number of districts to establish a date for the decree has been a prominent feature of the analysis of this section. Before 438/7, five districts existed on the tribute lists, as Caria stood separately from Ionia.[4] This arrangement suggested to those troubled by the redating occasioned by the publication of the Kos fragment that the Coinage Decree too must follow that date, since there is no provision for a herald to be dispatched to Caria.[5] Eventually the Kos fragment with its three-barred *sigmas* encouraged the main body of Attic epigraphists to promote a date in the early 440s. The "orthodox" view of the proponents of an early date was that four districts rather than five also existed in the period 450–46. The position was argued as early as Segre's editio princeps citing

[3] *IG* I³ 68.52–57: τὸς δὲ κέ[ρυκας *h*οσοι] ἄν τιν]|ες [ὅ]σ[ι] δς ἂν *ho*. πρυτάνες με[τὰ τε̃ς βολε̃ς *h*έλο|ντα]ι πέμφσαι ἐς τὰς πόλες ἐ[πὶ τε̃ς Κεκροπίδο|ς πρ]υτανείας *h*όπος ἂν αἱρε[θõσι *h*οι ἄνδρες *h*|οι] τὸ]ν φόρον ἐγλέχσοντες κ[αὶ ἀναγραφõσι ἐν| τõ]ι βολευτερί[ο]ι; *IG* I³ 71.4–6: πέμφσαι κέρυκας] ἐκ τõν [μισθοτõν *h*ος] ἂν χερο[τονέσει *he* βολὲ ἐς τὰ]|ς πόλες δύο [μὲν ἐπ' 'Ιονίαν καὶ Καρίαν] δύο δὲ ἐ[πὶ Θράικεν δύο δ]ὲ ἐπὶ Ν[έσος δύο δὲ ἐφ' 'Ελλέσπ]|οντον; cf. lines 38–42, 50–51. See Schuller, *Herrschaft* 58, 66–68 for the districts.

[4] Cf. *IG* I³ 269.III.34; 270.III.37; 271.I–II.63; 272.I–II.67; 273.IV.24.

[5] Tod *JHS* (1949) 105; Cavaignac, *RN* (1953) 2, responding to Segre 167–69; see also Robinson 324.

correspondence with Meritt, and was expounded in detail in *ATL*.[6] Segre had adduced the Congress Decree, an initiative of panhellenic reconciliation reported in Plutarch *Pericles* 17.1–4, where four sets of heralds are also dispatched. The Congress Decree played a major role in the subsequent discussion of the mission of the heralds in our decree and the division of the empire into districts. This was particularly unfortunate inasmuch as the Congress Decree is probably apocryphal and shows signs of fabrication in the fourth century.[7] Far more weighty points derived from the traces of an organization of the *arkhē* into four districts in the documents of the first tribute period, especially columns I and II of *IG* I³ 263.

Mattingly countered strongly by reopening the argument from the number of tribute districts.[8] Tod had already observed that the order in the Coinage Decree was the same as in the assessment of 425 itself, an observation which Mattingly emphasized as a proof that the Coinage Decree belonged in the 420s.[9] By the early 1960s that conclusion entailed a redating of the Kleinias Decree from the early 440s to the 420s as well. Meritt and Wade-Gery then answered Mattingly with a restatement of the "orthodox" position.[10] They rebuffed a downdating of the Kleinias Decree, tellingly rejecting Mattingly's contention that the provision for allies to send an offering of a cow and a panoply to the Panathenaia indicates a date after the reassessment of 425/4 (for Mattingly, that was the first imposition of the requirement). As for the order of the districts, Meritt and Wade-Gery noted that the reassessment of 425/4 and the attached list of specific assessments have different orders (compare *IG* I³ 71.4–6 with I.61, 110, II.161, 174, III.152, IV.124). Moreover, Mattingly had only achieved an ordered progression of the citation of districts on the quota lists by moving list 25 (*IG* I³ 281 [430/29]) to 426/5, but that entailed a radical and unlikely reconfiguration of the tribute lists of the seventh and eighth assessment periods.[11]

The next round of controversy on this subject (appearing in the mid-1960s) was marked by a further effort by Mattingly to date the Kleinias

6 *ATL* 3.30–32 (cf. 1.496).

7 See R. Seager, "The Congress Decree: Some Doubts and a Hypothesis," *Historia* 18 (1969) 129–40; cf. Meiggs 512–14. See also A.B. Bosworth, "The Congress Decree: Another Hypothesis," *Historia* 20 (1971) 600–616, esp. 601–605 on the mission of the envoys.

8 *Historia* (1961) 158–68, which concentrates on a redating of the Congress Decree after 438/7.

9 Note "Athenian Imperalism and the Foundation of Brea," *CQ* 16 (1966) 172–92, esp. 187–89 (with retractions of some earlier positions).

10 B.D. Meritt and H.T. Wade-Gery, "The Dating of Documents to the Mid-Fifth Century—I," *JHS* 82 (1962) 67–74, esp. 72–74.

11 See also Mattingly *BSA* (1970) 133–42.

Decree to the late 420s, with the suggestion that the Coinage Decree must follow that readjustment.[12] Furthermore, it still could not be accidental for Mattingly that the order that the Coinage Decree adopts appears in the reassessment of 425/4.[13] W.K. Pritchett also contributed to this debate.[14] Not unpersuasively he argued for clustering rather than a four-fold division of districts in the third assessment period (*IG* I³ 266–68) and considerable mixing in the lists of the second period instead of the four-district organization hypothesized by *ATL* (*IG* I³ 263–65). As one would expect, Meritt answered these critiques, stressing the discrepancies between instructions to the heralds in *IG* I³ 71.5–6 and the six districts that seem to be listed in the panels of allied names.[15] He also contended that Pritchett's comments on the disorder of the lists in the third period were partially marred by misidentification. Meritt closed his discussion by holding that he now saw no relevance in the number or order of districts for the shaping of formulas for the itineraries of heralds dispatched from Athens into the *arkhē*.

Thereafter, Erxleben revived the arguments of Mattingly and Pritchett, particularly criticizing Meritt on the significance of the six-fold list of the figures from the reassessment of 425/4.[16] Erxleben redated both the Coinage Decree and the Kleinias Decree to the late 420s, and he notes the similarity between their itineraries and the order of districts in list 32 (*IG* I³ 285), where he seems to believe that the organization was four-fold. In answer, Schuller has again restated the arguments for the "orthodox" dating.[17] E. Ruschenbusch explored the organization of list 5 of the second assessment period (449/8) and concluded that (despite mingling of entries) the Carian district existed during 450–46.[18] The Coinage Decree should then belong after 438.

12 *Ancient Society* 203; *BSA* (1970) 141–42.

13 See also "Formal Dating Criteria for Fifth Century Attic Inscriptions," *Acta of the Fifth International Congress of Greek and Latin Epigraphy, Cambridge, 1967* (Oxford 1971) 27–33, esp. 29–30. Note especially the counter-arguments of D.W. Bradeen and M.F. McGregor, *Studies in Fifth-Century Attic Epigraphy* (Norman, 1973) 20–23.

14 A. Georgiadès and W.K. Pritchett, "The Koan Fragment of the Monetary Decree," *BCH* 89 (1965) 400–441, esp. 428–38. Pritchett also directed criticism at the less probative use by the editors of *ATL* of Steph. Byz. s.v. Δῶρος (*Eth.* 255) as an indication of a five-fold division of the tribute lists in the first assessment period (cf. *ATL* 1.203–204, 483; 3.9–12).

15 See Meritt *GRBS* (1967) 121–26.

16 See Erxleben *AfP* (1971) 118–19, 148–51. Cf. Mattingly, *AJP* (1974) 284–85, who favorably comments on Erxleben's treatment, but states that he no longer holds that the itinerary of the Kleinias Decree need be restored as the same as that within this section of the Coinage Decree, citing his remarks in *Acta* 29–30.

17 Schuller, *Herrschaft* 212–13.

18 E. Ruschenbusch, "Zur Zahl der Tributbezirke des delischen Seebundes und zur Datierung des Kleinias- und des Münzdecrets (Meiggs-Lewis 45 und 46)," *ZPE* 26 (1977)

No firm conclusion about the dating of the Coinage Decree can be achieved based on the number of the heralds and their itinerary. The critics of the chronology of *ATL* are correct insofar as the existence of a four-district reckoning in the lists of the second period of assessment is far from established. An apparent weakness of the position of the downdaters is that their criticisms would force the redating of the Kleinias Decree, owing to its apparently parallel treatment. While some credence is owed the view that there were five districts until 438/7, suggestions that there was a consistency in the order of the listing of districts afterward necessitate massive reordering of the later lists, and few will find that rearrangement palatable. With both its different ordering of districts in the decree and in the roster of assessments and the six-fold organization of the panels (unsystematic though that may be), *IG* I^3 71 hints that we do not have enough data to decide whether such formulas are even significantly variable. For example, if the listing of assessments of the Pontic cities is held irrelevant for a four-fold division into districts of the *arkhē* by treating those cities as an appendix to the Thracian district, must we not then concede that the disposition of districts in such documents is also irrelevant for the actual journeys made by heralds? A practical itinerary would demand an attachment of the Pontic cities to the Hellespontine district.[19]

And then there is the problem that Caria is the one district out of five that is missing from the Coinage Decree. It is easy to conjecture on the basis of the irregularities of payment of tribute that have been outlined above (pp. 279–85) that the absence of Caria or its inclusion with Ionia, regardless of reigning convention on the contemporary tribute lists, might stem from its rather idiosyncratic monetary status. So enumeration and denomination of the tribute districts might have varied with the needs of the speaker, as the idiosyncratic listing in Thucydides 2.9.4 reminds us in its enumeration of tributary cities: καὶ ἄλλαι πόλεις αἱ ὑποτελεῖς οὖσαι ἐν ἔθνεσι τοσοῖσδε, Καρία ἡ ἐπὶ θαλάσσῃ, Δωριῆς Καρσὶ πρόσοικοι, Ἰωνία, Ἑλλήσποντος, τὰ ἐπὶ Θρᾴκης, νῆσοι ὅσαι ἐντὸς Πελοποννήσου καὶ Κρήτης πρὸς ἥλιον ἀνίσχοντα, πᾶσαι αἱ Κυκλάδες πλὴν Μήλου καὶ Θήρας. Note the characteristic emphasis on the ethnic affinity of allied states.

Consequently, our best course on this issue is to affirm a position rather like that of Lewis:[20] "I have never seen any necessary connection between the journeys and the way that tribute lists and assessments are

211–15. See also K. Meister, *Die Ungeschichtlichkeit des Kalliasfriedens und deren historische Folgen* (Wiesbaden 1982) 112.

19 Cf. Erxleben *AfP* (1971) 149.

20 Lewis, *Coinage and Administration* 59.

organized; I am perfectly prepared to contemplate the possibility that the Athenians varied their procedures and word-order without there being any particular significance to the variations."

One needs also to insist on a further corollary that highlights what one is actually dating by fixing the chronology of the formula attested in section ix. Section ix is attested by the Aphytis, Syme, and Siphnos (only in its provision for fining after *euthunai*) fragments of the decree and not by the Kos fragment with its three-barred *sigmas*. It may well be that the most logical assumption is that the heralds were dispatched only once, at the time of the first promulgation of the decree and contemporaneously with its first inscription. In the case, however, of a piece of legislation that might have been inscribed at different times over a considerable span (see pp. 455–57), it cannot be entirely excluded that the formula describing the mission of the heralds was modernized, perhaps almost unconsciously, and that such minor rewriting took place in disregard of the now forgotten actual experience of the heralds. This represents no more than a bare supposition but is worth remembering nonetheless.

The restoration in lines 4–5 of this section is guaranteed in its general import by the probable supplement ἀπ]οστειλάντ[ων.[21] The specific phrasing, derived from Segre and accepted by most subsequent editors, cannot truly to said to have built on a model; it does, however, belong to a pattern of restoring such loci. *IG* I³ 71.40–42 has been restored to read as follows: τὰ]ς δ[ὲ πορ]είας τοῖς κέρυχ[σι τοῖς ἰõσι χσυγγράφσαι κατὰ τ]|òν *hóρ*[κον τὸ]ς τάκ[τας *hέο*]ς τ[õ πο]ρε[υθέσ]αν[τα]ι *hίνα* μὲ αὐ[τοὶ |ἄτακτοι ἴοσι. *IG* I³ 127.34–35 is restored thus: καὶ τὴν πορείαν παρα||[σκευάσαι τοῖς πρέσβεσι τὸς στρατηγὸς ὡ]ς τάχιστα. . . . The term πορεία—its restoration in *IG* I³ 71 is strengthened by the likely appearance of the related verb—appears fairly secure, as a *terminus technicus* for the official conveyance of heralds during the *arkhē*. Notably, these two passages contain no punitive clauses.

Before we accept this reconstructed text, it is necessary to consider the apparent singular εὐθυ]νόσθω, the subject of which is unclear. An implied οἱ στρατηγοί remains a likely subject for a *plural* imperative from the standpoint of content. Various solutions have been proposed. For example, the proposer of the decree meant to say εὐθυ]νόσθων, or the plural was converted into a singular as the two suggestions of

[21] Hiller and Klaffenbach, *ZfN* (1924–25) 218, had offered ἀπ]οστειλάντ[ων αὐτὸς (number) ἡμερῶν, which lacks good parallels. Wilhelm, *AAWW* (1924) 162, suggested ἀπ]οστειλάντ[ων οὗ ἂν ἕκαστοι ἴωσιν, but that seems a little vapid as well as redundant. Note also Erxleben *AfP* (1969) 119.

Wilhelm offer.[22] Tod offers a similar set of options, namely, an error, understanding ἕκαστος αὐτῶν as the verb's subject[23] or treating this imperative as an alternative form for the plural. For the last, he had noted the form εὐ]θυνέσθο in *IG* I² 41.6 as a putative plural, but that has subsequently been restored as a singular (*IG* I³ 41.92).[24] Mattingly attempted to use the middle and passive imperatives as a criterion for dating imperial inscriptions: -οσθω/-οσθων are earlier than but overlap with -εσθω/-εσθων, although the Coinage Decree contained the assumed earlier form.[25] Meritt criticized this hypothesis, arguing for a much longer period for the overlap in the two sets of forms.[26] Mattingly later corrected his citations and was prepared to argue that no certain example of -εσθων preceded the Archidamian War, while forms in -οσθων lingered into the 420s.[27]

A number of cautionary comments are in order. The phrasing το[ύτοις δὲ τὴν πορείαν ἑκάστωι συγγράψαντες . . . does not inspire any great confidence. A frank recognition is also necessary that we do not know the precise denotation of the term πορεία. It may indeed mean something more than 'provision,' perhaps 'arrangements for the journey' or even 'conveyance.'[28] I am also unsure whether συγγράψαντες is correct, especially if it is to mean 'draw up a proposal' (cf. *IG* I³ 71.40–41). That this degree of punishment would be felt necessary in such an eventuality is hard to fathom. The punishment is a heavy one, and it is always assigned to an individual specifically when it is elsewhere meted out through *euthunē* (*IG* I³ 34.36–37; 61.38–39; 71.15–16, 37-38; 84.10, 20; 133.18; cf. 10.21–22; 63.4–5; 117.20–21). Although it is hard to gauge the seriousness of various official derelictions, the remaining examples of *euthunai* encompassing 10,000-dr. fines appear more serious than the mere failure to procure or propose the necessary funding for

22 Wilhelm *AAWW* (1924) 161–62; Erxleben, *AfP* (1969) 119, preferred to see an error.

23 Cf. Hiller and Klaffenbach *ZfN* (1924–25) 219.

24 Tod *GHI* 1.165. Erxleben, *AfP* (1969) 119, reaches a similar conclusion. *ATL* 2.64, also coming to similar conclusions, claims that εὐθυ]νόσθωμ [μ]υρ̣[ίαισι δραχμῆσι is the correct interpretation of what is actually visible on a squeeze of the Siphnos fragment, but that judgment has received little support from subsequent commentators.

25 Mattingly, *Ancient Society* 198–201.

26 See Meritt *GRBS* (1967) 131–32. The *ATL* (2.65) had earlier suggested ἀπ]οστειλάντ[ων· εἰ δὲ μή, καθ' ἕνα ἕκαστον εὐθυ]νόσθωμ μυρία[ισι δραχμῆσι]. Mattingly's second thoughts are found in *BCH* (1968) 468.

27 Mattingly, "Periclean Imperialism," as reprinted in G. Wirth (ed.) *Perikles und seine Zeit* (Darmstadt 1979) 312–49, esp. 319–22; see also *AJP* (1984) 357.

28 A.G. Woodhead, "ΠΟΡΕΙΑ," *Mnem.*⁴ 5 (1952) 94–107, esp. 98–99.

the dispatch of heralds.[29] As for the phrasing of the punishment, the formulation ἐὰν δὲ μή ... is attested while εἰ δὲ μή is not clearly evidenced. At the same time, ἐὰν δὲ μή and the conjunction ἤ are alike well represented in fifth-century punitive clauses, but ἤ is significantly more common.

Perhaps we would be justified in supposing that the *stratēgoi* were expected to assign one of their number to escorting each herald with a trireme. This *stratēgos* would be responsible for seeing that the herald could reach all the allied cities entrusted to him safely and so carry out his mission. As *IG* I^3 71.41 states, the risk was that the Heralds go ἄτακτοι, which probably means without proper military escort (cf. Hdt. 6.93; Thuc. 8.105.2–3). The heavy liability was appropriate for an official who was responsible for the success of the whole enterprise and not just for a herald's travel arrangements and financial support. Wilhelm wanted to understand "der Betreffende" 'the one concerned' as the subject, an idea that strikes about the right note.[30] Inasmuch as παρασκευάζω is used with τὴν πορείαν in *IG* I^3 127.34–35, it might be possible to restore: ... το[ύτος δὲ τὴν πορείαν ἑκάστωι παρασκευάσαντες οἱ στρατηγοὶ ἀ]|ποστειλάντ[ων ὡς τάχιστα ἢ ἕκαστος εὐθυν]όσθω μυρία[ισι δραχμῆσι. ...[31] We would be positing the alternative singular ending -οσθω (in parallel to the well attested plural -οσθων), which is not clearly attested among imperial inscriptions. This analogy does not represent much of a stretch of reasoning.

Just one more concluding point needs to be raised about this section of the decree: again one observes that the decree's focus is on controlling

29 *IG* I^3 34.36–37 has this penalty for *prytanes* who fail to bring (before the *Boulē*) *graphai* charging offenses concerning tribute collection; 61.38–39 threatens to punish the Hellespontophylakes for failing to allow unimpeded importation of grain from the Hellespont by Methone; 71.15–16 warns of retaliation for a failure of the *taktai* to establish assessments in accordance with *diadikasiai*; 71.37–38 handles *prytaneis* who fail to see that the assessment procedure is carried through; 133.18 provides deterrence against misuse of sacred funds. An exception might be *IG* I^3 84.10, 20 where the failure of the archon *basileus* and the *pōletai* on the leasing of land belonging to the cult of Kodros, Neleus, and the Queen is liable to the 10,000-dr. penalty.

30 Wilhelm *AAWW* (1924) 161–62.

31 These lines are represented solely by the Syme fragment, which is nonstoichedon with only the left part of the inscription preserved. Its restored line lengths are approximately as follows: (1) 59; (2) 59; (3) 56; (4) 61; (5) 58; (6) 57; (7) 58; (8) 57; (9) 61; (10) 60; (11) 59; (12) 56; (13) 62; (14) 12+ ?. Lines 1–5 are paralleled by the stoichedon Aphytis fragment, the second part of (7), ca. thirty-seven letters, through (14) are paralleled by the nonstoichedon Siphnos fragment, and (9) through (14) are paralleled by the Odessa fragment. I have given the letter counts for (6) and (7) on the basis of *IG* I^3. Nothing, however, bars the restoration proposed in the text, which has fifty-nine letters in (6) and fifty-eight letters in (7).

the behavior of Athenian officials and not on either deterring misdeeds by the allies or punishing them.

ix. κήρυκας δὲ ἑλέσθαι τὸ[ν δῆμον καὶ πέμψαι ἀπαγγελοῦντας IX.1
τὰ ἐψηφισμ]ένα, ἕνα μὲν ἐπὶ Νή[σους, ἕνα δὲ ἐπὶ 'Ιωνίαν,
ἕνα δὲ ἐφ' ῾Ελλήσπο]ντον, ἕν[α] δὲ ἐ[πὶ τὰ ἐπ]ὶ Θράικης·
το[ύτος δὲ τὴν πορείαν ἑκάστωι παρασκευάσαντες οἱ στρατηγοὶ
ἀπ]ποστειλάντ[ων ὡς τάχιστα ἢ ἕκαστος εὐθυν]όσθω μυρία[ισι
δραχμῆσι·

ix. The *dēmos* is to choose heralds and to send them to announce the measures that have been voted, one to the islands, and one to Ionia, and one to the Hellespont, and one to the Thraceward region. The generals having provided conveyance to each are to dispatch them as quickly as possible, or each should be fined 10,000 drachms when he undegoes his final scrutiny.

SECTION X

x. [ἀναγ]ράψαι δὲ τὸ ψήφισμα τ[όδε τὸς ἄ]ρχοντα[ς τ]ὸ[ς ἐ]ν X.1
ταῖσι πόλεσιν [καὶ θε͂ναι ἐν στή]ληι λιθίνηι ἐν τῆι ἀγορᾶι
[ἑκάστης] τῆ[ς πό]λεως καὶ τὸς ἐπιστ[άτας ἔμπροσθεν] το͂
ἀργυροκοπίο· ταῦτα δὲ ἐπ[. . . . . . . 16 . . . . ἐ]ὰμ μὴ αὐτοὶ
βόλωνται.

This section starts by setting out straightforward instructions both that the archons in the cities inscribe and erect copies of the decree in each allied city and that the *epistatai* of the mint see to its display in front of the mint in Athens.[32] As above in section iii, the archons in the cities should be Athenian officials established in the *arkhē*. If another argument in favor of that conclusion may be drawn from this context, one would note that it is more likely that Attic magistrates be paired (without ethnic denomination) with the *epistatai* of the Attic mint than

[32] The alternative restoration is καταθῆν]αι ... ἀναγράψαντας ἐν στήλαι λιθίναι, proposed by Wilhelm, *IG* XII.5 480 and *AAWW* (1924) 160; cf. *IG* I^2 p 295; and by Hiller and Klaffenbach *ZfN* (1924–25) 218. It is also accepted by *ATL*. Chabiaras read -γρα[ψ]αι, see *AE* (1922) 40 with Erxleben *AfP* (1969) 120. The alternative restoration also gives an unacceptably long line (8), ca. sixty-five letters, for the Syme fragment. These provisions are common, but the form of ἀναγράφω virtually always comes before the form of (κατα)τίθημι. For θῆναι (θε͂ναι) in such contexts, cf. *IG* I^3 118.27; 196.1.

that allied officials be so juxtaposed. That determination of the *arkhontes* raises a problem over the supplement 'Αθηναίος (acc. pl.) that has been offered in section x.4 (urged by Wilhelm and Hiller von Gaertringen and Klaffenbach and accepted by subsequent commentators). Although there is some sense in the proposition that resident Athenians might protect their city's interests by carrying out a task neglected by recalcitrant *allied* magistrates, it is unlikely that they intervened to fulfill responsibilities neglected by their own officials present in an allied city.

Hence some have assumed that these archons in the cities must be allied and not Athenian officers.[33] In that case, however, why did the Athenians not simply threaten allied officials with punishment? Moveover, the phrase ἐ]ὰμ μὴ αὐτοὶ βόλωνται seems a rather casual and permissive way to refer to recalcitrant allied officials. Admittedly, there is a risk of begging the question here inasmuch as no procedure for discipline is in fact attached to noncompliance with this instruction. That criticism, however, prompts our asking which group of officials was the more likely to have been allowed to opt out of erecting the decree. Once again, Attic officials are the probable answer.

Furthermore, no rationale comes readily to mind for these ordinary Athenians, who should certainly be identified in some specific fashion, being charged with fulfilling this function.[34] The provision seems to create unnecessary tinder for recriminations against allied *arkhontes* or the local Athenians, the former for disobediance and the latter for interference, thereby sowing disaffection among the allies and exposing the Athenians to danger. Are we to imagine that resident Athenians, emboldened by the possession (somehow) of a text of this decree, contracted for its inscription and then forced the allied leaders to find room for it in their marketplace? How did the Athenians enforce this intention to erect the decree? If Athens wanted to enlist Athenians living or traveling among the allies in seeing to display of this psephism, a clause that authorized ὁ βουλόμενος to proceed to legal action would have been the tried and true method (cf. *IG* I^3 34.31–35; 64.5–7; note also the restoration in 68.45–47).

It is more sensible to posit that the allies were directed to erect the decree by suggesting the restoration τὰς πόλες, if the Athenian

[33] They have followed Hiller and Klaffenbach *ZfN* (1924–25) 219.

[34] Some of these complications could be avoided if 'Αθηναίος connoted the Athenian state and not individual Athenians living or visiting abroad, as Mattingly, *Klio* (1977) 86–87, seems to suggest. It is hard to believe that the Athenian state could ever have been juxtaposed in this way with its own archons in the cities. Thus we are forced back on the *arkhontes* being allied officials and the mystery of the absence of a punitive clause.

officials (αὐτοί) were unwilling.[35] Some have accepted the restoration ἐ[πιτελεσάντον *hόσα* ἐν τῶι] ψηφίσματι οἱ ἄρχοντε[ς οἱ ἑκάστης τῆς πόλεως as one viable alternative in a parallel context in section iv above.[36] Nevertheless, the diction involving ἐπιτελέω may also give us a clue here, as this verb is not elsewhere used for the fulfillment of the political directives of the Athenian government by Athenian agents, unless the lacunose section of the regulations for Miletos contains a similar reference to the one suggested here (*IG* I³ 21.84). Its later utilization may provide a hint about the earlier valence of the word. The verb ἐπιτελέω is later used at Athens almost exclusively to denote the accomplishment of religious duties (*IG* II² 1035.27; 1338.5, 10, 23; 1368.111; 2788.17; cf. 1678.14). While it would be imprudent to imply that the allies were bound to obey Athenian orders as the Athenians were obligated to uphold ritual requirements, we might still conclude that ἐπιτελέω connoted in official parlance the carrying out of orders by those other than their makers.

The Athenians were willing to envisage that their own *arkhontes* might not undertake the duty of erection of a stele because their officials were not universally present in allied cities and had other responsibilities. They may have wanted their *arkhontes* to undertake the dissemination of the decree wherever they reasonably could, but did not insist on that action. Nor did they give specific instructions to *arkhontes* in certain cities to cover neighboring communities that had no Athenian official presence. This is the only instance out of the numerous mandates that stelai be erected which envisages a second stage. In other words, only this decree does not merely assume an implementation of the instructions of the *dēmos*. Therefore, I should understand section xi closely with this provision.

The role of individual Athenians has been useful anecdotally in scenarios that explain the "early" (or antiquated) appearance of the Kos fragment as the result of the enlistment of a retired stonecutter by private individuals (see below, pp. 449–50). It is, however, more sensible to suppose the Kos fragment was an inscription erected by transient

[35] For αἱ πόλες as the equivalent of οἱ σύμμαχοι, see, for example, *IG* I³ 34.32–33 (a probable restoration); 68.14; 71.45; 78.14–15.

[36] The word order differs inconsequentially among the fragments, although the existence of even minor differences may indicate the variations in how or when copies were inscribed (see pp. 451–53 below). Siphnos lines 4–5 has ἐν τῆι ἀγ[ορᾶι ἑκάστης | τῆς πό]λεως, which is duplicated by lines 1–2 of the Odessa fragment ἐν τῆι ἀγ|ορᾶι ἑκάστης] τῆ[ς πόλεως. Smyrna line 3 seemingly offers ἐν τῆι ἀγορᾶι τῆ[ς πόλεως ἑκάστης. Syme line 8 may lack the article τος in . . . τὸς ἄρχοντας τὸς ἐν ταῖσι πόλεσιν, that is restored on the basis of Smyrna line 2, cf. Siphnos line 3 (see Erxleben *AfP* [1969] note 3, p. 120), although restoring it would not give an impossibly long line (as *IG* I³).

(or resident) Athenian *arkhontes,* who supplied an itinerant stonecutter while the Koans provided the stele (apparently of island marble).

x. [ἀναγ]ράψαι δὲ τὸ ψήφισμα τ[όδε τὸς ἄ]ρχοντα[ς τ]ὸ[ς ἐ]ν X.1
ταῖσι πόλεσιν [καὶ θε͂ναι ἐν στή]ληι λιθίνηι ἐν τῆι ἀγορᾶι
[ἑκάστης] τῆ[ς πό]λεως καὶ τὸς ἐπιστ[άτας ἔμπροσθεν] τõ
ἀργυροκοπίο· ταῦτα δὲ ἐπ[ιτελέσαι τὰς πόλες, ἐ]ὰμ μὴ αὐτοὶ
βόλωνται.

x. The officials in the cities are to inscribe this decree and place it on a stone stele in the marketplace of each city and the *epistatai* are to place the decree in front of the mint; the cities are to carry out these instructions, if the officials are not willing.

SECTION XI

xi. δεηθῆναι δὲ αὐτῶν τὸγ κήρυκα τὸν ἰόντα ὅσα [κ]ελεύο[σιν] Ἀθηναῖοι. XI.1

The heralds were surely not policing the implementation of the whole decree in this section. That would have exceeded and jeopardized their traditional role as diplomatic intermediaries. The phrase ὅσα κελεύοσιν Ἀθηναῖοι should pertain only to the provisions for the recording and erection of the decree and not the entirety of its contents. The order to the Heralds to proclaim the contents had already been given in section ix.1–2, which has been restored: . . . ἀπαγγελοῦντας τὰ ἐψηφισμ]ένα. . . . The text of the decree instructed the allied citizens about the contents of the law and to suggest that the herald added some personal plea—"Hey guys! We mean it this time!"—strains credulity.

The wording δεηθῆναι δὲ αὐτῶν is not paralleled in other imperial decrees. If the relevant *comparanda* are drawn from Thucydides (note, for example, 1.27.2; 1.32.4, 5; 1.119; 5.37.3; 5.50.5), this phrase should mean "request of them through diplomacy," not "require of them."[37] The Athenians were ordering a herald dispatched to each district, on his arrival in a particular city (τὸγ κήρυκα τὸν ἰόντα) to request either of their officials in the area (if αὐτῶν here are the same people as αὐτοί

[37] Note Meritt *PAPS* (1975) 267; cf. Meiggs 405.

in section x.4) or of their allies, who are αὐτῶν in one of those sudden changes in perspective notable in inscriptions, what the Athenians were enjoining, namely, the inscription and erection of the decree. Many may prefer to see the request as being made of the allies.

The Athenians were eager to ensure the display of the decree in all allied cities, but foresaw an unwillingess or an inability on the part of their magistrates to carry out this intention. Officials were not *resident* in all the allied cities, and the Athenians may have envisaged difficulties, including the press of other duties that might hamper the arrangement for inscription and display during a visit by an *episkopos* (to take one example). Yet it was their expectation that the allies would be disposed to undertake publication in the stead of the *arkhontes*. Notwithstanding its Attic lettering, the island marble of the Kos fragment may hint at just such a cooperation.

The existence to date of six or even seven versions (if the two fragments from Syme derived from two stelai) indicates considerable diligence in the implementation of this provision. The fragments of the Coinage Decree from Syme, Siphnos, Aphytis, and Kos derived from cities without (on the basis of the present evidence) strong local practices of inscribing, while the true provenience of the Smyrna and Odessa copies is unknown. The Coinage Decree will have stood out in the marketplaces of such cities as one of the most prominent inscribed documents, if not, in some places, the most conspicuous public document on view (in light of our present knowledge).

xi. δεηθῆναι δὲ αὐτῶν τὸγ κήρυκα τὸν ἰόντα ὅσα XI.1
[κ]ελεύο[σιν] Ἀθηναῖοι.

xi. The herald arriving is to request of them as much as the Athenians are ordering.

SECTION XII

xii. προσγράψαι δὲ πρὸς τὸν ὅρκον [τ]ὸν τῆς βολῆς τὸν XII.1
γραμματέα τῆς [βολῆς {. . .} τα]δί· ἐὰν τις κόπτηι νόμισ[μα]
ἀργυρίο ἐν τῆσι πό[λεσι κ]αὶ μὴ χρῆται νομ[ίσμασιν τοῖς]
Ἀθη[να]ίων ἢ σταθμοῖς ἢ μέτ[ροις . . . . .12. . . . . νομίσμασι]ν
καὶ σταθμοῖς καὶ μέτροις, [. . . . . .21. . . . . κατὰ τὸ
πρότε]ρον ψήφισμα ὁ Κλέαρχ[ος εἶπεν].

The standard text of lines xii.4–5 that is printed by *ATL* is as follows:

'Αθη[να]ίων ἢ σταθμοῖς ἢ μέτ[ροις ἀλλὰ ξενικοῖς νομίσμασι]ν καὶ σταθμοῖς καὶ μέτροις, [τιμωρήσομαι καὶ ζημιώσω κατὰ τὸ πρότε]ρον ψήφισμα ὁ Κλέαρχ[ος εἶπεν]

As a final aspect of the enforcement of the decree, provision is made for the Bouleutai to swear to take action if a particular, one assumes central, condition of the decree is not respected.[38] This provision was probably laid out in greater detail elsewhere, either in a lost portion of this psephism or in another enactment, like the decree of Klearkhos, to be discussed momentarily. Oaths are a standard feature of Athenian hegemonic administration, as demonstrated by many inscriptions, but such oaths are customarily sworn by the officials or citizens of an allied city or, alternatively, by the Athenians and the citizens of an allied city.[39] In the customary picture of the decree as a measure of authoritarian control, one might expect the oath to be imposed on the officials of the allies from whom any putative violation would naturally have to originate. In the same spirit, however, as the Athenocentric preoccupations with deterrence and enforcement in the rest of the decree, this section of the decree is concluded by a clause added to the oath of the Athenian Bouleutai. That singular feature must be borne in mind throughout the following discussion.

The natural conclusion from this stipulation ought to be that the Athenians wanted to control the behavior of their own prospective legislators, who might not take enforcement of the mandate sufficiently seriously.[40] Superficially, the focus on the Athenian *Boulē* appears hard to square with the content of the clause added to the oath as it is normally restored and interpreted. Are we missing the legislation, either within or without the decree, that threatened allied citizens and officials with dire punishment? If it was promulgated in this psephism, it might surely be expected to be reiterated here, and perhaps in a sense it is, if we credit

[38] Wilhelm offered πρὸς τὴν γνώμην for Smyrna line 5 (*IG* XII.5 480; *AAWW* [1924] 160), but the reading in the text is now universally preferred (Hiller and Klaffenbach *ZfN* [1924–25] 219; cf. *IG* I² 295). His epigraphical discussion has been superseded by the input from the Odessa fragment. Another detour in the early commentary was the idea that the addition to the oath was added to the bouleutic oath of the allied cities; cf. Ziebarth, *Beiträge* 82.

[39] *IG* I³ 11 (Egesta), 21 (Miletos), 39 (Eretria), 40 (Chalcis), 54 (Leontinoi), 76 (Bottiaians), 89 (Perdikkas), 127 (Samos). Restorations: *IG* I³ 15 (Erythrai), 29, 37 (Kolophon), 48 (Samos), 53 (Rhegion), 62 (Aphytis), 75 (Halieis), and 123 (Carthage).

[40] Note the suggestion of Koch, *Volksbeschlüsse* 398, that the addition to the bouleutic oath was an amendment from the floor of the Assembly (citing the verb προσγράψαι). The intervention of an amender would intensify the impression that the resolve of the ordinary citizen serving as councilman needed stiffening.

certain interpretations of the phrase "earlier decree of Klearkhos." Indeed we must believe in the existence of a punitive procedure for policing allied behavior in this matter, if such pains were taken to ensure that the Bouleutai became involved.[41]

A vital clue toward an explanation, however, has been missed in the traditional reading of this clause. There may not be a general prohibition here against allied coining of silver: "if anyone coins money of silver in the cities and does not use the money, or the weights, or the measures of the Athenians but foreign (sic) money and weights and measures." The phrase ἢ μὴ χρῆται 'or does not use' was suggested by Hiller and Klaffenbach and has influenced interpretation ever since, perhaps by virtue of its appearance in the text of *ATL* D 14, beyond the degree to which it was supported by other commentators. The clause was restored with καὶ μὴ χρῆται quite early in our scholarship by Wilamowitz.[42] This particular restoration was accepted by Wilhelm and Segre and had been kept in some British commentary on the decree.[43] The Odessa fragment has now proved conclusively that καὶ is in fact correct.[44]

It is most striking that the possibility of a considerably different construal of the text has not been a subject for comment. Illegality is defined by two coordinate acts: (1) coining silver; and (2) not using Athenian money, weights, and measures (postponing discussion for a moment of the emended clause). In no sense could a refusal to utilize Attic money and standards be considered a corollary of coining local silver, as our discussion of various allied monetary regimes has demonstrated. So the two clauses do not state the same idea in converse ways. The alternative that is implied is perfectly feasible: one might coin silver *and still use* Attic coins, weights, and measures.

The framers of Attic psephisms were quite capable of expressing a series of equal and discrete objectionable activities in the protasis of a conditional sentence by connecting them with ἢ. An example appears in the Brea Decree, *IG* I³ 46.24-26: ἐ]ὰν δέ τις ἐπιφσεφίζει παρὰ τὲ[ν στέλ|εν ἒ ῥρέ]τορ ἀγορεύει ἒ προσκαλε͂σθα[ι ἐγχερ|ε͂ι ἀφαι]ρε͂σθαι ἒ λύεν τι το͂ν *h*εφσεφι[σμὲνον] . . . (for similar formulas: *IG* I³ 52B.17–19; 93.48–49; cf. 29.10; 63.1–2; 114.12–13 [restored]). Another formula

[41] We shall investigate below (pp. 400–403) whether there is any chronological conclusion is to be drawn from the role of the *Boulē* in enforcing the mandate affecting the allies.

[42] Cf. *AE* (1923) 117.

[43] H.T. Wade-Gery, "Studies in Attic Inscriptions of the Fifth Century B.C.," *BSA* 33 (1932–33) 101–36, esp. 118; Tod *GHI* 1.164 (cf. *ATL* 1.579 on T 69).

[44] See Meritt *GRBS* (1967) 128. Mattingly has an explicit comment, calling this one of "two small changes" (*Klio* [1977] 83).

is exemplified by *IG* I[3] 164.23–25: ἐ|ὰν δέ τ]ινας αὐτõν ἀπ[οκτένει βιαί|οι θαν]άτοι ἒ δέσει ἒ [ἄγει . . . (compare *IG* I[3] 55.12–13; 91.17–18; 105.8–9; 228.9–12) Another two similarly phrased culpable actions appear in *IG* I[3] 71.36–37: ἐὰν δ[ὲ μ]|ὲ ἐχσε[νέγ]κοσι ἐς [τὸν δε̃μ]ον ἒ [μὲ] δι[απρά]χσ[ο]σι ἐπὶ σφõν α[ὐτõν.[45]

There is nothing here that on superficial reading mandates the *exclusive* use of Athenian standards. If one credits the discussion above of the possible difficulties in exchanging local coinage for Attic tetradrachms in order to pay the tribute, it is easy to imagine how refusing Attic coins in the payment of local taxes might be a subject of considerable interest to the Athenian government in a way that merely coining local money might not. The local role of Attic money was therefore more problematical where local emissions coexisted. The contemporaneous use of two different systems seems indeed widespread, and in the relevant period the use of a single local currency exclusively was probably much less common.

But surely a traditionalist on the Coinage Decree would object that the exclusion of the option to use indigenous *and* Attic money and metrological standards is shown by the clarifying stipulation ἀλλὰ ξενικοῖς νομίσμασι]ν καὶ σταθμοῖς καὶ μέτροις 'but (uses) foreign money and weights and measures.' I am uncertain both about the effect of accepting this restoration and whether it should be accepted.

Let us consider then the restoration ἀλλὰ ξενικοῖς νομίσμασι]ν.[46] The term ξενικός must clearly mean 'non-Athenian' in an Athenian official document.[47] That would create no interpretative problems if this order operated within an exclusively Athenian context, where only the dichotomy Athenian/foreign could be activated, but it does not. In our unique context, ξενικός describes allied practices so that an allied interpreter is implicitly invited to view the word from his own perspective. For the ally, ξενικός could mean 'nonindigenous,' that is, alien not only to the Athenians but to the particular ally himself. This consideration

45 See also *IG* I[3] 104.26–27. In contrast, the assessment of 425/4 has a protasis with terms that have been restored as separated by καὶ, but they are in the negative, which is not directly comparable; *IG* I[3] 71.28–29: [ἐὰν δὲ *hoι* πρυτάνες μὲ τότε ἐσάγο]σι ἐ[ς] τὸν δε̃μον κ[αὶ μὲ φσεφίζονται δικαστ]έριον | περὶ τõ [φόρο καὶ μὲ τότε χρεματίζοσι ἐ]πὶ σ[φ]õν αὐτõν. . . . Even here it is a succession of steps that need to be taken to stay clear of liability.

46 *IG* XII.5 480 attributes these restored lines to B. Keil, but Wilamowitz in *AE* (1923) 117 is also credited.

47 Disregarding the appearances below in section xiii.1, xiv.4, note *IG* I[3] 383.308, 384; 384.2; 386.I.57; restorations in 388.13; 389.14; 409.22. See also *SEG* 26.72.8, for which see pp. 536–44 below.

may make ξενικός a poor choice for restoration here, unless we are prepared to hold that the provision merely forbade the use of the coins and standards of third parties, while permitting local coins and standards alongside Attic.[48] Nevertheless, this explanation of the clause seems a bit forced, despite having the advantage of congruance with the hypothesis that section xii.2–4 enjoined the use of Athenian standards on all who continued to coin silver.[49]

Accordingly, we must consider the possibility that the traditional restoration is incorrect. In doing so, a first necessary observation is that the restoration of ξενικός in section xii does not draw any great confirming strength from the appearance of the same word (ξενικόν) in section xiv.4, while its other appearance in section xiii.1 is in so fragmentary a context that the following strictures are valid a fortiori (see pp. 411–14 below). Although it might be conceded that slight support for restoration is gathered from repetition of any term in the decree, its usage in section xiv.4 would, unlike the phrase in section xii.4, cause no confusion of reference. The administrative context is Athens itself, with the *epistatai* of the mint (xiv.1, cf. 3) undertaking some action of recording or publication (xiv.2: ἀναγ]ράψαντες; cf. restored xiv.3: ἀνα]γραψάντων), and ξενικός having the unproblematical meaning of 'non-Athenian' pure and simple. The substantive qualified by ξενικόν is assumed to be τὸ ἀργυρίον and not τὸ νόμισμα. Both these points weaken the comparability of the two sections upon which the restoration of ξενικός in section xii could be thought to depend.

A more significant concern involves the pattern of conjunctivity in the adjacent clauses of the protasis of the provision added to the bouleutic oath. As it is customarily restored, the clause κ]αὶ μὴ χρῆται stipulates negatively what the clause ἀλλὰ ξενικοῖς ... reformulates (by implication) positively. The former states what the delinquent ally is not doing, namely, using Attic standards, while the latter describes what the ally is doing, namely, using ξενικός standards. It is important then to note that the two clauses are not in fact parallel since the conjunction ἤ joins the members of the first and negative description, but καὶ connects

[48] Translate: "if anyone coins money of silver in the cities and does not use the coins of the Athenians or weights or measures, but uses alien coins and weights and measures."

[49] If the intent was the steamline the process by which allies taxed their citizens in order to pay tribute in Attic coin, the prospect that an ally was accepting receipts in a foreign coinage may not have been pleasing to the Athenians. Similarly, allies providing correspondences between local measures and another (non-Attic) system (and not with Attic measures) might have aroused anxiety on the assumption that only an integration of metrological standards with the Athenians facilitated assessment.

the members of the second and positive description. The usage μὴ χρῆται . . . in the former is easily comprehensible; the failure to use any of the three Athenian metrological standards was improper for those who coined silver.[50] Accordingly, disobedience in any of the three metrological modes was equally inappropriate despite compliance in the other two.

In the second formulation, the appearance of the conjunction καὶ is certain (attested by both Siphnos and Odessa fragments): νομίσμασι]ν καὶ σταθμοῖς καὶ μέτροις. Why was such a variation necessary or attractive stylistically? As the clause is traditionally interpreted, it was the employment of any one of the three metrological modes (coins, weights, and measures) that needed to be excluded. The phrasing as usually restored, however, suggests that one had to use all three ξενικός standards to be truly blameworthy. That is not only inconsistent, but improbable historically. The lack of parallelism, in itself, not only undermines this specific restoration, but weakens any other that happens to contain ἀλλά. An Ibycus LEX search of Attic epigraphical material reveals no parallels in which a series of terms separated by ἤ is divided by ἀλλὰ from another series of which the terms are divided by καί.

The replacement of ἤ with καὶ in the second sequence of "coins, weights, and measures" should be taken as an indication that the two formulations are not equivalent and do not coordinate grammatically. Recognizing the ramifications of the usage of "and" instead of "or" encourages an important departure from past interpretations: the three metrological standards in the first list are separate modes of administrative supervision and control where the failure to use any one of the three is culpable, but the three items of the second list are envisaged as a collectivity (not individually). They are not then three areas of noncompliance, but a metrological unity that is seen as conjoined in some meaningful way. If the balance of the two clauses is correctly construed in these observations, we shall need to consider other restorations that subordinate the clause containing the second metrological sequence to the clause with μὴ χρῆται containing the first sequence. They are not merely two ways of describing the same behavior.

Restoration is, however, hampered by space restrictions. One possible restoration exploits the term καθάπερ, which we have already recognized as belonging to Athenian legislation on allied usage of coinage, weights, and measures from Aristophanes' *Birds* 1040–41: ἐάν τις κόπτηι

[50] Compare the description by Polybius of the legal and metrological policy of the Achaean League: . . . ἀλλὰ καὶ νόμοις χρῆσθαι τοῖς αὐτοῖς καὶ σταθμοῖς καὶ μέτροις καὶ νομίσμασι (2.37.10).

νόμισ[μα] ἀργυρίο ἐν τῆσι πό[λεσι κ]αὶ μὴ χρῆται νομ[ίσμασιν τοῖς] Ἀθη[ναί]ων ἢ σταθμοῖς ἢ μέτ[ροις καθάπερ ἑαυτõ νομίσμασι]ν καὶ σταθμοῖς καὶ μέτροις.... Such a restoration solves two dilemmas: it avoids both the ambiguity about the valence of ξενικός and the non-parallelism of the two clauses by insisting that the Attic standards possess equal currency or validity with local standards. We translate: "if anyone coins money of silver in the cities and does not use the coins of the Athenians or weights or measures just like his own coins and weights and measures." Like the legislation that we have envisaged as the background to the allusion in Aristophanes, this clause of the Coinage Decree is orienting allied metrological usage toward Athenian practice.

Another solution would also exploit phrasing that we find in Aristophanes, who has Pisthetairos quip: σὺ δὲ γ' οἷσπερ Ὠτοτύξιοι χρήσει τάχα (*Birds* 1042). Thus another restoration of this clause might be: ἐάν τις κόπτηι νόμισ[μα] ἀργυρίο ἐν τῆσι πό[λεσι κ]αὶ μὴ χρῆται νομ[ίσμασιν τοῖς] Ἀθη[ναί]ων ἢ σταθμοῖς ἢ μέτ[ροις οἷσ(περ) NAME νομίσμασι]ν καὶ σταθμοῖς καὶ μέτροις. Standing in our NAME slot would be some prestigious ally of Athens possessing an exemplary relationship with the Athenians in monetary or metrological matters, perhaps one that was established by *symbolai*. Examples might be οἱ Χῖοι or Σάμιοι.[51] We translate: "if anyone coins money of silver in the cities and does not use the coins of the Athenians or weights or measures which coins and weights and measures the NAME (use)." The citation of the name of the ally would serve the purpose of propaganda in showing that the Athenians were not mandating provisions that connoted low status but a privileged stance vis-à-vis the hegemonic power.

A third way to restore the clause also exploits the characteristic vocabulary associated with monetary legislation. The term δόκιμος is well attested in the meaning 'valid as tender or as a standard' (note Hesych. s.v. δοκίμον, δ 2126 Latte; cf. Pollux 3.86).[52] We find the phrase χρέματα

[51] Consider the role that such references play in two treaties connected with the Second Confederacy: *IG* II² 43.23–25 (the Decree of Aristoteles of 378/7): ... ἐπὶ | δὲ τ[οῖς] αὐτοῖς ἐφ' οἷσπερ Χῖοι καὶ Θηβαῖ|οι κα[ὶ] ἄλλοι σύμμαχοι; *IG* II² 41.67 (378/7 with Byzantion): ... τὴν [δὲ συμμαχίαν ἐ]|ναι αὐτ[οῖς καθάπερ Χίοις].

[52] See the citations and discussion in Figueira, *Aegina* 158–59 (note 74). Note Plut. *Mor.* 94D, 406B; Luc. *De conscrib. hist.* 10; Dio Chrys. *Or.* 66.28. See also H. Volkmann, "ΔΟΚΙΜΑ ΧΡΗΜΑΤΑ," *Hermes* 74 (1939) 99–102; T.V. Buttrey, "More on the Athenian Coinage Law of 375/4 B.C.," *NAC* 10 (1981) 71–94, esp. 83–88; O. Picard, "Sur deux termes des inscriptions de la trésorerie d'Aï Khanoum," in H. Walter (ed.), *Hommages à Lucien Lerat* (Paris 1984) 679–90, esp. 683–84. The terms δόκιμος and ἀδόκιμος were also terms of standard reference in judging the usefulness of ships and their equipment (for example, *IG* II² 1604–1608, 1610, 1627; cf. *IG* I³ 154.6), and δόκιμος was also used of stone and other building materials

| δόκιμα in an archaic law from Eretria (*IG* XII.9 1273/74.2–3).[53] The contrasting word ἀδόκιμος appears in the account, derived from Atthidography, of a demonetization of currency by the Athenian tyrant Hippias ([Arist]. *Oec.* 1347a8–11: τό τε νόμισμα τὸ ὂν Ἀθηναίοις ἀδόκιμον ἐποίησε).[54] In Plato *Laws* 742A, we have described for us how the citizens of the new city are to use money valid at home but τοῖς δὲ ἄλλοις ἀνθρώποις ἀδόκιμον 'invalid for the rest of mankind.' The contemporary usage of the term δόκιμος at Athens to describe valid tender may also be thought to be supported by the denomination as a δοκιμαστής of the slave who was to render judgment on the validity of coins submitted to him under the Attic law of 375/4 (see below, pp. 536–41).

Thus we might restore this section of the Coinage Decree as follows: ἐάν τις κόπτηι νόμισ[μα] ἀργυρίο ἐν τῆσι πό[λεσι κ]αὶ μὴ χρῆται νομ[ίσμασιν τοῖς] Ἀθη[να]ίων ἢ σταθμοῖς ἢ μέτ[ροις πρὸς δοκίμοις νομίσμασι]ν καὶ σταθμοῖς καὶ μέτροις. . . . We might then translate: "if anyone coins money of silver in the cities and does not use the coins of the Athenians or weights or measures in addition to valid coins and weights and measures."

The preposition πρός is, to be sure, more common in Attic inscriptions with the accusative. Yet its use with the dative is quite common too, and falls into two reasonably discrete categories. Its usage to convey spatial orientation is easily recognizable from its appearance with

---

(*IG* II^2 244.38, 66; 1670; 1678). Another parallel, not too distant in time from the Coinage Decree, is from Oropos (388–77), *IG* VII 235.22–23: . . . μὴ ἔλαττον ἐννεοβόλου δοκίμου ἀργ|υρίου. . . . As terms of monetary validation and invalidation, δόκιμος and ἀδόκιμος were common at Hellenistic Delos (for example, *IG* XI.2 144A.20 [before 301]; 287B.29 [250]; *ID* 3 1421A.b.I.5 [156/5]). At Hellenistic Arkesine on Amorgos: *IG* XII.7 67.9–11, 56 (= *SIG*^{3} 955); *IG* XII.7 69.22. For this set of related terms, see M. Cacciamo Caltabiano and P. Radici Colace, "ΑΡΓΥΡΙΟΝ ΔΟΚΙΜΟΝ . . . ΤΟ Δ' ΕΝΑΝΤΙΟΝ ΠΑΡΑΣΗΜΟΝ (Pollux 3,86)," *ASNP*^{3} 13 (1983) 421–47, esp. 423-28; D. Knoepfler, "Tétradrachmes attiques et argent 'alexandrin' chez Diogène Laërce, I," *MH* 44 (1987) 233–53, esp. 236–37.

53 Jeffery, *LSAG* 84 on "Eretria" #9 (p. 87) dates to ca. 550–500; see also E. Vanderpool and W.P. Wallace, "The Sixth Century Laws from Eretria," *Hesperia* 33 (1964) 381–91, esp. 389–90. F. Cairns, "ΧΡΕΜΑΤΑ ΔΟΚΙΜΑ: *IG* XII,9,1273 and 1274 and the Early Coinage of Eretria," *ZPE* 54 (1984) 145–55, argues that *khrēmata dokima* may be merely acceptable goods and not local monetary tender, a contention that he believes may better fit the chronology of the inscriptions and coins. This interpretation is condemned by its necessary corollary that the "10 staters" (of section 3, line 1 of the text of Vanderpool and Wallace) must become stathmic or weight staters. In Attica, ten weight staters were equivalent to a third of a stathmic talent, and it is hard to believe that they would be used to describe any "acceptable" goods other than metal. Must we then opt for a colossal fine in gold or silver or suppose that the Eretrian state was fining in bronze or iron? There is no specification in the surviving, albeit fragmentary, text. See also Cairns, "The 'Laws of Eretria' (*IG* XII.9 1273 and 1274): Epigraphic, Legal, Historical, and Political Aspects," *Phoenix* 45 (1991) 296–313, esp. 297–99.

54 See Figueira, *Excursions* 64–65, and the works therein cited in note 11 (p. 64).

characteristic verbal forms or with certain objects. The meaning 'in addition to' that has been suggested here is also attested on Attic inscriptions.[55] Perhaps another gauge of the possibility of πρός meaning 'in addition to' can be seen in the similar usage of the preposition by Thucydides.[56]

The rest of section xii offers the apodosis of the stipulatory clause added to the oath of the Bouleutai. The actual wording of the engagement made by the Bouleutai to take action against those who act in the manner proscribed in the protasis of the clause is missing. While there has been considerable agreement concerning the binding of the Bouleutai to take punitive action, controversy has surrounded both the wording of the responsibility for taking that action and the citation of the procedure to be utilized.[57]

The earlier restoration for the apodosis was τὴν τιμωρίαν ἔναι κατὰ τὸ πρότε]ρον ψήφισμα ὃ Κλέαρχ[ος εἶπεν].[58] That expression can be paralleled, although this phrasing chiefly occurs in clauses that ordain the same punishment for those harming favored non-Athenians as prevailed for Athenian citizens.[59] The text that is now generally accepted goes back to *ATL*, for its editors believed that they could see κα]ὶ ζ[ημιώσω in line 15 of the Siphnos fragment. While similar in content, this restoration has also the advantage of specifying the action of the Bouleutai in the first person terms likely in an oath (cf. *IG* I³ 40.25, 30–31). The verb ζημιόω is attested on fifth-century inscriptions (*IG* I³ 14.19; 65.21; 105.36; 153.18–19), appearing once in an oath in a negative injunction (*IG* I³ 40.7: . . . οὐδὲ φυγε͂ι ζεμιόσο . . .). If a *zeta* truly appears in line 15 of the Siphnos fragment, the restoration of ζημιώσω is probable. It is never, however, paired with τιμωρέω, which is very rare in Attic epigraphy in any case (cf. *IG* II² 2291a.44 [restored]). Thus, the restoration has illustrative value, with some other verb quite possibly appearing alongside ζημιόω.

Erxleben would like to restore ἐσαγγελέσθω ἐς τὴν βολήν, supporting his suggestion from an assertion that a *tau* (instead of]ιζ[) is visible

55 *IG* I³ 131.14; *IG* II² 73.3–4 (p. 657); 653.52; 1283.21; 1302.6; 10620a.2; *SEG* 24.151.26. Possible cases are *IG* I³ 86.17; *IG* II² 903.2; 1132.18.

56 1.31.3; 1.90.3; 2.7.2; 2.36.2; 2.52.1; 2.61.3; 3.39.8; 3.53.4; 3.57.1; 4.20.1; 4.24.1; 4.28.4; 4.87.1; 4.124.1; 5.6.4; 5.47.12; 5.75.5; 6.90.3; 6.104.1.

57 For the punitive powers of the *Boulē*, see P.J. Rhodes, *The Athenian Boule* (Oxford 1972) 179–207.

58 See *IG* XII.5 480; Hiller and Klaffenbach *ZfN* (1924–25) 219; *IG* I² p. 295. See Wade-Gery *BSA* (1932–33) 118, who notes the addition to the oath and suggests a first person form is required.

59 *IG* I³ 57.10–12; 156.15–17; 164.25–27; cf. 27.15–17; 28.15–16; 91.16–18; 161.3–5; 162.11–12; 227.23–24; 228.12–14.

in line 15 of the Siphnos fragment.[60] Lewis in *IG* I^3 agrees that the letter trace is likely to be a *tau*. Yet Erxleben's restoration has the disadvantage of not offering a first person form of the verb for the apodosis.[61] It may also be faulted on other grounds.[62] Anyone could initiate an *eisangelia*, so there is no rationale for a stipulation to be added to the oath of the *Boulē* in this fashion (note *Ath. Pol.* 45.2), and the Bouleutai did not have special responsibility for initiating such proceedings. Is there any reason to imagine that the Bouleutai did not hear (and then refer to a *dikasterion* or the Heliaia) any charge that was leveled that the law defined as falling within the process of *eisangelia*? Hence the addition to the oath seems otiose. Moreover, we are really looking here for some new action that specifically the Bouleutai could be *expected* to have taken thereafter.

Furthermore, Erxleben's restoration provides a basis for the argument, with chronological ramifications, that the scope of the powers of the *Boulē* implied by *eisangelia* here was limited to *probouleusis*.[63] Even if this restoration could be credited as probable (which I doubt), this entire approach goes much further than our evidence allows on the seriousness of violation of the provision alluded to in the addition to the bouleutic oath.[64] Once we lay aside our prejudices about the harshly punitive character of the Coinage Decree, it becomes uncertain that the punishment envisaged in this clause exceeded the mandate of the fourth-century *Boulē* (500 dr.), let alone its fifth-century predecessor. Nor is the comparison with section viii of the decree cogent, since the capital punishment that was envisaged there was not likely to lie within the discretion of the *Boulē* even in the 440s.

The suggestion of C. Koch keeps the pairing of the two verbs in a judicial context:[65] . . . καταγνώσομαι καὶ] τ[ιμήσω . . . 'I shall pronounce judgment and estimate the punishment.' The comparative material provides a number of similarities and several points of contrast, although restoration has played a sizable role for other imperial enactments. Note

60 See Erxleben *AJP* (1971) 125–26, citing (inappositely, to my mind) *IG* I^3 78.58–59.

61 Note Meritt *PAPS* (1975) note 4, p. 267.

62 Koch, *Volksbeschlüsse* 375, 398–99.

63 See Erxleben, *AJP* (1971) 151–52, where the restricted role of the *Boulē* in the Kleinias Decree is noted (*IG* I^3 34.37–39), but this is strictly an argument for the late dating of that decree and not of the Coinage Decree, as Erxleben goes on to argue (pp. 152–53) on the basis of the similarity of its letter forms to that of the Kleonymos Decree (*IG* I^3 68) and of Thoudippos' reassessment of 425/4 (*IG* I^3 71).

64 Cf. Schuller, *Herrschaft* 213–14. On additions to the oath, see, in general, Rhodes, *Boulē* 194–95.

65 Koch, *Volksbeschlüsse* 398–99.

first of all the Kleinias Decree (*IG* I³ 34.37–39; cf. 66–67): [*h*ὃ δ' ἂν]| καταγνὸι *h*[ε βολέ, μὲ τιμᾶν αὐτ]ο̣ῖ κυ̣ρία ἔστο [ἀλλ' ἐσ|φερέτο ἐς τ[ὲν ἐλιαίαν εὐθύς̣]. The Kleonymos Decree offers a similar formulation (*IG* I³ 68.50–52): ἐὰν δὲ το κα]|ταγνὸι τὸ [δικ]αστέριον τιμ̣[ᾶν ὅ τι χρὲ αὐτὸν π]|αθε̃ν ἒ [ἀπ]ο̣τεῖ̣σαι. A naval law of the Ionian War provides another instance of punishment (*IG* I³ 236.8–9): ... ἀποτινέτ]ο τοῖ δεμοσίοι *hó* τι ἂν τ^{v} ιμέσει τὸ δικαστέριον. Several contexts are heavily restored: *IG* I³ 21.50–51: ... τιμάτο δὲ τὸ] δ̣ικαστέριον *hó* τι ἂγ χ[ρε̃]ι̣ παθε̃ν ἒ ἀ[ποτεῖσαι; 41.95–97: ἐὰν δέ τι[ς κα|ταγνοσθε̃ι τότον καὶ τιμεθε̃ι, δεδέσθο] *ho halòs hεστιαίας hέοσπε*[ρ | ἂν ἐκτίσει.

If the action that the Bouleutai promise to take is to be limited to a judicial process, one must concede the considerable merits of this restoration. It has the interesting corollary that the punishment meted out by the *Boulē* might have been restricted in scope. It is known from the *Athenaion Politeia* that the *Boulē* had once possessed the power to punish up to the death penalty, but lost that power (*Ath. Pol.* 41.2, 45.1). A 500-dr. ceiling for punishment prevailed in the fourth century, and one may compare *IG* I³ 78.57–59 for the same fine under bouleutic discretion in the regulations for the Eleusinian *aparkhē* of ca. 422. Yet the punitive powers of the *Boulē* were not the same for non-Athenians, even allied citizens, as for Athenian citizens, as can be seen from a bouleutic condemnation of a Kean to death for murdering an Attic *proxenos* that is attested ca. 362 (Tod, *GHI* #142.36–41, 2.125–34). That could, however, be special jurisdiction. The Kleinias Decree has the *Boulē* acting only as a preliminary court for charges of improprieties involving the tribute that must be referred to the *Heliaia* (*IG* I³ 34.37–41).

Whether there is any trace of a letter or letters in the middle of line 15 of the Siphnos fragment is uncertain. On the basis of the foregoing discussion, several suggestions for restoration might be made, so long as we recognize that, beyond the overall sense of the clause, only an exemplary supplement may be contemplated. If we follow the editors of *ATL* in believing that]ι ζ[must be read in line 15 of the Siphnos fragment, one possibility might be αὐτὸν οὐκ ἐάσω καὶ ζημιώσω κατὰ τὸ πρότε]ρον ψήφισμα ὃ Κλέαρχ[ος εἶπεν].[66] This option is less redundant, establishing two modes of prospective bouleutic initiative, the administrative and the judicial. If one cleaves rather to Erxleben's

[66] Note *IG* I³ 89.31: ... καὶ οὐδένα κο]πέας ἐχσάγεν ἐάσο ἐὰμ μὲ 'Αθε[ναίο ...; cf. 65.21–23. Note also *IG* II² 111.64–66, from the oath of the Athenian *stratēgoi* and the allies toward the cities on Keos in 363/2: εἰ δέ τις μὴ βούλεται οἰ]κεῖν ἐγ Κέωι, ἐάτω αὐτὸν ὅποι ἂν βόλεται τῶ|[ν συμμαχίδων πολ]έων οἰκο̃ντα τὰ ἑαυτο̃ καρπο̃σθαι.

opinion that the traces of a *tau* appear in line 15, an alternative would be something similar to ἐάσομαι οὐδένα ταῦτα πο(ι)ε͂ν κατὰ τὸ πρότε]ρον ψήφισμα ὃ Κλέαρχ[ος εἶπεν].[67] As I have endeavored to establish in my discussion of monetary variety and the collection of the tribute, the most obvious lapse to which the Athenians yielded in monetary policy was to permit allied states on occasion to submit payment of their tribute in non-Athenian money (pp. 273–95). In any such concession, the *Boulē* would in all probability play a critical role in deciding whether to allow any dispensations in the mode of payment.

The clause that established the parameters for the intervention by the *Boulē* has also been a subject of considerable controversy. As we have already noted, the received restoration is κατὰ τὸ πρότε]ρον ψήφισμα ὃ Κλέαρχ[ος εἶπεν] 'in accordance with the earlier decree which Klearkhos proposed.' Much of this controversy was generated out of a appraisal of the historical role and impact of the Coinage Decree that we have found impossible to document numismatically or archaeologically. In this traditional view wherein it was a critical watershed, one can imagine the reluctance, especially among scholars working in the interpretative tradition of the editors of *ATL*, to place the psephism of Klearkhos in a sequence of Athenian legislation on monetary affairs. That supposition would raise the spectre of some decisive action in the history of Athenian imperialism (or more accurately in the history of Athenian supervision of allied administration) having occurred at an unknown date prior to the Coinage Decree, which was a document that could be dated, according to them, right in the midst of the supposed crisis of the empire around mid-century. And such a mid-century crisis figured prominently in the reconstruction of imperial history by the editors of *ATL* and by the influential Oxford historians such as Meiggs and Lewis who followed in their interpretative footsteps. Moreover, the possibility that the radical new policies attributed to this (fortunately) extant document by traditional scholarship belonged in fact to an entirely lost forerunner proposed by Klearkhos was received (most unsurprisingly) as disheartening.

In a revisionist reconstruction of the Coinage Decree, it need not stand as a turning point in Athenian relations with the allies. Rather its encouragement of the use of Attic coins, weights, and measures may be viewed as an outgrowth both of the economic factors set in motion by the organization of the system of tribute from its outset and especially by the requirement that tribute be paid in Athenian money (whenever

[67] Compare Perikles on the possibility of rescinding the Megarian Decree: . . . Μεγαρέας μὲν ὅτι ἐασόμεν ἀγορᾷ καὶ λιμέσι χρῆσθαι . . . (Thuc. 1.144.2).

that was stipulated). The Coinage Decree did not tighten Athenian control over the lives of their allies in any important way and cannot be seen as exploitative in any significant sense (for qualifications, see above pp. 257–58 and below pp. 553–57). If the Coinage Decree can, at its earliest first enactment, be placed in the 440s, its context is the lessening of military pressure on the Athenians and their allies through the quietening of active hostilities with Persia and the suspension of ongoing conflict between Athens and the Peloponnesians through the Five Years Truce of 451 (see below, pp. 457–63). In my reading of the decree and of the monetary history of the *arkhē*, a place can be given to the psephism of Klearkhos (or not, for that matter) without transforming the basic lines of this reconstruction and it is in this spirit that we may now survey the earlier work on the subject.

One reaction to the difficulties of positioning the psephism of Klearkhos relative to the Coinage Decree has been to assert that Klearkhos was himself the proposer of the extant decree, sometimes with the thought that the extant decree was Klearkhos' second piece of monetary and metrological legislation.[68] To affirm this position, one would have to consider that the adjective πρότε]ρον 'prior' in our document necessarily implies the notion of specific priority to the decree itself. Accordingly, the "priority" of the earlier legislation is justified, chiefly because this law was also a prosposal of Klearkhos. In this view, we have not only found out the name of the proposer of the Coinage Decree, but also have perhaps glimpsed momentarily and to a limited extent the richness and continuity of Attic lawmaking on monetary administration.

Various conclusions strike off tangentially from this early supposition of the commentators on the decree without necessarily conceding that Klearkhos had legislated on coinage and metrology previously. One approach, to my mind rather implausible, is to argue that the Coinage Decree itself could be considered "the prior psephism that Klearkhos proposed" when it is viewed from the perspective of the oath which it enjoins.[69] Meiggs-Lewis quite appropriately protested the superfluity of the term πρότε]ρον against such a background.[70]

Some other restorations deserve a mention in passing. Segre offered δεύτε]ρον or ὕστε]ρον, on the idea that Klearkhos was so active a proposer of important legislation in the *Boulē* (on various subjects?) that his

[68] This position is often maintained virtually in isolation from a discussion of the clause in question: Weil *ZfN* (1910) 356; Reinach *Mém. Acad. Ins. et Belles-Lettres* (1911) 355–56; Will, *Monde grec* 207–10.

[69] *ATL* 2.67; cf. Klaffenbach *DL* (1950) col. 35. See also Segre 173–74.

[70] See Meiggs-Lewis p. 114.

psephisms had to be differentiated in this way.[71] Yet there is no indication of such a careful method of citation elsewhere in surviving fifth-century legislation. Erxleben suggested ἡμέτε]ρον, which cannot be paralleled.[72] It would defeat the purpose of adding the clause to the oath of the *Boulē* because of the opportunity it would give to later misconstruction and dispute. How could future Bouleutai reaffirm a clause of an earlier decree through the use of the first person plural possessive adjective? Why would the Bouleutai appropriate a psephism passed by the *dēmos*? As Lewis observes in *IG* I[3] "sed decretum populi, non senatus foret," so that ἡμέτερον is not really an accurate descriptive term.

A more subtle solution to the problem that is perceived to lie in πρότε]ρον was presented by the editors of *ATL*, and it has been revived more recently by D.M. Lewis. They propose a mistake in the reading of the original and now lost Smyrna fragment by Baumeister, with the result that a *nu* was misread as a *rho*.[73] That would allow us to restore [γενόμε]ν̣ον, so that Klearkhos' legislation could become the Coinage Decree itself or some other piece of the same legislative program. This phraseology, however, while not by any means impossible, would still be unparalleled. The positing of such an error is a relatively desperate counsel, to which one ought not to accede unless more pressing reasons exist than have been offered heretofore.

Furthermore, it is also possible to sidestep a concession of the priority of Klearkhos' legislation by suggesting, as Tod has done, that the psephism of Klearkhos was not necessarily a piece of legislation on coinage, weights, and measures.[74] The responsibility of the Bouleutai to punish in accordance with his legislation could mean that his psephism dealt with penal issues or that he had proposed a law on judicial procedures in more general terms. Standing against this supposition is the failure of the citation of the psephism of Klearkhos to provide even so much as a hint of the

[71] Segre 175. In this case, Klearkhos could not be the Bouleutēs active in 408/7, since iteration of membership in the council cannot have taken place at so short an interval and the Coinage Decree cannot be this late. Note also Koch, *Volksbeschlüsse* 401–402.

[72] Erxleben *AfP* (1969) 126.

[73] *ATL* 2.67; Lewis, *Coinage and Administration* 59.

[74] Tod *GHI* 1.166; Cavaignac *RN* (1953) 5–6. Balcer, *Historia* (1976) 265–67, would posit "the Athenian Judicial Decree proposed by Klearkhos" as the major enactment that dealt with offenses against Attic *arkhontes* in tributary cities. He sees a further reference in the Chalcis decree (*IG* I[3] 40.74–76) and in Aristophanes *Birds* 1052 ("In that Aristophanes in 414 B.C. referred to the Currency Decree he could well have referred to a second decree promulgated perhaps that same morning, ca. 449 B.C. in the ekklesia"). See also Balcer, *The Athenian Regulations for Chalkis* (Wiesbaden 1978) 119, 140–42, for further elaboration; S. Cataldi, *La democrazia ateniese e gli alleati* (Padua 1984) 92–93.

procedure to be used.[75] Nevertheless, Lewis notes that there might be just enough room for a short reference to the contents of the psephism of Klearkhos at the end of line 10 of the Smyrna fragment.[76]

A certain determination on this hypothesis cannot be made in the present state of the evidence. At the same time, however, we must resist a prejudice against seeing the decree of Klearkhos as legislation on coinage and metrology, especially if our only reason for doing so is to guard the privileged place in our scholarship of the Coinage Decree as a crucial turning point in the evolution of Athenian imperialism. Rather, Klearkhos' *psēphisma* and the Coinage Decree may deserve to lose their status as radical departures toward tighter imperial control, the traces of which ought to be detectable archaeologically.

One ought, therefore, to oppose Tod's particular resolution to the question of the role of the prior psephism of Klearkhos. The two most likely injunctions laid on the Bouleutai in the new clause added to their oath are that they punish allies not using Attic money and standards—even if their exclusive use is not ordered—and that they refuse to cooperate with them, perhaps in their payment of tribute. It was not then enough to say that the Bouleutai were to take action, but a specification of what action in detail beyond that suggested in any restoration up to now appears to be called for. Thus, the decree of Klearkhos is likely to have detailed procedures, penalties, and provisos about monetary and metrological matters.

As soon as it is recognized that the Coinage Decree need not constitute any such decisive departure, we can admit the possibility that the psephism of Klearkhos was earlier legislation aimed at coping with problems of exchange and of fiscal management. This conclusion is indeed the most conservative reading of the evidence.[77] The evolution of Athenian policy on these matters is so obscure that we are hardly authorized to attach surely the name of Klearkhos to some earlier stage, like the requirement that allies pay tribute in Attic money (as did commentators early in the century) or even that the certain allies use Attic money and standards. Nor can we determine how long before the extant decree Klearkhos proposed his psephism; whether it is earlier by weeks

[75] Note Koch, *Volksbeschlüsse* 401–402.

[76] Lewis, *Coinage and Administration* 59–60, cites *IG* I^3 107.6–8: . . . καὶ τ]ἄλλα α[ὐτ]οῖν ἔναι κατὰ [τὸ πρότερον ψήφ|ισμα δ . . . ιπ]πος ε[ἶ]πε περὶ τῶν εὐεργ[ετῶν τõ δήμο τ|ῶν πρότερον] ἐξεληλυθότων ἐκ τῶν πό[λεων. . . . Cf. Klaffenbach *ZfN* (1924–25) 219.

[77] Some of the earliest commentary upheld this position, even though coupled with various now unlikely chronological, numismatic, and historical positions; see, for example, *SIG*^{3} 87, note 5, p. 111; Hiller and Klaffenbach *ZfN* (1924–25) 219.

or decades. Nevertheless, Klearkhos probably legislated about money and/or metrological standards, and this conclusion is not affected by the view that the Coinage Decree is the second of the *psēphismata* of Klearkhos himself on these issues. Nor does it affect the similar hypothesis that the addition of the bouleutic clause was an amendment that Klearkhos himself proposed, referring to his earlier legislation.

As for the identity of Klearkhos, our evidence fails us except for the attestations regarding two individuals. When the dating of this legislation was dominated by the chronological impressions made by the Ionic fragments and by Wilamowitz's reading of the presumed reference of Aristophanes in the *Birds*, the early editors identified Klearkhos with a *prytanis* of that name in 408/7 (*IG* I^3 515.25 = *DAA* 167.38; cf. *PA* #8479).[78] In *IG* I^3 112.2, dated by archon name to 408/7, where his name is restored Κλέ]αρχος, Klearkhos was serving as *grammateus* of the *Boulē* during the passage of a psephism, virtually completely lost, that mentioned the Hellespont. Nonetheless, proponents of earlier dates for the Coinage Decree and its precursors are not without a candidate for the Klearkhos of our inscription. A Klearkhos is attested as the master of a female slave, Gorgo, on a fragmentary list of the mid-fifth century (*SEG* 21.97B.17 = *IG* I^3 1037.40). The name is not uncommon later, although that matter is hardly relevant to us except to suggest that many fifth-century men named Klearkhos have been lost from our ken.

A final possibility, albeit a speculative one, would understand the allusion to the decree of Klearkhos in terms of the history of the inscription of this law. The Smyrna fragment in its line 6 (and possibly the Syme fragment at the same site) differs from the fragments of Siphnos and Odessa in its possession of an additional phrase (ca. ten letters in length) in the formula προσγράψαι δὲ πρὸς τὸν ὅρκον [τ]ὸν τῆς βολῆς τὸν γραμματέα τὸν τῆς [βολῆς------τα]δί. The editors of *ATL* restored ἐς τὸ λοιπὸν and Erxleben suggested καὶ τõ δήμο, which is most improbable.[79] In line 9, the Smyrna fragment has an inverted order, ... καὶ μ]έτροις κὰι σταθμοῖς. The extant portions of the Siphnos and

[78] See, for example, *IG* XII.5 480; Hiller and Klaffenbach *ZfN* (1924–25) 219; *SIG*^{3} 87, note 5, p. 111. Cf. Erxleben *AfP* (1971) 154.

[79] Erxleben, *AfP* (1969) 124–25, who cites *IG* II^2 1740.53 (before 388/7), cf. 1741.2 (378/7); *Agora* 15.39.18 (ca. 340) for the formula γραμματεὺς τῆι βουλῆι καὶ τῶι δήμωι, and *IG* II^2 1750.50–51 (334/3); 1751.62 (after mid-fourth) for the later formula γραμματεὺς τῆς βουλῆς καὶ τοῦ δήμου. The formula ὁ γραμματεὺς ὁ τῆς βουλῆς (and its relatives) appears either directly or in a probable restoration in ca. 52 sites in *IG* I^3, fascicle 1. In another ca. 18, it is restored with more or less credibility. Hence the restoration noting the *dēmos* is extremely unlikely, regardless of which date we accept for a fifth-century Coinage Decree.

Odessa fragments provide us neither with the reference to Klearkhos nor with the last two sections of the decree (xiii–xiv).

The possibility is then open to see the Smyrna fragment as working from a different master text. This version cited the decree that is attested in the other fragments with two significant differences. It provided the name of the *grammateus* of the *Boulē* who had added the clause to the bouleutic oath on the occasion of the first passage of the decree, thus fixing that addition chronologically and administratively. This version also provided the name of Klearkhos, who originally proposed the decree attested by the other fragments; giving, in other words, the clause of bouleutic oath not as it was to be sworn or was sworn on its first swearing but in the form in which it was sworn at the time of the Smyrna inscription. If this separation of the Smyrna fragment were valid, one could next extrapolate from the appearance of sections xiii–xiv after clauses moving toward closure in sections ix–xii. The Smyrna Decree was citing from the terms of the decree represented by the other fragments down through section xii. Thereupon the Smyrna decree presented another procedure, perhaps for converting foreign currency and bullion into Attic money. Thus sections xiii–xiv provide another initiative parallel to the one that we have suspected was enjoined in sections i–iii and the lost lines preceding them. Nevertheless, this line of interpretation is very speculative and is useful chiefly for its shaking our complacency about the unity and contemporaneity of the fragments.

Not enough emphasis has been put on the addition of this clause to the bouleutic oath as a technique for the implementation of the decree. However one restores the crucial provision in section xii.4–5, its genesis is shrouded. The assumption that it was promulgated in some lost portion of the opening of the decree is only one option, one that is untestable in the present condition of the fragments. It is also possible that this provision, whatever its character, preexisted this psephism (for example, in the psephism of Klearkhos). The clause added to the oath was intended either to enforce that injunction more rigorously or to promote it more energetically. Ignoring the controversies explored above, we find provisions for conversion of silver into coin, the creation of a protected fund, universal exposure for the law, and the binding of the Bouleutai to enforcement. All these actions are unusual enough so as to make intractable the decision between their inclusion in a first promulgation or their subsequent passage in the follow-up legislation represented by our decree. Nonetheless, the Athenians believed that adding religious sanction to the supervision of this provision by the *Boulē* would suppress permissive oversight.

Moreover, if the Athenians had merely been forbidding the coining of silver and the failure to use Athenian weights and measures by cities within the *arkhē*, it is odd that more of an apparatus for suppression of allied noncompliance was not set up in the decree (as far as we can determine). One would really expect instructions for *arkhontes*, *episkopoi*, and especially the *stratēgoi* instead of a sole focus on the initiative of the *Boulē*. This point may indicate that another mechanism for allied enforcement had been established earlier in other legislation or elsewhere. The *Boulē*, however, was initially responsible (among other functions connected with the *phoros*) for receiving allied requests concerning the implementation of the exaction of tribute and acting as an initial court regarding allied compliance; at least, these were its duties by 425/4 (*IG* I^3 71.12–26, 31–43; [Xen.] *Ath. Pol.* 3.2).[80]

The missing clause of the apodosis in section xii.5 is likely to have reminded the Bouleutai of what their appropriate reaction ought to be, perhaps not only in judicial review of offenses regarding failure to recognize as valid Athenian coins and standards, but also in the central role of the *Boulē*, *probouleusis* 'preliminary review and scheduling by the *Boulē*.' The Bouleutai were probably intended to rebuff efforts to allow the allies to circumvent the decree by proposals tendered to the *Boulē* by the allies themselves and supported by their *proxenoi*. The need to sacralize by oath-taking the responsibility of the *Boulē* in the area of coinage, weights, and measures implies that an expectation existed in the assembly that the Bouleutai might otherwise be induced or were inclined to allow greater latitude about allied behavior in these areas than either the law allowed or was prudent in general. How seriously the Athenians viewed the transgression that they wanted the *Boulē* to deter is unknown. We are in the dark because the parameters for the negative actions that the *Boulē* was authorized to take were outlined elsewhere by Klearkhos.

That expectation might well derive from past behavior, with which the *psēphisma* of Klearkhos could also have been connected. As we have seen above, some allied cities were undoubtedly sometimes in difficulty in paying their tribute in Attic coins. The new clause for the bouleutic oath might indicate that the allies had excused their own problems based on a deficiency of the Athenian money circulating in the local economy. The decree may then have tried to deter the resort to such excuses by ensuring that shortages of Attic coinage could not arise out of a wrong-headed or perverse refusal by the allies themselves to accept Athenian money as valid local tender.

80 See Rhodes, *Boule* 89–91.

xii. προσγράψαι δὲ πρὸς τὸν ὅρκον [τ]ὸν τῆ]ς βολῆς τὸν XII.1
γραμματέα τὸν τῆς [βολῆς τα]δί· ἐάν τις κόπτηι νόμισ[μα]
ἀργυρίο ἐν τῆσι πό[λεσι κ]αὶ μὴ χρῆται νομ[ίσμασιν τοῖς]
Ἀθη[να]ίων ἢ σταθμοῖς ἢ μέτ[ροις καθάπερ ἑαυτõ νομίσμασι]ν
καὶ σταθμοῖς καὶ μέτροις, [αὐτὸν οὐκ ἐάσω καὶ ζημιώσω κατὰ τὸ
πρότε]ρον ψήφισμα ὅ Κλέαρχ[ος εἶπεν].

xii. The *grammateus* ['secretary'] of the *Boulē* is to record an addition to the oath of the *Boulē* in the following terms: if anyone mints silver money in the cities and does not use the coins of the Athenians, or weights, or measures, in the same way as his own coins, and weights, and measures, I shall not permit him and shall penalize him in accordance with the earlier decree which Klearkhos proposed.

As I have observed, this section of the decree provides for various actions to be taken in the implementation of its provisions. Care should be exercised for the announcement of the decree through heralds and its inscription and erection. Athenian officials abroad are charged with this task, although it is also envisaged that the allies may choose to undertake the same duty. Past interpretation of the decree has been greatly affected by the absence of the clauses that lay out the purpose of the legislation. We work only from the shorthand reference included in the new provision for the bouleutic oath. This unique passage cannot be restored with assurance from comparable material. In contrast to earlier scholarship, arguing for a ban on allied minting of silver, we have seen that an imposition of the validity of Attic money and standards vis-à-vis allied and other money and standards is a viable alternative. There are at least the three ways presented above to express this idea.

15
THE COINAGE DECREE: PART IV AND CONCLUSION

SECTION XIII

xiii. [– – –ca. 26– – –]αι τὸ ξενιϰὸν ἀργύριον [– – –ca. 30– – – XIII.1
– – – – – – ὅ]ταμ βόληται· τὴν δὲ πό[λιν– – – – –ca. 28– – – – –
– – – – – – – αὑτὸν δὲ τὰ [ἑ]αυτõ ἕϰαστ[ον – – – –ca. 23– – – –
– – – – – – τὸ ἀργυ]ροϰόπιον.

As we saw in Chapter 14, the last part of the decree is attested only from the lost Smyrna fragment. Thus the possibility cannot be excluded that this inscription represents a closely related, but not identical, psephism to the one represented by the others.

The scant fragments of this part of the decree need to be approached with particular caution. As restored by Wilhelm, followed by Hiller von Gaertringen and Klaffenbach, and adapted by *ATL* to accommodate a longer line, provision was made in this section for private individuals to bring silver to the Athenian mint and receive Athenian money in return.

Wilhelm; Hiller and Klaffenbach:[1]

τὸς δὲ ἰδιώτας ἀποδõν]αι τὸ ξενιϰὸν ἀργύριον (a) [ἕϰαστον ὅ]ταμ βόληται· τὴν δὲ πό[λιν ϰαταλλάττεν, (b) ἀπογραψάντων δὲ τὰ αὑτõ ἕϰαστοι ϰαὶ ϰαταβαλόντων ἐς τὸ] ἀργυ]ροϰόπιον.

ATL:[2]

[ἐξε͂ναι δὲ ϰαὶ ὁτωιοῦν ἀποδίδον]αι τὸ ξενιϰὸν ἀργύριον (a) [ὃ ἂν ἔχηι ϰαὶ ϰαταλλάτεν ϰατὰ ταὐτὰ ὅ]ταμ βόληται· τὴν δὲ πό[λιν ἀνταποδõναι αὐτῶι νόμισμα ἡμεδαπὸν]· (b) αὑτὸν δὲ τὰ [ἑ]αυτõ ἕϰαστ[ον ϰομίζεν Ἀθήναζε ϰαὶ θε͂ναι ἐς τὸ ἀργυ]ροϰόπιον.

Erxleben:[3]

[τὸς δὲ ἰδιώτας ἐν τῆι πόλει αποδõν]αι τὸ ξενιϰὸν ἀργύριον (a) [ὃ ἂν ἔχωσιν, ἐπὶ ϰαταλλαγῆι ἕϰαστον ὅ]ταμ βόληται· τὴν δὲ πό[λιν

[1] Wilhelm, *IG* XII.5 480; *IG* XII Suppl., p. 216; Hiller von Gaertringen and Klaffenbach *ZfN* (1924–25) 219–20; cf. *IG* I^2 p. 295.
[2] *ATL* 2.66; cf. Erxleben *AfP* (1969) 127.
[3] Erxleben *AfP* (1969) 127.

ἀνταποδο͂ναι αὐτο͂ι νόμισμα ἡμεδαπὸν]· (b) αὐτὸν δὲ τὰ [ἑ]αυτο͂ ἕκαστ[ον ἀπογράψαι καὶ καταβαλε͂ν ἐς τὸ ἀργυ]ροκόπιον.

This section, in these reconstructions, disrupts the succession of concluding clauses that establish the promulgation (ix), publication (x–xi), enforcement by the *Boulē* (xii), and, afterward, a recording and display of a record of some operations of the mint (xiv). If all the fragments belong to a single decree, section xiii should not be a new stipulation, but should move the decree toward closure. Five clues for interpretation are certainly present: (1) τὸ ξενικὸν ἀργύριον 'foreign silver (money),' (2) ὅ]ταμ βόλεται 'whenever he/it wishes,'[4] (3) τὴν δὲ πόλιν 'the city,' (4) αὐτὸν δὲ τὰ [ἑ]αυτο͂ ἕκαστ[ον 'each . . . his own,' and (5) τὸ ἀργυ]ροκόπιον 'the mint.' Naturally, it is item 4 above that opens the possibility that private individuals are involved. The editors of this inscription have almost universally assumed that this mint is the Athenian mint, but that is not entirely certain.[5] A line length of ca. 50 (following *ATL*) needs to be adopted so that some of the restorations of Wilhelm, Hiller, and Klaffenbach can only be held as indicative of general context and of possible vocabulary.

Let us start by observing that there is no particular reason to see individuals outside the *arkhē* as the primary target of this clause, as the editors of *ATL* intend their version to indicate. It is hard to imagine a rationale for any Athenian interest in the monetary holdings of persons who lived outside their alliance, since that use of money did not affect tribute collection and disbursement of funds. Nor does one easily envisage any grounds for an encouragement of such persons' holding Attic money, in general or specifically in this decree, in preference to other currencies. Such an interpretation is a holdover from the unrealistic (and entirely unsupported) policies, in which some political advantage might be engineered by the Athenian state from a greater use by other Greeks of Athenian money or in which the Athenians were working a massive replacement of the monies in circulation.

A clause specifying that private individuals could bring silver to the mint and receive, after the requisite levies, newly minted coins is not an impossibility here. The mint was probably a money converter of last resort in any case, although it is difficult to understand why many

[4] *ATL* 2.66 presumably based its judgment of the "permissive aspect of this legislation" primarily on this clause and compared *IG* I[3] 78.30–34. Concomitantly, Ziebarth's suggestion that a surrendering of local money at the *local* mint was enjoined on individuals is highly unlikely (*Beiträge* 82).

[5] Reinach, *Mém. Acad. Ins. et Belles-Lettres* (1911) 355 also opted for the local mint.

people with foreign *coins* would resort to it. Could they not make a better deal elsewhere, since, in addition to fees (3–5 percent), the mint would probably treat any silver handed over as mere bullion? They lost any fiduciary value possessed by the foreign coins. It is not as though most people did not have the means at home to melt coins into bullion. The practices of the mint were probably of long standing and one is unsure why they needed to be specified here at all. Erxleben's addition of the phrase ἐν τῆι πόλει seems particularly unnecessary against this background. There is no reason why the Athenian government needed to call in foreign coinage that people were holding in Attica.[6] The currency law of 375/4 implies that people were compelled to accept only Attic coins approved as valid (*SEG* 26.72.3–4), but private persons could presumably undertake transactions by mutual agreement using any medium they chose. Moreover, Erxleben's restoration will give a fifty-three-letter line for Smyrna line 10, which length is at the upper level of feasibility.

Further specific objections may be raised to the received reconstructions on several grounds.

1. The reading τὴν δὲ πό[λιν ἀνταποδõναι is improbable, inasmuch as the *polis* specified as such is never treated as an agent in extant imperial decrees, and these would be dealings with *private* individuals. Even if the *polis* here could stand for the Athenian government, we would probably require τὴν δὲ πόλιν τὴν Ἀθηναίων (or τὴν δὲ πόλιν καὶ Ἀθηναίος). A more likely context for τὴν δὲ πόλιν would assume that an allied city was at issue.

2. The clauses marked (a) and (b) are likely to have been interwoven in the actual drafting of a decree. The idea that the decree would say anything as banal as clause (b) of *ATL* gives pause. In the restored context of *ATL* for the instruction αὐτὸν δὲ τὰ [ἐ]αυτõ ἕκαστ[ον κομίζεν Ἀθήναζε it is unclear why any mention of τὰ [ἐ]αυτõ is made. Why should the fact that the owner of the money was bringing his own property need such emphasis? One suspects that τὰ [ἐ]αυτõ must be truly emphatic in the text that we have lost. Erxleben has αὐτὸν δὲ τὰ [ἐ]αυτõ ἕκαστ[ον ἀπογράψαι καὶ καταβαλε̃ν ἐς] τὸ ἀργυ]ροκόπιον.[7] This comes closer to satisfying the requirement for emphasis, but provision for such an *apographē* seems far-fetched. Indeed the Athenian mint probably had a simple "book-keeping" procedure of long standing to allow itself and its

[6] The underlying idea, that these holdings needed conversion, because they had been demonetized in their cities of issuance in the *arkhē*, has been rendered inadmissible in our reconstruction not only of the main import of the decree but also of the numismatic evidence.

[7] Erxleben *AJP* (1969) 127–28.

"customers" to keep track of their transactions, a procedure that may not have needed enumeration here. In the simplest scenario, the *epistatai* probably had the public slaves of the mint weigh the silver in the presence of the "customer" and then returned the appropriate number of coins.

3. The phrase κατὰ ταὐτα (*ATL*) for the terms of conversion is also unlikely. They would in all likelihood require detailing, if this were the first presentation of a clause on individual conversion.

Any restoration here must be considered a free composition based on the restorer's vision of the sense of the whole decree, since this succession of clauses and terms is unique to this decree. A restoration that shows some continuity with the appearance of the *Boulē* in the previous section is preferable. The following is merely one example and adopts the hypothesis of a periodic opportunity granted to the allies for conversion purposes. Another alternative would surmise that a single city was at issue here.

xiii. ἡ δὲ βολὴ κελευέσθω τὰς πόλες δõν]αι τὸ ξενικὸν ἀργύριον XIII.1
[τοῖς ἐπιστάταις τõ ἀργυροκοπίο] ὅταμ βόληται· τὴν δὲ πόλ[ιν
ἑκάστην πρέσβες πέμψαι 'Αθήναζε]· αὐτὸν δὲ τὰ [ἑ]αυτõ ἕκαστ[ον
ἀπογράψαι καὶ καταθε͂ναι ἐς τὸ ἀργυ]ροκόπιον.[8]

xiii. Let the *Boulē* order the cities to give foreign money to the *epistatai* of the mint whenever it wishes; each city is to send envoys to Athens and each [envoy] is to register his own funds and deposit them at the mint.

SECTION XIV

xiv. ο[ἱ δ'] ἐπιστάτ[αι ------- ca. 31 -------] XIV.1
ἀναγ]ράψαντες κατα[θέντων] ----- ca. 12 ----- ἔμπροσθεν τõ
ἀργυροκο]πίο σκοπε͂ν τῶι βο[λομένωι------- ca. 33 -------
τό] ξενικόν, χω[ρὶς ------ ca. 41 ------
--------]ν ἀργύρι[ο ------- ca. 24 -------].

The general import of the concluding part of the decree is tolerably clear, and I shall note the restorations as printed by the *ATL*: ο[ἱ δ'] ἐπιστάτ[αι ἅπαντα τὰ παρ' ἑκάστων ἀποδοθέντα | ἀναγ]ράψαντες

[8] Note *IG* I³ 127.27–28: τὰ δὲ ὀνόματα τῶν τριηράρχων, ὧν ἦσαν αὗται αἱ νῆες, | ἀπογράψαι [τὸς πρέσ]βες τῶι γραμματεῖ τῆς βολῆς καὶ τοῖς στρατηγοῖς....

κατα[θέντων παρὰ τὴν στήλην ἔμπροσθεν τõ ἀργυ|ροκο]πίο σκοπε̃ν τω̃ι βο[λομένωι· ἀναγραψάντων δὲ καὶ ξύμπαν τὸ | νόμισμα τὸ] ξενικόν, χω[ρὶς τό τε ἀργύριον καὶ τὸ χρυσίον, καὶ ξύμ|παν τὸ ἡμεδαπὸ]ν ἀργύρι[ον.[9] The text of *IG* I^3, following a suggestion of Erxleben, substitutes τὸ ἀργύριον τὸ] ξενικὸν for τὸ νόμισμα τὸ] ξενικὸν. D.M. Robinson offered ἐπιχώριο]ν in Smyrna line 19 (= section xiv.5) instead of ἡμεδαπὸ]ν, and cited Plato *Laws* 742B.[10]

In accordance with his conviction that no "out-reach" to those beyond the *arkhē* is contemplated, Erxleben adapts the version of *ATL*: ο[ἱ δ'] ἐπιστάτ[αι τὰ παρ' ἑκάστων ἀποδοθέντα ἐς λευκώματα ἀναγ]ράψαντες κατα[θέντων παρὰ τὴν στήλην ἔμπροσθεν τõ ἀργυροκο]πίο ἀναγραψάντων δὲ καὶ ξύμπαν τὸ ἀργύριον τὸ] ξενικόν, χω[ρὶς τὸ ἐκ τῆς ὑπερορίας, χωρὶς τὸ ἐκ τῆς πόλεως πεπραγμένο]ν ἀργύρι[ον.[11] Is καὶ ξύμπαν, however, still acceptable with his rewording of the clause? And note that there is no sure evidence on extant Attic inscriptions for a usage in which the pattern χωρὶς . . . χωρὶς . . . appears, as Erxleben has restored (cf. *IG* I^3 101.41). Moreover, the phrase τὸ ἐκ τῆς ὑπερορίας does not sit comfortably as a way of expressing the official consignments of the allied cities that were converted.

Two relevant parallels are *IG* I^3 52A.22–24: . . . καὶ ἐν στέλει ἀναγραφσάντον μιᾶι ἅπαντα καθ' ἕκαστον τε | το̃ν θεο̃ν τὰ χρέματα *h*όποσα ἐστὶν ἑκάστοι καὶ συμπάντον κεφάλαιο|ν, χορὶς τό τε ἀργύριον καὶ τὸ χρυσίον; and *IG* I^3 259.VI.Postscript, 4–8: . . . ἀπαρχα|ὶ *h*οπόσαι τε̃ι θεõι ἀπὸ τὸ|μ πόλ]εον ἔ[σαν : χορὶς τό τε| ἀργύ]ριον : κ[αὶ τὸ χρυσίον]·| [τõ] ἀργυρίο : [κεφάλαιον ἔν]|. . . . As can be seen from these passages, there are a number of terms that can be imagined to be employed in such recapitulatory contexts.

The restored text is useful primarily for its help in visualizing the general configuration of this section and should not be taken as verifiable in detail. A publicly certifiable registration of some collection(s) of monies is promulgated here. Accordingly, there is no particular reason to opt for the exact formulation ἅπαντα τὰ παρ' ἑκάστων ἀποδοθέντα, which follows up on the restorations for section xiii, and has no independent standing. Tod is probably right in his objections to παρὰ τὴν στήλην

9 *IG* XII Suppl., p. 216 (cf. *IG* I^2 295) offers the earlier restoration with a shorter line that finds some support from *IG* I^3: οἱ δ' ἐπιστάτ[α. παραδεξάμενοι ἐς λευκώματα ἀναγ]ράψαντες κατα[θέντων ἔμπροσθεν τõ ἀργυροκο]πίο σκοπε̃ν τω̃ι βο[λομένωι· ἀναγράψαντες χωρὶς μὲν τὸ] ξενικόν, χω[ρὶς δὲ τὸ ἡμεδαπὸ]ν ἀργύριον. In contrast, *IG* XII.5 480 has lacunae after καταθέντων and χωρὶς δὲ.

10 Robinson *AJP* (1935) 154.

11 Erxleben *AJP* (1969) 128.

after κατα[θέντων (suggesting στήλην λιθίνην).[12] One would also much prefer to restore συμπάντον κεφάλαιον, if the framer of the decree truly intended to order a total, but that looks impossible.[13]

It is preferable to adopt wording that parallels the treatment of the conversion operations of the mint that are outlined in sections v–viii of the decree. As suggested in the restorations of section xiii, the prospect of the ordering of similar conversions in the future might have been envisioned. That theory would well fit the recapitulatory character of the closing sections. Something like the following would make minimal additional assumptions: ο[ἱ δ'] ἐπιστάτ[αι ἐξετάσαντες τὰ τῆς πόλεος ἑκάστης καὶ ἀναγ]ράψαντες κατα[θέντων] στήλην λιθίνην ἔμπροσθεν τὸ ἀργυροκο]πίο σκοπε̃ν τῶι βο[λομένωι· ἀναγραψάντων δ' ἐν τῆι στήληι τὸ νόμισμα] ξενικόν, χω[ρὶς τό (τε) χρυσίον καὶ τὸ ἀργύριον, καὶ τὸ σύμμειχτον ἄσημο]ν ἀργύρι[ον.[14] The word σύμμειχτον could also be spelled σύμμεχτον or σύμμιχτον. Alternatively, the final section might be ἀναγραψάντων δ' ἐν τῆι στήληι τὸ νόμισμα ξενικόν, χω[ρὶς τό τε σύμμειχτον ἐπίσημον καὶ τὸ σύμμειχτον ἄσημο]ν ἀργύρι[ον. This wording of the final clause exploits attested technical terminology on imperial inventories.[15]

The provision for public display for those wishing to examine the record is naturally indicative of the developed democracy. The decree of Teisamenos in 403 directs that the revised law code be exhibited in this way: Andoc. 1.83: οἵδε ᾑρημένοι νομοθέται ὑπὸ τῆς βουλῆς ἀναγράφοντες ἐν σανίσιν ἐκτιθέντων πρὸς τοὺς ἐπωνύμους σκοπεῖν βουλομένῳ. The phrase σκοπεῖν βουλομένῳ is repeated later in the same decree to denote the treatment of future *nomothesia* (Andoc. 1.84). One may also compare the decree on the cult of the Anakes (*IG* I[3] 133.9–11).[16] It appears a safe restoration that a similar clause appears in *IG* I[3] 60.31: ... σκο]πε̃ν τõ[ι βολομένοι ... and 140.7–8 is

[12] See Tod *JHS* (1949) 105.

[13] Cf. *IG* I[3] 52A.22–23 cited just above.

[14] For ἐξετάζω, note these postimperial inscriptions: *IG* II[2] 120.14, 17; 216.8; 217.8; 463.30; cf. *SEG* 33.77.3, 9, for possible usage of this word in Nikophon's Coinage Law of 375/4.

[15] Cf. *IG* I[3] 376.77–78: [ἀ]ργυρίο̣ν̣ [σύμμειχτον ἄσε]|μ̣ον καὶ ἐπ[ίσεμον; 383.384–87: [χ]σενικὸν ἀρ|[γ]ύριον σύμ[μ|ει]χτον ἐπίσ|[εμ]ον ...; cf. *IG* II[2] 1388.71–72: [ἀ]ργύριον σύμμειχτον ἄσημον.... On the general usage of the vocaculary, see M. Cacciamo Caltabiano and P. Radici Colace, "ΑΡΓΥΡΙΟΝ ΔΟΚΙΜΟΝ ... ΤΟ Δ' ΕΝΑΝΤΙΟΝ ΠΑΡΑΣΗΜΟΝ (Pollux 3,86)," *ASNP*[3] 13 (1983) 421–47, esp. 428–31.

[16] *IG* I[3] 133.9–11: ... κα[ὶ τὸ πλε̃θ]ος τὸ ἀργυρίο [χσύμπαντος ...7... ἀναγράφσαν]|τες ἐμ π[ιν]α̣κίοι μ̣[ετὰ τὲν] ἑορτὲν κατα[θέντον ....21.........]|[..]μίο [σχ]οπε̃ν τõι β[ολομένο]ι....

another possible use of the same formula ... σκοπε̃ν] | τõι βολομέ-[νοι.... Mattingly believes that this formula offers a criterion for dating, as the decree involving the cult of the Anakes (*IG* I[3] 133: after 434/3) is so strikingly similar to the Coinage Decree.[17] According to him, a later formula is found in the decree regarding the cult of Neileus (*IG* I[3] 84: 418/7).[18] The absence of sufficient parallel material renders such a conclusion unduly hypothetical.

The reference to gold, if it is correctly restored, could be owed to the mint's receipt of electrum coins in circulation in allied cities. Yet as Erxleben protests (received with sympathy by Lewis in *IG* I[3]), there is only a prohibition of silver in the decree. Once the idea that the decree determined to close allied mints is rejected, however, the reception of electrum becomes readily comprehensible. The Athenians envisaged receiving electrum coins for conversion, and then reminting the silver and reusing the gold. These electrum coins might otherwise have gone for the payment of assessed tribute, presumably collected from allies in instances where they had no other easy means of payment.

In the monetary environment implied by this interpretation of the decree, the Athenians, either on a single occasion or periodically, engaged to some degree in supplementing the stock of allied silver in circulation in the *arkhē* by managing a substantial conversion. On the conversion that seems to appear in the beginning of the extant decree and is perhaps the first such, this was probably done in connection with the tendering of the tribute by the allies. On later occasions, perhaps conversion was to occur in conjunction with the protected fund alluded to in sections vii and viii. In that case, there is no reason to think that they would not have received electrum coins as they sometimes had done in the regular collection of tribute and supplied silver that went to replace their normal revenues. They were merely generalizing a policy that had been previously implemented in piecemeal concessions to individual tributaries.

xiv. ο[ἱ δ'] ἐπιστάτ[αι ἐξετάσαντες τὰ τῆς πόλεος ἑκάστης καὶ XIV.1
ἀναγ]ράψαντες κατα[θέντων] στήλην λιθίνην ἔμπροσθεν

[17] H.B. Mattingly, "Formal Dating Criteria for Fifth Century Attic Inscriptions," *Acta of the Fifth International Congress of Greek and Latin Epigraphy, Cambridge 1967* (Oxford 1971) 27–33, esp. 29.

[18] *IG* I[3] 84.26–29 provides a slightly different formulation: τὸ δὲ φσέφισμα τόδε, ὅπος ἂν εἶ εἰδέναι τõ[ι] βολομένοι, ἀναγράφσα|ς ὁ γραμματεὺς ὁ τε̃ς βολε̃ς ἐν στέλει λιθίνει καταθέτο ἐν τõι Νελεί|οι παρὰ τὰ ἴκρια.

τõ ἀργυροχο]πίο σχοπε̃ν τω̃ι βο[λομένωι· ἀναγραψάντων δ' ἐν τη̃ι στήληι τὸ νόμισμα]
ξενικόν, χω[ρὶς τό (τε) χρυσίον καὶ τὸ ἀργύριον, καὶ τὸ σύμμειχτον
ἄσημο]ν ἀργύρι[ον.

xiv. The *epistatai* reviewing the submissions of each city and recording them in writing are to erect a stone stele in front of the mint for anyone wishing to scrutinize; and let them record on the stele the foreign money, separately [both] the gold and the silver, and the mixed, uncoined silver.

The final surviving section of the Coinage Decree presents us with an interesting problem of context. Two understandings of the general import of sections xiii and xiv have been offered: the traditional view that provision was made here for the exchange of monies by private individuals and my hypothesis that provision was made for future decisions by the *Boulē* to convert allied civic holdings of non-Athenian money. The difficulties in the former involve the improbability of a mass demonetization, the anomalous appearance of these clauses at this place in the decree, the unlikelihood of a provision for monetary exchange by non-allies (in the restoration of *ATL*), and the terminological idiosyncrasy and gratuitous character of some of the phraseology. My restoration suffers chiefly because section xiii.3 might entail a clumsy shift to the singular, if our assumption must be that single cities always dispatch multiple *presbeis* 'ambassadors' to deal with the Athenians.

It is also worth considering what these two sections might signify, if the Smyrna fragment actually represented a later decree that in its surviving opening is citing the decree that is contained on the other fragments. In that case, sections xiii and xiv might be the arrangements under which some individual *polis*, newly allied with Athens or recently returned to the *arkhē*, was allowed to convert a consignment of non-Athenian money and bullion into Attic currency. These sections follow the additional clause of the bouleutic oath, because of their parochial relevance. They seem to parallel what we suspect was being legislated at the beginning of the surviving decree and just before that beginning, because here was reenacted a similar project of monetary transformation. The discrepancies between the wording of the Smyrna fragment and the others are not sufficient in themselves to compel such a conclusion. It is equally true, however, that nothing in sections xiii and xiv as they stand conclusively militates against that conclusion.

CONCLUSION

Composite Restored Text

i. [– – – – – – – –]αι τὰ γ[ραμματεῖα....[8].... ἢ ἄρχοντες ἐν I.1
τῆσι π]όλεσι ἢ ἄρ[χοντες τῶν συμμάχων πεμπόντων].

ii. [οἱ] δὲ ἑλληνοταμ[ίαι τὰς τε πόλεις καὶ τὸ ἀργύριον II.1
ἀ]ναγραφόντων· ἐὰ[ν δὲ μὴ ὀρθῶς ἀναγράφωσι τὸ τῶν
π]όλεων
τινος, ἐσα[γόντων *h*οι ἐσαγογε͂ς τὰς δίκας ἐς τ]ὴν
ἡλιαίαν τὴν
τῶ[ν θεσμοθετῶν κατὰ τὸν νόμον· ο]ἱ δὲ θεσμοθέ[τ]αι
πε[νθ' ἡμερῶν δό]ντων [δίκας τοῖς φήν]ασι
ἕκαστον.

iii. ἐὰν δέ [τις ἄλλος τ]ῶν ἀρχόν[των ἐν τ]ῆσι III.1
πόλεσι μὴ
ποιῆι κα[τὰ τὰ συγκει]μένα ἢ τῶν [πολι]τῶν ἢ τῶν ξένων,
[ἄτ]ιμ[ος ἔστω καὶ τὰ χρή]ματα δημόσια [ἔσ]τω καὶ
τῆς θεο͂ τ[ὸ ἐπιδέκατον].

iv. [καὶ εἰ μ]ή εἰσι ἄρχοντες Ἀθηναίων, ἐ[π.μελήθεντων IV.1
τῶν
ἐν τῶι] ψηφίσματι οἱ ἄρχοντε[ς οἱ ἑκάστης τῆς πόλεως καὶ]
ἐὰμ μὴ ποιῶσι κατὰ τ[ὰ ξυγκείμενα?, ἔστω κατὰ τῶν
ἀρχ]όντων
τούτων πέρι ἀτ[ιμίας δίοξις Ἀθήνησι·

v. [ἐν δὲ τῶ]ι ἀργυροκοπίωι τὸ ἀργύ[ριον τὸ νῦν ὑπάρχον V.1
ἐπικόψαι μὴ ἔλ]αττον ἢ ἥμυσυ καὶ ἀ[πολαβε͂ν τὸ
ἀργύριον ὅσον
ἐσφέρουσ]ι αἱ πόλεις· πράττ[εσθαι δὲ ἐκ τούτο
νομίσματος τρε͂ς]
δραχμὰς ἀπὸ τῆς μν[ᾶς· τοὺς δ' ἐπιστάτας τὰ χρήματα
κατ]αλλάττεν ἢ ἐνόχο[υς ε͂ναι κατὰ τὸν νόμον]·

vi. [ὃ δὲ ἂν περιγ]ίγνηται ἀργυρίο[ῦ τοῦ κεκομμένου VI.1
σύμπαντος
ἀποδό]σθαι ἢ τοῖς στρατ[ηγοῖς ἢ τοῖς νέοις στρατηγοῖς.

vii. [ἐπε]ιδὰν δὲ ἀποδοθῆι, [οὗτοι ἐξαιρῶσι τὴν ἀπαρχὴν VII.1
τἀθην]άαι καὶ τῶι Ἡφαίσ[τωι ...

viii. καὶ ἐάν τ]ις εἴπ[ηι ἢ] ἐπιψηφίσηι περ[ὶ τῶν ἐξαιρέτων VIII.1
ἀναλῶσαι ἢ ἐς ἄλλο] τι χρῆσθαι ἢ δανε[ίζεσθαι, ἀπαγωγὴν
αὐτοῦ εἶναι πρὸς] τοὺς ἕνδεκα· οἱ δ[ὲ ἕνδεκα θαν]άτωι

ζ[ημιωσάντων· ἐὰν] δὲ ἀμφισβητῆι, ἐσ[αγαγόντων ἐς τὸ δικαστήρ]ιον.

ix. κήρυκας δὲ ἑλέσθαι τὸ[ν δῆμον καὶ πέμψαι ἀπαγγελοῦντας IX.1
τὰ ἐψηφισμ]ένα, ἕνα μὲν ἐπὶ Νή[σους, ἕνα δὲ ἐπὶ 'Ιωνίαν,
ἕνα δὲ ἐφ' 'Ελλήσπο]ντον, ἕν[α] δὲ ἐ[πὶ τὰ ἐπ]ὶ Θράικης·
το[ύτος δὲ τὴν πορείαν ἑκάστωι παρασκευάσαντες οἱ στρατηγοὶ
ἀπ]ποστειλάντ[ων ὡς τάχιστα ἢ ἕκαστος εὐθυν]όσθω μυρία[ισι
δραχμῆσι·

x. [ἀναγ]ράψαι δὲ τὸ ψήφισμα τ[όδε τὸς ἄ]ρχοντα[ς τ]ὸ[ς ἐ]ν X.1
ταῖσι πόλεσιν [καὶ θεῖναι ἐν στή]ληι λιθίνηι ἐν τῆι ἀγορᾶι
[ἑκάστης] τῆ[ς πό]λεως καὶ τὸς ἐπιστ[άτας ἔμπροσθεν] τõ
ἀργυροκοπίο· ταῦτα δὲ ἐπ[ιτελέσαι τὰς πόλες, ἐ]ὰμ μὴ αὐτοὶ
βόλωνται.

xi. δεηθῆναι δὲ αὐτῶν τὸγ κήρυκα τὸν ἰόντα ὅσα [κ]ελεύο[σιν] 'Αθηναῖοι. XI.1

xii. προσγράψαι δὲ πρὸς τὸν ὅρκον [τ]ὸν τῆ]ς βολῆς τὸν XII.1
γραμματέα τὸν τῆς [βολῆς τα]δί· ἐάν τις κόπτηι νομίσ[μα]
ἀργυρίο ἐν τῆσι πό[λεσι κ]αὶ μὴ χρῆται νομ[ίσμασιν τοῖς]
'Αθη[να]ίων ἢ σταθμοῖς ἢ μέτ[ροις καθάπερ ἑαυτõ νομίσμασι]ν
καὶ σταθμοῖς καὶ μέτροις, [αὐτὸν οὐκ ἐάσω καὶ ζημιώσω κατὰ τὸ
πρότε]ρον ψήφισμα ὃ Κλέαρχ[ος εἶπεν].

xiii. ἡ δὲ βολὴ κελευέσθω τὰς πόλες δõν]αι τὸ ξενικὸν ἀργύριον XIII.1
[τοῖς ἐπιστάταις τõ ἀργυροκοπίο] ὅταμ βόληται· τὴν δὲ πόλ[ιν
ἑκάστην πρέσβες πέμψαι 'Αθήναζε]· αὐτὸν δὲ τὰ [ἑ]αυτõ ἕκαστ[ον
ἀπογράψαι καὶ καταθεῖναι ἐς τὸ ἀργυ]ροκόπιον.

xiv. ο[ἱ δ'] ἐπιστάτ[αι ἐξετάσαντες τὰ τῆς πόλεος ἑκάστης καὶ XIV.1
ἀναγ]ράψαντες κατα[θέντων] στήλην λιθίνην ἔμπροσθεν τõ ἀργυροκο]πίο

σκοπε͂ν τῶι βο[λομένωι· ἀναγραψάντων δ' ἐν τῆι στήληι
τὸ νόμισμα]
ξενικόν, χω[ρὶς τό (τε) χρυσίον καὶ τὸ ἀργύριον, καὶ τὸ
σύμμειχτον
ἄσημο]ν ἀργύρι[ον.

Translation

i. . . . the registers . . . either officials in the cities or officials of the allies are to send.

ii. The Hellenotamiai are to register both the cities and the money. If they should not register correctly the entry of any of the cities, let the *Eisagōgeis* introduce the cases to the Heliaia of the Thesmothetai in accordance with the law, and the Thesmothetai should conduct the cases in five days for those informing in each instance.

iii. If some other one of the archons in the cities not act in accordance with the engagements either of the citizens or with the foreigners, let him be deprived of civic rights and let his property be exappropriated and a tithe belong to the goddess.

iv. And if there are no officials of the Athenians, let the officials of each city take care for the provisions of the decree; and if they do not act in accordance with the engagements(?), let there be a prosecution against these officials at Athens involving loss of civil rights.

v. Coin no less than half the silver now present in the mint and take in return the silver money so much as the cities contribute; out of this coinage levy three drachms from the *mna*; the *epistatai* are to exchange the money or be liable in accordance with the law.

vi. Whatever remains of all the silver that has been coined is to be handed over either to the *stratēgoi* or to the new board of *stratēgoi*.

vii. Whenever it has been handed over, they should reserve the *aparkhē* to Athena and to Hephaistos. . . .

viii. And if anyone speaks or moves a vote concerning the reserved monies to expend, or to use for any other purpose, or to loan, let there be a summary arrest of this person before the Eleven; the Eleven should punish him with death; but if he disputes his guilt, they are to bring him before a dicasteric court.

ix. The *dēmos* is to choose heralds and to sent them to announce the measures that have been voted, one to the islands, and one to Ionia, and one to the Hellespont, and one to the Thraceward region. The generals having provided conveyance to each are to dispatch them as quickly as possible, or each should be fined 10,000 drachms when he undegoes his final scrutiny.

x. The officials in the cities are to inscribe this decree and place it on a stone stele in the marketplace of each city and the *epistatai* are to place the decree in front of the mint; the cities are to carry out these instructions, if the officials are not willing.

xi. The herald arriving is to request of them as much as the Athenians are ordering.

xii. The *grammateus* ['secretary'] of the *Boulē* is to record an addition to the oath of the *Boulē* in the following terms: if anyone mints silver money in the cities and does not use the coins of the Athenians, or weights, or measures, in the same way as his own coins, and weights, and measures, I shall not permit him [to do this] and shall penalize him in accordance with the earlier decree which Klearkhos proposed.

xiii. Let the *Boulē* order the cities to give foreign money to the *epistatai* of the mint whenever it wishes; each city is to send envoys to Athens and each [envoy] is to register his own funds and deposit them at the mint.

xiv. The *epistatai* reviewing the submissions of each city and recording them in writing are to erect a stone stele in front of the mint for anyone wishing to scrutinize; and let them record on the stele the foreign money, separately [both] the gold and the silver, and the mixed, uncoined silver.

Interpretation

The interpretation of the Coinage Decree that has been developed in the preceding discussion departs radically from that in previous work. It could, however, be argued that it is a much more conservative reading of the extant text. There are several major features of earlier reconstructions that were not strongly grounded in the epigraphical evidence and constitute significant developments in the practices of Attic hegemony that are otherwise unknown in the remaining source material. A large-scale upheaval in the way the citizens of allied cities conducted their daily economic activities is absent from my interpretation. Non-Athenian money was not demonetized, recalled to Athens, or replaced. With the disappearance of a recall of allied money, the rationale for believing in movements of great consignments of superseded allied coins and of new Attic currency also evaporate.

In the place of a prohibition on the allies minting their own coins and the establishment of a monopoly for Attic money and metrological standards, we find a more modest provision that allies who still minted their own coins had to hold valid Athenian coins and standards as well. Rather than finding harsh punitive clauses that threatened the allies to gain compliance, we are faced with efforts to police the more limited reception of allied coin and its replacement in Athenian coffers. Both Athenian and allied officials were threatened with prosecution if they exploited this processs, or if they were negligent in its implementation, or perhaps if they executed their instructions without proper concern for the stipulations of other agreements. The punitive dimension of the decree culiminates in an attempt to strengthen the resolve of the *Boulē*. It is uncertain whether *bouleutai* were to swear to take both political and judicial steps to support the validity of Athenian coins and standards, or were merely to initiate a prosecution. Not only is the gravity of any such punition unknown, but the citation of the decree of Klearkhos raises the possibility that the mandates imposed on the allies and now to be supervised more conscientiously by the *Boulē* were not even innovative in this instance.

16

IG I³ 90 AND MONETARY LEGISLATION

A FRAGMENTARY stoichedon inscription in Pentelic marble (*IG* I³ 90 = *SEG* 10.87) that deals (in part) with coinage and *stathma* 'weights' has survived. The connections of this enactment with the Coinage Decree have been subjected to so much speculation that it will be necessary here to review in a most cautious spirit the state of our knowledge in order to explore the significance of this document for monetary history. The editio princeps was a wartime publication of Meritt, which I reproduce below.[1] The text of *IG* I³, which I also supply, has benefitted from the study of the inscription by Stroud.[2] Given the state of preservation and survival of the provisions of the inscription, the conservatism of the text presented by *IG* I³ is hardly surprising.

Meritt pointed out the similarity of the script to the alliance with Perdikkas (*IG* I³ 89), then dated to 423/2—hence dating to the known eighth prytany of Aiantis. The datings for *IG* I³ 89 have ranged considerably, with supporters for ca. 436, ca. 423/2, and ca. 416/5, or its date in *IG* I³ of 417–13(?).[3] Stroud conjectured a date of 440–20, while *IG* I³ dates ca. 416(?). Meritt restored a line of fifty-two letters. Note

[1] B.D. Meritt, "Attic Inscriptions of the Fifth Century," *Hesperia* 14 (1945) 117–33, esp. #11, pp. 119–22.

[2] See R.S. Stroud, "Three Attic Decrees," *CSCA* 7 (1974) 279–98, esp. 283–90, for which note *SEG* 26.13; Mattingly, *Klio* (1977) 83–100, esp. 84, who pronounced himself convinced by Stroud's corrections of Meritt.

[3] H.B. Mattingly, "Athenian Finance in the Peloponnesian War," *BCH* 92 (1968) 450–85, esp. 472–75 (on the comparison with the treaty with Perdikkas). On pp. 466–67, Mattingly notes a close similarity of lettering with *IG* I³ 467 (= *SEG* 10.215) dated by *IG* I³ to 430/29. Eventually, the dossier of inscriptions to be attributed to this stonecutter would also include the assessment decree of 422/1 (*IG* I³ 77); the Eleusinian first-fruits decree (*IG* I³ 78); the proxeny decree for Asteas (*IG* I³ 80: 421/0); regulations for the Hephaisteia (*IG* I³ 82: 421/0); the decree for Oiniades of Skiathos (*IG* I³ 110); the Golden Nikai record (*IG* I³ 467: 430/29). For these attributions see M.B. Walbank, "Criteria for the Dating of Fifth-Century Attic Inscriptions," in ΦΟΡΟΣ 161–69, esp. note 21, pp. 168–69 = *Athenian Proxenies of the Fifth Century* B.C. (Toronto and Sarasota 1978) 31–42, esp. note 21, p. 51. See also Mattingly *BCH* (1970) 142, 147; Mattingly, *Coinage and Administration* 71; Mattingly, "Some Fifth-Century Attic Epigraphic Hands," *ZPE* 83 (1990) 110–19, esp. 110–11. These affinities may have some weight against A.G. Woodhead's suggestion that *IG* I³ 90 belongs among the measures promoted by Perikles in anticipation of hostilities with the Spartans; cf. Woodhead, "Before the Storm," *Mélanges Helléniques offerts à Georges Daux* (Paris 1974) 375–88, esp. 384–85, but see his later thoughts in *Inscriptions: The Decrees*, *The Athenian Agora* 16, #17, pp. 22–23.

that the prytany of Aiantis is entirely a product of that line length so that . . . 'Ἀκαμ]ạντίδος would be another possibility (as Stroud points out).[4] Stroud opens the possibility of a much longer line (again, the valid parallel is *IG* I[3] 89).

Meritt:

[-----------------------------------]Ι̣
[-----------------------------------]Σ̣
[-----------------------------] Σ̣TAΟ̣
[---------------------------] Γ̣AΙ̣ [. .]Σ̣ḤO[.]
[-----------------------] Ẹ[. . .]EKATE[. .]AITO
[--------------------] ς π[ρυ]τανεί[ας τὸ]ν ἀ-
[-------καθάπερ κελευέι *h*ο] νόμος *h*ο Κ[α]λ̣λ̣[. .^{5}. .]
[. τὸν δὲ γραμματέα τε͂ς βολε͂ς ἀναγράφσαντα] τόδε τὸ φσ[έφι]σ[μα ἐν σ]
[τέλει καταθε͂ναι ἐμ πόλει· καταλλάττεν δὲ καὶ] το͂ χρυσίο πᾶν τὸ λο
[ιπὸν ἐάν τις βόλεται· τὸς δὲ πρυτάνες τε͂ς Αἰ]αντίδος πρυτανείας
[γνόμεν ἐχσενεγκε͂ν περὶ το͂ν μετάλλον το͂ν ἐ]πὶ Λαυρείọι *h*όπος ἂν [φ]
[σεφίσεται *h*ο δε͂μος ἐν τε͂ι πρότει *h*έδραι *h*]ότανπερ ε͂ι περὶ το͂ νο[μ]
[ίσματος· . . .^{6}. . . εἶπε· τὰ μὲν ἄλλα καθάπερ 'Ε]παίνετος· τοῖς δέ ἐπ[ισ]
[τάταις ἔστο χρυσᾶ νομίσματα παραδέχεσθα]ι καὶ καταλλάττεν ἀ[π]
[αρισθμεσαμένοις ἐναντίον τε͂ς βολε͂ς ἐμ πό]λει το͂ι αὐτο͂ι νόμισμ[α]
[τι χρομένοις *h*οίοι καὶ ἐς τὰ ἀργυρᾶ· ἐὰν δὲ] ἄλλο βόλονται νόμισ
[μα ----------------κρινέτο *h*ε βολ]έ· καὶ ἐάν τις ἄλλος [.]
[------------------------*h*]όπος ἂγ γίγνεται [.]
[----------------------]αι ἀπὸ το͂ν τραπ[εζ]
[ιτο͂ν--------------------] ΙΟ̣Ι· τὸς δὲ ἄρ[χον]
[τας------------------ κε]ραμεῖα· νῦν [δὲ.]

IG I[3] 90:

--Ι̣
--Σ̣
--Σ̣TAΟ̣
-------------------------------------Γ̣AΙ̣ [. .]Σ̣ḤO[.]
--------------------------------- Ẹ[. . .]EKATE[. .]AITO
------------------------------ ς π[ρυ]τανεί[ας τὸ]ν ἀ-
----------------------------ẸMΙ ΣΗΙ̣Κ[.]ΛΛ[. .^{5}. .]

[4] See Stroud *CSCA* (1974) 283. Contrast the further elaboration in Mattingly *BCH* (1968) 471.

[e.g. τὸν δὲ γραμματέα τε̃ς βολε̃ς ἀναγράφσαντα] τόδε τὸ
φσ[έφι]σ[μα ἐν σ]-
[τέλει λιθίνει καταθε̃ναι ἐμ πόλει· --------] τõ χρυσίο πᾶν τὸ λο-
[ιπὸν ------------------------ἐπὶ τε̃ς --]αντίδος πρυτανείας
[-------------------------------ἐ]πὶ Λαυρείοι *h*όπος ἂν [.]
[---------------------------*h*]ότανπερ ε̃ι περὶ τõ νο[μ]-
[ίσματος· ----εἶπε· τὰ μὲν ἄλλα καθάπερ] 'Επαίνετος· τοῖς δέ ἐπ[ισ]-
[τάταις --------------------------]σ[.]ι καὶ καταλλάττεν ἀ[.]
[---------------------------ἐμ πό]λει τõι αὐτõι νόμισμ[α]
[τι -------------------------ἐὰν δὲ] ἄλλο βόλονται νόμισ-
[μα --------------------------*h*ε βολ]έ· καὶ ἐάν τις ἄλλος [.]
[---------------------------------*h*]όπος ἂγ γίγνεται [.]
---------------------------------αι ἀπὸ τõν τραπ[εζ]
---------------------------------ιọι· τὸς δὲ ἄρ[. . .]
[τας------------------------------κε]ραμεῖα· νῦν [. . .]

Stroud saw more at the beginning of the stone and also offered some minor variants.[5] The effect of Stroud's variant readings is to call into question the suggested restorations of Meritt. Rhodes, in collaboration with D.M. Lewis, restores lines 10–12: τὸς δὲ πρυτάνες τε̃ς Αἰ]αντίδος πρυτανείας| [χρεματίζεν ἐπάναγκες περὶ τõν ἔργον ἐ]πὶ Λαυρείοι *h*όπος ἂν [φ|σεφίσεται *h*ο δε̃μος. . . .[6] To Rhodes, this procedure signals a nonprobouleumatic decree, that is, one passed in opposition to the wishes of the *boulē*. That conjecture is rather speculative.

The connection of the inscription with monetary and metrological matters is apparent from the references τõ χρυσίο πᾶν τὸ λο[ιπόν (lines 9–10); ἐ]πὶ Λαυρείοι (11); περὶ τõ νο[μίσματος (12–13); καταλλάττεν (14); τõι αὐτõι νομίσμ[ατι (15–16); ἐὰν δὲ] ἄλλο βόλονται νόμισ[μα (16–17); ἀπὸ τõν τραπ[εζ . . . (19); κε]ραμεῖα (21).[7] Possible similar restorations

[5] His first five line endings are: 1: . . .]IO[.]; 2: . . .]ATON; 3: . . .]Σ̣; 4: . . .] Σ̣TAΘ̣; 5: . . . παγ̣[τ]ος, *h*ος. His other minor variant readings (the more significant are discussed below) are as follows: line 8 (his 9): . . . τὸ φσ[έφ]ịσμ̣[α . . .; line 9 (10): . . . τõ χρυσίο πᾶν τὸ Λ[.]; line 11 (12): ἐ]πὶ Λαυρείοι *h*οπος ἂν μ̣; line 12 (13): . . . O *h*]ότανπερ ε̃ι περὶ TONO[.]; line 14 (15): line begins . . .]Σ[.]Α̣ καὶ . . ., with the *alpha* possible and also an assimilated *gamma* in place of *mu*; line 15 (16): the initial *lambda* was uncertain with only a part of a vertical to the left of the *stoichos* visible; line 20 (21): he sees the top of centered vertical in first space of . . . ιọι . . . and the second letter might have a central dot.

[6] P.J. Rhodes, *The Athenian Boule* (Oxford 1972) 259. Cf. Stroud *CSCA* (1974) note 17 on p. 288. Note *IG* I³: . . . πρυτανείας|[γνόμεν ἐχσενεγκε̃ν ἐπάναγκες. . . .

[7] The term has been interpreted as the plural nominative or more likely accusative of κεραμεῖον 'pottery shop (or business)' (note Aesch. 3.119). Cf. V. Grace, "Early Thasian

are το σταθ[. . . (4) and τοῖς δὲ ἐπ[ιστάταις (13–14).[8] Possible supplements for lines 19–20 are Meritt's ἀπὸ τõν τραπ[εζιτõν 'from the bankers' and Stroud's . . . τραπ[εζõν 'from the tables for exchange.' Clearly, this legislation about coinage also involved the mines at Laureion, exchange, money changers, a stock of gold, and the potting craft. The findspot of the inscription was in proximity to the proposed site of the mint, so that a similar mode of display to that stated in the Coinage Decree is a good conjecture (section x.3–4).[9] Woodhead suggests a building block of a large monument, a suggestion that is provocative for the way in which monetary legislation may have been displayed in Athens itself.[10]

Much else is controversial. Mattingly based much of his interpretation on reading in lines 5–6: δ]ὲ [οἱ δ]εκατε[υτ]αὶ τὸ | τέλος.[11] As Stroud observed and even Mattingly conceded, there are more options here than first appear feasible.[12] Meritt, followed by Mattingly, believed that the proposer of the main decree was probably a man named Epainetos, as we read in what was restored as a formula of amendment (line 13); Meritt also noted the clue offered by *h*]όταν περ ἔι περὶ τõ νο[μ|ίσματος. Stroud doubted the idea of an amendment formula and observed, as we can verify from the Coinage Decree itself, that there were other justifications for the citation of names in the nominative within an Attic psephism (cf. also *IG* I³ 35.7, 13; 78.60). This Epainetos is otherwise unknown, as the other known bearers of the name are not likely contemporaries of this inscription. Lines 8–9 appeared to Meritt to offer a formula for inscribing and display of the decree.[13] It is noteworthy that at least one clause was still to come even in a putative first decree on the stone. Stroud helpfully observes that a formula from an entrenchment clause is an equally likely

---

Stamped Amphoras," *AJA* 50 (1946) 31–38, esp. note 4, p. 31, who suggests a reference to the standard for vessel sizes.

8 Stroud *CSCA* (1974) 289 correctly observes that the restoration is far from secure, noting τοῖς δὲ ἐπ[ὶ NAME or τοῖς δε] ἐπ[ιμελεταῖς.

9 R.E. Wycherley, *Literary and Epigraphcial Testimonia, The Athenian Agora* 3 (Princeton 1957) 160–61; H.A. Thompson and R.E. Wycherley, *The Agora of Athens, The Athenian Agora* 14 (Princeton 1972) 78–79.

10 *Agora* 16.22. See pp. 309–11 above.

11 Mattingly *PACA* (1964) 35–53, esp. 49, who offers a citation from Antiphon fr. III.10 (B/T), from ἐν τῇ πρὸς τὴν Δημοσθένους γραφὴν ἀπολογίᾳ: δεκατευτὰς· ἀντὶ τοῦ τελώνας τοὺς τὴν δέκατην ἐκλέγοντας. Note also *BCH* (1968) 470–72

12 Stroud *CSCA* (1974) 284–85.

13 Compare Mattingly, *PACA* (1964) 50, who offered what he considered to be more conventional variants: fifty-two letters: [– – – – – – – καθάπερ κελεύει *ho* νόμος *ho* Κ[ά]λ̣λ̣[ιο· τὸς | δὲ ἐπιστάτας ἀναγράφσαι ἐστέλει λιθίνει] τόδε τὸ φσ[έφι]σ[μα πρό|σθεν τὸ ἀργυρικοπίο· ἔστο δὲ καταλάττεν καὶ] τὸ χρυσίο πᾶν τὸ λο[ι|πὸν . . . ; fifty-six letters: . . . τὸς | [δὲ ἐπιστάτας καταθε͂ναι πρόσθεν τὸ ἀργυρικοπίο τόδε τὸ φσ[έφι]σ[μα ἀνα|γράφσαντας ἐν στέλει λιθίνει· κατάλαττεν δὲ καὶ]. . . .

conjecture: [ἐὰν δέ τις ἒ ἄρχον ἒ ἰδιότες εἴπει ἒ ἐπιφσεφίσει παρὰ] τόδε τὸ φσ[έφισμα.... [14] Naturally, it is mere surmise that the same entrenched fund might be involved here as in the Coinage Decree.

Much attention has been focused on Meritt's reading of line 7, despite his tentativeness, because of his dependence on a squeeze and photograph: ... καθάπερ κελεύει *ho* νόμος *ho* Κ[α]λ̣λ̣[..⁵..], for it seemed to establish an allusion to a law famous enough to be known by the name of its proposer. Stroud, however, stated that he clearly saw NOM[.]Σ with a vertical stroke allowing either NOMTΣ (impossible, one supposes) or NOMIΣ. A *mu* or a mishapen *nu* seems to follow the *sigma*. In place of Meritt's two *lambdas*, Stroud saw the bottom of a vertical stroke for the first and the top of an approximately centered vertical for the second. Stroud prints] νόμ̣ισ̣μ̣[α] κ[α]ὶ [..⁵..]. *IG* I³ prints ...Ẹ̣MỊΣHỊK[.]ᒪᒪ.... That creates an extremely intractable sequence of letters to construe. Hence the cross reference to a law of a Kallias remains quite dubious, even before we proceed to the further speculation that the extant decrees of Kallias (*IG* I³ 52) are somehow involved.

In the much mutilated state of the inscription, anything beyond the observation that a related set of concerns to that exhibited in the Coinage Decree are evident would merely be speculation to suit our own historical assumptions.[15] We are, however, entitled to insist that the history of legislation on monetary policy seems to have been richer than the surviving documents indicate at first glance. The area of the mint was a locale for the public display of such enactments and it is unlikely that the Coinage Decree and *IG* I³ 90 were the only two documents displayed there.

A number of conclusions ought to be recognized as ill-grounded in the present state of our knowledge:

1. There is no evidence in the inscription itself for the view that this is another part of the same program of legislation as the Coinage Decree or is even a fragment of the decree itself.[16] Two important differences need to be emphasized. There is nothing preserved here that shows any application of the decree's provisions to allied states. Second, no certain

[14] Stroud, *CSCA* (1974) 287.

[15] Stroud, *CSCA* (1974) 290, observes drily: "Few, if any of the published supplements are as inevitable as their proponents have claimed and it is time to call a moratorium on historical speculation based on the missing parts of this undated text. Let us frankly admit that we cannot establish the length of the line and that this fragment preserves only tempting morsels of what was probably a long and detailed document."

[16] See Mattingly *PACA* (1964) 49–53; *Klio* (1977) 88; *Coinage and Administration* 70–71, for the view that *IG* I³ 90 was inscribed on the lower part of the same stele that bore the Athenian copy of the Coinage Decree. Shall we suggest alternatively: elsewhere on the same monument or building?

reference is made to minting; rather only a treatment of the mechanism of exchange can be positively substantiated.[17]

2. Anyone will concede that the restoration of lines 16–17 after Meritt to establish a procedure here by which the supposed prohibition of coining silver of the Coinage Decree is to be selectively suspended is to be adjudged particularly gratuitous.[18] All sorts of procedures for conversion, exchange, or minting could be hypothesized there.

3. The introduction of the decrees of Kallias is especially unwarranted and the use of the content of *IG* I^3 52 (for instance regarding the Treasury of the Other Gods) transcends the most speculative boundaries of discussion.[19] The only ground for such a conjecture is Meritt's decision to restore lines 14–16 based on *IG* I^3 52A.18–22. Moreover, to go further and suppose that *IG* I^3 90 carries through another of the massive repayments of sacred monies that were purportedly enjoined in the Kallias decrees may be acceptable as conjecture intending to show the explanatory potential of Mattingly's redatings, but it is hardly justified on the basis of the remains themselves.[20]

4. There is no way to tell at the moment in whose hands the gold of line 9 is residing; the Hellenotamiai or other officials standing in the normal flow of revenue, the allies, Athenian citizens (cf. ἐάν τις ἄλλος in line 18); Athenian treasuries (on the Acropolis?; cf. ἐμ πό]λει in line 15); or some reserve fund protected by entrenchment.[21]

[17] *IG* I^3 90, p. 108, however, offers tentatively in lines 20–21: . . . ἐν τõι ἀρ[γυροπίοι· τὸς δὲ ἀργυροκόπος. . . .

[18] Meritt (*Hesperia* [1945] 122) hesitantly offers the following for lines 16-17: ἐὰν δὲ] ἄλλο βόλονται νόμισ[μα κόπτεν *hαι* πόλες περὶ αὐτõ κρίνετο *hε* βολ]έ. The word order and syntax, while not impossible, are hardly elegant. See also *HCT* 3.627–28. Could the *Boulē* have really been given the latitude to decide on a matter of this significance as it is understood in the traditional interpretation of the Coinage Decree?

[19] Mattingly *PACA* (1964) 49–53; *BCH* (1968) 470, 475–76. Cf. L. Kallet-Marx, "The Kallias Decree, Thucydides, and the Outbreak of the Peloponnesian War," *CQ* 39 (1989) 94–113, for a healthy dose of skepticism not only on the chronology of *ATL*, but also on historical interpretation (much affecting Mattingly's work as well).

[20] Mattingly's revised restoration (*PACA* [1964] 52): τοῖς δὲ ἐπ[ισ|τάταις ἔστο τό χρύσιον τὸ τõν θεõν δέχεσθα]ι καὶ καταλλάττεν ἀ[π|αρισθμεσαμένοις ἐναντίον τε̃ς βολε̃ς ἐμ πό]λει τõι αὐτõι νομίσμ[α|τι χρομένοις οἷοι καὶ ἐς τὰ ἀργύριον· ἐὰν δὲ] ἄλλο βόλονται νόμισ|[μα. . . .

[21] Indeed the possibility that gold is being changed or is being accepted by the mint to be replaced with tetradrachms, if it were correct, would again direct us away from a control of allied minting toward facilitation of the collection of tribute and/or of other taxes. Gold was important not because the Athenians sought to regulate its circulation (see above pp. 230–31), but because some allies collected significant portions of tax receipts in electrum coins. Conversion of these assets into silver so that they could be spent by the Athenian government would then be a major issue. And this hypothesis does not even begin to consider the other aspects of conversion of gold dedications into silver for expenditure. It is suggested below

5. The reference to Laurion could relate to a wide range of contexts: state income from the mines, leasing arrangements, security matters in wartime, supervision of mining activity, or revenue from the Hephaistikon mine or some other mine under direct state exploitation (see above pp. 370–71).[22]

6. Even if we could be sure that the source(s) of the precious metal involved in this legislation were foreign, that need not further entail that the Athenians were legislating about the closure or reopening of allied mints or the conversion (on whatever scale) of allied holdings of non-Athenian coin.[23] The receipts of the 5 percent tax that replaced the tribute could be the source of the silver and gold. And if the Athenians were truly replacing the allied assets held in non-Attic coin, those assets could be the reserves of a single allied city that was adopting Attic money as legal tender in an agreement like those proposed on the basis of Aristophanes *Birds* 1040–41.

Nothing would be a more seductive prospect for anyone attempting to synthesize all the evidence on the monetary affairs of the fifth-century *arkhē* than to restore convincingly and synergistically *IG* I^3 90. There is, however, simply not enough go on in what survives on the stone or in other documents that might provide comparative phraseology.

---

that the Athenians decided to mint gold coins only when it was no longer practical to sell gold bullion in return for silver tetradrachms (pp. 511–21 below).

[22] Cf. Mattingly *Historia* (1961) 181–82 for an overhaul of the mining industry; also *BCH* (1968) 470.

[23] Cf. Mattingly *Klio* (1977) 83–84; Mattingly, *Coinage and Administration* 70–71.

17

THE DATING AND THE INSCRIPTION OF THE COINAGE DECREE

IT SHOULD NOT SURPRISE even a reader who is largely unaware of the bibliography on the Coinage Decree that the investigation of its chronology has been pervaded by assumptions about both its supposed imperialistic character and specifically its presumptive prohibition against the coining of silver by allied states. Thus, whether or not they made their reasoning on dating explicit, many commentators have tried to gauge at which point in the history of Athenian hegemony over their allies a policy initiative so nakedly intrusive could have been implemented. Furthermore, confirmation has been sought in the record restored from site archaeology and from numismatics for any date offered for this legislation.

THE STATE OF THE QUESTION

The natural tendency on the discovery of the first fragments of the Coinage Decree was to date them to the period just before the production of the *Birds* in 414, because the ever influential Wilamowitz was held to have implied that Aristophanes was making a specific allusion to this legislation. For example, Weil bracketed the Syracusan expedition with the decree of Klearkhos before and the Coinage Decree right afterward.[1] The state of knowledge about the epigraphy of Ionian inscriptions from the period of Attic hegemony stood as no impediment toward such a chronology.

The early hypothesis of a date for the epigraphical material in the 410s shortly yielded ground before Hiller von Gaertringen's and

[1] R. Weil, "Das Münzmonopol Athens im ersten attischen Seebund," *ZfN* 25 (1906) 52–62, esp. 56; also M. Romstedt, *Die wirtschaftliche Organisation des athenischen Reiches* (Leipzig 1914) 19. For comparable dates, see Cavaignac, *Études* 186–87, dating to the time of Peace of Nikias and seeing its cause in allied rebellion; Reinach, *Mém. Acad. Ins. et Belles-Lettres* (1911) 354–56, who dated this strong measure that anticipated further hostilities to 420–15; E. Babelon, "La politique monétaire d'Athènes au Ve siècle avant notre ère," *RN*[4] 17 (1913) 457–85, esp. 467–68, 480–81, who saw the decree as ending a tradition of similar legislation; also P. Gardner, "Coinage of the Athenian Empire," *JHS* 33 (1913) 147–88, esp. 150; J. Johnston, "An International Managed Currency in the Fifth Century," *Hermathena* 47 (1932) 132–57, esp. 147–49.

Klaffenbach's redating to the 420s and to the ascendancy of Kleon.[2] Klearkhos' legislation was placed at the outbreak of the Archidamian War. The presumed authoritarian character of the decree was felt to suit Kleon's management of the allies. Eventually, the decree would be held to be consonant with massive increases in tribute, the Kleonymos Decree (*IG* I³ 68), and the assessment of 425/4 (*IG* I³ 71).

Nothing in the fragments inscribed in the Ionic script served to repudiate a chronology in the 420s. Line 3 (our section x) of the Siphnos fragment had the older form of the dative article ταῖσι (line 7 of the Smyrna fragment: τῇσι), but that was taken to be only a slight indication of an earlier date, and then only a terminus ante quem of 420.[3] The appearance of a fragment from Aphytis did nothing to overcome prevailing judgment.[4] The Coinage Decree was redated only because the Kos fragment with its three-barred *sigmas* was announced so soon after the discovery at Aphytis. With the publication of the Kos fragment low dates in the 410s have been dropped from scholarly opinion (with the most notable recent exception being the editor of the Odessa fragment).[5]

Numismatists received this communis opinio on behalf of a date in the 420s conditionally. To them a date nearer to mid-century (which was sometimes perceived as the latest feasible placement) seemed most likely for a cessation or strong discouragement of minting in the *arkhē*, but for the moment, the postulate of earlier legislation with the same tendency toward the suppression of allied mints was their only recourse.[6] There was,

[2] Hiller and Klaffenbach *AE* (1923) 117; Hiller and Klaffenbach, *ZfN* (1924–25) 219; E. Cavaignac, "Le décret dit de Kléarkhos," *RN* 15 (1953) 1–7, esp. 2–3; Robinson *AJP* (1935) 151–52. See also Tod, *GHI* 1.165–66. The same position has more lately been argued in extenso by Erxleben *AfP* (1971) 159–61; also K. Meister, *Die Ungeschichtlichkeit des Kalliasfriedens und deren historische Folgen* (Wiesbaden 1982) 115.

[3] H.T. Wade-Gery, "The Financial Decrees of Kallias (*I.G.* I², 91–92)," *JHS* 51 (1931) 57–85, esp. 78–82. See also *IG* I² p. 95; *SIG*³ 87, note 1, p. 111; Cavaignac *RN* (1953) 2 (cf. K. Meisterhans, *Grammatik der attischen Inschriften*³ [Berlin 1900] 120–21). Cf. Tod *JHS* (1949) 105.

[4] See Chapter 12, note 6 above. Cf. D.M. Robinson, "Inscriptions from Macedonia, 1938," *TAPA* 69 (1938) 43–76, esp. 43.

[5] Other somewhat later proponents of a position on the chronology for the decree in the 410s comparable to that of Weil were H. Nesselhauf, review of B.D. Meritt and A.B. West, *The Athenian Assessment of 425 B.C.*, *Gnomon* 12 (1936) 296–301, esp. 298 (dating to 416) and H. Schaefer, "Beiträge zur Geschichte der attischen Symmachie," *Hermes* 74 (1939) 225–64, esp. 253–57, even in the face of the then recent announcement of the Kos fragment. Cf. B.D. Meritt, "The Early Athenian Tribute Lists," *CP* 38 (1943) 223–39, esp. note 24, p. 239.

[6] Babelon *RN* (1913) 467–69; see also Cavaignac, *Études* 186; Gardner *JHS* (1913) esp. 150; C. Seltman, *Greek Coins*² (London 1955) 111–12, cf. 144, 148–49, all identify this earlier legislation as the decree of Klearkhos. For Seltman's difficulties in homogenizing

after all, the citation of the psephism of Klearkhos in our section xii.5–6. In addition, there was a general tendency in the earliest numismatic discussions that reflected the discovery of the epigraphical evidence to see the growing predominance of the Athenian owls as an extended process.[7] While an appreciation of economic and especially fiscal factors was not entirely missing from their commentary, the early scholarship by numismatists on the epigraphical material tended to emphasize the growing predominance of Attic money as the result of a legislative process.

This first phase in studies on the dating of the Coinage Decree was brought to an end with the discovery of the Kos fragment with its use of three-barred *sigmas*.[8] Conventional wisdom urged that the three-barred *sigma* gave way definitively to the four-barred *sigma* by 446 (so that the dating of the Kos fragment created an almost immediate reconsideration of the date of the Aphytis fragment). The mainstream of epigraphical opinion acceded to Segre's redating, and Robinson restated the numismatic case for a date ca. 449.[9] In a sense, the early 440s date for the Coinage Decree remains the communis opinio even today, not only in terms of the chronology of the documents but also with regard to the use of the epigraphical evidence for historical analysis. Historical arguments were propounded to account for a mid-century date for what had so recently seemed to many scholars to belong to the heyday of Kleon.[10] Thereupon, Schuller, a recent champion of a date in the early 440s, could make a systematic attempt to see the Coinage Decree as an essential part of a Periclean reordering of the *arkhē*.[11]

Subsequently, there were a few other authorities who independently argued for later dates, even after Segre's publication of the Kos fragment (see note 5 above): Tod opted for a date shortly after 438 and Cavaignac

---

earlier theories on the decree and numismatic evidence, see G.K. Jenkins, review, *NC*[6] 15 (1955) 262–66, esp. 263.

[7] See note 1 above; also Romstedt, *Organisation* 19.

[8] Cf., for example, M.N. Tod, "The Progress of Greek Epigraphy, 1937–1938," *JHS* 59 (1939) 241–81, esp. 251–52.

[9] Robinson 339-40.

[10] Accordingly, proponents of a mid-century date such as Meritt (*PAPS* [1975] 269) or Schuller (*Herrschaft* 217) view Kleon as raising the burden of the allies within an elaborated and preexisting imperial system. Italian scholars had quickly drawn parallel conclusions from Segre's redating. G. DeSanctis was one of the first to utilize Segre's redating to see the Coinage Decree as an appropriate part of Periclean policies: see his review of A.W. Gomme, *The Population of Athens in the Fifth and Fourth Centuries* B.C., *RFIC* 55 (1937) 288–309, esp. 301. See also S. Accame, "Note per la storia della Pentecontaetia," *RFIC* 83 (1955) 146–74, esp. 159, where the Coinage Decree (unusually) is thought to bespeak panhellenism.

[11] Schuller, *Herrschaft* 70, 170–72, 177.

for the period of the Peace of Nikias.[12] Nevertheless, the dating of the decree became the centerpiece of an effort (or a series of efforts) by H.B. Mattingly to redate a group of important Attic documents concerning the allies from the 440s to the period of the Peloponnesian War. These redatings subserved a reconsideration of the evolution of Athenian imperialism that endeavored to see the more authoritarian and repressive features of Attic hegemony over the allies as products of the exigencies of war and of the influence of such demagogic and aggrandizing figures as Kleon. Mattingly has sustained his polemics in a blizzard of publications.[13]

While a number of other documents containing three-barred *sigmas* were featured in his general assault on the traditional system of epigraphical dating, the Coinage Decree has occupied a special place of prominence both in his scholarship and in that of those upholding what they consider to be the communis opinio.[14] Mattingly returned to the date of the Coinage Decree repeatedly and often in conjunction with his discussions of other inscriptions. A number of factors account for

[12] Tod *JHS* (1949) 105. See Cavaignac *RN* (1953) 6. Note in addition Jenkins, review of Seltman, *Greek Coins*², *NC* (1955) 263. Cf. A.G. Woodhead, *SEG* 15.4; J. Pouilloux, "Des rapports actuels de l'épigraphie et de l'histoire grecques,"*AC* 22 (1953) 32–49, esp. 38–39; Erxleben *AfP* (1971) 153–54.

[13] I list here the relevant works of H.B. Mattingly: "The Athenian Coinage Decree," *Historia* 10 (1961) 148–88; "Athenian Imperialism and the Foundation of Brea," *CQ* 16 (1966) 172–92, esp. 187–88 ; "Periclean Imperialism," in E. Badian (ed.), *Ancient Society and Institutions* (New York 1967) 193–223, esp. 193–96, 203–204; "Epigraphically the Twenties are Too Late . . . ," *BSA* 65 (1970) 129–49, esp. 133; "Formal Dating Criteria for Fifth Century Attic Inscriptions," *Acta of the Fifth International Congress of Greek and Latin Epigraphy, Cambridge 1967* (Oxford 1971) 27–33, esp. 29–31; "The Protected Fund in the Athenian Coinage Decree (*ATL* D 14, par. 7f)," *AJP* 95 (1974) 280–85; "The Second Athenian Coinage Decree," *Klio* 59 (1977) 83–100; "Coins and Amphoras—Chios, Samos and Thasos in the Fifth Century B.C.," *JHS* 101 (1981) 78–86; "The Athenian Coinage Decree and the Assertion of Empire," in I. Carradice (ed.), *Coinage and Administration in the Athenian and Persian Empires* (Oxford 1987) 65–71; "Methodology in Fifth-Century Greek History," *EMC* 7 (1988) 321–28, esp. 325–28; "Epigraphy and the Athenian Empire," *Historia* 41 (1992) 129–38, esp. 135; "New Light on the Athenian Standards Decree (ATL II, D 14)," *Klio* 75 (1993) 99–102. See also "The Methone Decrees," *CQ* 11 (1961) 154–65, esp. note 3, p. 156; "Athens and Euboea," *JHS* 81 (1961) 124–32, esp. 130; "The Growth of Athenian Imperialism," *Historia* 12 (1963) 257–73, esp. 266–67; "The Financial Decrees of Kallias (IG i² 91/2)," *PACA* 7 (1964) 35–53, esp. 48 with note 76 (pp. 48–49). The articles are collected in *The Athenian Empire Restored* (Ann Arbor 1996).

[14] To the best of my ability and with no certain claim to exhaustiveness, I have arranged Mattingly's redatings in the general order of their presentation in his writings to convey a sense of how his reconstruction of Athenian imperial history has ramified. See the appendix to this chapter for this material. I shall not attempt to repeat all the material usefully summarized by A.S. Henry, "The Dating of Fifth-Century Attic Inscriptions," *CSCA* 11 (1978) 75–108, esp. his table on p. 99, which provides an admirable and helpful listing and summary of Mattingly's redatings up to Henry's writing.

this emphasis, including the general acceptance of a later dating for the decree in earlier scholarship, based on the then extant inscriptions, the possibility of external corroboration, and the decree's presumably undeniable significance as a measure of unalloyed imperialism. Mattingly's suggested dates for the Coinage Decree were 425/4 and later 423/2.

Reactions have been split: there has been some sympathy toward the more modest readjustment of returning the Coinage Decree to the 420s (most notably by W.K. Pritchett) and general skepticism over systematic redating.[15] The most complete surveys of the epigraphical material by Meiggs and by Walbank tried to uphold the validity of the three-barred *sigma* as an indicator of a date prior to 446.[16] Nevertheless, Erxleben's detailed treatment of the decree settles on a date between 425/4 and 421/0, probably 425/4 or 423/2.[17] The inconclusiveness of traditional and solely numismatic arguments for chronology was illustrated by the virtually simultaneous argument for a mid-century date by H.A. Cahn.[18]

My comments above on the actual contents of the decree and its economic and fiscal context change the stakes and rules of the game vis-à-vis its chronology. If the decree did not ban coining by allied states and was not the massively intrusive gambit of an imperialistic state, the search for an archaeologically based chronology is unlikely to be fruitful. Moreover, impressions about how self-aggrandizing Athenian policy may have been in particular historical settings do not do much to determine chronology, especially if the Coinage Decree is no longer considered a marked watershed, dividing a less exploitative federal period in Athenian hegemony from an imperialist supremacy, but is viewed as a single item

[15] W.K. Pritchett, "The Three-Barred Sigma at Kos," *BCH* 87 (1963) 20–23; A. Georgiadès and W.K. Pritchett, "The Koan Fragment of the Monetary Decree," *BCH* 89 (1965) 400–40, esp. 425–27; G. Klaffenbach in U. Wilcken, *Griechische Geschichte*[9] (Munich 1962) 155, 346; R. Bogaert, "Le cours du statère de Cyzique aux Ve et IVe siècles avant J.C.," *AC* 32 (1963) 85–119, esp. 109. Cf. C.W. Fornara and L.J. Samons, *Athens from Cleisthenes to Pericles* (Berkeley 1991) 98–103.

[16] R. Meiggs, "The Dating of Fifth-Century Attic Inscriptions," *JHS* 86 (1966) 86–98, esp. 86–87, 96; M.B. Walbank, "Criteria for the Dating of Fifth-Century Attic Inscriptions," in ΦΟΡΟΣ 161–69 = *Athenian Proxenies of the Fifth Century* B.C. (Toronto and Sarasota 1978) 31–42; see also the *dicta* (especially on the Coinage Decree) of A.G. Woodhead in *SEG* 18.3, 19.7, 21.18.

[17] Erxleben *AJP* (1971) 145-62, and esp. 161, where he opts for 423/2 or the first months of the following year, a conclusion that was received with approval by J. and L. Robert, *BE* (1972) #113, p. 389 (*REG* 85). Meiggs commented while Erxleben's study was incomplete—his conclusions on dating were unavailable—and conceded that there was some force to his arguments (Meiggs 600–601). See also Meister, *Ungeschichtlichkeit* 109–12; S. Cataldi, *La democrazia ateniese e gli alleati* (Padua 1984) 91–93.

[18] H.A. Cahn, *Knidos: Die Münzen des sechsten und des fünften Jahrhunderts v. Chr.* (Berlin 1970) 16, 162–66. Cf. the review by E. Schönert-Geiss in *Gnomon* 44 (1972) 270–74, esp. 271.

in a chain of monetary legislation, itself constrained by economic forces and by their reflection in fiscal policy.

ARGUMENTS FOR THE CHRONOLOGY OF THE COINAGE DECREE

There are two series of arguments based on details of the Coinage Decree that offer defenses of, respectively, a date shortly after mid-century and a date after the beginning of the Peloponnesian War.

First we consider arguments that propose the later chronology. As already stated, Mattingly's redating of the Coinage Decree was part and parcel of his broader efforts to change the chronology of a number of imperial documents. While it is tempting to simplify our investigation by cleaving to the views of the majority of Attic epigraphists who have rejected Mattingly's rearrangement of these documents, the subset of Mattingly's arguments that specifically relates to the Coinage Decree nonetheless deserves to be discussed in order to understand the status of the case for a decree passed initially in the early 440s, as well as the later alternative.

1. Mattingly's general argument whether Perikles can have been this imperialistic fails in the face of the reinterpretation of the decree as nonaggrandizing in the conventional sense.[19] A specific example of this tendency is his extraordinary reading of the Athenian appeal to Chios in 425 (Thuc. 4.51) as traceable to Chian reaction to the Coinage Decree.[20] As I have argued elsewhere, there is no reason to believe that disagreements between Athens and Chios in the 420s constituted a genuine breach of Chian autonomy by the Athenians or acts of rebellion or noncompliance with Athenian leadership by the Chians.[21] Concomitantly, for Mattingly, the Coinage Decree is a document pervaded by the imperialism of Kleon.[22] That is another untenable position founded on analysis of the document, even if my more speculative restorations presented above are entirely ignored.

2. The argument from analogy was offered regarding a number of imperial documents held to be comparable by virtue of content or by their possession of other presumably late three-barred *sigmas*. The

[19] Mattingly *Historia* (1961) 148, 157–58; Mattingly *Historia* (1963) 271–73; cf. Schuller, *Herrschaft* 216–17.

[20] Mattingly, *Ancient Society* 204.

[21] See Figueira, *Excursions* 272–74.

[22] Mattingly *Historia* (1961) 181–88, where the climate of the times is illustrated by Arist. *Ach.* 515–59; *Clouds* 247–49; Plato Com., fr. 96 K = fr. 103, *PCG* 7.475–76 (the latter two mention the iron money of Byzantion; cf. also *Frogs* 718–32).

main examples adduced by Mattingly are cited in the Appendix to this chapter and the general issue is addressed again below on pp. 442–48. It is important to emphasize that the argument for later datings for three-barred *sigmas* is strictly ancillary to point 1 concerning the Coinage Decree. One would exploit epigraphical latitude about three-barred *sigmas* only when convinced that the contents of the Coinage Decree make it a distinctly inappropriate piece of legislation for the mid-century and for the supremacy of Perikles, since the majority of the documents with three-barred *sigmas* seem to antedate 446.

3. Erxleben supplemented Mattingly's dossier of evidence, following his lead on some documents that were not decrees.[23] He adduced the Samian *horoi* 'boundary stones' that marked a sacred precinct in honor of Athena Polias, the tutelary goddess of the Athenians, that supposedly were placed after the suppression of the Samian rebellion in 439, and the Aiginetan *horoi* for Athena, Poseidon, and Apollo that could perhaps be dated after the foundation of the Athenian colony on the island in 431.[24] Nonetheless, there is no particular reason to date the Samian *horoi* after the suppression of the Samian revolt, and Barron persuasively argues for a mid-century date.[25] The Aiginetan *horoi* are just as firmly counterindicative as they rightly belong in the early history of Aigina as a tributary state, when an element of the population of the island chose to advertize its identification with Athenian interests.[26] Finally, it is worth observing that the writing of private individuals was much less susceptible to a progression of styles than was that of professional stonecutters working for the public, so that personal documents provide inconclusive comparanda for public inscriptions.[27]

[23] Cf. Mattingly *Historia* (1961) 149.

[24] Cf. Erxleben *AfP* 156–59.

[25] See J.P. Barron, "Religious Propaganda of the Delian League," *JHS* 34 (1964) 35–48, esp 45–46.

[26] See J.P. Barron, "The Fifth-Century *Horoi* of Aigina," *JHS* 103 (1983) 1–12, esp. 9; Figueira, *Colonization* 115–20. Erxleben, *AfP* (1971) 157–58, sensibly concedes that it is only a possibility that some of the Attic *horoi* with three-barred *sigmas* that are collected under *IG* I^2 854–902a (now with noncontinuous *IG* I^3 numbers) and II^2 2505–2507 date after 446. As I shall suggest below, a few *horoi* or *ostraka* with archaising forms are not the foundation on which to build a redating of the Coinage Decree.

[27] Therefore, *ostraka* are little help: their social context differs so much from that of official inscriptions. Nonetheless, it is striking enough to note that the results of M. Lang's study of the Agora *ostraka* do not invalidate the conventional view of the obsolescence of the three-barred *sigma*: *Ostraka*, *The Athenian Agora* 25 (Princeton 1990) 12. Six of sixteen middle period (461–43) *ostraka* have three strokes, but none of seventeen from her later period (417–15). Cf. Erxleben *AfP* (1971) 158–59. H.R. Immerwahr, *Attic Script* (Oxford 1990) 157–58, discusses the evidence on vases for the transition from the three-barred *sigma* to the four-barred *sigma*: "Thus, while the vases basically agree with the standard chronology of the change from three- to four-stroke

4. The argument on the number and order of the districts to which heralds were dispatched is discussed above (pp. 381–85 on section ix). This represents Mattingly's strongest point in favor of dating once more to the 420s, although, as stated above, it is not conclusively probative, even under a considerably more favorable reception than the one with which I am comfortable. This argument may also entail some collateral redatings of enactments such as the tribute lists of the early 420s and the Kleinias Decree.

5. Another of Mattingly's points is the improbability of a Pontic copy like the Odessa fragment existing before the Periclean interest in the region ca. 435 and the likelihood that its imposition on the allies there would have followed a conciliatory period of interaction with the Pontic allies and other potential tributaries in the region.[28] Hence a dating to the 420s is supported. There are a considerable number of counterindications for this conclusion. The already mentioned (and substantial) possibility that the inscription in question derives from the Aegean holds the place of first honor among these points (see above p. 322). Other arguments also deal with the eventuality that the Odessa copy truly derives from Olbia or some other Pontic *polis* that was not tributary (to the best of our knowledge), so that the rationale for public display would be even more obscure.

It is also quite possible that our decree could have contained information that might be useful for *individuals* doing business among the states of the Delian league; for instance, a lost section of the decree might have listed those cities that were maintaining their mints. It might therefore have been worthwhile for Attic *proxenoi* and other pro-Athenians to erect a copy of the decree even in an independent allied or friendly state, if public display would disseminate valuable information about monetary conditions to those departing for the Aegean. Nor would the date of such an "informal" copy establish a chronology. Finally, there is no compelling reason why a city that allied itself with Athens might not have been encouraged (or compelled) to display a copy of the Coinage Decree and/or other legislation of relevance to daily life at the inception of its membership in the alliance. A decree that insisted on the legal standing of Attic coinage as local currency and imposed a consolidation of metrological standards—as the Coinage Decree did, in my interpretation—would have been of current relevance for the lifetime of its validity. The

---

sigma in period 455–440 . . . the change-over is much less complete on the vases than in official script. *Sigmas* with three strokes linger into the fourth century."

[28] Mattingly, *Ancient Society* 193–95; also Mattingly *Klio* (1993) 100–101.

memorialization of the legislation could then happen subsequent to its original enactment.

6. There is the similar possibility that the Syme fragment was put up after a supposed accession of the island to the league in 434.[29] Relevant again is the aforesaid obligation to display a copy after Syme's accession to Athenian hegemony. In any event considerable force attaches to the argument that an island such as Syme that must often have been passed by Athenian squadrons operating in Caria, was long a tributary state whose membership was obscured by its participation in the *syntely* of the Carian Chersonese.[30]

The argument based on the inception of tributary status of the Pontic allies and of Syme would admittedly have greater weight on the assumption that the Coinage Decree can only have had a limited period of validity. Thus all allies had to have erected their copies at about the same time. The evidence for the continuing minting activities of allied states might be held to force such a conclusion, particularly if we make the leap of faith entailed in believing that every active mint had a period of interruption and that all such periods coincided. Surely, however, the more sensible approach to the record of *noncontroversial* and seemingly uninterrupted coining is that the Coinage Decree did not forbid minting in the fashion that the traditional interpretation has proposed. Therefore, nothing a priori forces all the copies of the Coinage Decree to have been inscribed at the same time.

7. Erxleben's argument that the punitive powers of the Council of the Five Hundred are more appropriate in the 420s than the 440s is treated above on pp. 400–402. The disagreements over the restoration of the relevant sections of the decree create too great a spectrum of options for the powers of the *Boulē* to permit a conclusion.

8. Mattingly suggested that the clause establishing public display in section xiv can be dated to ca. 430, but that need not be concluded (see above, pp. 416–17).

9. The appearance of the phrase νομίσματος *hεμεδαπο̃* in the Kallias Decree (*IG* I[3] 52A.4) is used to suggest that the Coinage Decree had not yet been promulgated.[31] This terminology is problematical only on

[29] Mattingly, *Ancient Society* 195–96, who also admits the possibilities of a continued validity for the decree or a revival under Kleon. See also Mattingly *BSA* (1970) 141.

[30] See Meritt *GRBS* (1967) 129, where the possibility of earlier membership through a *syntely* is broached. With far less data from which to work than those offering later overviews of imperial coinage, Babelon, *RN* (1913) 469–77, posited the general phenomenon of cessation of coinage on entry to the league.

[31] Note Erxleben *AfP* (1971) 160. Cf. Cavaignac *RN* (1953) 5; Schuller, *Herrschaft* 214.

the conjecture of a demonetization and replacement of non-Athenian money throughout the *arkhē*. That supposition is most unlikely. In any case, it is notable that this phrase has a formulaic character and appears in accounts throughout the whole period (*IG* I^3 104.30–31? [409/8]; 372.2 [413/2?]; 376.32, 52, 68–69, 82–83, cf. 39, 41 [409/8?]; 383.98–99, 237–238 [429/8]). Moreover, even on the broadest construction of the impact of the Coinage Decree, coins from outside the *arkhē* were held within the *arkhē*, and there was, on everyone's reckoning, licit use (perhaps sometimes even for paying tribute) of electrum staters.

10. A difference has been alleged between the treatment of the coins held by the Treasurers of the Other Gods early in the Archidamian War and the notation thereafter. In the first stage, foreign coins were supposedly treated in their own terms, that is, without being considered as bullion.[32] *IG* I^3 383 (429/8) lists a wide variety of foreign coinage. In contrast, *IG* I^3 376 provides the accounts of the treasurers of Athena for a year that is perhaps 409/8. At that time, the gold and electrum foreign monies loaned are enumerated along with the amounts of Attic money to which they are equivalent (lines 60, 95–105; cf. 33–34, 55–56). Thompson argues, however, that it is inappropriate to compare lists of loans with inventories, observing that the *traditiones* of the Decelean War follow the supposedly earlier practice of mere enumeration without conversion in the cases where they have survived (note *IG* I^3 386–87).[33] Exactitude of accounting had gradually increased with the accounts for 418/7 and following years listing holdings in Cyzicenes with their Attic value and no citation of weight (*IG* I^3 370.65–66, cf. 13–14; cf. also 372.4–5).

11. Naturally, numismatic arguments have been mixed in with the arguments from observations about internal features of the Coinage Decree. For instance, the hypothetical provision of the decree that banned allied minting of silver was considered irreconcilable with the supposed existence of breaks in the coining of important Thracian mints during the mid-420s instead of the 450s.[34] Suffice it to repeat here that the issues of these mints do not yield to a simple interpretation in which changes in type, in standard, in output, and in denominations, as well as the cessations of minting activity, progressed in lockstep (see above pp. 176–79).

[32] Mattingly *PACA* (1964) 48–49; cf. Segre 176.

[33] W.E. Thompson, "Notes on Athenian Finance," *C&M* 28 (1967) 216–39, esp. 224–26.

[34] See Mattingly *Historia* (1961) 186–87; *ECM* (1988) 324–28; Erxleben *AJP* (1969) 112–15, (1971) 160. On Aigina: Mattingly, *BSA* (1970) 142–43; Samos: *BSA* (1970) 143–45; *JHS* (1981) 81–85; Chios: *JHS* (1981) 78–80; Thasos: *JHS* (1981) 85–86. Cf. Schuller, *Herrschaft* 214.

The evidence undermines any single, dramatic demarcating temporal boundary rather than a particular chronology for a closing of allied mints.

In the other series of arguments concerning the earlier dating of the Coinage Decree, Segre laid out the essential points for a date ca. 449.

1. The three-barred *sigma* was unsurprisingly advanced as the epigraphical criterion in the favor of an early date, a topic which will be discussed immediately below.[35]

2. Segre, basing himself on correspondence with Meritt, argued that a fourfold division of the *arkhē* was detectible on tribute documents of the second period (see above, pp. 381–82).[36] Segre was well aware of what he viewed as the disorder of the early lists: such lists of *aparkhai* could only be expected to bear traces of an actual division of the *arkhē*. This argument lacks persuasiveness.

3. Segre advanced another intrinsic argument based on the supposed repayment of debts to Athena and Hephaistos, which he and other commentators restored in section vii of the Coinage Decree (see above, pp. 369–70).[37] It is interesting to note that he attempted to put the decrees of Kallias in the same temporal setting, and others would turn the same argument against an early date after the majority opinion dated *IG* I^3 52 to 434/3 (while Mattingly dated to 422/1).

In their cumulative force neither the arguments, on the one hand, in favor of a date before 445, nor those, on the other, prompting a dating in the late 420s, are probative in support of a sure chronology. This judgment includes both considerations grounded in features intrinsic to the fragments and appeals to supposed aspects of the historical context. We cannot decide certainly between a mid-century date or an Archidamian War chronology; between Mattingly's later date or the communis opinio. Some of the earlier arguments outlined above imply scenarios (that are sometimes rather explicit) about the events surrounding the inscribing of individual copies of the Coinage Decree (for example, items 5–6). We shall return below to the subject of patterns and sequences of inscribing (pp. 449–54). At best, Mattingly's work on inscriptions with early or transitional Attic letter-forms opens a possibility that the Kos fragment of the Coinage Decree might be dated in the 430s or 420s.[38] Our next piece of business is to determine the magnitude of that possibility.

[35] Segre 165–67.
[36] Segre 167–69.
[37] Segre 169–71.
[38] Compare Schuller, *Herrschaft* 215.

THE THREE-BARRED *SIGMA* CONTROVERSY

The consensus among epigraphists on epigraphical criteria for dating imperial inscriptions has always been intrinsically fragile with reference to the Coinage Decree. There is only the Attic script of the Kos fragment by which to judge. Moreover, that inscription does not offer many letters on which diagnostics may be worked. There is only the three-barred *sigma*. The second edition of Meiggs-Lewis (1988) and *IG* I^3 show by their ascription of dates the conservatism of most epigraphists in the face of Mattingly's challenges. The surveys of fifth-century Attic letter-forms by Meiggs (1966) and Walbank (1974/1978) still hold sway, for the most part, with this constituency (see note 16 above). More recent scholarship on epigraphical criteria for chronology has largely provided further confirmation.[39] Yet, in contrast, all that was needed to dent this consensus was the appearance of a single public inscription containing a three-barred *sigma* that is securely dated to the period of the Peloponnesian war.

To take the prime example, Mattingly's redating of the treaty with Egesta (*IG* I^3 11) did draw significant support in the 1970s after its first presentation, although the majority of scholars did not accede to his chronology.[40] More lately, M. Chambers and two of his UCLA colleagues have attempted to apply laser technology and computer image enhancement to a reexamination of the stone.[41] The attempt, which is admirable and important for its deployment of new methodology, appears to have shown that the traces on the stone in the prescript (line 3) of the

[39] Henry, *CSCA* (1978), explores various linguistic features for their potential as chronological criteria (the moveable *nu*; hiatus and elision; assimilation of *nu*). Possibly late features do not, however, appear in the Kos fragment (pp. 100–101).

[40] See J.D. Smart, "Athens and Egesta," *JHS* 92 (1972) 128–46; T.E. Wick, "A Note on the Date of the Athenian-Egestan Alliance," *JHS* 95 (1975) 186–90: Wick, "The Date of the Athenian-Egestan Alliance," *CP* 76 (1981) 118–21; P. Green, *Armada from Athens* (Garden City, NY 1970) x; E. Ruschenbusch, "Die Verträge Athens mit Leontinoi und Rhegion von Jahre 433/2 v. Chr.," *ZPE* 19 (1975) 225–32, esp. 232. The force of these arguments did not fail to register on Meiggs (see Meiggs 599). See also O. Hansen, "The Date of the Alliance between Athens and Egesta (NR. 37 M.-L.)," *Hermes* 118 (1990) 376–77.

[41] M.H. Chambers, R. Gallucci, and P. Spanos, "Athens' Alliance with Egesta in the Year of Antiphon," *ZPE* 83 (1990) 38–57 = I. Worthington (ed.), *Acta of the University of New England International Seminar on Greek and Latin Epigraphy* (Bonn 1990) 38–63; M. Chambers, "Photographic Enhancement and a Greek Inscription," *CJ* 88 (1992/1993) 25–31; Chambers, "Reading Illegible Greek Inscriptions: Athens and Egesta," *Thetis: Mannheimer Beiträge zur Klassischen Archäologie und Geschichte Griechenlands und Zyperns* 1 (1994) 50–52. The reading has been accepted by J. Tréheux *BE* (1991) #228, p. 469 (*REG* 104); M. Vickers, "Fifth Century Chronology and the Coinage Decree," *JHS* 116 (1996) 171–74, esp. 171. See also S.E. Dawson, "The Egesta Decree *IG* I^3 11," *ZPE* 112 (1996) 248–52.

decree are only compatible with a citation as follows: 'Ἀντ]ιφõν ἔρχε. . . . Hence they would date the inscription to 418/7.[42]

It might still turn out that this process of enhancement has created a fallacious impression of what are in fact merely scratches or even subsurface fissures.[43] Yet Chambers and his collaborators have in my view shown that the alternative readings, of which *h*αβρ]ον (or *h*α]β̣ρ̣ον or *h*α]β[ρ]ον [*IG* I³in *apparatus*]), the archon of 458/7, is the most significant, are unlikely to be sustainable from the traces on the stone.[44] Consequently, a dating of 418/7 for the alliance with Egesta, for all the complications it creates for interpreting Thuc. 6.6.2, is, at the very least, as viable a possibility as an early date. Therefore, we must prudently consider that the point of demarcation beyond which documents carrying a three-barred *sigma*—and incidentally, the tailed *rho* that is irrelevant for the Kos fragment of the Coinage Decree—are not to be dated has been significantly lowered. Unsurprisingly, this demonstration has occurred in connection with an inscription for which the "orthodox" position had long been under strong attack.

What is the conclusion, however, that we must draw from this breaching of epigraphical orthodoxy, if we believe that that is what the new photographs of the Egesta decree signify? Is it that the Kos fragment and the Coinage Decree must also be redated?[45] Before coming to that determination, we must still consider the probabilities on the chronology of documents bearing three-barred *sigmas*, and these calculations are shaped by our decisions about the whole list of inscriptions for which Mattingly has offered redatings.[46] Let us start by recapitulating the

42 G. Németh, "Was sieht ein Epigraphiker?" *Acta Classica, Univ. Scient. Debrecen* 27 (1991) 9–14, reviews the history of the readings in light of the enhanced images.

43 Note A. Henry, "Through a Laser Beam Darkly: Space Age Technology and the Egesta Decree (I.G. i³ 11)," *ZPE* 91 (1992) 137–46, to which M. Chambers, "The Archon's Name in the Athens-Egesta Alliance (IG I³ 11)," *ZPE* 98 (1993) 171–74 responded. See, most lately, A. Henry, "Pour encourager les autres: Athens and Egesta encore," *CQ* 45 (1995) 237–40. D.M. Lewis, in his review of Worthington, *Acta* in *CR* 43 (1993) 460–61, also strongly counsels caution. For cogent criticisms of other aspects of the new restored text, see A.S. Henry, "Athens and Egesta (*IG* i³ 11)," *AHB* 7 (1993) 49–53.

44 Meiggs-Lewis pp. 81–82, 310 provides convenient discussion and references. See also Chambers *ZPE* (1990) 39–41.

45 Cf. Chambers *ZPE* (1990) 55–56; Mattingly *Historia* (1992) 129–30; Vickers *JHS* (1996) 171. Fornara and Samons called for a case-by-case review even before the Egesta redating (*Athens* 182–83).

46 I have used a number of standard rebuttals of Mattingly's redatings that are based on historical as well as epigraphical arguments: B.D. Meritt and H.T. Wade-Gery, "The Dating of Documents to the Mid-Fifth Century–I," *JHS* 82 (1962) 67–74; Meritt and Wade-Gery, "The Dating of Documents to the Mid-Fifth Century–II," *JHS* 83 (1963) 100–17; Meiggs *JHS* (1966); B.D. Meritt, "The Choregic Dedication of Leagros," *GRBS* 8 (1967) 45–52; D.W.

dated inscriptions with three-barred *sigmas* (using the tables and notes of Meiggs and Walbank). The condition of the inscriptions can sometimes be judged from my descriptions; in any case, I have marked with an asterisk those cases where there is little to work with historically.[47]

An Erechtheid casualty list (ca. 460): *IG* I^2 929 = Meiggs-Lewis #33 = *IG* I^3 1147
Tribute list for 454/3: *IG* I^3 259
Tribute list for 453/2: *IG* I^3 260
Tribute list for 452/1: *IG* I^3 261
Tribute list for 451/0: *IG* I^3 262
Tribute list for 450/49: *IG* I^3 263
Tribute list for 447/6: *IG* I^3 265 (so dated on the assumption that the missing list is 449/8)

We may then add the undated inscriptions bearing three-barred *sigmas* and dated after 478 and before 440 that have not been questioned by Mattingly or anyone else (to the best of my knowledge):

Eleusinian regulations (ante 460): *IG* I^3 6
Amphictyonic alliance (ca. 458): *IG* I^3 9
*A very fragmentary building account (465–50): *IG* I^3 13
*A fragment mentioning a phrourarch and an acropolis (ca. 450): *IG* I^3 16 (= *Agora* 16, #2)
*A very fragmentary inscription mentioning the *dēmos* (ca. 450): *IG* I^3 20
*A very fragmentary inscription mentioning the *dēmos* (ca. 450): *IG* I^3 22 (= *Agora* 16, #5)
An alliance with an unknown city (ca. 450): *IG* I^3 29 (= *Agora* 16, #3)
The decree for a Theraian (ca. 450): *IG* I^3 30
*A fragmentary inscription mentioning a *pompē* (ca. 450–45): *IG* I^3 33
*A very fragmentary decree mentioning *misthōsis* and *euthunē* (ca. 450–45): *IG* I^3 44 (= *Agora* 16, #6)
*A fragmentary *axon* (480–60): *IG* I^3 233
A sacred calendar (480–60): *IG* I^3 234

Bradeen, "The Athenian Casualty Lists," *CQ* 19 (1969) 145–59; Meiggs-Lewis pp. 92–93, 106, 109–11, and 124–25; Meiggs 519–23, 531–37, 599–601; A.G. Woodhead, "Reflections on the Use of the Literary and Epigraphical Evidence for the History of the Athenian Empire," *Akten des VI. Internationalen Kongresses für Griechische und Lateinische Epigraphik, München 1972* (Munich 1973) 345–54 (cf., however, the comments of J.D. Smart on p. 354); D.W. Bradeen and M.F. McGregor, *Studies in Fifth-Century Attic Epigraphy* (Norman 1973) 20–23, 65–70, 77–79; W.E. Thompson, "Linguistic and Stylistic Criteria for Dating Attic Inscriptions," *C&M* 32 (1971–1980) 75–86; cf. D.W. Bradeen, "The Kallias Decrees Again," *GRBS* 13 (1971) 469–83 (also responding to C.W. Fornara, "The Date of the Callias Decree," *GRBS* 12 [1971] 185–96). See also A.G. Woodhead, *Inscriptions: The Decrees, The Athenian Agora* 16 (Princeton 1997) esp. 4, 7.

[47] I have excluded *IG* I^3 26 and 235 as too fragmentary to list at all.

The deme decree of Melitenses (480–450): *IG* I^3 243
The deme decree of the Skambonidai (ca. 460): *IG* I^3 244
A decree by the *koinon* of the Supalettioi (470–60): *IG* I^3 245
A sacred law mentioning the Plynteria (470–50): *IG* I^3 246
*A decree of a *genos* or phratry (460–40): *IG* I^3 247
Accounts of Nemesis at Rhamnous, with three-barred *sigmas* in "I" and Ionic lettering (ca. 450-440): *IG* I^3 248
An Eleusinian building account (ca. 450-45): *IG* I^3 395
Accounts of *epistatai* of an unknown project, with a three-barred *sigma* in III, four-barred elsewhere (ca. 450): *IG* I^3 433
Accounts of Athena Promachos (ca. 450): *IG* I^3 435
The restored chariot monument (446/5): *IG* I^2 394 = *DAA* 173+ = *IG* I^3 501B
*The dedication of Epiteles and others: *IG* I^2 580 = *IG* I^3 873
A casualty list (perhaps of Drabeskos: 464): *Agora* 17, #1 = *IG* I^3 1144
*A very fragmentary casualty list (ante 450): *SEG* 21.118 = *Agora* 17, #2 = *IG* I^3 1145
A casualty list: *IG* I^3 1146 = 1144?
A casualty list (ca. 460): *IG* I^3 1147*bis* (= 1147?)
Casualty lists (*ante* 450): *IG* I^3 1150–52
A casualty list (*paulo ante* 450): *SEG* 10.409 = *Agora* 17, #6 = *IG* I^3 1153
A casualty list (ca. 450): *IG* I^3 1157
A casualty list (ca. 450): *Agora* 17, #8 = *IG* I^3 1158

Note that *IG* I^3 accepts a lower date in principle for two inscriptions with three-barred *sigmas*: a Hipparchic dedication: *IG* I^2 400 = *DAA* 135 = *IG* I^3 511 (450–30?); and an inventory of the deme Ikaria: *IG* I^3 353 (440–25).

The lists of *aparkhai* show the change in the style of *sigmas* with *IG* I^3 263 (450/49) and 265 (447/6) exhibiting three-barred *sigmas*, but *IG* I^3 264 (448/7) and 266 (446/5) showing the four-barred *sigma*. The casualty lists from the late 450s and 440s cannot be dated with the same assurance as the lists of the *aparkhai*. It is striking, however, that this sequence also indicates a shift to four-barred *sigmas* during the 440s, as casualty lists *IG* I^3 1159–64, all with four-barred *sigmas*, probably belong before the Thirty Years Peace of 446/5.

Admittedly, the lack of controversy in some of these cases is the byproduct of the brevity and fragmentary character of the document in question, so that citing them in this context betrays circular reasoning. The majority of these inscriptions also contain other putatively early letter forms. Yet granted the intensity of the controversy surrounding the use of epigraphical criteria for dating, it does take one a bit aback to realize the number of uncontroversial inscriptions there are that contain three-barred *sigmas*, some of which contain lettering that is not palpably more archaic than the Kos fragment, *IG* I^3 1453B (such as *IG* I^3 395 [perhaps], 435, and 1153). Once we concede that the use of three-barred *sigmas* might not give us a line of demarcation, it should also be admitted that the majority of inscriptions bearing this letter form still appear to precede 440. That determination must affect our willingness to assign any *one* inscription to the 420s.

Next we list the controversial inscriptions that Mattingly has sought to redate, but limit that list to only those inscriptions that contain three-barred *sigmas*:

The alliance with Egesta: *IG* I^3 11
The Erythrai decrees: *IG* I^3 14–15
The Sigeion Decree: *IG* I^3 17
A proxeny decree for some Parianoi or for Parianos: *IG* I^3 18
The proxeny decree for Acheloion: *IG* I^3 19
The Miletos Decree: *IG* I^3 21
The proxeny decree for the Delphians: *IG* I^3 27
The Hermione treaty: *IG* I^3 31
The decree on the Eleusinian *epistatai*: *IG* I^3 32
The decree for the priestess for Athena Nike: *IG* I^3 35
The Kolophon decrees: *IG* I^3 37, 42
The Aigina Decree: *IG* I^3 38
The Hestiaia Decree with four-barred *sigmas* except for line 55: *IG* I^3 41
The dedication(?) of the Messenians: *IG* I^3 148

Before we proceed to consider what the presence of the three-barred *sigmas* can tell us about the date of the Coinage Decree, it is important to say something about the likelihood of Mattingly having been correct in various of these redatings. Both S.V. Tracy and M.B. Walbank help us out here with their work on the identification of the hands of inscribers. Mattingly accepted Tracy's argument that the decree involving the priestess for Athena Nike derived from the same hand as the account of Athena Promachos (*IG* I^3 435).[48] The latter document seems to direct our attention firmly toward a date for this stonecutter around 450. Walbank suggests that the proxeny decree *IG* I^3 18 had the same inscriber as the Sigeion Decree (*IG* I^3 17), the treaty with Hermione (*IG* I^3 31), the Kolophon Decree (*IG* I^3 37), and a very fragmentary inscription

[48] S.V. Tracy, "Hands in Fifth Century B.C. Attic Inscriptions," in *Studies Presented to Sterling Dow*, *GRBS* Monograph 10 (Durham, NC 1984) 277–82, esp. 281–82.

(*IG* I^3 33).[49] While it is theoretically possible to follow Mattingly in dating all these inscriptions to the 420s and 410s, the dependence of such a wholesale change on many fragile arguments urges the more prudent course of retaining a chronology centered on the 440s for the products of these two inscribers.

I next offer a subjective ranking of the likelihood that any one of these inscriptions dates after 430. The issue whether or not the Coinage Decree can be pre-Peloponnesian War or Periclean is what interests us for the moment. In most cases, the differentiation between priority to 440 and priority to 430 is inconsequential, as the peaceful 430s are an unhappy context for many of these documents in any case. In the case where the significant chronological watershed falls elsewhere, I have annotated appropriately. The categories contain inscriptions listed in order of increasing probability of a later chronology.

Very unlikely (<10 percent):
The Erythrai decrees: *IG* I^3 14–15[50]
The decree for the priestess for Athena Nike: *IG* I^3 35[51]
The Aigina Decree: *IG* I^3 38 (not to be dated after 445)[52]

Quite unlikely (<20 percent):
The Kolophon Decree: *IG* I^3 37[53]
The Hermione treaty: *IG* I^3 31 (note *Agora* 16, #4)
The Hestiaia decree: *IG* I^3 41
The Sigeion Decree: *IG* I^3 17 (note *Agora* 16, #1)
A proxeny decree for some Parianoi or for Parianos: *IG* I^3 18[54]

Unlikely (<35 percent):
The proxeny decree for Acheloion: *IG* I^3 19[55]
The proxeny decree for the Delphians: *IG* I^3 27[56]

[49] M.B. Walbank, "Honors for Parianos of Issa and His Sons Athenodoros and Ikesios," *Hesperia* 42 (1973) 334–39; see also Mattingly *Phoenix* (1975) 284.

[50] See also H. Engelmann and R. Merkelbach, *Die Inschriften von Erythrai und Klazomenai* (Bonn 1972) 38–50.

[51] See B. Wesenberg, "Zur Baugeschichte des Niketempels," *JdI* 96 (1981) 28–54, esp. 52–53; also W.A.P. Childs, "The Frieze of the Temple on the Ilissos," *AM* 100 (1985) 207–51, esp. 208; cf. Fornara and Samons, *Athens* 183–85.

[52] Figueira, *Excursions* 120–26.

[53] See also Bradeen and McGregor, *Studies* 97–99.

[54] See Henry *CSCA* (1981) 86, where it is noted that this would be the earliest date of ἐπρυτάνευεν (noted for its movable ν) by almost a half a century.

[55] Meiggs 425–27.

[56] Ibid.

Some likelihood (35–55 percent)
The Miletos Decree: *IG* I^3 21[57]
The dedication of the Messenians: *IG* I^3 148
The decree on the Eleusinian *epistatai*: *IG* I^3 32 (possible date of 432/1)[58]

Significant probability (>55 percent):
The alliance with Egesta: *IG* I^3 11

When we consider the material as summarized in this fashion, it is understandable why the breaching of the orthodoxy on the three-barred *sigma* for one inscription should not necessarily lead to a stampede in redating other inscriptions. Even if we could be brought to admit that some examples of documents with three-barred *sigmas* extend down into the 420s or even into the 410s, the preponderance of instances would still make a date before 440 the presumptive favorite when dating any *single* inscription. We should be inclined to follow Mattingly in pleading for an exceptionally late date for the Coinage Decree only if the body of other evidence on monetary history rendered the decree highly improbable in its early setting. Neither the argument from the progression of Athenian imperialism nor the results of numismatic inquiries into the continuance of allied mints achieves anything approaching that level of evidentiary force.

The Coinage Decree also differs in another significant regard from the majority of the other inscriptions that Mattingly would redate. There is really nothing in the contents of the fragments that demands the passage of the decree at a time of international tension or conflict, unlike the inscriptions whose contents indicate the aftermath of hostilities or rebellion (for example, *IG* I^3 11, 14, 15, 21, 31, 37, 38, 41, 42, 148). If the redating of the Egesta treaty widens the "envelope" of possible dates for documents with three-barred *sigmas*, the late 440s and 430s represent plausible contexts for the Coinage Decree and are preferable to the 420s. Within the period 450–11, the widest limits of conceivable chronology, each succeeding period of five years is probably a little less probable for the enactment of the Coinage Decree than the preceding.

[57] See also Bradeen and McGregor, *Studies* 37–38, 54, 65–70; C.W. Fornara, "The Date of the 'Regulations for Miletus,'" *AJP* 92 (1971) 473–75; H.-J. Gehrke, "Zur Geschichte Milets in der Mitte des 5. Jahrhunderts v. Chr.," *Historia* 29 (1980) 17–31; S. Cataldi, "La secessione dei βέλτιστοι Milesî e le ξυγγραφαί Ateniesi per Mileto," in *Studî sui rapporti interstatali nel mondo antico* (Pisa 1981) 161–233; N. Robertson, "Government and Society at Miletus, 525–442 B.C.," *Phoenix* 41 (1987) 356–98, esp. 384–90. Cf. J.M. Balcer, "Miletos (IG I^2.22 [I^3.21]) and the Structures of Alliances," in *Studien zum attischen Seebund* (*Xenia* 8 [1984]) 11–30, esp. 27–28.

[58] K. Clinton, "The Date of the Classical Telesterion at Eleusis," Φιλια Επη εις Γεωργιον Ε. Μυλωναν (Athens 1987) 2.256–62; M.B. Cavanaugh, *Eleusis and Athens: Documents in Finance, Religion and Politics in the Fifth Century* B.C. (Atlanta 1996) 19–27.

PATTERNS IN INSCRIPTION OF THE FRAGMENTS

The chronological issue has been complicated by the application to its resolution of suggestions as to the circumstances surrounding the cutting of the Kos stone. In other words, the "archaic" or "obsolete" character of the Attic script of the Kos fragment could be explained on the basis of the hypothetical peculiarities of the context of its inscription. On account of the hesitant identification of the Kos fragment as Pentelic marble in Segre's *editio princeps*, conjecture was initially constrained by that "fact." An Attic inscription on Attic stone cried out for an Athenian frame of reference for its inscription. Tod's suggestion that an old stonecutter was pressed into service to help supply the large number of copies needed for the many allied cities that did not rush to erect their own inscriptions is one way to sidestep the epigraphical ramifications of the Attic script on the Attic stone of the Kos fragment, but the supposition is also patently ad hoc in character.[59]

A more fruitful line of approach was opened by Pritchett, who recognized that it was unlikely that the Kos fragment was Attic marble.[60] He went on to offer that an Athenian stonemason moved from Attica to Kos and maintained his Attic script style of the 440s into the 430s or 420s. One might with considerable justification protest that the emigration of any inhabitant of Attica, citizen or metic, to Kos (of all places) during the 440s was sufficiently improbable as to render the invocation of any *single* such individual for a historical causation an act of temerity. To complain in this vein, however, misses the spirit of this approach (and many related ones) to the Coinage Decree. The scenarios accounting for a supposed archaism of the Kos fragment take for granted that there is something desperately amiss about a Periclean, mid-century date for this legislation. Their authors are then entitled to implement extreme hypotheses in counteraction. Pritchett expanded his hypothesis by drawing on the petrological expertise of A. Georgiadès, who pronounced the Koan fragment to be Parian marble.[61]

Pritchett concluded that an inscription cut on non-Attic stone at Kos was free from any constraints of Attic epigraphical criteria and further believed that, discounting the three-barred *sigma*, the letter forms were more characteristic of the 420s.[62] A proponent of the mid-century orthodoxy might still counter by insisting on the improbability that the

59 See Tod *JHS* (1949) 105. Cf. Lewis, *Coinage and Administration* 57.

60 Pritchett *BCH* (1963) 20–23.

61 Georgiadès and Pritchett *BCH* (1965) 400–25; see also Meritt *GRBS* (1967) 126.

62 Georgiadès and Pritchett *BCH* (1965) 439–40.

Kos inscription was inscribed, not idiosyncratically (that might give further pause), but conventionally in a style 20+ years old, albeit the style of the youth of the inscriber.[63] The stonecutter had picked up no special quirks during his long residence on Kos. Must we gratuitously posit still further biographical details to explain how our wayward *Attikos* remained unaffected by subsequent epigraphical trends (whether Ionic or Attic)? Meiggs was indeed still prepared to offer the suggestion that an Attic stonecutter used a spare piece of Parian marble in Attica, in the absence of evidence that the Koans both imported Parian marble and would have preferred its cost to using local limestone.

Nevertheless, it is hard to avoid the conclusion that an Attic inscription must be judged in light of other inscriptions in the Attic script, regardless of its provenience, unless some internal characteristic betrays an anomalous status.[64] One should never deny the evidence of appreciations of the development of Ionic script for dating the Ionic copies of the Coinage Decree, but such conclusions are valid only for the particular Ionic fragment under investigation and not for the Kos fragment.[65] Even if one or all of the Ionic fragments of the decree could be incontrovertibly placed after the 440s, one is not thereby necessarily compelled to shift the Kos fragment from its date. In other words, epigraphical intuitions about the dates of Ionic versions that (moreover) lack comparanda do not really offset the indication of the three-barred *sigma* from Attic epigraphy (even if we now take it as not inevitably conclusive), since the Attic inscriptional tradition is the only one rich enough to allow for generalization.[66] In the present state of our knowledge, it is thoroughly counterintuitive to posit a non-Attic framework for the investigation of an inscription in Attic script. Invoking the inscription of the Kos fragment on non-Attic stone does not really circumvent this argument.[67]

Mattingly exploited the recognition that the stone of the Kos fragment was not Attic marble to propose a hypothesis on the pattern of

[63] I have rewritten the objections of Meiggs *JHS* (1966) note 41 (pp. 97–98) and Meiggs-Lewis p. 115 under the influence of the counter-objections of M.H. Jameson, review of Meiggs-Lewis, *AJP* 93 (1972) 474–80, esp. 478.

[64] Note Lewis, *Coinage and Administration* 58–59. Contrast *IG* I^3 1455, for which see Figueira, *Colonization* 32–35.

[65] Cf. Mattingly, *Ancient Society* 195–96. The opinion of the editor of the Odessa fragment that the letter forms were late, even to the point of suggesting an early fourth-century date, provides no new evidence. The Ionian fragments have always seemed late, but we lack the material, let alone a clear provenience, to submit this impression on the Odessa fragment to any real process of verification. See Erxleben *AfP* (1969) 123, countered by Schuller, *Herrschaft* 215.

[66] Note Lewis, *Coinage and Administration* 56.

[67] Cf. Erxleben *AfP* (1971) 159–60.

inscription of the various copies.[68] The Kos copy was shipped ready-made from Athens, a measure that spared the local Koan magistrates the odium of furthering Athenian ends so openly. The nearly equal line lengths of the Ionic fragments from Aphytis and Odessa prompt for him the conclusion that Athenian *arkhontes* undertook the duty of their inscription. The Syme, Siphnos, and Odessa fragments, with their various line lengths and some other discrepancies, were the work of local *arkhontes*. The merit of these suggestions is that they help us to clarify our thinking about the pattern and sequence of the inscription of the fragments by holding out the possibility of accounting for differences in the fragments by positing varying responsibilities for simultaneous inscription.

We respond first to his specific suggestions by doubting the restoration "Athenians" in section x.4, while further insisting that a contrast could never have been established in these terms between Athenian officials in the *arkhē* and the Athenian government at home (see above pp. 389–90). This conclusion suggests that Mattingly's explanation for the inscribing of the Kos fragment needs reformulation.

A word of caution is necessary before we proceed: we are without good evidence on the question of what *poleis* without strong traditions of civic inscribing did when they needed to cut and emplace an inscription at the behest of the Athenians. As my discussion of section x of the decree argues, there are really only two categories of potential inscribers: Athenian officials active in the *arkhē* and local officials of allied cities. It can be taken as fairly certain that any Attic copy belonged to the initiative of Athenian officials. In addition, that the majority of the fragments are in Ionic helps us to understand how the *kērukes* 'heralds' discharged missions such as the dissemination of the content of this psephism. It appears that they possessed Ionic transcriptions as well as an Attic original of the Coinage Decree.

A set of arguments supports this conclusion. First of all, the Athenians were striving for compliance, so that they would have endeavored to promulgate the Coinage Decree in a form most easily comprehensible, whether orally before the local assembly or council, in a written version provided to local magistrates, or, subsequently, through its inscription. An oral version in the Attic-Ionic dialect would better serve their interests, as the Ionic dialect was the local dialect of the majority of the allies and, undoubtedly, a lingua franca for the rest. On Doric-speaking Kos, however, a preference for Ionic script might have been less marked. In turn, the probable existence of a transcription in Ionic script for verbal

[68] *Klio* (1977) 86-89. Now see *Klio* (1993) 101.

or written dissemination by local officials who were less familiar with Attic-script texts speaks against the separate transcription by persons on the spot, be they Athenian or local officials.

Second, varying transcriptions would not have been in the interest of the Athenians, since transcriptions made by individual allies were vulnerable to various mechanical errors. There was no need to complicate the issue of compliance in this way. For example, the systematic variances in the lengths of the lacunae between the Kos and Aphytis fragments that create the possibility of different phrasing make best administrative sense the earlier they are thought to occur in the process of dissemination of the decree. Thus, Athenian officials in the *arkhē* would have had a choice between the original Attic text and a transcription carried by the *kērux* dispatched to the district of their assignment. That they would have often opted for the Ionic version can be understood by their desire for facility of communication along the lines already advanced. Thus some of the Ionic copies may be owed to Athenian *arkhontes*, just as Mattingly suggested for the Aphytis and Odessa inscriptions. Nevertheless, their line lengths are only approximately the same (42 and 41 letters respectively), and that is not a strong enough similarity to classify together two inscriptions that do not even overlap.

The hypothesis of official transcription into Ionic raises a further complication. Such a duty may have fallen to each herald, who was possibly supervised by the *stratēgoi* or a *stratēgos* assigned to convey him. Therefore the presence of the discrepancies listed above (also p. 327) might indicate the latitude assumed by the generals in their creation of official versions of psephisms for promulgation abroad. Proponents of a mid-century date may have no problem with seeing the board of *stratēgoi* dominated by Perikles and his faction acting in this manner. Thus, the Kos fragment would become the only version speaking to the Attic original, while the Ionic versions could be distributed among the four *kērukes*.

Let us next review the fragments, starting with those found in situ. The Aphytis fragment becomes an Ionic transcription of the herald sent to Thrace. The Syme fragment represents the version taken to Caria. It may then be the Ionic counterpart to the Kos fragment, with which it unfortunately does not overlap. The Siphnos fragment is the transcription of the herald dispatched to the islands. We have two stones that have wandered, the Smyrna and Odessa fragments. The Smyrna inscription shares with the Syme fragment an introduction to the clause added to the oath of *Boulē* that is different from those in the Aphytis and Siphnos fragments. Yet this convergence is expected if we suppose that the most likely origin for an inscription collected at Smyrna is a neighboring

Ionian city and that one herald seems to have visited both Ionia and Caria. The Siphnos and Odessa fragments are in complete agreement and vary in three places from the Smyrna fragment. That result is once again unsurprising since the most likely point of origin outside the Black Sea region for the Odessa fragment was an Aegean island (see above, p. 322). Was the stoichedon Odessa copy supervised by Attic *arkhontes* while the nonstoichedon Siphnos copy was the work of local officials?

One might next ask where we are left in our efforts to reconstruct the circumstances surrounding the inscription of the Kos fragment. The hypothesis of Ionic transcriptions carried by *kērukes* as the primary mode of dissemination of the Coinage Decree tells heavily against theories in which the Koan inscription is moved to Kos from Attica. Tod's suggestion of the conveyance of a stock of preinscribed copies also has the clumsiness and cost of such a procedure standing against it. Meiggs's suggestion of a Parian stone shipped out of Attica runs into much the same objections. In any case, it is easier to understand both the actual instructions of the decree and the variety of the inscriptions by assuming that the decision about inscription was made locally. That conclusion is telling against moving inscribed or fresh stones from Attica anywhere else in any scenario.

If we do not have stones being moved, does that necessarily entail that we must move an inscriber? Must a stonecutter have emigrated, as Pritchett argued? Meritt thought not and proposed a Koan inscriber using local stone and working from an Attic master copy, which he followed carefully.[69] This theory may be considered possible, but why in this one case was a decision made against transcribing? Surely there is an alternative that has been overlooked. It is known that providers of services accompanied Athenian military forces, and it is not impossible that an Attic stonecutter was dogging the tracks of the official conveyance of the herald dispatched to Ionia and Caria in the hopes of winning business. Whether he was an Athenian, a metic, or an ally in status, he would have sold his services as an individual experienced in inscribing Athenian official documents and would have naturally worked in the Attic script. We cannot expect such an individual to have reached many places and to have always (or even often) won work from the locals. The discharge of any commissions also took some time, and out of the way places may not have been reached at all, but surely Kos would be a reasonable stop. The Decree-seller of the *Birds* may then turn out to be a sort of composite figure, that is, an itinerant stonecutter fused with a corrupt demagogue.

[69] *PAPS* (1975) 267, 271–72.

Any explanation will also have to come to grips with the findspot of the Kos inscription in the north of the island at the site of the later city of Kos. This only became the primary settlement of this *polis* in 366/5, having been perhaps a secondary, but by no means insignificant, site previously, called Kos Meropis (DS 15.76.2; Strabo 14.2.19 C657). The contemporary political center and major concentration of population lay in the island's south at Astypalaia. Most commentators have cited a suggestion of G.E. Bean and J.M. Cook that an Athenian naval station may have been situated at the northern site.[70] Yet the military activity at this location is all during the Ionian War and understandable entirely in the context of the strategic situation then.[71] The presence of an Athenian base cannot in any case provide an argument for the inscription of the decree in Attic script there, as though advertizing Athenian imperialism was more fun in Attic. The placement of the inscription at a location other than the political center of the island could mean that a group of officials (Athenian and/or Koan) so construed the phrase "in the *agora* of each city" (section x.1–2) to mean in the marketplace of each substantial center of habitation.[72] Yet the relationship to each other of Astypalaia, Kos Meropis, and other centers of population in this period is quite obscure and was possibly complex in constitutional terms.[73] Thus there may have been a rationale in Koan terms for the placement of a copy of the Coinage Decree at Kos Meropis. The findspot of the Kos fragment is thus reconcilable with the hypothesis of an itinerant stonecutter of Attic-script inscriptions, following the path of the herald sent to Ionia and Caria.

70 "The Carian Coast III," *BSA* 52 (1957) 58–146, esp. 121–25.

71 Note Thuc. 8.41.2; 44.3, 108.2; cf. DS 13.42.3, 69.5; Xen. *HG* 1.5.1. The presence of a *horos* in a *temenos* of Athena Polias that may have wandered from Samos (*IG* I³ 1491, for which see S.M. Sherwin-White, *Ancient Cos: An Historical Study from the Dorian Conquest to the Imperial Period* [Göttingen 1978] 37–38) and the payment of odd amounts of tribute or its division into several payments do not constitute additional proof (cf. *IG* I³ 263.I.7, V.40 [450/49]; 264.III.10 [448/7]; 265.I.92, II.37, II.102 [447/6]; 280.I.36 [432/1]).

72 This hypothesis is preferable to Segre's suggestion that the site of the fifth-century *polis* was already at Kos Meropis (176–78). Rather, we should suppose that the increase in commerce during the Pentekontaeteia drew people to Kos Meropis, laying the foundation for the later synoecism there. See also J.P. Barron, "The Fifth-Century Diskoboloi of Kos," in C.M. Kraay and G.K. Jenkins, *Essays in Greek Coinage Presented to Stanley Robinson* (Oxford 1968) 75–89, esp. 86, who also concludes that Kos Meropis was the capital.

73 See Sherwin-White, *Ancient Cos* 44–58. On the placement of a copy of the Coinage Decree at Kos Meropis, she compares the erection of the Attic dispositions for Iulis of Keos at both Iulis and Karthaia (*IG* II² 111.19–23 = Tod, *GHI* #142: 363/2).

VARIANT DATING OF THE FRAGMENTS

Nevertheless, for those who believe that it is unlikely that all the Ionian fragments can be set in the 440s,[74] the existence of heraldic/*stratēgic* variations between fragments does not negate the hypothesis of some inscription at different times. An extreme proposition along these lines has already been suggested, namely, attributing the Smyrna fragment to a later decree that incorporated the original Coinage Decree (partly or wholly) before proceeding to mandate another conversion of non-Athenian currency (see above, pp. 407–409, 411). Some copies might have been erected at the time of the entrance of states into the league. An example might be the Odessa fragment, if it is seen as deriving from an ally in the Pontus. Other copies might have been inscribed at the moment of a change in status, like the dissolution of a *syntely* leading to the inscription of the Syme fragment, when the island first appears on the tribute lists in 434/3.

Other reasons for later inscription are possible, so that not all the copies of the decree need have the same date, if some clauses remained valid. The marketplaces of the many allied cities were subject to numerous vicissitudes by which inscriptions might be damaged. If the decree authorized some mints to continue, mandated a use of Attic coinage and standards, created a protected fund, or authorized the *Boulē* to convert allied silver on future occasions (all possible examples of continuing validity), a copy might be replaced or restored.

The foregoing treatment builds on the assumption that the Coinage Decree was promulgated at the time of the appearance of the first inscription. That was probably the Kos fragment, for which a date in the 440s is still the most likely. As a matter of probability, most of the other fragments were probably its near contemporaries. A period of continuous validity would encompass any of the Ionic fragments that date after 440.

One might object that a reimposition of the Coinage Decree during the Peloponnesian War is an equally likely assumption:[75] the Athenians had to give up the rigorous application of a Periclean ban on allied coining—the impact of which can supposedly be traced numismatically—because of allied recalcitrance. During the exigencies of the

[74] See Jeffery, *LSAG* 364, with particular emphasis on the Aphytis fragment.

[75] Cf. Lewis, *Coinage and Administration* 59, who envisages a measure that did not work on first promulgation and considered dividing the fragments over two decrees ("not recommending this line very strongly"). See also Jeffery, *LSAG* 364, note 1.

Peloponnesian War, when inhibitions against an autocratic posture toward the allies had weakened, the Coinage Decree was reimposed.[76] Such a punctuation was a leitmotif of Robinson's analysis of fifth-century minting among the allies.[77]

Yet as we have seen above, this punctuated prohibition does not indeed fit the numismatic evidence any better than a continuously valid decree. Monetary consolidation steadily progressed during the Attic hegemony, but allied cessation of minting was only one of its modes. No concentrated period or periods of interruption among the continuous mints can be made out. The prohibition of allied coining has usually been linked with a demonetization and replacement of allied currencies. In that case, more than a break of a few years in allied minting must have existed, as an ally could not simply issue a few new local coins to revert to the status quo ante. It had to demonetize and convert the Attic money in local circulation, a massive undertaking. Even if we eschew anything so radical as these successive demonetizations and conversions, some sizable issues of local coins would be needed to reach the status quo ante (for which there are no data: see pp. 189–94 above). Punctuated validity is also inferior to positing continuous validity on other grounds of administrative history. A reissue gives undue prominence to the Coinage Decree when there is a significant likelihood that the Attic legislative activity on coinage and metrology was a sustained enterprise. There are potentially the Klearkhos psephism, which is still most probably in the same tradition, *IG* I^3 90, and the reciprocal agreements with individual cities, the existence of which is implied by Aristophanes in the *Birds*.[78] A bilateral agreement promoting monetary and metrological consolidation was interestly conceivable in principle as late as 414.

Even if a late date for the three-barred *sigma* is admitted, there will be few takers for a date after 420. And the Siphnos fragment, with its long dative plural, looks more at home in the first half of the 420s at the latest rather than in the 410s. The numismatic investigations above neither substantiate or disprove a decree, promulgated in the early 440s, remaining valid in the 420s, and exemplifying an encouragement

[76] Cf. Mattingly *Klio* (1977) 89–90.

[77] See also E.S.G. Robinson, "Some Problems in the Later Fifth Century Coinage of Athens," *ANSMN* 9 (1960) 1–15, esp. 5, where *Birds* 1040 is introduced as an indication that the Coinage Decree was revived at this time (414), when the general tax on imports and exports was imposed in lieu of the collection of the tribute. Cf. also, for example, Cavaignac *Études* 186–87; Mattingly *Historia* (1961) 185–88.

[78] Hence, one may reject the superficially attractive argument that punctuated validity explains a number of later, Ionic fragments. We lack any comparative material of other psephisms to be erected throughout the *arkhē*. Cf. Cavaignac *RN* (1953) 2.

of monetary and metrological integration that was still living in 414. That remains the most likely option. There is no particular reason to believe that the Coinage Decree represented a unique or even a uniquely significant stage in this legislation merely on the basis of its substantial survival. That fate could be owed the careful arrangements made for its dissemination and memorialization.

CONCLUSION

My analysis has led to a partial decoupling of two chronological questions, the dating of every fragment of the Coinage Decree and the dating of the act of its legislation. When the decree is seen not to have compelled the extinction of allied mints, there is no longer any obstacle to accepting its continued validity, opening the possibility of versions inscribed over time. Moreover, enforcing the acceptance of Athenian monetary and metrological standards as locally valid gives a stronger continuing relevance to this legislation, so that it is easier to believe in the inscription of various copies over a span of time. If the Coinage Decree was nothing more than an order prohibiting the minting of silver, the motivations for an allied community to inscribe the psephism subsequently, on entering the alliance, or for replacing a damaged copy, would be weaker.

My inclination to keep the Kos fragment in the early 440s is complemented by a conviction that difficulties in exchange, perhaps assisted by a desire to simplify the appraisal of allied systems of taxation, motivated legislation that tried to consolidate standards. Not only does our evidence from the tribute lists direct us toward the mid-century rather than the period after the outbreak of the Peloponnesian War, but it also encourages us to hypothesize that the Coinage Decree is one item out of a long sequence of legislative activity. This lawmaking is by its very nature and responsivity to problems connected with tribute payment more likely to have started early than late. Thus, when we place the Coinage Decree late, we will always risk ignoring a preceding psephism that legislated significantly on the same issues.

Furthermore, the arguments in favor of a low dating, which cannot be definitively refuted in the present state of our evidence, appear motivated by an appreciation of the evolution of Athenian imperialism, which would like to "end-load" as many of its most authoritarian features as feasible. Any attempt (such as mine) that systematically calls into question the crudely visualized "details" within the fragments that are held to substantiate this imperialism reduces the impetus toward pitting

Kleon against Perikles as the guiding spirit of Athenian hegemonism. This is just as well: not only has it been difficult to assess or even approach most of the impressions that might cohere into a reconstructed Kleonean or demagogic context for the decree (at least, in the ambit of this work), but it is also hard to envisage how such an assessment could be mounted at all without undertaking a thorough reevaluation of the Archidamian War in its totality. The remarkable degree of institutional development that would be posited for these stressful war years appears problematical, not only intrinsically, but also in light of what actually appears in the narrative of Thucydides. Breaching the rule on the three-barred *sigma* does no more than offer the possibility of redatings of some epigraphical evidence after 430. In Mattingly's long struggle to urge a reconsideration of the usage of different forms of the letter *sigma*, it may well be a crowning irony that the work of Chambers and his associates in supporting a redating of the Egesta Decree, not only, at last, subverts the orthodoxy on epigraphical criteria, but also better exposes the absence in Mattingly's articles of a synthesis of the history of the *arkhē* that is able to stand up against the reconstruction of *ATL*. And I say this as one who has called many aspects of the *ATL* synthesis into question, both in this work and in others.

Any attempt to offer a most likely chronology for the promulgation of the Coinage Decree should exploit what has already been learned about the transfer of resources between the allies and the Athenians. When the evidence of the tribute lists of the first two assessment periods is considered, the Athenians seem to be seeking the payment of tribute in Attic coin, although it is unknown how early this policy existed. Indeed we may choose to coordinate the inception of the lists with some threshold that was reached in the monetary administration of the tribute system rather than in the movement of the treasury from Delos to Attica (which seems to belong earlier). We have already explored and rejected the initial stipulation of payment in Attic coin as marking the particular threshold in question, preferring to place that at the foundation of the alliance (pp. 266–69).[79] From our discussion of the fragments of the Coinage Decree, however, there has emerged the psephism of Klearkhos as a probable law on monetary policy that had an influential or even

[79] The question of the degree of compliance with such a stipulation is another issue. One suspects some latitude may have existed in the first decades of the alliance. If one cares to guess on the basis of availability of various coinages and their usefulness for military operations, a hierarchy of descending desirability in tendering the tribute could be imagined: Attic silver; Cyzicene electrum staters; Phocaic electrum *hectae*; Aiginetic silver; Persian silver; other local silver.

paradigmatic status. The decree of Klearkhos is then another candidate for constituting the threshold marked by the beginning of the tribute lists.

There are traces in the irregular *aparkhai* on the early lists both of the payment in non-Athenian coins and also of difficulties in acquiring the requisite amount of Athenian coinage. If we believe the traditional restoration of the postscript of the first list of *aparkhai*, a considerable sum of Cyzicene electrum was actually received as *aparkhē* (*IG* I^3 259, Postscript.8–13). The scale of that contribution to the *aparkhē* on the very first list may indicate that the amount of non-Attic money paid as tribute was probably at least as high in the period of the 450s before the lists as during the first two assessment periods. The anomalous payments of tribute appear to have been tolerated around mid-century, for nothing suggests punishment like fines in association with them. The Hellenotamiai, *Boulē*, and, in the last resort, the *Ekklēsia* and the diskasteric courts appear to have been making dispensations for allies who were unable to pay in Attic coin. In Chapter 10, reasons were conjectured why the allies may have received such toleration for irregularities of payment, assuming that the intent was present to pay the assessed sum in some monetary equivalent.

Nevertheless, manifestations of exchange problems in the early lists are cloaked by the reporting of all individual payments as though they were made in Attic money. The reckoning of the *aparkhai* in Attic silver, however, may be more than an accounting convention. It is only Cyzicene electrum that stands as an exception on the first list and not Phocaic electrum, although we have seen that the early lists themselves may betray payment of some tribute in Phocaic *hectae* as well. Moreover, the separate notation for Cyzicenes is never repeated after 454/3.[80] It is as if we have caught the Athenians in transition from one level of rigor in the enforcement of payment in Attic coin to another. In the final stage of an earlier dispensation, Cyzicenes were allowed to form part of the *aparkhē*, while any allied silver and Phocaic electrum paid as tribute were not. Thereafter only Attic silver went to pay the *aparkhē*, regardless of the medium in which the ally paid the whole or part of its tribute. It would surprise no one if the Athenians were more fastidious about the symbolic aspects of their hegemony over their allies so that Athena received her due only in coins bearing her image while coins intended for secular use were still more disparate (cf. Hesych. Πάλλαδος πρόσωπον,

[80] As far as can be determined, tribute lists of the first stele either have no postscripts on the adjoining sides of the stone (the first postscript is to the right of the first list) or are preserved below their last column where such a postscript might have appeared.

π 228 Latte).[81] Yet the exchange undertaken by the Athenian government to protect the homogeneity and integrity of the *aparkhai* would not differ from the other exchange operations that can be imagined to lie hidden among the irregular figures for the tribute payments in the first and second assessment periods, when foreign coins were exchanged for expenditure.

In the Coinage Decree, as it has been reconstructed above, the Hellenotamiai are seen to be registering what were probably payments of monies from the allies. These sums will eventually be introduced into the revenue stream that flows to the *stratēgoi* (and perhaps to the *apodektai*). It was argued above that money that goes from the allies to the Athenian *stratēgoi* through the agency of the Hellenotamiai should be the assessed tribute or some amount that took its place. This conclusion may be endorsed even in the absence of an assent to the various restorations that would make its character more explicit.

Nevertheless, the mint and its *epistatai* are involved in this transfer of resources; in my particular reconstruction they are minting a part of their silver stock and taking allied silver and electrum in return for it. It is also obvious that a protected fund of money is being created either from the transferred funds or from an equivalent amount that comprises newly minted silver from bullion previously held in the mint. An *aparkhē* for a fund under the protection of Athena and Hephaistos has been hypothesized to account for the diversion of monies in this next stage of the decree. Since the decree has at its heart an act of conversion, it may then be true that the Athenians were extending their individual and occasional policy of receiving tribute payment in non-Attic coin to the entirety of the alliance for one year. They were permitting their allies to clean out their public holdings in currencies other than Athenian coins and perhaps in bullion and worn Attic coins. It is even possible that the allies might have taken in some coins in private hands, if the Athenian terms were sufficiently favorable and they could easily collect such holdings.

It is uncertain who would create a permanent record of the sums handled pursuant to this enactment; it could be the Hellenotamiai on the basis of the act of registration that opens the extant decree, or the *epistatai*

[81] Nor should this hypothesis lead us to expect that the tribute should previously have been tendered in coins bearing the image of Apollo. In the first place, there were not enough Delian coins to handle monetary transfers of this magnitude. Second, the cult of Apollo of Delos was a common possession of all the Ionians; tendering an *aparkhē* to Apollo could not reinforce the recognition of Athenian hegemony that dedicating the *aparkhē* to Athena signified. The decision to tender the *aparkhai* to Athena changed the act of dedication to an expression of the recognition of the hegemony of the Athenians and their goddess. That is presumably why it had to come through a Samian proposal (Plut. *Arist.* 25.3).

who are seen as recording sums in the last section of the decree. Yet it is likely that any memorializing of this operation would not be included among the accounts of the *aparkhai* on the first stele recording the yearly payments but on some other monument near the mint (perhaps as an adjunct to the lost Athenian copy of the Coinage Decree).

This last point becomes particularly provocative when it is recalled that one of the tribute lists from the early 440s does not appear to exist.[82] I am of course accepting the prevailing view, which is not without its own complexities and controversy.[83] It is most likely that this list is the record of *aparkhai* for 449/8,[84] although the possibility that it is the list for 448/7 or for 447/6 does not affect my argument.[85] There are at least four ways to understand how the Coinage Decree as restored above might necessarily lead to the absence of one list from the first stele of the accounts of the *aparkhai*.

First, it is likely that the Athenians were accepting monies in lieu of tribute that went to the mint and not to the treasury of the Hellenotamiai (even though the Hellenotamiai were monitoring the process). Second, the money was not good Attic silver and may not therefore have been suitable for the *aparkhē* to the patroness of the city. After the first list, the *aparkhē* has been hypothesized to have been otherwise exclusively Athenian coin that bore the image of the goddess. Third, it is possible

[82] H.T. Wade-Gery, "Studies in Attic Inscriptions of the Fifth Century B.C.," *BSA* 33 (1932–33) 101–36, esp. 112–13; Wade-Gery, "The Question of the Tribute in 449/8 B.C.," *Hesperia* 14 (1945) 212–29, esp. 212–15; *ATL* 1.133, 175; 2.13 with bibliography; Meiggs-Lewis #50, pp. 133–36.

[83] W.K. Pritchett maintained in a series of articles that the *lapis primus* (first tribute stele) bore a crowning member that held the missing list on its rear. See "The Height of the *Lapis Primus*," *Historia* 13 (1964) 129–34; "The Top of the *Lapis Primus*," *GRBS* 7 (1966) 123-29; "The Location of the *Lapis Primus*," *GRBS* 8 (1967) 113–19; "Lucubrationes Epigraphicae," *CSCA* 5 (1972) 153–81, esp. 153–59; also *The Liar School of Herodotus* (Amsterdam 1993) note 124 (pp. 155–57). Cf. R.I. Sealey, "Notes on the Tribute-Quota-Lists 5, 6, and 7 of the Athenian Empire," *Phoenix* 24 (1970) 13–28; Sealey, *A History of the Greek City-States: ca. 700–338 B.C.* (Berkeley and Los Angeles 1976) 278–82. In rebuttal, see B.D. Meritt, "The Top of the First Tribute Stele," *Hesperia* 35 (1966) 134–140; Meritt, "The Tribute Quota List of 454/3," *Hesperia* 41 (1972) 403–17, esp. 403–405. On the sculptural arguments see, most recently, C. Lawton, "Sculptural and Epigraphical Restorations to Attic Documents," *Hesperia* 61 (1992) 239–51, esp. 244–46. The presence of a crowning block does not, of course, necessitate that its rear face was inscribed.

[84] The dominant opinion is that the first list on the rear bears the denotation, ἐπὶ τε̃ς ἀρχε̃ς τε̃ς] ἐγ[άτες *he̅ι* . . . (*IG* I^3 266.1). See also D.M. Lewis, "Notes on Attic Inscriptions," *BSA* 49 (1954) 17–50, esp. 25–29; M.F. McGregor, "The Ninth Prescript of the Attic Quota-Lists," *Phoenix* 16 (1962) 267–75.

[85] See, most recently, M. Piérart, "Athènes et son empire: la crise de 447–445," in J. Servais, T. Hackens, and B. Servais-Soyez (eds.), *Stemmata: Mélanges de philologie, d'histoire, et d'archéologie grecques offerts à Jules Labarbe* (Louvain-le-Neuve 1987) 293–303.

that any money withdrawn from this process of conversion for the purpose of dedication went to a cult of Athena and Hephaistos rather than to the cult of Athena Polias that was administered by the Treasurers of Athena. Finally, the memorialization of transfers of funds connected with this legislation ought to have been made in the vicinity of the mint, where the Athenian copy of the Coinage Decree was erected, and not on the Acropolis. Therefore, the date for the first promulgation of the Coinage Decree might be one of the three years in the early 440s for which the list of the *aparkhai* could be missing.[86]

This hypothesis constitutes a departure from current scholarly views. It is not, however, radical in its interpretation of the historical evidence, but rather a more conservative reaction to the absence of a list than are the prevailing treatments. The absence of the list is not hereby traced to some vast political upheaval but to a conversion of monies that everyone concedes took place (although there is dispute about its scale). Conventional thinking would attempt to connect the absence of a list with the absence of tribute collection and a crisis of the "empire," either a refusal of the allies to pay or an Athenian hesitation to continue collection. That is used to buttress the historicity of the dubious Peace of Kallias,[87] as though the Athenians or the allies would consider dismantling a defense establishment that would take many years to rebuild in return for an agreement that could be abrogated at a moment's notice.[88] Accordingly, there is something about the conventional thinking that defies the realities of war and peace in the fifth century. The implication of the Coinage Decree for the absence of one list of *aparkhai* admirably responds to the misgivings about a cessation of tribute collection for even one year by those who consequently speculated about the assignment of a whole

[86] There are permutations, whose elaboration is unnecessary here, in which a short list on the back of a sculptured finial block could be assimilated to our hypothesis.

[87] Particularly influential were two articles of H.T. Wade-Gery, *Hesperia* (1945) esp. 216–24; Wade-Gery, "The Peace of Callias," *Essays in Greek History* (Oxford 1958) 201–32. See also *ATL* 3.230–31, 275–79; D.M. Lewis, *CAH*² 5.121–27. On the Peace of Kallias, see Meiggs 487–95, 598–99; G.E.M. de Ste. Croix, *The Origins of the Peloponnesian War* (London 1975) 310–11; Meister, *Ungeschichtlichkeit*. The efforts to move the Peace of Kallias into the 460s have the same decoupling effect (from the missing list) as do doubts about the historicity of the agreement; see E. Badian, "The Peace of Callias," *JHS* 107 (1987) 1–39 = *From Plataea to Potidaea* (Balimore 1993) 1–72, 187–201; J. Walsh, "The Authenticity and the Dates of the Peace of Callias and the Congress Decree," *Chiron* 11 (1981) 31–63. S. Accame, review of B.D. Meritt, *Documents on Athenian Tribute*, in *RFIC* 66 (1938) 409–16, esp. 413–14, offers a different crisis as cause, namely, the insurrections against pro-Athenian governments of 447/6.

[88] Vigorously and acutely expressed by de Ste. Croix, *Origins* 311–14.

year's tribute for a special purpose like the building of the temple of Athena Nike.[89]

It would be reckless to predict the changes in our interpretation of Attic monetary policy if the complete text of the Coinage Decree came into our possession. It is important, however, to emphasize that a later date for the promulgation of the decree, even one in the 420s, need not compel substantial changes in our understanding of the purport of this legislation. The Coinage Decree was not a unique measure but probably one of a number of initiatives that promoted monetary consolidation. Hence, a later date for the enactment merely extends the period of evolution toward the stronger sanction that is represented by the addition of a clause to the bouleutic oath. The injunction embedded in the clause may have preceded that insertion, constituting the chief contribution of the earlier psephism of Klearkhos. Our investigation has isolated three points of general demarcation in monetary policy: the inception of the inscribed lists of *aparkhai*, the Decree of Klearkhos, and the Coinage Decree. The shortest time frame is to collapse the first two points in 454/3, and to date the Coinage Decree to the year of the missing list in the early 440s. Longer chronologies in which the three stages are spread over the period 454–11 are, of course, viable in the present state of our knowledge. Their apparent and relative lack of explanatory power compared with the hypothesis of a shorter evolution could be the result of the dearth of our evidence.

APPENDIX: REDATING OF ATTIC INSCRIPTIONS OF THE PENTEKONTAETEIA

These citations follow this format:
Document title (*IG* I³ Number: *IG* I³/*SEG* Date | Mattingly date): work of Mattingly

1. The Kleinias Decree (*IG* I³ 34: 448/7 | 425/4): *Historia* (1961) 150–55; *CQ* (1966) 188–90; *BSA* (1970) 129–33; *Acta* 27–29; "Vocabulary Change and Epigraphic Dating," *Mnem.*⁴ 30 (1977) 66–69; *Coinage and Administration* 66–68; "Epigraphy and the Athenian Empire," *Historia* 41 (1992) 129–38, esp. 135.
2. The appointment of the priestess for Athena Nike (35: ca. 448 | 427–24): *Historia* (1961) 169–71; "The Peace of Kallias," *Historia* 14 (1965) 273–81, esp. 278–80; *AJP* (1974) 284; withdrawn in *Coinage and Administration* 68.

[89] Meiggs 152–54; 496–503.

3. The decree on the Eleusinian *epistatai* (32: ca. 449–47 | 432/1): *Historia* (1961) 171–73; "Athens, Delphi and Eleusis in the Late 420s," *PACA* 9 (1966) 61–76, esp. 69–74; "Athens and Eleusis: Some New Ideas," in ΦΟΡΟΣ 90–103, esp. 97–98; *AJP* (1984) 347; *Coinage and Administration* 69–70.
4. Hermione treaty (31: ca. 450 | 425/4): *Historia* (1961) 173; *Historia* (1963) 261; *Ancient Society* 211–12; review *IG* I³, *AJP* 105 (1984) 340–57, esp. 348–49; *Historia* (1992) 133–34.
5. The Miletos Decree (21: 450/49 | 426/5): *Historia* (1961) 174–81; *Historia* (1963) 257–58; *Ancient Society* 207–209; *BSA* (1970) 145–47; *Acta* 31–32; ΦΟΡΟΣ 98–101; "Three Attic Decrees," *Historia* 25 (1976) 38–44, esp. 40–42; "The Athenian Decree for Miletus (*IG* I², 22 = *ATL* II,D 11): A Postscript," *Historia* 30 (1981) 113–17; *AJP* (1984) 340–42, 346–48; *Coinage and Administration* 68–70.
6. The Kolophon Decree (37: 447/6 | 427/6 or 425/4): *Historia* (1961) 179-80, cf. *Historia* (1963) 266–67; *Ancient Society* 209–13; *Historia* (1992) 131–32.
7. The decrees regarding the Euboian cities, Eretria (39: 446/5 | 424/3), Chalcis (40: 446/5 | 424/3), and Hestiaia (41: ca. 446/5 | post 428/7): *JHS* (1961) 124–32; *PACA* (1966) note 21, pp. 64–65; *Ancient Society* 201–202; *Historia* (1976) 38–40; *Historia* (1992) 132–33, 135–37.
8. The Brea Decree (46: ca. 445 | 426/5): *Historia* (1963) 258–60; *CQ* (1966) 172–86; *AJP* (1984) 352–53.
9. The Koroneia epigram (*IG* I³ 1163d–f: ca. 446 | 424): *Historia* (1963) 261–62; *CQ* (1966) 191–92.
10. The proxeny decrees *IG* I³ 19, 27, and 28 (all 450–40 | 420s): *Historia* (1963) 263-66, *Ancient Society* 205–207; *AJP* (1984) 345–46.
11. The Erythrai decrees (14–15: ca. 450 | 430s): *Historia* (1963) 271; withdrawn in *Ancient Society* 206–207.
12. The Sigeion Decree (17: 451/0 | 418/7): *Historia* (1963) 267–68; *JHS* (1966) 95; *AJP* (1974) 282–84; *AJP* (1984) 346, 348–349; *Historia* (1992) 129–31.
13. The alliance with Egesta (11: pre-450 | 418/7) and the alliance with Halikyai (12: ca. 433/2 | 418/7): *Historia* (1963) 268–73; *Historia* (1965) 274–75; "Athens and the Western Greeks: C. 500–413 B.C.," in *La circolazione della moneta ateniese in Sicilia e in Magna Grecia*, *AIIN* Suppl. 12–14 (Rome 1969) 201–222, esp. 204–205 (with some recantation, itself later recanted in note 7 of *Chiron* [1986]); *AJP* (1974) 284; *Historia* (1976) 42–44; *AJP* (1984) 344–47; 349; "The Alliance of Athens with Egesta," *Chiron* 16 (1986) 167–70; "Some Fifth-Century Attic Epigraphic Hands," *ZPE* 83 (1990) 110–19, esp. 117; *Historia* (1992) 129.

14. The Kallias Decrees (52: 434/3 | 422/1): *PACA* (1964), cf. "Two Notes on Athenian Financial Documents," *BSA* 62 (1967) 13–17, esp. 14–17; "Athenian Finance in the Peloponnesian War," *BCH* 92 (1968) 450–85, esp. 450–56; *BSA* (1970) 147–49; ΦΟΡΟΣ 94–97; "The Mysterious 3000 Talents of the First Kallias Decree," *GRBS* 16 (1975) 15–22; *AJP* (1984) 355–57; *ZPE* (1990) 113, 117–19.
15. The Phaselis Decree (10: 469-50 | 425/4): *PACA* (1964) 37–39.
16. The Prytaneion Decree (131: ca. 440–32? | 423/2): *PACA* (1966) 63–66
17. The Aigina Decree (38: 457-45 | 432): "Athens and Aigina," *Historia* 16 (1967) 1–5, with recantation in "Athens and Aigina: A Palinode," *Historia* 26 (1977) 370–73; *AJP* (1984) 346, 348.
18. Dedication of the Messenians (148: fifth century | 426): *AILN* Suppl. 12–14, 214
19. The proxeny decree (for Parianoi?) (18: ca. 450 | 420s): "The Athenian Proxeny Decree, *IG* I^2 30 + 23 (*SEG* 10.20)," *Phoenix* 29 (1975) 284–86.
20. A special place among these inscriptions is occupied by the treaty with Perdikkas (*IG* I^3 89) which was once dated in the mid-430s. Mattingly argued for the later date of 423/2. See *BCH* 472–75; *Klio* (1977) 84; *AJP* (1984) 353. *IG* I^3 now dates to 418–13 (see above, p. 424). This document has no relevance for the dating of the Coinage Decree.

These publications of H.B. Mattingly have now been collected in *The Athenian Empire Restored* (Ann Arbor 1996).

PART V

SYNTHESIS

18

MONETARY INTEGRATION

THIS and the following chapters attempt to assess the monetary system of the *arkhē* during the second half of the fifth century. Naturally, much will flow through extrapolation out of the conclusions that have already emerged in the course of our earlier investigations.

This consolidation of monetary usage was the premier manifestation of the history of money during the fifth century. Monetary consolidation was the process by which a growing number of cities came to depend on and use currencies other than those struck in the mint under the control of the local political authority. As an explicit change such as adopting the Euboeic/Attic standard suggests, monetary consolidation among the allies of the Athenians tended to work in favor of Athenian money, although care should be taken to concede (at least in principle) that other panhellenic or regional currencies may also play a role in the process. The discussion above has outlined the case for seeing special roles in monetary consolidation for Cyzicene electrum, Phocaic electrum, and Aiginetic silver both in particular parts of the *arkhē* and for specific economic functions. In actuality, both the concerns over procuring Attic coins for paying tribute and the sheer scale of Athenian mint activity (when compared to that of others) suggest that most of the monetary consolidation that occurred among Athenian allies of the fifth-century *arkhē* featured an adoption of or an intensification of an employment of Attic money.

The late archaic monetary order achieved a certain degree of integration through the production and utilization together of coins struck on a common standard. The clearest manifestation is the record of the adoption of the Aiginetic standard and the widespread reception of Aiginetan coins. In distinction, fifth-century or classical monetary integration is a more elusive phenomenon. The growth of the service of money changing in market activities provided a more subtle means of integration.

At the fall of the Athenian hegemony the dominance of Attic owls is confirmed incidentally in the tradition that the Spartan general Gylippos had embezzled some of the 1,500T of booty the victorious navarch Lysander had dispatched to the home government after Aigospotamoi. Gylippos had opened a seam in the bottom of the sacks in which the coins were conveyed. Although the Spartans were mystified when the contents did not tally with the written inventories, they did not move against Gylippos until they received the intelligence that "many owls were roosting under his roof tiles," which was decoded to mean Athenian coins (Plut. *Lys.* 16.1–2; cf. DS 13.106.8–9; [Plut.] *Mor.* 10B). For the story to make sense (even for a fabrication), everyone involved must have assumed that the majority of the booty was in Attic coins.

ASSESSING MODES OF MONETARY CONSOLIDATION

It is axiomatic that a particular amount of tribute must in general reflect a comparable proportion of the income in taxes of the cities within the *arkhē*, as well as a similar percentage of the economic activity underlying taxation. Admittedly, the Athenians may have miscalculated from time to time, with the result that they gave some allied cities heavier or lighter burdens of tribute in relation to the assessments of others. Some scholars argue for a punitive aspect in certain changes in assessment.[1] Even if we are skeptical about the hypothesis that punitive assessment was ever a deliberate, consistent, and coherent policy, it will not affect the discussion below much, if it is conceded that hostile or amicable attitudes among the Attic *dēmos* always conditioned the assessment process. Nevertheless, assessments probably convey the relative size of allied economies, especially when short-term variations are deemphasized in favor of longer term levels or trends.

As the earlier discussion has attempted to show, the dominant aspect of monetary consolidation was the absence of minting within economic contexts in which significant monetization is likely to have existed either on the basis of direct evidence or through analogy. It has already been shown that about 60 percent of the allies did not coin either before or during the period of Attic hegemony. While the influence of the Athenian government or economy and the impact of the circulation of Attic money cannot naturally be implicated in the failure to begin coining before 478/7, the fact that many of these cities would mint coins in some later period of their history is notable. The existence of a large political unit (the Delian League) militated against the inauguration of minting activity among the allies who had not coined previously.

A more direct effect has been traced in the considerable number of allied states that ceased minting activity. Clearly, this process had started even before the creation of the alliance. The ramifications of the federal system of revenues and expenditures, however, probably played its part

[1] Cf. Figueira, *Colonization* 193–94.

in sustaining or accelerating decisions by allied cities to stop producing their own coinage. The increased degree of economic integration among the allies through commerce had an underlying influence that is hard to assess in the present state of the evidence, but was doubtless significant.

Table 2.1 (pp. 54–55 above) reported the compilation of the data on the minting activity of the tributary allies. One is reminded that about four fifths of the tributaries were not coining in 445. Accordingly, a little over half of the economic and taxational activity of the subject allies was being conducted in cities that did not mint their own money. In many contexts it is indeed possible to imagine the existence of a laissez-faire situation in private transactions in which participants in the local market were relatively free to determine the media by which transactions were to be conducted.[2] There must, however, have been a legal specification of the currency or currencies in which taxes were to be paid in most locales.

The revisionist interpretation urges that the Coinage Decree established Athenian money as the recognized and valid medium for allies who continued to strike silver coins. In any event, whether or not such a provision has been correctly restored and interpreted in the inscriptions, the reality that the Athenians received (or tried to receive) payments of tribute in Attic tetradrachms would have acted strongly in favor of such a recognition of Attic money even by nonminting allies. The variety of dates at which cities appear to stop coining is a bit obscured by the conventional thresholds, marked by dates like 479 or 465, that have been adopted in numismatic research and consequently in the treatments of individual mints that are referenced above. Nevertheless, the evidence seems to imply that most mint closings were separate incidents, whether they were taken on local initiative or implemented in consort with the Athenians.

The role of the cessation of minting has long been noted, although it has been studied more for the light it was expected to shed on the date of the Coinage Decree than for its intrinsic importance. The removal, however, of the shibboleth of a prohibition on allied minting not only helps us to envisage the significance of the decisions of city after city to close its mint, but also leads us toward other aspects of monetary consolidation. Chief among these other processes of consolidation is the shift to a minting of smaller denominations exclusively. When states that had not minted (category II) and states that had previously minted (with examples mainly in category IV but also scattered throughout our

[2] See, in general, pp. 56–58 above and pp. 544–47 below for the evidence of the Silver Coinage Law of 375/4.

classifications) concentrated on minting drachms and lighter coins, it is unlikely that their monetary practices had changed so dramatically that staters and the like were no longer required at all. Hence, other coins and especially Athenian tetradrachms began or continued to perform the previous functions of heavier coins.

Congruent with the limiting of the size of the denominations coined is the parallel tendency of many allied mints to decrease the scale of their coining as the century proceeded. Sadly, evidence is lacking for full documentation of the level of minting in all (or even the majority) of the allied mints, but those for which there is appropriate source material lowered their rate of emission of coins or held it (less frequently) relatively constant. Once again the likely outgrowth of the slackening output of local coins among the tributaries was an augmented circulation of Attic money. If the total extra-Attic economy of the *arkhē* grew during the Pentekontaeteia, there was a conspicuous failure by allied mints to increase their output of coins accordingly. The end result may well have been a situation in which Attic coins mediated a larger proportion of a rising level of business activity within a growing Aegean economy. Given the injections of enormous amounts of silver into the Aegean economy from the mines of Laureion, it is possible that the total money supply, of which Attic coins comprised an increasing proportion, had outstripped the (rising) output of other goods. The *arkhē* may have experienced inflation, but extraordinarily this was an inflation of prices because of an increased money supply of *higher* quality coins (see the Endnote to this chapter, pp. 493–95 below).

The coiners of electrum can be thought of in terms similar to the drachm/fractional minters. The cities minting electrum either never minted silver (Phokaia), or cease minting silver coins of more than fractional weight (Kyzikos, Lampsakos, and Mytilene). Silver was probably the medium of exchange for much of the internal economies of these allied *poleis* including most smaller transactions. Their tax receipts were taken in both electrum and silver, depending on whether taxes drew on business and commerce conducted in electrum or they did not. Capitations, levies on global income of *oikoi*, and taxes on capital like the Attic *eisphorai* may also have elicited payments in electrum, especially when their exaction was extraordinary or they otherwise drew on savings. Just as electrum and silver did not necessarily compete as media for conducting business (but perhaps only as media for saving or for hoarding), each dominating in its own sphere, the allied mints striking electrum were not in competition with the Attic mint or with any other silver-minting authority. Electrum was problematical, only insofar as those allies who had significant tax receipts in the metal were tempted to endeavor to pass electrum coins on to the Athenians as tribute.

The shift to drachm/fractional minting is comparatively well attested when compared to its converse, the restriction of minting to heavier coins. That is unsurprising since Attic tetradrachms traveled farther than drachms and fractions, as illustrated by the hoard evidence. The presence of Attic tetradrachms in the *arkhē* lessened or removed the need for local coins in the stater range of weights. When an allied city coined only staters or tetradrachms, it must be assumed that foreign fractions were present in sufficient numbers to fulfill the role of accommodating retail business. That must be true, unless we accept that such transactions were not mediated monetarily in those particular cities. That conclusion has nothing to recommend it in comparative terms. If there was enough international or regional currency in circulation in lighter denominations in a particular allied state, a satisfactory supply of heavier coins from abroad may also be supposed to have penetrated the local economy in most instances.

Thus, a city like Kos that minted only staters (tetradrachms or triple-*sigloi*) in its last fifth-century monetary phase may have implemented a special conduit for the dispersion of its tetradrachms. Cities like Maroneia may also have had special modes of dissemination or constituencies in mind during the period in which their output was solely in the form of heavier coins. For some cities, a role for heavier denominations (in preference to lighter coins) may have been reserved by reason of facilitating cooperation with non-Greeks, for whom those coins had traditional relevance in business or politics.

A hypothesis of special channels of dissemination of coins raises again the possibility of a role for coins as documents intended to convey messages to their users. Their types fostered the solidarity of the community by invoking a characteristic badge with which citizens experienced a sense of identity. Types, whether the civic badge or not, drew on the religious, mythological, and historical traditions of the issuing state so that the circulation of coins bearing them promoted the psychological integration of the community.

Thus, we may happily concede that the continued emission and use of local coinage both bespoke and reinforced local patriotism. As expressions of shared values, the local issues of Athenian allies could be understood as ideologically charged documents, and even as a form of propaganda, the precise terms of which cannot now always be clearly deciphered. This determination does not, however, make of the continuing activities of certain allied mints acts of defiance of Athens, nor does it render these series of coins necessary tokens of local autonomy. It is in this context of public ideology that changes of coin type to Atticizing images are also to be understood, for surely they indicate that assertions of local tradition, if not patriotism, could still occur in the context of an avowal of loyalty to Athens. The usage of such types is another mode of monetary consolidation, albeit one operating on the symbolic side of the ledger of costs and benefits that was involved in the decision whether to mint and which type of coins were to be minted.

As in any large political entity that has been formed from smaller units that not only possessed a heritage of independence but also persisted as components of the larger unity, the Athenian *arkhē* was typified by prioritizing gestures from the hegemonic authority that were intended to instill an affiliation with Athens. A nonexhaustive list would include the portrayal of the allies as colonists of Athens (their *mētropolis*), the assertions of an institutional convergence of allied *dēmoi* with the Athenian *dēmos*, the celebration of the Athenian-led panhellenic crusade of liberation from Persia, and the declaration of allied cultural dependency on the Athenians, starting from the Attic origin of agriculture. Countervailing gestures embodied localism within the *arkhē*, and there should be no hesitation in recognizing that local coining could, in principle, be among them.

These same considerations may also contribute to explanations of why allied states that made their break from Athens during the Ionian War resumed coining. Admittedly, by virtue of their break with the Athenians and (often) ensuing Attic military operations that were aimed at retaliation or recovery, some allies experienced a diminution of the amount of Athenian coinage that flowed into their local economy. A renewal of minting remedied that shortfall in the money supply. Rebels also faced practical concerns in having to coordinate their military operations with those of their new Peloponnesian allies.[3] Hence the pattern is attested in which former Athenian allies began to coin on the Aiginetic or the Chian standard. Notwithstanding these practical motivations, it is not improbable that the new oligarchic regimes of 411 and the years thereafter sometimes opted to offer their citizens a reminder of local traditions through the types of their revived emissions of money.

Moreover, after the defeat of the Athenians at Aigospotamoi and the "liberation" of the allies by Sparta, there are the monetary requirements of the Lysandrian order to be considered. Not only did Lysander assign *harmosts* to supervise strategic locations and implant *decadarchies* as governing authorities, he also assessed a tribute of 1,000T on the

[3] Cf. Kraay *ACGC* 92, 155, 157, 159, 248.

former allies within the Attic *arkhē* (DS 14.10.2; cf. Isoc. 12.67–69; Polyb. 6.49.10). Naturally, this tribute was not paid in Spartan money, any more than the Peloponnesian fleet had conducted its affairs in the cumbrous mode of iron bars. The Spartans with their primitive fiscal apparatus and perennial financial embarassments were prepared to receive subventions in whatever form the donors chose. During the Ionian War, Chian, Aiginetic, and Athenian coins seem to have bulked large in their disbursements.

The coins bearing the legend ΣYN and the type of an infant Herakles can be seen as alluding to Lysander's victory over the Athenians.[4] These coins can be attributed to seven or eight East Greek mints: Byzantion, Ephesos, Iasos, Knidos, Kyzikos, Rhodes (lacking ΣYN), and Samos; a Lampsacene gold issue (also lacking ΣYN) is questionable. The coins are minted on the Chian/Rhodian standard—most are tridrachms that would be equivalent to Aiginetic didrachms—that would be appropriate in this historical context. The coins could also easily be expended to support military operations.

This coinage probably reflects a need to tender tribute to Sparta that turned out to be of a short duration, because the Spartan government acted to curtail the hegemonic arrangements of Lysander (Xen. *HG* 3.4.2 for the dissolution of the decadarchies).[5] Hence the ΣYN-coinage, surviving in a few examples, does not appear to have been long-lasting, although the twelve surviving obverse dies indicate a relatively sizable output. This conjecture would be strengthened if an attractive suggestion of Kraay were correct, namely, that the ΣYN legend is not an archaism for συνμαχικόν, but abbreviates the Greek word σύνταξις or συντέλεια (terms denoting taxation).[6] In its brief life, other cities under Spartan hegemony might have availed themselves of this coinage in an effort to avoid a recourse to Attic tetradrachms, so redolent of Attic hegemony, in tendering assessed sums to the Spartans. As noted above, the Spartans had no inhibition against receiving booty and *phoros* in Attic tetradrachms.

[4] S. Karweise, "Lysander as Herakliskos Drakonopnigon ('Herakles the Snake-Strangler')," *NC* 140 (1980) 1–27. Earlier work opted for a date during the Corinthian War: G.L. Cawkwell, "A Note on the Heracles Coinage Alliance of 394 B.C.," *NC*[6] 16 (1956) 69–75. Note that any anti-Spartan alliance in a Corinthian War setting involving these cities would have been under Attic sponsorship and almost necessarily would have worked within an Attic monetary context. See also Kraay, *ACGC* 248–49, 259; E. Schönert-Geiss, *Griechisches Münzwerk: Die Münzprägung von Byzantion* (Berlin 1970) 31.

[5] Adducing a fiscal rationale is preferable to a hypothesis in which honorific purposes were solely operative. Cf. Karweise, *NC* (1980) 13–15.

[6] C.M. Kraay, "Greek Coinage and War," in W. Heckel and R. Sullivan (eds.), *Ancient Coins of the Graeco-Roman World: The Nickle Numismatic Papers* (Waterloo, Ontario 1984) 3–18, esp. 8–9.

The decadarchic oligarchs, however, may have wished to dispel any appearance that nothing save the recipient of their citizens' tribute had changed by deploying the powerful visual symbolism of the ΣΥΝ issues.

TO MINT OR NOT TO MINT

While Attic hegemony was unchallenged, calculations of the costs and benefits associated with minting silver seem to have been conditioned by the ease of conducting business and administration in Attic coin and thus there was a movement toward monetary consolidation. The analysis of advantages and debits, however, varied from ally to ally. On the basis of the present state of the data, we can merely determine which mints closed or remained active and speculate about the factors militating against or in favor of monetary consolidation. This judgment is particularly valid regarding the form of consolidation that most interests us, that is, the acceptance of Attic coins as locally valid. A group of factors have turned up repeatedly in the investigation of allied minting activities in Part I: proximity to Athens, susceptibility to interaction by sea, and the size of the local economy.

Coining and Monetary Standard

The standard on which the local government coined was also fairly clearly a factor, although it has been suggested above that it seems to play different roles in two separate contexts. Earlier in the fifth century, mints with small outputs on the Euboeic/Attic and Aiginetic standards appear to have terminated their production of coins. Note the attrition in those minting on these standards that is so apparent in Table 18.1. While coining Euboeic/Attic-weight silver would still be a breach of the supposed prohibition on minting engineered by the Coinage Decree (in the traditional interpretation), it provides an excellent example of the type of monetary consolidation that our interpretation posits.

In the second half of the century, when few allies were minting at all and fewer still minted coins heavier than a drachm, the employment of the Euboeic/Attic standard or of the Aiginetic standard, either of which were in general interstate use, and the ease with which local coins could be exchanged with coins on these standards may have helped sustain some minting activity. The Aiginetic standard had been important in the monetary systems of the Cycladic islands. It is quite possible that Aiginetic coins not only continued to be hoarded in the islands during the Attic hegemony, but that coins on the Aiginetic standard retained validity in some places (one suspects alongside Athenian money). That

Table 18.1 The Decline of Silver Mints on Important Standards among Athenian Allies

* = minting of lighter denominations

A. Cities Minting on the Aiginetic Standard

Pre-480	*After 478*	*After 465*	*After 445*	*After 430/Before 411*
Aigina	Aigina	Aigina	Aigina	Kebren*
Andros	Astypalaia?	Ialysos*	Ialysos*	Knidos*
Astypalaia?	Iulis	Kameiros	Kameiros*	Koressia*
Iulis	Kameiros	Karthaia	Kebren*	Siphnos*
Kameiros	Karthaia	Kebren*	Knidos*	Teos?
Karthaia	Kebren*	Knidos*	Teos	
Khersonesos?	Khersonesos?	Siphnos*		
Knidos*	Knidos*	Teos		
Koressia	Koressia			
Kos	Paros			
Kyme	Siphnos			
Naxos	Teos			
Paros				
Seriphos				
Siphnos				
Tenos				
Teos				
Thera				

B. Cities Minting on the Euboeic/Attic Standard

Pre-480	*After 478*	*After 465*	*After 445*	*After 430/Before 411*
Aineia	Aineia	Aineia	Aineia*	Aineia*
Akanthos	Akanthos	Akanthos	Akanthos	Akanthos
Astypalaia?	Astypalaia?	Dikaiopolis	Aphytis*	Aphytis*
Chalkis	Chalkis	Klazomenai	Dikaiopolis*	Elaia*
Delos	Delos	Kos?	Elaia*	Ialysos*
Dikaiopolis	Dikaiopolis	Mende	Halikarnassos*?	Kalkhedon*
Eretria	Eretria	Miletos*	Kalkhedon*	Kameiros*
Karystos	Karystos	Poteidaia	Klazomenai*	Mende*
Khersonesitai*	Klazomenai	(S)kapsa*	Lindos*?	Miletos*
Klazomenai	Kos?	Skione	Mende	Samos (<12>)
Peparethos	Mende	Torone	Miletos*	Thasos?
Poteidaia	Miletos*		Poteidaia*	Torone*
Sermylia	Poteidaia		Torone*	
(S)kapsa*	Sermylia			
Skione	(S)kapsa*			
Stageira	Skione			
Tenedos?	Stageira			
Torone	Tenedos?			
	Torone			

acceptance would explain why Koressia on Keos and Siphnos may have resumed minting fractions on the Aiginetic standard after ca. 420. They were supplementing a straitened supply of Aiginetic fractions, depleted after the closing of the Aiginetan mint. During the Ionian War, as some cities entered their post-alliance periods, the Aiginetic standard may have been adopted by mints such as Abdera and Maroneia, although the metrology is controversial.

The same process of attrition in the mints coining on the Euboeic/Attic standard can also be detected, although it is less marked than among the mints coining on the Aiginetic standard. This is because cities minting on the Euboeic/Attic standard produced coins that could circulate in their local markets at parity with Athenian coins. For similar reasons, there was stability in the number of mints using the Attic standard after 430, when some cities shifted their production (mainly of fractions) to the Euboeic/Attic standard. The activity of these mints (in the last column on the right in Table 18.1B) does not connote rivalry with Athens, but reflects a policy of complementary monetary activity.

Other standards such as the Chian, Samian, Phocaic, or Milesian had fewer representatives among the states in the Delian League to start. None of these standards was immune to monetary consolidation so that a similar pattern of attrition could be documented for each. It suffices to draw attention to the end result of this evolution.

After the outbreak of the Peloponnesian War, Samos was the only state still exclusively minting on the Samian standard down to its conversion to the Euboeic/Attic standard in 412, but some Methymnian issues have been classified as Samian. Chios was similarly the primary mint using the Chian/Rhodian standard, which was to undergo so major a revival after 411, although the later fifth-century fractions of Miletos may also be on the Chian standard (alternatively on reduced Persic). A surviving representative of the Milesian standard was Ephesos. On the Phocaic standard was Mytilene. The Phoenician standard had a minter of smaller denominations in Neapolis. Abdera and Maroneia employed for a time what modern scholars have called various versions of the Thraco-Macedonian standard. Least affected was the Persic standard in use at Antandros, Aspendos, Dardanos, Erythrai, Kelenderis, Kolophon, Kyzikos and possibly Ainos, and Methymna. Just as coining itself tended to survive in areas where the alliance abutted upon or interacted with different monetary or economic zones, the Persic standard alone maintained a number of minters within the *arkhē* by virtue of its use in Persian controlled Asia Minor.

It will be explained shortly that the size of the local economy as revealed by tribute assessments is a good predictor whether a city would continue to mint. Yet there is no extended influence from the mints of the larger economies like Samos and Chios toward other cities using their coin standard or even toward their neighbors who might have adopted their standard. In other words, there were no minting blocs within the *arkhē.* The absence of such groups might be considered a confirmation of the fiscal or taxational role of the tribute system in encouraging monetary consolidation. The tribute system was not the only influence on decisions to cease or scale back minting operations, but it was a factor strong enough to discourage monetary integration with any economy and monetary system save the Athenian. While using money on the same standard as a large neighbor did facilitate any commercial dealings with the citizens or resident aliens of that neighbor, it did not address the problem of acquiring enough Attic coin expeditiously so that the assessed tribute could be payed on time. The happenstance of sharing coins of the same standard with the larger neighbor had no impact on the task of gathering enough tetradrachms through taxation. The patchiness of survival of mints on standards that did not possess many mints in the regions adjacent to the *arkhē* also helps support the hypothesis that the requirement for payment in Attic coin greatly influenced monetary policy among the allies.

H.A. Cahn investigated the interaction of Greek coin standards in the eastern Aegean and in Asia Minor in connection with his study of the mint at Knidos, which produced coins in our period on the Aiginetic standard.[7] His perspective on standards was innovative because he considered the role of coins of specific denominations minted on one standard for their particular relevance to different standards. Thus, if the Aiginetic tetrobol weighs 3.8 g, the diobol, 2 g, trihemiobol, 1.5 g, and the obol, 1 g, he would classify all the mints that produce coins of that weight ca. 500 as having a relationship to the Aiginetic standard for economic purposes, regardless of the relationship of other Aiginetic denominations to the rest of the coins of the mint in question.

The results yielded the following correspondences for the various Aiginetic denominations: tetrobol: Parion, Skepsis, Phokaia; diobol: Skepsis, Miletos, Poseidion (Karpathos?); Samos(+); Kebren(-); trihemiobol: Abydos; obol: Kebren, Samos. Note that some coins fall

[7] H.A. Cahn, *Knidos: Die Münzen des sechsten und des fünften Jahrhunderts v. Chr.* (Berlin 1970) 178–95; cf. Cahn, "Étalons monétaires en Asie-mineure jusqu'au Ve siècle," in *Congresso internazionale di numismatica* (Rome 1961–65) 2.19–23.

somewhat above or below the norm for the weight of the respective Aiginetic denominations. That complicates any assumption that the coins were equivalent in terms of market value. The same analysis when applied to the Euboeic/Attic standard offers these equations ca. 500 (in the view of Cahn): didrachm (8.5 g): Methymna; tetrobol (2.8 g): Methymna, Teos; hemidrachm (2.1 g) = Aiginetic diobol; diobol (1.4 g): Teos, Erythrai, Klazomenai, Kameiros, Methymna(-), Samos; trihemiobol (1.05 g) = Aiginetic obol.

This analysis is valuable chiefly as a reminder, as Cahn urges us, that Greek coins circulated as currency and not as bullion among Greek *poleis*. Despite the confusions created by a plethora of different series emitted by various political units, there were a significant number of intersections between various coin standards that, in principle, may have been exploited to mitigate the difficulties associated with exchange. Notice also how the salient aspect of such equivalencies was perhaps the usefulness of these assorted issues in transactions undertaken in economic environments dominated by the Aiginetic and secondarily the Euboeic/Attic standards. Insofar as some of the correspondences noted by Cahn continued into the fifth century, they may also have been factors in the persistence of certain mints, although there is no reason to believe that they can have possessed a predominant influence.

Caution is advisable before overestimating the economic impact of these intersections or their role in policy-making. One obvious objection is that frequency tables do not really create exact correspondences but merely bands of rough equivalence. The overlap of two such bands or a single equivalence does not guarantee interchangeability or a recognition of validity between the coins of two independent cities.

It is also difficult to appraise the economic significance of these analogies. They did not much affect merchants who would have exchanged moderate to large sums in order to do business. It is hard to imagine visitors to a city using a coinage on the Euboeic/Attic standard stocking up on just their own fractional coins that happened to weigh the same as Aiginetic diobols to conduct business there without recourse to exchange. Some correspondences between standards were more important (as has been noted above where appropriate). Yet even the equivalence between the Euboeic/Attic hemidrachm and the Aiginetic diobol and between the Euboeic/Attic trihemiobol and the Aiginetic obol were presumably subsumed into the general ratio of 3:2 that sometimes prevailed between the value of the coins of the two standards by their bullion weight.[8] Even this ratio was only one conventional guide, subjected in specific situations to market forces sensitive to time, place, and nature of transaction.

Other Factors in Decisions to Mint

As for the reasons why allied states continued coining, factors of an economic or fiscal nature appear a good deal more credible as causation than does legislative enactment. The further away from Attica an allied community is situated the later in the period of the Attic hegemony it is likely to have continued minting or never to have ceased at all. And distance from Attica is not merely real distance but distance measured in terms of the time of the average round trip in different seasons of the year. Cities whose citizens carried on commerce with the non-Greeks on the fringes of the Aegean world were also more likely than those who did not to continue coining either in silver or in electrum. As just noted, facility of monetary interaction with those using the Euboeic/Attic standard also typified some allies that continued minting activity. The access of some allies to sources of silver, especially those cities in proximity to the silver mines of Mt. Pangaion and others elsewhere along the Thracian littoral, may help explain the persistence of coining in that region. Finally, and certainly not least significant, was the size of the economy of the allied state.

A little more can be said about this last subject synthetically. Table 18.2 collects the evidence on the size of allied economies as suggested (n.b.) by their payments of tribute. Ten talents of tribute has been used as a minimum threshold for inclusion during periods 1–7 and 20T for period 8 (according to the divisions of assessments used in this work, for which see the Appendix). Not only was the ability to maintain autonomy a function of size,[9] but literary testimonia also distinguish the autonomous cities from the rest of the allies for their wealth.[10] According

[8] Fourth-century evidence speaks in favor of the ratio of 70:100 between Aiginetic and Euboeic/Attic coin. This ratio was enshrined in the accounting conventions of the period where the Aiginetic talent had 4,200 Aiginetic dr. See Figueira, *Excursions* 69–71.

[9] See Figueira, *Colonization* 170–71, 251–53; Figueira, *Excursions* 264–66, especially on the hypothesis that contribution of ships became the more efficient means for Athens to draw on the military assets of the ally as the size and wealth of the allied state increased.

[10] On Chios, note Thuc. 8.24.4: Χῖοι γὰρ μόνοι μετὰ Λακεδαιμονίους ὧν ἐγὼ ᾐσθόμην ηὐδαιμόνησάν τε ἅμα καὶ ἐσωφρόνησαν, καὶ ὅσῳ ἐπεδίδου ἡ πόλις αὐτοῖς ἐπὶ τὸ μεῖζον, τόσῳ δὲ καὶ ἐκοσμοῦντο ἐχυρώτερον; on Samos, note Ion *FGH* 392 F 16 in Plut. *Per.* 28.7 on Perikles' reduction of Samos: θαυμαστὸν δέ τι καὶ μέγα φρονῆσαι καταπολεμήσαντα τοὺς Σαμίους φησὶν αὐτὸν ὁ Ἴων, ὡς τοῦ μὲν Ἀγαμέμνονος ἔτεσι δέκα βάρβαρον πόλιν, αὐτοῦ δὲ μησὶν ἐννέα τοὺς πρώτους καὶ δυνατωτάτους Ἰώνων

Table 18.2 Minting and Level of Assessment

Cities actively minting in silver or electrum appear in capitals; nonminters in lower case. Those states in parentheses are not specifically attested in the period in question, but the amounts assigned to them are likely to have been their actual assessments. The lists are headed (in brackets) with Chios, Samos, Mytilene (and its Lesbian allies taken collectively), and Methymna, although these were autonomous or, at least, nontributary islands.

454/3–451/0 (1)	*450/49–447/6 (2)*	*446/5–443/2 (3)*	*442/1–439/8 (4)*
[CHIOS]	[CHIOS]	[CHIOS]	[CHIOS]
[SAMOS]	[SAMOS]	[SAMOS]	[SAMOS]
[MYTILENE]	[MYTILENE]	[MYTILENE]	[MYTILENE]
AIGINA/30	[METHYMNA]	[METHYMNA]	[METHYMNA]
ABDERA/15	AIGINA/30	AIGINA/30	AIGINA/30
(Byzantion)	ABDERA/15	ABDERA/15	ABDERA/15
AINOS/12	AINOS/12	(Lampsakos?)	Lampsakos?/12
LAMPSAKOS/12	Byzantion/15	Byzantion)	(Byzantion)/15+
Andros/12	LAMPSAKOS/12	AINOS/10	AINOS/10
Kyme/12	IALYSOS/10	LYKIOI/10	Perinthos/10
(Perinthos)	LINDOS/10	Perinthos/10	
	MILETOS/10		
	Perinthos/10		

438/7–435/4 (5)	*434/3–431/0 (6)*	*post 429 (7)*	*ATL A9–13, T31–49 (8)*
[CHIOS]	[CHIOS]	[CHIOS]	[CHIOS]
[SAMOS]	[SAMOS]	[SAMOS]	[SAMOS]
[MYTILENE]	[MYTILENE]	[MYTILENE]	[METHYMNA]
[METHYMNA]	[METHYMNA]	[METHYMNA]	ABDERA/75
ABDERA/15	Byzantion/18	THASOS/30	THASOS/60
(Lampsakos?)	THASOS/30	Byzantion/15	Paros/30
MARONEIA/10	ABDERA/15	(Perinthos)/15	MARONEIA/21
(Byzantion)	POTEIDAIA/15	Lampsakos?/12	AINOS/20
Perinthos/10	(Lampsakos?)	ABDERA/10	KYZIKOS/20
	ERYTHRAI/10		
	LINDOS/10		
	MARONEIA/10		
	Perinthos/10		

to the tribute figures, there was a striking correlation between the size of the local economy and the persistence of minting. The impression of Table 18.2 is even more striking, if one is prepared to understand the nonminting of the cities at the straits to the Black Sea, Byzantion and Perinthos as special cases. One may also note a number of continuing minters of fractions such as Kalkhedon and Kameiros that just miss the lower end of these lists (in these two cases with tribute payments of 9T).

ἑλόντος. On Mytilene and the other Lesbian rebels, compare Figueira, *Colonization* 196 for the size of the Lesbian economy. Methymna probably possessed a smaller economy than any of these three; at a guess, an economy comparable to one of the Rhodian cities.

THE IMPLEMENTATION OF MONETARY CONSOLIDATION

While the evidence for the actual minting patterns of Greek *poleis* allied with the Athenians indicates the existence and the significance of monetary consolidation, direct evidence about how allies decided to attune their internal usage of money to Athenian practices is considerably more obscure. In discussing the problem, the first *desideratum* is that we not overlook the obvious. Members of the Delian League decided to undertake the various steps that have been described as modes of monetary consolidation in a variety of chronological contexts. Moreover, some states made a succession of decisions, for example, reducing their coining to fractions and then ceasing altogether, combining changes in standard or in standard coin with alterations in coin weight, or altering the intensity of minting. Therefore, many allied cities may have decided on their own to accept Attic coins as valid for the different reasons of economic and administrative advantage that have been outlined above. With the paucity of surviving inscribed laws from allied states during the Attic hegemony, these choices in policy lack direct testimony at the present and will probably continue to do so, unless a series of lucky and unanticipated epigraphical finds takes place.

One indirect light is cast on the arrangements that were made concerning the validity of foreign coins in Greek cities. The terminology of coinage, which is so highly developed and various with reference to plating and counterfeiting, lacks an equivalent vocabulary to signify coins of substandard weight and the attempts by the unscrupulous to exploit them.[11] Either coins were often conceded a fiduciary value as token money or foreign coins circulated abroad as mere bullion, a possibility that neither the hoard evidence nor common sense recommends.[12] Through what is likely to have been a combination of official arrangements and private initiatives that used means such as countermarks, it is probable that foreign coins were either changed into local money to be spent (with the coins themselves recirculated to areas where they had legal value) or utilized directly with a value established by market forces. The participants in individual deals doubtless haggled over prices with an eye toward the quality and identity of the monetary medium to be used

[11] Note Pollux 3.86 with the commentary in M. Caccamo Caltabiano and P. Radici Colace, "ΑΡΓΥΡΙΟΝ ΔΟΚΙΜΟΝ ... ΤΟ Δ' ΕΝΑΝΤΙΟΝ ΠΑΡΑΣΗΜΟΝ (POLLUX, 3, 86)," *ASNP*[3] 13 (1983) 421–47, esp. 447; Cf. Caccamo Caltabiano and Radici Colace, "ΑΡΓΥΡΙΟΝ ΕΥΔΟΚΙΜΟΝ (Pollux, 3,87)," *ASNP*[3] 15 (1985) 81–101, esp. 81.

[12] The predominance of the semantics of counting over those of weighing also urges this conclusion. See O. Picard, "Sur deux termes des inscriptions de la trésorerie d'Aï Khanoum," in H. Walter (ed.), *Hommages à Lucien Lerat* (Paris 1984) 679–90, esp. 680–82.

(cf. Diphilus fr. 66 K = fr. 67, *PCG* 5.92),[13] but the government may have customarily been an "arm's length" monitor in many transactions.[14]

A passage in Plato's *Laws* (742A–B) illustrates the underlying economic (n.b.) situation in which some currencies acquired a significance that transcended the borders of their *polis* of origin. Plato envisages the arrangements to be made by a *polis* using an idiosyncratic, token money at home. That practice is, of course, a technique for controlling social differentiation by circumscribing individual initiatives that result in upward or downward mobility, including claims to higher status. Sparta's rejection of gold and silver coinage in favor of its cumbersome money of iron bars lies in the background of Plato's thinking on the subject.[15] The *polis* of the *Laws* must, however, conform to general Greek usage when its citizens travel abroad. Consequently, Plato enjoins the usage of ἑλληνικὸν νόμισμα 'Greek money,' by which he presumably means one of the currencies commonly recognized by the citizens of many cities.

As we can see from Plato's treatment of money in the *Laws*, no amount of local legislation could entirely nullify the need to conform to the employment of coinages of international validity. And the theoretical statesmen of the *Laws* deployed more efficacious methods of achieving compliance than any actual fifth-century politician can be imagined to have had at his disposal. It is the existence of "Greek" or panhellenic monies that permitted cities that ceased minting to eschew coining their own money, while maintaining a monetary economy. Plato writes within an economic context wherein it is likely that Attic coinage played a significant role in many local economies. This passage supplements the material presented above about the validity of Aiginetan and Aiginetic-standard money beyond the borders of Aigina (see above, pp. 36–38, 125–27, 255–56). We have already seen how Aiginetan and Aiginetic coins circulated with a recognized usage that transcended their value as bullion.

On any interpretation of the Coinage Decree, one would concede that it shows the Athenians implementing measures in support of

[13] If the *kolakretai* levied a fee themselves on the *agio* charged by money changers when they exchanged coins, as a scholion to Aristophanes suggests (ΣArist. *Wasps* 788b; cf. 787a–c), it was to the advantage of a casual or small-scale purchaser attempting to use foreign coins to reach an accommodation with the other party to a transaction.

[14] Even when the Olbians are careful to restrict the rate at which the Cyzicene is to be exchanged (*SIG*[3] 218.23–26: τὸ δὲ χρυσίον πωλεῖν καὶ ὠνεῖσθ[αι τ]|ὸν μὲν στατῆρα τὸν Κυζικηνὸν [ἐνδεκ]|ά (or δωδεκ]|ά) ἡμιστατήρο, καὶ μήτε ἀξιώτερο[ν | μή]τε τιμιώτερον . . .), they allowed unconstrained agreements about other coinages (lines 26–29: τὸ δ' ἄλλο χρυσίον τὸ [ἐ|πίσ]ημον ἅπαν καὶ ἀργύριον τὸ ἐπίση[μον | πωλεῖν καὶ ὠνεῖσθαι, ὡς ἂν ἀλλήλους πείθωσι . . .).

[15] Note Figueira, *Aegina* 76–79.

monetary and metrological consolidation. In the traditional interpretation of the document, the decree preempts or excludes the necessity for the other means of consolidation, because it enacts the monopoly of Attic money, *metra*, and *stathma* by a single act. Nonetheless, even in the more modest law, reconstructed above, the Athenians were acting to ensure that those allies still striking silver coins treated Athenian money as legal tender in their own jurisdictions.

Unlike the traditional interpretation in which a prohibition on minting could have its impact measured (at least, in the abstract) by the number of states still coining, exhausting the ramifications of the decree in the revisionist interpretation does not only depend on ascertaining the roster of states still minting (at different times during the lifetime of the Delian League) that might have had to yield acceptance to Athenian money. It should also depend on specifying the cities that were not already accepting Attic coins as valid tender for the payment of taxes at the time of the promulgation of the decree. Unfortunately, a determination of that matter is thoroughly impractical. Therefore, in light of the reconstruction that is explored above, it is impossible to establish the magnitude of the consequences of the stipulation that is illustrated in the addition to the oath of the Attic *Boulē* that forbade (with uncertain sanctions) an acquiescence in allied intransigence toward Attic coin and standards. Indeed the law may only *promote* through religious scruple a provision that may already have existed before the Coinage Decree, perhaps in the decree of Klearkhos. It is thus possible that the emphasis in the inscribed law lay not only on the imposition of terms on allied minting but on the provisions for the conversion or exchange of a large consignment of monies from the allies in order to facilitate future payments of tribute in Attic money.

It is possible to take a more direct approach to the issue of the movement toward monetary consolidation when it was a matter of official arrangement between states. The reference to Athenian monetary legislation in the *Birds* of Aristophanes has been interpreted above to offer testimony on one mode of Attic intervention in allied monetary affairs. The Athenians were conjectured to have addressed issues of the usage of monetary and metrological standards when new states were incorporated into their alliance. The historical paradigm lying behind the humor of Aristophanes is one in which the Athenians established a pattern of metrological practices for the new ally on the model provided by their agreement with another, presumably favored, allied state. The passage in the *Birds* can also be understood to some extent as the Athenians imposing thereby the validity of their own weights and measures on Cloudcuckooland. That interpretation might give a more imperialistic resonance to Attic monetary and metrological policy, but it does not much affect our conclusion here: the Athenians probably organized the monetary and metrological affairs of a new ally pursuant to their induction into the alliance, just as they believed themselves authorized to assess a new ally and make military arrangements for a common defense.

We have a later example of the sort of clause in which one *polis* agreed to use the coinage of another hegemonic city-state. It occurs in a treaty of alliance and *sympoliteia* between Smyrna and the *katoikoi*, who controlled Magnesia at Sipylos (*OGIS* 229 = *SVA*[2] 3.492).[16] The historical context is the so-called "War of the Brothers" between Seleukos II and Antiochos Hierax or its aftermath in which Smyrna supported the cause of Seleukos (246–41). Right after the involved clauses that implement the registration and incorporation of those in Magnesia that are to receive Smyrnaian citizenship (lines 45–53), the treaty introduces the legal standing of the Magnesians: the newly enrolled Magnesians are to use the laws of the Smyrnaians regarding *synallagmata* 'contracts' and *enklēmata* 'accusations' that involve Smyrnaians (lines 54–55). There next appears the clause involving money: δέχεσθωσαν δὲ καὶ ἐμ Μαγνησίαι τὸ νόμισμα τὸ τῆς πόλεως [ἔνν]ομον 'and let them also accept in Magnesia the authorized money of the city' (line 55).[17] Inasmuch as Magnesia had no coins in this period, the agreement was establishing that the Magnesians recognize the coins of Smyrna as legal tender.[18]

Where they already existed (or where administrative latitude was allowed for their negotiation), *symbolai* between allied cities or between an ally and Athens may have addressed issues about the exchange of currencies, about the standing in the marketplace of different systems of weights and measures, and about the acceptability of any respective coinages. If the restoration of a reference to *symbolai* in the Coinage Decree is correct, that would be important confirmation that monetary and metrological practices were addressed in *symbolai* just like other concerns involving commerce, taxation, and the adjudication of disputes between persons conducting private affairs. There would then be a context for an evolution of monetary and metrological relations within the ambit of negotiating and revising *symbolai*. Such diplomacy might travel on a parallel track to Athenian enactments regarding coins, *metra*, and *stathma*. Relations of the Athenians with autonomous states were particularly

16 See T. Ihnken, *Die Inschriften von Magnesia am Sipylos* (Bonn 1978) #1, esp. 23–42 for text, context, and dating.

17 See Ihnken, *Inschriften von Magnesia* 80–81.

18 For the mint of Smyrna, Head[2] 592.

deferential even in the full-fledged *arkhē* toward earlier *symbolai* that were the product of less constrained negotiation.

Furthermore, there may well have been agreements of a more exclusively monetary character between those states that continued to mint in the second half of the fifth century that ordained the manner in which their currencies were to be treated on each others' territory. These agreements supplemented Attic mandates and *symbolai* to which Athens was a party. We are not much better off on this topic than on the matter of Attic *symbolai*, but we do have one important document in the inscribed evidence. This is a monetary compact between Phokaia and Mytilene in the form of an inscription in the Aeolic dialect that constitutes the Mytilenean copy of the pact (Tod, *GHI* #112 = *IG* XII.2 1+).[19]

After an initial clause that seems to have provided for amendment on mutual agreement of the two states, the surviving portions of the law dealt with the supervision of the person, presumably a public slave, who was charged with mixing the electrum to be used in the issuance of coins by either of the signatories. Depending on his performance of his duties either in Mytilene or in Phokaia, he was to be tried by a special tribunal in which the magistrates of the city of his official actions provided the majority of the jurors. Deliberate dilution of the mixture was a capital offense, while inadvertent adulteration received punishment at the discretion of the court. The city where the crime occurred was to be held blameless. This alternation of judicial venue for the minting and the final statement of the inscription telling us that Mytilene won the allotment to go first indicates that minting was to alternate between the two cities. The minting practices implied by the agreement are consonant with the reconstruction of the means for achieving the proportions of metal in Phocaic *hectae* and with their possession of a token value that were investigated in Chapter 3 above.

That cooperation would have gone along with an equivalency of Phocaic-weight *hectae* for both Mytileneans and Phokaians. This same conclusion about the interchangeability of Mytilenean and Phokaian

[19] See C.T. Newton, "On a Greek Inscription at Mytilene, Relating to the Coinage of that City and Phocaea," *Trans. of the Royal Soc. of Lit.* [2] 8 (1866) 548–58; W. Clemm, "Zum Münzvertrag zwischen Mytilene und Phokaia," *RhM* 33 (1878) 608–10; C.D. Buck, *The Greek Dialects* [2] (Chicago 1955) #25, pp. 213–14; Tod, *GHI* 2.34–36; J.D. Kontis, *AA* (1940) 288; J.F. Healy, "Notes on the Monetary Union Between Mytilene and Phokaia," *JHS* 77 (1957) 267–68; *SVA* [2] #228, 2.174–76; R. Hodot, "Notes critiques sur le corpus epigraphique de Lesbos," *Études d'archéologie classique* 5 (1976) 17–81, esp. 19–20; L. Burelli, "L'accordo monetale tra Focea e Mitilene (I.G., XII, 2, 1)," *NAC* 7 (1978) 43–51; F. Bodenstedt, *Die Elektronmünzen von Phokaia und Mytilene* (Tübingen 1981) 29–31; A.J. Heisserer, "IG XII, 2, 1 (The Monetary Pact between Mytilene and Phokaia)," *ZPE* 55 (1984) 115–32.

hectae can also be reached from a consideration of the references in Attic epigraphy and in classical literary testimonia to the *hectae*, where they are specified as "Phocaic" apparently without regard to whether struck on Lesbos or at Phokaia. Moreover, there is little doubt of the equivalency of these *hectae* a little later in the fourth century. The historian Callisthenes relates the story that the lyric poet Persinos spoke of getting a better exchange rate for his Phocaic *hectae* at Mytilene than at Atarneus (Callisthenes *FGH* 124 F 4 *apud* Poll. 9.93). That was perhaps because Phocaic weight *hectae* had a fixed relation to silver both at Mytilene and at Phokaia.[20] Their lower value at Atarneus and in neighboring cities may have been reached by monetary market forces.

The inscription is usually dated to the early fourth century by virtue of its letter forms.[21] Yet there are indications that such cooperation, whether or not in this precise fashion of alternating years in minting, preceded the date of the inscribed agreement. In the first place, there is the already mentioned lack of differentiation in our sources between *hectae* from Mytilene and Phokaia. Second, Bodenstedt has identified several "master-hands" responsible for cutting fifth-century dies who worked for both the Mytileneans and the Phokaians.[22] The earliest of those he has identified is placed 509–491. Finally, it has been argued that the agreement that was inscribed in the early fourth century was a revival of an earlier fifth-century compact.[23] On the basis of his review of the letter forms, A. Heisserer went so far as to take the position that the inscription itself could date ca. 440–10.[24]

We glimpse in this inscription that the monetary relations between Mytilene and Phokaia were themselves complex, having their own diplomatic history. This exceptional discovery might hint at a wealth of evidence concerning reciprocal arrangements made by Attic allies that have not survived. In addition, there may have been another monetary pact that involved Phokaia. J.M. Balcer has argued that the Phokaians and the Teians cooperated in coining after their revolt from Athens in 411,

[20] Note Clemm *RhM* (1878) 609, who dates the episode ca. 360.

[21] W. Wroth, *Catalogue of the Greek Coins of Troas, Aeolis, and Lesbos* (London 1894) lxv: ca. 400; W. Paton, *IG* XII.2, pp. 1–2: not much before 350; Head[2] lxxxiii: ca. 400; *SVA*[2] #228, 2.174–76: pre-394; Bodenstedt, *Elektronmünzen* 30: ca. 394.

[22] Bodenstedt, *Elektronmünzen* 38–45.

[23] See Bodenstedt, *Elektronmünzen* 30, who dates the original pact as early as ca. 521, with strengthened sanctions ca. 478. Note also his *Elektron-Geld* 48, 87; cf. Heisserer *ZPE* (1984) 124–27. See also Healy *JHS* (1957) 268; cf. Burelli *NAC* (1978) 46.

[24] See Heisserer *ZPE* (1984) 119–22, where he prefers a dating right after the Mytilenean revolt in ca. 426.

adducing the Aiginetic staters that bear the inscription THION along with the small swimming seal badge of the Phokaians.[25]

Nonetheless, there are objections to treating the agreement between Mytilene and Phokaia as paradigmatic. It is uncertain whether the arrangement (or hypothetically two arrangements) entered on by the Phokaians is indicative of a rich lost diplomacy that organized the acceptance of foreign monies in Greek *poleis*. It is possible that the peculiar situation of Phokaia made its efforts at numismatic diplomacy exceptional. The Phokaians were a great commercial power of the sixth century that in the fifth century possessed an economy at the lower middle ranks among the allies. They specialized during the life of Attic hegemony in minting "noncivic" electrum money and produced no silver coinage.

CORINTH AND MONETARY HEGEMONY

The *polis* of Corinth stands in provocative juxtaposition to Athens as a hegemonic power during the fifth century whose leadership subsumed a monetary policy.[26] Inheriting a legacy of early archaic colonization conducted by the city's Bacchiad aristocracy that encompassed such notable foundations as Syracuse and Corcyra, the archaic Corinthian tyrants and especially Periander had endeavored to create a network of satellite colonies mediated through the persons of members of their Cypselid family. Taking this accomplishment as a precedent, the fifth-century Corinthians exerted hegemony over a number of these former colonies. These efforts flourished mainly in northwest Greece, far from the regular haunts of Athenian naval forces and away from concentrations of Attic allies, although the exception of Poteidaia (on the Pallene peninsula of the Chalcidice) may be noted where the institution of receiving Corinthian officials (*epidamiourgoi*) continued even during that city's period of alliance with Athens (Thuc. 1.56.2). Corinthian expansion in the Ionian Sea led to the Epidamnos dispute with Corcyra into which Athens itself was drawn with such important ramifications for the movement of the Peloponnesians toward war (Thuc. 1.24–55).

Numismatic evidence allows us to glimpse some of the details of Corinthian administrative policy toward allied states. In our exploration of the hoard evidence, the predominance of Corinthian coins and other coins minted on the same standard was noted for the territory of Corinth

[25] J.M. Balcer, "Phokaia and Teos: a Monetary Alliance," *SNR* 49 (1970) 25–34; cf. Burelli *NAC* (1978) 50. I shall pass over Balcer's intriguing (but rather speculative) suggestions about a fixed exchange between Teian silver staters and Phokaic *hectae* (p. 31).

[26] In general, see Kraay, *ACGC* 78–88.

and its dependencies during the fifth century (see above, pp. 35–36). Notably, Corinthian satellites went beyond Attic practice, not only minting on the Corinthian standard but using the same design of the obverse (Pegasus) and the reverse (a head of Athena). The *koppa* (an equivalent of *kappa*) appears between the legs of Pegasus for Corinth, while other initials are used for various allied cities. For the fifth century, such variants are attested for Ambrakia (A), Anaktorion (F), Epidamnos (E), Leukas (Λ), and Poteidaia (Π).[27] This pattern begins about 490 at Leukas, where an earliest phase is followed by an issue used to support participation in the struggle against Xerxes in the late 480s. The corresponding Ambrakiot emission (an isolated striking) exhibited the sharing of reverses by Ambrakiot and Corinthian obverses, and thus was probably struck at Corinth.[28]

Leukas like Corinth appears to have continued regular emissions during the Pentekontaeteia. Resumed coining at Ambrakia is associated with the crisis of the 430s, starting from the sending of troops to Epidamnos by Corinth, Ambrakia, and Leukas in early 435 (Thuc. 1.26.1).[29] Stylistic links beween Ambrakiot coins and those of Corinth and Leukas suggest a simultaneous intensification at these two mints also. Implicated here (to some degree) is the large buildup for the expeditionary force that eventually met the Corcyreans at the Sybota islands. Its preparations saw a tripling of the ships deployed by Corinth and Ambrakia (Thuc. 1.46.1). A small issue with a *digamma* associated with Anaktorion may also be noted for this same context.

Kraay originally assigned the issue marked with an *epsilon* to Epidamnos and to the same military and political context, but later had qualms over the production of these coins as early as 435.[30] Jonathan Kagan will soon argue most persuasively for a return of this issue to Epidamnos, while adducing a slightly earlier looking coin once in the

[27] Kraay, *ACGC* 84–85, 123–30; R. Calciati, *Pegasi* (Mortara 1990) 2.355–57, 383–98, 433–52, 477–81, 564–67.

[28] C.M. Kraay, "The Earliest Issue of Ambracia," *NAC* 6 (1977) 35–52; cf. O. Ravel, *The "Colts" of Ambracia* (New York 1928), *NNM* 37, 22–58, 86–97. The suggestion that this was a coining of booty is far less likely than the supposition that this emission was intended to subsidize the defensive effort, possibly through disbursements to sailors who were needed to man ships supplied to these allies by Corinth (Hdt. 8.45; 9.28.5 for Leukas and Ambrakia).

[29] C.M. Kraay, "The Coinage of Ambracia and the Preliminaries of the Peloponnesian War," *NAC* 8 (1979) 37–59; *Id.*, *Nickle Numismatic Papers* 9. Cf. Ravel, *Colts* 87–112. Corinth, Leukas, and Ambrakia had also been the three largest contributors to the earlier Corinthian fleet defeated by the Corcyreans at Leukimne (Thuc. 1.27.1–2).

[30] Compare *ACGC* 84 with *NAC* (1979) 57–58. His other possibilities were Ephyre or Elea (Elaos) in Thesprotia in Epiros (cf. Thuc. 1.46.3–4).

collection of the Marquis de la Goy.[31] At least, one of the obverse dies associated with this series had its *epsilon* altered to a *koppa* for Corinth (the British Museum specimen). Kagan draws the necessary conclusions: the dies never left Corinth and any minting after 435 is to be connected with the outlays for the Corinthian colony that reinforced Epidamnos (Thuc. 1.27.1).

Kraay associated the *pi* issue with Poteidaia, wavering between 432, when Corinthian forces intervened to support rebellion there (Thuc. 1.60.1–3), or 433, as a Poteidaian contribution to the costs of the force that fought the Corcyraeans at Sybota.[32] If the Poteidaians had wished to make a contribution to the Corinthians they would hardly have needed or waited to strike a new issue to do so; local money or Attic coins, in which their tax receipts and tribute were presumably paid, would have been appropriate. A special issue was a needless provocation at a time when the Poteidaians made initial efforts to allay Attic fears (Thuc. 1.58.1), and even paid their *phoros* in spring 432 (*IG* I^3 279.II.70). The most likely explanation is that the Corinthians minted these coins and sent them out with Aristeas to defray the expenses of his 2,000 "volunteers" (Thuc. 1.60.2–3), although stylistic affinities complicate this supposition.[33]

Any reconstruction of the political context for these minting patterns is perforce speculative. The establishment of the venue for the period II Ambrakiot emission and the Epidamnian issue of the 430s at Corinth itself should be given considerable emphasis. In contrast, the mint at Leukas was independent of the metropolitan mint during the Pentekontaeteia, although its output was much more modest. As has been observed elsewhere in this volume, spikes in the production of coins are to be associated with increased governmental expenditure. For the Corinthian sphere of influence in the 430s, these outlays were obviously military. The expenses for the expeditionary forces mounted by the Corinthians

[31] J.H. Kagan, "Epidamnos or Ephyre (Elea): A Note on the Coinage of Corinth and her Colonies at the Outbreak of the Peloponnesian War," forthcoming in the memorial volume honoring M.J. Price (I thank the author for allowing me to consult this important contribution). A corresponding change would move the period II, group A coins of Ambrakia to 440–36 and tentatively associate them with the Attic expedition under Phormio to Akarnania (Thuc. 2.68.7–8). The weight of the historical arguments falls heavier in favor of a date before the Thirty Years Peace for this campaign. See *HCT* 2.416; J.B. Salmon, *Wealthy Corinth* (Oxford 1984) 422–23; cf. *HCT* 1.198–99, 2.202; Meiggs 204; S. Hornblower, *A Commentary on Thucydides* (Oxford 1991) 1.353–54.

[32] Kraay, *ACGC* 84–85; *NAC* (1979) 58.

[33] Kagan in "Epidamnus . . ." brings out the ramifications of an earlier date (perhaps as early as 435) for Athenian policy toward Poteidaia.

during these years were twofold in nature, capital outlays for ships and other equipment, and pay for personnel with consumable supplies. In any case, expenses of the former category were almost all incurred at Corinth (or in Peloponnesian dockyards), inasmuch as Leukas or Ambrakia hardly had the commercial infrastructure for naval building programs.

The Corcyreans make considerable point to the Athenians of the Corinthian hiring of military personnel from the *arkhē* and the rest of Greece (Thuc. 1.35.3–4). The Corinthians, therefore, needed additional ships' crews to man their many new triremes. One suspects, however, that allied personnel from the *arkhē* probably sought payment in tetradrachms. Coins minted in Corinth but bearing the initial letters of dependencies were probably reserved for paying the citizens of the Corinthian satellites who manned the ships provided to their states by the Corinthian government. In contrast, the permanent military establishment of the Athenians and their allies had mastered these administrative techniques early in the Pentekontaeteia. What was for the Corinthians an extraordinary mobilization was for the Athenians the regular business of hegemonic power projection.

When the opportunity of intervening at Epidamnos appeared after no great warning in 435, the Corinthians, Leukadians, and Ambrakiots probably minted the coins associated with Kraay's Ambrakiot period II, group A—the die-linked Ambrakiot component being so striking as a revival of that city's coining. These coins probably were used to pay for the garrison sent to Epidamnos (Thuc. 1.26.1–3). The intensive coining associated with Ambrakiot period II, groups B and C were the issues connected with the mobilization for Leukimne (1.29–30) and the beginning of the buildup for Sybota. Provision was made early in this sequence for subsidizing any help that would come from Anaktorion, which turned out to be a single disappointing trireme at Sybota, although troops from Anaktorion may well have earlier marched with the land force meant to relieve Epidamnos (Thuc. 1.46.1; 1.55.1). Note the Corinthian seizure and colonization of Anaktorion in the aftermath of the battle of Sybota. The first Epidamnos coins subsidized colonists serving as infantry in that same land force that marched in conjunction with the Corinthian and allied fleet toward the beleaguered city. As the general program of Corinthian coining advanced, coins were accumulated for the pay chests of the allied force that sailed to Sybota, which included 150 ships and at least 30,000 naval personnel. It is even possible that the later Epidamnos coins (that Kraay and Kagan link with Ambrakiot period II, group D) may follow Sybota, if the Corinthians kept intact the colonists for Epidamnos. Some of them may have helped colonize and hold Anaktorion.

Athenian allies after mid-century contributed their *phoros* and served as paid personnel in the Athenian fleet. The few exceptions were the large autonomous cities, commercial states that were capable of furnishing their own squadrons. Corinthian allies were much smaller states whose contribution was manpower in the form of ships crews and companies of hoplites. The resources to underwrite their operations, even on campaigns over moderate distances, may often have come from Corinth itself, just like the ships to be manned by Leukas (probably) and by Ambrakia (almost certainly). The form of such payments was a uniform coinage much of which was probably struck in Corinth despite its variant ethnic markers. This pattern appears almost the converse of the Athenian monetary situation: the majority of the Athenian allies supplied money for use by Attic forces. While the Leukadians and Ambrakiots satisfied an important criterion of autonomy by their military service, their expression of individuality through coinage was much less marked than many of the tributary allies of the Athenians. It is likely that these satellites used Corinthian money (along with their own) in their home economies, but the exclusivity of that usage is now unknowable.

Corinth provides an alternative model for a fifth-century hegemonistic state that chose to exploit the symbolic possibilities of coins as a means for an expression of its ideology of leadership. This exercise occurred in an administrative environment that was much less problematical, for it lacked large-scale, regular transfers of resources through *phoros* and the recirculation of military pay. And the Corinthians need not have worried over commercial relations with large economies of equal complexity, unlike the Athenians, who were faced with the needs of the Chians, Samians, and Aiginetans.

ENDNOTE: FIFTH-CENTURY INFLATION

The working hypothesis should be that the massive issues of Athenian coins during the fifth century led to an increased supply of silver money in the *arkhē* and in Attica, even after coins removed from circulation and those passing overseas are taken into account. It is also unlikely that increases in output, whether calculated globally or per capita, rose proportionately to the rise in the money supply. These conditions ought to have led to price inflation. Comparative prices have not survived in adequate number to allow an estimation of the rate of fifth-century inflation or even (frustratingly) to prove conclusively that inflation existed.

Some data are, however, available on the price of grain, for which observe the following ratios of nutritive value: 1 *medimnos* (*med.*) of barley = 0.65 *med.* of wheat; 1 *med.* of *alphita* 'barley groats' = 0.72–0.82 *med.* of wheat. See Figueira, "Mess Contributions and Subsistence at Sparta," *TAPA* 114 (1984) 87–109, esp. 92–93. One must start with controversy, as it is uncertain whether we can find a base figure for the cost of grain in Plut. *Solon* 23.3, which seems to state the amounts of monetary income needed for eligibility to the Solonian census classes as equivalences to the original levels of income in *medimnoi* of grain. So the figure of 1 dr. for a *medimnos* of grain (more probably barley?) could be taken (unfortunately, only with emendation) to provide an early fifth-century price for grain. See Figueira, *Colonization* 177.

Later in the century, Aristophanes (*Wasps* 300–302 with scholia, produced in 422) might imply a price for *alphita* of ca. 2 dr., 4 ob. per *med.* (not 1 dr., 2 ob., as Heichelheim suggested). In Plut. *Mor.* 470F, Socrates observes that *alphita* is inexpensive at 2 dr. per *med.* Thus, the price of 2 dr. may be a favorable one. During the stay in Athens of Diogenes the Cynic, *alphita* could still be valued at 2 dr. per *med.* In contrast, note [Aris.] *Oec.* 1347a32–34 (possibly dating from the Ionian War and specifically from 410/9); it has *alphita* at 4 dr. per *med.* at Lampsakos before the arrival of a large fleet. At an uncertain date ca. 400–350, *alphita* was valued at Athens at 4 dr. (*IG* II^2 1358.II.45, 50).

Wheat was not only more nutritious than barley or *alphita* for an equivalent volume and weight but was much preferred by consumers. On the "Attic Stelae," the accounts of the *pōletai* of sales of confiscated property, *phormoi* 'man-loads' of wheat (~ *medimnoi* in size) are sold for 6 dr., 3 ob.; 6 dr.; 6 dr., 1 ob. (*IG* I^3 421.137–39). *IG* II^2 1356.2, 21 presents a price for wheat of 6 dr. at the beginning of the fourth century. In Aristoph. *Ecclesiazousae* 547–48 (of 393) wheat has a cost of 3 dr. per *med.*, but that might be a humorously good price. In the early 380s, the price of wheat per *medimnos* could vary over a 1 dr. during a day, a situation that probably implies price levels of at least ca. 6 dr. (Lys. 22.12). The equivalences for the Solonian census classes reported by Pollux (8.129–30) might reflect the course of fifth-century inflation: Pentekosiomedimnoi: 500 measures, with 1T financial responsibility; Hippeis: 300 measures, with 3,000 dr.; Zeugitai: 200 measures, with 1,000 dr.

On grain prices, see L. Spaventa (de Novellis), *I prezzi in Grecia e a Roma nell' antichità* (Rome 1934) 49–55; F. Heichelheim, "Sitos," *RE* Suppl. 6.819–92, esp. cols. 887–90; W.K. Pritchett, "The Attic Stelai, Part II," *Hesperia* 25 (1956) 178–328, esp. 196–98; also A. Jacob, "Preis (I): Preisgeschichte," *Handwörterbuch der Sozialwissenschaften* 8 (Tübingen/Göttingen 1964) 459–76, esp. 462–65. As for other prices, only a few words can be ventured. The price of gold measured in silver is possibly consistent with general price inflation before the Peloponnesian War, but gold lost value relative to silver after 431. See pp. 511–17 below.

Ideally, one would hope for a series of testimonia on private sector wages to balance the aforesaid prices of grain. Military pay and allowances and pay for political activity seem to have risen during the second half of the fifth century.

Jury pay rose from 2 to 3 dr. in ca. 425 (Arist. *Wasps* 682–85; Σ*Wasps* 88a, 300b–c; *Ath. Pol.* 62.2). A pay of 4 obols per day was allotted for the *epistatai* of the Eleusinian cult (*IG* I^3 32.38–39) and for Attic personnel at Miletos during the Athenian intervention there (*IG* I^3 21.13). In the "Springhouse Decree" an administrator was, however, receiving 1 drachm daily (*IG* I^3 49.4). *IG* I^3 21 and 32 have a consensus date around mid-century, and *IG* I^3 49 is dated 440–32. It must be conceded, however, that the controversy concerning the chronology of these inscriptions makes problematic the hypothesis that a general rise in salaries is attested here. There is also the problem that we may be comparing unlike responsibilities. See U. Kahrstedt, *Untersuchungen zur Magistratur in Athen: Studien zum öffentlichen Recht Athens* Teil II (Stuttgart 1936) 181–83; M.M. Markle, "Jury Pay and Assembly Pay at Athens," in P.A. Cartledge and F.D. Harvey (eds.), *Crux: Essays Presented to G.E.M. de Ste. Croix on His 75th Birthday* (London 1985) 265–97, esp. 293–97; W.T. Loomis, *Wages, Welfare Costs and Inflation in Classical Athens* (University of Michigan Press [Ann Arbor] forthcoming), esp. chapter 15.

As for military stipends, we must note that any upward trend is obscured by lower wages under the constraining circumstances during the Ionian War. The best wage for sailors and hoplites at the beginning of the Peloponnesian War was 1 drachm daily. For earlier allowances, note the telltale figure of 2 ob. a day mentioned by the aged Philokleon about an earlier expedition to Paros (ca. 454–46?) in *Wasps* 1188–89. See W.K. Pritchett, *The Greek State at War* 1 (Berkeley and Los Angeles 1971) 14–24. Increases in political stipends may have as their background a general rise in prices. Since political and military forces condition such prices, however, it would be imprudent to treat them as proportionate to the rise in the cost of living.

On late fifth-century inflation, see also H.-D. Zimmermann, "Freie Arbeit, Preise und Löhne," in E.C. Welskopf (ed.), *Hellenische Poleis* 1 (1974) 92–107; L. Gallo, "Salari e inflazione: Atene tra V e IV sec. a.C.," *ASNP*[3] 17 (1987) 19–63; M. Bar, "Le pouvoir d'achat de la monnaie à Athènes à la fin du Ve et au début du IVe siècle avant notre ère," *CENB* 5 (1968) 43–53; *CENB* 6 (1969) 1–2. The literature on price cycles is enormous. Worth considering for a start is the vivid and well-documented recent work of D.H. Fischer, *The Great Wave: Price Revolutions and the Rhythm of History* (Oxford 1996). For a statement of the quantity theory of money, see M. Friedman, "The Supply of Money and Changes in Prices and Output," in K.R. Leube (ed.), *The Essence of Friedman* (Stanford 1987) 304–21.

19

HEGEMONY AND MONETARY DISINTEGRATION: THE HOME FRONT

THE MONETARY CONSOLIDATION achieved by the Athenians and their allies during the Pentekontaeteia was put under great stress by the Peloponnesian War. The high level of production of the silver mines at Laureion had led to massive issues of Attic coins. A larger Aegean economy was thus provided with a larger money supply within which Attic coins probably played a greater role than previously. Athenian money also flowed out of the *arkhē* and, indeed, out of the Greek world into Egypt and the Near East. These coins not only paid for imports from abroad but helped to monetize non-Greek economies (however imperfectly). The high quality of Athenian coins was zealously guarded—their silver was as pure as prevailing technology could achieve.

An explanation of the breakdown of the hegemonic monetary system will offer us insights of two types. Clearly, we can perceive therefrom elements of the monetary situation of the period following the Athenian hegemony during the fourth century. Yet more important for our purposes in this work is that the decay of the hegemonic order in the Ionian or Decelean War allows us to appreciate some of the characteristics of fifth-century monetary policy that are not visible to us until they became problematized by crisis. There are two major spheres of monetary affairs into which our investigation may be organized: internal Athenian consequences and the reactions of the users of Attic money abroad. The former will be examined in this chapter and the latter is reserved for Chapter 20.

In the period of the Peloponnesian War, during which Athens fell under increasing financial pressure, the Athenians reacted to changed monetary conditions by diverging from their previous exclusive dependence on high-purity silver coinage. Let us start by considering the earlier divergence, one into the minting of bronze coins, before examining gold coinage later in the chapter.

BRONZE MONEY DURING THE PELOPONNESIAN WAR

Bronze money made its first appearance among the western Greeks around 450, with Akragas and Himera likely to have been the first mints to issue bronze fractions.[1] At Athens, the context for the introduction of bronze money during the Peloponnesian War and the nature of the issues themselves are vexed questions.

The first sign of the use of currency in base metals by the Athenians was during the late 420s, when references began to appear to the *kollybos*.[2] Along with its multiples, the *dikollybon* and *trikollybon*, the *kollybos* appears not only from context but from lexical material to be a coin of little value.[3] Theophrastus gives us the seemingly numismatic sequence *krithē* 'coin (or amount) like a barley grain,' *kollybos*, *tetartēmorion* 'quarter-obol,' and *hēmiōbolos* 'half-obol' (*De lapibus* 46). Even if this listing is merely a series of weights, it establishes the *kollybos* as a natural subdivision of the obol.[4] The numismatic meaning for *kollybos* is related to its fiscal connotation in the sense of *agio*, which is money levied by the exchanger in a conversion of currencies, because the *agio* in many such transactions was worth only a small fractional coin.[5]

It is tempting to connect the earliest references to *kollyboi* to the tradition about Dionysios ὁ Χαλκοῦς 'the Copper' or 'the Brazen.' He

[1] I have depended greatly on the surveys of M.J. Price, "Early Greek Bronze Coinage," in C.M. Kraay and G.K. Jenkins (eds.), *Essays in Greek Coinage Presented to Stanley Robinson* (Oxford 1968) 90–104; Price, "The Function of Early Greek Bronze Coinage," *AIIN* Suppl. 25 (1979) 351–65. On the dating of early Sicilian bronze issues, see also C. Boehringer, "Bemerkungen zur Sizilischen Bronzeprägung im 5. Jahrhundert v. Chr.," *SM* 28 (1978) 49–65.

[2] Arist. *Peace* 1198–1202 (421) with scholia (1200); fr. 3 K = fr. 3, *PCG* 3.2.36; from the *Aiolosikon* (Pollux 9.63); Eupolis fr. 233 K = fr. 247, *PCG* 5.438–39 from the *Poleis*; cf. *Com. Adesp.* fr. 1167 K = fr. 811, *PCG* 8.233. The literary and epigraphical evidence for the term κόλλυβος was collected by M.N. Tod, "Epigraphical Notes on Greek Coinage," *NC*[5] 5 (1945) 108–16.

[3] Cf. Hesych. s.v. κολλυβιστής, κ 3348 Latte; τρικόλυβον, τ 1385; Poll. 6.165, 9.72; ΣArist. *Peace* 1200. For other uses of the terms, see Call. *Iamb.* fr. 191 Pf.; Origen *Comm. in evang. Joann.* 10.29.183. A κολλυβιστής is a lender of petty sums; note Hesych. s.v., κ 3348; ἀργυραμοιβοί, α 7058; τραπεζίτης, τ 1255 Latte; Poll. 7.170; *Suda*, s.v. κολυβιστής, κ 1971.

[4] J.H. Kroll, *The Greek Coins*, *The Athenian Agora* 26 (Princeton 1993) 25 with note 8, cites D.E. Eicholz, *Theophrastus: De Lapibus* (Oxford 1963) 119, who sees κόλλυβος as an interpolation from a list of weights. His grounds are not palaeographical, but arise from the impracticality that any touchstone (for that is the subject of the passage) could actually distinguish between a *krithē* and a *kollybos*. Yet we cannot exclude such infeasible claims prima facie, merely on the grounds of modern scientific knowledge.

[5] Note, for example, Pollux 3.84, 7.170; *IG* XII.5 817.4; *SIG*[3] 672.32; Cic. *ad Att.* 12.6; *Verr.* 3.78.181.

was an elegiac poet, who is reported to have urged the adoption of a currency of base metal on the Athenians, hence earning his nickname (Athen. 15.669D).[6] A date in the 420s would suit Dionysios, who is otherwise known to have participated in the foundation of Thourioi in 446/5 (Plut. *Nic.* 5.3; Phot. s.v. θουριομάντεις [as emended: τῷ χαλκιδεῖ to τῷ χαλκῷ]). He may well have brought the idea of bronze money back from the west, where it had a generation's headstart on the Greek homeland. Yet it is unclear from the references whether Dionysios' suggestions won official (or any wide) acceptance. As shall become clear from the discussion below, Dionysios' proposal may only have put forward the right of merchants to make small change legally with their own tokens.

Accordingly, it is far from assured that the *kollybos* was a bronze coin, since numismatists have not provided us with any likely survival from an early fractional bronze coinage that is marked with any characteristic Athenian design. Nonetheless, one could equate the *kollyboi* with the bronze tokens of various types (numbering at least 600–700 in all) that have been found found in various Attic archaeological settings, starting from the late fifth or the early fourth century, as, for example, J.N. Svoronos and E.S.G. Robinson urged.[7] There is, however, no certain evidence to put the small bronze tokens early enough to account for the literary references and no intrinsic feature of theirs establishes a monetary usage. J. Kroll reminds us that these small bronze tokens have their strongest affinities with the larger lead tokens of allotment, used as devices for allocation in a variety of political procedures.[8] Therefore some prefer to view them as nonmonetary.[9] Thus, some might choose to follow T. Reinach in seeing the *kollybos* as a small silver coin.[10] But Attic examples have not been as yet discovered.

[6] Cf. fr. 1–4 W *apud* Athen. 15.668e–669e; fr. 5 *apud* Athen. 10.443c; fr. 6 *apud* Athen. 15.702b; fr. 7 *apud* Aris. *Rhet.* 1405a32–34, with Athen. 13.602b–c.

[7] See J.N. Svoronos, "ΟΙ ΚΟΛΛΥΒΟΙ," *JIAN* 14 (1912) 123–60; E.S.G. Robinson, "Some Problems in the Later Fifth Century Coinage of Athens," *ANSMN* 9 (1960) 1–15, esp. 6–7. The first systematic treatment was A. Postalakas, "Κερμάτια συμβολικά," *AE* 3 (1884) 1–20. See also T. Reinach, "KOLLYBOS," *RN*[4] 31 (1928) 145–60, esp. 145–52.

[8] See M. Crosby in M. Lang and M. Crosby, *Weights, Measures and Tokens*, *The Athenian Agora* 10 (Princeton 1964) 76–85; J.H. Kroll, "Some Athenian Armor Tokens," *Hesperia* 46 (1977) 141–46. For discussions of the dicasteric *symbola* mentioned in *Ath. Pol.* 65.2, 68.2, see Rhodes, *CAAP* 711–12, 731; most recently A. Boegehold et al., *The Lawcourts at Athens*, *The Athenian Agora* 28 (Princeton 1995), esp. 69–76, 82–90.

[9] Kroll, *Agora* 26, 24, who cites as additional supporters on the nonmonetary character of the tokens, P. Gardner, *A History of Ancient Coinage: 700–300 B.C.* (Oxford 1918) 296–97; Crosby, *Agora* 10, 84 with note 32. An unavoidable degree of numismatic esthetics must be conceded: the discovered "*kollyboi*" seem insufficiently coinlike for some experienced eyes.

[10] See Reinach *RN* (1928) 154–60.

Counterbalancing these arguments is a reference in the *Ecclesiazousae* of Aristophanes (performed in 393 or 392: vv. 815–22). Here an anonymous male character has his mouth filled with bronze coins in the marketplace—when they are demonetized in favor of silver coins—these must then be small fractions, as the parallel passages referring to silver coins held in the mouth show.[11] In addition, the fragment from the *Aiolosikon* (fr. 3 K) also speaks of a diobol kept in the mouth that became a *dikollybon*. There does not seem to be much chance that the silverplated bronze drachms and tetradrachms (discussed below) could account for these references; they were inappropriate for carrying in the mouth.

Robinson tried to obviate this dilemma, in which the numismatic evidence and the literary testimony are in conflict over the date and character of the *kollyboi*, by positing a possible third base metal currency at the end of the fifth century (in addition to the aforesaid noncivic "tokens" and to the plated coins discussed immediately below).[12] Robinson originally suggested a dating during the Peloponnesian War for a series of diobols (marked with two pellets) and obols (marked with one pellet), made distinctive by their spelling of the abbreviation ΑΘΕ with the letters ΑΘΗ and the positioning of the owl of the reverse on a wheat kernel. He would assign the references in the *Ecclesiazousae* and in the *Aiolosikon* of Aristophanes to this issue. Robinson noted that the fragment of the *Aiolosikon* could illustrate an eventuality where a diobol like the coin marked by the two pellets was transformed into a *dikollybon*. He tried to explain that eventuality as a demonetization of a fiduciary bronze diobol so that it was worth only its weight in metal.

The collection of additional evidence, both from the Agora excavations and from elsewhere, has not been kind to this hypothesis. Subsequently, Robinson and M.J. Price independently conceived that a later context was more appropriate for the earliest of these bronze coins. Writing together, they assigned them to the bronze coinage that was struck by the Athenian *stratēgos* Timotheos during his operations in the Chalcidice in 363–59 (n.b. [Aris.] *Oec.* 1350a23–30).[13] This identification

[11] Arist. *Wasps* 609 has a triobol held in the mouth. *Wasps* 787–95 describes Philokleon carrying a drachm in his hand in order to break it into obols; when he attempts to put three obols into his mouth, he finds that they have been switched for fish scales (from a gray mullet). Arist. *Birds* 502–503: an obol accidentally swallowed; fr. 48 K = fr. 48, *PCG* 3.2.55 from the *Anagyros* speaks of a trihemiobol in the mouth. See also Theophr. *Characters* 6.9; Alexis fr. 123 K = fr. 128, *PCG* 2.92.

[12] Robinson, *ANSMN* (1960) 13–15, following H.B. Earle Fox, "Some Athenian Problems," *NC*[4] 5 (1905) 1–9, esp. 1–5.

[13] E.S.G. Robinson and M.J. Price, "An Emergency Coinage of Timotheos," *NC*[7] 7 (1967) 1–6.

was encouraged by the fact that six out of the eleven pieces known to Robinson and Price were found in the excavations at Olynthos.[14] The wheat kernel connoted the use of the coins by soldiers to purchase grain for subsistence. Robinson and Price assigned the examples to two classes, approximating the silver triobol and trihemiobol in appearance. The first category is likely to be the double of the second in any event (one pellet = trihemiobol; two pellets = triobol). The northern Aegean provenience is now less striking, as eight coins have been found in the Agora, one on the Pnyx, and three have been purchased at Thebes (along with some further finds in Macedonia).[15] No one, however, has recently challenged the thesis that these coins belong in a fourth-century context.

Furthermore, Kroll has argued that the coins fit best with the activities of Timotheos, because stylistic features like the modeling of Athena's profile eye and the heavy foliage of the olive sprays point to the fourth century. The lettering is a deliberate departure from tradition in favor of the contemporary Ionic alphabet. Against A. Giovannini's attempt to revive the first hypothesis of Robinson (see below), Kroll raised other objections to the placement of the bronze money with the inscription ΑΘΗ in the fifth century. They have appeared in no dated archaeological context within the Agora excavations that precedes the later 300s. Excavations have, however, revealed other early bronze issues, the first of which has the reverse type of a double-bodied owl whose silver analogues belong around mid-century.[16]

Complicating the issue of fixing the relationship of the *kollyboi*, the bronze noncivic "tokens," and the literary allusions in the *Ecclesiazousae* and elsewhere is the undeniable fact that another, very different coinage utilizing base metal was initiated toward the end of the Peloponnesian War. Our best evidence is from the *Frogs* of Aristophanes.

> πολλάκις γ' ἡμῖν ἔδοξεν ἡ πόλις πεπονθέναι
> ταὐτὸν εἴς τε τῶν πολιτῶν τοὺς καλούς τε κἀγαθοὺς
> εἴς τε τἀρχαῖον νόμισμα καὶ τὸ καινὸν χρυσίον.
> Οὔτε γὰρ τούτοισιν οὖσιν οὐ κεκιβδηλευμένοις,
> ἀλλὰ καλλίστοις ἁπάντων, ὡς δοκεῖ, νομισμάτων
> καὶ μόνοις ὀρθῶς κοπεῖσι καὶ κεκωδωνισμένοις
> ἔν τε τοῖς Ἕλλησι καὶ τοῖς βαρβάροισι πανταχοῦ
> χρώμεθ' οὐδέν, ἀλλὰ τούτοις τοῖς πονηροῖς χαλκίοις

[14] D.M. Robinson and P.A. Clement, *Excavations at Olynthus. Part III. The Coins Found at Olynthus in 1928* (Baltimore 1931) 41 (on #82); Robinson and Clement, *Excavations at Olynthus. Part VI. The Coins Found at Olynthus in 1931* (Baltimore 1933) 46 (on #59–61).

[15] Kroll, *Agora* 26, 25–26, and 39, with #35a–g, #36 for the examples from the Agora.

[16] See Kroll, *Agora* 26, 31–32, 41–42.

χθές τε καὶ πρώην κοπεῖσι τῷ κακίστῳ κόμματι.
Τῶν πολιτῶν θ' οὓς μὲν ἴσμεν εὐγενεῖς καὶ σώφρονας
ἄνδρας ὄντας καὶ δικαίους καὶ καλούς τε κἀγαθοὺς
καὶ τραφέντας ἐν παλαίστραις καὶ χοροῖς καὶ μουσικῇ,
προυσελοῦμεν, τοῖς δὲ χαλκοῖς καὶ ξένοις καὶ πυρρίαις
καὶ πονηροῖς κἀκ πονηρῶν εἰς ἅπαντα χρώμεθα
ὑστάτοις ἀφιγμένοισιν, οἷσιν ἡ πόλις πρὸ τοῦ
οὐδὲ φαρμακοῖσιν εἰκῇ ῥᾳδίως ἐχρήσατ' ἄν.
Ἀλλὰ καὶ νῦν, ὠνόητοι, μεταβαλόντες τοὺς τρόπους
χρῆσθε τοῖς χρηστοῖσιν αὖθις· καὶ κατορθώσασι γὰρ
εὔλογον, κἄν τι σφαλῆτ', ἐξ ἀξίου γοῦν τοῦ ξύλου,
ἤν τι καὶ πάσχητε, πάσχειν τοῖς σοφοῖς δοκήσετε.

We have decided that the city has often suffered
the same thing both regarding the *kaloi k'agathoi* ['elite males']
and regarding the traditional money and the new gold.
For these pieces that were not subjected to fraudulence,
but the most beautiful of all coins—in my view—
and alone struck properly and well jingling
both among the Greeks and the barbarians everywhere,
we do not use, but these wretched *khalkia* ['bronzes'],
the ones struck yesterday and the day before with the worst metal.
Those of our fellow citizens whom we know to be well born and moderate
men and just and *kaloi k'agathoi*
and reared in the palaestras and the choruses and with musical training,
we discard, and the *khalkoi* ['brazen'] and the *xenoi* ['alien'] and red-headed
and wretched born from wretches, most lately parvenus
we use for everything, men whom the city previously
would not have readily used as scapegoats in all likelihood.
But indeed now, dummies, exchanging your practices,
use the *khrēstoi* ['the good and useful'] again. If you are successful
the praise will be yours and if you miscarry you will hang from good wood,
and if you suffer, you will appear to wise men to suffer misfortune.

In the extended metaphor developed in these verses, the use of poorly struck *ponēra khalkia* 'wretched bronzes' that lack the long history and the traditional acceptance of the previous *kallista nomismata* 'most fair coins' is compared with a failure to entrust policy and leadership to members of the traditional, hereditary elite who had received the conventional upper-class education. On the contrary, lower-class individuals of alien extraction and recent naturalization were achieving prominence.

As Robinson observes, the points of comparison are sharpened even more if we suppose both that the silver plating for the base metal drew somewhat on imported silver (with Laureion silver less available) and that the wearing down of their silver envelope imparted a reddish tinge to these coins.[17] Thus they could well be compared to the brazen (χαλκοῖς), foreign (ξένοις), and redheaded (πυρρίαις) parvenu politicians.

Unlike the references to the brazen coins that follow, the minting of a gold currency at the end of the Peloponnesian War raises no problems numismatically. Thus, two new currencies were of recent innovation in 406/5 when the *Frogs* was first performed. The scholia add some detail drawn from Atthidography. The gold money had been introduced in the archonship of Antigenes (407/6) in the year preceding the *Frogs* (ΣArist. *Frogs* 720, 725), and the bronze coins the next year, according to Hellanicus (*FGH* 323a F 26) and Philochorus (*FGH* 328 F 141). Aristophanes chose to pair the ancient silver and the recent gold and hold them up to contrast with τούτοις τοῖς πονηροῖς. His contrast has the greatest point, however, in juxtaposing the new bronze and the old silver (as has been noted), but the new gold by virtue of its intrinsic worth and esthetic quality may be equated with the earlier owls (cf. ΣArist. *Frogs* 717).[18]

These plated coins appear to have been drachms and tetradrachms, as initially suggested by Head.[19] The coins were first described systematically by Svoronos on the basis of a Peiraieus hoard (*IGCH* #64).[20] The Eleusis hoard of 1902 (*IGCH* #46) appeared to contain quite a number of these same coins, when scholarly opinion accepted that it was indeed a separate hoard.[21] It is now very likely that the Peiraieus hoard, which was

[17] Robinson *ANSMN* (1960) 11.

[18] The passage should not be complicated by reading a contrast between the long-traditional silver and the new gold in these lines. Both τἀρχαῖον νόμισμα and τὸ καινὸν χρυσίον are the antecedents of τούτοισιν in line 721. Note W.E. Thompson, "The Functions of the Emergency Coinages of the Peloponnesian War," *Mnem.*[4] 19 (1966) 337–43, esp. 340.

[19] Head[2] 373. These coins may also appear in fourth-century inventories (*IG* II[2] 1453.3–4, 1487.25 [restored]).

[20] J.N. Svoronos, "La monnaie d'or attique," *JIAN* 21 (1927) 147–70, esp. 157-58.

[21] J.H. Kroll, "Aristophanes' πονηρὰ χαλκία: A Reply," *GRBS* 17 (1976) 329–41; Kroll, *Agora* 26, 7–8, 25–26; M. Oeconomides-Caramessini, "Note on the Piraeus Hoard of 1902 of

never fully presented, was converted into an Eleusis hoard by a confused reference, a mistake perhaps encouraged by the fact that that one and the same large deposit had been broken up and scattered in purchase. In any case, the plated coins are stylistically close to the gold coinage with which they are contemporary. Both Svoronos and Kroll consider them to have been produced by the same die-cutters who produced the late fifth-century gold and silver issues. Nevertheless, the references to the *kollyboi* and to the coins mentioned in the *Ecclesiazousae* and the *Aiolosikon* cannot be explained by this coinage.

Aristophanes in the *Ecclesiazousae* and the *Aiolosikon* does not mention plated coins and some issue of fractions is required to account for the references to change that could be carried in the mouth.[22] A. Giovannini would retain the bronze coins in which the owl is turned to the left as an issue that belongs in the fifth century rather than attributing them to Timotheos. They should also be the coins to which Aristophanes refers in the *Frogs*. Giovannini's further attempts to throw doubt on the official standing of the plated tetradrachms by seeing the "Eleusinian" hoard as *private* forgeries are particularly problematical, especially because of their apparent technical affinity with official issues.[23] The size of the issue also tells against the hypothesis of forgery, as does the fact that they were hoarded.[24] No ploy was employed to disguise that the plated coins would naturally turn out lighter than the earlier silver tetradrachms so that plated coins could be readily distinguished by their users.[25] That outcome would defeat any intention to deceive.

Nor does Giovannini really confront the arguments of Robinson that suggest that Aristophanes in the *Frogs* was hinting at the plated quality of these coins by the terms of his comparison with the political parvenus. In further support, Giovannini had cited the Hekatompedon

Athenian Plated Coins," *CH* 7 (1985) 40–41, who provides some further details and confirms the equation of Peiraieus Hoard and *IGCH* #46, "Eleusis, 1902." For a later issue of plated coins, see A.S. Walker, "Some Plated Coins from the Agora at Athens," in T. Hackens and R. Weiller (eds.), *Proceedings of the 9th International Congress of Numismatics. Berne, September 1979* (Luxemburg 1982) 1.133–36, who dates them to the crisis atmosphere of 338. J.H. Kroll, "The Piraeus 1902 Hoard of Plated Drachms and Tetradrachms (*IGCH* 64)," ΧΑΡΑΚΤΗΡ, *Festschrift M. Oikonomidou* (Athens 1996) 139–45, discusses the hoard in detail, confirming the identity of *IGCH* #46 and #64 (I thank the author for allowing me to consult this piece in advance of publication).

22 See A. Giovannini, "Athenian Currency in the Late Fifth and Early Fourth Century B.C.," *GRBS* 16 (1975) 185–95, esp. 185–90.

23 Cf. Giovannini *GRBS* (1975) 189, note 13.

24 Kroll, *Agora* 26, 7, notes six separate known die pairs; Kroll, *Festschrift Oikonomidou* 140–41, specifies two dies for tetradrachms and five for drachms.

25 Kroll *GRBS* (1976) 335 corrected by *Agora* 26, 9, note 32.

inventory entries that mention ἀργύριον κί]βδηλον τὸ 'Ε[λ]ευσινόθεν (*IG* II^2 1393.33–34 [ca. 398/7], also 1400.53; 1401.39; 1445.16–17; cf. *IG* II^2 1388.53–54 [398/7]). Yet it is more likely that these coins are issues of the rump government of the Thirty at Eleusis (Xen. *HG* 2.4.38, 43). His suggestion that the emission of bronze coins necessarily requires that silver fractions be demonetized also exceeds the evidence. Consequently, one should resist the temptation to remove the plated tetradrachms and drachms as an official issue. The bronze coinage lettered ΑΘΗ cannot be moved back into the fifth century.[26] The plated drachms and tetradrachms are the coins that Aristophanes was thinking of when he composed his lament for the decline of Attic silver in the *Frogs*.

The usage of *kollyboi* is difficult to pin down because they were probably not initially official issues of the government but constituted money created by those doing business in Attica who needed to make change in transactions but lacked sufficient silver fractions to do so.[27] That would explain why the bronze tokens, the presumptive *kollyboi*, lack the official device of the state, are often without any sign of their value, and are otherwise so various in their appearance. Private issuers may have felt it unacceptably presumptuous to do anything more than make their bronze tokens identifiable to and by themselves, avoiding devices such as imposing a specific equivalence with the official coinage or linking their emissions with the state ideology by type. The single letters and pellets that occasionally appear on the tokens would represent inoffensive identifying features of private valuation (akin to countermarks). This same reticence, however, has unfortunately convinced some numismatists of their nonmonetary character. On the contrary, the proposition that the *kollyboi* mentioned in literary contexts could have begun as the private money created by various people in business and recognized by extragovernmental convention should not be resisted in principle, if it saves us from the seeming contradictions in the evidence. The three denominations *kollybon*, *dikollybon*, and *trikollybon* might have stood for the quarter-, half-, and three-quarter-obol. That might help account for the later two-fold nomenclature of the obol, into *khalkoi* of which there were eight and into quarters (for example, τεταρτημόριον 'quarter-obol'; cf. Pollux 9.65–67; Vitruv. 3.1.7). On this hypothesis, the Athenians were permitting considerable latitude to private agents in reaching accommodations to facilitate nongovernmental transactions during the 420s.

26 Contrast also Kroll, *Agora* 26, 33–34, 40 and #50.
27 Note Price *AIIN* Suppl. 25 (1979) 356.

Dionysius ὁ Χαλκοῦς may have defended this proposition on the basis of his diplomatic experiences among the western Greeks.

This phenomenon of private money may have been limited at Athens to a single chronological context, as it has left little impression on the historiography of coinage save for a short discussion of the term σύμβολον in the *Onomasticon* of Pollux (9.70–72). Pollux describes the *symbolon* as a small coin or ἡμίτομον νομίσματος 'half of a coin.' He then illustrates the usage of the term with a number of passages from Old Comedy, starting with Hermippus. Fragment 61 K (= fr. 61, *PCG* 5.590) from the *Phormophoroi* usefully establishes the private and retail nature of the *symbolon*; Hermippos has a character stating παρὰ τῶν καπήλων λήψομαι τὸ σύμβολον 'I will take a *symbolon* from the shopkeepers.' The title, which plays on the status of the allies as *phorophoroi* 'tribute-bearers,' belongs in the early or mid-420s with its references to Corcyra, Perdikkas, and Sitalkes (fr. 63.7–8, 10–11 [= fr. 63, *PCG* 5.591–94]). As a coin of little value, a *symbolon* could be juxtaposed with two obols as change that has been dropped in a fragment from the *Anagyros* of Aristophanes.[28] Archippus in another passage speaks of a member of the elite who does not possess a *symbolon*, an index of deep impoverishment.[29]

Pollux was clearly working from another fragment of Hermippus (from the *Dēmotai*), which he cites when he speaks of the *symbolon* as being struck on one face or cut in half: οἴμοι, τί δράσω σύμβολον κεχαρμένος; (fr. 14 K = fr. 13, *PCG* 5.568). For something of such small value, the token idea wherein a half is held by each party to a deal is less attractive (but cannot be excluded: cf. pp. 253–54 above). Considering the bronze tokens actually discovered, a small token with one face struck seems a better option. It should be emphasized that all four citations from the comic poets appear best dated during the Peloponnesian War.

Nonetheless, the *Ecclesiazousae* and the *Aiolosikon* seem to imply an officially recognized fractional bronze coinage. Kroll's answer to this conundrum is to note the existence of four plated triobols in coin collections in Berlin, Munich, and Athens.[30] Although Kroll initially raised the possibility that even smaller plated denominations (diobols, obols, and even hemiobols) might in time be discovered—their lower rate of

[28] Fr. 44 K = fr. 41, *PCG* 3.2.52: τοῦτ' αὐτὸ πράττω, δύ' ὀβολὼ καὶ σύμβολον | ὑπὸ τῷ 'πικλίντρῳ.

[29] Fr. 8 K = fr. 8, *PCG* 2.540–41: ἀνδρῶν ἄριστος καὶ μάλιστ' ἐμοὶ ξένος,| ἀτὰρ παρ' ἐμοί γ' ὧν εἶχεν οὐδὲ σύμβολον. Archippus' first victory was in 415–12 (*Suda* s.v. Ἄρχιππος, α 4115 Latte).

[30] Kroll *GRBS* (1976) 334–335. Kroll, *Festschrift Oikonomidou* 142–43, discusses the likely candidates as official plated triobols.

survival being owed to their low value—he now doubts whether such small plated coins would have been worth the effort. The plated diobol did not exist outside the "banter of comic dialogue." If this view consigns all references to the *kollyboi* as small fractions to a realm of phantasm, those troubled by that decision will probably transcend literalists about comedy by several degrees.

The plated triobols may indeed be the solution to the enigma of the literary references, if indeed some subclass of these coins are genuine state issues out of the many private forgeries. That hypothesis would still not lack its difficulties. The comment in the *Aiolosikon* about the diobol suddenly converted into a *dikollybos* implies that the coin would have the recognized status and value of a *dikollybos* when the process was done. That raises the question whether a plated diobol (of which there are as yet no known examples) would retain the value of a *dikollybos* in the marketplace. Why should the private issuers and users of tokens recognize the putative plated diobol as being worth anything at all save its raw metallic value? Is it also not more likely that a plated diobol might still be overvalued as a *dikollybos*?

These questions, to which the answers may still turn out favorably for Kroll's resolution of the issue, open the possibility that Athenians might also have imparted an artificial value like that of the obol, diobol, or triobol to some of the *kollyboi* that originated among private issuers, at some point after they had recognized the ability of private participants in transactions to impart a value to their *kollyboi* in excess of their worth as metal. As radical a measure as this might appear, it would not be surprising during the despair of the siege of the city, for instance, when efforts could have been made to get resources into the hands of poorer citizens. One might expect silver fractions to have been withdrawn quickly by their holders from circulation as precious metal became a logical choice as a hedge against an uncertain future. Later, with a general demonetization of bronze issues these *kollyboi*, once officially enhanced, would lapse back to their earlier value as initially established by their private issuers, unless exchanged for silver fractions. The *kollyboi* were superseded by new silver issues some of which were produced in very small fractions (down to a *hemikhalkous* or $\frac{1}{16}$ of an obol).[31]

In contrast, the purpose for the issuance of plated tetradrachms and drachms in 406/5 can be reconstructed with the aid of the episode in

[31] See E. Pászthory, "Zwei Kleinmünzen aus Athen," *SM* 29 (1979) 1–6, esp. 4–6. Speculatively, the base metal *kollyboi* could be seen as precursors of these fractions, but the chronology of their introduction is not secure.

the campaign of Timotheos against Olynthos in 363–59, to which there has already been allusion.[32] According to the *Oeconomica* attributed to Aristotle (1350a23–30), Timotheos lacked sufficient silver to pay his men.[33] He accompanied his minting bronze with instructions to the merchants doing business with his camp (*emporoi* and *agoraioi*) that his bronze would be valid tender not only for soldiers' purchases of necessary supplies but also for the products of the Olynthian *khōra* and for booty. Any excess could be redeemed for silver with him, presumably when a merchant withdrew from the Olynthian theater of the hostilities. Though few examples of these coins have survived—Robinson and Price studied eleven specimens and Kroll mentions fifteen more—the issue was fairly sizable. Robinson and Price estimated three obverse and eight reverse dies for their type 1 and two obverse and three reverse dies for their type 2. One is reminded that the campaigns in the north were expensive, with the cost not limited to the notoriously costly and futile attempts to recover Amphipolis.

Timotheos used the official obverse design of a helmeted Athena and a reverse with an owl; we have already remarked on the pecularities of design (some leftward-facing Athenas and the legend ΑΘΗ). That the owl stands on a wheat grain on some of the coins perhaps shows that the central purpose of the coining was to allow members of Timotheos' expeditionary force to procure food from merchants. It is also important to note that Timotheos, operating as an Athenian *stratēgos*, seems to have had no reluctance either about creating a locally valid token money or about ordering the stamping of money with the official *kharaktēr*. Polyaenus reports another occasion on which Timotheos undertook similar action. In a war against Perdikkos of Macedonia, he melted down Macedonian coins that he adulterated with an admixture of Cypriot bronze to create *episēmon* 'stamped' silver (*Strat.* 3.10.14).[34] The term *episēmon* shows that these coins, of which none have survived (to my knowledge), were adaptations of official coinage just like the bronze coins issued at Olynthos.

Both the *kollyboi* and the plated bronze, just like Timotheos' emergency coinage, were likely to have been a true token money, especially if

[32] See Robinson and Price *NC* (1967) 1–6.

[33] Similar financial manipulations by Timotheos are reported in [Aris.] *Oec.* 1350a30–b15; Polyaen. *Strat.* 3.10.9–11. In a comparable but nonmonetary exploitation of his authority as *stratēgos*, Timotheos exchanged his *sphragis* 'seal' for money from the merchants that accompanied his forces (Polyaen. *Strat.* 3.10.1).

[34] Although an Attic-standard issue could be envisaged for this coining, it is also possible that Timotheos coined on the Aiginetic standard, as the term *pentedrakhmia* is used by Polyaenus. See pp. 158–59 above.

Price is correct in that even low-denomination bronze coins were regularly overvalued in terms of metallic content.[35]

If the reconstruction above is correct, plated coins were tetradrachms, drachms, and perhaps triobols, while the previously private *kollyboi* (less than an obol in value) were permitted at some juncture to assume values up to the diobol or possibly the triobol within Attica itself. No attempt was made to disguise the plated issues which Kroll found weighed 15–20 percent less than their silver counterparts. Many forgeries, however, are intended to approximate genuine silver coins in weight. Since Athenian plated bronze coinage of the late Peloponnesian War should be considered to have circulated at a value far exceeding its metallic content, as a token coinage it could only have held value in Attica and in places where governmental authority sustained its value.[36]

The issuance of bronze money during the Peloponnesian War and especially the later phase of the Decelean/Ionian War probably fulfills the dual function of Timotheos' intervention. The minting of the plated tetradrachms allowed the Athenian government to pay bills that it could not if forced to use silver exclusively. As discussed earlier in this work, output of the silver mines of Laureion had been grievously affected—some have thought a virtual shutdown—after 413 (see above pp. 228–29). Bronze money (both plated coins and the *kollyboi*) was also a reaction to the realization that there was insufficient money in circulation to cope with daily retail transactions.[37] The existence of "private" money in the form of *kollyboi* betrays that this realization had penetrated the popular consciousness first, for their only purpose can have been to create change to facilitate transactions.

Nonetheless, care must be exercised to avoid sketching these monetary circumstances in contours that are too sharply drawn. There is no evidence to suggest that Attic silver was demonetized, and it is hard to imagine a rationale for doing so.[38] Individuals would happily pay

[35] Price, *Robinson Festschrift* 103, basing himself on the weight of the heaviest bronze coins of Akragas and Himera and the prices for copper and tin in *IG* I³ 472.139–45.

[36] See Thompson *Mnem.* (1966) 337–38. Note the other examples from the *Oeconomica* attributed to Aristotle: the city of Klazomenai introduced a token iron coinage during a crisis of public debt (1348b17–32; cf. Pollux 7.105); Dionysios of Syracuse attempted a token coinage of tin during a crisis of finances (1347a27–33; cf. Pollux 9.79).

[37] See M.R. Cataudella, "Aspetti e strumenti della politica monetaria ateniese fra V e IV secolo," *Sileno* 12 (1986) 111–35, but the recourse to the concept of bimetallism takes us in the wrong direction.

[38] This conclusion is supported by the succession of silver issues and bronze equivalents in several fourth-century mints such as Thasos. See O. Picard, "Innovations monétaires dans la Grèce du IVᵉ siècle," *CRAI* (1989) 673–87.

the state in plated coins if they had no choice but to receive them in payment from the state, while private individuals could never be stopped from using the remaining silver coins in circulation. If silver had been demonetized, Aristophanes would probably have made something of this action in his *Frogs*. It is also reasonable to avoid overly neat divisions such as seeing bronze money exclusively for home consumption and the gold coins emitted solely for foreign trade. Naturally, silver and gold coins would have gravitated toward those persons who were in the strongest position in transactions, such as foreign suppliers of essential goods with alternative customers and the sailors in the fleet (and any other paid individuals needed for the war effort). It would be of the greatest historical interest to learn whether the rowers of the fleet were ever paid in anything except silver and gold coins. The ability of the Spartans to build up the fleet that won at Aigospotamoi would appear under a rather new light if the historicity of an Athenian recourse to plated tetradrachms for military pay was established. One suspects, however, that plated tetradrachms were not paid to military personnel and would not be accepted by the merchants accompanying Attic expeditionary forces.

Naturally, fresh silver tetradrachms might have had more value in many settings even within Attica itself than their plated successors. Bad money may have served to drive out the good, and Aristophanes' reaction to the new monetary conditions reflects that reality. A significant part of the good silver will also have been withdrawn into hoards as a hedge against uncertainty. The power of the state would have to have been applied liberally to keep silver and plated tetradrachms near parity. That authority is illustrated in the law of 375/4 regarding the *dokimastēs*, where significant jurisdiction is shown to have existed for punishing merchants who refused validated coins. One must keep in mind, however, that the need for enough coins to undertake daily business served to counterbalance the unattractiveness of the plated tetradrachms.

Nevertheless, the "good" silver was probably not suddenly or completely driven from the marketplace by the plated silver. It may well have been that some stated prices would have been reformulated to allow for payment in plated owls, while discounts could be offered for paying in older silver, much as today there are so often (informal?) discounts for paying cash. It is doubtful whether the *agoranomoi* and other officials would have had the coercive ability to impose anything more than an acceptance of plated coins. One suspects that their authority would have fallen short of an imposition of a thoroughgoing parity of old silver and plated silver under the conditions of the war. Nor is there any rationale for arguing that plated money could not have been used in the areas of the *arkhē* where Attic hegemony and democratic pro-Athenian governments held sway. Its recipients will merely have endeavored to recirculate plated coins back to Attica with the greatest expedition.

Given the various crises confronted by the Athenian state during the Ionian War, the recourse to bronze and plated money was a prudent response to dire circumstances. The deliberate effort to avoid an incremental debasement of the silver content of the main series of drachms and tetradrachms illustrates the Athenian appreciation of the value to the Attic economy and state of the reputation of those coins for their purity of composition. There is no evidence suggesting that the Athenians were ever so desperate, even when confronting defeat and enslavement, as to put at risk the acceptance and validity of their silver coins. Nevertheless, the Attic monetary hegemony in the Aegean had been heavily dependent on the high production of the mines at Laureion and a strong annual outflow of new issues of silver. The inauguration of official bronze money at the end of the Peloponnesian War marked the lower boundary of this important epoch.

As we have already learned from the *Ecclesiazousae* of Aristophanes, the Athenians demonetized their bronze sometime before the date of that play (393 or 392) in a manner consistent with its standing as token money.[39] The *Aiolosikon* was performed twice (after 402 and ca. 386), so that a demonetization of bronze would be conceivable either right after the war (my preference) or after the revival of Athenian military fortunes when Konon returned from Persian service.[40] Yet we know from Lysias 19.11 that as late as 390/89 a speaker could refer to σπάνιν ἀργυρίου 'shortage of money.' Even if the abruptness of the change in the Aristophanic passages is owed to comic exaggeration, it may be that silver coins had once again been minted and were circulating in sufficient amounts before any such demonetization of the bronze was to take place.[41] That

[39] Cf. Giovannini *GRBS* (1975) 189–90 with note 19 (pp. 190–91); Kroll *GRBS* (1976) 335–38.

[40] Kroll, *Agora* 26, 8 (cf. *GRBS* [1976] 338–41), opts for a demonetization of the bronze by the time of the restoration of the democracy in 403/2, while a resumption of the minting of silver may have had to wait for Konon (spring or summer 393) and Persian subsidization at the end of the decade. The first appearance of fourth-century owls is in Sicilian hoards: *IGCH* #2117, "Lentini" (ca. 390?), #2119, "Contessa" (390–80), #2121, "Manfria" (390–80). Yet they give us no certain chronology: all three hoards might well reflect the circumstance of coins carried westward by the sailors of the Syracusan and Italiot squadrons that were active in the Aegean at the end of the Corinthian War, at which time Athens might already have been striking coins for a decade.

[41] See Kroll, *GRBS* (1976) 338–41, who also observes that the gap in silver issues need not have been longer than one or two years. That judgment is most compatible with the

is another strike against there ever having been an earlier demonetization of silver coins. The desperate measures undertaken to ward off defeat at Spartan hands were replaced with a strong movement back toward monetary normality. As so often for fourth-century Athenians, that normality was to be defined by the practices of the fifth-century *arkhē*.

SILVER AND GOLD VALUES IN HISTORICAL CONTEXT

The ratio of the value of gold to silver represents another means for us to envisage the monetary conditions of the late fifth century. The relative volume of the two metals in daily circulation as coinage and bullion had a great effect on their value relative to each other. So too did the relative supply of and demand for gold and silver for other modes of consumption. The value ratio was strongly influenced by the ongoing hostilities. Because of its greater basic valuation by human beings and its greater rarity, gold will always be more valuable than silver in a society characterized by near-subsistence agriculture and some degree of economic differentiation. How much more valuable gold stands than silver is dependent on demand, supply, and the volume of the two metals in circulation.

Herodotus gives us literary evidence for a lower valuation of gold, speaking of a 1:13 ratio, than prevailed later in the century (3.95.1). Scholarly opinion is in general agreement about the ratio of the two metals before the Peloponnesian War, namely, 1:14, based on a number of epigraphical documents. *IG* I^3 458.15–18 (440/39) from the accounts of *epistatai* of the chryselephantine statue of Athena equates a purchase of 6T, 1,618 dr., 1 ob. of gold with a silver amount of 87T, 4,652 dr., 5 obols.[42] That equation implies a gold:silver ratio of 1:14. The way in which the specific price slightly varies from the presumably conventional ratio (at that time) of 1:14 demonstrates that this is probably a true market price. *IG* I^3 449.389–91 (434/3) offers us the next bit of price information. Here the *epistatai* of the Parthenon are selling (in all probability) 98 dr. worth of gold and receiving in return 1,372 dr. of silver, with a gold:silver ratio of 1:14.[43]

---

hypothesis of no demonetization of earlier Attic silver and of a fluid circulation of silver, gold, and plated currencies in company with each other during the last years of the war.

[42] W.E. Thompson, "Gold and Silver Ratios at Athens during the Fifth Century," *NC*^{7} 4 (1964) 103–23, esp. 103; D.M. Lewis, "New Evidence for the Gold-Silver Ratio," *Festschrift Robinson* 105–10, esp. 105.

[43] Thompson *NC* (1964) 103; Lewis, *Festschrift Robinson* 105. A restoration is necessary to engender the generally accepted result, for which see W.B. Dinsmoor, "Attic Building Accounts," *AJA* 17 (1913) 53–80, esp. 74–76.

Hence, although the loss in value of silver cannot be characterized as dramatic, there is some indication of the monetary inflation that is indicated by changes in grain prices (see above pp. 493–94). Nonetheless, gold began to lose value relative to silver after the Peloponnesian War began. Establishing the historical ratios in value, however, depends on using more fragmentary documents, and the rather technical discussion has been relegated to Endnote A to this chapter. The value ratio of gold to silver seems to have bottomed out at approximately 1:10. Accordingly, it is indeed possible that the lexical notices that speak of a gold stater that was worth twenty Attic silver drachms are to be related to the value of the Attic gold didrachms of the end of the Peloponnesian War.[44] A gloss of Harpocration that gives the same information, equating the value of the Attic gold stater with that of the Daric gold stater, might be taken to suggest an earlier rather than a later date for the gold stater at issue in the main lexical tradition (s.v. Δαρειкός).

D.M. Lewis has exploited another source of information on gold and silver ratios during the Peloponnesian War. He suggested that one could utilize the tendency of the Athenians to order gold crowns and other dedications in stereotypical, round numbers of silver drachms. The methodology is discussed in Endnote B, and the results are summarized in Table 19.1. Even with the reservations that are explored in Endnote B, the ratios implied by these dedications do seem to peak in the late 430s and then to chart a downward course for the value of gold as measured against silver. If one were to equate (necessarily crudely) the higher ratios at the beginning of this list with the 1:14 relationship that is derived from the earliest epigraphical documentation (450–431), the lowest ratios on this list could be recalculated to yield the 1:11 or 1:10 ratios that are suggested by the lowest estimates based on the epigraphical documents of the Peloponnesian War. Moreover, the early fourth-century literary evidence also suggests that gold had fallen in value since the beginning of the Archidamian War, although it may have rebounded from its lowest value that was reached during the Decelean War.[45] Lysias 19.39–40 speaks of the financial arrangements carried out on the death

[44] See Hesych. s.v. χρυσοῦς, χ 804 Latte, cf. s.v. δραχμὴ χρυσίου, δ 2353 Latte.

[45] The fourth-century material on the gold:silver ratio is reviewed by P. Marchetti, "Quelques réflexions sur les équivalences entre l'or et l'argent," in T. Hackens and P. Marchetti (eds.), *Histoire économique de l'antiquité* (Louvain 1987) 135–49; Marchetti, "Le Cours du Cyzicène au IVe siècle," *RBN* 122 (1976) 35–58, esp. 54–57. For further material, see S. Lauffer, "Das Bergbauprogramm in Xenophons Poroi," *MIGRA* 1 (1975) 171–205, esp. 176–77. For discussion and bibliography, note also R. Bogaert, "Le cours du statère de Cyzique aux Ve et IVe siècles avant J.-C.," *AC* 32 (1963) 85–119, esp. 91–100.

TABLE 19.1 Gold Dedications and the Gold to Silver Ratio

* = not on Lewis' list

DATE	OBJECT	GOLD WEIGHT	COST IN SILVER	RATIO	REFERENCE
434/3	**phialai* (2)	1344??	3.5T?	15.6*	*IG* I³ 317.4–5
	stephanos	60	1,000	16.7	*IG* I³ 343.4
	phiale	1200	3T	15	*IG* I³ 317.7–8
432/1	*stephanoi* (2)	40 × 2	600 × 2	15	*IG* I³ 319.20
429/8	*stephanos*	33.5	500	14.9	*IG* I³ 297.22–23
428/7	**phialai* (3)	ca. 848 × 3	2T × 3	14.2	*IG* I³ 323.48–49 with 325.5–6; 326.17
	stephanos?	60	1,000	16.7	*IG* I³ 323.50–52 with 327.30–31
427/6–423/2	*stephanos*	33.33	500	15	*IG* I³ 325.9
	stephanē	63	1,000	15.9	*IG* I³ 325.9–10 with 326.21
	stephanoi (4)	135.33	2,000	14.8	*IG* I³ 325.10 with 330.25
	**stephanos*	18.5	250/300	13.5/16.2	*IG* I³ 351.21
	**stephanos*	29	400/500	13.8/17.2	*IG* I³ 351.21
	stephanos	33	500	15.2	*IG* I³ 351.22
	stephanos?	33	500	15 2	*IG* I³ 351.23
422/1	*stephanos*	18.5	250/300	13 5/16.2	*IG* I³ 325.11
420/19	*stephanos*	26.5	400	15.2	*IG* I³ 328.48
418/7	*stephanos*	1250	3T	14.4	*IG* I³ 329.13–14
	stephanos	35	500	14.3	*IG* I³ 329.14–15
417/6	*stephanoi* (2)	53	750	14.2	*IG* I³ 330.29–30
415/4	*stephanos*	72	1,000	13.9	*IG* I³ 339.16 = *SEG* 10.181
414/3	*stephanos?*	724??	10,000?	13.8	*IG* I³ 333.15 with 339.16–17
399/8	*stephanos*	272.5	3,000	11	*IG* II² 1388.29–30
	stephanos	85	1,000	11.8	*IG* II² 1388.36–37
398/7	*stephanos*	245.25	3,000	12.2	*IG* II² 1388.67

of Konon, where one item is 5,000 gold staters out of a total amount equivalent to 40T of silver in all. To make the requisite contribution toward the 40T, each of these gold staters needed to have been of equal value to ca. 22 Attic silver drachms (that is, a ratio of 1:11). [Plato] *Hipparchus* 231D (of the 380s?) gives the gold to silver ratio as 1:12.

Another method for investigating the history of the gold to silver value relationship is provided by an examination of the exchange ratio between the Cyzicene electrum stater and the Attic silver drachm, since Cyzicenes were one of the most important currencies containing gold (see Table 19.2).[46] Thus, their relationship to Athenian money could be reflective of the underlying ratio in value between the two metals. One must naturally proceed with caution, since there is evidence that electrum coins were also items of consumption (for hoarding) and that different electrum coin series might have had somewhat different values. Moreover, there was variation in the gold content of issues within the same electrum mint that were presumably circulated at parity. The specialist discussion may be consulted by those interested in Endnote C. One would not describe the results of these investigations as very satisfactory. Nevertheless, they do seem to support the calculations from the other bodies of evidence that gold fell in value relative to silver during the period 420–400 and rebounded in the early fourth century.

TABLE 19.2 The Value of the Cyzicene Stater

Date	*Bogaert*	*Other Authorities*
Mid-fifth century	27–28 dr.?	
ca. 415	25–26 dr.	25 dr., 4½ ob./Thompson
ca. 409/8	25–26 dr.	25 dr., 4½ ob.(–)/Thompson
Beginning of fourth century	27 dr.	
370–350	21 dr., 4 ob.??	30 dr./Marchetti
Mid-fourth century	25 dr.??	
ca. 327	21 dr., 4 ob.	28 dr./Marchetti

Had we none of the foregoing evidence, we could have speculated very differently about the value ratio of gold to silver during the Peloponnesian War, for it would have been an easy assumption to have made that silver *depreciated* relative to gold and other goods because of the thousands of talents of silver previously held in public reserve (and private savings) that were spent by the Athenians for their war effort.[47] In other words, our hypothetical prewar appreciation of the value of gold would have persisted. The additional Attic money put into circulation caused the

[46] Bogaert, *AC* (1963) 85–119, initiated the recent consideration. For the earlier scholarship, see op. cit. 86 with notes 5–12.

[47] M.H. Vickers, "Artful Crafts: The Influence of Metalwork on Athenian Painted Pottery," *JHS* 105 (1985) 108–28, esp. 112–17, draws our attention to the substantial accumulation of gold and silver plate by the Attic elite during the *arkhē*. Taxes during the war drew down these holdings. The description in Thucydides of the deception practiced by the Egestans on an Attic embassy shows ordinary Attic expectation (6.8.1–2; 46.1, 3–5; cf. 6.6.2–3): large private holdings of plate were a (if not the) primary source for underwriting a war. See also M. Vickers, "Golden Greece: Relative Values, Minae, and Temple Inventories," *AJA* 94 (1990) 613–25.

money supply to grow, with price inflation the predictable result, so that the same amount of silver bought less of other goods including gold.[48] Moreover, it has also been pointed out above that Attic money no longer circulated during the Peloponnesian War as far abroad as it had previously done, so that the money supply could also have increased through a retention of tetradrachms within the *arkhē*. More of the economy of the Aegean basin was geared toward the hostilities, so recipients of spending who contributed to the war effort had a relatively greater number of coins coming their way than those who did not and than persons living outside the *arkhē* in Egypt and the Levant.

One way to account for the appreciation of silver relative to gold would be that the supply of available silver, both monetary and nonmonetary, did not in fact expand so much despite the radically increased expenditures of the Athenians and their allies on the war. Less silver was probably being produced both at Laureion and in the north. More old coins were being also drawn off to satisfy nonmonetary uses for silver and for hoarding. Such subtractions balanced the augmentation of the money in circulation through expenses for the war. Silver could also have been drawn off from the more integrated Aegean economy to noncombatant states to pay the expenses for the war. In this regard, Thompson noted the costs of the Syracusan expedition and of the Decelean War.[49] Yet, if the impression garnered from the dedications is correct, gold was already in decline during the Archidamian War. And then there is the risk in such a hypothesis of overestimating the flow of Attic silver outside the *arkhē*, when Egypt and the Near East may already have been so hungry for Attic tetradrachms. Could the non-Greek suppliers of timber and pitch in Macedonia and Thrace and grain in the Pontos have drained off the greatest part of the increased expenditure of silver and created a static or shrinking money supply?

It cannot be excluded that the economies of the *arkhē* continued their prewar expansion at least during the Archidamian War. A war that is largely financed by already minted silver coins that were held in nonproductive storage could give a boost to economic activity.[50] While the Greeks were consuming their hoarded savings, a process with long-term deleterious effects, they were also eliciting for the moment the creation of new goods and services. A larger output of goods and services soaked up the added silver, creating a situation of relative price

[48] See the Endnote to Chapter 18.
[49] Cf. Thompson *NC* (1964) 113–23.
[50] Cf. Figueira, *Aegina* 107–14, 332–35.

stability during the Archidamian War, but one in which gold depreciated in relation to silver.

In time, however, any such "sinks" that existed to draw off an increased amount of Attic silver coins circulated by Athenian expenditures would be balanced by the divergence of manpower from peacetime activities to military service in an economy without sophisticated artificial means of production. The eventual effect of the war would have been to cause nonmilitary economic activity to contract, with the result that the supply of silver coins probably grew in relation to the scale of the economy of the *arkhē* as the war continued. There was also the plague, which had an analogous effect on Attic output; it killed productive workers of all political statuses. Over time, as the *eisphorai* proceeded from draining savings to drawing on resources needed to expand or replace productive assets, any early economic boomlet created by the spending of reserves would have spent itself. Hence other goods experienced price inflation: silver had less buying power for most goods but, surprisingly, more buying power to purchase gold.

Consequently, other factors must be elicited as determinants of the fall in the value of gold relative to silver during the last decades of the fifth century, for it is hard to see why the price of gold lost ground with reference to silver rather than simply holding its own. It is possible that the nonmonetary utilization of gold changed after the outbreak of the war. The prewar demand for gold may have been shaped by its employment in craft industries. After the beginning of hostilities, both public and private consumers of craft goods were inhibited from buying as many gold objects by rising taxes, the stress of personal dangers, and more cautious attitudes in general. Demand for gold contracted at the same time that both the Athenian government and private individuals sold their gold plate to pay their expenses. With much gold entering a depressed market, gold became less valuable in relation to silver. After 411, the Persians may have made some of their subsidization of the enemies of the Athenians in the form of gold Darics and may have bought silver coins for expenditure on the Peloponnesian war effort with gold bullion.[51] Those actions also put more gold into circulation in the Aegean and onto the market for precious metals.[52] Finally, when gold coins began to be minted in Athens from 407/6, a large amount of gold, heretofore reserved, that was now

[51] Note Thompson *NC* (1964) 120–23; Thompson, "The Official Tariff of the Kyzikene Stater at Athens," *AC* 40 (1970) 574–88, esp. 587.

[52] Although the wages of Peloponnesian seamen were probably reckoned in terms of Attic or Aiginetan drachms and paid in those currencies and Chian staters ("fortieths"), it is possible that they may in fact have been paid on some occasions in gold Darics.

liquidated could have caused gold to lose even more of its value. All these were temporally restricted effects and gold rebounded in terms of silver in the early fourth century.

GOLD COINAGE

The downward movement in the value of gold during the Peloponnesian War shows the liquidation of large stocks of the metal. Private individuals sold their silver and gold plate to pay for the tetradrachms with which to pay taxes and to subsidize their military service. The Athenian state is known to have melted down public holdings of gold and silver, especially those in cult treasuries. The emission of gold coins, however, indicates a more radical departure from past practice.

As observed above, Aristophanes in *Frogs* 718–26 gives literary witness to the context for the minting of an Athenian gold coinage at the end of the fifth century. Examples of this emission of coins are known in the denominations of didrachm, drachm, triobol, and diobol. The didrachm or stater is attested epigraphically from the end of the century.[53] The hemiobol denomination is attested on *IG* II^2 1414.6. As seen from the Aristophanic scholia, the gold coins were first minted in 407/6 (Hellanicus *FGH* 323a F 26; Philochorus *FGH* 328 F 141).[54] Philochorus adds the detail that the metal for the coins was drawn from the gold statues called Nikai 'Victories' (cf. the restoration in *IG* II^2 1408.11–13). The emphasis on the use of the Nikai may indicate that most other famous gold dedications had already been utilized. The delicacy needed for asking the Athenians to break up the Nikai for the war is illustrated by the transformation of the initiative into an exemplary occasion for euphemism in rhetorical treatises (Demetrius, *On Style* 5.281; Quintil. 9.2.92).

There had been at least eight Nikai which had been dedicated in pairs (cf. *Ath. Pol.* 47.1; 49.3).[55] The golden exterior was mounted in the form of plates that could be detached for inspection and weighing

[53] *IG* I^3 379.48–49, 59–60 (~ *IG* II^2 1686.18–25); 382.7–8 = *IG* II^2 1687+, where lines 14 and 16 are restored.

[54] Svoronos *JIAN* (1927) 152–56; W.E. Thompson, "The Date of the Athenian Gold Coinage," *AJP* 86 (1965) 159–74, esp. 159–65, adequately disposes of the theory of W.S. Ferguson, *The Treasurers of Athena* (Cambridge MA 1932) 87–95 with pp. 8–15, that the coinage belongs to the next year. See also T. Fischer, "Zu den Athener Goldmünzen von 407/06 v. Chr.," *MMB* 17 (1977) 383–88.

[55] For details on the construction and weighing of the Nikai, see D.B. Thompson, "The Golden Nikai Reconsidered," *Hesperia* 13 (1944) 173–209. A fundamental study drawing on epigraphical evidence is A.M. Woodward, "The Golden Nikai of Athena," *AE* (1937) 159–70, esp. 169–70. See also D. Harris, *The Treasures of the Parthenon and the Erechtheion* (Oxford 1995) 272–75.

(in separate batches), and in extremis for melting down and expenditure. Seven of the eight Nikai were utilized in this way, since in the early fourth century only one statue remained intact, while the χαρακτῆρες 'frames' for the others survived (as listed in inventories of the holdings in the Opisthodomos of the Old Temple and later in the Chalcotheke: *IG* II^2 1424a.120, cf. 378; 1425.374: 1469.107–108; *SEG* 19.129.24–25 [restored] = *IG* II^2 1438.48; 1471.56–57; cf. 1408.11–13; 1409.5–6).

The history of the Nikai can now be viewed somewhat better through the accounts edited for *IG* I^3 by W.E. Thompson (*IG* I^3 467–71).[56] Their first appearance, however, is in the second of the Kallias decrees (*IG* I^3 52B.3, with a consensus date of 434/3). *IG* I^3 467 reports a Nike that was fashioned by Deinocrates ca. 430/29. Another Nike may have preceded it in the enumeration. *IG* I^3 468 records a Nike dedicated in 426/5 and the possibility cannot be entirely excluded that a second Nike is also mentioned in lines 28ff. of the same inscription.[57] Thompson believes that *IG* I^3 469 (apparently of 407/6), containing references to two Nikai, indicates that they had just been completed, basing himself on the phrase *epistatai* of Nikai (dual) in line 26. Nevertheless, this would be a surpassingly foolish time to have relegated such resources to this purpose, but this observation does not rule out the possibility entirely. Thompson believes that the same two statues were almost immediately melted down for gold currency. Inasmuch as the context for the mention of the *epistatai* is lost—perhaps they were noted simply to help in the identification of the statue(s)—it may be that these Nikai date from the commemoration of an earlier victory. *IG* I^3 470 (ca. 406/5) mentions a Nike that was probably consigned to the mint for conversion into money.

After their introduction, gold coins continued to be minted, through the end of the war. Thompson argues that the appearance of the term ἀμφιδέ[αι in *IG* I^3 380.25 indicates that one of the golden Nikai was in the process of being turned into gold coins in 404/3, the date of that inscription, inasmuch as the same term is used in connection with the Nikai elsewhere (*IG* I^3 468.19; 469.25–26; 470.9–10).[58] From the previous year (405/4), he also notes that Nί]κας ἐπιχ[ρύ]|[σος appeared among the list of the items loaned by the Treasurers of Athena along with natural products, a variety of silver objects, gold Darics, and

[56] Cf. Thompson *AJP* (1965) 170–74; Thompson, "The Gold Nikai and the Coinage of Athens," *NC*^{7} 10 (1970) 1–6.

[57] Cf. *IG* II^2 403.8–12, with Thuc. 3.108–12; 4.46–48, 49.1. See Woodward *AE* (1937) 169–70.

[58] Cf. Thompson *Mnem.* (1966) 341–43.

Attic gold staters (*IG* I^3 379.43–44 = *IG* II^2 1686.13–14).[59] It is assumed that each of the Nikai weighed 2T of gold (*IG* I^3 467.2–3), meaning that at least 14T from seven Nikai were converted to provide the metal for the gold issue of 407/6.[60] Some of the dies for minting this coinage appear on the inventories of the Treasurers of Athena. Four anvil (obverse) dies and twenty-two punch or striker (reverse) dies are recorded.[61] There is, however, no guarantee that there were not other dies used in this issue that became so worn out through usage that they were not preserved.

Other gold dedications from the acropolis were also melted down for coining, with the exception that the gold from the great Pheidian Athena was spared the crucible.[62] The necessary transfers from inventories have left traces on the epigraphical record (*IG* I^3 469.1–11; 470.11–15). Moreover, *IG* I^3 316 has been read to mark the consignment to the foundry of the dedications of the *pronaos* 'fore-temple' of the Parthenon, although the inscription is too fragmentary for certainty. The total amount of other offerings that went to supplement the gold from the Nikai is unknown. As we have seen, the estimates for the productivity of an obverse die vary on a range from 8,000 to 30,000 coins; the corresponding figures for a reverse have been estimated along the range from 4,000 to 10,000 coins. The four anvils dies listed on inventories would thus coin 32,000–120,000 coins; the twenty-two reverse dies, 108,000–220,000 coins. The contribution of discarded dies and the distribution of the dies among various weights is of course unknown. Therefore, it is clear that the gold coinage whose production must be compressed into 407/6, 406/5, and 405/4 (possibly with 404/3) was massive. Robinson estimated the issue as representing the equivalent of 100,000 gold dr., and Thompson estimated 104,000 dr.[63] Those may well be underestimates. Compare also the figure of over 500T for the amount of unminted gold and silver dedications that Athens possessed on the eve of the war (Thuc. 2.13.4).

59 For other fourth-century inventories mentioning the surviving Nike and additions/restorations of other Nikai, note *IG* II^2 1370 + 1371.13–18; 1388.16–24; 1393.6–11; 1400.8–12; 1407.8–11; 1424a.50–62; 1425.45–62; 1428.9–41; 1431.1–13; 1440.40–45.

60 Thompson *Mnem.* (1966) 338–39.

61 *IG* II^2 1424a.119; *SEG* 19.129.24–25 [restored] = *IG* II^2 1438.48–49; 1469.107–108; cf. 1408.11–13; 1409.4–6; 1471.56–57. The question whether a religious rationale accounts entirely for the preservation of dies is complicated by the appearance of two hammers along with them.

62 Robinson *ANSMN* (1960) 12; D. Hossis. "Gold and Silver on the Athenian Acropolis: Thucydides 2.13.4 and the Inventory Lists," *Horos* 8–9 (1990–91) 75–82 (esp. on *IG* I^3 316).

63 Robinson *ANSMN* (1960) 12; Thompson *NC* (1970) 6.

Let us again consider why the Athenians did not sell gold dedications in return for silver tetradrachms to support the war effort, as they may have done earlier in the war.[64] If they did not do so for exclusively financial reasons, we would have to recognize this as powerful testimony to the depression of the Attic economy and the private impoverishment of the Athenians. They could expect no buyers in Attica for such amounts of gold at acceptable prices. And that judgment would perhaps also hold good for potential overseas customers (at least within the *arkhē*). The recourse to a gold coinage would indicate that the only feasible means for putting so much gold on the market was through disbursements to a wide spectrum of the recipients of state funds.

As noted above in connection with the contemporary bronze issues, there is no reason to consider Attic gold as aimed only toward a foreign clientele. It may well have been needed to pay all those whose position in business with the Attic state was so strong that they would take payment only in the best coin. It is likely that the expenses of Athenian *stratēgoi* for paying crews and suppliers of the fleet provided the most well-traveled route by which gold staters were expended and circulated. The train of merchants accompanying Attic expeditionary forces may have constituted an absorbant medium for stocks of gold disseminated through the gold coinage, one with an osmotic ability to transfer gold to a wider Greek and non-Greek clientele.

The management of a bimetallic stock of money is inherently difficult. During the closing years of the Peloponnesian War, the usage of one or two coinages in base metal (the plated tetradrachms/drachms and the validated *kollyboi*) complicated monetary conditions. The recourse to gold coinage at the end of the war is another, conclusive sign of the unraveling of the hegemonic monetary system based on the prevalence of Attic silver. Using gold and silver coins fully interchangeably requires that they stand in a fixed relationship to each other, when many factors caused the two metals to vary in value over time and various contexts, as our previous discussion has demonstrated. Much of the variability lay outside governmental ability to influence. Although Athens had a huge economy for a city-state, the proportional scale of the economies of modern nation-states is of another order. This sheer scale imparted opportunities for stabilization lacking in the case of Ionian War Athens. By the desperate end of the Peloponnesian War, using large stocks of gold

[64] It is likely that, since the outbreak of the war, private individuals had been converting their own holdings in gold plate into coin to pay taxes, and this contributed to depressing the price of gold (see note 47 above).

and silver—assuming they had existed—to buy and sell the metals as needed to keep them in the same value-ratio would have been inconceivable. Nothing in Attic financial records hints that any such effort was even attempted. Rather, precious dedications poured toward the mint for rapid conversion into expendable media.

The Athenians appear to have essayed a four-tier monetary system during the last years of the war: gold hemiobols through didrachms, silver coins in the customary range from fractions upward to tetradrachms (in circulation even if no longer being minted), plated bronze in drachms (also perhaps in triobols) and tetradrachms, and *kollyboi* as smaller bronze change. If nothing else, the overlaps in denomination and value in these coinages will disabuse us of any illusion that this was a fully coordinated system. Thus a certain degree of monetary disorder must have characterized these years. In desperate times, the Athenians took a series of improvisational measures, the interactions of which are most uncertain from a modern vantage point. Regardless, of our guesses about their effect, they are still remarkable for their absence of any intent to deceive the users of Attic money. The Attic government showed remarkable forebearance against the temptation to adulterate its silver issues, when even minor debasement would have reaped appreciable benefits. Aristophanes, *Frogs* 718–37 speaks to the pride of the average Athenian in the quality and status of their owls. In a democracy, where any alteration to established minting procedures needed to pass the council and assembly, the protective attitude against cheapening their coins was the best guarantor of sound money.

ENDNOTE A: EPIGRAPHICAL EVIDENCE ON THE GOLD TO SILVER RATIO

There is much debate over the specific evolution of the value of gold and silver during the Peloponnesian War. An entry from the accounts of the treasurers of Athena, *IG* I^3 376.112–16 (409/8), preserves traces of a lower ratio between gold and silver than the prewar 1:14. Wade-Gery restored this relationship to be *h*ενδεκασ]τάσιοṿ (1:11), while Thompson, building on Wade-Gery's work, argued for δοδεκασ]τάσιοṿ (1:12), based on an examination of the number of likely *stoichoi*.[65] Wade-Gery tentatively offered as amounts underlying his ratio of 1:11, 2,800 dr. of gold (the extant numerals) and 5T, 800 dr. of silver. Another, even more damaged, context in the same inscription (*IG* I^3 376.54–56) offers

[65] H.T. Wade-Gery, "The Ratio of Silver to Gold during the Peloponnesian War: I.G. I^2, 301," *NC*^{5} 10 (1930) 16–38, 333–34. See also Thompson *NC* (1964) 105–108; cf. Lewis *Festschrift Robinson* 106.

]δεκαστά[σ]ιο[ν in line 54 and the same word is restored in line 56. This takes us nowhere directly, save undercutting the present validity of the earlier 1:14 ratio, but the associated numeral in line 55 has been read and restored as 1T, 3,370 dr. (Wade-Gery) and 1T, 3,460 dr. (Thompson, followed by Lewis in *IG* I³, p. 355). Wade-Gery's supplementation of the line gives a figure that would be congruent with an amount in silver of 15T, 3,700 dr. at a ratio of 1:10. He would restore this amount in line 109, where the appropriate last six numerals are extant. Thompson would sunder the two contexts. If there are two ratios for gold and silver in this inscription, it is worth remembering (as Thompson notes) that these are not records of purchases or sales but accounting records reporting shifts of assets between Athenian officials.

It has also been argued that *IG* I³ 386.173–83 (408/7) and 387.14–17 (407/6: from the Eleusinian accounts) have 2,000 dr. of gold exchanged for 3T, 2,000 dr. of silver (the surviving figure), a ratio of 1:10.[66] Thompson and Lewis believe that a figure for the amount of gold cannot be restored with this degree of confidence, owing to doubts over the placement of the figure on the stone.[67] For Thompson, it is not possible to choose between ratios of value of 1:10 or 1:12 for this context. Literary evidence from this period is not strong enough to help us to a conclusion.[68]

It has also been stated that the gold coinage minted during the period from 407/6 to the end of the war took for granted a 1:12 ratio for the value of gold to that of silver.[69] Each attested denomination could thus be easily converted into a whole drachm equivalent in silver coinage, starting with the hemiobol worth 1 dr. up to the didrachm stater equaling 24 silver dr. in value. Yet that equivalence is merely an outgrowth of the traditional sixfold division of the drachm in the Attic monetary system, and that principle of organization would not have been altered regardless of the ratio of gold to silver in their current value.

ENDNOTE B: GOLD DEDICATIONS AND THE GOLD TO SILVER RATIO

There are numerous examples of the following formula and its successors that give instructions for crowning honorands with crowns of specified costs: καὶ τὸν δε̃μ̣[ο]ν τὸν 'Αθεναίο||[ν στεφανõσαι αὐτὸν χρύσõι στε]φάνοι, ποιε̃σα||[ι δὲ τὸν στέφανον ἀπὸ χιλίον δρ]αχμõν (*IG* I³ 102.9–11). Fourth-century and later instances are too numerous for it to be worthwhile to cite exhaustively (cf., for

66 Cf. Ferguson, *Treasurers* 85–95.

67 See Thompson *NC* (1964) 105; Lewis *Festschrift Robinson* 106 (followed in *IG* I³, p. 380).

68 Bogaert *AC* (1963) esp. 94, 97–99, believes that Ael. *VH* 1.22, drawing on Ctesias, implies a rate of exchange between Attic drachms and Persian Darics that was equivalent to a gold:silver ratio of 1:13.6.

69 Robinson *ANSMN* (1960) 10; Thompson *NC* (1964) 111–12; Fischer *MMB* (1977) 384–86.

example, *IG* II^2 103.28–30; 207.7–8; 233.23–26). The Athenians regularly standardized their honors in terms of cost to the treasury rather than through a necessarily subjective standardization of the finished product that might vary in the amount of gold employed and in the cost of production. Such gold crowns were dedicated subsequently (*IG* II^2 212.33–39). Thereafter they appear in Attic cult inventories where they are often listed by weight (n.b.). D.M. Lewis hypothesized from the surviving evidence on the weight of crowns (and a few other comparable dedications) conventional totals in round numbers for the amounts of silver drachms that were authorized for the preceding act of honoring the individual who later made the dedication.[70]

There are several impediments toward using such a procedure. First of all, the cost of production, however modest that is assumed to be, must be taken into account, so that the resulting gold article will always be more expensive than unprocessed gold of the same weight. Thus the finished product is the equivalent of the cost of the raw material and the labor. Therefore the ratios derived from such artifacts are more appropriately compared with each other than with the value ratios for gold and silver generated from other data. Second, crowns of the same weight presumably varied in workmanship and therefore in their price. This makes it unfruitful to compare specific artifacts with each other individually since differences in price because of perceived quality differentials, unrelated to the ratio in value of gold to silver, can overwhelm the presumed changes in the value ratios of the metals. Rather, we must look to general trends.

Next, the method by which Lewis estimates the magnitude of the original cost in silver of the dedication is problematical. Almost all the crowns with which benefactors of the Attic *dēmos* were honored cost 500 or 1,000 dr. except for the unusual 300-dr. crowns of *IG* II^2 2b.8 (of 403/2, n.b.) and of *IG* II^2 1255.9 (which is not a crowning by the *dēmos*). There is not much difficulty in imagining that special dedications could be considerably more expensive, ranging from 0.5T to 3T, but the crowns under 500 dr. in cost that Lewis must hypothesize cause some reason for caution and concern, since they are otherwise rare and appear only in the two clusters of 300 dr. dedications. Can we be certain that these were not more elaborate artistic works in which a larger proportion of the cost (than the 2.5–6 percent suggested by Lewis) was value added by the craftsman? In that eventuality, calculations of ratios of value based on these cases would be undermined.

70 Lewis *Festschrift Robinson* 106, following a suggestion of U. Köhler on *IG* II^2 1496.52–61 in "Aus der Finanzverwaltung Lykurgs," *Hermes* 5 (1871) 223–27, esp. 225–26. M. Vickers, "Persian Gold in Parthenon Inventories," *REA* 91 (1989) 249–57, takes a very different approach to the weights of dedications, attempting to explain them in terms of *weight* (n.b., not monetary or exchange) equivalences with other standards (chiefly the Persic, but also the Thraco-Macedonian). Most of the objects in question are in silver; his equivalences in Darics for the gold dedications do not appear definitive (pp. 254–55). See also Vickers *AJA* (1990) 620–23.

In addition, we must assume that dedications that are aggregated represent a single act not only of dedication but also of honoring. Thus one can work back to a single cost that reflects the ratio in value of silver to gold at the time of production. If individuals, on the contrary, dedicated *stephanoi* acquired at different periods, then there is no reason to divide their total weight among artifacts of equal weight. Accordingly, there is also no guarantee that the crowns dedicated were fashioned in the same context for the values of the two metals. Finally, one can never be entirely sure that crowns were dedicated shortly after their manufacture. Otherwise, delays, even if they only lasted a year or two, create false impressions about the ratio of gold to silver at the time that the dedications first appear in our accounts. With these conditions fresh in mind, the material collected by Lewis, by W.E. Thompson (reported in *IG* I^3 pp. 305–306, 318, 331–2), and by D. Harris,[71] is presented with augmentation, correction, and modernization of citations in Table 19.1 on p. 513 (including the information on gold *phialai* for comparative purposes).

ENDNOTE C: EXCHANGE RATES FOR CYZICENE STATERS

Determining the rate at which Cyzicene staters exchanged with Attic drachms is important both for an interpretation of certain irregular amounts found on the tribute lists, already discussed in Chapter 10, and for its evidence for the value ratio between gold and silver. Unfortunately, the issue is much disputed.[72]

IG I^3 376 (= I^2 301+: 409/8?) can be variously restored in its crucial lines 99–102. Following the restoration of Woodward, the coins in question would be Cyzicenes in the amount of 10,955 st. valued at 43T, 4,920 dr. of silver.[73] This entry is preceded by another entry, one surely refering to Lampsacenes, where the amounts need be less radically supplemented to reach 408 st., 4 *hectae* and silver equivalence of 5T, 388 dr. That entails granting each type of electrum stater an exchange rate of 1:24 with Attic drachms. Bogaert, however, was skeptical of this equation and offered two alternatives for the equivalences of the Cyzicenes:[74] under the first, there were 10,471 st., a silver equivalent of 43T, 3,775 dr., and an exchange rate of 1:25; under the second, 10,078 st., 43T, 4,028 dr., and an exchange rate of 1:26. Lampsacenes were lighter on average than Cyzicenes according to standard metrological works, so that the Cyzicenes

[71] Harris, *Treasurers* 269–71 (with some errors), including a scatter chart of the values of the gold to silver ratio over time.

[72] The recent debate has been dominated by a few scholars with repeated contributions, starting from Bogaert *AC* (1963) 85–119. For an overview, see R. Bogaert, "Le cours du statère de Cyzique à Athènes aux Ve et IVe siècles avant J.-C.: état de la question," *RBN* 123 (1977) 17–39. See also M. Laloux, "La circulation des monnaies d'électrum de Cyzique," *RBN* 117 (1971) 31–69.

[73] A.M. Woodward, "Notes and Queries on Athenian Coinage and Finance," *JHS* 34 (1914) 276–92, esp. 278–80.

[74] Bogaert *AC* (1963) 105–108.

ought to have possessed a higher exchange rate and Lampsacenes to have been less valuable.[75]

According to Bogaert, a ratio higher than 1:24 is also proven by *IG* I³ 370.13–14 (418/7). In a badly fragmented setting, a number of Cyzicenes ending in an amount of *hectae* is matched with an equivalent of silver of which only the final 2 ob. survive. That result would be impossible if the exchange rate were 1:24, since a 1:24 ratio would yield a round number. W.E. Thompson made the same observation independently, and further pointed to lines 57–58 (from the accounts of 416/5) where a number of Cyzicenes has a silver value that ends in 3 ½ ob.[76] He also noted *IG* I³ 376.124–26, where a silver equivalent for what is probably an amount of Cyzicenes ends in 2 ob. (his preference and the reading of *IG* I³) or 100 dr. Thompson not only agrees that the Cyzicene could not have exchanged with the Attic drachm at 1:24 in these contexts, but further concludes that a fractional rate of exchange is demanded by the figure ending in 3 ½ ob. He believes that a fractional value ca. 25 Attic dr. is likely and fits the weight differential between the Cyzicene and the Lampsacene. His final conclusion would be that Cyzicenes were not the second coinage listed in *IG* I³ 376.99–101, which would have been Darics or Phocaics, but the third coinage listed later in lines 101–105, since their silver equivalent ends in 12 dr., 1 ob.

S.K. Eddy attempted to pin down Thompson's estimate, working from the weight and the gold content of the Cyzicene.[77] He suggested that *IG* I³ 376.124–26 actually ends with the notation of 4 ob. for the silver equivalent of what must have been a round number of Cyzicenes (there is no room for restoring a number of *hectae*). Attic values for the stater of 24 dr., 4 ob. or 24 dr., 5 ob. are the only alternatives that meet these conditions. Unfortunately, this judgment leads to the improbable result that *IG* I³ 376.105 cannot feature a numeral ending, as it seems, with the sign for 1 ob. Thus, Eddy emended in that locus to produce a value for the Cyzicene of 24 dr., 5 ob. before proceeding to sugggest how the other passages noted above may be restored in accordance with this same value ratio. Subsequently, Thompson countered by noting that Eddy's reasoning depended both on the value ratio not involving a fraction of an obol and not diverging much from ca. 25 dr. to (for example) 23 dr., 3 ob. or 26 dr., 3 ob.[78] Thompson took a hint from the value of the Lampsacene stater which he would place at 24 dr., and the heavier weight of the Cyzicene to place a "floor" under the value of the Cyzicene at 25 dr. Thompson suggests that the most probable value for the Cyzicene in Attic drachms in *IG* I³ 376 is 25 dr., 4 ½ ob. (with 26 dr., 3 ob. his next choice).[79]

75 Cf. W.E. Thompson, "The Value of the Cyzicene Stater," *NC*⁷ 3 (1963) 1–4; esp. 2–3.

76 Thompson, *NC* (1963) 2–4.

77 S.K. Eddy, "The Value of the Cyzicene Stater at Athens in the Fifth Century," *ANSMN* 16 (1970) 13–22.

78 Thompson *AC* (1970) 578–83.

79 Thompson *AC* (1970) 574–78.

Determining the value of the Cyzicene earlier in the fifth century demands an indirect approach, and one over which many may experience discomfort, inasmuch as there is a danger of confusing stathmic and numismatic units of measurement and equating equivalences from different periods. Herodotus states that the Babylonian talent of 5,400 *sigloi* was equivalent to 70 Euboeic/Attic *mnai*, or 7,000 dr. (Hdt. 3.89.2, unemended; cf. Pollux 9.86). Hence a Daric equivalent to 20 *sigloi* was worth about 26 Attic dr. (citing Xen. *Anab.* 1.7.18), and the next question becomes the value of the Cyzicene to the Daric. Bogaert argued that the Cyzicene was more valuable than the Daric, ca. 28 dr.[80] J.C. Guépin countered that the Cyzicene was equivalent to the Daric.[81] After the articles and counter-articles of Bogaert and Guépin, the analyses published by Bodenstedt made the most substantial contribution, not only for his investigation of the composition of a small number of Cyzicenes but for his suggestions on the correction of the results of other methods.[82] His conclusions supported Bogaert in his view on the superiority of the Cyzicene to the Daric. Therefore, the Cyzicene had fallen in value during the Peloponnesian War in comparison to the Attic silver drachm, exactly the result predictable from the change in the gold to silver ratio in favor of silver.

As for the later fourth-century value of the Cyzicene, several passages shed light on the subject. Some have believed that Attic silver drachms exchanged with Cyzicenes at a value ratio of 28:1 in the northern Pontos, as implied by an inscribed and official rate of exchange between Olbian (Aiginetic) drachms and Cyzicenes early in the fourth century (*SIG*³ 218). It is also quite possible that a similar rate of 1:28 prevailed at Pantikapaion in 327/6 according to [Dem.] *Against Phormio* 34.23–26.[83] In a rather more speculative vein, Marchetti argues that the same speech hints at a contemporary rate at Athens of 1 Cyzicene st. to 30 Attic silver dr. Care must be observed, however: another interpretation of the same speech renders a ratio of value of 21 dr., 4 ob.[84]

Caution is sensible in this matter. Clearly, the intrinsic value of the gold (especially) and the silver in electrum coins at a particular moment created boundaries within which value ratios may have varied. Nonetheless, other market forces played their role, and the intrinsic value of the constituent metals may have been chiefly significant in establishing a basic worth below which

[80] Bogaert *AC* (1963) 91–94; Bogaert, "Encore le cours du statère de Cyzique aux Ve et IVe siècles avant J.-C.," *AC* 33 (1964) 121–28; Bogaert, "Méthodes d'analyse et numismatique: Le problème du Cyzicène III," *AC* 34 (1965) 204–13.

[81] J.P. Guépin, "Greek Coinage and Persian Bimetallism," *Jaarboek voor Munt- en Penningkunde* 49 (1962) 1–19, esp. 12–13; Guépin, "Le cours du Cyzicène," *AC* 34 (1965) 199–203. I do not believe that Xen. *Anab.* 7.6.30, 37 contributes anything toward a conclusion. Note Bogaert *AC* (1963) 91; *AC* (1964) 126; Guépin *AC* (1965) 202; Marchetti *RBN* (1976) 37–40; Bogaert *RBN* (1977) 26–27.

[82] F. Bodenstedt, *Phökaisches Elektron-Geld von 600–326 v. Chr.* (Mainz 1976) 39–41. See also Bogaert *RBN* (1977) 33–35.

[83] Marchetti *RBN* (1976) 40–51.

[84] Cf. Bogaert *AC* (1963) 99–104; *RBN* (1977) 27–33.

coins seldom dropped. The interaction of the proportion of gold content and other market forces may explain why it was necessary to mint *hectae* with a higher proportion of gold than the corresponding staters (as Bodenstedt's analyses seem to suggest). In addition, one cannot be certain that the essential figures that are missing from our inscribed evidence have been or even can be correctly restored. And there is particular doubt regarding *IG* I^3 376 where to look in the document for the crucial anticipated reference to Cyzicene staters.

As our epigraphical data comes from more than one year, there is no certainty that the value of the Cyzicene did not change in terms of Attic drachms within a few years.[85] Furthermore, as discussed above in reference to the reception by the Athenians of electrum coins in the collection of the tribute, it cannot be excluded that a rate of 1 electrum st. equaling 24 dr. may have been used for Phocaic electrum *and* Cyzicene electrum (and possibly a common ratio of 1 to 27 dr. at other junctures). In the case of the Cyzicene stater such a value ratio would have been particularly favorable to the Athenian government. This differential might be indicative of the discrepancy between the "buy" rate for Cyzicenes (where they were permitted to replace Attic tetradrachms in tribute payment) and the higher "sell" rate at which Cyzicenes were carried on Athenian accounts. This supposition adds a further cautious note to what is necessarily a speculative survey of work on the value of the Cyzicene stater and other electrum coins. In Table 19.2 (p. 514), Bogaert's exchange ratios for Cyzicene staters have been annotated in order to suggest the state of current scholarship.[86]

[85] Thompson, *AC* (1970) 587–88, notes that *IG* I^3 370 may embody a different ratio of value, one prevailing before the massive expenditures of the Decelean War.

[86] *AC* (1964) 212, as emended and supplemented by *RBN* (1977) 35–36.

20

IMITATIONS OF ATTIC COINS

THE EVOLUTION of the imitation of Athenian coinage allows us a means of ingress into the subject of how the unraveling of Athenian hegemony affected the use of money in the Aegean basin and more widely in the eastern Mediterranean. The phenomenon of coins that copied the type of Athenian coinage with varying degrees of fidelity is surprisingly widespread.[1] Many thousands of imitations of Attic tetradrachms that circulated alongside genuine Attic coins in the Near East and Egypt were minted. The existence of these good-quality copies of Attic tetradrachms was not always owed to an intent to deceive recipients, inasmuch as the issuer often possessed a near approximation of the requisite silver (sometimes supplemented by gold) to implement his program of minting or any other emission with an appropriate weight and value for his coins.[2] And that is not to mention the cases in which these coins have a deliberately caricatured appearance that suggests that no particular effort was being made to dupe their users.[3] Accordingly, the purpose of

[1] Many of these coins were discussed in E.T. Newell, *Miscellanea Numismatica: Cyrene to India*, *NNM* 82 (New York 1938) 53–55, 59–75, 82–88. An excellent survey of the utilization of the owl of Athena as a coin type by non-Athenians is provided by H. Nicolet-Pierre, "L'oiseau d'Athena, d'Égypte en Bactriane: Quelques remarques sur l'usage d'un type monétaire à l'époque classique," in L. Kahil, C. Augé, and P. Linant de Bellefonds (eds.), *Iconographie classique et identités régionales*, *BCH* Suppl. 14 (1986) 365–76.

[2] This estimation of the quality of pseudo-Attic coinage is based on the research of J. Diebolt and H. Nicolet-Pierre, "Recherches sur le métal de tétradrachmes à types athéniens," *SNR* 56 (1977) 79–91, where the results of analysis by neutron activation of several groups of Attic and pseudo-Attic coins are summarized. The salient feature of pseudo-Attic coins is their greater variability when compared with probable authentic issues of the Athenian mint. Coins from the second half of the fourth century that betrayed their non-Attic provenience by legend or caricatured style were compared with a group of contemporary coins likely to be genuine. The imitations possessed a markedly higher proportion of copper. It is hard, however, to estimate the effect of such variation on the intrinsic value of the coins, since they also often contained higher percentages of gold. If these coins are assessed in terms of their bullion value, their higher proportions of gold more than offset the adulteration with copper of their component of silver. Most are at least as valuable as contemporary emissions of the Attic mint. When the anonymous pseudo-Attic coins of the late fifth and early fourth centuries are juxtaposed with their fifth-century stylistic analogues, the higher proportion of copper is again noticeable, although it is less than that of the fourth-century imitations. The proportion of gold is lower than in the fourth-century pseudo-Attic coins and more than likely genuine issues. Some of these coins may be slightly less valuable than their authentic analogues.

[3] The continuum of imitation spans faithful reproductions of Attic coins struck in Egypt to pieces like the Gazan tetradrachms of ca. 400 that use the Euboeic/Attic standard and

these coiners of pseudo-Attic currency often does not seem to have been to exploit the users of Attic coinage, but to supplement the stock of Attic coins in circulation. In many other cases, however, those issuing copies of Attic coins intended their coins to circulate alongside genuine Attic money without calling attention to themselves. The division between the faithful and the perfunctory imitators seems to have resided in the degree of regular penetration by genuine Attic coins into the local economy of the minter. Perfunctory minters had no incentive to minimize differentiation of their own imitations from the few Attic coins in local circulation; they merely strove to offer currency in a familiar, widely accepted form. Their handiwork is notably of less interest to us, because perforce it has less to do with Aegean monetary conditions.

In general, the need to provide copies of Attic coins necessarily implies that there were economic contexts in which the expectation of the partners to an exchange of goods was that the proper monetary medium was to be Athenian coins. That some parties to such exchanges were forced to go to the trouble and expense of minting imitations of Athenian coins demonstrates that a sufficient amount of Attic money could not be acquired through normal commercial means. A further corollary may be that the flow of Attic coinage toward such users had slackened or failed to keep pace in the late fifth and early fourth centuries so that the supply of Attic money could not be maintained or expanded in proportion to a growing scale of monetized transactions. By the early fourth century, the range of transactions that could be mediated by pseudo-Attic coins extended to relatively modest transactions, as is shown by the minting of pseudo-Attic obols outside Greece.

Although the imitation of Athenian owls is a complex phenomenon that has not yet been subjected to exhaustive review,[4] the phenomenon of the minting of pseudo-Attic coins was widespread throughout the Near East during the entire fourth century.[5] Sometimes pseudo-Attic

---

borrow the symbol of a owl, idiosyncratically posed, for the *obverse*. See Nicolet-Pierre, *Iconographie* 367.

[4] The most useful surveys are D. Schlumberger, "L'argent grec dans l'empire Achéménide," in R. Curiel and D. Schlumberger, *Trésors monétaires d'Afghanistan*, *Mémoires de la délégation archéologique française en Afghanistan* 14 (Paris 1952) 1–64, esp. 19–25; Nicolet-Pierre, *Iconographie* 365–76. esp. 367.

[5] On Palestinian imitations with Aramaic legends, see Newell, *Miscellanea* 54–55. On fourth-century pseudo-Attic money minted at Babylon and used in Mesopotamia, see Newell, *Miscellanea* 82–88; G. Le Rider, "Tetradrachmes 'au lion' et imitations d'Athènes en Babylonie," *SM* 22 (1972) 1–7 (cf. *IGCH* #1752–53). Most appear to follow Alexander and are marked by an eclecticism of style in which pseudo-Athenian coins of Egyptian provenience are themselves stylistic intermediaries. See also Nicolet-Pierre, *Iconographie* 374. On a Phoenician imitation, see G. Le Rider, "Monnaies grecques récemment acquises par le Cabinet des Medailles," *RN*[6] 3 (1961) 1–26, esp. 13–14. On the later, parallel minting of

coins bear symbols engraved on their dies that reveal their origin; others have Aramaic letters as the only distinguishing marks.[6] Still others show that their provenience was not Attic by the stylistic variations that cannot be paralleled on Attic issues. For example, Newell placed the earliest imitations with Aramaic legends on the reverse at the very beginning of the fourth century. The border lands of the *arkhē* in Persian Asia Minor and in Egypt were the testing grounds for an adaptation of the Greek monetary regime in which Athenian coins aided in monetizing economies.

The manifestations of this phenomenon that are more significant for our discussion are good imitations of late fifth-century Attic tetradrachms of Egyptian (or "pharaonic") or Syrian derivation.[7] Although the best foreign die cutters carefully copied genuine Athenian coins, they were conservative in their treatment. Thus, we can never be certain that the imitations of Attic issues of the fifth century are contemporary with their models. The weight of the evidence, however, does seem to support the view that significant imitation (at least in Egypt) began in the last two decades of the fifth century. We even possess a reverse die that was found in Egypt (with *IGCH* #1663, "Tel el Athrib" [fourth century]) that was used to strike pseudo-Attic tetradrachms of the very category of coins with which it was found.[8] G. Dattari linked the die with the

---

Athenian tetradrachms (from the fourth century) with Aramaic legends and found in Arabia, see P. Naster, "Remarques au sujet des imitations des monnaies d'Athènes dans la presque'ile Arabique," in I. Gedai and K. Biró-Sey (eds.), *Proceedings of the International Numismatic Symposium* (Budapest 1980) 31–36. There was often considerable independent evolution of stylization in these issues. See also Nicolet-Pierre, *Iconographie* 370–71. On imitations found in Bactria, see Nicolet-Pierre, "Monnaies grecques trouvées en Afghanistan," *RN*[6] 15 (1973) 35–42; Nicolet-Pierre and M. Amandry, "Un nouveau trésor de monnaies d'argent pseudo-athéniennes venu d'Afghanistan (1990)" *RN*[6] 26 (1994) 34–54.

[6] Cf. Nicolet-Pierre, *Iconographie* 369–70.

[7] E.S.G. Robinson, "The Tell El-Mashkuta Hoard of Athenian Tetradrachms," *NC*[6] 7 (1947) 115–21, provides basic discussion, while noting typological oddities such as a tetradrachm with an owl with outstretched wings (or dual olive sprays) that is perhaps Philisto-Arabian in origin. See also J. Mavrogordato, "Was there a Pre-Macedonian Mint in Egypt?" *NC*[4] 8 (1908) 197–207 (including descriptions of several obols); Newell, *Miscellanea* 59–62 (including, among 3 ob., one where NAU, for Naukratis, had usurped AΘE); Robinson, "Coins from the Excavations at Al-Mina (1936)," *NC*[5] 17 (1937) 182–96, esp. 186; J.G. Milne, "The Currency of Egypt under the Ptolemies," *JEA* 24 (1938) 200–207, esp. 200–201, who would limit the usage of such coins to mercenaries; G.K. Jenkins, "Greek Coins Recently Acquired by the British Museum," *NC*[6] 15 (1955) 131–56, esp. 144–50; J.W. Curtis, "Coinage of Pharaonic Egypt," *JEA* 43 (1957) 71–76. See also Nicolet-Pierre, *Iconographie* 369, dating the first of these coins in the fifth century.

[8] G. Dattari, "Comments on a Hoard of Athenian Tetradrachms Found in Egypt," *JIAN* 8 (1905) 103–11, esp. 110–11. See also J.G. Milne, "The Beni Ḥasan Coin-Hoard," *JEA* 19 (1933) 119–21; Nicolet-Pierre, *Iconographie* 372. Cf., for the hypothesis of a thief, I.N. Svoronos, "Σφραγὶς Ἀθηναϊκοῦ τετραδράχμου," *Corolla Numismatica* (New York 1906) 285–95, esp. 293–95; for the theory of dies sent officially by the Athenians to their Egyptian

financial policy of the Pharaoh Takhos, acting on the instance of the Athenian general Khabrias who was serving with his forces (cf. [Aris.] *Oec.* 1350b33–1351a17).[9]

The relevant hoards containing the earliest specimens of such material are *IGCH* #1243, "Karaman" (ca. 400–390): 42 tetradr. with a Tissaphernes tetradrachm; #1259, "Cilicia" (ca. 380): 3 tetrdr. and 1 coin fragment; #1487, "Al Mina, 1936" (ca. 375): 18 Attic and pseudo-Attic tetradr.; #1488, "Al Mina, 1936" (ca. 375): 26 Attic and pseudo-Attic tetradr.; #1490, "Aleppo" (ca. 400–350): pseudo-Attic fractions; #1649, "Tell el Maskhouta" (either fourth-century or ca. 330); #1830, "Cabul" (ca. 380).[10] The poorly described *IGCH* #1484, "Marash" (fifth century), a hoard from Commagene, contains a range of pseudo-Athenian variants including some that are rather caricatured and self-betraying in their style.[11] Some examples of pseudo-Attic coins have even been found at Athens itself (see immediately below).[12]

Buttrey has recently reviewed the Egyptian material both in light of a large hoard (of 347 Attic tetradrachms) of the early fourth century that was found at Karanis in the Fayum and through a revisiting of *IGCH* #1649, "Tell el Maskhouta."[13] He has identified two classes of such imitations that he calls style X and style B, both numerous in Egyptian hoards. They possess a high degree of silver fineness. Style B is somewhat finer in

allies, see Curtis *JEA* (1957) 71–72. For the die from Tel el Athrib and several others found in Egypt, see also C.C. Vermeule, *Some Notes on Ancient Dies and Coining Methods* (London 1954) 10–12 on #2–4. According to G.F. Hill, "Ancient Methods of Coining," *NC*[5] 2 (1922) 1–42, esp. 14, two similar dies from Sais were exhibited in the British Museum in 1910.

[9] Milne *JEA* (1933) 119–21; Curtis *JEA* (1957) 71–76; E. Will, "Chabrias et les finances de Tachôs," *REA* 63 (1960) 254–75, esp. 262–65.

[10] See also *IGCH* #1504, "Nablus" (ca. 332); #1662, "Semenood" (fourth century), with coins of Sabakes; *IGCH* #1663, "Tel el Athrib" (fourth century); #1752, "Hillah" (shortly before 310); #1753, "Babylonia?, 1954" (shortly before 310), with coins of Mazakes in both of the latter; #2165, "Sicily, before 1890" (late fourth century). Note these later hoards, also containing coinage of Alexander: *IGCH* #1421, "Cilicia, 1964" (ca. 320); #1436, "Asia Minor, ca. 1966" (ca. 323); #1507, "Abu Shusheh" (ca. 330); #1514, "Tel Tsippor" (after 311); #1761, "Babylonia, ca. 1900?" (ca. 280).

[11] Nicolet-Pierre, *Iconographie* 368–69, notes a tetradrachm with the satrapal obverse and standard reverse (if this is not an error), a coin with an Arabic or Aramaic letter, one with a transposed owl reverse, one with an obverse of Athena of non-Attic style, and several examples of Egyptian pseudo-Attic tetradrachms (see below).

[12] See J.H. Kroll, *The Greek Coins, The Athenian Agora* 26 (Princeton 1993) 6–7, 17 (for *#8f–h*).

[13] T.V. Buttrey, "Pharaonic Imitations of Athenian Tetradrachms," in T. Hackens and R. Weiller (eds.), *Proceedings of the 9th International Congress of Numismatics. Berne, September 1979* (Luxemburg 1982) 1.137–40; Buttrey, "Seldom What They Seem: The Case of the Athenian Tetradrachm," in W. Heckel and R. Sullivan (eds.), *Ancient Coins of the Graeco-Roman World: The Nickle Numismatic Papers* (Waterloo, Ont. 1984) 292–94. Buttrey's point that we must reevaluate the late fifth-century Attic imperial mint in light of a considerable proportion of its output being in fact Egyptian and fourth-century is an interesting one, but his suggestion will need more examination of the die links of coins appearing in Egyptian hoards.

quality of execution and has often been mistaken for genuine issues of the Attic mint. It perhaps belongs to the fourth century, and constituted a massive emission of coins (124 known obverse dies from the Fayum; 70 more known from a partial study of *IGCH* #1649).

An appraisal of Buttrey's observation that these imitations were an official coinage of Egypt will depend on how we understand the engagement of the authorities with such coins (beyond the decision to strike them). It is likely that the coins served as a medium for the discharge of governmental financial responsibilities (especially to Greeks). Insofar as the Egyptian government received payments in coin (a most obscure proposition), the usage by any "taxpayers" (of indirect levies) of such pseudo-Attic issues along with genuine Athenian money would have been welcome. Nonetheless, the independent regimes of fourth-century Egypt were presumably operating within a predominantly natural economy. Moreover, the anonymity of these issues excluded the ideological and propagandistic functions sometimes associated with an official coinage. Finally, the imitations obviously claimed no status as exclusive legal tender that was not already held by genuine Attic coins established through market forces. The trade port of Naukratis, where Ionian and Aiginetan traders predominated, linked Egypt with the Aegean economy.[14] The establishment of Attic coins as a preferential monetary medium in Egypt was initially an outgrowth of the practices and predilections of the Naukratite commercial community, whether resident or transient.

Buttrey also adduces a tetradrachm from a find or a group of hoards from Iraq (*CH* 1.78 = *CH* 3.22) that bears the legend in demotic Egyptian of "Artaxerxes pharaoh" that stylistically belongs to style B and was probably produced around the time of the Persian reconquest of Egypt in 343. The coin was accompanied by many other imitation Attic tetradrachms of Mesopotamian or Egyptian provenience (probably fourth-century).[15] That would constitute another indication that style B was issued by independent Egyptian leaders of the earlier fourth century, perhaps (in part) to pay Greek mercenaries.[16] The expectation of early

[14] Figueira, *Excursions* 311–23.

[15] See O. Mørkholm, "A Coin of Artaxerxes III," *NC*[7] 14 (1974) 1–4 with A.F. Shore, "The Demotic Inscription on a Coin of Artaxerxes," *NC*[7] 14 (1974) 5–8.

[16] In addition to Artaxerxes, the last two Persian satraps of Egypt, Sabakes and Mazakes, were also emitting pseudo-Attic tetradrachms. See Newell, *Miscellanea* 62–75; H. Nicolet-Pierre, "Les monnaies des deux derniers satrapes d'Égypte avant la conquête d'Alexandre," in O. Mørkholm and N.M. Waggoner (eds.), *Greek Numismatics and Archaeology: Essays in Honor of Margaret Thompson* (Wetteren 1979) 221–30; M.J. Price, "New Owls for Pharaoh," *Minerva* 1 (1990) 39–40.

fourth-century mercenaries to be paid in Attic coins exemplified the sort of precedent from the late fifth-century Aegean economy that was exported to Egypt. In contrast, style X derived from late fifth-century minting activity.[17] Care must be observed in dating any pseudo-Attic issue, as they remain faithful to the style of the massive, genuinely Attic issues of the second half of the fifth century long into the fourth century, as Nicolet-Pierre notes about the "Artaxerxes coin."[18]

Furthermore, the practice of Near Eastern imitation of Attic coins can be given a more specific basis of origination. Peloponnesian fleets worked within a logistical milieu sustained by private merchants acting comparably to the pattern first established with the fleets of the Delian League. That logistical framework has already been described as a microcosm of the Aegean economy that had earlier probably worked in terms of Athenian money (pp. 261–63). A series of Attic tetradrachms bear various representations of Persian authorities as additional items along with the usual type.[19] These are heads of the Great King (with tiara), presumably Dareios II, and an unbearded figure (n.b., also with tiara) who may represent Kyros the Younger, portrayed as Karanos or regent for Asia Minor. Various Aramaic letters also appear on coins exhibiting the same style of treatment of the conventional features.[20] These additional items are placed on the cheek of Athena (where they are usually almost too small for identification) or at the left foot of the owl on the reverse. These coins were minted by Kyros to assist the Peloponnesian war effort after his arrival in Asia Minor in 407, and particularly to pay the monthy wages of sailors in the fleet (Xen. *HG* 1.5.1–7). It was not only advantageous for the enemies of Athens to offer equal or preferably higher salaries to entice defectors from Athenian service, but also for them to provide payment in a familiar medium, tetradrachms on the Attic standard. Indeed, we have a passing remark of Thucydides on just such a financial situation when he reports that the Spartans sought pay for their sailors in Athenian coinage in 412 (8.5.5, 29.1–2; cf. Xen. *HG* 1.5.6–7). Thus the pseudo-Attic coinage in question seems to precede Aigospotamoi and belong to the Ionian War.

Inasmuch as there are many superficially "Athenian" tetradrachms that have strong affinities with the coins that betray their Persian

[17] See also Nicolet-Pierre, *Iconographie* 369, dating the first of the Egyptian imitations in the fifth century. Cf. Curtis *JEA* (1957) 76, dating them to 392–80.

[18] See Nicolet-Pierre, *Iconographie* 371.

[19] For full discussion, see W. Weiser, "Die Eulen von Kyros dem Jüngeren zu den ersten Münzporträts lebender Menschen," *ZPE* 76 (1989) 267–96, esp. 267–78.

[20] Weiser *ZPE* (1989) 276–78, puts the coins with an *alef* for Artaxerses II and a *kaf* for Kyros in 404–401, after the death of Dareios II.

provenience by typology, Weiser suggests that these coins also derived from the mint of Kyros at Sardis. He would identify as such many of the Attic tetradrachms in *IGCH* #1255, "Cilicia, 1957" (ca. 400: the "Celenderis Hoard").[21] Kyros may have brought some of the 500T given to him by Dareios for the war and his own resources in bullion and other media that he chose to coin or recoin (Xen. *HG* 1.5.2–3). When Xenophon tells us that he promised the Spartans to κατακόψειν the throne of gold and silver on which he sat, we are meant to understand the verb to mean 'would strike into coins' (cf. Hdt. 3.96.2; DS 16.56.6).

There also exists an owl of normal weight, but with the usual reverse inscription ΑΘΕ replaced by ΒΑΣ to signify a royal issue and with the usual obverse replaced by a portrait of a Persian satrap, perhaps Tissaphernes (in *IGCH* #1243, "Karaman, Lycaonia, 1946," ca. 400–390).[22] This money was probably minted by Tissaphernes to pay those who expected payment in Attic coinage. Robinson placed the minting activity of Tissaphernes at Miletos in 412–11.[23] Paradoxically, our broadening awareness of the prevalence of high-quality pseudo-Attic coinage has complicated this chronological determination. *IGCH* #1243 was dated by virtue of its apparently fifth-century Attic tetradrachms that may in fact be pseudo-Attic coins of Egyptian origin that were minted in the early fourth century in the style of earlier Attic coins. In that case, *IGCH* #1243 may be downdated either to 375–50 or closer to mid-century. In the former case, one may still choose to attribute to Tissaphernes and date to 401–395, but sever any linkage with Miletos and the fleet operations against the Athenians (as does Weiser who bases himself on similiarities with the *chalkoi* bearing the legend ΤΙΣΣΑ). Or we may agree with Price to make an association with some other satrap.[24]

[21] Weiser *ZPE* (1989) 276–78. Cf. C.M. Kraay, "The Celenderis Hoard," *NC*[7] 2 (1962) 1–15, esp. 1.

[22] Weiser *ZPE* (1989) 284 locates the hoard not at ancient Laranda in Lykaonia (Robinson followed by Schlumberger, *L'argent grec* 9) but at Marash, ancient Antiochia in Commagene (see H. Seyrig as cited in the *IGCH*). Northern Asia Minor is an alternative locale for his coining. See the comment of A.J. Johnston in Nicolet-Pierre, *Iconographie* 375.

[23] E.S.G. Robinson, "Greek Coins Acquired by the British Museum 1938–1948. I," *NC*[6] 8 (1948) 43–59, esp. 48–56. For analysis, see also Robinson *ANSMN* 9 (1960) 4; cf. H.A. Cahn, "Dynast oder Satrap?," *SM* 25 (1975) 84–91. See also S. Hurter, "Der Tissaphernes-Fund," *Festschrift Thompson* 97–108, esp. 100–101, 108; H.A. Cahn, "Le monnayage des satrapes: iconographie et signification," *REA* 91 (1989) 97–105, esp. 99–100.

[24] Weiser *ZPE* (1989) 283–86; see the comment of M.J. Price in Cahn *REA* (1989) 106. On the early fourth-century coinage (401–395), with portraiture of Tissaphernes from Astyra in Mysia, see H.A. Cahn, "Zwei griechische Miszellen," in R. Margolis and H. Voegtli (eds.), *Numismatics: Witness to History* (Wetteren 1986) 12–14.

CONCLUSION

It should be concluded that these imitations of Attic currency started from the period of the Peloponnesian War and doubtless reflect the economic and fiscal conditions of the Decelean/Ionian phase of the war. Not only had the production of the Attic silver mines fallen off markedly, but the Athenian government had now far less resources with which to conduct military activity. Fewer tetradrachms were being issued. The enemies of the Athenians operating in the eastern Aegean were the first to feel the need for procuring more Attic coins than could be acquired through normal means, but they were hardly the last. Those in Egypt (and later in the Levant) who chose to use Attic money for *some* transactions confronted circumstances in which more of a smaller output of tetradrachms were being spent for the war in the Aegean basin and fewer were being circulated to non-Greeks.[25] The entire phenomenon is a strong reminder of the characteristic flow of silver during the *arkhē*. Athens and its allies balanced their purchases of goods from the Near East and Egypt (especially after the mid-century waning of hostilities with the Persians) by exporting silver, much of it in the form of tetradrachms.

Furthermore, it is likely that less grain was coming from Egypt to the *arkhē*, grain that would often be paid for in silver, either because hostilities made the conveyance of grain from Egypt impractical or the Persian authorities in Egypt preempted the loading of cargoes for Attica. Thus the Athenians had been made more dependent on their friends, the Spartokids of the Crimea, for wheat. Non-Greeks who were accustomed (like the Egyptians or the Persian authorities in Egypt) or were compelled by reasons of state (like Tissaphernes and Kyros the Younger) to conduct business in tetradrachms made efforts to supplement the Attic coinage then in circulation with their own imitations. As shall be seen shortly, these imitations circulated to individuals, like mercenaries and merchants following in the wake of armies of the period, who would in their turn carry them toward the Aegean or even toward Attica. The arrival of good quality reproductions of Attic tetradrachms on the territory of the mother city of their models created difficulties for the definition of legal coinage. That development stood as a further, curious legacy of the prominence of Attic money during the fifth-century political hegemony.

[25] M.J. Price, "Darius and the Daric," *REA* 91 (1989) 9–14, comments "the Attic tetradrachm represented a ready-made two shekel piece" (p. 11), which helps explain some of the initial popularity of the coin in monetizing economies of the Near East.

21

THE COINAGE LAW OF 375/4

THE COLLAPSE of the fifth-century Attic hegemony and the monetary arrangements that were correlated with it find important retrospective illumination in Nikophon's law on coinage of 375/4, found on stone in the Agora.[1] The inscription, which does not deal with the rationale for contemporary monetary policy, sets down the practical conditions for the functioning of the Dokimastes 'Validator,' a public slave charged with the duty of approving the coins to be used in the marketplace (cf. [Plato] *Virt.* 378D–E; Men. fr. 581 K/Th.).[2] It will be necessary to cite the inscription in full before proceeding; I follow the editio princeps of Stroud, an admirable treatment on which this discussion and the work of others greatly depends. The text printed in *SEG* 26.72 has been used.

ἔδοξε τοῖς νομοθέταις, ἐπὶ Ἱππο[δάμαντος]
ἄρχοντος: Νικοφῶν εἶπεν·
τὸ ἀργύριον δέχεσθαι τὸ Ἀττικọ̀ν ὅτ[αν δεικνύητ?]-
αι ἀργυρõγ καὶ ἔχηι τὸν δημόσιογ χα[ρακτῆρα. ὁ δὲ]
δοκιμαστὴς ὁ δημόσιος καθήμενος με[ταξὺ τῶν τρ]-
απεζῶν δοκιμαζέτω κατὰ ταῦτα ὅσαι ἡ[μέραι πλὴν]
ὅταν ἧ[ι] χρημάτωγ καταβολή, τότε δὲ ἐ[ν τῶι βολευτ]-
ηρίωι. ἐὰν δέ τις προσενέγκηι ξ̣[ε]ν[ικὸν ἀργύριον?]
ἔχον τὸν αὐτὸγ χαρακτῆρα τῶι Ἀττι[κῶ]ι̣, ἐ[ὰν καλόν],
ἀποδιδότω τῶι προσενεγκόντι. ἐὰν δὲ ὑπ[όχαλκον]
ἢ ὑπομόλυβδον ἢ κίβδηλον, διακοπτέτ̣ω πα[ραυτίκ]-

[1] See R.S. Stroud, "An Athenian Law on Silver Coinage," *Hesperia* 43 (1974) 157–88. For complete reviews, see S. Alessandri, "Il significato storico della legge di Nicofonte sul *dokimastes* monetario," *ASNP*^{3} 14 (1984) 369–93; G. Stumpf, "Ein athenisches Münzgesetz des 4. Jh. v. Chr.," *JNG* 36 (1986) 23–40. Good reviews of the scholarship down to their dates of composition are provided by Stumpf *JNG* (1986) 23–26; T.R. Martin, "Silver Coins and Public Slaves in the Athenian Law of 375/4 B.C.," in D.M. Metcalf (ed.), *Mnemata: Papers in Memory of Nancy M. Waggoner* (New York 1991) 21–47, esp. 21–24 with notes 2–3.

[2] See A. Giovannini, "Athenian Currency in the Late Fifth and Early Fourth Century B.C.," *GRBS* 16 (1975) 185–95, esp. 195. T.V. Buttrey, "The Athenian Currency Law of 375/4 B.C." *Festschrift Thompson* 33–45, esp. 38–39; Buttrey, "More on the Athenian Coinage Law of 375/4 B.C.," *NAC* 10 (1981) 71–94, esp. 83–88, for discussion of the lack of "testing" by the Dokimastes and of the inapposite translation (after Stroud) of "Tester" for the official. The procedures of testing and evaluation of coins are surveyed by R. Bogaert, "L'essai des monnaies dans l'antiquité," *RBN* 122 (1976) 5–34. The advantages for control and accountability in having a public slave as Dokimastes are partially addressed by Martin, *Mnemata* 28–47.

α καὶ ἔστω ἱερὸν τῆς Μητρὸς [τ]ῶν θεῶγ καὶ κ[αταβαλ]λέτω ἐς τὴμ βολήν. ἐαν δὲ μὴ καθῆτ[α]ι ὁ δοκι[μαστὴ̣ς] ἢ μὴ δοκιμάζηι κατὰ τὸν νόμον, τυπ̣[τ]όντων [αὐτὸν ο]ἱ τõ δήμο συλλογῆς πεντήκοντα πληγὰς τ[ῆι μάστι]γι. ἐὰν δέ τις μὴ δέχηται τὸ ἀ̣[ρ]γ[ύρ]ιον ὅ τ[ι ἂν ὁ δοκι]μαστὴς δοκιμάστηι, στερέσθω ὧν ἂμ [π]ωλῆτ̣[αι ἐκεί]ηι τῆι ἡμέραι. φαίνειν δὲ τὰ μὲν ἐν [τ]ῷ̣ι σ̣[ίτωι πρὸς] τὸς σιτοφύλακας, τὰ δὲ ἐν τῆι ἀγορᾶι κ[α]ὶ [ἐν τῶι ἄλ]λωι ἄστει πρὸς τοὺς τὸ δήμο συλλογέ[ας], τὰ [δὲ ἐν τῶ]ι ἐμπορίωι κὰι τῶι Πει[ρ]αιεῖ πρὸς τοὺ[ς ἐπιμελητ]ὰς τοῦ ἐμπορίο πλὴν τὰ ἐν τωῖ σίτωι, τὰ δὲ [ἐν τῶι σί]τωι πρὸς τοὺς σιτοφύλακας. τῶν δὲ φανθέ[ντων, ὁπό]σα μὲν ἂν ἦι ἐντὸς δέκα δραχμῶν, κύριοι ὄ[ντων οἱ ἄ]ρχοντες διαγιγνώσκειν, τὰ δὲ ὑπὲρ [δ]έ[κ]α [δραχμάς], ἐσαγόντων ἐς τὸ δικαστήριον. οἱ δὲ θε[σμ]οθ[έται π]αρεχόντων αὐτοῖς ἐπικληρõντες δικα[στήριον ὅ]ταμ παραγγέλλωσιν ἢ εὐθυνέ̣σθω[ν .] δραχ[μαῖς. τῶι] δὲ φήναντι μετέστω τὸ ἥμισυ, ἐ[ὰ]ν ἕληι ὁ̣ [ὠνόμενος] ἐ̣ὰν δὲ δõλος ἦι ὁ πωλῶν ἢ δόλη, ὑπ⟨α⟩ρχέτω̣ μ[ὲν αὐτῶι] τύπτεσθαι 𐅄 πληγὰς τῆι μάστιγι ὑπὸ [τῶν ἀρχόντω]ν οἷς ἕκαστα προστέτακται. ἐὰν δέ τις [τῶ]ν ἀ[ρχόντ]ων μὴ ποιῆι κατὰ τὰ γεγραμμένα, εἰσαγ[αγέτω αὐτὸ]ν ἐς τὴμ βολὴν Ἀθηναίων ὁ βολόμενος οἷς [ἔξεστιν]. ἐὰν δὲ ἁλῶι, ὑπαρχέτω μὲν αὐτῶι πεπαῦσθ[αι ἄρχον]τι καὶ προστιμάτω αὐτῶ[ι] ἡ βολὴ μέχρι [𐅅 δραχμῶν. ὅ]πως δ' ἂν ἦι καὶ ἐμ Πειραιεῖ δοκιμαστὴς [τοῖς ναυκ]λήροις καὶ τοῖς ἐμπόροις καὶ τοῖς ἄλλο[ις πᾶσιν], καταστησάτω ἡ βολὴ ἐκ τῶν δημοσίων ἐὰ̣[ν ὑπάρχηι] ἢ ἐσπριάσθω, τὴν δὲ τιμὴν οἱ ἀποδέκται [μεριζόντ]ων. οἱ δὲ ἐπιμεληταὶ τοῦ ἐμπορίο ἐπιμελ̣έ[σ]θω[ν ὅπ]ως ἂγ καθῆται πρὸς τῆι στήληι τοῦ Ποσειδῶνο[ς κα]ὶ χρήσθων τῶι νόμωι καθάπερ περὶ τọ̃ ἐν ἄστ[ει δοκ]ιμαστõ εἴρηται κατὰ ταὐτά. ἀναγράψαι δὲ ἐν σ[τήλ]ηι λιθίνηι τὸν νόμον τόνδε καὶ καταθεῖναι ἐν [ἄσ]τει μὲμ μεταξὺ τῶν τραπεζῶν, ἐμ Πειραιεῖ δὲ πρό[σ]θεν τῆς στήλης τοῦ Ποσει[δ]ῶνος. ὁ δὲ γραμματε[ὺ]ς [δ] τῆς βολῆς παραγγειλάτω μίσθωμα τοῖς πωλ[ηταῖς]. οἱ δὲ πωληταὶ ἐσενεγκόντων ἐς τὴμ βολήν. τ[ὴν δὲ μ]ισθοφορίαν εἶναι τῶι δοκιμαστῆι τῶι ἐν τῶι [ἐμπ]ορίωι ἐπὶ μὲν Ἱπποδάμαντος ἄρχοντος ἀφ' οὗ̣ [ἂν κα]ταστάθῆι, μεριζόντων οἱ ⟨ἀ⟩ποδέκται ὅσομπερ τ̣[ῶ̣ι]

ἐν ἄστει δοκιμαστῆι, ἐς δὲ τὸν λοιπὸγ χρόν[ον ἔνα]-
ι αὐτῶι τὴμ μισθοφορίαν ὅθεμπερ τοῖς ἀργυ[ροκό]-
ποις. εἰ δέ τι ψήφισμα γέγραπται πο ἐστήληι πα̣[ρὰ τ]-
όνδε τὸν νόμον, καθελέτω ὁ γραμματεὺς τῆς βολ[ῆς].

Resolved by the *Nomothetai* ['Legislative Board'], in the archonship of Hippodamas: Nikophon proposed: receive Attic silver money when it is shown to be of silver and it has the *dēmosion kharaktēra* ['public type']. Let the *dēmosios* Dokimastes ['public Validator'] validate in accordance with the following every day, sitting among the tables of the bankers and money changers, except when there is a deposit of monies (to the state), when he shall validate in the Bouleuterion. And if someone submits *xenikos* ['foreign'] money that has the same *kharaktēr* as Attic money, if it is good(?) let him return it to the person submitting it. But if it has a bronze core or a lead core or is fraudulent, let him cut it through immediately and let the money be sacred to the Mother of the Gods and let it be deposited with the *Boulē.* But if the Dokimastes does not sit or does not validate in accordance with the law, let the *Syllogeis* ['Collectors'] of the *dēmos* strike him thirty lashes with the whip. Moreover, if someone does not accept the silver money which the Dokimastes validates, let him be deprived of whatever goods he was selling on that day. For offenses concerning grain, let there be a denunciation to the *Sitophulakes* ['Guardians of the grain supply']; but for sales in the Agora and in the rest of the city let there be a denunciation before the *Syllogeis* of the *dēmos*; but in the *emporion* ['commercial harbor'] and in the Peiraieus let there be a denunciation before the *Epimelētai* ['Supervisors'] of the *emporion* except for matters in connection with grain, but those concerning grain before the *Sitophulakes.* Regarding those of the denounced goods that are worth less than 10 drachms, let the archons ['officials'] be authorized to render a verdict; regarding those over 10 drachms let them refer to a dikasteric court. The *Thesmothetai* ['Legal Archons'] are to assign a dikasteric court to them by allotment whenever they make a request, or the *Thesmothetai* are to be subject to a fine of ?? drachms at their *euthunai* ['final scrutinies']. Let a share of half go to the one making the denunciation if the one selling is convicted, but if the seller is a male or female slave let him or her be subjected to be beaten fifty lashes with a whip by the archons to whom the various spheres of responsibility are assigned. Moreover, if any of the officials does not act in accordance with these written provisions, let anyone who wishes of the Athenians for whom it is permitted hale him before the *Boulē* of the Athenians, and if he is convicted, let him be subjected to cessation of his office and let the *Boulē* fine him 500? drachms. In order that there be also a Dokimastes in the Peiraieus for the *nauklēroi* ['shipowners'] and for the *emporoi* ['merchants'] and for all others, let the *Boulē* establish one from the public slaves, if there is one suitable, or let it buy one. And let the *Apodektai* ['Receivers of public revenue'] provide the cost. The *Epimelētai* of the *emporion* are to supervise that he sit at the stele of Poseidon and let them use the law in the same manner as is stated concerning the Dokimastes in the *astу* ['town of Athens']. Inscribe this law on a stone stele and erect it in the town among the tables of the bankers and money changers and in the Peiraieus in front of the stele of Poseidon. Let the Secretary of the *Boulē* report the price to the *Pōlētai* ['Sellers']. The *Pōlētai* are to provide the money to the *Boulē*. Let there be a salary for the Dokimastes in the *emporion* in the archonship of Hippodamas from which time he is appointed and let the *Apodektai* provide the same amount as for the Dokimastes in the town. And for the future let there be a salary for him from the same source as for the mint-workers. If there is any psephism anywhere on a stele contrary to this law, let the Secretary of the *Boulē* destroy it.

At the outset of our exploration of this document, it is important to note that the law is dated too late to be seen merely as a corrective for monetary problems that came into being during the latter part of the Peloponnesian War. There is a good chance, not only on prima facie grounds internal to the inscription but also based on the likelihood of conservatism in monetary legislation, that the law of Nikophon had a broadly traditional character. Lines 55–56 of the decree instruct the Grammateus of the *Boulē* to destroy any inscribed psephism that contravenes this law, which is an indication of the place of this legislation within such a rich tradition.

Let us begin with some preliminaries that are uncontroversial. The references to the archon Hippodamas in lines 1 and 51 date the decree to 375/4. The prescript, which does not mention any initiatives by the *Boulē* or the assembly, indicates the participation of the Nomothetai in the genesis of the legislation. That fact might also be taken to suggest the traditional quality of the provisions, especially if one supposes that the Nomothetai had been involved in a review of Attic law on commerce. Nikophon is a common name, and nothing about various contemporary bearers of the name is helpful in interpreting the decree.

Although it is not the only solution to the question of the timing of the law, one may suspect that the intention to provide a Dokimastes to work exclusively in the Peiraieus, either for the first time or as a resumption after a period when the state could not afford two such officials, could have prompted this particular proposal. Lines 52–55 order that the salary of the Dokimastes in the Peiraieus is to be the same as that of his colleague in the *asty* 'town,' implying that a Dokimastes had existed in the *asty* for some time. Possibly, a single slave may have split his time between the *asty* and Peiraieus prior to 375/4. Alessandrì argues that wholesale citation of a preceding law is a characteristic of nomothetic lawmaking.[3] He would then split the law of Nikophon at line 36 with the formula ὅπως ἄν, which he believes is characteristic of the transition to new material in nomothetic legislation.

Accordingly, the departure from current practice made by this decree was the provision for a second Dokimastes. The original Dokimastes was a public slave, whose existence had been previously suspected on the basis of *IG* II^2 1492.137 of 305/4 (cf. line 111). He was stationed daily among the tables of the money changers and bankers in the Agora (except when his services were required in the Bouleuterion: lines 4–8); his counterpart in the Peiraieus sat before the stele of Poseidon (line 42). This psephism of 375/4 was to be publicly displayed in both these places and contains arrangements for its own inscription and erection (lines 44–47). Stroud suggests that an inventory for the Hecatompedon of 398/7 may indicate the earlier existence of a Dokimastes, saying that the phrase στατῆρες κίβδηλοι ἐν κιβωτίωι σεσημασμένοι οἱ παρὰ Λάκωνος may mark reception from a Dokimastes, a public slave named Lakon (*IG* II^2 1388.61–62).[4] Although he does not subscribe to this hypothesis on the identity of Lakon, Alessandrì believes that the inventory indicates that the Dokimastes already existed and consequently dates the law that was the basic material for the reworking of Nikophon to 402–399. In that case the Dokimastes either did not exist or, more probably, had his activities suspended or radically reshaped during the last days of the war, when various desperate monetary devices were tried that could now be laid

[3] See Alessandrì, *ASNP* (1984) 376–81, who provides a number of compelling arguments. Contrast Buttrey, *NAC* (1981) 73–75, who suggests that the new feature was that the Dokimastes was to function in the market for the first time. His point, however, about the imperative character of the participle καθήμενος (derived from E. Badian) would equally fit the case where the Dokimastes of the *asty* was henceforward limited to the station in the Agora.

[4] Note *Suda* s.v. διακέκοπται: οἷον ἀδόκιμον ἔστι. διέκοπτον γὰρ τὸ ἀδόκιμον νόμισμα οἱ παλαιοί (δ 573 Adler). Consider *IG* II^2 1453.7: διακεκομένα; cf. 1443.158, 160; 1457.4; 1459.4. For the dedicated staters associated with Lakon, see *IG* II^2 1388.61–62; 1400.57; 1401.44–45; 1415.19–20; 1424a.311–12; 1428.149; 1443.207–208; cf. 1407.43. See Stroud *Hesperia* (1974) 176–77; Alessandrì *ASNP* (1984) 391; cf. Alessandrì, "Gli stateri falsi παρὰ Λάκωνος," *ASNP*^{3} 12 (1982) 1239–54, esp. 1252–54.

to rest (like the plated tetradrachms and the governmental recognition of private retail change in the form of *kollyboi*). The reestablished democracy restored the pre-crisis legal situation for money, perhaps only when minting silver was begun again and the bronze coinages were demonetized. Therefore, one should be reluctant to identify any individual clause in lines 3–36 of the law as innovative without a good reason. Moreover, there is also no need to find a specific crisis behind the promulgation of the legislation in its main body.[5]

It is striking that the decree envisages one particular facet of economic interaction that requires the intervention of the Dokimastes; that is, the situation in which someone offering goods for sale refuses to accept the coinage offered in payment. It is a testimony to the willingness to allow market forces to predominate in sales that the opposite eventuality is not a subject for legislation here or elsewhere (to the best of our knowledge): no legal necessity appears to have compelled transactors to use Attic currency exclusively in exchanges, even in Attica.[6] Thus, hypotheses arguing for an elaborate demonetization of foreign coinage during the fifth century and the prohibition of any employment of non-Attic coinage by allied citizens (which traditional interpreters of the Coinage Decree have seen as the goals of Athenian monetary policy) may not be disproved by the provisions of the law of Nikophon, but they are quite out of keeping with its actual content. They apply a more exclusive status for Athenian money in the *arkhē* than prevailed in fourth-century Athens itself.

In contrast, the Dokimastes had to be present in the Bouleuterion on the days that payments were made to the government, presumably to validate the coins used in payment to the state (lines 8–9; cf. *Ath. Pol.* 47.5–48.2). The state had an abiding interest, based on fiscal efficiency, in being paid in validated Attic coinage. That function for the Dokimastes probably preceded any fourth-century innovations and may indeed be a crucial inheritance of the fifth-century fiscal regime.[7]

Thus, while it is undoubtedly true that Attic coins mediated the vast majority of transactions occurring on Athenian territory, we have

5 Buttrey, *Festschrift Thompson* 40–45; cf. Stroud *Hesperia* (1974) 186–88. Relative to the motivation of the law, Alessandrì, *ASNP* (1984) 381–91, has a skeptical review of the relevance of the historical and economic context.

6 F. Bourriot, "Note sur le texte de la loi athénienne de 375/4 concernant la circulation monétaire (la loi de Nikophon)," *ZPE* 50 (1983) 275–82, esp. 277; Alessandrì *ASNP* (1984) 374–76; cf. H. Engelmann, "Wege griechischer Geldpolitik," *ZPE* 60 (1985) 165–76, esp. 172–73.

7 The law demonetizing plated tetradrachms and *kollyboi* may be parallel to that (re)establishing the functions of the Dokimastes, as Alessandrì, *ASNP* (1982) 1253–53; *ASNP* (1984) 391-92, believes.

already seen that Chian coins may have been legally usable in Attica (pp. 161–63, 484–85) and that Athenians, like so many other Greeks, occasionally used Aiginetan coins and Aiginetic weights (pp. 314–15). This phenomenon is exhibited in the anecdote in Diphilus about buying in Aiginetic obols and receiving Attic obols in change, indicating that the use of non-Attic money was not prohibited in Attica (fr. 66 K= fr. 67, *PCG* 5.92). That anecdote presumably contains too casual a reference to be an intentional misrepresentation. The references to Cyzicenes in late fifth- and fourth-century literature probably indicate that Athenians made loans and conducted other business in terms of these coins for trade with the Propontis and Black Sea region. It was presumably left to the private parties to individual business deals to decide among themselves the monetary terms for their completion.[8]

From our understanding of the sessions of the Dokimastes in the Bouleuterion, from our earlier discussion of the tribute system, and from the absence of any alternative provision in extant Attic law, it is necessary to conclude that the Athenian government demanded payment only in Attic coin. In contrast, there was only a single problematic aspect of *private* business that fell under the jurisdiction of the Dokimastes. That was a determination whether a coin was to be accepted in private commerce because it could be validated as a genuine issue of the Athenian mint. Money changers, bankers, and merchants themselves also carried out evaluations similar to the official scrutiny of the Dokimastes (witness the phenomenon of countermarking), but their review had only restricted private relevance.[9] Any slaves who were purchased would presumably come from the ranks of these private-sector evaluators (cf. DL 2.34: ... εἴ τις τετράδραχμον ἓν ἀποδοκιμάζων τὸν ἐκ τῶν τοιούτων σωρὸν ὡς δόκιμον ἀποδέχοιτο). At an unknown juncture, the state may have established or extended its services of public validation probably because high-quality pseudo-Attic tetradrachms minted in Egypt had reached Athenian consumers in some numbers. Their presence complicated the task of private validators and thereby undermined public faith in Attic coins.

[8] That is probably why the Athenians appear from the wording of the law to have been unconcerned about sorting out forgeries of foreign coins and ensuring their absence from circulation. Cf. Buttrey *NAC* (1981) 88–89. In any case, they could never have expected the Dokimastes to have adequate expertise based on experience to perform evaluation for foreign series analogous to his appraisals of doubtful Atticizing coins.

[9] See, for example, Plut. *Mor.* 421A; Epict./Arrian *Discourses* 1.20.7–9, 2.3.2–3. Cf., for example, 1.1.1; 1.1.6; 1.7.6–8; 3.6.10.

The sanction of this law bore down heavily on the person offering goods in the Agora or Peiraieus who refused to accept valid Attic coin. We recognize δέχεσθαι as the appropriate technical term from Aristophanes' usage of it in *Ecclesiazousae* 821–22.[10] The central and longest portion of the law deals with the responsibility for the adjudication (through the procedure of *phasis*) of charges of refusal to accept valid Attic currency.[11] Valid currency has a simple definition; it is made of silver and bears the public type: τὸ ἀργύριον δέχεσθαι τὸ 'Αττικὸν ὅτ[αν δεικνύητ]|αι ἀργυρõγ καὶ ἔχηι τὸν δημόσιογ χα[ρακτῆρα (3–4; with the restoration δεικνύηται going back to Stroud).[12] The punishment was a stringent one, confiscation of all the goods offered for sale on the same day, and, as an added punishment for slaves, a flogging. The buyer was the person naturally envisaged as the one who would appeal to the Dokimastes against the seller, and Stroud's restoration of the end of line 29 would make the point more explicit (ἐ[ὰ]ν ἔληι ὁ [ὠνόμενος] or [ἀγοράζων]). Other clauses guaranteed swift punishment by the *Boulē* of magistrates who failed to administer the provisions of the law.

The Dokimastes had two licit options when coins deemed to be unacceptable were submitted for his evaluation. The second of the two is better preserved in the inscription. If the coin in question had a bronze or lead core (ὑπόχαλκος or ὑπομόλυβδος) or was κίβδηλος 'counterfeit' or 'fraudulent,' he was to cut it through, whereupon it was dedicated to the Mother Goddess and was deposited in the Metroon (10–13).[13] It is mainly private frauds that are envisaged here. Athens' own plated coins had been demonetized by 393–92, at the latest, although one supposes it barely possible that well-preserved examples might have been used inadvertently

[10] Stroud *Hesperia* (1974) 164 cites *SIG*³ 729.3–4 = *FD* 3.2.139; *IC* 4.162.

[11] Controversy surrounds the procedure for the official who transgresses the law, with εἰσαγ[γελλέτω μὲ]ν being offered in place of εἰσαγ[αγέτω αὐτὸ]ν (lines 33–34) of Stroud *Hesperia* (1974) 182. See M.H. Hansen, *Eisangelia* (Odense 1975) 28; P. Gauthier, "Sur une clause pénale de la loi athénienne relative à la monnaie d'argent," *RPh*³ 52 (1978) 32–36; J. Robert and L. Robert, *BE* (1980) #196 (= *REG* 93); H. Wankel, "Bemerkungen zu den athenischen Münzgesetz von 375/4," *ZPE* 52 (1983) 69–74, esp. 72–73. On the phraseology of punishment in the decree, see also H. Wankel, "Zur Formulierung von Strafbestimmungen in dem neuen attischen Münzgesetz," *ZPE* 21 (1976) 149–50.

[12] The other suggestions are the following: T. Fischer, "Das athenische Münzgesetz von 375/4 v. Chr.," *Hellenika: Jahrbuch für die Freunde Griechenlands* (1981) 38–42: ὅτ[αν ἧι ἀληθεῖ]αι; Wankel, *ZPE* (1983) note 15, p. 71: ὅτ[αν ἐξετάζετ]αι.

[13] Buttrey, *Festschrift Thompson* 33–35; *NAC* (1981) 75–76, suggests that all counterfeits, regardless of origin, are at issue. All counterfeits may have been forfeit and to be dedicated in the Metroon, but none would be confiscated by the Dokimastes in this procedure except those of the standard Attic type.

and very occasionally at the time of this law. The Dokimastes cut through or cut in two (παραυτίκα 'immediately') the coins he confiscated, thus putting his evaluation to a final destructive test.[14] Not only was such treatment a traditional means for removing a coin from circulation, but it had the additional advantage of helping the Athenians to avoid any hint of their using the evaluations of the Dokimastes to confiscate sound coins for the profit of the state. Should this bisection or cutting across have revealed a sound Attic coin, one suspects that its owner would have appealed to the Syllogeis, who supervised the Dokimastes, in order that they might punish him as laid out in lines 14–16 of the inscription. Their authority could also be another innovation either of the law of 375/4 or (more probably) of a predecessor passed in the years right after the Peloponnesian War.

The other class of unacceptable coins was not submitted to this punitive regimen. It is clear that they had the same *kharaktēr* 'type' as Attic coin. Stroud's probable conjecture was that foreign money was at issue (line 8: ξ[ε]ν̣[ικὸν ἀργύριον]). Even if these coins may not have met the standards of the Attic mint, the phrase in line 10, ἐ[ὰν καλὸν] (if it is correct) suggests that they were struck from a sufficient amount of silver that an intent to defraud could not be casually assigned to their minter and (more importantly) to the person attempting to spend them.[15] The Dokimastes gave these coins back to the person submitting them (line 10: ἀποδιδότω τῶι προσενεγκόντι), but not in order that their owner use them as validated. That interpretation is excluded because the law has already stipulated in line 4 that the coin necessarily accepted is 'Αττικόν, to which the coin handed back in line 10 is contrasted by virtue of its being ξενικόν. A further contrast with the "Attic" is marked by the distinction that it has the same type as an Attic coin (line 9).

[14] The alternative is πα[ραχρῆμα (cf. Dem. 24.42), for which see R. Bogaert, *Epigraphica* 3 (Leiden 1976) #21, pp. 23–25; Wankel *ZPE* (1983) 69; Wankel, "Nachtrag zu dem athenischen Münzgesetz von 375/4," *ZPE* 53 (1983) 94 (citing *SEG* 30.60B, fr. a 12).

[15] See Buttrey *NAC* (1981) 81–83. Engelmann *ZPE* (1985) 170–71, suggests . . . ἔ[μμετρον, which has similar connotations, but differentiation of "good" coin by weight is rare. F. Sokolowski, "The Athenian Law Concerning Silver Currency (375/4) B.C.," *BCH* 100 (1976) 511–15, sees a division between private Atticizing coins and the emissions of mints which were returned to the owner. He restores line 9 to ἔχον τὸν αὐτὸγ χαρακτῆρα τῶι 'Αττι[κῶ]ι ἐ[κ τõ νόμο]. If that must imply that other cities had the right to mint using the official type of the Athenians, it takes us in the wrong direction. Bourriot, *ZPE* (1983) 279–83, suggests . . . ἐ[πισήμωι, but that seems redundant. Wankel, *ZPE* (1983) 70–72, reviews earlier suggestions and offers ἐ[ξετάσας. That has stylistic advantages but does not much alter the construal of the text. Cf. Stumpf *JNG* (1986) 26–27.

Stroud himself adduced the phenomenon that has been discussed in the preceding chapter, namely, the existence of Egyptian and Near Eastern imitations of Attic tetradrachms.[16] This second class of coins that could not be validated were returned to their owners, who could not demand their compulsory acceptance by merchants but who could try to use them again with someone prepared to accept them without resistance or attempt to exchange them.[17] I emphasize that this legislation did not forbid a seller to take such coins in payment, but merely that he was not required to receive them as he would be required in the case of genuine Athenian coins, approved by the Dokimastes (lines 16–17). It is true that the penalty for counterfeiting was death (note Dem. 20.167; 24.212), but such sanctions had no practical role where the counterfeiter was a vast distance away at the head of a long string of intermediation.

The purview of the Dokimastes does not seem to have extended to an examination of coins for their weight. Such calculations may have been left to negotiations between buyers and sellers. Perhaps prices were quoted with the understanding that good-quality Attic coins were to be tendered, and subsequent adjustments were held appropriate when either of the parties produced a worn, damaged, or clipped coin. Nevertheless, it is quite possible that Attic law prescribed a token value for all denominations of valid Attic money until coins had lost some significant amount of their weight. Theophrastus in the *Characters* 4.13 describes as one of the offensive traits of the *agroikos* 'boor' that he refuses coin as too *lepreos* 'rough' (that is, worn). Presumably, social norms condemned such a practice.[18] There are also some valuable insights to be gained from Jewish law as reflected in the Talmud.[19] The monitoring

[16] See also Buttrey *NAC* (1981) 76–78.

[17] Giovannini *GRBS* (1975) 191–94; Bourriot *ZPE* (1983) 276–77; Buttrey, *Festschrift Thompson* 35–41, but his views on the exclusive use of Attic coinage in Attica are unacceptable. See also E.E. Cocchi, "Il controllo statale sulla circolazione di moneta straniera nella città greche," *RSA* 12 (1982) 53–59; O. Mørkholm, "Some Reflections on the Production and Use of Coinage in Ancient Greece," *Historia* 31 (1982) 290–305, esp. 293–96; Cataudella *Sileno* (1986) 132–33. Cf. Stroud *Hesperia* (1974) 169; J. Robert and L. Robert *BE* (1980) #195 (= *REG* 93).

[18] See C.J. Howgego, "Why did Ancient States Strike Coins?" *NC* 150 (1990) 1–25, esp. 16–17 on *IG* XII.7 69.21–23 and Suet. *Nero* 44.2

[19] Various rabbinical authorities describe varying percentages at which coins may be deficient and still not open their users to an charge of fraud (with one twenty-fourth the lowest deficiency and one sixth the largest). Coins having lost half their weight had to be treated in certain specified ways to avoid any subsequent fraudulent misrepresentation. Note, for example, J. Neusner (trans.), *The Talmud of the Land of Israel: A Preliminary Translation and Explanation* 29 (1982) 95–96. See E. Lambert, "Les changeurs et la monnaie en Palestine du

of the acceptance of worn coins might have fallen to the *agoranomoi* when the participant in a transaction attempted to push the "envelope" of social convention too far, either by demanding very fresh coins or by pressing payment in badly worn coins.

As Buttrey has sensibly observed, there was no guarantee of the silver content of these coins rejected by the Dokimastes.[20] The Athenian government had not collaborated in their production, but, unlike private forgeries, governmental resources in Egypt or the Near East had been applied to produce sophisticated copies. Their holders were not to be penalized for their acquisition, possession, and attempted use beyond the limited loss that was contingent on carelessly acquiring a coin that may have had a lower percentage of silver than a coin issuing from the Attic mint.

Ordinary individuals were not expected to be experts on the parameters for a genuine Attic coin as compared to good imitations of sophisticated technique, but they were subjected to confiscation of fraudulent or counterfeit coins, presumably because they were expected to exercise adequate caution against their casual acquisition and because confiscation subjected their holders to no additional loss since the coins were themselves worthless. The Dokimastes defaced *kibdēlos* 'counterfeit' or 'fraudulent' coins and deposited them in the shrine of the Mother Goddess in a part of the Old Bouleuterion called the Metroon. As Stroud first outlined, there is considerable parallel evidence for the relegation of counterfeit coins in temples.[21] Some counterfeits were found in temple inventories prior to 375/4, showing the practice to have had a previous history, notwithstanding any innovation enacted by this law.

Two points deserve to be emphasized in closing our discussion of the law of Nikophon. First of all, it is noteworthy that the status of the Attic owls as the dominant currency of the largest Greek political entity in the fifth century had profound effects in Egypt and the Near East as economies monetized under the influence of interaction with the Greeks. Athenian money achieved a supranational standing as a natural monetary medium of administration. The decline of the hegemonic economy prompted efforts at supplementation of the reduced supply of Athenian coins. Postimperial Athens was left to grapple with that situation, since it attracted back to itself successor, imitative coinage. The situation might have needed intervention in 375/4, a period when

---

Ier au IIIe siècle de l'ère vulgaire d'après les textes talmudiques (suite et fin)," *Revue des études juives* 52 (1906) 24–42, esp. 30–34.

[20] See Buttrey *NAC* (1981) 79–83; Stumpf *JNG* (1986) 31–32. Compare Chapter 19, note 2 above.

[21] Stroud *Hesperia* (1974) 173–78; also Bogaert *RBN* (1976) 23.

the flow of Atticizing coins to Athens may have increased after the creation of the Second Athenian Confederacy, although the arrangements laid out on the inscription could well have originated in similar contexts earlier in the century (such as ca. 400 or at the return of Konon to Attica in 392).

Second, the modesty of the Athenian provisions about legal tender outlined in this law is noteworthy. They do not intend to specify the monetary medium for all business in Attica or by Athenian citizens. Rather, they intervene to correct a circumscribed difficulty, namely, the heightened suspicions of merchants that were created by the presence in the money supply of good imitations of Attic coins that nonetheless may have been at times somewhat inferior in silver content. By affording a governmental validation through the Dokimastes in the Peiraieus, they chose to allay those suspicions, while upholding the principle that Attic coins ought always to be received in Attica as valid instruments of business transactions. Copies of good quality received neither validation of their public function nor invalidation of their private function. Those who would posit more intrusive policies for the Athenians of the *arkhē* will find no comfort in the law of Nikophon.

22

FINAL THOUGHTS

HEGEMONY AND MONETARY POLICY

IT IS UNCERTAIN whether it was someone endowed with political authority acting on behalf of his community or an individual acting on his own behalf who conceived the idea of coinage, which, for our purposes, may be defined as standardized weights of precious metal (at first electrum), arranged in a hierarchy of values, and stamped with some particularizing symbol, be it expressive of authority, ownership, or appropriation. Any private innovator soon yielded to the state as the social agent most concerned with the benefits that control of a coinage conferred. Chief among these advantages was the ability that coins afforded their issuers for managing disbursements of assets. Coins expedited, simplified, and regularized outlays of resources in a manner easily represented to the members of a community and readily evaluated in terms of equity. They permitted a more sophisticated recirculation of goods, mediated through the government, among the members of society in a manner that allowed more continuity of policy. Such recirculation enhanced social cohesion.

The mental revolution worked by the commencement of coined money was hardly less momentous. Indeed, it would be tempting to call it a spiritual transformation, except that the pairing of money and soul appears paradoxical to our present sensibilities. Money provided a single, simple scale of valuation against which all other aspects of human existence could be held up for better or worse. The abiding worth of gold and silver (which preceded their monetary usage) lent a solidity and permanence to such appraisals. Money gave to each person a powerful tool for analyzing the institutions and interactions surrounding him, for monetary evaluation of material or social goods was intensely individual and at the same time easily communicated. To be sure, the despairing cry of χρήματ' ἄνηρ 'money is the man' reveals how the reorientation that was worked by thinking (and even feeling) in terms of money could be corrosive of traditional social relations,[1] but it also bespeaks the liberating and individualizing effects of the monetary sensibility for the purposive

[1] See Alc. fr. 360 L/P; cf. Apostolius 12.31b, *CPG* 2.550.

optimization of personal happiness.[2] The emergence of entrepreneurial activity and the differentiation of economic behavior and socioeconomic roles that typify late archaic Greece rests on monetary foundations.

The inauguration of minting in silver (ca. 560?) signified another watershed, scarcely less important than the initiation of coinage itself. The lesser value of this metal extended the number of transactions that could be mediated monetarily, especially as silver fractions became more prevalent toward the end of the sixth century. The purity of objects in silver, including coins, could be judged much more easily by physical means, visually or by touchstone, than electrum.[3] The importance of the authority of a governmental issuer in guaranteeing the value of his coin was thereby lessened, while the range of utilization by the individual user was extended. That opened for coinage less stereotypical interactions, a wider range of transactors, and a depersonalization of business. So market forces, including competition, had a greater impact within the silver economy than in the barter, premonetary standard (for example, tripods, cattle, or raw metal),[4] and gold/electrum economies that had gone before.

Throughout the Greek mainland and the Cyclades, Aiginetan coins played a critical role in monetizing compartmentalized local economies. The activities of Aiginetan retailers within the "capillaries" here of interregional commercial networks introduced silver coins as a monetary medium. Local political elites looked on Aiginetan staters as a primary means for treasurizing wealth and for the accumulation of familial reserves that could be used in the face of political vicissitudes. Furthermore, the possession of savings or surpluses converted into Aiginetan coins allowed members of the elite to tap stocks of prestige trade goods like jewelry, fine pottery, metalwork, luxury goods of Near Eastern provenience, and slaves. The acquisition of such distinguishing articles established a presumptive claim to elite status. Secondarily, fiscal and symbolic motivations prompted the same local elites to initiate their own minting, often using the Aiginetic standard.

[2] Note Figueira, "*Khrēmata*: Acquisition and Possession in Archaic Greece," in K.D. Irani and M. Silver (eds.), *Social Justice in the Ancient World* (Westport CN 1995) 41–60. See also T.R. Martin, "Why Did the Greek *Polis* Originally Need Coins?" *Historia* 45 (1996) 257–83.

[3] Note, for example, Theognis 117–18; 119–26; 415–18; also *Adespota Elegiaca* fr. 22 W; cf. Theognis 963–70. Gold coins could also be evaluated by touchstone: Theognis 447–52; 1105–1106, where the addition of the epithet ἄπεφθος 'refined' to χρυσός is telltale. Yet gold coins were not an alternative/competitor to silver money in the sixth-century economy. Testing by fire was not an option for merchants (cf. Theognis 499–500), but only for authorities sampling from large payments.

[4] Compare Figueira, *Aegina* 72–77.

Moreover, the circulation of sufficient silver coinage of recognized value within a community supported the mediation of more types of transactions through money. The governments of *poleis* could then devise taxes that corresponded to each mode in which people interchanged goods. In the administration of the late archaic city, these indirect taxes balanced the levies of personal service that supported military activity and political participation.[5] The utilization of indirect taxes promoted social cohesion, both because these taxes cushioned hereditary elites from the effects of levies on assets and because they did not impede the upwardly mobile as much as levies on production or income.

During the late sixth century and first decades of the fifth century, it is probable that the amount of trade rose not only absolutely but proportionately in relation to other sectors of communal output.[6] Commercial activity was particularly suitable for the imposition of indirect taxes like harbor levies, transit fees, and tariffs on imports and exports. That judgments may have been made (sometimes erroneously) that the incidence of commercial imposts fell substantially on those outside the citizen body of the taxing community would only have increased their attractiveness. The evolved arsenal of indirect taxes of the *polis* permitted a truly monetized administration, one drawing on many streams of revenue that in their aggregate were sufficient to undertake the large public endeavors that typified the late archaic city-state, such as fortifications, fleets of triremes, religious and civic complexes of buildings, and elaborate public celebrations. A final, additional fiscal benefit conferred by coining was the levying of charges on the process of striking coins itself.

A program for the minting of silver coinage also conferred symbolic or ideological advantages that were especially helpful in a late archaic political context dominated by aristocratic or oligarchic constitutions and influences. The act of producing a state coinage expressed the unity of the community, and the very playfulness of some coin types with their punning allusions may have subserved this purpose. Coins could also invoke cultic, mythological, patriotic, and historical symbolism that enhanced the integration of the community. Ideological ends were best served by a variety of type and by a thematic richness, but variation did not contribute to the breadth of acceptance for a coinage. The static or slowly evolving types of the Aiginetans and Athenians were coupled with processes producing coins of a high standard of purity and presumably

[5] The list in *SIG*³ 4 from sixth-century Kyzikos is an invaluable early witness, especially when it is remembered that these are only the taxes not exempted for the honorands. Note also Arist. *Wasps* 655–60.

[6] This is one great lesson of the *Arkhaiologia* of Thucydides (for example, 1.13–14).

consistency of weight. Hence, the stability of these types was a guarantor of consistent quality. The ubiquitous owls of Athens and the turtles of Aigina expressed the power and wealth of their coiners. The lack of dramatic discontinuity in the sequence of emissions in the early fifth century mirrored the solidity of the social integration of these two societies, the same social compact that was celebrated respectively by Aeschylean tragedy for the Athenians and Pindaric choral lyric for the Aiginetans.

In the fifth century, other mechanisms became more available for fostering the cohesion of the inhabitants of a *polis*, especially those exploiting literacy such as inscription and display of laws and the composition of local histories. Coinage was therefore less important as a medium for ideological communication in the classical period. This judgment is particularly valid for the states of the *arkhē*, where the Attic model for social integration through populist ideology was often emulated or adapted.

The advantages, however, for the administration of the *polis* in a monetized economy did not now entail that the local government emit coins in its own name. While many governments may have initiated coinage as the surest means to guarantee that their citizens would have an appropriate volume of money out of which to pay their taxes, the maintenance of a mint had real costs. To these were to be added any difficulty that may have existed (especially for those without mines or easy interaction with mining districts) over accumulating and holding the requisite amount of silver for coinage. The greater the monopoly or exclusivity preserved for the local coinage, the greater were the efforts necessary to provide a sufficient money supply for the size of the local economy. To the extent that local money held exclusive sway in the marketplace or for taxation, problems making exchanges into other currencies affected both private individuals and the state.

Undoubtedly, once a foreign currency or currencies was recognized as a valid means for conducting business and paying taxes, the pressures associated with maintenance of the mint and procurement of silver were eased. The profession of money changing had become prominent for the purpose of expediting the conversion of monies. At the same time, however, the motivation for having a state mint at all was also diminished. As has been seen, the tendency of early fifth-century mints to terminate operations was manifested even before the commencement of the Attic hegemony. Some local currencies were in retreat before more regional coinages barely a generation after their inception. Nor should it be forgotten that any conjectured primacy of fiscal considerations in decisions to retain or to close the local mint had to be balanced against the likely preference of any persons doing business across political boundaries that monetary and metrological standards be consolidated.

Therefore, the history of minting during the fifth century is one of both consolidation of monies, weights, and measures and greater economic integration. These processes were given a more powerful impetus after the establishment of Athenian hegemony in the Delian League. As a plentiful and significant regional coinage, drawing on an ample supply of silver from the massive production of the mines at Laureion, Attic owls had already been a beneficiary of monetary consolidation before the creation of the alliance. The period of Athenian hegemony richly illustrates the various modes of consolidation like termination of coining, amalgamation of coin standards, concentration on minting smaller denominations, minting for restricted channels of circulation, and reconciliation of metrological usage that have been presented extensively above. The questions whether to coin and what to coin were conditioned by the geographcial and economic context of each allied city. Factors such as the commutation of allied military service to payment of tribute, the incorporation of large numbers of salaried allied sailors into the Attic fleet, and the relocation of allied merchants and craftsmen to Attica to live as metics all influenced monetary and metrological consolidation and economic integration in synergy with the system for the collection of tribute and the administration of the military forces of the alliance.

The costs created by having to exchange different currencies were borne by all those individuals conducting business across political boundaries, a spectrum of participants in trade spanning, on one pole, the Athenian innkeeper providing lodging at modest cost to allied visitors to Athens for conducting political activity and, on the other, the Ionian merchant shipowner conveying large cargoes of wheat from Egypt to the Aegean (with considerable amounts of capital invested in these activities). Many of those most affected by the costs of exchange were already or became Athenian metics during the Pentekontaeteia. Whenever they did not sever links with their home cities, their use of Athenian coins in Attica stimulated broader utilization by those connected with their communities of origin. Any consolidation of standards and currencies facilitated daily business throughout the *arkhē*, so that the influence of myriad individual business decisions was inevitably in favor of progressive monetary and metrological unification. Inasmuch as the background to monetary decision making goes unreported in our sources, there is no way at present to evaluate directly the role of facilitation of exchange by and for individuals in the formulation of measures furthering consolidation of currencies and standards.

If the primary purpose of the Athenians was to make gestures expressive of their hegemony over their allies/subjects, it is possible to conceive of a number of patterns of allied minting that could have been formulated to fulfill this goal, at least as well as the Coinage Decree in its traditional interpretation. To take just one alternative, the Athenians could have mandated that each allied state mint their own coins on the Athenian standard and that only coins of their standard could be used legally among the allies. The allied coins could have had the head of Athena modeled on the Attic type on the obverse and a local type on the reverse.[7] Such legislation would have promoted the hegemonic symbolism of expressing the incorporation of allied cities into a single political body led by the Athenians. But this and other similar gambits were not desirable because they ran counter to the economic forces militating both for a termination and restriction of minting in allied cities and against further complications to exchange caused by the need to take on trust the commonality of the emissions of different mints.

The chronology of the adjustments in allied minting implies that many of the decisions in monetary policy were made by the allies themselves, probably without the direct intervention of the Athenian government. Nevertheless, the Athenians clearly promoted monetary and metrological consolidation by their initiatives. There is the evidence from Aristophanes that they often settled at least the tenor, if not the specific pattern, of an ally's monetary and metrological practices at the inauguration of its membership in the alliance (*Birds* 1040–41). Here also there is some evidence that a role was played in these arrangements by paradigmatic dispensations previously established by the Athenians and some favored or high-status allied state. The further hypothesis that monetary pacts and monetary clauses in *symbolai* played a part in advancing monetary consolidation may be supported by the evidence for the collaboration of Mytilene and Phokaia (among others). The relations of Chios and Athens may be another instance of the significance of reciprocal agreements although we know much less of them than we would like. Some have even supposed that the intervention of *symbolai* in the creation of monetary policy is a supposition that is needed for interpreting the Coinage Decree itself.

Finally, there was the impact of general Athenian hegemonic legislation, of which the only extant representatives, the fragments of the Coinage Decree, have absorbed much of our attention above. The

[7] One might term this pattern the Corinthian model for monetary hegemony. See pp. 489–93 above.

discussion of the background to Attic monetary legislation of general application directed attention toward problems of exchange as potential areas of dysfunction within the system for the collection of the tribute. That indication was amply borne out by the evidence of the tribute lists themselves both for the acceptance of non-Athenian electrum coins and for the toleration of irregular amounts of payment. The latter were taken to reveal problems in acquiring the requisite amount of Attic money for payment of the tribute or in consummating the exchange of local money for Attic tetradrachms in a timely and appropriate manner. The lists of *aparkhai*, recording the sixtieths dedicated to Athena, were seen to hint at some of the payments tendered in non-Athenian coin, but they did not reveal all such payments because others may have been cloaked in unexceptional round numbers. Nothing suggests, however, that the underlying irregularities that have been detected on the lists of *aparkhai* were instances for punishment by the Athenians or that they were not in fact officially tolerated to some considerable degree. Nonetheless, the *aparkhai* seem to have been reckoned and probably paid exclusively in Attic coin after the first list of 454/3 regardless of the nature of the payments of the tribute of which they were the first fruits.

Some significant threshold in the monetary history of the alliance was crossed in 454/3 at the beginning of the inscription of lists of the *aparkhai*, and this threshold is unlikely to have been the transfer of the treasury. Some have thought that it was the first promulgation of the principle that the allies ought to pay their *phoros* in Attic tetradrachms. It may rather have been the passage of the decree of Klearkhos that, suggested by the contents of the Coinage Decree, may have promoted the acceptance and recognition of Attic money and applied punitive sanctions (for the first time?) for lack of cooperation in monetary discipline in the payment of the tribute. On the basis of that conjunction, Klearkhos may also have heightened the rigor surrounding the tendering of the *aparkhai* in Attic silver. This hypothesis is even reconcilable with the view that the inauguration of the "tribute lists" was owed to the *aparkhai* being tendered to Athena for the first time, and not to Apollo, in 454/3. In the period of the mid-century, the understanding of Athena as the tutelary deity of the alliance and emphasis on the tendering of the tribute in the tetradrachms that bore her images may have dovetailed. With its clause added to the bouleutic oath, the Coinage Decree may subsequently have acted to further adherence to the strictures promulgated by Klearkhos.

The epigraphical evidence fulfills the expectations created by analyses of the finances and economics of the *arkhē*. Monetary legislation, the majority of which has not reached us through the vicissitudes of preservation, seems to have formed a significant class of lawmaking for the Athenians. The connection of the Coinage Decree with the system for collecting tribute is illustrated by the role of the Hellenotamiai in the fragments. The sensitivity of exchange into Athenian money is seen in the provision made for the minting and conversion into Attic coins by the *epistatai* of the mint. It has been suggested in the body of this work that at the moment of the first promulgation of the decree a consignment composed of non-Athenian coins levied from the allies was tendered in lieu of the annual tribute or alternatively that some amount of allied monies that was assimilated to tribute payment was processed under the provisions of the decree. Reserves in the mint were ordered to be coined and distributed to Athenian officials such as the *stratēgoi* to maintain the (normal) flow of resources to confederate forces. A fund, perhaps for use in future monetary exchange, that was consecrated to Athena and Hephaistos was established and protected against encroachment by Athenian officials and legislators. This line of analysis also led us to the hypothesis that at the time of promulgation of the decree allies were allowed to submit the annual *phoros* in non-Athenian money for that one particular year. That provision would have helped them to relieve themselves of the non-Athenian money in allied treasuries and would have injected more Attic money into circulation in the *arkhē*. Indeed, alternative mechanisms for affecting the Attic proportion of the allied money supply may not have been available to policy-makers.

Much of the analysis of the Coinage Decree's place in history has turned on the interpretation of the clause added to the oath of the *Boulē*, and, specifically, in determining the status that was implied therein for Athenian coinage. The provision that was reflected in the additional clause of the bouleutic oath probably did forbid allied decisions to continue minting silver while refusing to accept the validity of Athenian money, weights, and measures. The lost context for such a stipulation was a situation where most cities that did not mint their own coins were already using Athenian silver to some degree. The gradual retreat of local minting throughout the *arkhē*, which is substantiated through the numismatic evidence, parallels the growing acceptance and even dominance of Athenian money, which was minted in vastly greater amounts on a continual basis than were even those allied emissions that their cities chose to continue.

Those who continued to coin their own silver were not being harassed in that activity (as far as we can now discern). Again, it is the numismatic evidence that demonstrates the uncontroversial persistence of local coinages and the deposition of these coins in hoards. We have glimpsed the existence of several categories of factors that induced cities to maintain their minting of coins in specific denominations; chief among them was satisfying the expectations of non-Greek trading partners. Those who continued to coin were obliged, however, to recognize Attic money as locally valid. The legal standing accorded to Attic money made it more likely that enough Athenian coins would be circulating in a local economy to render the amassing of the assessed tribute in tetradrachms relatively free from trouble. Monetary and metrological consolidation also made the practical tasks of assessment of the income of allied states easier and more likely to be perceived as fair.

There was no provision made in the decree about the coining of electrum. The cities minting electrum were not intrinsically free from difficulties of exchange in acquiring the requisite amount of Attic coins, as the tribute lists show. Rather, because electrum was a specialized form of money, Attic and other silver coinages were already accepted as locally valid to cover much intra-*polis* circulation and administration in the cities minting electrum.

In this understanding, the Coinage Decree was a significant piece of legislation whose impact is hard to judge because it is unknown whether the rule encapsulated in the added clause to the bouleutic oath was an innovation or merely an attempt to strengthen a provision of some history, one that a (now irrecoverable) subset of the allies had been transgressing. Some questions now defy our answering, although they can be posed for the first time after the foregoing discussion. Had the Athenians been overly indulgent to those allies who had failed to recognize Attic money and metrological standards? Did they trace that latitude to successful attempts by allied delegations to engineer permission to pay their tribute in non-Athenian coins?

The Athenocentric content of the decree and the lack of authoritarian rhetoric focused explicitly on the allies subverts interpretations that see the Coinage Decree as a watershed in the movement from alliance to empire. Dealing with allies unable to pay their tribute in Attic money inconvenienced Athenian administration, but the Athenians seem to have been prepared to make some exceptions from time to time. Although the apodosis of the conditional sentence that described the new injunction to the *Bouleutai* is partially lacunose, the fact that the stipulation was added to their oath is significant. The *Boulē* was the likely initial recipient of requests for such exceptions and the Athenians were probably hoping to restrict their number and scope by hardening the resolve of the ordinary Athenians alloted to serve on the Council.

Most of the judicial or disciplinary attention in the decree from the Athenian perspective fell on the possibility that Athenian magistrates would be remiss in their implementation of this legislation. The allies also come into the picture, as their officials were expected to join in carrying out the wishes of the *dēmos*. There may be a further concern that both allied and Athenian officials conduct the implementation of the decree in a fashion that does not disrupt other incidentally relevant agreements. Athenian heralds were to look for allied help in the publication of the decree. Following the revisionist interpretation of the Coinage Decree presented here, that expectation of cooperation was a reasonable one.

In contrast, from the allied perspective, the chief expense as well as the onus of blame at home for an inability to pay the tribute in the requisite amount of Attic money probably fell on local magistrates. There were inherent authoritarian aspects to a hegemony over an alliance of tributaries that ought not be glossed over. Nevertheless, the insistence on the part of the Athenians that their money be valid even for those coining locally had the effect of removing any pressure on local officials from those who might try to color monetary affairs, making them an issue of defiance, local pride, or autonomy.

A review of the whole constellation of literary and epigraphical evidence on the dating of the fragments of the Coinage Decree does not lead to a conclusive judgment on its chronology. The theory deserving the greater credence, however, is that the decree was a piece of legislation that was first passed in the 440s, as indicated by the Kos fragment and by the clustering of irregularities on the tribute lists, but that remained in force for some decades thereafter, possibly generating some of the other fragments. While the allusion in the *Birds* of Aristophanes to monetary agreements is not a direct reflection of the inscribed decree or decrees, its character is consonant with a still-valid Coinage Decree, as interpreted in Part IV above.

If it is true that in a year early in the 440s the allies were permitted to pay their tribute in any available specie, it is then sensible to locate this payment in the year without a list, probably in 449/8. The timing is appropriate to this supposition: the Athenians acted soon after fighting with the Persians had subsided, when there would be less external pressure on the regular process of revenue collection and disbursement.

There may have been a practical disincentive to the tendering of the *aparkhai* to Athena in the year in which the tribute was replaced by the aggregation of non-Attic silver and electrum from the allies, namely, its resulting in the collection of a disparate set of coins and bullion, cumbrous in accounting and difficult to use in an emergency. The coinage collected from the allies may have been needed in its entirety to replace the reserves that had been held in the mint and had just been ordered coined by the decree. Additionally, it may have been perceived as lacking in propriety to dedicate to Athena coins bearing the images of other gods and heroes. That would have been quite a different thing from her treasurers receiving more anonymous and less programmatic or ideological electrum issues from time to time, if they truly ever did so in the form of *aparkhai* after 454/3 (which I doubt).

For all the significance that has been found above in the Coinage Decree, a conservative reading of its contents does not provide substantiation for the vast projects of confiscation, demonetization, and replacement of allied coinages that have sometimes been conjectured. The majority of the specie in Greek *poleis* lay in the hands of private individuals and not in the possession of the state. The calling in of existing coins for the purpose of their shipment to Attica for reminting would have represented a marked intrusion in the private lives of the allies. The only attested demonetizations in this period occurred during crises and were engineered by more authoritarian regimes (cf. pp. 120–21 with note 30). Perceptions of intrusiveness would have conditioned the presence or absence of cooperation. Not only do we lack any numismatic traces of such an upheaval in the usage of money in the *arkhē*, as witnessed by hoards, but indications are alike absent both of the huge administrative apparatus necessary to carry through such a project and of the equally extensive punitive machinery to cope with the inevitable resistance.

The factors driving monetary and metrological consolidation emerged from the evolving integration of the Aegean economy, in which the largest single item of inter-*polis* transfer of resources was the payment of the annual *phoros* by the allies to the Athenians. The dispositions about minting and coinage made either by the allies acting individually or by the Athenians through diplomacy or hegemonic dispensation could be no more or less imperialistic than the terms of the tribute system, which constrained the policy of everyone. Once the virtually demilitarized allied states became subsidizers of Attic military (and political) activities, the potential for (and perhaps the inevitability of) Attic intrusiveness was established. Athenian monetary policy was symptomatic of this disparity in military, political, and economic power, but it by no means constituted its driving force.

While many features of the fifth-century *arkhē* were revived during the Second Confederacy of the fourth century, like a network of colonial holdings and the raising of allied contributions toward the subsidization of a common fleet, no later analogue to the Coinage Decree existed, whether it is understood in its traditional interpretation or explained in our terms. The decree of Aristoteles (378/7) is our best evidence on the basic ground rules of the alliance. The decree excluded explicitly the exaction of tribute (*IG* II^2 43.23 = Tod, *GHI* #123: μήτε φόρον φέροντι; cf. *IG* II^2 44.24). Common expenses were to be defrayed through *syntaxis* 'contribution' by allied cities, a differentiating term that, according to Theopompus, was suggested by the Attic statesman Kallistratos (Harp. s.v. σύνταξις; Theopompus *FGH* 115 F 98). Rather than assessed by the *hēgemōn*, the *syntaxeis* were probably set by the *synhedrion* 'council' of the allies and perhaps eventually approved by the Athenian assembly (*IG* II^2 233.15–17; 404.10?; Aesch. 3.91–94; cf. *IG* II^2 44.24), although Athenian generals may have had an initial role when cities were first "liberated" and joined the alliance (cf. [Dem.] 58.37–38).[8] Thus, the process of individual assessment and the comparison of assessments that was arguably expedited during the *arkhē* by a consolidation of money and standards had been shifted to the *synhedrion*, where a multiplicity of perspectives was an unavoidable fundamental condition.

The rhetoric surrounding the *syntaxeis* seems to emphasize their commonality; note especially the phrase τῶν κοινῶν συντάξεων in [Dem.] 49.49. Since the allies set each others' *syntaxeis* reciprocally, it is possible that allied cities could declare their *syntaxis* in terms of any currency they chose and then pay accordingly. The *syntaxeis* probably accrued to a common treasury of the allies, and not to the Attic treasury (*IG* II^2 43.45–46; cf. 125.14–17). If the joint coinage of various Spartan allies ca. 400 was marked with ΣΥΝ for σύνταξις, this *syntaxis* would serve as a precedent for the use of the term in the Second Confederacy. The precedent would establish collaterally that *syntaxeis* might be paid in local money, albeit, in this case, of a common standard and type (see pp. 475–76 above). Conversely, nothing suggests that the *syntaxeis* were compulsorily tendered to the Athenians exclusively in Attic coins. Aeschines spoke of the insular *syntaxis* as amounting to 60T under duress (2.71), and Demosthenes refered to 45T raised in advance from the same

[8] In general, see F.H. Marshall, *The Second Athenian Confederacy* (Cambridge 1905) 38–42, 115; S. Accame, *La lega ateniese del sec. IV. A.C.* (Rome 1941) 134–35; P. Brun, *Eisphora—Syntaxis—Stratiotika* (Paris 1983) 74–142; F. Mitchel, "The Assessment of the Allies in the Second Athenian League," *EMC* 28 (1984) 23–37. Other ancient references to *syntaxis*: Isoc. 7.2; 8.29, 36; 15.113, 123; Aesch. 3.91–102; Hyperid. fr. 71 Jensen; Plut. *Phoc.* 7.1–2; *IG* II^2 123.7–21; 126.15–16; 207c.13; 213.13–14; also Xen. *HG* 6.2.1, 9 (who does not use the term in this connotation); cf. *IG* II^2 111.5–17; where the precise message of our documentation is unclear. See also immediately below for further citations.

allies (18.234). Even if these sums are conceded to have been paid in Attic money, that determination gives us little help in discerning whether payment in Attic coin was a legal obligation. The islanders were predominantly using Attic money anyway (see above, pp. 65–70). We should dearly like to know (as we do not now) in what coin minters such as Abdera, Byzantion, Maroneia, and Thasos were contributing. Amid this collection of minting and nonminting allied states, the status of Athenian coinage in various locales is unfortunately obscure. Although the Attic economy was markedly smaller and the output of the silver mines distinctly depressed, economic influence probably continued to promote some acceptance of Athenian coin among the allies to a certain extent.

The fourth-century Athenians became unpopular not by virtue of the now defunct procedures of assessment in the mode of the fifth-century *arkhē*, but in part because of their willingness to allow *stratēgoi* on campaign to enforce the payment of the *syntaxeis*.[9] The chronic penury of fourth-century Attic military operations that is dramatized by so many anecdotes in the *Oeconomica* attributed to Aristotle and in handbooks of military strategems meant that irregular and possibly extortionate exactions were tolerated (cf. also Isoc. 15.108). Thus, Attic monetary legislation was never revived, not because the Athenians resisted what had represented one of the abuses of the fifth-century *arkhē*, but because, in the absence of an assessment of *phoros*, it lacked any appropriate rationale in an expediting of tribute collection.[10]

Revival of the requirement that has been seen by us as embedded in the Coinage Decree had to wait for a time when features of Attic hegemonic policy might be absorbed into the common cultural heritage of all Greeks. The acceptance of Attic money then could be promoted for panhellenic patriotic reasons after it had lost any role as a facet or a symbol of political allegiance to Athens. Remarkably, the Amphictyones of Delphi used their religious authority at the end of the second century B.C. to mandate that all Greeks accept as valid (δέχεσθαι) the

9 Plut. *Phoc.* 7.1–2; Isoc. 8.29, 36; 15.123, cf. 113. To this may be added the anxieties over Athenian campaigns aimed at recovery of their fifth-century colonial holdings (for which, see Figueira, *Colonization* 241–49).

10 The disintegration of the dichotomy, "contribution of men/ships = no contribution of monies" or "no service in person = contribution of money," is attested in the conduct of the Second Confederacy (cf. on Thebes: Xen. *HG* 6.2.1, 9; [Dem.] 49.48–49); on Euboia: Aesch. 3.91–94; on Corcyra: Xen. *HG* 6.2.9. The beginnings of the fourth-century practices can be seen in the grants of autonomy during the Ionian War, and the replacement of the *phoros* by the 5 percent tax on imports and exports in 413 may be implicated (note Thuc. 7.28.4). See Figueira, *Excursions* 262–64, 285.

Attic tetradrachm.[11] Slaves were threatened with flogging for failing to obey; free men and women with a 200-dr. fine (with half to the accuser). The Amphictyones instructed the officials in the Greek cities or at major religious festivals to handle enforcement, while threatening a trial before themselves for those who failed to take action. A separate clause appears to threaten *trapezitai* 'bankers' with punishment for noncompliance. The Hieromnemones were to bring sealed copies of the decree to their home cities. The secretary of the Amphictyones was ordered to convey it to all the Greeks, and to see to the erection of copies at the Attic treasury in Delphi (the surviving version) and probably on the Acropolis at Athens.

Such a revivification of hegemonic legislation as a noncoerced gesture of cultural solidarity is not unparalleled. The provision that all Athenian colonies and subsequently all allied *poleis* were to supply an ox and a panoply at the quadrennial Panathenaic festival signified political subordination during the fifth-century *arkhē*. Yet, it was not so unremittedly resented that some Ionian communities did not agree to adhere to this principle after Athens had ceased to be their main military protector (*IPriene* #5.2–6, 10–13 [ca. 325]; *IG* II² 456b.5–10 for Kolophon [307/6]).

When the Amphictyones acted ca. 100, the motivating force for enhancing the status of Attic tetradrachms was unlikely to have been economic, although New Style Attic silver was much admired for its quality (setting a standard for the coins expected in payment of indemnities to Rome: Polyb. 21.32.8, 43.19).[12] The Athenian economy was a minor factor in the economics of the mainland Greeks. An Amphictyonic decree of 117 reveals a similar nostalgic and patriotic sentiment. Confirming the honors of the theatrical specialists working at Athens, amid references to Attic religious and cultural benefactions, the decree describes the Attic *dēmos* as the ἀρχηγός 'author' or 'founder' of all goods(?) for mankind (*FD* 3.2.69.11–12).

The Amphictyonic decree on coinage is so overreaching in its claims to international jurisdiction—it being so difficult to envisage a local *archon* actually being tried for violating it before the Amphictyonic council—that

[11] *FD* 3.2.139 (ca. 100) = *SIG*³ 729 (105–96) = Pleket, *Epigraphica* #13 (dating to 125–100). See also T. Reinach, "L'anarchie monétaire et ses remèdes chez les anciens Grecs," *Mém. Acad. Ins. et Belles-Lettres* 38 (1911) 351–64, esp. 357–64.

[12] Cf. M. Rostovzeff, *The Social and Economic History of the Hellenistic World* (Oxford 1941) 2.743, 3.1503–1504, where economic influences are foremost. The prevalence of New Style Attic coins saved the provisions of the decree from irrelevance, but can hardly be considered to have compelled that a decree urging the validity of Attic coinage be issued. For the hoard evidence, note *IGCH*, pp. 41–53.

it practically begs to be submitted to an ideological analysis, along with the just-mentioned *FD* 3.2.69 on the rights of theater personnel. It is doubtful whether the Amphictyony would have enacted such a decree even after an Athenian request, unless its provisions were somehow traditional. Whether declaration of the validity of Attic money had an earlier history in this particular form at Delphi itself is unknown. The Delphic decree did indeed establish the validity of Attic money alongside other (including local) issues in precisely the same manner as the reinterpretation of the Coinage Decree that has been argued above.

APPENDIX

ATHENIAN ALLIES: COINAGE AND TRIBUTE

The name of the allied state is followed by assessment period/estimated assessment for each assessment period. Variant payments are listed in parentheses after or below entry. Doubtful amounts are followed by a question mark. A plus sign indicates that the payment probably exceeded the amount noted.

1 = 454/3–451/0	5 = 438/7–435/4
2 = 450/49–447/6	6 = 434/3–431/30
3 = 446/5–443/2	7 = 430/29 and after
4 = 442/1–439/8	8 = Assessment A9–10, 13 (*IG* I³ 71, 77, 100) or list 34–40 (*IG* I³ 285–90)

I. NONMINTING ALLIED STATES

The symbol * = first coining after 400.

IONIA

ASTYRA

1: 500	2: —	3: 500	4: 500	5: —	6: —	7: —	8: —

BOUTHEIA

1: 3	2: —	3: —	4: 1000	5: —	6: —	7: 1000	8: —

DIOSERITAI

1: 1000	2: 1000	3: —	4: 500	5: —	6: 500	7: —	8: 500

ELAIA

1: 1000	2: —	3: 1000	4: 1000	5: —	6: 1000	7: —	8: —

*ELAIOUSA

1: —	2: —	3: 100	4: 100	5: —	6: —	7: –	8: 1

*GRYNEION

1: 1000	2: 1000	3: 1000	4: 1000	5: —	6: 2000	7: 2000	8: —

HAIRAI

1: 3	2: 3	3: 1	4: 1	5: —	6: 1	7: —	8: —

ISINDA
1: — 2: — 3: 1000 4: 1000 5: — 6: 1000 7: — 8: —

*LARISA ——No amounts have survived——

LEBEDOS
1: 3 2: 3 3: 1 4: 1 5: — 6: — 7: — 8: —

LEROS
1: 3 2: — 3: — 4: — 5: — 6: — 7: — 8: —

MAIANDRIOI
1: 4000 2: — 3: 4000 4: — 5: — 6: — 7: — 8: —

MARATHESION
1: — 2: — 3: — 4: 3000 5: — 6: 2000 7: — 8: —

MYOS
1: 1.3000 2: 1 3: — 4: 1 5: — 6: 1.3000 7: — 8: —

*MYRINA
1: 1 2: 1 3: 1 4: 1 5: — 6: 1 7: 1 8: —

*NISYROS
1: 1.3000 2: — 3: — 4: 1 5: — 6: 1 7: — 8: —

NOTION
1: 2000 2: 2000 3: 2000 4: 2000 5: — 6: 2000 7: — 8: 2000

OINAIOI ON IKAROS
1: 1.2000 2: 1 3: 4000 4: 4000 5: — 6: 1 7: — 8: —

POLIKHNA
1: — 2: — 3: 4000 4: 4000 5: — 6: — 7: 1 8: —

*PRIENE (early minting in electrum?)
1: 1 2: 1 3: — 4: 1 5: — 6: — 7: — 8: —

PTELEON
1: — 2: — 3: — 4: 100 5: — 6: — 7: — 8: —

PYGELA
1: — 2: — 3: 1 4: 1 5: — 6: 1.3000 7: — 8: —

SIDOUSA
1: — 2: — 3: — 4: 500 5: — 6: — 7: — 8: —

TEIKHIOUSSA ——No amounts have survived——

THERMAIOI ON IKAROS
1: 3000 2: 3000 3: — 4: 3000 5: — 6: 3000 7: — 8: —

HELLESPONT

AKHILLEION ——No amounts have survived——

*ALOPEKONNESOS

1: — 2: 3240 3: — 4: 1000 5: — 6: 2000 7: — 8: —

ARISBA

1: 2 2: — 3: — 4: 2 5: — 6: 6 7: — 8: —

ARTAIOTEIKHITAI

1: — 2: — 3: — 4: — 5: — 6: — 7: — 8: 1000

ARTAKE

1: 2000 2: 2000 3: 2000 4: 2000 5: 2000 6: 2000 7: 2000 8: 4000

ASTYRA TROIKA ——No amounts have survived——
(see also Astyra in Mysia [Ionia])

AZEIA

1: 400 2: — 3: — 4: 400 5: 400 6: 400 7: 400 8: —

BERYSIOI

1: 1000 2: 1000 3: 1000 4: — 5: — 6: — 7: — 8: —

*BISANTHE

1: — 2: — 3: — 4: — 5: — 6: — 7: — 8: 2

BRYLLEION

1: — 2: — 3: — 4: — 5: — 6: 3000 7: 3000 8: —

BYSBIKOS

1: — 2: — 3: — 4: — 5: — 6: 3000 7: — 8: —

DAREION ——No amounts have survived——

DASKYLEION

1: 500 2: 500 3: — 4: — 5: — 6: 500 7: 500 8: —

DAUNOTEIKHITAI

1: 1000 2: 1000 3: 1000 4: 1000 5: 1000 6: 1000 7: 2.4000 8: 2

DIDYMOTEIKHITAI

1: 1000 2: 1000 3: 1000 4: 1000 5: 1000 6: 1000 7: 1000 8: —

*ELAIOUS

1: — 2: 3000 3: 3000 4: 3000 5: 3000 6: 3000 7: 3000 8: —

EURYMAKHITAI

1: — 2: 1000 3: — 4: — 5: — 6: — 7: — 8: —

*GENTINIOI

1: 500 2: 500 3: 500 4: — 5: — 6: — 7: — 8: —

*HARPAGION
1: — 2: 300 3: 300 4: 300 5: 300 6: 300 7: 300 8: —

*ILION
1: — 2: — 3: — 4: — 5: — 6: — 7: — 8: 2

KALLIPOLIS
1: — 2: — 3: — 4: — 5: — 6: 1000 7: 1000 8: —

*KIOS
1: 1000 2: 1000 3: 1000 4: 1000 5: 1000 6: 1000 7: 1000 8: —

KOLONAI ——————No amounts have survived——————

*KOLONE
1: — 2: — 3: — 4: — 5: — 6: — 7: — 8: 1000

LARISA
1: — 2: — 3: — 4: — 5: — 6: — 7: — 8: 3

LIMNAI
1: — 2: 2000 3: — 4: 500 5: 500 6: 1000 7: — 8: —

*MADYTOS
1: — 2: — 3: — 4: 500 5: 2000 6: 2000 7: 2000 8: 2000

MARKAIOI ——————No amounts have survived——————

METROPOLIS NEAR PRIAPOS
1: — 2: — 3: — 4: — 5: — 6: — 7: — 8: 1

*MILETOPOLIS ——————No amounts have survived——————

MYSOI
1: 2000 2: — 3: — 4: — 5: — 6: — 7: — 8: —

NEAPOLIS
1: — 2: — 3: — 4: 300 5: — 6: 300 7: — 8: —

*OPHRYNEION
1: — 2: — 3: — 4: — 5: — 6: — 7: — 8: 5

OTLENOI
1: — 2: — 3: — 4: — 5: — 6: — 7: — 8: 2000

PAISOS
1: 1000 2: 1000 3: 1000 4: 1000 5: 1000 6: 1000 7: 1000 8: —

PALAIPERKOTE
1: 500 2: 500 3: 500 4: 500 5: — 6: 1500 7: 500 8: —

PALAMEDEION
1: — 2: — 3: — 4: — 5: — 6: — 7: — 8: 5

*PERINTHOS
1: — 2: 10 3: 10 4: 10 5: 10 6: 10 7: 10 8: —

PERKOTE
1: 1000 2: 1000 3: 1000 4: 1000 5: — 6: — 7: 1000 8: —

PETRA
1: — 2: — 3: — 4: — 5: — 6: — 7: — 8: 2

POLIKHNE ——No amounts have survived——

*PRIAPOS
1: 500 2: 500 3: 500 4: 500 5: 500 6: 500 7: 500 8: —

PYTHOPOLITAI
1: — 2: — 3: — 4: — 5: — 6: — 7: — 8: 100

*RHOITEION
1: — 2: — 3: — 4: — 5: — 6: — 7: — 8: 8

SERIOTEIKHEION ——No amounts have survived——

*SESTOS
1: — 2: — 3: — 4: 500 5: 1000 6: 1000 7: 1000 8: —

*SIGEION
1: — 2: 1000 3: 1000 4: 1000 5: — 6: 1000 7: 1000 8: 1

SOMBIA
1: — 2: — 3: — 4: — 5: — 6: — 7: — 8: 4000

TEREIA ——No amounts have survived——

*THYMBRA
1: — 2: — 3: — 4: — 5: — 6: — 7: — 8: 1.3000

TYRODIZA
1: 1000 2: — 3: 500 4: — 5: — 6: — 7: — 8: —

*ZELEIA ——No amounts have survived——

THRACE

AIGE
1: 3000 2: 3000 3: 2000 4: 2000 5: 3000 6: 3000 7: 3250 8: —

AIOLEION
1: — 2: — 3: — 4: — 5: — 6: 500 7: 500 8: 500

AKROTHOOI ——No amounts have survived——

ASSERA
1: 2400 2: 2400 3: 2400 4: — 5: 3000 6: 3000 7: — 8: —

BERGE

1: 2880	2: 3240	3: —	4: —	5: 3120	6: 3120	7: —	8: —

BORMISKOS

1: —	2: —	3: —	4: —	5: —	6: —	7: —	8: 1000

DION

1: 1	2: 1	3: 1	4: 1	5: 1	6: 1	7: 1	8:—

DRYS NEAR SERRES

1: —	2: —	3: —	4: —	5: —	6: —	7: —	8: 1

GALE

1: —	2: —	3: —	4: —	5: 800	6: 3000	7: —	8: 10 dr.!

GALEPSOS

1: 1.3000	2: 1.1200	3: 1.3000	4: 3000	5: —	6: 1000	7: 1000	8: —

GIGONOS ——————(See Smilla)——————

HAISA ——————(See Smilla)——————

HAISON

1: 1500	2: 1500	3: 1500	4: 1500	5: 1500	6: 1000	7: 1000	8: —

*HAMAXITOS

1: —	2: —	3: —	4: —	5: —	6: —	7: —	8: 4

HERAKLEION

1: —	2: —	3: —	4: —	5: —	6: —	7: —	8: 1000

*IKOS

1: 1500	2: 1500	3: 1500	4: 1500	5: 1500	6: 1500	7: 1500	8: —

KAMAKAI

1: —	2: —	3: —	4: —	5: —	6: —	7: —	8: 600

KHEDROLOS = ERODIOI

1: —	2: 500	3: —	4: —	5: 500	6: 1000	7: —	8: —

KITHAS ——————(See Smilla)——————

KLEONAI

1: —	2: —	3: —	4: —	5: —	6: 500	7: 500	8: 100

KOSSAIOI ——————No amounts have survived——————

KYSTIROS

1: —	2: —	3: —	4: —	5: —	6: 300	7: —	8: —

MEKYBERNA

1: 2.1880	2: 1	3: 4000	4: 4000	5: 1	6: 1	7: —	8: 10 dr.!

*METHONE

1: —	2: —	3: —	4: —	5: —	6: 3	7: 3	8: 5

MILTOROS
1: — 2: — 3: — 4: — 5: 1000 6: 3000 7: — 8: —

NEAPOLITAI IN CHALCIDICE
1: 3000 2: 3000 3: 3000 4: 3000 5: 3000 6: 3000 7: 3000 8: —

OLOPHYXOS
1: 2000 2: 1500 3: 2000 4: 2000 5: 2000 6: 2000 7: 2000 8: 1

OTHOROS
1: — 2: — 3: 500 4: 700 5: 700 6: 500 7: — 8: 1000

PERGAMOTEIKHEION ——No amounts have survived——

PHARBELOS
1: 1000 2: 1000 3: 1000 4: 1000 5: 1000 6: 500 7: — 8: 500

PHEGETOS
1: 1600 2: 1600 3: 1000 4: 1000 5: 1000 6: — 7: — 8: —

PIERES NEAR PERGAMOS ——No amounts have survived——

PILOROS
1: — 2: — 3: — 4: — 5: — 6: 600 7: — 8: —

PISTASOS
1: — 2: — 3: — 4: — 5: — 6: 500 7: — 8: 500

PLEUME
1: — 2: — 3: — 4: — 5: — 6: 1000 7: 1000 8: —

POLIKHNE ——No amounts have survived——

POSEIDEION
1: — 2: — 3: — 4: — 5: — 6: — 7: — 8: 1000

SALE
1: — 2: — 3: — 4: — 5: — 6: — 7: — 8: 3000

SANE
1: 2.2000 (1) 2: 1 3: 4000 4: 4000 5: 1 6: 1 7: 1000 8: —

SARTE
1: — 2: — 3: — 4: — 5: — 6: 1500 7: 1500 8: 100

SERME
1: — 2: 500 3: 500 4: 500 5: 500 6: 500 7: — 8: 500

SINGIS
1: 4 2: 2 (1.5000) 3: 2 4: 2 5: 3 6: 2 (1) 7: — 8: 10 dr.!

SINOS
1: — 2: — 3: — 4: — 5: — 6: 1500 7: — 8: 800

SKABALA
1: — 2: 3000 3: 2000 4: 2000 5: 3000 6: 3000 (1500) 7: — 8: —

*SKIATHOS
1: — 2: 1000 3: 1000 4: 1000 5: 1000 6: 1000 7: 1000 8: —

SMILLA
1: — 2: — 3: — 4: — 5: — 6: 3000 7: — 8: 3000
(with Gigonos, Haisa, Kithas, and Tinde = Poleis Krossidas)

STOLOS
1: — 2: 5000 (4000) 3: 4000 4: 4000 5: 1 6: 1 7: — 8: —

STREPSA
1: 1 2: 1 (5) 3: 1 4: 1 5: 1 6: 1 7: — 8: —

THERAMBOS
1: — 2: — 3: 1000 4: 1000 5: 1000 6: 1000 7: 1085 8: —

THESTOROS ————No amounts have survived————

THYSSOS
1: 4000 2: 1.3000 3: 1 4: 1 5: 1 6: 1 7: 1 8: —

TINDAIOI ————(See Smilla)————

TRIPOAI
1: — 2: — 3: — 4: — 5: — 6: — 7: — 8: 800

ZEREIA
1: — 2: — 3: — 4: — 5: — 6: — 7: — 8: 500

ZONE NEAR SERRES
1: — 2: — 3: — 4: — 5: — 6: — 7: — 8: 2

CARIA

*ALINDA (?)
1: 1.0600(+) 2: — 3: — 4: — 5: — 6: — 7: — 8: —

AMIOI
1: — 2: — 3: — 4: — 5: — 6: 2250 7: — 8: —

*AMORGOS
1: — 2: — 3: — 4: — 5: — 6: 1 7: 1 8: —

AMYNANDA
1: 3050 2: — 3: 3000 4: — 5: — 6: — 7: — 8: —

ARKESSEIA
1: — 2: 1000 3: — 4: 1000 5: — 6: 1000 7: 1000 8: —

ARLISSOS(?) ——No amounts have survived——

AULIATAI
1: 500 2: 500 3: 500 4: 500 5: — 6: 500 7: — 8: 500

*BARGYLIA
1: 1000 2: 1000 (4000) 3: 1000 4: 1000 5: — 6: — 7: — 8: —

BOLBAI
1: 1030 2: — 3: — 4: — 5: — 6: — 7: — 8: —

BRIKINDARIOI ON RHODES
1: — 2: — 3: — 4: — 5: — 6: — 7: — 8: 1

BRYKOUNTIOI
1: — 2: 500 3: — 4: — 5: — 6: — 7: — 8: 500

DIAKRIOI ON RHODES
1: — 2: — 3: — 4: — 5: — 6: — 7: — 8: 2

ERINES
1: 4130 2: 3240 3: 1000 4: — 5: — 6: — 7: — 8: 1

ETEOKARPATHIOI
1: — 2: — 3: — 4: — 5: — 6: 1000 7: — 8: —

*EUROMOS
1: — 2: 2500 3: 2500 4: 2500 5: — 6: — 7: — 8: 6

HIERA ——No amounts have survived——

HYBLISSOS
1: 1060 2: — 3: — 4: — 5: — 6: — 7: — 8: 2000(+)

HYLIMA(?) ——No amounts have survived——

*IASOS
1: — 2: 1 3: —(1) 4: 1 5: — 6: 1 7: — 8: 3000

ITYRA
1: — 2: — 3: — 4: — 5: — 6: — 7: — 8: 4000

KALYDNA = KLAYNDA
1: — 2: — 3: 1 4: — 5: — 6: — 7: — 8: —

KARBASYANDA
1: 1000 2: 1000 3: 1000 4: 1000 5: — 6: 1000 7: — 8: —

*KARYANDA
1: 1000 2: 500 3: 500 4: 500 5: — 6: 500 7: — 8: 1000

KARYE
1: — 2: — 3: — 4: — 5: — 6: — 7: — 8: 1

KASOLABA
1: 2500 2: 2500 3: — 4: — 5: — 6: — 7: — 8: —

KASOS
1: — 2: — 3: — 4: — 5: — 6: 1000 7: 1000 8: 1000

KEDREAI
1: 3000 2: 3000 3: 3000 4: 3000 5: — 6: 2000 7: — 8: —

*KERAMOS
1: 1.3000 2: 1.3000 3: 1.3000 4: 1.3000 5: — 6: — 7: — 8: —

KHALKE
1: — 2: 3000 3: 2000 4: 2000 5: — 6: 2000 7: 2000 8: 2000

KHALKETOR
1: 2000 2: 2100 3: 2100 4: 2100 5: — 6: — 7: — 8: 2(+)

KHIOI IN CARIA
1: 2000 2: 2000 3: — 4: — 5: — 6: — 7: — 8: 2(+)

KILLARA
1: 1000 2: — 3: — 4: — 5: — 6: — 7: — 8: 2

KINDYE
1: 1 2: 1 3: — 4: 1 5: — 6: — 7: — 8: 4?

KODAPES
1: 1000 2: 1000 3: 1000 4: — 5: — 6: — 7: — 8: 2000(+)

KROUSA ——No amounts have survived——

KRYE
1: 2000 2: 2000 3: 2000 4: 2000 5: — 6: 2000 7: — 8: —

KYDAI
1: 400 2: 400 3: — 4: — 5: — 6: — 7: — 8: 2000

KYLLANDOS
1: 2 2: 2 3: — 4: — 5: — 6: — 7: — 8: —

KYRBISSOS
1: 2000 2: 2000 3: 2000 4: — 5: — 6: — 7: — 8: 2000(+)

LATMOS
1: 1 2: 1 3: 1 4: 1 5: — 6: 1 7: — 8: —

*LEPSIMANDOS
1: 1500 2: 1500 3: 1000 4: 1000 5: — 6: — 7: — 8: 2000(+)

MADNASA
1: 2 2: 1 3: 1 4: 1 5: — 6: 1 7: — 8: —

MILYAI ——No amounts have survived——

MYDONES
1: 1500 2: 1500 3: 1500 4: 1500 5: — 6: — 7: — 8: —

*MYNDOS
1: 500 2: 500 3: 500 4: 500 5: — 6: 500 7: 500 8: 1000

NARISBARA
1: 1000 2: 1000 3: 1000 4: 1000 5: — 6: — 7: — 8: —

NAXIA
1: 1000 2: 500 3: 500 4: 500 5: — 6: 500 7: — 8: —

OIAI
1: 3300 2: — 3: — 4: — 5: — 6: — 7: — 8: —

OURANION
1: 1030 (500) 2: — 3: — 4: — 5: — 6: — 7: — 8: —

PARGASA
1: — 2: 1000 3: 500 4: — 5: — 6: — 7: — 8: —

PARPARIOTAI
1: 1000 2: 1000 3: 1000 4: 1000 5: — 6: — 7: — 8: —

PASANDA
1: 3000 2: 3000 3: 3000 4: 3000 5: — 6: — 7: — 8: —

PEDASA
1: 2 2: 1 3: — 4: — 5: — 6: — 7: — 8: 3000

PEDIEIS IN LINDOS
1: — 2: 2000 3: 100 4: 100 5: — 6: 5000 7: — 8: 1

PELEA
1: 4000 2: 3000 3: 3000 4: 3000 5: — 6: 3000 7: — 8: —

PERGE ——No amounts have survived——

PLADASA
1: — 2: 2000 3: — 4: 2000 5: — 6: — 7: — 8: —

POLIKHNAIOI
1: 1000 2: — 3: — 4: — 5: — 6: — 7: — 8: —

PYRNOS
1: 1000 2: 1000 3: 1000 4: 1000 5: — 6: 1000 7: — 8: —

SAMBAKTYS
1: 1 2: — 3: — 4: — 5: — 6: — 7: — 8: —
(1.0400)

SAROS
1: — 2: — 3: — 4: — 5: — 6: — 7: 300 8: 200

SILLYON ——————No amounts have survived——————

SILOI
1: 1500 2: — 3: — 4: — 5: — 6: — 7: — 8: —

*SYANGELA (later mint uncertain)
1: 3000 2: 1 3: 1? 4: 1 5: — 6: 1 7: 1800 8: —

*SYME
1: — 2: — 3: — 4: — 5: — 6: 1800 7: 1800 8: 3000

TARAMPTOS ——————No amounts have survived——————

TARBANA
1: 1030 2: — 3: — 4: — 5: — 6: — 7: — 8: 1000

TELANDRIA
1: 1 2: 3000 3: 3000 4: 3000 5: — 6: — 7: — 8: —

*TELMESSOS (later mint uncertain)
1: — 2: — 3: 1 4: — 5: — 6: — 7: — 8: —

*TELOS
1: — 2: — 3: — 4: — 5: — 6: — 7: — 8: 2

THASTHARA
1: 500 2: 500 3: 500 4: 500 5: — 6: — 7: — 8: —

THYDONOS
1: 1000 2: — 3: — 4: — 5: — 6: — 7: — 8: —

TYMNESSES ——————No amounts have survived——————

YDISSOS
1: 1200 2: 1 3: — 4: — 5: — 6: — 7: — 8: —

YMISSOS
1: 1200 2: 1200 3: — 4: — 5: — 6: — 7: — 8: 6
(with Edries, Kyromes)

ISLANDS

BELBINA
1: — 2: — 3: — 4: — 5: — 6: — 7: — 8: 300

DIADES
1: 2000 2: 2000 3: 4000 4: 2000 5: — 6: 2000 7: — 8: 1

DIAKRES
1: — 2: — 3: — 4: — 5: — 6: 800 7: 800 8: 2000

DIAKRIOI IN EUBOIA
1: — 2: — 3: — 4: — 5: — 6: — 7: 1.2000 8: 1.2000

DION
1: 1000 2: 2000 3: — 4: 2000 5: 2000 6: 2000 7: — 8: —

GRYNKHE
1: 1000 2: 1000 3: 1000 4: 1000 5: — 6: 1000 7: 1000 8: 2000

*HESTIAIA
1: — 2: 1000 3: — 4: 2000 (Attic colony)

*IMBROS
1: — 2: 3300 3: — 4: 1 5: 1 6: 1 7: 1 8: 1

*IOS
1: 1 2: 840 3: — 4: 3000 5: — 6: 3000 7: 3000 8: 1 (3000)

*KIMOLOS
1: — 2: — 3: — 4: — 5: — 6: — 7: — 8: 1000

*KYTHERA (see Thuc. 4.57.4)
1: — 2: — 3: — 4: — 5: — 6: — 7: 4 8: —

*KYTHNOS
1: — 2: 3 3: 3 4: 3 5: — 6: 3 7: — 8: 6

*LEMNOS
1: 9 2: 4? 3: 4.3000 4: 4.3000 5: 4.3000 6: — 7: — 8: 4

*MYKONOS
1: 1.3000 2: 1.3000 3: 1.3000 4: 1 5: — 6: 1 7: 1 8: 2

*PHOLEGANDROS
1: — 2: — 3: — 4: — 5: — 6: — 7: — 8: 2000

POSEIDEION
1: — 2: — 3: — 4: — 5: — 6: — 7: — 8: 1000

RHENAIA
1: 1000 2: 300 3: — 4: 300 5: — 6: 300 7: 1000 8: 1000

*SIKINNOS
1: — 2: — 3: — 4: — 5: — 6: — 7: 1000 8: 1000

STYRA
1: — 2: 1 3: 1 4: 1 5: 1 6: 1 7: 1 8: 2

*SYROS
1: 1500 2: 1000 3: 1000 4: 1000 5: — 6: 1500 7: 1500 8: 1

II. ALLIED STATES INITIATING COINAGE DURING THE *ARKHĒ*

APHYTIS (fraction only: Attic standard; then Milesian)
1: 3 2: 3 3: 1 4: 1 5: 3 6: 3 7: 3 8: —
Refs.: Head[2] 209–10; Babelon 2.4.635–44, #1031–32; Gaebler, *Münzen* 44; Erxleben *AfP* 107

BOTTIAIOI (fr. only: Phocaic; Mil.)
Spartolos
1: 2 2: 2 3: 2 4: 2 5: 2 6: 3.0500 7: — 8: —
Prassilos
1: — 2: — 3: — 4: — 5: — 6: — 7: — 8: 900
Refs.: Head[2] 213; Babelon 2.4.589–94, #954–55; Gaebler, *Münzen* 50–51 (432>); Erxleben *AfP* 107–108

BYZANTION (dr./fr. only; Persic)
1: 15 2: 15 3: — 4: 15.4300 5: — 6: 18.1800 7: 15? 8: —
Refs.: Head[2] 266–70; Babelon 2.4.973–86; Robinson 333; Erxleben *AfP* 95–96; Kraay, *ACGC* 238, 259; E. Schönert-Geiss, *Griechisches Münzwerk: Die Münzprägung von Byzantion* (Berlin 1970) esp. 35–51

ELAIA (fr. only; Euboiec/Attic)
1: 1000 2: — 3: 1000 4: 1000 5: — 6: 1400 7: — 8: —
Refs.: Head[2] 554–55; Babelon 2.2.1188–90; Erxleben *AfP* 77

GARGARA (fr. only: Persic)
1: 4500 2: 4500 3: — 4: 4660 5: — 6: — 7: 4500 8: —
Refs.: Head[2] 545; Babelon 2.2.1259–64, #2283–91; Erxleben *AfP* 107–108

IDYMA (fr./dr.: Rhodian or Phoenician)
1: 1.0890 2: 5200 3: 2000 4: — 5: — 6: — 7: — 8: —
Refs.: Head[2] 621; Babelon 2.2.995–1000; Erxleben *AfP* 84–85

LAMPONEIA (fr./dr.: Lesbian)
1: 1000 2: 1000 3: 1000 4: 1000 5: — 6: 1400 7: 1400 8: —
Refs.: Head[2] 547; Babelon 2.2.1263–66, #2292–97; Erxleben *AfP* 98

NEANDREIA (fr. only)
1: 2000 2: 2000 3: 2000 4: 2000 5: — 6: 2000 7: — 8: —
Refs.: Head[2] 547; Babelon 2.2.1295–1300, #2283–91; Erxleben *AfP* 99

PITANA (fr. only)
1: 1000 2: 1000 3: 1000 4: 1000 5: — 6: 1000 7: — 8: —
Refs.: Head[2] 537; Erxleben *AfP* 81

PORDOSELENE/NESOS (fr./dr.: Phocaic; Chian)
—— No amounts have survived ——
Refs.: Head[2] 563; Babelon 2.2.1247–52, #2272–74; Erxleben *AfP* 102

PROKONNESOS (fr./dr.?: Persic)
1: — 2: 3 3: 3 4: 3 5: 3 6: 3 7: 3 8: —
Refs.: Head[2] 537–38; Babelon 2.2.1478–80, #2831–36; M. Thompson, "The Coins of Proconnesus," *RN*[6] 7 (1965) 30–35 (c. 450>); Erxleben *AfP* 99

TRAGILOS (fr. only: Phoen.)
1: — 2: — 3: — 4: — 5: — 6: — 7: — 8: 1
Refs.: Head[2] 217; Babelon 2.4.753–58, #1191–92; Gaebler, *Münzen* 131–32; Erxleben *AfP* 122–23

III. ALLIED STATES THAT CEASED MINTING OPERATIONS DURING THE *ARKHĒ*

Later revival of coining = *

A. Allies Ceasing Minting before 478

*ANAPHE (Milesian = Phoenician)
1: — 2: — 3: — 4: — 5: — 6: — 7: 1000 8: 1000 (with Keria)
Refs.: F. Imhoof-Blumer, *Griechische Münzen* (Munich 1890) 19; D.H. Cox, in A.R. Bellinger, "Greek Coins from the Yale Numismatic Collection," *YCS* 11 (1950) 307–16, esp. 307–308; L. Robert, "Monnaies dans inscriptions grecques," *RN*[6] 4 (1962) 7–24, esp. 13–17; Erxleben *AfP* 69–70

*ANDROS (Aiginetic)
1: 12 2: 6 3: 6 4: 6 5: — 6: 6 7: 6 8: 15
Refs.: D.P. Pachales, «ΝΟΜΙΣΜΑΤΙΚΗ ΤΗΣ ΑΡΧΙΑΣ ΑΝΔΡΟΥ», *JIAN* 1 (1898) 299–366, esp. 344–46; Head[2] 482; Babelon 2.1.1275–78; S.W. Grose, *Catalogue of the McClean Collection of Greek Coins*, v. 2 (Cambridge 1926) 515–16; Robinson 329; Erxleben *AfP* 70; cf. Imhoof-Blumer, *Münzen* 13–14 (assigning to Karthaia on Keos); C.T. Seltman, *Athens: Its History and Coinage before the Persian Invasion* (Cambridge 1924) 7–8 (assigning to Athens); Kraay, *ACGC* 45, 49.
Hoard evidence: *IGCH* #6, "Cyclades" (ca. 500); #7, "Santorin" (ca. 500–490); #1165, "Asia Minor" (ca. 500); *CH* 8.19?, "Asia Minor?, 1989" (ca. 500). See also J.H. Kagan, "An Archaic Greek Coin Hoard from the Eastern Mediterranean and Early Cypriot Coinage," *NC* 154 (1994) 17–52, esp. 22.

*KALYMNA (= Kalydnioi: various standards: Babylonian; Persic; Milesian; Euboeic)
1: 1.3000 2: 1.3000 3: 1.3000 4: 1.3000 5: — 6: 1.3000 7: — 8: —
Refs.: Babelon 2.1.435–40; Head^2 631 (is doubtful); Kraay, *ACGC* 38; R. Dus, "Un statère rarissime de Kalymna," *JEListeFPL* 106 (1988) 2–4.
Hoard evidence: *IGCH* #1874, "Taranto" (ca. 508); cf. #1216, "Calymna, 1823" (ca. 355).

KARPATHOS (= Poseidion?; Phoenician-Milesian)
1: — 2: — 3: 1000 4: 1000 5: — 6: 1000 7: — 8: 500
Refs.: F. Imhoof-Blumer, "Beiträge zur Münzkunde und Geographie von Alt-Griechenland und Kleinasien," *ZfN* 1 (1874) 93–162, esp. 153–62; Head^2 631; Babelon 2.1.446–48; Price and Waggoner 93; Kraay, *ACGC* 38; N.M. Waggoner, *Early Greek Coins from the Collection of Jonathan P. Rosen, Ancient Coins in North American Collections* 5 (New York 1983) 41. Cf. H. Cahn, "Poseidion on Karpathos?," *NC*^{6} 17 (1957) 11–12; S. Boutin, "Essai de classement de monnaies archaïques de la mer égée au type des deux delphins," in R. Margolis and H. Voegtli (eds.), *Numismatics: Witness to History* (Wetteren 1986) 1–10.
Hoard evidence: *IGCH* #1644, "Asyut" (ca. 475); #1645, "Zagazig" (ca. 470); #1790, "Malayer" (ca. 375); *CH* 8.48, "Elmali, Lycia, 1984" (ca. 460).

*KAUNOS (Persic)
1: 3000 2: 3000 3: 3000 4: 3000 5: — 6: — 7: — 8: 10
Refs.: Head^2 612–13 (<480); cf. E. Keckman, "Zwei Fundmünzen aus Kaunos in Karien," *SM* 31 (1981) 34–35.
Hoard evidence: *IGCH* #1790, "Malayer" (ca. 375); *CH* 8.9?, "Unknown Findspot, 1983" (ca. 525).

*KHERSONESITAI (Euboeic/Attic; fr. only?)
1: 18 2: 13.4840 3: 1 4: 1 5: 1 6: 1 7: — 8: —
Refs.: Erxleben *AfP* 83; Kraay, *ACGC* 158; cf. Babelon 2.1.1231–34; Head^2 257–58 (<493, but also 480–350); cf. G. LeRider, *Deux trésors de monnaies grecques de la Propontide* (Paris 1963) 52–54.
Hoard evidence: *CH* 1.15, "Black Sea, ca. 1970" (ca. 425).

*KYME (Aiginetic)
1: 12 2: 9 3: 9 4: 9 5: — 6: 9 7: — 8: —
Refs.: Head^2 552–54; Babelon 2.1.331–40, 2.2.1170–71 (<470); Erxleben *AfP* 81.
Hoard Evidence: *IGCH* #1167, "Vourla" (ca. 500–490); #1183, "Colophon" (ca. 450?).

*NAXOS (Aiginetic; see also Anaphe)
1: — 2: 6.4000 3: 6.4000 4: 6.4000 5: — 6: 6.4000 7: — 8: 15
Refs.: Head^2 488; Babelon 2.1.1311–17 (#1950–52: <490); R.R. Holloway, "The Crown of Naxos," *ANSMN* 10 (1962) 1–8; Erxleben *AfP* 73; Kraay, *ACGC* 45, 49; Price and Waggoner 80; cf. J.G. Milne, "A Group of Coins Attributable to the Revolt of Naxos in 467," *NC*^{5} 20 (1940) 76–88.
Hoard evidence: *IGCH* #7, "Santorin" (ca. 500–490); #11, "Isthmia, 1954" (ca. 480); #1636, "Mit Rahineh" (ca. 500); #1637, "Demanhur" (500); #1639, "Sakha" (early fifth century?); #1640, "Benha el Asl" (ca. 485); #1644, "Asyut" (ca. 475); #1874,

"Taranto" (ca. 508); *CH* 7.12 = 6.4–5 = 8.45, "Syria, 1978/9" (ca. 475). See also J.H. Kagan, "An Archaic Greek Coin Hoard from the Eastern Mediterranean and Early Cypriot Coinage," *NC* 154 (1994) 17–52, esp. 22–23.

*PEPARETHOS (Euboeic/Attic)
1: 3 2: 3 3: 3 4: 3 5: 3 6: 3 7: 3 8: —
Refs.: Head^{2} 312–13 (<480); W. Wroth, "Peparethus and its Coinage," *JHS* 27 (1907) 90–98; Erxleben *AfP* 116; J.M. Balcer, "Peparethos: The Early Coinage Reconsidered," *SNR* 46 (1967) 25–33 (<500); Balcer, "Peparethos: Further Notes," *SNR* 54 (1975) 33–36 (<490); Price and Waggoner 49 (who assign some "Peparethian" coins to an unknown northern mint); Kraay, *ACGC* 119–20.
Hoard evidence: *IGCH* #1173, "Cos" (ca. 480); #1644, "Asyut" (ca. 475); #1874, "Taranto" (ca. 508); *CH* 8.48, "Elmali, Lycia, 1984" (ca. 460).

*SERIPHOS (Aiginetic)
1: 2 2: 1 3: 1 4: 1 5: — 6: 1 7: 1 8: 2
Refs.: J.N. Svoronos, «ΒΑΤΡΑΧΟΣ ΣΕΡΙΦΙΟΣ», *JIAN* 1 (1898) 205–11, esp. 205; Head^{2} 480, 490; Babelon 2.1.1303–1306; Erxleben *AfP* 73.
Hoard evidence: *IGCH* #4, "Cythera" (525–500).

*TENOS (Aiginetic; mainly fr.)
1: — 2: 3 3: — 4: 2 5: — 6: 2 7: 2 8: 10
Refs.: Imhoof-Blumer, *Münzen* 23–24; J.N. Svoronos, «ΝΟΜΙΣΑΤΙΚΗ ΚΑΙ ΙΣΤΟΡΙΑ ΤΗΣ ΑΡΧΑΙΑΣ ΜΥΚΟΝΟΥ», *BCH* 17 (1893) 455–501, esp. 476–77; Head^{2} 492–93 (<500); Babelon 2.1.1295–98 (<479); Erxleben *AfP* 74; Kraay, *ACGC* 49; L. Artemis-Gyselen, "Les monnaies archaïques de Ténos," *RBN* 123 (1977) 5–15.
Hoard evidence: *IGCH* #1874 (ca. 508); *IGCH* #1185 = *CH* 8.21 (ca. 450); the Tenian stater in the "Asyut" hoard (*IGCH* #1644) is questionable; for which see Price and Waggoner 82; cf. Artemis-Gyselen *RBN* (1977) 8–9.

TERMERA (Persic; frs. only)
1: 2.3000 2: 2.3000 3: — 4: 3000 5: — 6: — 7: — 8: —
Refs.: Head^{2} 627 (<450–40); Erxleben *AfP* 93–94; M.J. Price, "Histiaeus, sonn an Tymnes, tyrann i Termera i Karia" = "Histaeus, son of Tymnes, Tyrant of Termera, Caria," *NNF-NYTT* 3 (1979) 4–7 and 8–11 (<475). See also "Other Carians ruled by Tymnes".

*THERA (Aiginetic)
1: — 2: — 3: — 4: — 5: — 6: — 7: 3 8: 5
Refs.: Head^{2} 493 (doubtful of attribution); Babelon 2.1.1323–30; L. Forrer, *The Weber Collection*, v. 2 (London 1924) 575–76; K. Regling, "Zur griechischen Münzkunde. IV. (Thera.–Bithynium.–Lycia)," *ZfN* 25 (1905) 39–51, esp. 39–44; Erxleben *AfP* 74; S. Boutin, "Essai de classement de monnaies archaïques de la mer égée au type des deux delphins," in R. Margolis and H. Voegtli (eds.), *Numismatics: Witness to History* (Wetteren 1986) 1–10.
Hoard evidence: *IGCH* #1, "Matala" (ca. 550–25); #6, "Cyclades?, ca. 1889" (ca. 500); #7, "Santorin" (ca. 500–490); #68, "Peloponnesus?, ca. 1924" (ca. 350–25); #1185

= *CH* 8.21, "Rhodes" (ca. 450); #1483, "Massyaf" (ca. 425–20); #1874, "Taranto" (ca. 508).

TINDE (Babylonian)

1: — 2: — 3: — 4: — 5: — 6: 3000@ 7: — 8: —

@ = assessed with Kithas, Smilla, Gigonos, Haisa

Refs.: Robinson 336; Erxleben *AfP* 122; Gaebler, *Münzen* 211–12 (seeing these coins as forgeries), cf. Kraay, *ACGC* 140

Hoard evidence: *IGCH* #1482, "Jordan" (ca. 445), for which see C.M. Kraay and P.R.S Moorey, "Two Fifth Century Hoards from the Near East," *RN*^{6} 10 (1968) 181–238, esp. 183.

B. Allied States Ceasing Minting 478–65

*ASTYPALAIA (Persic?, Aiginetic?, Euboeic/Attic?; possibly only frs.)

1: 2 2: 2 3: 2 4: 1.3000 5: — 6: 6 7: — 8: —

Refs.: Robinson 330 (assigning to Astypalaia, not Astyra); see also G.E. Bean and J.M. Cook, "The Carian Coast III," *BSA* 52 (1957) 58–146, esp. note 143, p. 95 (no community of Astyra!); cf. Head^2 630; Babelon 2.2.975–78 (assigning to Astyra); Erxleben *AfP* 83 (doubtful over amphora/oenochoe obv. coins; accepts authenticity of Helios obv.).

*CHALKIS (Attic/Euboic)

1: — 2: 5 3: — 4: 3 5: 3 6: 3 7: 3 8: 10

Refs.: Head^2 357–58 (<507); Babelon 2.1.663–73; Erxleben *AfP* 75; Kraay, *ACGC* 89–91 (ca. 465); H. Chantraine, "Zur Münzprägung von Chalkis im 6/5 Jahrhundert," *JNG* 9 (1958) 7–19 (<465); W.P. Wallace, "The Early Coinages of Athens and Euboia," *NC*^{7} 2 (1962) 23–42, esp. 38–42 (<490).

Hoard evidence: *IGCH* #3, "Euboea" (530–10); #1640, "Benha el Asl" (ca. 485). Cf. *CH* 8.74 = *IGCH* #42, "Euboea (or Boeotia), 1951" (ca. 400).

*DELOS (Euboeic/Attic) ———— NONTRIBUTARY ————

Refs.: Head^2 485 (<478); Babelon 2.1.1297–1304; cf. 2.3.834–38 (<480); Erxleben *AfP* 75; Kraay, *ACGC* 45, 46, 49; T. Hackens, "Les monnayage de Délos à l'époque archaïque," in *Études déliennes*, *BCH* Suppl. 1 (1973) 209–26; Hackens, "Les monnaies," in P. Bruneau and J. Ducat, *Guide de Délos* (Paris 1983) 107–11 (<478).

Hoard evidence: *IGCH* #1482, "Jordan" (ca. 445); #1637, "Demanhur" (500).

DIKAIA IN THRACE (Thraco-Macedonian; Phoencian)

1: 3000 2: 3000 3: 2000 4: — 5: 3000 6: 3000 7: — 8: 75 (with Abdera)

Refs.: Head^2 252; Babelon 2.1.1209–14; J.M.F. May, "The Coinage of Dikaia-by-Abdera: c. 540/35–476/5 B.C.," *NC*^{7} 5 (1965) 1–25; Erxleben *AfP* 110; E. Schönert-Geiss, *Griechisches Münzwerk: Die Münzprägung von Bisanthe: Dikaia: Selymbria* (Berlin 1975) 15–29 (<476/5); Kraay, *ACGC* 153–54; Price and Waggoner 37–38; Schoenhammer 170–84.

Hoard evidence: *IGCH* #1185 = *CH* 8.21, "Rhodes" (ca. 450); #1636, "Mit Rahineh" (ca. 500); #1637, "Demanhur" (500); #1638, "Delta" (ca. 500); #1639, "Sakha" (early fifth); #1644, "Asyut" (ca. 475); #1820?, "Balkh" (ca. 390–80); *CH* 1.4, "South Anatolia, 1971" (ca. 500); *CH* 8.19, "Asia Minor?, 1989" (ca. 500). See also J.H. Kagan, "An Archaic Greek Coin Hoard from the Eastern Mediterranean and Early Cypriot Coinage," *NC* 154 (1994) 17–52, esp. 19.

*ERETRIA (Euboeic/Attic)

1: —	2: 6	3: —	4: 3	5: 3	6: 3	7: 3	8: 15

Refs.: Head^{2} 360–62; Babelon 2.1.673–94 (<490); W.P. Wallace, "The Early Coinages of Athens and Euboia," *NC*^{7} 2 (1962) 41–42; Erxleben *AfP* 75; Kraay, *ACGC* 91–92; Price and Waggoner 54–56 (<490); A. Geiser, "Le trésor de monnaies classiques trouvé en 1981 sur l'agora d'Éretrie," in I.A. Carradice (ed.), *Proceedings of the 10th International Congress of Numismatics* (London 1986) 41–44 (<449).

Hoard evidence: *IGCH* #2 = *CH* 8.13, "Athens, ca. 1788" (ca. 525–515); #5 = *CH* 8.15, "Eleusis" (ca. 525–500); #9, "Eretria" (500–480); #10, "Pascha" (ca. 500–480); #11, "Isthmia" (ca. 480); #1483, "Massyaf" (ca. 425–20); #1639, "Sakha" (early fifth); #1640, "Benha el Asl" (ca. 485); #1644, "Asyut" (ca. 475); *CH* 1.7, "Egypt, ca. 1955" (480?); 1.18, "Chalcidice, ca. 1962" (late fifth); *CH* 8.48, "Elmali, Lycia, 1984" (ca. 460); 8.69, "Eretria, Euboea, 1981" (ca. 411).

*KARYSTOS (Euboeic/Attic)

1: 7.3000	2: 5	3: —	4: 5	5: —	6: 5	7: 5	8: 5

Refs.: Head^{2} 356–57; Babelon 2.1.691–94; S.W. Grose, *Catalogue of the McClean Collection of Greek Coins*, v. 2 (Cambridge 1926) 2.331–32; Wallace *NC* (1962) 41–42; Erxleben *AfP* 75; Kraay, *ACGC* 92 (<475–65?); Price and Waggoner 55.

Hoard evidence: IGCH #1644, "Asyut" (ca. 475); 6.4 = 8.45, "Homs, Syria" (ca. 480–75).

*KEOS = Iulis (Aiginetic); tribute split with Karthaia

1: —	2: 4	3: 4	4: 4	5: —	6: 3	7: 3	8: 10

Refs.: Imhoof-Blumer, *Münzen* 18–19; Head^{2} 484; Babelon 2.1.1233–90; L. Forrer, *The Weber Collection*, v. 2 (London 1924) 558–60; Erxleben *AfP* 71–72. Cf. C. Papageorgiadou-Banis, "Koinon of the Keians? The Numismatic Evidence," *RBN* 139 (1993) 9–16.

Hoard evidence: *IGCH* #6, "Cyclades, ca. 1889" (ca. 500); #7, "Santorin" (ca. 500–490).

*MYLASA?? (Persic)

1: —	2: 1	3: 5200	4: 5200	5: —	6: —	7: —	8: —

Refs.: Babelon 2.1.455; Robinson *NC* (1961) 114; Kraay, *ACGC* 274; Price and Waggoner 91; cf. p. 64 above with note 27, also pp. 281–82 above.

Hoard evidence: *IGCH* #1177, "Asia Minor" (ca. 480); #1644, "Asyut" (ca. 475); *CH* 8.38 = *IGCH* #1170, "Kisebüku (Alâkilise), Caria, 1955" (ca. 480); *CH* 8.48, "Elmali, Lycia, 1984" (ca. 460).

*PARION (Persic)

1: 1	2: —	3: —	4: 2000	5: 1	6: 1	7: 1	8: —

Refs.: Head^{2} 531 (500–400); Babelon 2.1.387–90, cf. 2.2.1383–88; S.W. Grose, *Catalogue of the McClean Collection of Greek Coins*, v. 3 (Cambridge 1929) 58; E.S.G. Robinson,

"A Hoard of Archaic Greek Coins from Anatolia," *NC*^{7} 2 (1962) 107–17, esp. 113; Erxleben *AfP* 99; Price and Waggoner 84.

Hoard evidence: *IGCH* #695, "Krusevo" (ca. 475); #697, "Tekirdag" (ca. 480–50); #734, "Ioan Corvin" (ca. 330–20); #1177, "Asia Minor (ca. 480); #1644, "Asyut" (ca. 475); *CH* 2.21, "Turkey" (fifth); *CH* 6.7, "Akandjievo, Pazardjik, Bulgaria" (ca. 450); *CH* 8.48, "Elmali, Lycia, 1984" (ca. 460); cf. *CH* 8.71, "Asia Minor, 1984" (ca. 400).

*PAROS (Aiginetic)
1: — 2: 16.1200 3: 18 4: 18 5: — 6: — 7: — 8: 30 (18)

Refs.: Head^{2} 489–90; Babelon 2.1.1309–12 (<489); Erxleben *AfP* 73; Kraay, *ACGC* 45; Price and Waggoner 80–81, 119–20; Kagan, *Coinage and Administration* 26.

Hoard evidence: *IGCH* #6, "Cyclades, ca. 1889" (ca. 500); #7, "Santorin" (ca. 500–490); #13 = *CH* 7.13, "Paros, 1936" (early fifth); #1636, "Mit Rahineh" (ca. 500); #1637, "Demanhur" (ca. 500); #1639, "Sakha" (early fifth?); #1644, "Asyut" (ca. 475); #1645, "Zagazig" (ca. 470); *CH* 8.48, "Elmali, Lycia, 1984" (ca. 460).

SELYMBRIA (octobol largest issue; Thraco-Macedonian; Euboeic/Attic?)
1: 6 2: 6 3: — 4: 5 5: 900 6: 900 7: 9 8: —

Refs.: Head^{2} 450; Babelon 2.1.1221–24, 2.4.971–74; Erxleben *AfP* 100; E. Schönert-Geiss, *Griechisches Münzwerk: Die Münzprägung von Bisanthe: Dikaia: Selymbria* (Berlin 1975) 37–49 (493–90 to 473–70; 425–20 to 411/10).

*SERMYLIA (Euboeic/Attic)
1: 7.4320 2: 3 3: 5 4: 5 5: 4.3000 6: 4.3000 7: — 8: —
(5.5500)

Refs.: Head^{2} 207 (ca. 500); Babelon 2.1.1163–66; Gaebler, *Münzen* 106–107; Erxleben *AfP* 117; Price and Waggoner 46–47.

Hoard evidence: #1638, "Delta" (ca. 500); #1644, "Asyut" (ca. 475).

STAGEIRA (Euboeic/Attic)
1: 1000 2: 1000 3: 1000 4: 1000 5: 1000 6: 1000 7: 1000 8: —

Refs.: Gaebler, *Münzen* 110–11; H. Gaebler, "Die Münzen von Stagira," *SPAW* (1930) 293–304; Erxleben *AfP* 120; Kraay, *ACGC* 133; Price and Waggoner 42–43; H.A. Cahn, "Skione–Stagira–Akanthos," *Zur Griechischen Kunst, Antike Kunst* Beiheft 9 (1973) 7–13; Cahn, "Stagira in Tel-Aviv," in A. Houghton, S. Hurter, P.E. Mottahedeh, J.A. Scott (eds.), *Festschrift für Leo Mildenberg* (Wetteren 1984) 43–50.

Hoard evidence: *IGCH* #1185 = *CH* 8.21, "Rhodes, 1880" (ca. 450); #1478, "Ras Shamra" (ca. 525–20); #1637, "Demanhur" (500); #1644, "Asyut" (ca. 475); *CH* 8.19, "Asia Minor?, 1989" (ca. 500). See also J.H. Kagan, "An Archaic Greek Coin Hoard from the Eastern Mediterranean and Early Cypriot Coinage," *NC* 154 (1994) 17–52, esp. 20.

*TENEDOS (Phocaic; Euboeic/Attic)
1: 4.3000 2: 4.3000 3: 4.3000 4: 2.5280 5: 2.5280
6: 2.5280 7: 2.5280 8: —

Refs.: Head^{2} 550–51; Babelon 2.1.365–74; Grose, *McClean Collection* 3.89–90; Erxleben *AfP* 100; Kraay, *ACGC* 39; Schoenhammer 272–73 (<450).

Hoard evidence: *IGCH* #1188, "Troas, 1969" (ca. 450); #1483, "Massyaf" (ca. 425–420).

C. Allied States Ceasing Minting 465–45

*ABYDOS (Persic; Dr./Fr. only)

1: 4.2260 2: 4 3: 4.0315 4: 4 5: — 6: 6 7: 5 8: —

Refs.: Head[2] 538–40; Babelon 2.2.1322–34; Erxleben *AfP* 94–95; Kraay 245; cf. Price and Waggoner 84–85.

Hoard evidence: *IGCH* #1165, "Asia Minor, before 1893" (ca. 500); #1644, "Asyut" (ca. 475).

ARGILOS

1: 1.3000 2: — 3: 1 4: 1 5: 1 6: 1000 7: 1000 8: —

Refs.: K. Liampi, "Argilos—History and Coinage," *Nomismatika Khronika* 13 (1994) 21–36.

*ERYTHRAI (Milesian; Persic)

1: — 2: 9 3: 7 4: 7 5: — 6: 10.1100 7: — 8: —

Refs.: Head[2] 578–79; Babelon 2.1.301–306, 2.2.1135–42; Erxleben *AfP* 78–79; P. Kinns, *Studies in the Coinage of Ionia: Erythrae, Teos, Lebedus, Colophon: ca. 400–30* B.C. (Diss., University of Cambridge 1980) 8–9 (<450); cf. P. Kinns, "The Pattern of Coinage during the Last Century of the Persian Empire," *REA* 91 (1989) 183–93, esp. 186.

Hoard evidence: *IGCH* #1183?, "Colophon" (ca. 450); #1184 = *CH* 7.21 = 8.49, "Erythrae" (ca. 455); #1252, "Asia Minor, before 1912"; #1830, "Cabul" (ca. 380).

*KARTHAIA (Aiginetic); see also Keos; tribute split with Iulis

1: — 2: 4 3: 4 4: 4 5: — 6: 3 7: 3 8: 10

Refs.: Head[2] 483; Babelon 2.1.1279–82; Erxleben *AfP* 71; Kraay 45–46; S. Hurter and E. Pászthory, "Archaischer Silberfund aus dem Antilebanon," in A. Houghton, S. Hurter, P.E. Mottahedeh, J.A. Scott (eds.), *Festschrift für Leo Mildenberg* (Wetteren 1984) 111–25, esp. 117, with the excursus of H. Bloesch, pp. 124–25. Cf. C. Papageorgiadou-Banis, "Koinon of the Keians? The Numismatic Evidence," *RBN* 139 (1993) 9–16.

Hoard evidence: *IGCH* #1874, "Taranto" (ca. 508): *CH* 8.45 = 6.4, "Antilebanon, 1978" (ca. 475).

*KOS (Aiginetic; Euboeic/Attic?; Persic?)

1: 5 2: 5 3: — 4: 5 5: — 6: 5 7: — 8: —

Refs.: Head[2] 632–34; Babelon 2.1.439–44, 2.2.1031–42; Erxleben *AfP* 87–88; J.P. Barron, "The Fifth-Century Diskoboloi of Kos," in C.M. Kraay and G.K. Jenkins, *Essays in Greek Coinage Presented to Stanley Robinson* (Oxford 1968) 75–89 (<450 or <442); H.A. Cahn, *Knidos: Die Münzen des sechsten und des fünften Jahrhunderts v. Chr.* (Berlin 1970) 164; Kraay, *ACGC* 245–46; Price and Waggoner 93–94; S.M. Sherwin-White, *Ancient Cos: An Historical Study from the Dorian Conquest to the Imperial Period* (Göttingen 1978) 22–23, 34–35.

Hoard evidence: *IGCH* #6, "Cyclades?" (ca. 500); #1165, "Asia Minor, before 1893" (ca. 500); #1636, "Mit Rashineh" (ca. 500); #1637, "Demanhur" (500); #1638, "Delta" (ca. 500); #1644, "Asyut" (ca. 475); *CH* 8.48, "Elmali, Lycia, 1984" (ca. 460); cf. (for example) #1207, "Asia Minor, before 1856" (ca. 370).

LINDOS (Milesian; Euboeic/Attic)

1: 9 2: 10 3: 6 4: 6 5: — 6: 10 7: — 8: 15

Refs.: Head^2 637; Babelon 2.1.473–78; H.A. Cahn, "Die archaischen Silberstatere von Lindos," in K. Schauenburg (ed.), *Charites: Studien zur Altertumswissenschaft* (Bonn 1957) 18–26; Erxleben *AfP* 92–93; Kraay, *ACGC* 35, 245; Price and Waggoner 95–96; Kagan, *Coinage and Administration* 25.

Hoard evidence: *IGCH* #1644, "Asyut" (ca. 475); #1790, "Malayer" (ca. 375); *CH* 5.2, "Asia Minor, before 1965" (480?); *CH* 8.19, "Asia Minor?, 1989" (ca. 500); *CH* 8.48, "Elmali, Lycia, 1984" (ca. 460). See also J.H. Kagan, "An Archaic Greek Coin Hoard from the Eastern Mediterranean and Early Cypriot Coinage," *NC* 154 (1994) 17–52, esp. 24.

OULE??

1: 1030 2: — 3: — 4: — 5: — 6: — 7: — 8: —

Refs.: M. Thompson, "Some Noteworthy Greek Accessions," *ANSMN* 12 (1966) 1–18, esp. 8–9; Kraay, *ACGC* 274.

*SAMOTHRACE (Babylonian)

1: 6 2: 6 3: 6 4: 6 5: 6 6: 6 7: 2 8: 15

Refs.: Head^2 263 (accepting only post-imperial issues); W. Schwabacher, "Ein Fund Archaischer Münzen von Samothrake," in *Transactions of the International Numismatic Congress 1936* (London 1938) 109–20, esp. 119–20; Erxleben *AfP* 117; Kraay, *ACGC* 158; Schoenhammer 265–66.

Hoard evidence: *IGCH* #696, "Kiourpet" (ca. 470).

(S)KAPSA (Euboeic/Attic; frs. only)

1: 1000 2: 1000 3: 1000 4: 1000 5: — 6: 1000 7: — 8: —

Refs.: Head^2 212; Babelon 2.1.1118–44; Gaebler, *Münzen* 66–67; Erxleben *AfP* 111.

*SKIONE (Euboeic/Attic; Phoenician)

1: 6 2: — 3: 6 4: 6 5: 15 6: 4 7: 9 8: —

Refs.: Head^2 210; Babelon 2.1.1145–48; J. Babelon, "Protésilas à Scioné," *RN*^{5} 30 (1951) 1–9; H. Bloesch, "Die Löwen von Skione," *SNR* 38 (1957) 5–10; Bloesch, "Noch einmal Skione," *SM* 13–14 (1964) 59–61; Erxleben *AfP* 117–20; H.A. Cahn, "Skione–Stagira–Akanthos," *Zur Griechischen Kunst, Antike Kunst* Beiheft 9 (1973) 7–13; Bloesch, "Stagira" in *Antike Kunst*, Beiheft 9 (1973) 7–13; Kraay 133–34; Price and Waggoner 43; U. Westermark, "The Coinage of the Chalcidian League Reconsidered," *Studies in Ancient History and Numismatics Presented to Rudi Thomsen* (Aarhus 1988) 91–103, esp. 97 (later tetrobols fourth-century); Schoenhammer 84–92.

Hoard evidence: *IGCH* #360, "Nea Cassandra" (ca. 400); #1637, "Demanhur" (500); #1644, "Asyut" (ca. 475); *CH* 1.18, "Chalcidice, ca. 1962" (late fifth); *CH* 8.63, "Scione, 1991" (ca. 425). Cf. *CH* 8.76, "Homolion, Greece, early 1993" (400–375).

OTHER CARIANS RULED BY TYMNES

1: — 2: 3000 3: 3000 4: — 5: — 6: — 7: — 8: —

Refs.: Head^{2}627; Babelon 2.1.417–18; Erxleben *AfP* 93–94; Kraay 37–38; M.J. Price, "Histiaeus, sonn an Tymnes, tyrann i Termera i Karia" = "Histaeus, son of Tymnes, Tyrant of Termera, Caria," *NNF-NYTT* 3 (1979) 4–7 and 8–11 (<475).

IV. OTHER STATES ISSUING DRACHMS AND FRACTIONAL COINS

A. Smaller Denomination Mints Ceasing Minting 445–20

*AINEIA (Euboeic/Attic; Phoenician)
1: 3   2: 3   3: 3   4: 3   5: 3   6: 3   7: 1000   8: —
Refs.: Head^2 214; Babelon 2.1.1111–14, 2.2.571–74; Gaebler, *Münzen* 20–22 (430>); Robinson 334; Erxleben *AfP* 103–104; Kraay, *ACGC* 134; Price and Waggoner 43–44; Price, *Coinage and Administration* 46 (into third quarter of century); Westermark, *Thomsen Festschrift* 96–97 (moving Athena head/bull standing with averted head to fourth century).
Hoard evidence: *IGCH* #369, "Nea Cassandra" (ca. 400); #1634, "Egypt, before 1879" (500); #1635, "Fayum" (500); #1644, "Asyut" (ca. 475); *CH* 8.45 = 6.4, "Antilebanon, 1978" (ca. 475); cf. *IGCH* #377, "Olynthus, 1931" (ca. 348).

*ASSOS (Rhodian?)
1: 1   2: 1   3: 1   4: —   5: —   6: —   7: 1   8: —
Refs.: Head^2 542; Babelon 2.2.1265–70; Erxleben *AfP* 76.

ASTAKOS (Persic)
1: 1.3000   2: 1000   3: 1000   4: —   5: —   6: —   7: —   8: —
Refs.: Head^2 510; Babelon 2.2.1489–91; Robinson 332–33; Erxleben *AfP* 95.

DIKAIOPOLIS = Dikaia (Euboeic/Attic)
1: 4   2: 1   3: 1   4: 1   5: 1   6: 1   7: 1   8: —
Refs.: Head^2 213; Babelon 2.1.1125–30, cf. 2.4.923–26; G.K. Jenkins, "Greek Coins Recently Acquired by the British Museum," *NC*^{6} 15 (1966) 131–56, esp. 136; Erxleben *AfP* 110; E. Schönert-Geiss, *Griechisches Münzwerk: Die Münzprägung von Bisanthe: Dikaia: Selymbria* (Berlin 1975) 30–34; Kraay, *ACGC* 134, 153–54.
Hoard evidence: *IGCH* #1645, "Zagazig" (ca. 470); *CH* 1.18, "Chalcidice, ca. 1962" (late fifth).

*HALIKARNASSOS (Persic; Aiginetic??; Euboeic/Attic?; Rhodian)
1: 1.4000   2: 2   3: 1.4000   4: 1.4000   5: —   6: 1.4000   7: —   8: —
Refs.: Head^2 617–19; Babelon 2.1.419–24, 2.2.999–1001; Robinson 328; Erxleben *AfP* 84; cf. Kraay, *ACGC* 23.

KHERSONESOS (Aiginetic or Milesian)
1: 3   2: 3   3: 2.4200   4: 2.4200   5: —   6: 3   7: —   8: —
Refs.: Erxleben *AfP* 83; Head^2 614; Babelon 2.1.433–34; H.A. Cahn, *Knidos: Die Münzen des sechsten und des fünften Jahrhunderts v. Chr.* (Berlin 1970) 200–11; Kraay, *ACGC* 38; Schoenhammer 292–94.
Hoard evidence: *IGCH* #1174, "Datca, ca. 1966" (ca. 480); #1202, "Marmaris?" (390–80).

*KLAZOMENAI (Milesian; Euboeic/Attic)
1: 1.3000   2: 1.3000   3: 1.3000   4: 1.3000   5: —   6: 1.3000   7: —   8: —
Refs.: Head^2 567–69; Babelon 2.1.305–12, 2.2.1143–58; Erxleben *AfP* 97; C.M. Kraay, "Monnaies provenant du site de Colophon," *SNR* 42 (1962/63) 5–13 (assigning Milne group IC to Klazomenai); Kraay, *ACGC* 39; S. Hurter, "42 Tetradrachmen von

Klazomenai: Ein Fundbericht," *SNR* 45 (1966) 26–50. Cf. E. Işik, *Elektronstatere aus Klazomenai: Der Schatzfund von 1989* (Saarbrücken 1992).

Hoard evidence: *IGCH* #1167, "Vourla" (ca. 500–490); #1183, "Colophon" (ca. 450?); #1184 = 8.49, "Erythrae" (ca. 455); #1189, "Asia Minor, before ca. 1930" (ca. 450); #1252, "Asia Minor, before 1912" (ca. 430); #1482, "Jordan" (ca. 445); #1639, "Sakha" (early fifth); #1644, "Asyut" (ca. 475); #1790, "Malayer" (ca. 375); cf. #1210, "Vourla, 1964" (ca. 360).

*PHASELIS (Persic; Euboeic-Attic?)

1: 6 2: 3 3: 3 4: 3 5: — 6: 6 7: — 8: 6

Refs.: Head^{2} 696–97; Babelon 2.1.513–22; 2.2.963–70; Erxleben *AfP* 88–90; Kraay, *ACGC* 273; C. Heipp-Tamer, *Die Münzprägung der lykischen Stadt Phaselis in griechischer Zeit* (Saarbrücken 1993) 39–47 (<ca. 446/411>); cf. E.S.G. Robinson, "A Find of Archaic Coins from South-West Asia Minor," *NC*^{5} 16 (1936) 265–80; D.J. Blackman, "Brief History of the City, Based on Ancient Sources," in J. Schäfer (ed.), *Phaselis* (Tübingen 1981) 31–37, esp. 32.

Hoard evidence: *IGCH* #1180, "Caria, 1932" (ca. 460); #1182, "Asia Minor, 1963" (ca. 460); #1185 = *CH* 8.21, "Rhodes, 1880" (ca. 450); #1482, "Jordan" (ca. 445); #1637, "Demanhur" (500); #1640, "Benha el Asl" (ca. 485); #1644, "Asyut" (ca. 475); #1645, "Zagazig" (ca. 470); #1820, "Balkh" (ca. 390–80); *CH* 5.2, "Asia Minor, before 1965" (480?); *CH* 6.4 = 8.45, "Homs, Syria" (ca. 480–75); 6.5, "Latakia, 1979" (ca. 480); *CH* 8.10, "Western Asia Minor" (ca. 525); 8.19, "Asia Minor?, 1989" (ca. 500). See also J.H. Kagan, "An Archaic Greek Coin Hoard from the Eastern Mediterranean and Early Cypriot Coinage," *NC* 154 (1994) 17–52, esp. 24.

*POTEIDAIA (Euboeic/Attic)

1: — 2: — 3: 6 4: 6 5: 6 6: 15 7: — 8: —

Refs.: Head^{2} 212; Babelon 2.1.1147–54; J.A. Alexander, *Potidaea: Its History and Remains* (Athens, GA 1963) 50–63, with notes, pp. 110–12; Erxleben *AfP* 116; Kraay, *ACGC* 134; Price and Waggoner 45–46.

Hoard evidence: *IGCH* #360, "Nea Cassandra" (ca. 400); #1636, "Mit Rahineh" (ca. 500); #1644, "Asyut" (ca. 475); #1645, "Zagazig" (ca. 470); #1874, "Taranto" (ca. 508); *CH* 8.48, "Elmali, Lycia, 1984" (ca. 460); 8.63, "Scione, 1991" (ca. 425).

B. Resuming Lighter Coinage

*ANTANDROS (Persic)

1: — 2: — 3: — 4: — 5: — 6: — 7: — 8: 15 (8?)

Refs.: Head^{2} 541; Babelon 2.2.1255–60; Erxleben *AfP* 101–102.

DARDANOS (Milesian?; Persic?)

1: 1.3000 2: 1 3: 1 4: 1 5: 1 6: 1 7: 1 8: —

Refs.: Head^{2} 544; Babelon 2.2.1315–22; Robinson 333; Erxleben *AfP* 96–97; Kraay, *ACGC* 30; cf. W. Wroth, *Catalogue of the Greek Coins of Troas, Aeolis, and Lesbos* (London 1894) xlii.

Hoard evidence: *IGCH* #6?, "Cyclades, ca. 1889" (ca. 500); #7?, "Santorin" (ca. 500–490): #1167?, "Vourla" (ca. 500–490).

*KNIDOS (Aiginetic)

1: 1 2: 5 3: 3 4: 3 5: — 6: — 7: 2 8: —

Refs.: Head^2 614–17; Babelon 2.1.425–34, 2.2.977–91; Erxleben *AfP* 85–87; H.A. Cahn, *Knidos: Die Münzen des sechsten und des fünften Jahrhunderts v. Chr.* (Berlin 1970) 162–66 (<449/430>); Kraay, *ACGC* 246–47; Price and Waggoner 90–91; cf. J.H. Nordbo, "The Coinage of Cnidus after 394 B.C.," in I.A. Carradice (ed.), *Proceedings of the 10th International Congress of Numismatics* (London 1986) 51–56.

Hoard evidence: *IGCH* #1163, "Rhodes?, before 1941" (ca. 525–500); #1174, "Datca" (ca. 480); #1186, "Bodrum" (ca. 450); #1193, "Caria?, ca. 1966" (ca. 410); #1200, "Caria?, ca. 1925" (ca. 394); #1202, "Marmaris?" (390–80); #1252, "Asia Minor, before 1912" (ca. 430); #1483, "Massyaf" (ca. 425–420); #1644, "Asyut" (ca. 475); *CH* 7.11, "Caria, Turkey, 1967" = *IGCH* #1202? (early fifth); *CH* 8.48, "Elmali, Lycia, 1984" (ca. 460); cf. *IGCH* #1790, "Malayer" (ca. 375); #1820, "Balkh" (ca. 390–80).

*KOLOPHON (Persic; Milesian?; Chian/Rhodian)

1: 3 2: — 3: 1.3000 4: 1.3000 5: — 6: 3 7: 500 8: 500

Refs.: Head^2 569–71; Babelon 2.2.1109–19; J.G. Milne, *Kolophon and Its Coinage: A Study*, *NNM* 96 (New York 1941) 36–49 (<460/430>); C.M. Kraay, "Monnaies provenant du site de Colophon," *SNR* 42 (1962/63) 5–13 (assigning Milne group IC to Klazomenai); Erxleben *AfP* 80; Kraay, *ACGC* 244; cf. P. Kinns, "The Pattern of Coinage during the Last Century of the Persian Empire," *REA* 91 (1989) 183–93, esp. 187–88.

Hoard evidence: *IGCH* #1183, "Colophon" (ca. 450?); #1189, "Asia Minor, ca. 1930" (ca. 450); #1190, "Asia Minor, ca. 1936" (ca. 450); #1639, "Sakha" (early fifth); *CH* 8.10, "Western Asia Minor, 1985" (ca. 525); 8.14, "Colophon, ca. 1968" (ca. 510); 8.68, "Ionia"(ca. 415); cf. *IGCH* #1218, "Pademlik" (ca. 330); *CH* 1.23, "Ionia, 1972" (early fourth); *CH* 4.17, "Asia Minor, 1976" (late fifth).

KORESSIA (Aiginetic)

1: 2.1500 2: — 3: — 4: — 5: — 6: — 7: — 8: —

Refs.: Imhoof-Blumer, *Münzen* 14–18; Head^2 483; Babelon 2.1.1284–96; Erxleben *AfP* 71; Kraay, *ACGC* 45–46. Cf. C. Papageorgiadou-Banis, "Koinon of the Keians? The Numismatic Evidence," *RBN* 139 (1993) 9–16.

*NEAPOLIS (Babylonian; Phoenician)

1: 1000 2: 1000 3: 1000 4: 1000 5: 1000 6: 1000 7: 1000 8: —

Refs.: Head^2 196–97; Babelon 2.1.1191–96, 2.4.733–42; Gaebler, *Münzen* 79–83 (St. <480; Dr./Fr. 424>); Robinson 335; Erxleben *AfP* 114; Kraay, *ACGC* 150; Schoenhammer 264–64.

Hoard evidence: *IGCH* #363, "Chalcidice, ca. 1936" (ca. 400–375); #364, "Aidhonokhorion" (ca. 400–375); #1185 = *CH* 8.21, "Rhodes, 1880" (ca. 450); #1637, "Demanhur" (500); #1638, "Delta" (ca. 500); #1639, "Sakha" (early fifth); #1640, "Benha el Asl" (ca. 485); #1646, "Fayum" (ca. 460); #1874, "Taranto" (ca. 508) = *CH* 7.10; *CH* 2.10, "Egypt, 1971/72" (500); 7.12 = 6.4–5, "Syria, 1978/9"; *CH* 8.16, "Pontolivado, Kilkis, 1971" (ca. 510); *CH* 8.44 = *IGCH* #1644, "Asyut" (ca. 475); cf. *CH* 8.75, "Drama, Macedonia, 1983" (ca. 400).

*OLYNTHOS AND CHALCIDIAN LEAGUE (Euboeic/Attic; Phoenician)
1: 2.4000 2: 2 3: 2 4: 2 5: 2 6: 2 7: — 8: —
(2)

Refs.: Head^2 207–209; Babelon 2.1.1153–60, 2.4.575–88; Gaebler, *Münzen* 84–89; Robinson 335; D.M. Robinson and P.A. Clement, *Excavations At Olynthus. Part IX: The Chalcidic Mint and the Excavation Coins Found in 1928–1934* (Baltimore 1938) 112–42, 292–98; Erxleben *AfP* 101–10, 114–15; H.A. Cahn, "'Olynthus' and Syracuse" in C.M. Kraay and G.K. Jenkins, *Essays in Greek Coinage Presented to Stanley Robinson* (Oxford 1968) 47–52 (questioning the attribution of early tetradrachms to Olynthus); Kraay, *ACGC* 135, 138; Price and Waggoner 45; Westermark, *Thomsen Festschrift* 91–103 (Ol. Fr. 430>; Chal. St./Fr. 400>); C.C. Lorber, *Amphipolis: The Civic Coinage in Silver and Gold* (Los Angeles 1990) 165–75.

Hoard evidence: *IGCH* #359, "Olynthus, 1931" (ca. 421); #364, Aidhonokhorion (ca. 400–375); #1644, "Asyut" (ca. 475). Cf. *CH* 8.76, "Homolion, Greece, early 1993" (400–375).

*SIPHNOS (Aiginetic)
1: — 2: 3 3: 3 4: 3 5: — 6: 3 7: 3 8: 9

Refs.: Head^2 491; Babelon 2.1.1305–10; Erxleben *AfP* 73–74; Kraay 46–47.

Hoard evidence: *IGCH* #6, "Cyclades, ca. 1889" (ca. 500); #7, "Santorin" (ca. 500–490).

C. Continuous Minters of Small Denominations

IALYSOS (Milesian?; Aiginetic?; Lydian?; Euboeic/Attic)
1: 10 2: 10 3: — 4: 6 5: — 6: 6 7: 10 8: 5

Refs.: Head^2 636–37; Babelon 2.1.467–74, 2.2.1007–10; Erxleben *AfP* 90–91; Robinson 329; H.A. Cahn, *Knidos: Die Münzen des sechsten und des fünften Jahrhunderts v. Chr.* (Berlin 1970) 180–85, 190; Kraay, *ACGC* 35, 245; Price and Waggoner 94–95.

Hoard evidence: *IGCH* #1185 = *CH* 8.21, "Rhodes" (ca. 450); #1195, "Ionia, before 1940" (fifth); #1637, "Demanhur" (500); #1639, "Sakha" (early fifth?); #1644, "Asyut" (ca. 475); *CH* 8.19, "Asia Minor?, 1989" (ca. 500). See also J.H. Kagan, "An Archaic Greek Coin Hoard from the Eastern Mediterranean and Early Cypriot Coinage," *NC* 154 (1994) 17–52, esp. 23.

KALKHEDON (fr. only: Euboeic/Attic?; Phocaic?; Persic?; Chian/Rhodian)
1: 7.3010 2: 9 3: 9 4: 9 5: - 6: 6 7: 6 8: —

Refs.: Head^2 511; Babelon 2.2.1491–1500; Grose, *McClean Collection* 3.23; Erxleben *AfP* 97; cf. G. LeRider, *Deux trésors de monnaies grecques de la Propontide* (Paris 1963) 45.

KAMEIROS (Aiginetic; Euboeic/Attic)
1: 9 2: 9 3: — 4: 6 5: — 6: 6 7: — 8: 10

Refs.: Head^2 636; Babelon 2.1.459–64, 2.2.1005–1008; L. Forrer, *The Weber Collection*, v. 3.1 (London 1926) 3.1.408; Erxleben *AfP* 91–92; Cahn, *Knidos* 180–85, 190; Kraay, *ACGC* 35, 245; Price and Waggoner 94; N.M. Waggoner, *Early Greek Coins from the Collection of Jonathan P. Rosen, Ancient Coins in North American Collections* 5 (New York 1983) 42; Kagan, *Coinage and Administration* 25–26.

Hoard evidence: *IGCH* #1163, "Rhodes?, before 1941" (ca. 525–500); #1639, "Sakha" (early fifth?); #1644, "Asyut" (ca. 475); #1645, "Zagazig" (ca. 470); *CH* 2.10, "Egypt, 1971/72" (500); *CH* 8.48, "Elmali, Lycia, 1984" (ca. 460).

*KEBREN (fr. only; Aiginetic)

1: 3	2: 3	3: —	4: —	5: —	6: —	7: —	8: —

Refs.: Head[2] 543; Babelon 2.2.1277–86; Erxleben *AfP* 97; cf. L. Lazzarini, "Note sulle monete bronzee di Kebren nella Troade," *RIN* 88 (1986) 27–35.

Hoard evidence: *IGCH* #1188, "Troas, 1969" (ca. 450); *CH* 8.10, "Western Asia Minor" (ca. 525); cf. *IGCH* #1228, "Sigeum" (fourth); #1229, "Troas, before 1882" (fourth).

*MILETOS (Milesian; Euboeic/Attic)

1: —	2: 10	3: —	4: 5	5: —	6: —	7: —	8: 10

Refs.: Head[2] 584–86; Babelon 2.1.265–72, 2.2.1047–52; Robinson 331; K. Welz, "Kleinmünzen aus Milet," *SM* 11 (1961) 99–101; Welz, "Ein neuer Münzfund aus Milet," *SM* 15 (1965) 1–2; Erxleben *AfP* 81; Kraay, *ACGC* 37; Price and Waggoner 86, 90, 117; G. Moucharte, "À propos d'une découverte de Milet," *RBN* 130 (1984) 19–35; F. Becker, "Ein Fund von 75 milesischen Obolen," *SNR* 67 (1988) 5–33; cf. B. Pfeiler, "Zur Münzkunde von Milet," *SM* 12 (1962) 20–21; Pfeiler, "Die Silberprägung von Milet im 6. Jahrhundert v. Chr.," *SNR* 45 (1966) 5–25; B. Deppert-Lippitz, *Die Münzprägung Milets vom vierten bis ersten Jahrhundert v. Chr.* (Aarau 1984) 13–14.

Hoard evidence (excluding sixth-century electrum): *IGCH* #6, "Cyclades?" (ca. 500); #7, "Santorin" (ca. 500–490); #8, "Melos" (ca. 500–490); #1164, "Asia Minor 1960" (ca. 520); #1165, "Asia Minor, before 1893" (ca. 500); #1168, "Asia Minor, ca. 1962" (ca. 500–490); #1175, "Asia Minor, 1961" (ca. 480); #1183, "Colophon" (ca. 450); #1195, "Ionia, before 1940" (fifth); #1196, "Asia Minor, before 1894" (fifth); #1199, "Asia Minor, before 1960" (ca. 400); #1252, "Asia Minor, before 1912" (ca. 430); #1482, "Jordan" (ca. 445); #1637, "Demanhur" (500); #1638, "Delta" (ca. 500); #1644, "Asyut" (ca. 475); *CH* 1.23, "Ionia, 1972" (early fourth); *CH* 7.15, "Turkey, 1980" (475); *CH* 8.10, "Western Asia Minor" (ca. 525); 8.14, "Colophon, ca. 1968" (ca. 510); 8.22, "Near Izmir, Turkey, 1982" (ca. 500); 8.36, "Western Asia Minor, 1970" (ca. 490); *CH* 8.48, "Elmali, Lycia, 1984" (ca. 460); 8.54, "Caria, 1987" (ca. 450); 8.72, "Ionia, 1989" (ca. 400). Cf. *IGCH* #1205, "'Gherelli'" (ca. 375); #1259, "Cilicia, before 1914" (ca. 380).

*TORONE (Euboeic/Attic; Phoenician)

1: 12	2: 7.5440 (12+)	3: 6	4: 6	5: 6	6: 6	7: 12	8: 15(+)

Refs.: Head[2] 206–207; Babelon 2.1.1159–64; C.M. Kraay, "Greeks Recently Acquired by the Ashmolean Museum, Oxford," *NC*[6] 14 (1954) 9–17, esp. 10–15; Erxleben *AfP* 120–21; Kraay 134–35; Price and Waggoner 47–49; U. Westermark, "The Coinage of the Chalcidian League Reconsidered," *Studies in Ancient History and Numismatics Presented to Rudi Thomsen* (Aarhus 1988) 91–103, esp. 96–97 (Fr. *). The presence of an Attic colony on Torone from 421 would probably exclude any late fifth-century minting. See Figueira, *Colonization* 220, 224.

Hoard evidence: *IGCH* #356, "Olynthus, 1928" (ca. 479); #366, "Olynthus, 1934" (379), for which see D.M. Robinson and P.A. Clement, *Excavations At Olynthus. Part IX: The Chalcidic Mint and the Excavation Coins Found in 1928–1934* (Baltimore 1938) 315–16; #375, "Olynthus, 1934" (348), for which see *Olynthus IX* 179–83; #1634, "Egypt, before 1879" (500); #1640, "Benha el Asl" (ca. 485); #1644, "Asyut" (ca. 475); #1645, "Zagazig" (ca. 470); #1790, "Malayer" (ca. 375), for which see C.M. Kraay and P.R.S. Moorey, "Two Fifth Century Hoards from the Near East," *RN*^{6} 10 (1968) 181–238, esp. 222–28, 232–33; *CH* 1.18, "Chalcidice, ca. 1962" (late fifth); *CH* 8.45 = 6.4, "Antilebanon, 1978" (ca. 475); *CH* 8.48, "Elmali, Lycia, 1984" (ca. 460). Cf. *CH* 8.76, "Homolion, Greece, early 1993" (400–375).

V. INTERRUPTED MINTS

*METHYMNA (Milesian?; Euboic-Attic; Persic?; Samian?)

——————NONTRIBUTARY——————

Refs.: Head^2 558–59; Babelon 2.1.115–18, 2.2.1241–46; Robinson 331–32; Erxleben *AfP* 101; P.R. Franke, "Zur Münzprägung von Methymna," in H.-G. Buchholz, *Methymna* (Mainz 1975) 163–76 (<460/450–40>).

Hoard evidence: *IGCH* #1187, "Lesbos, before 1892" (ca. 450).

*SKEPSIS (Persic; Phocaic?)

1: 1 2: — 3: — 4: 1 5: — 6: — 7: — 8: —

Refs.: Head^2 548–49; Babelon 2.2.1286–94; Erxleben *AfP* 100; cf. J.H. Kagan, "Hellenistic Coinage at Scepsis after its Refoundation in the Third Century B.C.," *ANSMN* 29 (1984) 11–24.

Hoard evidence: *IGCH* #1188, "Troas, 1969" (ca. 450); cf. *IGCH* #1229, "Troas, before 1882" (fourth).

*THASOS (Thraco-Macedonian; Babylonian = Euboeic/Attic?; Chian/Rhodian)

1: 3 2: 3 3: 30 4: 30 5: 30 6: 30 7: 30 8: 60

Refs.: Head^2 263–66; Babelon 2.1.1195–99, 2.4.701–32; Robinson 335–36; J. Pouilloux, *Recherches sur l'histoire et les cultes de Thasos*, v. 1 (Paris 1954) 106–108, 116–17; (<463/430>); Erxleben *AfP* 121–22; G. LeRider, "Les monnaies Thasiennes," in *Guide de Thasos* (Paris 1968) 185–91 (<463/435>); Kraay, *ACGC* 149–50; Price and Waggoner 34–36 (skeptical on attribution of coins 510–480); O. Picard, "Problèmes de numismatique thasienne," *RA*^{5} 1 (1982) 169–74; Picard, "Monnayage thasien du Ve siècle av. Jésus-Christ," *Académie des Inscript. et Belles Lett., Comptes Rendus* (1982) 412–24; Picard, "Monnaies et gravure monétaire à Thasos à la fin du Ve siècle," ΦΙΛΙΑ ΕΠΗ ΕΙΣ ΓΕΩΡΓΙΟΝ Ε. ΜΥΛΩΝΑΝ (Athens 1976–1989) 2.150–63; cf. A.B. West, *Fifth and Fourth Century Gold Coins from the Thracian Coast, NNM* 40 (New York 1929) 33–36; O. Picard, "L'organisation de l'atelier de Thasos au IVe siècle," in T. Hackens and R. Weiler, *Proceedings of the 9th International Congress of Numismatics: Berne, September 1979* (Louvain-La-Neuve 1982) 123–28.

Hoard evidence: *IGCH* #691, "Venkovec, Bulgaria" (ca. 500–475); #692, "Nevrokop, Bu." (ca. 500–475); #695, "Krusevo, Bu." (ca. 475); #701, "Vaksevo, Bu." (fifth); #702, "Benkovski, Bu." (fifth); #703, "Pazardzik, Bu." (fifth); #710, "Thasos?, before 1912" (ca. 400); #711, "Goljamo Belovo, Bu." (ca. 400); #712, "Dupnica, Bu." (ca. 400); #713, "Sofia" (ca. 400); #1182, "Asia Minor, 1963" (ca. 460); #1185 = *CH* 8.21, "Rhodes, 1880" (ca. 450); #1277 = *CH* 8.43?, "Cyprus, 1934–35" (ca. 425–400); #1482, "Jordan" (ca. 445); #1483, "Massyaf" (ca. 425–420); #1637, "Demanhur" (500); #1638, "Delta" (ca. 500); #1639, "Sakha" (early fifth); #1640, "Benha el Asl" (ca. 485); #1644, "Asyut" (ca. 475); #1645, "Zagazig" (ca. 470); #1830, "Cabul" (ca. 380); #1874, "Taranto" (ca. 508); *CH* 1.11, "Pontolivado" (ca. 475); 1.18, "Chalcidice, ca. 1962" (late fifth); *CH* 2.10, "Egypt, 1971/72" (500); *CH* 4.15, "Tigourovo, Bulgaria, 1971" (475–50); *CH* 5.2, "Asia Minor, before 1965" (480?); *CH* 6.7, "Akandjievo, Pazardjik, Bulgaria" (ca. 450); 6.8, "Plovdiv"; *CH* 7.12 = 6.4–5, "Syria, 1978/9" (480); 7.25, "Gotze, Deltchev, Bulgaria" (400); *CH* 8.16, "Pontolivado, Kilkis, 1971" (ca. 510); *CH* 8.19, "Asia Minor?, 1989" (ca. 500); 8.42–43 = *IGCH* #1272?, "Larnaca, Cyprus, 1933" (480–70); 8.45 = 6.4, "Antilebanon, 1978" (ca. 475); *CH* 8.48, "Elmali, Lycia, 1984" (ca. 460); 8.70, "Thasos, 1982" (400–350); 8.75, "Drama, Macedonia, 1983" (ca. 400). See also J.H. Kagan, "An Archaic Greek Coin Hoard from the Eastern Mediterranean and Early Cypriot Coinage," *NC* 154 (1994) 17–52, esp. 20.

VI. ELECTRUM MINTS

*KYZIKOS (Phocaic; Milesian; Persic; Chian/Rhodian)

1: — 2: 4320 3: — 4: 9 5: 9 6: 9 7: 9 8: 20

Refs.: Head[2] 522–28; Babelon 2.1.149–80, 389–92; 2.2.1389–1472; H. von Fritze, "Die Elektronpragung von Kyzikos. Eine chronologische Studie," *Nomisma* 7 (1912) 1–38; von Fritze, "Die Silberprägung von Kyzikos," *Nomisma* 9 (1914) 34–56; K. Regling, "Die griechische Goldschatz von Prinkipo," *ZfN* 41 (1931) 1–46; Erxleben *AfP* 98; Robinson 333; Kraay, *ACGC* 260–67; L. Mildenberg, "The Cyzicenes: A Reappraisal," *AJN*[2] 5–6 (1993–1994) 1–12. Cf. D. Rouvière, "Notes techniques sur les statères de Cyzique," *SNR* 38 (1957) 11–20; T. Caruso, "Alcuni tipi dei *Ciziceni*," *ASNP*[3] 4 (1974) 741–51.

Hoard evidence: *IGCH* #7, "Santorin" (ca. 500–490); #8, "Melos" (ca. 500–490); #43, "Elis, 1919" (EL.: ca. 400); #47, "Piraeus, 1882" (ca. 400–380); #714, "Dubnica, Bulgaria" (EL.: ca. 400); #1002, "Olbia, 1966" (450–400); #1168, "Asia Minor, ca. 1962" (ca. 500–490); #1171, "Chios" (EL.: ca. 480); #1175, "Asia Minor, 1961" (ca. 480); #1183, "Colophon" (ca. 450); #1188, "Troas" (ca. 450); #1194, "Vourla?" (EL.: ca. 410–400); #1234, "Isiklikőy, Bithynia" (EL.: ca. 460); #1638, "Delta" (ca. 500); #1644 (*CH* 2.16), "Asyut" (ca. 475); *CH* 1.18, "Chalcidice, ca. 1962" (late fifth); *CH* 2.1., "A Field in Western Thrace," (500–480); 2.7, "Sveti-Blas, Burgas, Bulgaria" (550–500); *CH* 4.14, "Gemlik Bursa, Turkey 1972" (mid-fifth); *CH* 8.24, "La Castella, Croton, 1956" (500–450); cf. electrum hoards from the fourth century: *IGCH* #1011; #1012; #1013; #1045; #1248.

*LAMPSAKOS (Phoen.; Persic; Chian/Rhodian)

1: 12 2: 12 3: — 4: 12 5: — 6: — 7: 12 8: —

Refs.: Head[2] 529–31; Babelon 2.1.183–88, 375–86; 2.2.1363–84; A. Baldwin, *The Electrum Coinage of Lampsakos* (New York 1914) 30–34; Baldwin, "Lampsakos: the Gold

Staters, Silver and Bronze Coinages," *AJN* 53.3 (1924) 55–62 (<470 or <490 for dr./fr.) = *Lampsakos; the Gold Staters, Silver and Bronze Coinages* (New York 1924); Erxleben *AfP* 98–99; Kraay, *ACGC* 244–45; Price and Waggoner 83; cf. J.F. Healy, "The Gold Staters of Lampsakos: a Preliminary Investigation," in I.A. Carradice (ed.), *Proceedings of the 10th International Congress of Numismatics* (London 1986) 45–50.

Hoard evidence: *IGCH* #1165, "Asia Minor, before ca. 500" (EL.: ca. 500–490); #1183, "Colophon" (ca. 450); #1188, "Troas" (ca. 450); #1194, "Vourla?" (EL.: ca. 410–400); #1644, "Asyut" (ca. 475); #1830, "Cabul" (ca. 380).

*MYTILENE (Milesian?; Phocaic) ——————NONTRIBUTARY——————

Refs.: Head^2 558–59, 561–63; Babelon 2.1.114–15, 339–62; 2.2.1207–42; Robinson 332; Erxleben *AfP* 100–101; Kraay, *ACGC* 260–61, 266–67; J.F. Healy, "A New Light on the Unique Stater of Mytilene," *ANSMN* 8 (1958) 1–9; F. Bodenstedt, "Studien zur Elektronprägung von Phokaia und Mytilene," *SNR* 52 (1973) 17–35, esp. 27–35 (El. Fr. 525>); Bodenstedt, *Phökaisches Elektron-Geld von 600–326 v. Chr.* (Mainz 1976) esp. 17–19, 28–31, with reviews of H. Küthmann, *JNG* 26 (1976) 151–53; P. Arnold, *Erasmus* 30 (1978) 359–64; J. Guèpin, *JHS* 99 (1979) 217–18; R. Laffineur, *RBPh* 57 (1979) 475–76; Bodenstedt, "Observations on Some Early Electrum Types of Mytilene and Phocaea," *ANSMN* 22 (1977) 1–7; Bodenstedt, *Die Elektronmünzen von Phokaia und Mytilene* (Tübingen 1981) with reviews of C.M. Kraay, *Gnomon* 54 (1982) 499–500; P. Naster, *RBN* 129 (1983) 216–18; cf. J.F. Healy, "The Composition of Mytilenean Electrum," in J. Babelon and J. LaFaurie (eds.), *Congrès international de numismatique: Paris 6–11 Juillet 1953* (Paris 1957) 2.529–36; Healey, "Alexander the Great and the Last Issue of Electron Hektai," *NC*^{7} 2 (1962) 65–71.

Hoard evidence: *IGCH* #1184 = 8.49, "Erythrae" (EL: ca. 455); #1188, "Troas, 1969" (ca. 450); #1221 = *CH* 8.30, "Chios, 1931" (EL: fifth–fourth); *CH* 1.22, "Bergamo?, 1971/2" = 3.15, "Pergamum, Turkey, 1976" (400–395); *CH* 2.23, "N.W. Turkey" (fifth); *CH* 3.5, "Lesbos, 1960–69" (480).

*PHOKAIA (Phocaic)

1: 3	2: 3	3: 1.5250	4: 2	5: —	6: —	7: —	8: —

Refs.: Head^2 587–90; Babelon 2.1.94–114, 331–330; 2.2.1161–66, 1195–1200; Kraay, *ACGC* 39, 260–61, 265; Bodenstedt *SNR* (1973) 17–27, 34–35; Bodenstedt, *Phökaisches Elektron-Geld*, esp. 17, 19, 20–27; Bodenstedt, *AMSMN* (1977) 6–7; Bodenstedt, *Die Elektronmünzen von Phokaia und Mytilene* (Tübingen 1981) with reviews of C.M. Kraay, *Gnomon* 54 (1982) 499–500; P. Naster, *RBN* 129 (1983) 216–18.

Hoard evidence: *IGCH* #1153, "Ephesus, 1905" (EL.: ca. 600–590); #1165, "Asia Minor, before 1893" (ca. 500); #1183, "Colophon" (ca. 450?); #1184 = 8.49, "Erythrae" (ca. 455); #1185 = *CH* 8.21?, "Rhodes, 1880" (ca. 450); #1221 = *CH* 8.30, "Chios, 1931" (fifth–fourth); #1874, "Taranto" (ca. 508); #2352, "Auriol" (470–60); CH 1.22, "Bergamo?, 1971/2" = 3.15, "Pergamum, Turkey, 1976" (400–395); 2.23, "N.W. Turkey" (fifth).

VII. CONTINUOUS MINTERS

* = minted in fourth century.

A. Independent Mints

*AIGINA

1: 30 2: 30 3: 30 4: 30 5: — 6: 14 7: — 8: —

Refs.: Head[2] 394–98; Babelon 2.1.643–64, 2.3.151–66; H.B. Earle Fox, "The Early Coinages of European Greece," *Corolla Numismatica: Numismatic Essays in Honour of Barclay V. Head* (Oxford 1906) 34–46; Robinson 329; W.L. Brown, "Pheidon's Alleged Aeginetan Coinage," *NC*[6] 10 (1950) 177–204; E.S.G. Robinson, "A Hoard of Archaic Greek Coins from Anatolia," *NC*[7] 1 (1961) 107–17; R.R. Holloway, *The Elder Turtles of Aegina* (Diss., Princeton University 1960); Holloway, "An Archaic Hoard from Crete and the Early Aeginetan Coinage," *ANSMN* 17 (1971) 1–21; S. Grunauer-von Hoerschelmann, "Zwei Schatzfunde archaischer Statere von Aigina," *Chiron* 5 (1975) 13–206; Kraay, *ACGC* 41–49; Price and Waggoner 69–76; H. Nicolet-Pierre, "Remarques sur le monnayage d'Egine au VIe et au Ve siècle d'après la trouvaille de Mégalopolis de 1936," in V. Kondic (ed.), *Frappe et Ateliers monétaires dans l'antiquitée et Moyen Age* (Belgrade 1976) 5–12; F.F. Jones, "Fifteen Turtles and Tortoises," *Greek Numismatics and Archaeology: Essays in Honor of Margaret Thompson* (Wetteren 1979) 115–18; M. Caramessini-Oeconomides, "The 1970 Myrina Hoard of Aeginetan Staters," *Festschrift Thompson* 231–39; L. Beer, *The Coinage of Aegina: A Chronological Reappraisal Based on Hoards and Technical Studies* (Diss., Oxford University 1980) 195–98. M. Caramessini-Oeconomides, "Deux trésors de statères éginétes du Cabinet des médailles d'Athènes," *SM* 30 (1980) 81–90; F. Michaux-van der Mersch and F. Delamare, "Évolution de la technique de frappe des statères éginétiques," *RBN* 133 (1987) 5–38. D. Gerin, A. Kyrou, and P. Requier, "Une trouvaille de quatre fractions d'argent à Porto Heli," *SM* 149 (1988) 4–8; M. Oeconomides-Caramessini, "À propos du trésor de Lappa *IGCH* 35," *Kraay-Mørkholm Essays* 9–22; M. Oeconomides, "The IGCH 101 Hoard and the Circulation of the Tortoise in the Peloponnesus," in *Florilegium Numismaticum: Studia in honorem U. Westermark edita* (Stockholm 1992) = *NM* 38 (1992) 307–12. Cf. Oeconomides, "À propos du trésor de Zougra (Noe 1186)," *RBN* 114 (1968) 132–37. See also J.H. Kagan, "An Archaic Greek Coin Hoard from the Eastern Mediterranean and Early Cypriot Coinage," *NC* 154 (1994) 17–52, esp. 21–22.

Hoard evidence: *IGCH* #1, "Matala" (ca. 550–25); #6, "Cyclades?" (ca. 500); #7, "Santorin" (ca. 500–490); #11, "Isthmia" (ca. 480); #15, "Olympia" (ca. 470); #21, "Koumares" (ca. 450); #28, "Chavari" ca. 450–400?); #30, "Peloponnesus, 1935" (ca. 425–400); #35, "Lappa" (fifth); #36, "Porto Cheli" (fifth); #37, "Agrinion" (fifth?); #40, "Arcadia?" (late fifth); #44, "Olympia, ca. 1859" (ca. 400?); #45, "Thessaly, ca. 1966" (late fifth–early fourth); #1177, "Asia Minor, before 1961" (ca. 480); #1182, "Asia Minor, 1963" (ca. 460); #1185 = *CH* 8.21, "Rhodes" (ca. 450); #1252, "Asia Minor, before 1912" (ca. 430); #1482, "Jordan" (ca. 445); #1483, "Massyaf" (ca. 425–420); #1636, "Mit Rahineh" (ca. 500); #1637, "Demanhur" (500); #1639, "Sakha" (early fifth?); #1640, "Benha el Asl" (ca. 485); #1644, "Asyut" (ca. 475); #1645, "Zagazig" (ca. 470); #1646, "Fayum" (ca. 460); #1647, "Naucratis" (450–25); #1789,

"Persepolis" (before 511); #1874, "Taranto" (ca. 508); #2352, "Auriol" (470–60); *CH* 1.5, "Aegina, 1973" (ca. 500); 1.8, "Greece, 1944" (ca. 480); 1.12, "Aegina?, 1965"; 1.14, "North Syria, 1974" (mid-fifth); 1.25 = 3.12 = 5.11, "Myrina, Karditsa, 1970" (400); *CH* 2.10, "Egypt, 1971/72" (500); 2.13, "Babes, Olympia, 1958–60" (480); 2.24, "Eirini, Paros" (470); *CH* 3.9, "Angistri, Aegina, 1975" (450?); 3.10 = 8.60, "Megalopolis" (430); *CH* 6.4, "Homs, Syria" (ca. 480); 6.5, "Latakia, 1979" (ca. 480); *CH* 7.26, "Peloponnese?" = *IGCH* #30? (400); *CH* 8.19, "Asia Minor?, 1989" (ca. 500); 8.20, "Aegina?, Greece, 1986/87" (ca. 500); 8.35, "Selinunte, Sicily, 1985" (ca. 490); 8.45 = 6.4, "Antilebanon, 1978" (ca. 475); 8.48, "Elmali, Lycia, 1984" (ca. 460); 8.67, "Hollmn, village of Qinam, S.E. Albania, 1991" (end of fifth). *N.B.* fifth-century coins are common in later hoards. See Oeconomides, *Florilegium Numismaticum*, note 8, p. 311 for a listing of 19 fourth-century hoards with tortoises, some with early coins, and Beer, *Coinage* 107–108 (note 2), 110 with note 2 for the mixture of coins in later hoards.

*ASPENDOS (Persic) ——————No amounts have survived——————

Refs.: Head² 699; Babelon 2.1.523–34; 2.2.941–56; *SNG* Copenhagen 31, #153–89; Erxleben *AfP* 82; C.M. Kraay, "The Celenderis Hoard," *NC*⁷ 2 (1962) 1–15, esp. 7–8; Kraay, "Notes on the Mint of Side in the Fifth Century B.C.," *NC*⁷ 9 (1969) 15–20, esp. 17–18; N. Olçay and O. Mørkholm, "The Coin Hoard from Podalia," *NC*⁷ 11 (1971) 1–29, esp. 16–22, 28–29; Kraay, *ACGC* 276–77 (an interval in the late fifth century is possible).

Hoard evidence: *IGCH* #1253, "Asia Minor, before 1948" (ca. 420); #1254, "Selimiye" (ca. 400); #1257, "Asia Minor, 1966" (ca. 390); cf. #1830, "Cabul" (ca. 380).

*EPHESOS (Phoen.; Milesian?; Chian/Rhodian?)

1: 7.3000 2: 7.3000 3: 6 4: 6 5: — 6: 7.3000 7: — 8: —

Refs.: Head² 571–78, cf. Head, *The Coinage of Ephesos* (London 1880); Babelon 2.1.271–78; 2.2.1085–1110; Robinson 330–31; Erxleben *AfP* 77–78; Kraay, *ACGC* 244 (few issues, possibly intermittent); Fried, *Coinage and Administration* 6–7.

Hoard evidence: *IGCH* #1153, "Ephesus" (EL.: 600–590); #1155, "Asia Minor, 1935–36" (EL.: 600–590); #1159, "Asia Minor, before 1933" (EL.: ca. 575–60); #1165, "Asia Minor, before 1893" (ca. 500); "1168, "Asia Minor, ca. 1962" (ca. 500–490); #1182, "Asia Minor, 1963" (ca. 460); #1482, "Jordan" (ca. 445); #1636, "Mit Rahineh" = *CH* 3.2 (ca. 500); *CH* 1.23, "Ionia, 1972" (early fourth); *CH* 8.45 = 6.4, "Antilebanon, 1978" (ca. 475); *CH* 8.48, "Elmali, Lycia, 1984" (ca. 460).

*KELENDERIS (Persic)

1: — 2: — 3: — 4: — 5: — 6: — 7: — 8: 2

Refs.: Head² 718–19; Babelon 2.1.544–54; 2.2.897–908; C.M. Kraay, "The Celenderis Hoard," *NC*⁷ 2 (1962) 1–15; Erxleben *AfP* 82; Kraay, *ACGC* 278–79; A. Lemaire, "Remarques à propos du monnayage cilicien d'époque perse et des légendes araméens," *REA* 91 (1989) 141–56, esp. 153.

Hoard evidence: *IGCH* #1255, "Cilicia, 1957" (ca. 400); #1258, "Bereket" (ca. 390–80); #1820, "Balkh" (ca. 390–80); #1830, "Cabul" (ca. 380); *IGCH* #1255 = *CH* 1.21, "Cilicia, 1957" (late fifth); *CH* 1.23, "Ionia, 1972" (early fourth).

*LYCIAN STATES (Persic; various indigenous standards)

1: — 2: — 3: 10 4: — 5: — 6: — 7: — 8: —

Refs.: Head[2] 688–94; Babelon 2.1.479–514; 2.2.173–343; Erxleben *AfP* 88; O. Mørkholm, "The Classification of Lycian Coins before Alexander the Great," *JNG* 14 (1964) 65–76; N. Olçay and O. Mørkholm, "The Coin Hoard from Podalia," *NC*[7] 11 (1971) 1–29; O. Mørkholm and J. Zahle, "The Coinage of Kuprlli," *Acta Archaeologica* 43 (1972) 57–113; Kraay, *ACGC* 269–73; Price and Waggoner 98–103; J. Spiers, "Lycian Coins in the 'Decadrachm hoard'" in Carradice, *Coinage and Administration* 29–37; J. Zahle, "Politics and Economy in Lycia during the Persian Period," *REA* 91 (1989) 169–79; cf. W. Schwabacher, "Lycian Coin Portraits," in C.M. Kraay and G.K. Jenkins, *Essays in Greek Coinage Presented to Stanley Robinson* (Oxford 1968) 111–24.

Hoard evidence: *IGCH* #699, "Lemnos" (ca. 450); #1185 = *CH* 8.21, "Rhodes" (ca. 450); #1259, "Lycia, 1954" (ca. 450); #1251, "Lycia, 1961" (440–30); #1277, "Cyprus" (ca. 425–400); #1482, "Jordan" (ca. 445); *IGCH* #1636, "Mit Rahineh" = *CH* 3.2 (ca. 500); #1637, "Demanhur" (500); #1638, "Delta" (ca. 500); #1639, "Sakha" (early fifth?); #1644, "Asyut" (ca. 475); #1645, "Zagazig" (ca. 470); #1646, "Fayum" (ca. 460); #1647, "Naucratis" (450–25); #1747, "Mesopotamia" (390–85); *CH* 1.4, "South Anatolia, 1971" (ca. 500); 1.6 = 8.40, "Lycia, 1972" (ca. 480 or later); 1.15, "Black Sea, ca. 1970" (ca. 425); *CH* 2.18, "Lycia, 1970" (470) = 5.3, "Lycia, 1970" (480–60); 2.27, "Lycia, 1970" (440–30); *CH* 3.15, "Turkey, 1976" (400); *CH* 4.9, "Lycia, Turkey, 1976" (480); 4.12, "Fethiye, Turkey, 1977" (475); *CH* 8.9, "Unknown Findspot, 1983" (ca. 525); 8.10, "Western Asia Minor" (ca. 525); 8.11, "Lycia, 1985"; 8.19, "Asia Minor?, 1989" (ca. 500); 8.32, "Western Lycia/Eastern Caria, 1992?" (500–400); 8.39, "Lycia, 1982/83" (ca. 480); *CH* 8.45 = 6.4, "Antilebanon, 1978" (ca. 475); *CH* 8.48, "Elmali, Lycia, 1984" (ca. 460); *CH* 8.57, "Egypt, before 1879" (450–20). cf. *IGCH* #1790, "Malayer" (ca. 375). See also J.H. Kagan, "An Archaic Greek Coin Hoard from the Eastern Mediterranean and Early Cypriot Coinage," *NC* 154 (1994) 17–52, esp. 25–27.

*TEOS (Aiginetic; Chian/Rhodian)

1: 6 2: 6 3: 6 4: 6 5: — 6: 6 7: — 8: —

Refs.: Head[2] 595–96; Babelon 2.1.311–22; 2.2.1121–36; Forrer, *Weber Collection* 2.574; J.M. Balcer, "The Early Silver Coinage of Teos," *SNR* 47 (1968) 5–50 (<449/412>); Erxleben *AfP* 82; Kraay, *ACGC* 243; Price and Waggoner 86–87 (lowering Balcer's dates by 10–15 years); Kinns, *Studies in the Coinage* 163–64 (long after 450); S. Hurter, "Teos over Tanagra," *Florilegium Numismaticum: Studia in honorem U. Westermark edita* (Stockholm 1992) = *NM* 38 (1992) 171–73 (<440, at least); D. MacDonald, "A Teos/Abdera Overstrike," *SM* 44 (1994) 37–40; H.B. Mattingly, "A New Light on the Early Silver Coinage of Teos," *SNR* 73 (1994) 5–9; D. MacDonald, "A Note on *CH* VIII, No. 47: Ionia 1983," *NC* 155 (1995) 321–23.

Hoard evidence: #1165, "Asia Minor, before 1893" (ca. 500); #1183, "Colophon" (ca. 450); #1188, "Troas" (ca. 450); #1189, "Asia Minor, ca. 1930" (ca. 450); #1190, "Asia Minor, ca. 1936" (ca. 450); #1637, "Demanhur" (500); #1643, "Memphis" (ca. 480); #1644, "Asyut" (ca. 475); #1645, "Zagazig" (ca. 470); *CH* 1.23, "Ionia,

1972" (early fourth); *CH* 8.14, "Colophon, ca. 1968" (ca. 510); 8.47, "Ionia, 1983" (ca. 460).

B. Northern Aegean Mints

*ABDERA (Abderite = Phoen.?; Thraco-Macedonian; Aiginetic)

1: 15 2: 15 3: 15 4: 15 5: 15 6: 15 7: 10 8: 75 (with Dikaia)

Refs.: Head[2] 253–57, 891; Babelon 2.1.1203–10, 2.4.875–924; H. von Fritze, "Die Chronologie der autonomen Münzprägung von Abdera," in M.L. Strack, *Die Antiken Münzen von Thrakien* 1.1 (Berlin 1912) 19–127; G. Kleiner, "Zur Chronologie der Münzen von Abdera," *JNG* 2 (1950/51) 14–20; J.M.F. May, *The Coinage of Abdera (540–345 B.C.)* (London 1966): <449/8/439/8>, with the review of E.J.P. Raven, *NC*[7] 7 (1967) 289–97; Erxleben *AfP* 102–103: Kraay, *ACGC* 152–53, 154–56; Price and Waggoner 36–37; Schoenhammer 141–69.

Hoard evidence: *IGCH* #694, "Kârdžali, Bulgaria" (ca. 490–80); #698, "Abdera" (ca. 460–50); #708, "Sokolovci, Bu." (late fifth); #1177, "Asia Minor, before 1961" (ca. 480); #1182, "Asia Minor, 1963" (ca. 460); #1478, "Ras Shamra" (ca. 525–20); #1482, "Jordan" (ca. 445); #1637, "Demanhur" (500); #1639, "Sakha" (early fifth?); #1644, "Asyut" (ca. 475); #1789, "Persepolis" (ca. 511); *CH* 2.1., "A Field in Western Thrace," (500–480); *CH* 5.2, "Asia Minor, before 1965" (480?); *CH* 6.4 = 8.45, "Homs, Syria" (ca. 480–75); *CH* 8.19, "Asia Minor?, 1989" (ca. 500); *CH* 8.21 = *IGCH* #1185, "Rhodes?, before 1880" (ca. 500); 8.35, "Selinunte, Sicily, 1985" (ca. 490); *CH* 8.48, "Elmali, Lycia, 1984" (ca. 460); *CH* 8.57, "Egypt, before 1879" (450–20); cf. *IGCH* #715, "Thrace?, 1910–11" (ca. 385–75); *CH* 2.35, "Abdera, 1971" (375–50). See also J.H. Kagan, "An Archaic Greek Coin Hoard from the Eastern Mediterranean and Early Cypriot Coinage," *NC* 154 (1994) 17–52, esp. 19.

*AINOS (Persic-based?)

1: 12 2: 12 3: 10 4: 10 5: 4 6: — 7: — 8: 20

Refs.: Head[2] 246–48; Babelon 2.4.949–66; H. von Fritze, "Die autonomen Münzen von Ainos: Eine chronologische Studie" *Nomisma* 4 (1909) 16–32; von Fritze, "Die Chronologie der autonomen Münzen von Ainos," in M.L. Strack, *Die Antiken Münzen von Thrakien* 1.1 (Berlin 1912) 143–72, esp. 144–45; J.M.F. May, *Ainos. Its History and Coinage: 474–341 B.C.* (Oxford 1950) 8–172 with the review of P. Naster in *RBN* 96 (1950) 231–33 and the joint comment of May and Naster in *RBN* 97 (1951) 157; Erxleben *AfP* 104–105; Kraay, *ACGC* 155, 158–60; Schoenhammer 211–30.

*AKANTHOS (Euboic/Attic; Phoenician)

1: — 2: 5 3: 3 4: 3 5: 3 6: 3 7: 3 8: —

Refs.: Head[2] 205–208; Babelon 2.1.1165–86, 2.4.659–72; Gaebler, *Münzen* 23–29; J. Desneux, "Les tétradrachmes d'Akanthos," *RBN* 85 (1949) 5–122, with reviews of J. Babelon, *RN*[5] 12 (1950) 233–34; J.M.F. May, *NC*[6] 20 (1950) 155–58; J. Desneux, "A propos de la chronologie du monnayage d'Akanthos," *RBN* 98 (1952) 113–15; Robinson 334; Erxleben *AfP* 106; H.A. Cahn, "Skione–Stagira–Akanthos," *Zur Griechischen Kunst, Antike Kunst* Beiheft 9 (1973) 7–13; Kraay, *ACGC* 133–36; Price and Waggoner 40–42; Schoenhammer 93–125.

Hoard evidence: *IGCH* #357, "Hierissos" (ca. 480–50); #359, "Olynthus, 1931" (ca. 421); #360, "Nea Cassandrea" (ca. 400); #364, "Aidhonokhorion" (ca. 400–375); #1177, "Asia Minor, before 1961" (ca. 480); #1182, "Asia Minor, 1963" (ca. 460); #1479, "Djeble, Seleucis" (500–490); #1480, "Seleucis" (500–480); #1482, "Jordan" (ca. 445); #1483, "Massyaf" (ca. 425–20); #1639, "Sakha" (early fifth?); #1640, "Benha el Asl" (ca. 485); #1644, "Asyut" (ca. 475); #1645, "Zagazig" (ca. 470); #1646, "Fayum" (ca. 460); #1820, "Balkh" (ca. 390–80); #1874, "Taranto" (ca. 508); #2065, "Messina" (489–79); #2066, "Gela" (ca. 485); #2071, "Monte Bubbonia" (475–70); *CH* 1.14, "North Syria, 1974" (mid-fifth); 1.15, "Black Sea, ca. 1970" (ca. 425); *CH* 4.10, "North Greece, 1977" (480); *CH* 6.5, "Latakia, 1979" (ca. 480); 6.9, "Hierissos, Greece" (ca. 450); *CH* 8.45 = 6.4, "Antilebanon, 1978" (ca. 475); *CH* 8.48, "Elmali, Lycia, 1984" (ca. 460); *CH* 8.57, "Egypt, before 1879" (450–20); *CH* 8.63, "Scione, 1991" (ca. 425); cf. *IGCH* #1790, "Malayer" (ca. 375); #1830, "Cabul" (ca. 380); *CH* 8.76, "Homolion, Greece, early 1993" (400–375).

*MARONEIA (Thraco-Macedonian; Aiginetic; Phoenician)
1: 1.3000 2: 1.3000 3: 1.3000 4: 1.3000 5: 10 6: 10 7: 3 8: 21(+)
Refs.: Head[2] 248–52; Babelon 2.1.1215–22, 2.4.925–48; A.B. West, *Fifth and Fourth Century Gold Coins from the Thracian Coast*, *NNM* 40 (New York 1929) 55–145; Kraay, *ACGC* 154, 157; J.M.F. May, "The Coinage of Maroneia: c. 520–449/8 B.C.," *NC*[7] 5 (1965) 27–56 (<449/8); Erxleben *AfP* 111–12; E. Schönert-Geiss, *Griechisches Münzwerk: Die Münzprägung von Maroneia* (Berlin 1987); Schoenhammer 185–210.
Hoard evidence: *IGCH* #709, "Haskovo, Bulgaria" (late fifth); cf. #715, "Thrace?, 1910–11" (ca. 385–75).

*MENDE (Euboeic/Attic; Phoenician)
1: 8 2: 15 3: 5 4: 9 5: 8 6: 8 7: 8 8: —
Refs.: Head[2] 210–12; Babelon 2.1.1129–44, 2.4.597–630; Gaebler, *Münzen* 72–78; K. Regling, "Mende," *ZfN* 34 (1924) 7–35, esp. 15–16; S.P. Noe, *The Mende (Kaliandra) Hoard*, *NNM* 27 (New York 1926); Erxleben *AfP* 112–13; Kraay, *ACGC* 134, 136–37; Price and Waggoner 44–45, 117–19; F. Michaux, "Les tétroboles de Mendé," *RBN* 127 (1981) 5–18.
Hoard evidence: *IGCH* #358, "Kaliandra, 1913" (ca. 423); "360, Nea Cassandra" (ca. 400); #361, "Kaliandra, 1892" (ca. 400 or later); #1173, "Cos" (ca. 480); #1185 = *CH* 8.21, "Rhodes, 1880" (ca. 450); #1480, "Seleucis" (ca. 500–480); #1638, "Delta" (ca. 500); #1640, "Benha el Asl" (ca. 485); #1644, "Asyut" (ca. 475); #1645, "Zagazig" (ca. 470); #1446, "Fayum" (ca. 460); #1874, "Taranto" (ca. 508); *CH* 1.18, "Chalcidice, ca. 1962" (late fifth); *CH* 8.48, "Elmali, Lycia, 1984" (ca. 460); 8.63, "Scione, 1991" (ca. 425); cf. *CH* 8.76, "Homolion, Greece, early 1993" (400–375).

C. Autonomous Mints

*CHIOS ——— NONTRIBUTARY ———
Refs.: Head[2] 599–602; Babelon 2.1.295–302, 2.2.1129–42; A. Baldwin, "The Electrum and Silver Coins of Chios," *AJN* 48 (1914) 1–60 = *The Electrum and Silver Coins of Chios* (New York 1915); J. Mavrogordato, "A Chronological Arrangement of the Coins of Chios," *NC*[4] 15 (1915) 1–52; "A Chronological Arrangement . . .; Part II," *NC*[4] 15

(1915) 361–432; "A Chronological Arrangement . . . ; Part III," *NC*[4] 16 (1916) 281–353; Erxleben *AfP* 76–77; J.P. Barron, *The Silver Coins of Samos* (London 1966) 86–87; Kraay, *ACGC* 242–43; Price and Waggoner 87–89; N.M.M. Hardwick, *The Coinage of Chios from the Sixth to the Fourth Century* B.C. (Diss. Oxford University 1991); Hardwick, "The Coinage of Chios from the VIth to the IVth Century B.C.," in T. Hackens and G. Moucharte (eds.), *Proceedings of the XI International Numismatics Congress* 1 (Louvain-la-Neuve 1993) 211–22; Hardwick, "The Solution to Thucydides VIII 101.1: The 'Chian Fortieths'," *NAC* 25 (1996) 59–69.

Hoard evidence: *IGCH* #6, "Cyclades?" (ca. 500); #21, "Koumares" (ca. 450); #1165, "Asia Minor, before 1893" (ca. 500); #1167, "Vourla" (ca. 500–490); #1171, "Chios, 1890" (ca. 480); #1172, "Chios, 1919" (ca. 480); #1177, "Asia Minor, before 1961" (ca. 480); #1179, "Chios?, ca. 1933" (ca. 460); #1184 = 8.49, "Erythrae" (ca. 455); #1191, "Phanae on Chios" (ca. 450–440); #1252, "Asia Minor, befoe 1912" (ca. 430); #1482, "Jordan" (ca. 445); #1483, "Massyaf" (ca. 425–420); #1636, "Mit Rahineh" (ca. 500); #1637, "Demanhur" (500); #1638, "Delta" (ca. 500); #1639, "Sakha" (early fifth?); #1640, "Benha el Asl" (ca. 485); #1644, "Asyut" (ca. 475); #1645, "Zagazig" (ca. 470); #1646, "Fayum" (ca. 460); #1647, "Naucratis" (450–25); #1874, "Taranto" (ca. 508); *CH* 7.20? = *IGCH* #1179 , "Chios?"; *CH* 2.10, "Egypt, 1971/72" (500); 6.4 = 8.45, "Homs, Syria" (ca. 480–75); 5.15 (with unlisted Chian coins); 7.14, "Chios?, 1980" (475); *CH* 8.48, "Elmali, Lycia, 1984" (ca. 460); *CH* 8.57, "Egypt, before 1879" (450–20).

*SAMOS ——————— NONTRIBUTARY ———————

Refs.: Head[2] 602–606; Babelon 2.1.278–96, 2.2.1059–84; Gardner, *JHS* (1913) 160–61; Robinson 331; J.P. Barron, *The Silver Coins of Samos* (London 1966) 47–101 with the reviews of J.F. Healy, *Gnomon* 39 (1967) 315–17; C.M. Kraay, *JHS* 87 (1967) 196–97; L. Lacroix, *RPh* 45 (1967) 497–500; H. Plommer, *CR* 81 (1967) 212–14; and C. Boehringer, *JNG* 20 (1970) 251–55; Erxleben *AfP* 82; Kraay, *ACGC* 240–42, 332–34; Price and Waggoner 89–90.

Hoard evidence: *IGCH* #1004, "Kerch" (late fifth–early fourth); #1157, "Priene" (EL.: ca. 575–60); #1158, "Samos, 1894" (EL.: ca. 575–60); #1167, "Vourla" (ca. 500–490); #1183, "Colophon" (ca. 450); #1198, "Samos, ca. 1953" (ca. 400); #1201, "Durasalar" (ca. 390); #1637, "Demanhur" (500); #1638, "Delta" (ca. 500); #1639, "Sakha" (early fifth?); #1644, "Asyut" (ca. 475); #1645, "Zagazig" (ca. 470); #1647, "Naucratis" (450–25); #1747, "Mesopotamia" (390–85); #1790, "Malayer" (ca. 375); #1830, "Cabul" (ca. 380); *CH* 2.10, "Egypt, 1971/72" (500); 7.12 = 6.4–5 = 8.45, "Syria, 1978/9" (ca. 475); *CH* 8.48, "Elmali, Lycia, 1984" (ca. 460).

SELECT BIBLIOGRAPHY

Note that the bibliography associated with individual civic mints is to be found in the entries of the Appendix.

Allen, W.R. "Mercantilism." In J. Eatwell, M. Milgate, and P. Newman (eds.). *The New Palgrave: A Dictionary of Economics* (London 1987) 445–49.

Alessandrì, S. "Il significato storico della legge di Nicofonte sul dokimastes monetario." *ASNP*[3] 14 (1984) 369–93.

Ardaillon, E. *Les mines du Laurion dans l'antiquité* (Paris 1897).

Babelon, E. "La politique monétaire d'Athènes au Ve siècle avant notre ère." *RN*[4] 17 (1913) 457–85.

Badian, E. "The Peace of Callias." *JHS* 107 (1987) 1–39 = *From Plataea to Potidaea* (Baltimore 1993) 1–72, 187–201.

Balcer, J.M. "Imperial Officials in the Athenian Empire." *Historia* 25 (1976) 257–87.

Barron, J.P. "Chios in the Athenian Empire." In J. Boardman and C.E. Vaphopoulou-Richardson (eds.). *Chios: A Conference at the Homereion in Chios 1984* (Oxford 1986) 89–103.

———. *The Silver Coins of Samos* (London 1966).

Baumeister, A. *Bericht über die Verhandlungen der Königl. Preuss. Akad. der Wissenschaften* (Berlin 1855) 186–99.

Beer, L. *The Coinage of Aegina: A Chronological Reappraisal Based on Hoards and Technical Studies* (Diss., Oxford University 1980).

Beer, L., N.H. Gale, W. Gentner, G.A. Wagner, and J. Price. "Archaic Greek Coinage: Silver." *Metallurgy in Numismatics* 1 (1980) 1–54

Bodenstedt, F. *Die Elektronmünzen von Phokaia und Mytilene* (Tübingen 1981).

———. *Phökaisches Elektron-Geld von 600–326 v. Chr.* (Mainz 1976).

Bogaert, R. "L'essai des monnaies dans l'antiquité." *RBN* 122 (1976) 5–34.

———. "Le cours du statère de Cyzique à Athènes aux Ve et IVe siècles avant J.-C.: état de la question." *RBN* 123 (1977) 17–39.

Bon, A.-M. and A. Bon, with V. Grace. *Les timbres amphoriques de Thasos*, *Études thasiennes* 4 (Paris 1957).

Bourriot, F. "Note sur le text de la loi athénienne de 375/4 concernant la circulation monétaire (la loi de Nicophon)." *ZPE* 50 (1983) 275–82.

Boutin, S. "Essai de classement de monnaies archaïques de la mer égée au type des deux delphins." In R. Margolis and H. Voegtli (eds.). *Numismatics: Witness to History* (Wetteren 1986) 1–10.

Bradeen, D.W. and M.F. McGregor. *Studies in Fifth-Century Attic Epigraphy* (Norman, OK 1973).

Brashinsky, J.B. *Afiny i Severnoe Prichernomor'e* (Moscow 1963).

Burelli, L. "L'accordo monetale tra Focea e Mitilene (I.G., XII, 2, 1." *NAC* 7 (1978) 43–51.

———. "Metaphore monetali e provvedimenti finanziari in Aristophane." *ASNP*³ (1973) 767–86.

Buttrey, T.V. "The Athenian Currency Law of 375/4 B.C." In O. Mørkholm and N.M. Waggoner (eds.). *Greek Numismatics and Archaeology: Essays in Honor of Margaret Thompson* (Wetteren 1979) 33–45.

———. "More on the Athenian Coinage Law of 375/4 B.C." *NAC* 10 (1981) 71–94.

———. "Pharaonic Imitations of Athenian Tetradrachms." In T. Hackens and R. Weiller (eds.). *Proceedings of the 9th International Congress of Numismatics. Berne, September 1979* (Luxemburg 1982) 1.137–40.

Cacciamo Caltabiano, M. and P. Radici Colace. "ΑΡΓΥΡΙΟΝ ΔΟΚΙΜΟΝ ... ΤΟ Δ' ΕΝΑΝΤΙΟΝ ΠΑΡΑΣΗΜΟΝ (Pollux, 3,86)." *ASNP*³ 13 (1983) 421–47.

———. "ΑΡΓΥΡΙΟΝ ΕΥΔΟΚΙΜΟΝ (Pollux, 3,87)." *ASNP*³ 15 (1985) 81–101.

———. "Darico persiano e nomisma greco: differenze strutturalli, ideologiche e funzionali alla luce del lessico greco." *REA* 91 (1989) 213–226.

Cahn, H.A. "Étalons monétaires en Asie-mineure jusqu'au Vᵉ siècle." In *Congresso internazionale di numismatica* (Rome 1961–1965) 2.19–23.

———. *Knidos: Die Münzen des sechsten und fünften Jahrhunderts v. Chr.* (Berlin 1970).

Carter, G.F. "A Simplified Method for Calculating the Original Number of Dies from Die Link Statistics." *ANSMN* 28 (1983) 195–206.

Cataldi, S. *Symbolai e relazione tra le città greche nel v secolo a.C.* (Pisa 1983).

Cataudella, M.R. "Aspetti e strumenti della politica monetaria ateniese fra V e IV secolo." *Sileno* 12 (1986) 111–35.

Cavaignac, E. *Études sur l'histoire financière d'Athènes au Vᵉ siècle* (Paris 1908).

———. "Le décret dit de Kléarkhos." *RN*⁵ 15 (1953) 1–7.

Chabiaras, N. "Σποράδων ἐπιγραφαί." *AE* (1922) 39–52.

Chambers, M.H., R. Gallucci, and P. Spanos. "Athens' Alliance with Egesta in the Year of Antiphon." *ZPE* 83 (1990) 38–57.

Cocchi, E.E. "Il controllo statale sulla circolazione di moneta straniera nell cittá greche." *RSA* 12 (1982) 53–59.

Conophagos, C.E. *Le Laurium antique* (Athens 1980).

Crosby, M. "The Leases of the Laurion Mines." *Hesperia* 19 (1950) 189–312.

Davesne, A. "La circulation monétaire en Cilicie à l'époque achéménide." *REA* 91 (1989) 157–68.

Depeyrot, G., T. Hackens, and G. Moucharte (eds.). *Rythmes de la production monétaire de l'antiquité à nos jours* (Louvain 1987).

Descat, R. (ed.). *L'or perse et l'histoire grecque, REA* 91 (1989).

Diebolt, J. and H. Nicolet-Pierre. "Recherches sur le métal de tétradrachmes à types athéniens." *SNR* 56 (1977) 79–91.

Dunbar, N. *Aristophanes Birds* (Oxford 1995).

Earle Fox, H.B. "The Early Coinages of European Greece." *Corona Numismatica* (Oxford 1906) 34–46.

———. "Some Athenian Problems." *NC*⁴ 5 (1905) 1–9.

Eddy, S.K. "Some Irregular Amounts of Athenian Tribute." *AJP* 94 (1973) 47–70.

———. "The Value of the Cyzicene Stater at Athens in the Fifth Century." *ANSMN* 16 (1970) 13–22.

Empereur J.-Y. and Y. Garlan (eds.). *Recherches sur les amphores grecques, BCH* Suppl. 13 (Paris 1986).

Engelmann, H. "Wege griechischer Geldpolitik." *ZPE* 60 (1985) 165–76.

Figueira, T.J. "*Autonomoi kata tas spondas* (Thucydides 1.67.2)." *BICS* 37 (1990) 63–88.

———. "Karl Polanyi and Ancient Greek Trade: The Port of Trade." *Ancient World* 10 (1984) 15–30.

———. "*Khrēmata*: Acquisition and Possession in Archaic Greece in Archaic Greece." In K.D. Irani and M. Silver (eds.). *Social Justice in the Ancient World* (Westport CT 1995) 41–60.

———. "Population Patterns in Late Archaic and Classical Sparta." *TAPA* 116 (1986) 165–213.

———. Review of E.E. Cohen, *Athenian Economy and Society: A Banking Perspective* (Princeton 1992) in *Bryn Mawr Classical Review* 5.2 (1994) 109–13.

———. "*Sitopolai* and *Sitophulakes* in Lysias' Oration 'Against the Grain-dealers.' " *Phoenix* 40 (1986) 149–71.

———. "The Ten *Archontes* of 579/8 at Athens." *Hesperia* 53 (1984) 447–73.

———. "A Typology of Social Conflict in Greek Poleis." In A. Molho, K. Raaflaub, and J. Emlen (eds.). *City States in Classical Antiquity and Medieval Italy* (Stuttgart 1991) 289–307.

Finley, M.I. *The Ancient Economy* (Berkeley and Los Angeles 1973).

———. "The Athenian Empire: A Balance Sheet." In *Economy and Society in Ancient Greece* (New York 1982) 41–61.

Fischer, D.H. *The Great Wave: Price Revolutions and the Rhythm of History* (Oxford 1996).

Fornara, C.W. and L.J. Samons. *Athens from Cleisthenes to Pericles* (Berkeley 1991).

Fried, S. "The Decadrachm Hoard: An Introduction." In I. Carradice (ed.), *Coinage and Administration in the Athenian and PersiaEn Empires* (Oxford 1987) 1–9.

von Fritze, H. "Sestos: Die Menas-Inschrift und das Münzwesen der Stadt." *Nomisma* 1 (1907) 1–13.

Gale, N.H. "Lead Isotopes and Archaic Greek Silver Silver Coins." In *Proceedings of the 18th International Symposium on Archaeometry and Archaeological Prospection, Bonn, 1978, Archaeo-physika* 10 (1979) 194–208.

———. "Some Aspects of Lead and Silver Mining in the Aegean." *MIGRA* 2 (1979) 9–60.

Gallo, L. "Salari e inflazione: Atene tra V e IV sec. a.C." *ASNP*³ 17 (1987) 19–63.

Gardner, P. "Coinage of the Athenian Empire." *JHS* 33 (1913) 147–88.

Gauthier, P. *Un commentaire historique des Poroi de Xénophon* (Geneva/Paris 1976).

———. *Symbola: Les étrangers et la justice dans les cités grecques* (Nancy 1972).

Gentner, W., O. Müller, G.A. Wagner, and N.H. Gale. "Silver Sources of Archaic Greek Coinage." *Naturwissenschaften* 65 (1978) 273–84.

Georgiadès, A. and W.K. Pritchett. "The Koan Fragment of the Monetary Decree." *BCH* 89 (1965) 400–41.

Giovannini, A. "Athenian Currency in the Late Fifth and Early Fourth Century B.C." *GRBS* 16 (1975) 185–95.

Grace, V. *Amphoras and the Ancient Wine Trade* (Princeton 1961).

———. "Exceptional Amphora Stamps." In G. Kopcke and M.B. Moore (eds.). *Studies in Classical Art and Archaeology* (Locust Valley, New York 1979) 117–27.

———. "Standard Pottery Containers of the Ancient Greek World." In *Commemorative Studies in Honor of Theodore Leslie Shear, Hesperia* Suppl. 8 (1949) 175–89.

Guépin, J.P. "Greek Coinage and Persian Bimetallism." *Jaarboek voor Munt- en Penningkunde* 49 (1962) 1–19.

Hackens, T. "La circulation monétaire, questions de méthode." *Études d'archéologie classique* 4 (1975) 213–22, *Annales de l'Est, Univ. de Nancy II*, #44.

———. "L'apport de la numismatique à l'histoire économique." In T. Hackens and P. Marchetti (eds.). In *Histoire économique de l'antiquité* (Louvain 1987) 151–69.

———. "Rythmes de la production monétaire: les monnayages archaïques et classiques de Grèce." In G. Depeyrot, T. Hackens, and G. Moucharte (eds.). *Rythmes de la production monétaire de l'antiquité à nos jours* (Louvain 1987) 1–13.

Healy, J.F. "A New Light on the Unique Stater of Mytilene." *ANSMN* 8 (1958) 1–9.

Henry, A.S. "The Dating of Fifth-Century Attic Inscriptions." *CSCA* 11 (1978) 75–108.

Hiller (von Gaertringen), F. "Ἀττικὸς νομισματικὸς νόμος ἐκ Σύμης." *AE* (1923) 116–17.

Hiller von Gaertringen, F. and Klaffenbach, G. "Das Münzgesetz des ersten athenischen Seebundes." *ZfN* 35 (1924–1925) 217–21.

Hopkins, K. "Taxes and Trade in the Roman Empire (200 B.C. to A.D. 400)." *JRS* 70 (1980) 101–25.

Hopper, R.J. "Interstate Juridical Agreements in the Athenian Empire." *JHS* 63 (1943) 35–51.

Howgego, C.J. "Why Did Ancient States Strike Coins?" *NC* 150 (1990) 1–25.

Hurter, S. and E. Pászthory. "Archaischer Silberfund aus dem Antilibanon." In A. Houghton, S. Hurter, P.E. Mottahedeh, and J.A. Scott (eds.). *Festschrift für Leo Mildenberg* (Wetteren, Belgium 1984) 111–125.

Johnston, J. "An International Managed Currency in the Fifth Century." *Hermathena* 47 (1932) 132–57.

Kagan, J.H. "An Archaic Greek Coin Hoard from the Eastern Mediterranean and Early Cypriot Coinage." *NC* 154 (1994) 17–52.

———. "The Decadrachm Hoard: Chronology and Consequences." In I. Carradice (ed.), *Coinage and Administration in the Athenian and Persian Empires* (Oxford 1987) 21–28.

———. "IGCH 1185 Reconsidered." *RBN* 138 (1992) 1–24.

Kallet-Marx, L. *Money, Expense, and Naval Power in Thucydides' History 1–5.24* (Berkeley and Los Angeles 1993).

Karyshkovsky, P.O. *Materialy po arkheologii Severnogo Pricheromor'ia, Odessa 3* (1961).

Kraay, C.M. "À propos de monnaies divisionaires de Croton." *SM* 8 (1958) 99–102.

———. "Archaic Owls of Athens: New Evidence for Chronology." *MIGRA* 1 (1975) 145–60.

———. "The Asyut Hoard: Some Comments on Chronology." *NC*[7] 17 (1977) 189–98.

———. "Greek Coinage and War." In W. Heckel and R. Sullivan (eds.). *Ancient Coins of the Graeco-Roman World: The Nickle Numismatic Papers* (Waterloo, Ontario 1984) 3–18.

———. *Greek Coins and History* (London 1969).

———. "Hoards, Small Change and the Origin of Coinage." *JHS* 84 (1964) 76–91.

Kraay, C.M. and V.M. Emeleus. *The Composition of Greek Silver Coins: Analysis by Neutron Activation* (Oxford 1962).

Kraay, C.M. and G.K. Jenkins. *Essays in Greek Coinage Presented to Stanley Robinson* (Oxford 1968).

Kroll, J.H. "Aristophanes' πονηρὰ χαλκία: A Reply." *GRBS* 17 (1976) 329–41.

———. *The Greek Coins, The Athenian Agora* 26 (Princeton 1993).

Lacroix, L. "La monnaie grecque et les problèmes de la circulation monétaire." *BAB*[5] 55 (1969) 169–80.

Laloux, M. "La circulation des monnaies d'électrum de Cyzique." *RBN* 117 (1971) 31–69.

Lang, M. and M. Crosby. *Weights, Measures, and Tokens, The Athenian Agora* 10 (Princeton 1964).

Lauffer, S. "Das Bergbauprogramm in Xenophons Poroi." *MIGRA* 1 (1975) 171–205.

Leppin, H. "Die ΑΡΧΟΝΤΕΣ ΕΝ ΤΑΙΣ ΠΟΛΕΣΙ des delisch-attischen Seebundes." *Historia* 41 (1992) 257–71.

Le Rider, G. "Contremarques et surfrappes dans l'antiquité grecque." In J.-M. Dentzer, P. Gauthier, and T. Hackens (eds.). *Numismatique antique: problèmes et méthodes, Annales de l'Est* 44 (Nancy-Louvain 1975) 27–56.

Lewis, D.M. "The Athenian Coinage Decree." In I. Carradice (ed.), *Coinage and Administration in the Athenian and Persian Empires* (Oxford 1987) 53–63.

———. "Entrenchment-Clauses in Attic Decrees." In D.W. Bradeen and M.F. McGregor (eds.). ΦΟΡΟΣ: *Tribute to Benjamin Dean Meritt* (Locust Valley, New York 1974) 81–89.

———. "New Evidence for the Gold-Silver Ratio." In C.M. Kraay and G.K. Jenkins (eds.). *Essays in Greek Coinage Presented to Stanley Robinson* (Oxford 1968) 105–10.

Lyon, C.S.S. "The Estimation of the Number of Dies Employed in a Coinage." *NCirc* 73 (1965) 180–81.

Marchetti, P. "Le Cours du Cyzicène au IVe siècle." *RBN* 122 (1976) 35–58.

Martin, T.R. "Silver Coins and Public Slaves in the Athenian Law of 375/4 B.C." In D.M. Metcalf (ed.). *Mnemata: Papers in Memory of Nancy M. Waggoner* (New York 1991) 21–47.

———. *Sovereignty and Coinage in Classical Greece* (Princeton 1985)

Mattingly, H.B. "The Alliance of Athens with Egesta." *Chiron* 16 (1986) 167–70.

———. "Athens and the Western Greeks: C. 500–413 B.C." In *La circolazione della moneta ateniese in Sicilia e in Magna Grecia, AIIN* Suppl. 12–14 (Rome 1969) 201–222.

———. "Epigraphy and the Athenian Empire." *Historia* 41 (1992) 129–38.

———. "The Growth of Athenian Imperialism." *Historia* 12 (1963) 257–73.

———. "New Light on the Athenian Standards Decree (ATL II, D 14)." *Klio* 75 (1993) 99–102.

Meiggs, R. "The Dating of Fifth-Century Attic Inscriptions." *JHS* 86 (1966) 86–98.

Meritt, B.D. "Attic Inscriptions of the Fifth Century." *Hesperia* 14 (1945) 117–33.

———. "The Early Athenian Tribute Lists." *CP* 38 (1943) 223–39.

———. "Perikles, the Athenian Mint, and the Hephaisteion." *PAPS* 119 (1975) 267–74.

Meritt, B.D. and H.T. Wade-Gery. "The Dating of Documents to the Mid-Fifth Century—I." *JHS* 82 (1962) 67–74.

———. "The Dating of Documents to the Mid-Fifth Century—II." *JHS* 83 (1963) 100–17.

Michaelis, A. "The Metrological Relief at Oxford." *JHS* 4 (1883) 335–50.

Mørkholm, O. "Some Reflections on the Production and Use of Coinage in Ancient Greece." *Historia* 31 (1982) 290–305.

Müller O., and W. Gentner. "On the Composition and Silver Sources of Aeginetan Coins from the Asyut Hoard." In *Proceedings of the 18th International Symposium on Archaeometry and Archaeological Prospection, Bonn, 1978, Archaeophysika* 10 (1979) 176–93.

Nicolet-Pierre, H. "L'oiseau d'Athéna, d'Égypte en Bactriane: Quelques remarques sur l'usage d'un type monétaire à l'époque classique." In L. Kahil, C. Augé, and P. Linant de Bellefonds (eds.). *Iconographie classique et identités régionales, BCH* Suppl. 14 (1986) 365–76.

———. "Monnaies grecques trouvées en Afghanistan." *RN*[6] 15 (1973) 35–42.

Patterson, C.C. "Silver Stocks and Losses in Ancient and Medieval Times." *EHR*[2] 25 (1972) 205–35.

Picard, O. "Innovations monétaires dans la Grèce du IVe siècle." *CRAI* (1989) 673–87.

Postalakas, A. "Κερμάτια συμβολικά." *AE* 3 (1884) 1–20.
Pouilloux, J. "Des rapports actuels de l'épigraphie et de l'histoire grecques." *AC* 22 (1953) 32–49.
———. *Recherches sur l'histoire et cultes de Thasos, Études Thasiennes* 3, 5 (Paris 1954, 1958)
Price, M.J. "The Coinages of the Northern Aegean." In I. Carradice (ed.), *Coinage and Administration in the Athenian and Persian Empires* (Oxford 1987) 43–51.
———. "Early Greek Bronze Coinage." In C.M. Kraay and G.K. Jenkins (eds.). *Essays in Greek Coinage Presented to Stanley Robinson* (Oxford 1968) 90–104
———. "The Function of Early Greek Bronze Coinage." *AIIN* Suppl. 25 (1979) 351–65.
Price, M. and N. Waggoner. *Archaic Coinage: The Asyut Hoard* (London 1975).
Pritchett, W.K. "The Attic Stelai, Part I." *Hesperia* 22 (1953) 225–99.
———. *The Greek State at War* (Berkeley and Los Angeles 1971–1991).
———. "The Koan Fragment of the Monetary Decree." *BCH* 89 (1965) 400–40.
———. "The Three-Barred Sigma at Kos." *BCH* 87 (1963) 20–23.
———. "The Transfer of the Delian Treasury." *Historia* 18 (1969) 17–21.
Raven, E.J.P. "The Amphictyonic Coinage of Delphi: 336–334 B.C." *NC*[5] 10 (1950) 1–22.
Reinach, T. "L'anarchie monétaire et ses remèdes chez les anciens Grecs." *Mém. Acad. Ins. et Belles-Lettres* 38 (1911) 351–64.
———. "KOLLYBOS." *RN*[4] 31 (1928) 145–60.
Rhodes, P.J. *The Athenian Boule* (Oxford 1972).
Robinson, D.M. "A New Fragment of the Athenian Decree on Coinage." *AJP* 56 (1935) 149–54.
Robinson, E.S.G. "A Find of Archaic Coins from South-West Asia Minor." *NC*[5] 16 (1936) 265–80.
———. "A Hoard of Archaic Greek Coins from Anatolia." *NC*[7] 1 (1961) 107–17.
———. "Some Problems in the Later Fifth Century Coinage of Athens." *ANSMN* 9 (1960) 1–15.
———. "The Tell El-Mashkuta Hoard of Athenian Tetradrachms." *NC*[6] 7 (1947) 115–21.
Robinson, E.S.G and M.J. Price. "An Emergency Coinage of Timotheos." *NC*[7] (1967) 1–6.
Romstedt, M. *Die wirtschaftliche Organisation des athenischen Reiches* (Leipzig 1914).
Rutter, K. "Athens and the Western Greeks in the Fifth Century B.C.: The Numismatic Evidence." In G. Le Rider, K. Jenkins, N. Waggoner, and U. Westermark (eds.). *Kraay-Mørkholm Essays: Numismatic Studies in Memory of C.M. Kraay and O. Mørkholm* (Louvain-la-Neuve 1989) 245–57.
———. "Early Greek Coinage and the Influence of the Athenian State." In B. Cunliffe (ed.). *Coinage and Society in Britain and Gaul: Some Current Problems* (London 1981) 1–9.

Schlumberger, D. "L'argent grec dans l'empire Achéménide." In R. Curiel and D. Schlumberger (eds.). *Trésors monétaires d'Afghanistan* (Paris 1953) 1–64.

Schoenhammer, M. "Some Thoughts on the Athenian Coinage Decree." In T. Hackens and G. Moucharte (eds.). *Proceedings of the XI International Numismatic Congress* 1 (Louvain-la-Neuve 1993) 187–91.

Schönert-Geiss, E. "Einige Bemerkungen zu den präemonetären Geldformen und zu Anfängen der Münzprägung." *Klio* 69 (1987) 406–42.

———. "Die Geldzirkulation Attikas." *Klio* 56 (1974) 377–414.

———. "Die Geldzirkulation Attikas im 4. Jahrhundert v. u. Z." In E.C. Welskopf (ed.). *Hellenische Poleis* 1 (Berlin 1974) 531–50.

———. "Die Wirtschafts- und Handelbeziehungen zwischen Griechenland und der nordlichen Scharzmeerküste im Spiegel der Münzfunde (6.–1. Jh. v. u.Z.)." *Klio* 53 (1971) 105–17.

Schubiger, P.A., O. Müller, and W. Gentner. "Chemical Studies of Greek Silver Coins from the Asyut Hoard." In E.A. Slater and J.O. Tate (eds.). *Proceedings of the 16th International Symposium on Archaeometry and Archaeological Prospection, Edinburgh, 1976* (Edinburgh 1976) 164–76.

Schwertheim, E. "Ein Dekretfragment aus dem 5. Jh. v. Chr. aus Hamaxitus." *Araştirma Sonuçlari Toplantisi* 6 (1988) 283–85.

Sokolowski, F. "The Athenian Law Concerning Silver Currency (375/4) B.C." *BCH* 100 (1976) 511–15.

Sommerstein, A.H. *Birds* (Warminster 1987).

Starr, C.G. *Athenian Coinage: 480–449 B.C.* (Oxford 1970).

———. "New Specimens of Athenian Coinage 480–449 B.C." *NC* 142 (1982) 129–34.

Stroud, R.S. "An Athenian Law on Silver Coinage." *Hesperia* 43 (1974) 157–88.

———. "Three Attic Decrees." *CSCA* 7 (1974) 279–98.

Stumpf, G. "Ein athenisches Münzgesetz des 4. Jh. v. Chr." *JNG* 36 (1986) 23–40.

Svoronos, J.N. "La monnaie d'or attique." *JIAN* 21 (1927) 147–70.

———. "ΟΙ ΚΟΛΛΥΒΟΙ." *JIAN* 14 (1912) 123–60.

Thompson, D.B. "The Golden Nikai Reconsidered." *Hesperia* 13 (1944) 173–209.

Thompson, H.A. and R.E. Wycherley. *The Agora of Athens, The Athenian Agora* 14 (Princeton 1972).

Thompson, W.E. "The Chian Coinage in Thucydides and Xenophon." *NC*⁷ 11 (1971) 323–24.

———. "The Date of the Athenian Gold Coinage." *AJP* 86 (1965) 159–74.

———. "The Functions of the Emergency Coinages of the Peloponnesian War." *Mnem.*⁴ 19 (1966) 337–43.

———. "Gold and Silver Ratios at Athens During the Fifth Century." *NC*⁷ 4 (1964) 103–23.

———. "The Gold Nikai and the Coinage of Athens." *NC*⁷ 10 (1970) 1–6.

———. "The Protected Fund of Athena and Hephaistos." *AJP* 98 (1977) 249–51.

Tobey, L. Beer and A.G. Tobey. "Experiments to Simulate Ancient Greek Coins." *Metallurgy in Numismatics* 3 (1993) 28–33,

Tracy, S.V. "Hands in Fifth Century B.C. Attic Inscriptions." In *Studies Presented to Sterling Dow, GRBS Monograph* 10 (Durham, North Carolina 1984) 277–82.

Vanderpool, E. and W.P. Wallace. "The Sixth Century Laws from Eretria." *Hesperia* 33 (1964) 381–91.

Vickers, M. "Artful Crafts: The Influence of Metalwork on Athenian Painted Pottery." *JHS* 105 (1985) 108–28.

———. "Fifth Century Chronology and the Coinage Decree." *JHS* 116 (1996) 171–74

Viner, J. "Economic Thought: II. Mercantilist Thought." In D.I. Sills, *International Encyclopedia of the Social Sciences* (New York 1968) 4.435–43.

Wade-Gery, H.T. "The Peace of Callias." *Essays in Greek History* (Oxford 1958) 201–32.

———. "The Question of the Tribute in 449/8 B.C." *Hesperia* 14 (1945) 212–29.

Walbank, M.B. *Athenian Proxenies of the Fifth Century* B.C. (Toronto and Sarasota 1978).

———. "Criteria for the Dating of Fifth-Century Attic Inscriptions." In D.W. Bradeen and M.F. McGregor (eds.). ΦΟΡΟΣ: *Tribute to Benjamin Dean Meritt* (Locust Valley, New York 1974) 161–89.

Wallace, M.B. "Progress in Measuring Amphora Capacities." In J.-Y. Empereur and Y. Garlan (eds.). *Recherches sur les amphores grecques*, *BCH* Suppl. 13 (Paris 1986) 87–94.

———. "Texts, Amphoras, Coins, Standards and Trade." *Ancient World* 10 (1984) 11–14.

Wallace, W.P. *The Euboian League and Its Coinage*, *NNM* 134 (New York 1956) 49–50, 137–39.

Weil, R. "Das Münzmonopol Athens im ersten attischen Seebund." *ZfN* 25 (1906) 52–62.

———. "Das Münzrecht der ΞΥΜΜΑΧΟΙ im ersten attischen Seebund." *ZfN* 28 (1910) 351–64.

Weiser, W. "Die Eulen von Kyros dem Jüngeren zu den ersten Münzporträts lebender Menschen." *ZPE* 76 (1989) 267–96.

Wesenberg, B. "Zum metrologischen Relief in Oxford." *Marburger Winckelmann-Programm* (1975–1976 [1976]) 15–22.

Westermark, U. "The Coinage of the Chalcidian League Reconsidered." In *Studies in Ancient History and Numismatics Presented to Rudi Thomsen* (Aarhus 1988) 91–103.

von Wilamowitz-Moellendorff, U. *Aus Kydathen* (Berlin 1880), *Philol. Untersuchungen* 1.

———. *Reden und Vorträge* (Berlin 1901).

Wilhelm, A. "Epigraphischer Bericht aus Griechenland." *JOAI* 1 (1898), "Beiblatt." cols. 41–50.

———. "Zu jüngsten Veröffentlichungen griechischer Inschriften." *AAWW* 61 (1924) 149–62.

Will, E. *Le monde grec et l'orient* (Paris 1972).

Woodhead, A.G. "Before the Storm." *Mélanges Helléniques offerts à Georges Daux* (Paris 1974) 375–88.

———. *Inscriptions: The Decrees, The Athenian Agora* 16 (Princeton 1997).

———. "Reflections on the Use of the Literary and Epigraphical Evidence for the History of the Athenian Empire." *Akten des VI. Internationalen Kongresses für Griechische und Lateinische Epigraphik, München 1972* (Munich 1973) 345–54.

Wycherley, R.E. *Literary and Epigraphical Testimonia, The Athenian Agora* 3 (Princeton 1957).

Ziebarth, E. *Beiträge zur Geschichte des Seeraubs und Seehandels im alten Griechenland* (Hamburg 1929).

INDEX LOCORUM

Note: Underlining is used as a typographic device for distinguishing items within entries.

A. INSCRIPTIONS

B. LITERARY SOURCES

Note: Σ = *Scholia*

GENERAL INDEX

NOTE: Page numbers followed by "n" (for example, 53n) indicate that discussion of the entry is confined to a footnote or footnotes on the enumerated page(s). Entries that name individual cities are to be understood to include the mint of that city. Hence, "Abdera" is understood to connote "Abdera and its mint." Tables 2.2 and 2.3 on pp. 84–91 contain information on allied minting activity. The Appendix (pp. 563–98) may be consulted for further information on individual mints.

www.ingramcontent.com/pod-product-compliance
Lightning Source LLC
LaVergne TN
LVHW091514200926
848483LV00005B/418/J